Taiwan
in
Modern Times

edited with an introduction by
Paul K.T. Sih

Asia in the Modern World Series, No. 13

Published by the

St. John's University Press

under the auspices of the

Center of Asian Studies

Copyright 1973 © St. John's University
Library of Congress Catalog Card Number 72-94212

Library of Congress Catalog Information
lists the editor's name also as
Hsüeh, Kuang-ch'ien
according to the Wade-Giles system of romanization.

Dedicated to the inauguration

of

Dr. Sun Yat-sen Memorial Hall

Contents

Map

Introduction

BY PAUL K.T. SIH

In all considerations -- ethnical, cultural, geographical and historical — Taiwan is an integral and inalienable part of China. Anyone who claims that Taiwan can be separated from and independent of China is denying historical facts as well as present-day realities. The substantiation of this premise is the purpose of the present work. The contributors to this volume, four American and six Chinese, are scholars and specialists whose research and study in their own fields have included the historical background or current development of Taiwan, making them eminently qualified for their present contributions.

Furthermore, three of the Chinese scholars, Drs. Chan Lien, Parris H. Chang and Yung Wei, were either born or reared in Taiwan. Their Chinese ethnic and cultural heritage, Taiwan homeland consanguinity and advanced American education lend a special competence to them in the discussion of the problems of Taiwan, past or present.

Various approaches to the general theme are undertaken in different chapters, but they are synthesized to achieve the unified and total effect, that Taiwan is inseparable from the Chinese land, state, and nation. The most convenient yet convincing way, we believe, to state our factual argumentation is by a two-phase presentation. Accordingly, this series of essays can best be grouped in two sections. The first section, Chapters I to VII, seeks to answer these questions: When and how did Taiwan become populated exclusively by Chinese? How did Taiwan become an integral part of China by undergoing a two-century development under the Manchu Imperial government? The second section, Chapters VIII to XI, aims to answer the following questions: How does the Taiwan of colonial status under Japanese rule compare with Taiwan as a province of China after its restoration in 1945. Is the political, economic, social and cultural progress brought to Taiwan in the post-war period a blessing that would never have come had Taiwan not been restored to China? Would such progress have been brought about, had Taiwan still remained under Japanese rule? Although space does not allow full details and discussion, the essays adequately answer these central questions.

Chapter I, "The Physical Setting of Taiwan," serves as an introduction to both sections. Dr. Chiao-min Hsieh, Professor of Geography at the University of Pittsburgh, covers his subject from twelve aspects: Location, Origin, Landform, Coast, Temperature, Rainfall, Winds, Typhoons, Hydrography, Soil Groups. Natural Vegetation, and Mineral Resources. He finds that

> . . .from these bits of evidence — the contrasting curvature between the Ryukyu arc, the Philippine archipelago, and Taiwan; the structural alignment and rock correlation with the mainland; the character of the Strait's submarine configuration; the simple and smooth coast line of the island, and the existence of extensive basalt masses formed through fissure emption — we may conclude that the island of Taiwan has long been in existence and was actually a part of the Chinese mainland during early geological periods. Not until the Pleistocene epoch, when the Strait sank and formed a rift valley, was Taiwan separated from the continent and isolated as an island.

The fact that the Chinese were the first who came to Taiwan is pointed out by Professor Ting-yee Kuo, noted historian and a member of Academia Sinica, Republic of China. In Chapter II, "Early Stages of the Sinicization of Taiwan, 230-1683," Professor Kuo identifies the development of Taiwan by early Chinese as not a matter of political conquest or economic colonization, but as a demonstration of pioneering efforts which brought about hundreds of years of reclamation and settlement. In his words:

> The Chinese who first moved into Taiwan from across the sea were almost all South Fukienese and Hakkas. They were Chinese with full national consciousness and strong pioneering spirit. They crossed the sea and carried with them into Taiwan Chinese traditions and cultural and technical backgrounds. Yet their achievement in planting the roots there was not easy; it was an accomplishment built in slow accumulation of days into months and months into years. . . .

While the Chinese people migrated on a large scale to Taiwan, the Dutch followed with their ships and guns in the wake of their East Indian Company conquests. The Dutch presence in Taiwan lasted nominally for thirty-eight years (1624-1662). Constantly under Dutch oppression, the Chinese settlers rose in revolt in 1652. In 1662, Cheng Cheng-kung (Koxinga) succeeded in ousting the Dutch from Taiwan and restored the land to Chinese rule. This is discussed in Chapter III, "Brief Episodes -- Dutch and Spanish Rule," by Dr. George M. Beckmann, Dean, College of Arts and Sciences, University of Washington, Seattle. He records the last struggle of the Dutch for the recovery of their interests in Taiwan in these words:

> For several years, after the fall of Zeelandia, they [the Dutch] cooperated with the Manchus against Koxinga and in 1663 landed a force of two hundred men at Keelung. However, because of the lack of trade, they departed again in 1668. Formosa had come to the end of another era of its history and for the Dutch it was the end of the dream of linking together trade with China and Japan through Formosa.

From 1662 to 1683, Taiwan was under the rule of Cheng Cheng-kung. This is dealt with in Chapter IV, "Cheng Cheng-kung (Koxinga) and Chinese Nationalism in Taiwan, 1662-1683," by Parris H. Chang, Associate Professor of Political Science at the Pennsylvania State University. In evaluating Cheng Cheng-kung's achievements, Dr. Chang has this to say:

> Although Cheng Cheng-kung did not succeed in ousting the Manchus from the mainland and in restoring the Ming dynasty, his liberation of Taiwan from the Dutch colonial yoke was nonetheless a splendid achievement and made him China's national hero. His movement of the Chinese people to Taiwan and his nation-building undertakings, which laid the foundation for Taiwan's future development, distinguished himself as the maker of Taiwan. Moreover, his restoration of Taiwan to the Chinese and transformation of Taiwan into a Chinese community produced historical consequences which were to affect international relations of East Asia in the 19th century and even to the present day; as such, he is immortal.

From the Manchu restoration of Taiwan to Imperial rule in 1683 to the year 1874, when China and Japan concluded their first treaty over Taiwan, China had a series of external relations involving Taiwan as the center of interest. A detailed account of these international relations is found in Chapter V, "Taiwan in China's External Relations, 1683-1874," by Dr. Chan Lien, Professor and Chairman, Department of Political Science, National Taiwan University. According to Dr. Lien, under the Manchu rule Taiwan was first involved in external relations in the Opium War period. In the aftermath of the Treaty of Nanking in 1842, the British began to take steps to test the enforcement of its terms, and among such measures the future trading possibilities in Taiwan were explored. When their new treaty rights were ignored, especially in the opening of the city of Canton, the British prepared to make war against China.

Encouraged by the British policy, Peter Parker, American Chargé d'Affaires in China at that time, suggested that a concerted action with Britain be taken so that a privileged position for the United States be secured in Taiwan. This the United States government refused to consider. In his reply to Parker, Secretary of State William L. Marcy stated, as quoted by Dr. Lien in his essay, that:

> The President does not believe that our relations with China warrant the "last resort" you speak of, and if they did, the military or naval forces of the United States could only be used by the authority of Congress. The "last resort" means war, and the executive branch of this government is not the war-making power. ...For the protection and security of Americans in China and the protection of their property, it may be expedient to increase our naval force on the China station, but the President will not do it for aggressive purposes.

In similar situations, wherein the subject of Taiwan became one of great interest to certain Americans in seeking territorial gains or acquiring special privileges, the United States government always remained disinterested and never gave any serious consideration or support to their aggressive attempts. "This (American) policy had, no doubt," as Dr. Lien put it, "terminated all ambitions that certain Americans might have harbored over Taiwan in the late 40's and early 50's of the nineteenth century."

As a result of the *Locha Arrow* War (1856-1860), Western nations, notably Britain and France, secured more privileges from

China at the expense of the latter's sovereignity. Tamshui in Taiwan, for instance, was made one of the treaty ports open to all Powers which enjoyed the most-favored-nation clause in their treaties with China. China's next major confrontation involving Taiwan was with Japan. In 1874, an agreement on Taiwan was finally signed between China and Japan after five months of hostilities and negotiations. China had to pay monetary compensations in exchange for the withdrawal of Japanese forces from the island.

From 1683 to 1891, Taiwan underwent a great period of internal development and eventual modernization under the Manchu government. In Chapter VI, "The Internal Development and Modernization of Taiwan, 1683-1891," Professor Ting-yee Kuo, the aforementioned historian and author of books and articles on the history of Taiwan, details in four sections China's efforts in developing and modernizing Taiwan: (1) The Maturity of Sinicization (1683-1874); (2) The Beginnings of Modernization (1874-1883); (3) The Defense of Taiwan (1884-1885), and (4) The Rapid Advancement of Modernization (1885-1891).

The two centuries of sustained development in Taiwan from 1683 to 1894 have definitely and unquestionably established the historical fact that Taiwan was an integral part of China at the time of its cession to Japan in 1895.

About 1683, there were only a few hundred thousand Chinese in Taiwan. By 1890, there were more than three million. In 1683, the local administrative units decreed by Emperor Kang-hsi was one prefecture *(fu)* with three districts *(hsien)*, all in the present-day Tainan area. Two centuries later, in 1885, an Imperial decree proclaimed Taiwan a "province" *(sheng)*, the twentieth province of China. The new province consisted of three prefectures, with eleven districts, one special district *(chou)*, and six sub-prefectures *(t'ing)*, very much the same as Taiwan today. This expansion in population and settled areas forms the keynote of this two-century development. Professor Kuo's essay accounts for this period of history of the Chinese migration, reclamation and settlement in Taiwan, taking note of government policy, administrative leadership, welfare programs for aborigines (population about 200,000), local cultural development, and other factors.

Next in importance, as presented in Kuo's essay, is the period of modernization of 1874-1891. Following the wars between 1840 and 1860, national self-strengthening became the order of the day in China. Taiwan was involved in this movement because it stood at the forefront of China's coastal defense. In the post-1860 period it was the first to face invasions. The Japanese landed a small force on its east coast in 1874, and the French navy attacked Keelung and took Penghu in the Sino-French War of 1884-85. Each episode spurred Peking's efforts in the building up of Taiwan. Men of renowned ability and leadership were assigned to the task. In 1874-1875 it was Shen Pao-chen, and in 1884-1891, Liu Ming-chuan. When Liu left in 1891, Taiwan was able to record the following achievements: a railroad line and inter-port and overseas steamship lines, a coal mine to supply these lines, manufacturing and mining by machinery, modern naval vessels and fortifications for coastal defense, an arsenal and magazine to supply the regular forces and militia, staple export crops like rice, sugar, and camphor, introduction of cotton and tea planting, telegram and postal services, and, above all, modern public schools. None of the mainland provinces, except Chihli, which shelters Peking, had achieved such an array of accomplishments. "Liu Ming-chuan's accomplishment was unique and outstanding in that he promoted Taiwan to the most advanced province of China." This was Taiwan's status at the time of its annexation by Japan.

Although Taiwan was ceded to Japan in 1895 by the Treaty of Shimonoseki, the Chinese people of the island were not subdued. Under the leadership of Tang Ching-sung, then Acting Governor of Taiwan Province, the Republic of Taiwan was proclaimed. This was followed by a war of resistance against Japan. In Chapter VII, "A Short-Lived Republic and War, 1895: Taiwan's Resistance Against Japan," Dr. Harry J. Lamley, Associate Professor of History, University of Hawaii, stresses the significance of this episode by stating: "The rise of the Taiwan Republic and the ensuing war of resistance were extraordinary episodes since they came to pass without the sanction of the Ching court and in defiance of both the Japanese military power and the terms of the peace treaty."

It may be noted that the resistance movement was not an independence movement, but a protest against the cession of Taiwan by China to alien rule. It defied the treaty entered into by the Ching government, yet without the least intention of being disloyal to the Imperial Regime. Thus, Dr. Lamley writes:

> On the whole, they [Taiwan leaders] appear to have been sincere in their allegiance, for they still linked their fate to that of China and the Ching dynasty. Thus, Tang Ching-sung in his memorials and proclamations, and both Chiu Feng-chia and Liu Yung-fu in their petitions and oaths, constantly made it clear that they did not wish to sever their ties with the mainland no matter how much the weak and vacillating Ching court had disappointed them.

In 1895, Taiwan was ceded to Japan by the treaty of Shimonoseki. It was not returned to China until the end of World War II in 1945. For fifty years, Taiwan was under the colonial rule of Japan. Chapter VIII, "Taiwan's Japanese Interlude, 1895-1945," therefore serves as a dividing line between the two sections of this book. In this chapter, Dr. Hyman Kublin, Professor of History, Brooklyn College of the City University of New York, surveys what Japan did in Taiwan in the half century, and pointed out that ". . . the correlated and long-range Japanese colonial policy in Taiwan was to insure that the island contribute to the larger national interests of the mother country." Thus, ". . . Taiwan and not the Taiwan people represented the greatest concern of Japan."

Chapter IX, "Taiwan's Movement into Political Modernity, 1945-1972," Chapter X, "Economic Development of Taiwan," and Chapter XI, "Taiwan: A Modernizing Chinese Society," form the substance of the second section of the book. They provide studies of the development and progress of Taiwan in its political and economic, and social and cultural aspects from the end of World War II to the present time.

Dr. Richard L. Walker, James F. Byrnes Professor of International Relations, University of South Carolina, discusses the theme "Taiwan's Movement into Political Modernity, 1945-1972" in five sections: (1) Kuomintang Rule; (2) Official Ideology; (3) Two-Tiered Government; (4) Military Emergency, and (5) Custodial Rule. Commenting on the remarkable progress in Taiwan, Dr. Walker attributes this achievement to the capability of the Kuomintang (KMT) leaders who are also political leaders and experts in the government of the Republic of China (GRC):

The important point which has been all too often forgotten or overlooked in studies of the Taiwan scene is that the remarkable progress in social, educational, economic and other fields could not have been possible without *political* direction and thrust from a capable élite. The GRC under the one-party rule of the KMT has been characterized by a group of modernizers who were able to see the interrelationships of all aspects of life on the island. The same KMT leaders who managed to maintain a stable currency in Taiwan (in contrast to the disastrous inflationary spiral which helped to spell Nationalist doom on the Chinese mainland) and who worked with intensity on the modernization and industrialization of the economy were political leaders and Party members as well as economic and planning experts.

Because of the presence of such a capable élite in the GRC, there developed a continuity in the political process in Taiwan, a continuity, in the words of Dr. Walker, "which stood in marked contrast to some of the violent fluctuations in policies and regimes in other developing countries." "It is this continuity in leadership at the national level," the American Professor continues, "which has tended to obscure some of the major political changes which have been taking place in the politics of Taiwan within all of the major areas which can be singled out in significant and distinguishing features of Nationalist Rule."

Taking note of Premier Chiang Ching-kuo's appointment of an increased number of young people and Taiwanese to national executive positions, he observed some of the essential trends toward political modernization and development of Taiwan, emphasizing that ". . .political direction in Taiwan begins passing to a young élite with different perspectives," and that there is the fact of ". . .the increasing involvement of Taiwanese in top positions, national as well as provincial." Thus in his concluding passage, the American scholar hopefully remarks:

With the passing of the older élite and the rise to the very top positions of those who have been responsible for Taiwan's social and economic progress, the way was open for further political development and modernization.

The next chapter, "Economic Development of Taiwan, " Dr. Anthony Y.C. Koo, Professor of Economics at Michigan State University, devotes himself to a detailed description of Taiwan's post-war economic growth in seven sections: (1) Economic

Heritage; (2) Battle Against Inflation; (3) United States Aid; (4) Land Reform Since Retrocession; (5) Economic Achievements of the Domestic Section; (6) The Foreign Trade Sector, and (7) From the Seventies On and Beyond.

It is most obvious that economic success in Taiwan has been considered a spectacular performance by a twentieth century developing area. "Whatever Taiwan economy has accomplished," Dr. Koo states "is now a matter of record." Two developments are particularly impressive: (1) United States aid and land reform, and (2) industrial build-up and foreign trade growth. In spite of tremendous achievements, however, Taiwan still has future economic problems, although they are problems of success, not of failure. In the words of Dr. Koo:

> . . .in a resource scarce and labor abundant economy such as Taiwan, the task to continuously improve the standard of living of the people by sustaining a high rate of economic growth is not an easy one. Thus, the achievement in Taiwan so far is truly remarkable in view of the constraints. In the last analysis, however, short of a reduction of birth rate and development and mastery of modern and advanced techniques of production, the problem of sustaining rapid economic growth will be a constant challenge. Fortunately, it is being squarely met on both fronts: Family planning and improvement of the quality of labor force on the one hand and promotion of new technology industries on the other. The outcome of this concentrated effort deserves our foremost attention because of the implication beyond Taiwan. The struggle, if successful, will be a beacon of hope and a source of inspiration to all who are faced with the same kind of economic problems as Taiwan.

In Chapter XI, "Taiwan: A Modernizing Chinese Society," Dr. Yung Wei, Associate Professor of Political Science, Memphis State University, discusses Taiwan's process of modernization under five topics: (1) Modernization: A Clarification of the Concept; (2) Modernization on Taiwan: The Historical Background and the Stage of Post-War Developments; (3) Modernization on Taiwan: An Examination of Its Various Aspects; (4) The Impact of Modernization Upon the Social Structure, Attitude, and Behavior of the People in Taiwan, and (5) The Modernization Process in Taiwan: Some Reflections and Projectives.

After detailing the efforts of the Republic of China in

reconstructing Taiwan as a modern society, Dr. Wei makes a comparison of the performance of the GRC with that of the Communists on the Chinese mainland. He stated:

> In comparison with Mainland China, Taiwan is a far more industrialized society, with much higher per capita income, calory intake, and radio and telephone possession for its people. Given this kind of wide gaps between the society on Mainland China and that on Taiwan, it is inconceivable for the people of Taiwan to accept the authority of a communist regime which has thus far failed to demonstrate the superiority of their formula for modernization over the model that has been successfully tried out in Taiwan during the past twenty-five years. It is safe to say, therefore, that the primary concern of all the people in Taiwan, including both the Taiwanese and Mainlanders, is how to defend the fruits of their modernization efforts against the threat of the Chinese Communists.

He concludes his study by declaring convincingly that "by all indications, the progress made by the people of Taiwan toward modernization will continue at an even faster pace."

Taking encouragement from these scholarly works, I feel strongly that this combined effort of American and Chinese scholars may help clarify the following points which seem to have long remained doubtful in Western minds:

1. Taiwan has been, in population and in culture, in geography and in history, an integral part of China. It had been one of the most modernized provinces of China before it was annexed by Japan.

2. Since its retrocession to China after World War II in 1945, Taiwan, as a province of the Republic of China, has been enjoying continued and sustained progress which serves as a model to other developing countries of the world.

3. There were popular revolts and uprisings in the history of Taiwan, notably the revolt of 1662 led by Cheng Cheng-kung and the revolt of 1895 led by Tang Ching-sung. Both were under Chinese leadership, however, and both were calculated not to break from but to remain under Chinese sovereignty. In the case of Cheng Cheng-kung, he wished that Taiwan, being freed from the Dutch, might be restored to Imperial Ming rule; and in the case of Tang Ching-sung, he desired that Taiwan not be ceded to Japan but remain as a part of China. Tang's attempt for a "Taiwan

Republic" was an improvised scheme to save Taiwan from imminent Japanese takeover and no contemplation of any real independence of the island was in evidence.

4. Any movement for "Taiwan Independence," is, therefore, without any truthful cause, real basis, genuine dedication, or intrinsic merit. The so-called "Mainlanders" and "Taiwanese" are but convenient designations of two groups of one and the same people, all Chinese in origin and in culture. The "Taiwanese" are only the earlier Chinese of Taiwan while the "Mainlanders" are new Chinese who came after World War II. As Dr. William L. Tung, Professor of Political Science at Queens College of the City University of New York, has pointed out very pertinently:

> A small number of Westerners and Taiwanese residing abroad have been in favor of the establishment of an independent state of Taiwan by and for the Taiwanese. This equally unrealistic plan is based upon the current misconception in the West that the Taiwanese and the Mainlanders are of two different races. Actually the only native people in Taiwan are the aborigines living mostly in mountainous areas. This tiny group has neither the capacity nor the ambition to form a new state even with the assistance of foreign adventurers. As to the Taiwanese, they were born in Taiwan but are of Chinese race and culture. Their ancestors came to Taiwan earlier than the so-called Mainlanders today. If any distinction must be made between the Taiwanese and the Mainlanders, it is the time of arrival and the place of birth. *

There are Western writers who choose to say that certain differences do exist between Taiwanese and Chinese. They imply that fifty years of Japanese rule necessarily made the Taiwanese different. A careful reading of Dr. Kublin's essay (Chapter VIII) makes it obvious that the Japanese had given the vast majority of the Taiwanese nothing but a police state and colonial economy, leaving them with neither a new culture, a new life, nor a new faith nor new aspirations. The only thing they did to the benefit of a tiny minority of Taiwanese was to provide some education in the Japanese language imposed upon the colony. This created a Taiwansese élite of two categories: first, scholars who enjoyed the ability to imbibe knowledge or ideas and to appreciate philosophy

---

*The Political Institutions of Modern China (The Hague: Martinus Nijhoff, 1964), p. 235.

and literature written or published in Japanese; and second, leaders in government and society who enjoyed the privileges derived from the positions made accessible to them by their higher education. Yet no Taiwanese scholar of perceptive mind, nor Taiwanese leader of real quality, will value their lost privileges so much as to wish for a return to their former status of serving somebody else's interests, though this time only as protégès.* Furthermore, as Dr. Wei observes:

> The successful "National Language Movement" has practically eliminated the communication barrier between the Taiwanese and Mainlanders. Nowadays, one can hardly tell the youngsters of these two provincial groups apart by listening to the way they talk, for both groups are speaking the Mandarin language with hardly any differences in pronunciation and intonation.

Finally, I would like to borrow another passage from Dr. Wei in which he expresses his faith and confidence in the future of Taiwan, a confidence I believe everyone who has read these essays will share:

> Despite a series of setbacks suffered by the Republic of China in international politics, there has been little indication that this has seriously and adversely affected the process of economic development. The extent of calmness and self-assurance demonstrated by the people of Taiwan after the seating of Communist China in the United Nations has left a deep impression on western observers. It is safe to say, therefore, that with this kind of confidence and determination, the people of Taiwan will build an even more prosperous society on the island in the near future, which will remain as a living testimony to the people of the world of what the Chinese people could achieve in an open, free and competitive system.

In editing and making this volume available to the American reading public, I am most grateful to all the contributors for their kind cooperation. Special thanks are due to Dr. Robert A. Scalopino, of the University of California at Berkeley, for his

*Voters of free China went to the polls December 23, 1972 to elect 182 representatives to national, provincial and local offices. Of the eighty-nine named to the National Assembly and Legislative Yuan, all but ten were natives of Taiwan province.

counsel and advice, particularly at a time when the project was in its formative stage. Professor Kuang-huan Lu, my colleague at the Center of Asian Studies, was most helpful in carefully reading the whole manuscript. To Mrs. Dorothy Canner, I wish to record my appreciation for her unfailing secretarial assistance.

I must also express my sincere thanks to the Very Reverend Joseph T. Cahill, C.M., President of St. John's University, Reverend Joseph I. Dirvin, C.M., Vice President for University Relations and Secretary of the University, Reverend John V. Newman, C.M., Special Assistant to the President, Dr. Paul T. Medici, Dean of the Graduate School of Arts and Sciences, for their constant guidance, and to Dr. Frank L. Kunkel, Editorial Director, Mrs. Julia Barone, Production Director, and the entire staff of the University Press for their sustained cooperation and assistance in bringing this project to completion.

Paul K. T. Sih

Assistant to the President for
International Studies and Education
and
Director of the Center of Asian Studies
St. John's University

January 1973

Chapter I

The Physical Setting of Taiwan

BY CHIAO-MIN HSIEH

I
Location

The island of Taiwan lies 100 miles east of mainland China. It is some 700 miles south of Japan, and 200 miles north of the Philippine Islands. Taiwan is thus midway between Japan and the Philippines and halfway between Shanghai and Hong Kong.

In earlier centuries, the intervening Ryukyu archipelago in the north formed stepping stones to Japan. To the south, the Bataan island arcs led to the Philippines. These three connections — with the coastal provinces of China to the West, with Japan to the North, and with the Philippines to the south -- have lured to Taiwan many different cultural groups, including Malayan aborigines, Chinese, Japanese, Spanish, and Dutch. All of these groups have helped to shape the history of Taiwan.

Thus Taiwan is not only saliently positioned between the Philippines and Okinawa, but also is an important strategic point in the festoon of islands running from the frozen Arctic along the Asiatic coast to the South China Sea along the western rim of the Pacific Ocean.

Taiwan includes as its administrative areas sixteen *hsien*, or counties, and five municipalities -- Taipei (the capital), Tainan, Keelung, Kaohsiung, and Taichung.

The shape of Taiwan is roughly that of a long oval, approximately 240 miles long from north to south, and ninety-eight miles wide from west to east at its broadest point. No place

1

in Taiwan is more than sixty miles from the sea. Its smooth coastline, totaling 708 miles in length, is bathed by the warm waters of the Kuroshio current (Japan current). Taiwan covers an area of 13,884 square miles, which is about one-third the size of the American state of Virginia, one-half the size of Ireland, a little larger than the Netherlands, and a trifle smaller than Switzerland. Latitudinally, it lies astride the Tropic of Cancer in a position comparable to that of Cuba.

II
Taiwan's Origin

Taiwan lies at the intersection of the Ryukyu and Philippines Islands arcs. These islands are curved so that their concave side faces the Asian continent. The mountain chain of Taiwan also forms an arc; however, its concavity faces not the continent but the Pacific. This striking contrast in curvature between Taiwan and the other islands of the festoon has kindled much interest and curiosity among geologists and geographers. Some believe that many years ago Taiwan was part of the continent and that the main mountain chain of Taiwan was virtually a coastal range on the China mainland, with the eastern border of the island being the real continental margin.

The structural alignment of Taiwan with the continent is the result of the thrust faulting which sliced the island into longitudinal belts. These overthrusts came from the southeast over the Pacific, and not from the northwest over the continent as they did both in the Ryukyu and the Philippines. While it is easy to see the disagreement of the structural form between the islands along the Asian continent, it is not surprising to find that the Neo-Cathaysian trend on the continent also shows a slight curvature facing inland, as manifested by the mountain ranges in the western part of Fukien province. When Taiwan suffered rather severe orogenic movements during the Tertiary and Quaternary periods, the arc became more pronounced. The fact that Taiwan cannot be grouped together with the Ryukyus and the Philippines is further illustrated by its rock formations. The oldest rocks in the Ryukyus are of the Paleozoic era; the rock basis of the Philippines consists of diorite (which is not as old as the Paleozoic). In Taiwan, the core of the cordillera is composed of schists, quartz, and gnesis, which can easily be linked with the old land mass of the Archean rocks in Fukien.

Physiographically, Taiwan is not bordered by deep ocean as are the Ryukyus and the Philippines. Taiwan Strait, which separates the island from the mainland, is a rather shallow sea, being from twenty to forty fathoms deep generally, and nowhere exceeding fifty fathoms. The continental coast, though rich in minor identations that are due to drowned valleys, indicating a relatively recent submergence of land, is generally straight; it apparently follows a dislocation line, as is suggested by its simple, straight, and relatively steep submarine slope. The west coast of Taiwan is occupied by flat alluvial plain and the shoreline is simple and straight. As indicated by the rather close submarine contour lines and their straightness, the west coast is also guided essentially by dislocation. Thus Taiwan Strait is a rift valley or grabem intervening between the Asiatic continent and Taiwan. This tectonic depression took place before the submergence of the land. Prior to this submergence, the sea floor was probably land surface of low relief, situated between the Taiwan coastal range and the old land of Fukien.

The rift valley of Taiwan Strait evidently resulted from restlessness of the earthy's crust, while faulting stretched the surface and created fissures in the crust. There are fissure eruptions in the Strait, issuing large amounts of lava and flooding the surface of the Strait bottom. They are characteristically bedded, so that successive floods have spread over the preceeding flows. The flat-lying sheet of lava was solidly cemented and rose only a little above sea level. The Penghu Islands (the Pescadores) are just such a dissected mesa of basalt.

From these bits of evidence — the contrasting curvature between the Ryukyu arc, the Philippine archipelago, and Taiwan; the structural alignment and rock correlation with the mainland; the character of the Strait's submarine configuration; the simple and smooth coast line of the island, and the existence of extensive basalt mesas formed through fissure eruptions — we may conclude that the island of Taiwan has long been in existence and was actually a part of the China mainland during early geological periods. Not until the Pleistocene epoch, when the Strait sank and formed a rift valley, was Taiwan separated from the continent and isolated as an island.

III
Landform Region

Taiwan is a mountainous island. About two-thirds of the area consists of rugged mountains. A tilted block traverses from northeast to southwest, forming a kind of backbone. The central part of the island is made up of four parallel anticlinal ranges which thrust up forty-eight peaks of 9,850 feet or more in height. Since the mountain chain is nearer to the eastern seaboard, the eastern half has many crags and steep slopes. The sea cliffs rise perpendicularly for 295 feet or more and then slope to heights as great as 9,850 feet; the western part has gentler slopes and less relief. It is on the western part of the island that many of the rivers cut the land into successive terraces and further build the alluvial plains sloping gently to the sea. Toward the north, the western plains gradually become narrower and higher; in the south, the plains are broader and more level. Because of the heavy rainfall in the subtropical climate, the rivers of Taiwan have been endowed with vigorous erosinal power. In the western part of the island, nearly all the rivers have precipitous upper valleys, incised meanders in the middle part, and characteristic terraces along the lower valley. On reaching the coastal area, the streams deposit their debris and build the alluvial plains.

Physiographically, Taiwan has three types of surface configurations, namely: mountains, which occupy about 8,886 square miles in area, forming 64 per cent of the whole island; plains and basins, 3,332 square miles covering 24 per cent of the island; and hills and tablelands the remaining 12 per cent of the total area.

The Taitung rift valley, the most conspicuous geologic feature of the island, is an elongated grabed in structure, lying between the eastern coastal rolling hills and the Central Mountains. The trench lies roughly northeast-southwest and meets the sea at both ends. This rift valley is seventy-seven miles long, yet in width averages only from five to ten miles. It appears like a deep slash into the mountainous surface of the island. The great fault scarp

LANDFORMS OF TAIWAN

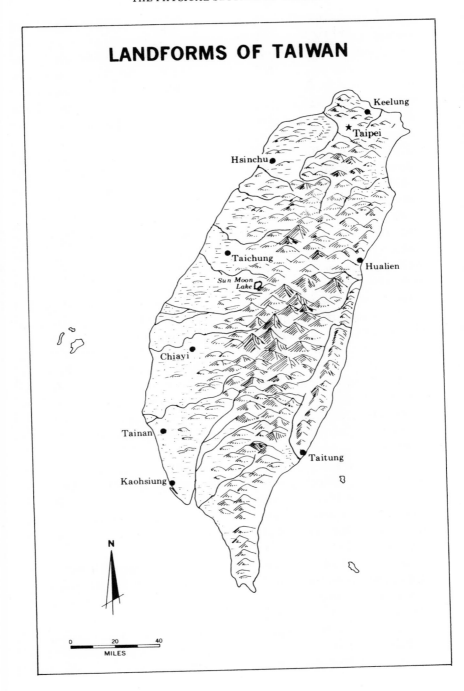

of the western edge of the depression, which is 3,936 to 4,592 feet in altitude, has been cut by many consequent rivers and has transported much debris to the foothills. Thus, it forms an irregular line at the foothills. Its many triangular facets penetrate the western side of the scarp. These triangular facets may have been caused by their being remnants of the former river valleys that were interrupted by the fault. The famous Tailukuo gorge is the representative feature of the valley. On the eastern edge of the trough, the fault line is not so prominent. The floor of the trough is covered by thick deposits of alluvial material brought down from the mountains by rivers that have cut sharp gorges and have formed alluvial fans.

The Taipei basin extends over an area of 155 square miles, with the shape of a triangle. The three sides of the basin are marked by fault lines. The basin is drained by the Tamshui River and its tributaries, the Keelung and the Shintien. The Keelung River flows from the northeast, meets the Shintien River, which comes from the south at the middle of the basin, and is led by the Tamshui which flows out of the basin at the northwest corner, and empties into the ocean. It is evident that the Taipei basin is a tectonic depression. Also, it was reported that in 1697 A.D. the center of the basin was still waterlogged. Therefore, it is believed that in a former geological period the basin was a lake. Later, as a consequence of the uplifting of this part of the earth's crust, the lake gradually disappeared. The floor of the basin is covered by a thin layer of alluvium, deposited by the Tamshui River and its tributaries.

In the central part of Taiwan, there is a depressed tract of relatively low relief, surrounded by rugged mountains that are about 100 feet high. The depressed tract is occupied by a series of intermontane basins, arranged lineally in a northeastern-south-western direction. The most important intermontane basin is that of Sun Moon Lake.

Sun Moon Lake, or Lake Candidius as it is also known, is the largest fresh-water lake in Taiwan and is noted for its beautiful scenery and water-power development. Lavish hotels, restaurants, and souvenir shops flourish along the lake shores.

The lake has an irregular outline, narrow and lozenge-shaped. The inflow from the river is barely sufficient to maintain the water level in the lake, and there was at one time danger of the lake becoming extinct. Recently, however, it has been used as the reservoir for generating electricty. A dam was constructed at the outlet and the water level was raised from 2385 to 2640 feet. This resulted in an expansion of 60 per cent in the size of the lake and is expected to prolong its life.

The western coastal part of Taiwan is in general a flat land consisting of low alluvial plains. It extends from Keelung in the north to Pingtung in the south. This area is about 200 miles long and ranges from five to twenty-five miles in width. When the rivers originate in the Central Mountains and flow out of the interior foothills into the plain, parallel with one another, their debris is deposited and forms a large number of alluvial fans. The plain is thus the coalescence of many alluvial fans and is underlain by recent alluvium. Flowing with a low gradient on the broad alluvial plain, the rivers meander sluggishly across it to the sea.

The coastal plain is monotonously flat and when it reaches the sea, the shore is marked by wide tidal flats. Especially in the south, from Kaohsiung Peninsula to the Choshui River, shore currents have built up spits, off-shore bars, marshes, and many shallow lagoons. The lagoon at Kaohsiung, with its complete shelter and spacious holdground, has been used as an important naval base.

The coastal plain is narrow in the northern part of the island and gradually becomes wide as it extends into the south, especially near Tainan. According to the well-drill record near Hsinchu, the sand deposits extend as deep as 250 feet, without reaching bedrock. The strong winds, the heavy deposits of sand, and the early colonial development of the region, all of which led to the disappearance of the original vegetation, favor the development of sand dunes and barchanes which extend from two to four miles and with an average height of sixty-five feet. These barchanes are subject to migration. The survey indicates that a barchane migrated 1640 feet in the eight years from 1926 to 1933, averaging 205 feet for every year.

The coastal plain is still rising. The land is being elevated, and the parallel rivers from east to west are becoming extended rivers which produce new alluvial fans. There thus appear some complex fans, combining old alluvial fans with new ones.

The western coastal plain ends at the city of Pingtung, which is located on a plain extending from north to south thirty-one miles long and twelve miles wide, forming a rectangle. The plain is bordered on the east by the Chaochow fault line. These alluvial fans also pushed the lower Tamshui River to the westward.

While the eastern coast is precipitous cliff, the Ilan plain, which is the delta of the Ilan River, is the most conspicuous alluvial plain in eastern Taiwan. The plain forms an equilateral triangle, each side of which is about ninety-eight feet long. The base of the plain is formed by part of the coast and its apex penetrates the Central Mountains. The Ilan River originates in the Central Mountains and bisects the plain from its apex to the sea. The apex is about 525 feet high, and the Ilan River radiates from it for about fourteen miles; the radius of the fan is about twelve miles in length. On this alluvial fan, part of the water seeps underground and reappears at the end of the fan.

IV
Coast

The characteristics of the coasts of Taiwan are the result of seawave erosion. They present a variety of aspects. In some places, many inlets, bays, and islands are to be found; in others, long stretches of unbroken coast are in evidence. Some of these coasts are bordered by stretches of low-lying sand; others are rockbound. Along some coasts deep water is found, and along others very shallow marshes are seen. Variations in type of rock, in geological structure, in quantity of river deposits, and in stability of the earth's crust all act to bring about these different forms of coastline.

The coasts of Taiwan are of four types: the eastern coast presents a fault coast line; the western, a raised coast line; the northern, a rias submergent type; and the southern, a coral reef type.

The Eastern Fault Coastline

Starting from Santienlin at the northeastern tip of the island, and ending at the Hengchun peninsula at the south end, the eastern Taiwan coast is rather straight.

The eastern coast is composed of hard rocks, such as sandstone, slate, and limestone. The strike of these rocks is parallel to the coast. Along the coast are found marine terraces and abrasion benches; earthquakes occur frequently; all this indicates that the eastern coast is unstable along a dislocation line.

The Western Raised Coasts

In the western part of Taiwan appears a raised coastline, which is straight, monotonous, and flat; as a result the coast lacks harbors. The shallowness of the water prevented the sea waves from approaching the coast; thus there is no wave erosion, except where the waves have pushed the sand to build up off-shore bars, splits, lagoons, and marshes. The lagoons of Taiwan are used to raise fish; the marshes are used to raise weeds.

Starting from the south bank of the Tamshui River, and ending at Fonglien in the south, the western coastal line is 255 miles in length. This coast is composed of gravel, sand, and clay. As a result of the large amount of sand together with strong winds in this rain-shadow dry area, many sand dunes have developed. There are sometimes from 650 to 1000 feet in length and attain a height of several feet. Tidal flats have also developed, sometimes two and a half or three miles in length, bounded by offshore bars, spits, and sandbars. Shallow lagoons form, usually less than three feet in depth; their water is not brackish, but is sea water, and they are usually used for fishing ponds and as salt fields.

Although most of the western coastline is straight and flat, there is in the southwestern part a drowned valley, at the Lower Tamshui, which presents an important coast landform. This valley was not formed by waves or tidal forces; it can be explained only as the result of drowning.

The northern drowned coasts

The drowned coasts of northern Taiwan extend for fifty-three miles from Santienlin in the northeastern corner of the island to the mouth of the Tamshui River. The rocks of those coastal areas include slate, sandstone, and shale. The strike of these rocks and the structure alignment is at a right angle with the coast line; therefore the coasts are irregular and are made up of peninsulas and bays, which form rias types of coasts. The port of Keelung is

in the rias coast, full of abrasion benches, sea caves, wave-cut
arches, notch stacks, and chimneys. Elevated coastal phenomena
such as coastal terraces, raised mushroom rocks, and raised
wave-cut arches also appear. These features all indicate that the
coasts in northern Taiwan have experienced much eustatic change.

The south coral reef coasts

The coral reefs appear all around the south coasts of Taiwan.
They also appear in the north near Keelung and on the eastern and
western coasts. However, conditions such as rocky shores, clear
water and high temperature of the water, all combine to favor the
growth of coral reefs along the south coast. These fringing reefs
surround the southern tip of the island.

V
Temperature

Taiwan's climate is characterized by high temperatures, heavy
rainfall, and strong winds. The factors which control the climate
are the island's position relative to ocean and the Asian continent,
the arrangement of its mountains, and ocean currents.

Summer in Taiwan is long and hot, but winter is very short
and mild. Throughout the island, the annual mean temperature is
no more than seventy degrees. The isotherms mean annual
temperature run from west to east, bisecting the island and
running parallel to the latitudes. As the latitudes decrease, the
annual temperatures increase. Thus, there is little difference in
annual temperature between east and west, but there is a great
difference between north and south. For example, Keelung, on the
northern coast, has an annual average temperature of 71.2 degrees,
while the annual average temperature found in Hengchun at the
southern tip of the island is 75.9 degrees. As one travels from
north to south, with each degree of latitude one finds an increase
of 1.5 degrees in temperature.

July is Taiwan's hottest month, and the heat is practically as
great in the north as in the south. For that month, the average
temperature at Keelung is 82.7 degrees while at Hengchun it is
81.5 degrees, showing a difference of less than 1.2 degrees. Also,
the July temperature is not too much different between the east

coast and the west coast of the island. Maximum temperatures in excess of 102.2 degrees have been recorded.

In January and February, the coldest months, the temperature differs greatly from north to south, Keelung have a monthly average of 59.3 degrees and Hengchun, 68.9 degrees, showing a difference of 9.6 degrees. Snow is rarely seen in the lowlands although the summits of the lofty mountains are covered with snow for a short time. The maximum temperature in January can reach more than 86 degrees.

In January and February the temperature varies not only from north to south, but also from east to west, being higher in the east than in the west. This is because the ocean current is stronger on the eastern coast than along the western coast.

VI
Rainfall

Taiwan has abundant rainfall throughout the year. Many stations have an average annual rainfall of 98.5 inches. But the rainfall in Taiwan is by no means evenly distributed. In general, the eastern coast has more rainfall than the western coast, and lowlands receive less rain than mountain slopes, where the air masses are forced to ascend and discharge their moistures. The isohyets indicating 78.98 inches coincide with many places on the 1,600 feet contour lines. The east coast has a heavier rainfall (more than 78.8 inches) than the west coast, owing partly to the prolonged winter rains and partly to the rugged terrain. The areas receiving more than 148 inches of annual rainfall are found in the northern and southern extremities and on some of the high mountain peaks of the Central Mountain ranges. Houshaoliao, on the northern tip of Taiwan near Keelung, has recorded for the past thirty-eight years an average annual rainfall of 258.9 inches with a recorded maximum of 331.28 inches in 1912, making it one of the wettest spots in East Asia.

The most striking feature of Taiwan's rainfall is that the dry and rainy seasons occur in the north and in the south at opposite times. In the north, the rainy season is from October to March as in the cities of Keelung, Ilan, and Taipei. During this period, Keelung has a precipitation of sixty-four inches which is 56 per cent of the total rainfall of 114 inches. On the other hand, during these months the south enjoys continually fine and delightful weather and irrigation is a necessary agricultural practice. In the south, the rainy season lasts from April to September as in the cities of Hengchun, Tainan, and Taitung. During these months, Hengchun has a rainfall of seventy-nine inches which makes up 88 per cent of its total rainfall of ninety inches.

As the air rises over the mountains, condensation causes clouds and rain. The winds that reach the south during these months have lost the greater portion of their moisture and so bring clear dry weather.

During the summer months, from April to September, the southwest monsoon prevails over southern Taiwan. The southwest monsoon is light and weak. Under the hot sun, frequent local thunderstorms occur, bringing abundant rainfall to southern Taiwan. Strong winds occur only during the occasional typhoons. It is during this period that the northern part is rather dry.

Not only is the rainy season opposite in north and south, but the character of the rainfall is also different. In the north, the rainfall, brought by the northeast monsoon, seldom comes in torrents but generally falls at a moderate rate. The cold, drizzling rains are depressing. Consequently, rainy days are many and drawn out. It is due to these rainy days that Keelung is called "rainy port." The rainfall in the south, caused by local convectional storms and typhoons is characterized by frequent thunderstorms and tremendous downpours. On the east coast, south of Hualien, the northeast monsoon blows nearly parallel to the shore, and brings hardly any rain in spite of the dull weather. The western coastal plain lies within the rain shadow of the Central Mountains, and as a result, the central part of the west coast is the driest part of the island.

VII
Winds

Being located on the eastern side of the great land mass of Asia and on the western edge of the Pacific Ocean, Taiwan's wind patterns are largely determined by the monsoons. In winter the cold Asiatic continent develops an immense thermal anticyclone from which great surges of dry and cold air spread oceanward; this is the northwest winter monsoon of China. Owing to the deflection force caused by the earth's rotation in Northern Hemisphere, these northwest winds become a northeast monsoon bringing moisture from the ocean by the time it reaches Taiwan. In summer, on the other hand, a thermally-induced low pressure replaces the winter anticyclone over Asia. The pressure gradient is consequently the reverse of that which prevails in winter and moist tropical and subtropical maritime air masses originating over the low latitudes of the Pacific Ocean converge upon eastern Asia. This is China's weaker and more intermittent southeast summer monsoon. This southeast wind changes to a southwest monsoon when it reaches Taiwan, due to the deflection force of the earth's rotation. Therefore, the winds in Taiwan prevail from the northeast, having originated over the cold land mass of eastern Siberia (throughout the winter months, from the end of October to the end of March). During this period the northeast winds coincide with the northeast trade winds and the velocity increases immensely, especially in the north coastal region. These strong winds cause much damage to crops. In the northwest coastal area of Taiwan, which is directly exposed to the northeast gales, the farmers have set up lines of windbreaks composed of trees in order to protect their crops.

In summer (from the early part of May to the later part of September) the winds in Taiwan are from the southwest, having originated over tropical areas. The wind velocity of this southwest wind is far less than that of the northeast monsoon. Since the southwest monsoon is gentle and brings with it some rainfall, it has a favorable effect on the crops in this dry area.

VIII
Typhoons

Typhoons are tropical cyclones of a certain degree of intensity. In North and Central America they are known as *hurricanes*, and in India as *cyclones*. In the Philippines these storms are called *bayuios*, and in Australia, *willy-willies*. The Chinese name for typhoons is *chu-feng*, meaning "wind from all quarters."

Despite the different names, these tropical cyclones all have essentially the same origin, structure, and behavior. They are small low-pressure areas forming revolving storms and are very nearly circular in shape. They are the most violent storms experienced by the mariner.

As to monthly distribution, typhoons are most frequent from July to October. This four-month period is commonly referred to as typhoon season in East Asia.

The occurrence of typhoons has had certain effects on the rainfall pattern in Taiwan. Although the wide variation in the amounts of annual rainfall and even the monthly means are sufficient to mask any correlation between it and typhoon occurrences, further investigation using the five-day means of rainfall shows that such a correlation does exist.

Typhoons are the most destructive natural force, apart from earthquakes, in the island of Taiwan. Their destructiveness is due to strong winds and heavy rainfall. Horizontal pressures during squalls may reach 100 pounds per square foot and typhoons may carry two quarts of rain per cubic yard of air.

The combination of strong winds, low barometric pressures, and the pounding force of the typhoon generates sea swells and destructive waves which cause major damage in coastal areas.

The sudden heavy rainfall brought by typhoons makes many rivers flood, destroying houses, damaging crops, and even causing injury to persons. In Taiwan hardly a year passes without the occurrence of typhoons which brings tremendous rain to the rice crop. No other rice cultivation area in the Far East has suffered so much from typhoons as has Taiwan. It is impossible to prevent typhoons from visiting the island, but it is possible to make accurate forecasts of their coming, and to predict the routes they will take.

VIIII
Hydrography

Since the general configuration of Taiwan is that of a tilted block with all the streams originating from the high Chungyang Shan, the island presents a radial drainage pattern. With less than sixty miles between the high mountain peaks and the coastal margins, the rivers in Taiwan are naturally short and swift. The Choshui, the longest river in Taiwan, is only 105 miles long. Only six rivers exceed sixty miles in length and only twenty are more than thirty miles long. Among these twenty rivers, sixteen flow toward the west and only four toward the east. Since the main divide of the island lies near the eastern coast, and since the surface of the eastern part is much steeper than that of the western part, the rivers of the east are shorter and swifter than those of the west. The rivers of Taiwan are shorter even than those of Japan, which are notoriously lacking in length. The shortness of the rivers is an important characteristic of Taiwan.

A second characteristic of the rivers in Taiwan is their steepness. Most rivers in Taiwan originate from peaks of more than 6,000 feet elevation, and empty into the sea within a short distance from their source. A steep gradient and a high velocity result as a consequence of this fact. Thus the gradient of the rivers in Taiwan may be the greatest in the world.

The third characteristic of the rivers of Taiwan is the distinct seasonal change of hydrography. Except in the northeastern part of the island, the rainfall is concentrated in the summer, and the water level in the river rises to its highest level from June to September, and reaches its lowest point from December to January. In the summer, the stormy nature of rainfall, aided by the steep gradient of the rivers, causes great flooding of all the rivers.

On the contrary, during the winter season, the rainfall decreases and the water level in rivers is also lowered, the rivers thus becoming dry creeks. Because of this seasonal change of hydrography, the rivers in Taiwan are not navigable and the lack of water in winter is a great handicap in irrigation.

Another characteristic of Taiwan's rivers is that they contain a great volume of sand. On this subtropical island, the stormy rainfall, together with the fragile rock base and the destruction of the forest cover in mountain areas all combine to create a great erosive force. The rivers contain a great volume of sand and gravel during flood time. In mountain areas the rivers cut deep gorges and waterfalls and rapids often occur. On reaching the gentle slopes, the velocity of the rivers decreases and the carrying capacity of the rivers also diminishes. Thus, the rivers deposit their debris and build up alluvial fans in the outlets of the mountain area and in the delta near the sea. On the western coast along the mouths of the rivers, there are sand deposits of various widths, from 1.5 to three miles. This indicates that deposition is still in process.

In summary, the rivers of Taiwan are short, swift, flooded, and sandy. All these characteristics are unfavorable for navigation. With the exception of the Tamshui, which is navigable for a small steamboat of fifty tons between Tamshui and Taipei, none of the other rivers in Taiwan is navigable. In spite of the fact that the rivers of Taiwan are difficult to manage, as these rivers descend rapidly from steep slopes, they are, on the other hand, able to supply a large amount of power for the production of electricity, an important factor in the industrial development of Taiwan. Also, the rivers have been utilized to the benefit of agriculture, that is, by providing the means for irrigation. The southwestern plain of Taiwan is noted as the island's granary, but the dry season during the winter has prevented it from producing large amounts of agricultural products. From the early days, the rivers in this part of Taiwan have been used efficiently for irrigation. The Chianan irrigation system is a good example of the utilization of the waters of Tsengwen river and the Choshui river.

Three broad ground-water regions in Taiwan can be recognized: the mountain region, the foothill area, and the coastal plains. The storage of ground water is limited in the mountain region and the foothill area, making the coastal plains the sole storehouse for ground water. In the mountain region and foothill area not only is the reservoir of ground water limited, but also cultivated land and settlement are sparse. Thus, these two areas have less demand and less value for developing ground water, while on the coastal plain the rich ground-water reservoir, together with the large population and great amounts of cultivated acreage, make the area promising for the development of underground water resources.

X
Soil Groups

The interplay of different soil-forming factors gives the soils in

Taiwan a great diversity. However, as a result of the island's landforms the soils vary more according to vertical zonation than horizontal. In traveling from the western coast to the Central Mountain area eleven various soil groups are encountered. In the west are encountered first salines (solonchaks) and planosols (paddy soils), then alluvial soils. Next, we cross the hills and terraces where the lateritic soils are found. Proceeding ahead, the red and yellow soils are seen, and after climbing this hilly land, it will be noticed that the podzolic profile is more prominent, recognizing the characteristic gray-brown soils. When the top of the mountainous area is finally reached, podzolic and stony mountain soils are encountered.

Because of the various soil groups which exist in this cross-section, land use differs accordingly, from the coastal flatlands to the interior mountains. In the west to east journey, one sees only salt fields and some fish culture along the coast; proceeding inland sugar cane, rice and paddy fields, citrus fruit, and barren steep slopes are encountered; climbing to the high mountains one is surrounded by huge forests or waste lands.

Soil fertility in Taiwan can be briefly summarized as follows: cultivated soil in Taiwan is mainly of the alluvial type. The fertility of this alluvial soil is rather high and its physical properties are well-suited for growing crops. As to the soil texture, loamy soil occupies a large area, while the extent of sandy soil is limited. The area occupied by clay soil is by no means small, but the clay soil is somewhat loamy in texture; thus it does not have the disadvantage of being too heavy. In Taiwan there are no soils which are excessively acidic or alkaline, most of them ranging from slightly acidic to neutral in reaction. The organic content of the soil is, in most places, around 2 per cent, which cannot be considered low. In general, then, Taiwan's soils are in good condition. If these soils are well managed, they can provide a sound foundation for increased development of agriculture.

The less productive soils in Taiwan are the lateritic and the red and yellow soils which are distributed in the Hsinchu and Taichung foothills along the western side of the Chungyan Shan area. Of the two, lateritic soil is the poorer. Having developed in a hot and humid climate, its base content has been thoroughly leached, and it is strongly acidic. In addition, the calcium, potash, and phosphorus content is a reliable index of the soil's productivity. The low productivity in southern Taiwan soil is mainly due to their deficient supplies of organic matter. However, with proper treatment this soil still can be made fertile. The soils along Taiwan's coastal areas are also low in productivity, mainly because of their strong alkalinity.

The most productive soils in Taiwan are the alluvial soils, which show a slightly acidic or neutral reaction. Some examples of these soils are found along river banks in Taichung and Kaohsiung, and in the plains of Pingtung. These fertile soils have these three very salutary qualities: first, they range from slightly acidic to neutral; second, they have a high organic content -- around 3 per cent. With these three characteristics, these soils are structurally sound and have an abundance of effective plant nutrients, including calcium, potash, and phosphorus.

The soils of Taiwan react very well to nitrogen, phosphorus, and potash fertilizers. The soils which react most noticeably to phosphorus are the lateritic and salt soils, while those which can be effectively treated by potash fertilizer are the lateritic and the red and yellow soils.

Farmers in Taiwan have long suffered from the heavy texture of the marine-deposited soils, for these heavy soils are rather difficult to work. During sunny weather they become muddy and sticky. Along with the improvement of the irrigation systems to meet the water shortage, the structure of this marine-deposited soil could be improved by adding lime organic matter. The introduction of agricultural machines may also greatly help in solving the different problem of plowing.

The soils of southern Taiwan are very low in organic matter content, and this is the main reason for their low productivity. Therefore, green manure should be widely used in order to maintain a level of organic matter ncessary to raise the capacity of the soil to support plant growth.

XI
Natural Vegetation

With high mountains, high temperature, and abundant rainfall, Taiwan has a rich flora. However, different groups of settlers, who came to the island at various times, cleared the natural vegetation from all western plains suitable for agriculture. At present, approximately 68 per cent of the island, estimated at 6,158,975 acres, is still forested. About 80 per cent of this forested acreage is covered with trees, while the remaining 20 per cent is covered by shrubs.

Four main types of vegetation are dominant, namely, broad-leaved evergreen forests, mixed forests, coniferous forests, and steppe and shrub and bamboo. The total number of species of commercial importance reaches about 100, ranging from tropical hardwood growing at sea level to spruce, hemlocks, and firs occurring at higher elevations.

Of the total forest area in Taiwan (4,563,115 acres), the broad-leaved evergreen forest has an area of 3,356,235 acres or 73 per cent of the total. Next comes the mixed forest which has 665,157 acres or 14 per cent of the total. The coniferous forest, which is the most important economically, represents only 417,967 acres, or 10 per cent of the total. The bamboo has the least area in the total forest in the island, with 123,755 acres, or about 3 per cent.

The vertical distribution of Taiwan's forests demonstrates an unusual rich variety and distinct zonations, which include the tropical, sub-tropical, temperate, and cold temperate zones. Because of the latitudinal extension of the island, the climatic condition in Taiwan is quite different between the north and south.

XII
Mineral Resources

The main resources of Taiwan are agricultural rather than mineral. The chief minerals produced on the island are coal, gold, and sulphur; other mineral resources of importance include copper, petroleum, and salt. While agricultural production depends on climatic conditions and soil fertility, the mineral resources are related to geological basis. The low mineralization in Taiwan is chiefly due to lack of widespread igneous intrusion, which is usually assoicated with mineralforming processes. Despite the diligent survey by the Japanese under their colonial policy between the years 1920 and 1940, and the efforts of today's

Chinese geologists to discover more mineral wealth, the wide-spread distribution of sedimentary rock of recent age which might have more petroleum reserve makes it unlikely that important mineral reserves still remain to be discovered. The most important rock formations in terms of minerals are the Tertiary beds of shale and sandstone. Bituminous coal is found interbedded with shale and pools of petroleum and reserves of natural gas. Gold veins are located in the extreme northeast's metamorphic rock; copper reserves are found in the crystalline schist formation on the east flank of the central Mountains; and sulphur in economic quantities is available throughout the areas of volcanic rocks.

Chapter II

Early Stages of the Sinicization of Taiwan, 230-1683

BY TING-YEE KUO

The vast expanse of the territories of China, though one and the same in being integral parts of China, varied in their periods of development. Taiwan, on account of its geographical location, has been somewhat late in its entering into the Chinese entity. But still it has been a part of China for at least more than three hundred years; and towards the end of the nineteenth century, the rapid development of this late comer has made it more modernized than its older fellow-members. The Chinese who first moved into Taiwan from across the sea were almost all South Fukienese and Hakkas. They were Chinese with full national consciousness and strong pioneering spirit. They crossed the sea and carried with them into Taiwan Chinese traditions and cultural and technical backgrounds. Yet their achievement in planting the roots there was not easy; it was an accomplishment without any official or governmental support or encouragement. It was an achievement entirely by these early Chinese, built with sustained and persistent efforts, built in slow accumulation of days into months and months into years, a growth of unceasing struggle and endless toil marked by their blood and sweat.

The earliest date of China's influence spreading into Taiwan was in the times of Wu, one of the three states of the post-Han Three Kingdoms period, a state founded in the Lower Yangtze area. In the year 230 A.D., Sun Ch'uan, first emperor of Wu, was recorded as having sent a commander leading an expeditionary force into Taiwan. Nothing came out of the expedition, but the record shows that the knowledge or information about the island was quite accurate at that time, which called it by the name of I-chou. In the beginning of the 7th century, Yang-ti, second Emperor of the Sui Dynasty, having repeatedly failed to bring the island to submission by persuasion, finally had to resort to force. He sent an expedition of over ten thousand men to land at the middle west coast of the island, and had the islanders beaten in three successive battles. But the effort led to naught as the Sui government soon undertook campaigns in Korea, which was followed by internal uprisings that brought the dynasty to an end.

The Tang Dynasty was strong and successful in the early decades, but its attention was concentrated to the northeastern and northwestern frontiers, and nothing was planned on Taiwan, which, since the Sui times, was renamed Liu-chiu (same Chinese characters as the Ryukyu Islands), a name to be used in the following period, for about seven hundred years. In the early part of the 9th century, mainland people in increasing numbers moved to live on the Penghu Islands (the Pescadores). Shih Chien-wu, a Tang poet, moved there with his clansmen from the present day Chekiang area of the mainland coast, keeping up correspondence with his friends and relatives of his native land from time to time.

In the 12th century, the southern Sung court moved the capital of China to the city of Hangchou, hence the development of the coastal areas of southeast China and the expansion of overseas trade became the steady policy and active enterprise of the central government. Chao Ju-kua, well-known author then in charge of shipping and trade duties of the port of Chuanchou of Fukien, recorded that at the time Penghu was considered a part of the district of Chin-chiang of the prefecture of Chuanchou, and therefore as Chinese territory, and that the inhabitants there were close neighbors to the villages of Taiwan, and contacts between them were becoming increasingly more frequent.[1]

In the 13th century, when the North China Juchen state of Chin was conquered by the Mongols, many of the Chinese people inhabiting the Yellow River valley, fleeing from the scourge of war, took the sea route to move south, and rough seas often sent their ships to Taiwan, "henceforth they settled there, lived on farming the soil, and some might have moved and failed to maintain contact with the parent group, thus after a few generations would fail to keep track of their own origin, except that the tongue they spoke would remain unchanged."[2] Those were probably the earliest mainland Chinese who came to settle in Taiwan. On the fall of Southern Sung, more Chinese moved to Taiwan to flee from the hazards of war.

In the 13th century, the Mongol government of China installed a local administrative official, the *hsun chien ssu*, or sub-district magistrate, at Penghu, thus an office formally representing political authority was established there. This also shifted Penghu to be part of the district of T'ung-an of the prefecture of Chuanchou, and record shows that it had a population of about 200 households, equivalent to about 1,000 heads. Wang Ta-yuan, a man with rich overseas travelling experience, wrote at the time that these poeple were mostly natives of Chuanchou, and that they lived in thatched roof huts, making a living as handicraftsmen or tradesmen, carrying Taiwan products, such as sulphur, beeswax, golddust, millet, and the skin or furs of deer, leopard and doe to the mainland and mainland products to Taiwan, bringing closer ties between the two and greatly improving the economic life of Taiwan, a land which Wang had visited in person.[3] Kublai Khan, Mongol Emperor of China, sent an envoy to Taiwan to try to win the allegiance of the people and thus to make the island officially Chinese territory, but he failed to gain any of his desired results.

In the early years of the Ming Dynasty, Tai-tsu, the founder, in view of that the Mongols were still a threat to the northern frontier, and that a lesson should be learned from the disastrous failures Kublai Khan suffered from his sea adventures in Japan, took a passive attitude in his policy towards the high seas, and no active undertakings were entertained towards oversea lands, which naturally included Taiwan. (At this time, the Liu-chiu or Ryukyu Islands of today had become the vassal state of the Ming Empire. Thus Taiwan, then under the name of Liu-chiu, as mentioned above, was renamed Hsiao-liu-chiu, or Minor Liu-chiu. Other names were also applied to identify Taiwan, such as Chi-lung shan (Hen-roost Mountain), Pei-kang (North Port), Tung-fan (East Barbarians), or other phonetic equivalents of Taiwan such as T'ai-yuan, Ta-wan, Ta-yuan or T'ai-wan).

Then when the Japanese pirates (wo-k'ou) infested the Chinese coast, the Ming government ordered the closing of the coast. Penghu was thought of as uneasy to protect and control, and plans of moving the people from the island were contemplated. Along the coast from Shantung in the north to Fukien in the south, walled garrison forts were built and garrison forces posted to defend against the Japanese. In 1388, the Penghu local administrative office was abolished and the people there moved to Changchou and Chuanchou on the Fukien coast. This was to deprive the raiders of convenient places to fall upon for supplies, a policy similar to the closing of the coast, which means moving people and supplies from the coast while keeping strong garrison posts there.

In the beginning of the 15th century, Emperor Cheng-tsu ascended the throne, and revoked his father's policies. This change brought about the famous overseas voyages of Cheng Ho, with the Taiwan Strait serving as the route for everyone of his seven trips. Although Cheng Ho himeslf might not have visited Taiwan, some of his ships and men surely had. Thus there were left in Taiwan a number of anecdotes related to Cheng Ho and his lieutenant Wang San-pao (Ching-hung).

Chinese endeavours in long voyages over the high seas began not later than the 2nd century B.C. In the 8th century A.D. there were Chinese establishing rule and claiming authority in the South Sea Islands. In the 13th and 14th centuries, the navigation of the Indian Ocean was almost completely dominated by the Chinese. The influence of the voyages and activities of Cheng Ho was not limited to the revival of Chinese overseas trade and the restoration of Chinese prestige, it also gave encouragement to the people of the coastal regions to renew their interest in oversea adventures. This of course was also influenced by the stimulus given by the appearance of Europeans along the coast of Kwangtung, Fukien and Chekiang in the 16th century.

In 1558, the main force of the Japanese raiders shifted to the Fukien coast. The Chinese sea adventurers of the Fukien-Kwangtung area, traditionally called pirates, responded to the occasion with a corresponding burst of activities, led by such leaders as Wu P'ing, Lin Tao-ch'ien and Lin Feng, and made the seas of the Taiwan-Penghu area their favorite rendezvous or preying grounds. When Lin Tao-ch'ien and Lin Feng were each being routed by government forces, both took the course of retreating to the central or southern parts of Taiwan, to ports such as Pei-kang or Luerhmen, each with followers numbering several thousand, thus drawing Ming government forces to frequent the area for patrol and suppression.

After the suppression of two Lin's, the Ming government restored the sub-magistrate office *(hsun-chien-ssu)* of Penghu, with garrison forces installed in the warm season, thus reviving the Chinese authority there. In the beginning of the 17th century, the pirate being still very active, the Ming government decided to place a permanent garrison force in Penghu, with reinforcements in battle duty and patrol duty units for the use of guarding Taiwan.

The most prominent leader active in the Fukien coastal seas at this time was one by the name of Yen Ssu-ch'i. He was a native of the district of Hai-ch'eng of the prefecture of Changchou. Being oppressed by the mighty and persecuted by officials, he took refuge to the high seas, and his ability in handling ships and trade soon promoted him to wealth and prominence, which he in turn made use of to help the needy and to win friends. Among his partners one most noted was Cheng Chih-lung (I-quan), native of the district of Nanan of the prefecture of Chuanchou. They owned a number of ships engaged in trade between Fukien and Japan.

In 1620, they made the port of Pei-kang in central Taiwan their permanent base. Four years later, the Dutch occupied what is present day Anping in Taiwan, but their influence was limited to what is the present day Tainan area in southwest Taiwan. At the time there were Chinese living in Taiwan by several tens of thousands engaged in farming or trade, all from the Changchou and Chuanchou area, native lands of Yen and Cheng. In 1625 Yen Ssu-ch'i died and Cheng Chih-lung became the top leader, in command of several hundred ships and several thousand followers. His wise and winning leadership spread his fame and attracted more of his kinsmen, clan members, and fellow natives to cross the sea to join him, thus rapidly increasing his influence and holdings in Taiwan.

In 1628, Cheng accepted the authority of the Ming government and claimed allegiance to the Ming Empire. Thus Taiwan was definitely joined to the mainland, and contact between the two was made easier and more frequent. Cheng "undertook to move by seagoing ships people suffering from hunger by several tens of thousands to settle in Taiwan. He gave each man three taels of silver, and every three men a draft cow, in order that they might start opening up arable lands for farming and move on the road to self-sustainment. Thus villages and towns soon came into being."[4]

This shows that the Chinese government had engaged in large

scale planned migration of people to Taiwan. It also shows therefore that the authority of the Chinese government had by that time been established in Taiwan. At this time, the Dutch in Taiwan numbered about 2,000. They lived inside the city while the Chinese farmed in the rural areas.

The Dutch presence in Taiwan lasted nominally for thirty-eight years (1624-1662). Their actual rule was limited to Hung-mao-ch'eng (Zeelandia, also called *Tai-wan-ch'eng* or *Ch'ih-kan-ch'eng*, which is the Anping of today), Ch'ih-kan-chieh (Sakum, which is the Tainan of today), and several strongholds in the present day Keelung area. The rest, vast rural areas, were all inhibited by Chinese engaged in farming or trade, paying part of the rice and sugar they raised to the Dutch East India Company. Constantly under the oppression and exploitation of the Dutch, they rose in 1652 in revolt under the leadership of Kuo Huai-i. The up-rising failed and 8,000 of them died.

In 1662, Cheng Cheng-kung (Koxinga), the son and successor of Cheng Chih-lung, succeeded in ousting the Dutch from Taiwan and restored the land to the Chinese. He made the city of Ch'ih-kan-chieh the east capital, or the prefectural capital of the prefect of Ch'en-t'ien. The district of T'ienhsing was established in the north (present day district of Chia-i) and the district of Wannien was established in the south. A sub-magistrate, *an-fu-ssu*, was installed in Penghu. This marks the beginning of the division of Taiwan into Chinese local administrative units, and the establishment of local administrative government there.

Cheng Cheng-kung also arranged for the settlement of the officers and men taking part in the war against the Dutch. He engaged them in the opening up of virgin lands, in forestry and fishery projects, and in the organization of military farms in the Chinese tradition, combining garrison duty to farm work. The Manchus, in conquering the Ming government of the Chinese, became the enemy of Cheng who refused to shift his allegiance.

The Manchu government of the Ching Dynasty therefore committed themselves to the policy of "continental embargo" to isolate Taiwan, ordering all people of the coastal area to move inland to behind a certain demarcation line, and prohibiting even a single piece of board to be sent adrift in the sea. In spite of such measures, more people from Fukien and Kwangtung, being uprooted from their homesteads, moved to Taiwan to join Cheng.

He arranged for the settlement of everyone of them, exhorting them "to keep their faith in loyalty, to face hardships with courage, to follow the call of righteousness, and to live and work with fellow members in harmony."[5]

Cheng maintained discipline among his followers, was prompt and fair in awarding reward and punishment, and everyone became public spirited and law abiding. Many leaders of the native tribes came to express their allegiance. He treated them with parties and showered them with gifts, and visited the native areas in person to show the government's appreciation. It was recorded that "the natives, men and women, swarmed the road in coming out to greet him." The natives were backward in their farming, knowing not how to use farm implements. He took the advice of Yang Yin, his director of finance, and sent iron plows, hoes, and harrows, together with trained farm draft cows, to all native tribes, with experienced farmers to teach them plowing, planting and harvesting.[6] This increased their crops and improved their livelihood, and made them more glad and willing to follow the government.

Unfortunately Cheng died a premature death, but what he did had laid the political and economic foundations for the later development of Taiwan. His son, Cheng Ching, succeeded to the leader's chair with Ch'en Yung-hua serving as chief adviser, carried out the unfinished work by developing the institutions and measures initiated by the deceased leader to their consummation.

Cheng Cheng-kung based his administration upon rigorous and unrelenting discipline, while Ch'en, the succeeding chief adviser, shifted to leniency, with judgments passed upon and punishments dealt all tending to be fair and forgiving. This won the gratitude of the people, and everyone heartily turned to be good and refrain from offenses, until lost things picked up were always returned, and market prices offered were always fair without overcharging. In economic policies, the new administration emphasized population census and tax registration, and the encouragement of farming and sericulture. This led to the disappearance of loafers, the gradual extension in the opening up of the virgin land of the natives, and the increase in acreage in cultivated fields. It also encouraged the planting of sugar cane and the production of sugar. It reformed the process for the manufacture of salt. This increased the revenues of the government and enriched the supplies of the people's dining table.[7]

The natives were thus led to appreciate further the value of "industry in farming and the necessity of savings, and such practices led to more households with substantial coffers. Many native areas displayed well grown trees shading clean and adequately roomed houses, comparing not unfavorably with mainland villages."[8] In trade, the new administration expanded overseas trading, encouraged the importation of goods from the mainland to be re-shipped to the South Seas and to Japan. A trade agreement was signed with the English East India Company allowing the Company trade advantages, indicating that it had a more enlightened attitude than the Manchu government. In culture and education, a Confucian temple was built and schools were founded for developing the talented and nourishing leadership. A higher academy was established at the capital Ch'en-t'ien-fu and lower level schools were installed in local and native centers. Civil service examinations were held at designated regular intervals.[9] Youths of the native tribes studying in rural schools were entitled to certain privileges such as exemption from corvee service. Thus the cultural level of the natives was raised, and native tribes closer to the city were especially noticeable in their better cultural standing.[10]

In a word, in the twenty-two years under the government of the Cheng's (1662-1683), Taiwan's relationship with China had begun a new page, and Taiwan's construction and development had entered a new era. Chinese from the mainland had migrated into Taiwan in great numbers, and a definite link was formed between people inhabiting the island and people of the continent. In blood kinship, in social traditions, and in instutions and culture, Taiwan had been totally sinicized. In political status, Taiwan was still a living part of the deceased Ming Empire, Cheng Cheng-kung's title of His Royal Highness the Infeudated King of Yen Ping *(Yen p'ing chun wang)* was conferred by the Ming court, and was held without change after the passing of Ming rule. The official calendar observed by the Cheng's still maintained in it the reign title of the Ming Emperor. These evidently indicated that their ambition was not aimed at a final declaration of independence to set up a sovereign state in Taiwan maintaining a separate entity over the high seas disconnected with the mainland Empire. Rather, their ambition and intentions were using Taiwan as a base for the restoration of Ming rule on the Chinese continent.

Notes to Chapter II

(For convenience sake, the editions used are as many as available from the Bank of Taiwan's *Taiwan Historical Literature Series*, Taipei, Taiwan, 1957-1900 (Tai-wan yin-hang, *T'ai-wan wen-hsien ts'ung-k'an*—shown here as TWT.)

1 Chao Ju-kua, who wrote *Chu fan chih*, completed 1225. (English translation — Hirth and Rockhill, *Chau Ju-kua: His Work on the Chinese and Arab Trade in the 12th and 13th Centuries*, New York, Paragon reprint, 1967).

2 Yu Yung-ho, *Pai-hai chi-yu* (A Journey to Taiwan), Vol. 2, p. 33, TWT ed.

3 Wang Ta-yuan, who wrote *Tao-i chih-lueh* (Islands and Natives) at c. 1335-1349.

4 Huang Tsung-hsi, *Tz'u hsing shih-mu* (Chronicles of Koxinga and other Late Ming Royalties), p. 6, TWT ed.

5 Lien Heng, *T'ai-wan t'ung-shih* (General History of Taiwan), ch. 6, p. 134, TWT ed.

6 Yang Yin, *Ts'ung-cheng shih-lu* (Eyewitness Records of the Campaigns of His Royal Highness), p. 193, TWT ed.

7 Lien, *T'ai-wan t'ung-shih, op. cit.* ch. 29, pp. 755-756.

8 Yu, *Pai-hai chi-yu, op. cit.*, Vol. 2, p. 17.

9 Lien, *T'ai-wan t'ung-shih, op. cit.*, ch. 11, p. 268.

10 Yu, *Pai-hai chi-yu, op. cit.*, Vol 2, p. 17.

Chapter III

Brief Episodes - Dutch and Spanish Rule

BY GEORGE M. BECKMANN

The history of the Dutch on Taiwan (Formosa) is intimately related to the maritime expansion of Europe in Asia in the sixteenth and seventeenth centuries. The Portuguese overcame Arab sea power and overran strategic Arab bases, ultimately establishing a commercial empire that extended from Lisbon around Africa and through Asia all the way to Japan. Spain established control over Luzon in the Philippines and undertook to pacify the entire archipelago. The Dutch did not participate in the initial phase of this expansion and for a long time were content to play a role as trade intermediaries in Europe. They sent their small ships to Lisbon to exchange the grain, fish, and wood of northern Europe for the wine, olive oil, and fruits of southern Europe and the products of Asia. Although engaged in a prolonged war for independence with Spain, the Dutch continued to trade at Lisbon after Philip II of Spain extended his domains to include Portugal in 1580. The Dutch did not want to give up the substantial financial gain derived from this trade, and the Spanish, like the Portuguese, needed the Dutch as freight carriers. But in 1594 Philip II banned the Dutch from Lisbon.

The stage was set for the Dutch to go directly to Asia. Dutch officials and merchants became convinced that they could compete successfully with the Spanish and Portuguese. In 1594 a Dutch merchant group founded the Company of the Far Regions and announced its intention to send two expeditions to the East Indies. Other groups of merchants formed companies with similar objectives. In 1595 Cornelis de Houtman, who had served with the Portuguese for several years, sailed for the Indies with three large ships and 294 men. He returned in 1597 with only one third of the expedition intact, but he had reached his destination and had a rich cargo of spices. Although the total cost of the expedition was not met, the promise of profits to be gained in the future was great. Some twenty-two ships outfitted by five Dutch companies sailed to the East in 1598; fourteen fleets including sixty-five ships left for the East by 1602.

I
The Dutch East India Company

Competition with Portugal and Spain forced the Dutch to consolidate their efforts under one larger and more powerful company. The Dutch originally were not primarily interested in attacking directly the interests of Portugal in Asia. They wanted to establish commercial relations with regions beyond Portuguese control. Portugal was to be regarded as a neutral power, not a hostile state; however, it proved impossible to maintain that posture so long as their rivals regarded them as pirates and treated them accordingly. By 1602, the Dutch and Portuguese were actively at war. These difficulties with the Portuguese forced the union of the various Dutch trading companies into one, the East India Company, to which the States-General of the Dutch Republic gave exclusive rights for trading between the Cape of Good Hope and the Strait of Magellan, establishing Dutch colonies, declaring and conducting war, and concluding treaties with native rulers. Although unstated, it was clear that the founding of the united company was aimed at weakening Spanish-Portuguese power. However, the company was established for other reasons as well. For one thing, the Dutch wanted to avoid unnecessary competition among themselves. Money and lives were being wasted through such competition. Moreover, the Dutch wanted to maintain a more effective balance between supply and demand of spices in order to keep prices as high as possible. Finally, the Dutch were motivated to act by the example of the English who in 1600 had founded the English East India Company and sent out a company armed fleet.

The Dutch East India Company was a joint stock company, with all the inhabitants of the Dutch Republic having the right to buy shares in it. The Dutch believed they had to tap the resources of as many prosperous citizens as possible. At the same time, they wanted to prevent concentration of control in the hands of a few. In case more money was offered then could be used, those who had subscribed for more than 30,000 guilders would be obliged to reduce their subscriptions so that others with more modest means would be able to purchase shares in proportion to their means. For investors the early years of the Company's activities were particularly profitable. Dividends declared by the Company during the first two decades averaged well over 60 per cent paid in money, debentures, and spices. Dividends declined during the subsequent several decades but remained high by contemporary standards. For the period of Dutch control of Formosa, the low was 12½ per cent in cash in 1653 and 1659; and the high, 47½ per cent in cash in 1646. Later, dividends were reduced further but until 1700 still averaged over 20 per cent.

The history of Dutch expansion in Asia is too well known to be repeated in detail here, but it is essential to remember that the heart of the Dutch commercial empire in Asia was Batavia on the island of Java. This site was for 300 years the capital of the Dutch colonial empire in the East. Dutch sea power was able to establish and maintain Dutch supremacy in Ceylon, the Straits of Molucca, the Indies, and extend Dutch trade to Japan. The first Dutch ship had reached Japanese shores in 1600, and trade was regularized with the establishment of a trading base in 1609 at Hirado, an island off Kyushu in southwest Japan. Here the Dutch successfully competed for Japanese favor against the Portuguese and Spanish. The Dutch were also able to face the challenge of the English in the Indies and, despite a treaty commitment in 1619 to the English to share in the spice trade, they succeeded in depriving the English of all but a small share of that trade with the result that the English shortly thereafter abandoned the area to concentrate on India.

II

Early Relations with China

The lure of trade with China was another great incentive to the Dutch East India Company. Portugal had successfully opened European trade with Ming China at Canton in 1514 and established a permanent commercial base at Macao in 1557. At Macao the Portuguese exchanged Chinese silks, porcelain, lacquerware, and gold for spices, sandalwood, drugs. and dyes. Chinese merchants at Canton also engaged in trade on a small scale — two ships a year — with the Portuguese after 1578, and although the Portuguese expanded the Canton trade later, Macao continued to be the more important base for them. Spain also was able to secure Chinese goods through trade based at Manila. The Dutch were anxious to gain a share of the China trade and to supplant the Portuguese as they were able to do elsewhere.

The first Dutch ship appeared in Chinese waters in 1601 and encountered Portuguese opposition in the form of hostile advice to the Chinese. In 1603 two Company ships bombarded Macao but had to retire in the face of strong resistance, after having destroyed one Portuguese galleon. The Company also tried to open negotiations for commercial privileges with the Chinese. It made two such attempts in 1604. First, the Company sent a Dutch emissary to Peking in the entourage of a Siamese tribute mission, but that tactic failed. Second, it sent an expedition to south China under Admiral Wybrand van Warwyk, but a typhoon forced it to seek refuge in the Pescadores, where it remained for five months. From there, the admiral sent a letter to the Fukien authorities asking for commercial privileges. This effort, too, came to nothing.

However, the Dutch desire for trade with China increased as the market in Europe for Chinese goods, particularly silk, increased. The silk cargo of the captured Portuguese carack, *St. Catherine*, yielded greater profits to the Dutch than did spices. The cargo was taken to Amsterdam, where it was sold at public auction in August, 1604, with merchants from all over Europe flocking to the sale. The Company made another unsuccessful effort in 1607 when it dispatched Cornelis Matelief de Jonge with letters from the Prince of Orange for the King of Siam, asking for his assistance in securing trade with China, and for the Emperor of China himself. This was the last serious attempt by the Dutch until 1622 because of their preoccupation with the situations in the Indies and Japan. Yet the desire remained alive. In 1609 the Company instructed the governor-general at Batavia to promote the silk trade with China directly, and again in 1617 it reiterated these instuctions.

The Company seriously turned its attention to China again,

beginning in 1622 when it ordered Cornelis Reyerszoon to attack Macao. His fleet of sixteen ships bombarded Fort St. Francis for five days (July 19 to July 24) and then landed 800 men out of an expeditionary force of 2,000 soldiers. The Dutch captured the fort on the 24th but were unable to overcome the resistance of the Portuguese when they marched on Macao. They were forced to retire to their ships and abandon the attack. The Chinese regarded the attack as an act of hostility against China and assisted the Portuguese in repairing Macao's fortifications. The Dutch accused the Chinese of aiding the Portuguese and complained that they did not enjoy commercial privileges.

With the failure of the expedition against Macao, the Dutch shifted tactics again, deciding to take steps to force the Chinese to grant rights. Reyerszoon proceeded to the Pescadores, where he began construction of a large fort in August, 1622. He forced some 1,500 Chinese to provide labor for the enterprise, treating them badly. Many died, and the survivors were sent to the Indies and sold into slavery. The Pescadores provided the Dutch with an excellent strategic location. It lay at the center of principal trade routes. From it, the Dutch could easily intercept Portuguese commerce between Macao and Japan and Chinese commerce between Amoy and Manila. Moreover, it was a convenient staging area for an attack on Macao or for harassment of the China coast.

Chinese officials saw well these dangers and became willing to enter into negotiations with the Dutch in order to get them to leave the Pescadores. Negotiations began at Chuanchou in Fukien and were continued in the Pescadores. The chief Chinese delegate offered the island of Formosa to the Dutch in exchange for the Pescadores; he had no objection to their fortifying it. He promised that if the Dutch accepted this arrangement, he would refer the Dutch request for trade to the Emperor and his council. The Dutch had established a small temporary base on Formosa in the summer of 1622 and had found some Chinese settled there for trading purposes. They considered the Chinese proposal and rejected it. And when the Chinese departed, they ordered their ships to pillage and burn south China coastal villages. The Dutch and Chinese engaged in hostilities between October, 1622 and the spring of 1623.

Fighting gave way once again to negotiations, first at Amoy with the Chinese reiterating the condition of the need for the

Dutch to give up the Pescadores for Formosa, and subsequently at Foochow and at Chuanchou, where an agreement was reached in November, 1623. The Chinese officials may have been influenced by a large contingent of merchants from Amoy who expressed concern over the ruin of the coastal trade because of Dutch harassment. Under the terms of the settlement, the Chinese agreed to send to the Dutch on Formosa as much silk as wanted and that four or five junks, filled with silk and other merchandise, would be sent to Batavia under the escort of Dutch ships, accompanied by a Chinese official who would negotiate a more permanent commercial relationship. Reyerszoon agreed to inform the governor-general at Batavia that it was absolutely indispensable for the Dutch to abandon the Pescadores. Chinese on Formosa were to be permitted to remain there, and new immigrants from China were to be allowed to settle there and enter trade.

For some reason, while waiting for a reply from Batavia, the Chinese suddenly shifted tactics and attempted to burn the Dutch squadron anchored in the river. They set fire to three ships, of which one was completely destroyed. The remaining Dutch ships fled down river, destroying junks as they went, and returned to the Pescadores in April, 1624. The Chinese, fearing retaliation because of their attack, made new overtures based on the earlier agreement. However, they were resolved to fight if the Dutch would not leave the Pescadores. The Chinese realized that the Dutch position was not strong and blockaded the Pescadores base with a large fleet of war junks. When Maarten Sonk arrived in August to relieve Reyerszoon of his command, he accepted the Chinese terms. The Dutch, assisted by Chinese troops, dismantled the fort and transported most of the materials to Formosa, where they were to establish a permanent base in the expectation of engaging in trade with China.

III
Establishment of Fort Zeelandia

The Dutch led by Sonk, who served as the first governor, established their base on a small isle situated off the southwest coast of Taiwan. The isle, which extended northwest to southeast, was one and a half miles long and slightly more than a half mile wide. It was a sand reef with vegetation confined to a sparse growth of wild trees. Its northern point was about two and a half miles from the shore; the southern extremity was only the distance of the range of an arrow shot and was joined to the shore by a sandbar which at low tide was passable. On the mainland opposite was the village of Sakkam, near a river bank and containing approximately one hundred dwellings. The isle is now joined to the mainland because of river silting and constitutes the town of Anping, which is situated at the entrance to the harbor that serves the present city of Tainan.

The Dutch proceeded to build their installations on the northern extremity of the isle. The central building was Fort Zeelandia, constructed of Chinese cut stone and bricks from Batavia, and named after the ship which brought Governor Sonk. Zeelandia was also the name generally used for the isle itself. By 1634, the fort had been enlarged and contained the residence of the governor, a church, prison, and storehouses for arms and provisions. Chinese and Dutch merchants settled on the north side of the fort and founded a non-walled trade quarter. Before the fort, on high ground near the sea, the Dutch built another stone enclosure called Utrecht. On this side of Fort Zeelandia were warehouses, arms works, offices, and between them and the higher ground were a market place and a place for executions. The extrance to the harbor was relatively easy from the ocean side, and the Dutch took steps to make it more protective. They filled six or seven old transports with rocks and placed them in the passage so that to enter the harbor it was necessary to pass under the fire of the fort. If they did not, ships ran the risk of running against the stationed transports or running aground on the sandbar. Unfortunately, however, the harbor entrance would only accommodate light ships of twelve to fourteen-foot draft; but once inside the harbor, ships were sheltered from winds. With these precautions, the Dutch were convinced that the harbor was impregnable against attack from the sea.

IV
Trade with China

The main purpose of establishing the base at Zeelandia was to develop trade with China. The Dutch quickly succeeded in achieving that objective; however, maintaining that trade over a period of time proved to be difficult. The Dutch sent money to Amoy to purchase merchandise to be sold or traded in Japan, the Indies or Europe. Chinese officials, bribed by presents, closed their eyes to this trade at Amoy but refused officially to open other ports to Dutch ships. Chinese merchants came also to Zeelandia to sell merchandise but not at great profit to the Dutch. Junks filled the port and exchanged silk and other goods for spices, cotton cloth, and silver ingots. It was more profitable for the Dutch to trade directly at Amoy. The principal items purchased there by the Dutch were raw silk and bolts of silk; the raw silk was destined principally for Japan, and the bolts for Batavia and Europe. In 1627, five cargoes of silk, valued at 621,855 guilders, or 1,295,534 francs, were sent to Japan; and in the same year, two cargoes, valued at 559,493 guilders, or 1,165,610 francs, were sent to Batavia and Holland. This trade returned a 100 per cent profit in 1627 and 1628. With all expenses for the colony deducted, there was still a huge annual profit for the Dutch. Moreover, employees of the Company also engaged in trade, largely because they were so poorly paid. In the early years, some employees made great fortunes.

Chinese officials, especially those at Peking, remained wary of the Dutch. They were convinced that while the Portuguese at Macao had no hostile intentions, the Dutch were different and had definite aggressive designs against China. To them, the establishment of Dutch trading stations in the Indies and on Formosa appeared to be the prelude of a Dutch attempt to conquer and colonize China. The Chinese, threatened by the Manchus in the north, prepared to deal with the southern threat by allying with the powerful pirate leader, Cheng Chih-lung. They hoped that Cheng's fleet could attend to the Dutch menace in the south. Negotiations between the Chinese government and Cheng were begun at Amoy. Ts'ai Shan-chi, the official envoy, asked for Cheng's assistance against the Dutch, explaining that Peking would then be able to deal with the Manchus. Cheng was receptive to the proposal, especially as Ts'ai assured him that Peking wanted to force the Dutch out of Formosa. This appealed to Cheng because he saw in Formosa a base for his own operations. However, Cheng delayed making any commitment until there was some guarantee of his own position when the Dutch were driven out of Formosa.

The Dutch meanwhile continued their efforts to expand their trade in South China; but their methods, quite unscrupulous, had the opposite result. Their actions helped to bring about the alliance between the Chinese government and Cheng. Pieter Nuyts, the third governor of Formosa, sought in 1628 to negotiate an agreement with the governor-general of Fukien to expand the trade. Moreover, on learning of the meetings between Cheng and Ts'ai, he became determined to gain Cheng's support for such an agreement. Nuyts paid a visit to Cheng at Amoy and was received cordially and suitably feasted, In return, he invited Cheng to meet with him on board the Dutch warship. There Nuyts forced Cheng to grant the Dutch rights to trade in all South China ports.

This bold act proved unwise. It precipitated Cheng's acceptance of Ts'ai's proposal. Cheng agreed to cooperate with the Chinese government against the Dutch. He was appointed Commander of the Imperial Fleet in South China, with his official headquarters at Amoy. Cheng then formulated his plans to expel the Dutch from Formosa. Dutch ships in the waters north of the Indies were to be seized and their cargoes confiscated; migration from South China to Formosa was to be encouraged, and Formosa was to become part of the Chinese empire with Cheng's family ruling the island. Cheng waited for the opportune time to implement his plans.

Dutch policy continued to be aggressive. Hans Putmans, who arrived in Zeelandia in 1629 as successor to Pieter Nuyts, was deeply committed to using force to open Chinese ports. However, he was not able to force the issue for several years. In 1663, he surprised Cheng's fleet, at anchor in Changchou Bay, and destroyed most of it. He then proceeded to force Cheng into an agreement. He offered military assistance against the Manchus if Cheng would agree to the establishment of a Dutch trading post at Foochow and permit freedom of trade with other South China ports. Cheng rejected the proposal; and he directed his remaining ships, under cover of night, to set fire to the Dutch warships that were blockading Amoy harbor. Putmans was forced to retire to Zeelandia. There, fearing that the Chinese might close all trade to the Dutch, he became more conciliatory and was able to negotiate with Cheng an agreement maintaining trade between Zeelandia and Foochow provided Chinese junks were used as transports. This arrangement enabled Cheng to keep informed of the state of Dutch defenses at Zeelandia.

Cheng never realized his ambitions regarding Formosa. Developments in China increasingly commanded his attention. Yet he kept alive the idea that in event of the Manchus gaining control of China, Formosa could serve as a strategic base from which China could be recovered.

V

Trade with Japan

As noted above, Zeelandia played an important role in the general Dutch trade with Japan. Ships from Zeelandia carried a great variety of products to Japan: raw silk, silk cloth, sugar, deerskins, lead, tin, spices, ivory, and woolen cloth. These were exchanged for gold and gold objects, silver coins and silverware, copper and copper goods, camphor, grains, lacquerware, and porcelain. The overall annual profit for the Dutch in the Japan trade amounted for a time to some 500,000 guilders, which greatly surpassed that derived by the Dutch from their trade with any other country in Asia. However, the volume of the Japan trade ultimately fluctuated greatly because of Dutch difficulties in getting Chinese silk and problems created by Dutch policies regarding the Japanese on Zeelandia.

Zeelandia was the site of a considerable trade between China and Japan, a neutral port where the ships of the two countries met. At this time, the Japanese government encouraged foreign commerce and licensed vessels to trade chiefly with Southeast Asia. Until the coming of the Dutch, this trade had been entirely exempt from all charges and taxes. However, from the first year of their occupation, the Dutch decided to levy a tax on the sugar and rice which were exported to China in great quantities and on all Japanese goods. The Chinese merchants made no objections to this tax, but the Japanese refused to pay. This resulted in the seizure of several Japanese vessels and confiscation of their cargoes to the profit of the Dutch. The Japanese sent an expedition to Zeelandia in 1627 in order to investigate the situation and negotiate a change in Dutch policy. The commander, an officer of the *shogun*, failed to sway the Dutch. He returned to Japan, accompanied by sixteen

Formosan natives, whom he had persuaded to petition the Japanese government to take over rule of the island. Learning of this plan, the Dutch dispatched Pieter Nuyts to Edo in July, 1627; and by dispensing large sums of money among the *shogun's* retainers, he was able to influence the Japanese ruler not to accept the natives' offer. Nuyts then returned to Zeelandia and assumed the post of governor of the colony.

On Zeelandia, the Dutch still continued to make life difficult for the Japanese. Exasperated by Nuyts' repeated acts of discrimination, the Japanese finally decided in June, 1628 to depart. However, Nuyts and the Japanese could not agree on the terms of their departure. In desperation, the Japanese decided boldly to seize the governor to protect themselves and to force him to accept their terms. They attacked the fort, entered it without difficulty, and imprisoned Nuyts. The attack had been so sudden that the small garrison was unable to defend itself. Casualties were light, but several persons were killed on both sides. Nuyts, with his life threatened, was forced to agree to let the Japanese leave peacefully with a substantial amount of silk or its money equivalent. The infuriated Nuyts did get the opportunity to exact reprisals. Shortly thereafter, when two Japanese vessels came to Zeelandia, he seized and ransomed them, not releasing them until a year later.

These difficulties had important implications for the Dutch trade in Japan. Nuyts himself recognized this. In reporting the incident of the Japanese attack to the government in the Indies, he recommended that the Japanese be given a share of the China trade at Zeelandia and not be taxed. He pointed out the possibility of Japanese reprisals against the Dutch trade in Japan and, of course, he was correct in his judgment.

When the Japanese authorities learned what had happened at Zeelandia, they quickly placed an embargo on nine Dutch vessels at Hirado, impounded them, and suspended all commerce with the Dutch. This measure alarmed the Dutch at Batavia, who desired to remain on good terms with the Japanese. The Dutch who had succeeded in 1609 in obtaining permission to establish a small trading post at Hirado did not want to lose that trade and sought to resolve the difficulty but to no avail. The situation remained unchanged for three years. At last, in 1631, the authorities in Batavia, increasingly concerned about the return of their ships, sent a vessel to Japan to discover what had happened. The Japanese permitted the ship to discharge its cargo at Hirado and to take on goods for Batavia but did not release the other ships and did not explain to the Dutch the motives behind their actions.

Meanwhile, Nuyts was recalled to Batavia and imprisoned; he was blamed for all the difficulty with the Japanese because of his earlier detention of the Japanese ships. Nuyts asked the authorities to carry out a thorough investigation, and he proposed to go to Japan to prove his innocence. He was sent to Japan in 1632 but to be turned over to the *shogun*. On his arrival in Japan, he was arrested and imprisoned by the Japanese government. Reparations thus made, commercial relations were resumed. The unfortunate Nuyts remained incarcerated for several years. In 1636, however, a Dutch embassy with gifts for the *shogun* arrived in Japan and secured a pardon for him. He was released and returned to Batavia. Three years later, in 1640, the Dutch succeeded in obtaining from the Tokugawa government a European monopoly of the Japan trade, with the exclusion of the Spanish and Portuguese. However, they were confined to the island of Deshima in Nagasaki harbor. The only other foreigners who also traded at Nagasaki were the Chinese. At the same time, the Tokugawa government withdrew the licenses for trade with foreign countries that had been granted to numerous Japanese vessels. It was forbidden to build in Japan vessels above a size that would be large enough for long sea voyages. The Dutch were therefore in an advantageous position so long as they remained in the favor of the Tokugawa rulers.

VI
The Spanish on Formosa

The Dutch Republic was not the only European power to establish a base on Formosa. From their stronghold in the Philippines, the Spanish were able to gain a foothold on the northwest coast. They made their initial contact with the island in 1580, the year of the reunion of Spain and Portugal under Philip II and the end of national commercial rivalry between the two states. In that year, the Spanish governor at Manila sent Jesuit Alonzo Sanchez to Macao to inform the Portuguese authorities there of that reunion and to receive their oath of loyalty to Philip.

After completing his mission, Sanchez planned to return by way of Japan but was shipwrecked on the coast of Formosa, where he was enchanted by its natural beauty. He returned to Macao on a Chinese fishing junk and soon thereafter returned to Manila. The Spanish subsequently sent a small expedition from the Philippines to take possession of the island. But it was caught in a typhoon; two ships were dashed to pieces and a third foundered and sunk. The Spanish thereafter abandoned their plans.

Spanish interest in Formosa revived with the success of the Dutch in establishing their base at Zeelandia. They began to be concerned about possible Dutch interference with their own ships, especially those bound for Japan. The governor at Manila, Don Fernando de Silva, decided therefore to send an expedition to establish a colony on the northern coast of Formosa. The small fleet set sail in February, 1626, and several months later, after exploring stretches of the coast, disembarked troops at Keelung and built a fort nearby. Dominicans who accompanied the expedition were able to overcome the fears of the native population, who had fled at the sight of the Spanish, and persuaded them to return to Keelung. Several years later the Spanish founded a second base to the northwest at the mouth of the Tamshui River and built another fort to protect it. They showed little inclination to enlarge their small colonies in the years that followed. Their purpose was primarily to protect their trading ships and secondarily to convert natives to Catholicism.

The Dutch at Zeelandia were much disturbed by these actions. Governor Nuyts in 1628 urged Batavia to send an expedition against the Spanish at Keelung. He argued that the Spanish were in a strategic position to intercept Dutch vessels trading on the China coast. According to Nuyts, a single prize vessel taken by the Spanish would constitute a loss to the Company equivalent to the cost of a six-month expedition against Keelung. The governor also expressed concern that the Spanish would become a more active trade rival, attracting Chinese merchants and merchandise to Keelung. Wouldn't it be more profitable to have a monopoly of the Formosa-based China trade? Finally, Nuyts relayed his fears that the Spanish might attempt to incite the natives against the Dutch. He pointed out that, without the friendship of the natives, the Dutch would be unable to remain on Formosa unless they augmented their forces, which would increase expenses and thereby curtail profits — a good business argument. The Dutch authorities at Batavia did not act on this advice; and since the Spanish were not aggressive as predicted by Nuyts, the Dutch and their rivals enjoyed peace for over a decade.

Not until 1641, a year after Spain and Portugal were separated once again, did the Dutch attempt to oust the Spanish from Formosa. The immediate pretext for this shift in policy was a rebellion in 1640 against the Dutch for which the Spanish were blamed. Paulus Tradenius, sixth governor at Zeelandia, sent to Gonsalo Portilio, commandant of the Spanish fort at Keelung, a letter dated August 26, 1641 which declared his intention to drive out the Spanish. If they did not go peacefully, Tradenius threatened hostilities. Portilio replied on September 6, 1641 courteously and firmly that he would not surrender the fort but would defend it.

Both sides then prepared for the fight. The Dutch sent an expedition against the Spanish later in 1641, but it was driven off by fierce resistance. They then planned to mount a larger force. The Spanish meanwhile asked Manila for reinforcements, but the governor had his forces engaged in operations against Mindanao and Sulu. He could send only some provisions, a small quantity of arms, and eight Spanish soldiers. The second Dutch expedition appeared before Tamshui on August 3, 1642: four frigates, a large cutter, nine small ships, and several transports. The Dutch quickly disembarked and overwhelmed the defenders. They then marched on Keelung, where the Spanish resisted stubbornly until the fort fell on August 24. The Dutch spared the vanquished Spanish but confiscated all their goods and property. They sent their captives first to Zeelandia and then on to Batavia, and ultimately dispatched them to Manila. By these victories, the Dutch gained control of the northern coast and became the sole European master of Formosa.

The Spanish smarted under these defeats. They lamented the loss of these advance bases situated between China and Japan and considered whether they should try to retake them. In the end, they decided against it, perhaps because of rumors that the seizure of Tamshui and Keelung were preliminary to an attack by the Dutch on Manila. A Dutch squadron did appear off Manila but only to intercept Spanish ships. It was met by a Spanish fleet and soon disappeared. This altercation did have the effect of ending serious Spanish discussion of a possible return to Formosa.

VII

Dutch Rule and the Native Population

By 1642 the Dutch were supreme in Formosa; yet their position was limited to Zeelandia and the west coast, and the former Spanish forts in the north, which they maintained with garrisons of about forty men each. They gradually expanded their control of the western and northern coasts through the establishment of small military posts. By the end of 1650, there were twenty-five such posts. Keelung and Tamshui remained military bases with no commercial activity and had little influence on the country outside of their immediate vicinities. The east coast was practically unknown to the Dutch.

Dutch military might and law ruled the island, and the governor and council were supreme. However, while the Dutch had control and introduced some laws among the native tribesmen, they had each village or town designate its own headman who would administer its affairs with the right of appeal to the governor at Zeelandia. The Dutch gave each headman, as mark of his office, a silver staff on which was engraved the arms of the Company. This symbol of authority was transferred to each newly confirmed headman. Because of the convenience of continuity, the Dutch preferred to reappoint able and cooperative headmen. The governor convened the headmen in annual assemblies at which time they reported on village affairs. On these occasions, he called on them to treat Dutch clergymen and schoolmasters with respect and to encourage native attendance at church services and school in order to make them more amenable to direction by the Company. The assemblies were also social occasions, usually terminating with much feasting and drinking. Dutch control of the natives was generally indirect in approach, but it was an effective means to collect tribute, carry on trade, and to control the movement of the natives from village to village and at the same time check on the activities of the Chinese settlers.

The introduction of Christianity and rudimentary education was also part of the Dutch impact on Formosa and the native tribesmen. However, it should be pointed out that the missionary objectives of the Dutch clergy on Formosa (Calvinists of the Reformed Church) were aspects of a more general concept of service. The Company sent clergymen to Formosa primarily to act as chaplains to Dutch officials, soldiers, and families resident there; and local officials employed them as interpreters, civil officers in collecting tribute, selling hunting licenses, and trading for local produce, especially animal skins, with salt, cloth, and beads. The objective of establishing and building up Christian congregations, although regarded as worthwhile and encouraged by the governor, was not of comparable importance. Clergymen were under the control of the governor and his council. Specifically, the Zeelandia officialdom located them in their service posts, determined the nature of teaching in church and schools, and had the authority to suspend or dismiss them, although disputes regarding suspension of dismissal could be referred for final settlement to the Council at Batavia and even to the Supreme Council in the Netherlands. Perhaps the primary reason for Company restrictions on clergymen was the fear of offending the Japanese who persecuted Christians, which fact might lead to their own explusion from Japan as was the case of the Portuguese and Spanish. Company officials were generally ambivalent regarding the missionary activities of the clergymen and generally did not give them the assistance they needed.

The first clergymen to be recruited by the Company for service on Formosa were George Candidius (1627) and Robert Junius (1629). Assisted by catechists, they preached a simple Christianity, applied what medical competence they had, and introduced very rudimentary education. They were successful and their influence expanded; and clergymen who followed them built on the solid foundations of their work. In all, some thirty-two clergymen served in Formosa from 1627 until 1662. Their purpose, from the Company's point of view, was to transform the natives into profitable servants of the Company; however, the enterprising clergymen were not satisfied with this definition of their role. Ultimately they were able to support themselves and attempted to act independently of the Company. The number of churches grew and natives attended in increasing numbers. In 1650 the number of baptized members of the native church was recorded as over 7,000. The small school that Junius established expanded into a network of schools with swelling enrollments. Yet on major issues the clergymen had to bow to the will of the Company. On one occasion, they declared the worship of native tribal gods a criminal offense to be punished by public whipping and banishment. Once a month, it was obligatory for all villagers to assemble and hear a reading of a proclamation setting forth the manner of this punishment. The Company reacted against this practice and instructed the governor in Formosa not to implement this policy. The Calvinist conscience of the clergymen may have been stunned, but the order of the Governor was reluctantly accepted. On another occasion, the clergymen decided to establish a seminary for the training of native clergy, but the Company opposed this action and again prevailed. It seemed for a time that the clergymen were on the point of breaking with Company, but pressure from some source prevented this. These "civilizing" efforts of the Dutch had no lasting impact on the natives, although some vestiges of Dutch teaching were discovered in the late 19th century in the form of native documents written in Dutch letters.

VIII
Chinese Insurrection of 1652

While the native tribesmen were on the whole submissive, the Chinese settlers, mostly immigrants from Fukien and Kwangtung provinces, were alien to Dutch control. One of the principal Chinese complaints was the obligation to pay a capitation tax from which the Dutch obtained substantial funds for administrative expenses. Moreover, as the capitation tax increased, so did the hostility of the Chinese population. In one year alone, this tax yielded 300,000 guilders, more than all the expenses of the Dutch. The Chinese were also exploited as labor in warehouses and in rice and sugar cane fields owned by the Dutch. As their resentment grew, the Chinese, on several occasions, rose up against the Dutch but to no avail.

The largest of these insurrections took place in 1652. A certain Fayet (Kuo Huai-yi), chief of the village of Smeerdorp situated several miles from Sakkam, plotted a surprise attack against Fort Zeelandia. He planned to invite the governor, Nicholas Verburgh, his officers, and the principal Dutch merchants to a feast celebrating the full moon and to massacre them during the festivities. He would then march with his men on the fort, pretending to escort the governor's party home, and seize it. But Fayet's brother, a chief who lived in a village near Zeelandia, alarmed at the consequences should the plot fail, opposed it and refused either to participate in it or to remain neutral as his brother asked him. He decided to inform the governor of the plot. On Sunday, September 7, he went to the fort in the morning and asked to see the governor on urgent business. Verburgh was then at church with his officers. The sentry at first refused to inform the governor of the request, but, then, when the Chinese insisted, he complied. Forewarned of the plot, Verburgh immediately dispatched troops to Smeerdorp. En route, they learned that the insurrection had broken out and that the insurgents were moving in force toward Sakkam. They returned to Zeelandia to consult with the governor.

Meanwhile, the small Dutch community (some thirty persons in number) which lived at Sakkam took flight to Zeelandia. Those who lived in the countryside also fled to the fort. Fayet, meeting no resistance, put Sakkam to fire, sparing no one. He then left the scene before the Dutch forces arrived. Verburgh dispatched a Captain Danker with 120 men in a war sloop and small auxiliary ship. The two ships quickly passed the bay between Zeelandia and Sakkam and disembarked troops on the bank, confronting some 1,000 insurgents who did not make a move to oppose them. Fayet had given the order to let the Dutch land with the idea of surrounding and decimating them. Danker and his men moved forward and in the first exchange of gunfire killed Fayet. Without their leader, the insurgents were no match for the disciplined Dutch troops; in fear, they fled for their safety. The Dutch pursued them as far as Sakkam and recaptured it. Before nightfall, two thousand tribesmen Christians, called into action by the governor, continued the pursuit and, catching up with the insurgents, massacred a large number of them. The remainder, commanded by a lieutenant of Fayet, retired to an inaccessible mountain area.

Eight days later, this lieutenant was captured when he ventured to the plains. The Dutch decided to make an example of him, and his execution was especially brutal. He was trampled under horses' hoofs and dragged about Zeelandia. After he expired, his head was cut from his body and implanted on the end of a pole at the gate of the fort. The Dutch executed many other insurgents after frightening punishments. In fifteen days, the rebellion was crushed and several thousand Chinese killed, but the discontent of the Chinese was not overcome. It remained a potential source of danger to the Dutch. The Dutch recognized this and took steps to improve their defenses. It was at this time that they constructed Fort Provintia, at Sakkam, two miles east of Zeelandia.

IX
Relations with China, 1653-1660

Expansion of the China trade remained a matter of great concern to the Dutch. They continually considered ways to gain access to Chinese ports. In 1653, information brought from China by the Jesuit, Martin Martini, raised their hopes anew. Martini, who had lived in China for some ten years, arrived in Batavia on his way home to Europe. He suggested to the Dutch that the situation had changed with the fall of the Ming Dynasty and the establishment of the new regime under the Manchus. The Dutch authorities at Batavia therefore resolved to make new overtures to the Manchu government and ordered Governor Verburgh at Zeelandia to send an ambassador to Canton. The governor selected the merchant, Frederic Schedel, "a prudent man endowed with a brave spirit," for this important and delicate mission. Schedel was well received by the governor-general at Canton, who permitted him to disembark and sell his merchandise, and to establish a commercial base. These concessions caused the Portuguese at Macao, fearful of having a rival so close, to complain, painting Schedel and the Dutch in the blackest color as pirates. Meanwhile, the governor-general was replaced and his successor, conceding to the Portuguese, informed Schedel that as a local official he did not have sufficient authority to conclude an agreement. He gave Schedel a letter for Governor Verburgh in which he advised the Dutch to send a mission to Peking with rich presents as the only way to negotiate the right to trade at Canton. Verburgh informed the authorities at Batavia of this outcome, and they, in turn asked the Company officials in Holland for instructions. Meanwhile, they sent Schedel with two large ships back to Canton to renew the request for trade. Influenced by the Portuguese, the governor-general rebuffed the mission under the pretext that the Dutch had not furnished letters or presents for the emperor.

Instructions from the Company in Holland in 1655 authorized sending an embassy to Peking, and the Batavian authorities selected Pierre de Goyer and Jacob de Keyser for this purpose. Their mission consisted of fourteen persons, including a steward, surgeon, interpreter, guardsmen, a trumpeter and drummer, and two merchants. The presents, especially selected for the Manchu emperor, included telescopes, mirrors, and armor. De Goyer and de Keyser proceeded to Canton, where they transmitted their request to the Manchu imperial court at Peking through the governor-general. However, they were not able to establish a friendly relationship with the governor-general. They had several quarrels with him, but he nevertheless threated them as official guests. At last, the emperor's reply came. His majesty agreed to permit them to proceed to the capital with a flotilla of junks charged to escort them and carry the Company's presents. The mission made the trip from Canton to Peking and was welcomed to the capital by officials representing the emperor. They were received at court in audience in the same way as emissaries from Korea, Siam, and Annam, and presented with gifts. The Manchus regarded the ambassadors as tribute bearers, coming to offer to the emperor the homage of their ruler. They were therefore invited to come and pay their respects to the emperor on a regular basis at fixed periods like the Koreans and other neighboring peoples. Thus the mission secured no commercial advantages for the Dutch. In the judgment of De Goyer and de Keyser, the opposition of the Jesuits, especially the vernerable Adam Schall who had been in Peking for over thirty years, was an influence on the Manchus.

Dutch relations with China were complicated because of the threat to Zeelandia posed by Cheng Cheng-kung, who succeeded to his father's (Cheng Chih-lung) ambitions in South China. Called Koxinga by the Dutch (from the popular title Kuo-hsing-yeh: "Lord of the Imperial Surname") he rallied to the desperate Ming cause against the conquering Manchus. When Foochow fell to the Manchus and his father was taken to Peking, he established his base on island strongholds in Amoy harbor and continued resistance on behalf of the former dynasty. Koxinga's plans for Formosa were reported to the Dutch from a variety of sources. The first intimation of this design came from the Dutch trading base in Japan in 1646 with the result that the directors in the Netherlands resolved that Zeelandia should not have fewer than 1,200 defenders even in times of peace. The Jesuit Martini warned the officials at Batavia that Koxinga was purposely influencing the behavior of the Chinese on Formosa. Verburgh, retiring as governor and returning to Batavia in 1654, reported that Koxinga was likely to attempt the conquest of Formosa if he was driven from South China in the struggle against the Manchus. Cornelis Caesar, his successor, was also concerned because of the halt of the junk trade from South Chinese ports and inferred that Koxinga had cut off the trade and was planning a surprise attack. Caesar stored as many provisions as he could in anticipation of a long siege and requested reinforcements from Batavia.

Frederik Coyett, who replaced Caesar in 1656, sought to restore the trade and entered into negotiations with Koxinga in 1657. In a message to Coyett, Koxinga declared that he had no other intention than to maintain a friendly relationship with the Dutch. He explained that the trade had been interrupted by rebellious subordinates and promised to remove the prohibition. The trade was not only resumed, but it expanded dramatically. Dutch profits from the China trade in 1658 were larger than any previous year. Moreover, the Chinese community on Formosa was peacefully submissive to Dutch regulations.

Despite the improved situation, the Dutch at Zeelandia remained fearful of Koxinga. Coyett recommended rebuilding several dilapidated fortifications and adding some new ones; and although these needs were recognized in Batavia, the officials there, far removed from any danger, declined to act. They explained that they could not afford large expenditures on Formosa. It seems that these officials did not believe Koxinga had the courage to fight the Dutch. They appear to have been confident that the name of the Dutch East India Company was sufficient to deter him. By 1659, Koxinga's position in South China had deteriorated, and there were constant rumors of his intention to attack Zeelandia. Moreover, the number of refugees bound for Formosa swelled. Seeing the Chinese settling in increasing numbers, the Dutch became alarmed. Chinese merchants on Zeelandia in March, 1660 warned of an attack. They were exporting more goods than they were importing and were removing goods and property from Formosa to China. The Dutch prepared as best they could for an attack and placed numerous controls on the Chinese community. But by May, with the situation still peaceful, they relaxed those controls.

X
Koxinga and the Dutch Collapse

In 1660 Koxinga finally made the decision to move his base from Amoy to Formosa and halted the trade again, and in the summer of that year the Dutch began to carry out a more positive policy toward him. In response to a pressing request from Coyett regarding Koxinga's war preparations at Amoy, Batavia sent to Zeelandia in July, 1660 a dozen ships and 600 men under the command of Admiral Jan van der Laan with orders to help defend Zeelandia in the event of attack. But if Koxinga made no such move, van der Laan had orders to seize Macao. Decisions regarding the disposition of these forces were to be made by Coyett. The expeditionary force called at Macao on the way to Zeelandia to take on water and, of course, aroused the suspicions of the Portuguese. It arrived at Zeelandia in September with many of the troops quite ill.

Coyett and van der Laan could not agree on a course of action. The latter refused to believe reports of Kaxinga's intentions and belittled him. A Dutch account of these events published in 1675 has characterized the admiral as a "brusque and impudent man, given to boasting, careless, proud, senseless, stubborn, and having a very obstinate and uncivil demeanor, all these qualities in him having been noticed by everyone who had spent an hour or two in his company." Van der Laan argued for an expedition against Macao, but Coyett and his council asked that it be postponed until there was more reliable information regarding Koxinga. Van der Laan reluctantly agreed and with Coyett sent a mission with a conciliatory letter to Koxinga in late October. The mission was politely received by Koxinga, who professed great friendship for the Company and declared willingness to enter into negotiations in order to put the trade on a more secure basis. He stated that he had not the least thought of war against the Company. He explained the need for halting the flow of trade from the mainland to Formosa on the ground that he needed the junks for the transportation of his men.

In a letter to be returned to Coyett, for which he kept the mission waiting twenty days, Koxinga said that he was preparing his forces for a campaign against the Manchus, and he promised that once they were repulsed, he would give orders for the trade to be resumed. Soon thereafter, he reopened the trade. But again his position deteriorated, and he was confined to the offshore islands near Amoy. The danger to Zeelandia was greater than ever before. Coyett and the council decided by majority vote to cancel the Macao expedition and that van der Laan's militia should be retained for the defense of Zeelandia. The Dutch reimposed controls on the Chinese, and the native assembly was postponed for the second consecutive year so that in event of a sudden attack, the natives would not be deprived of the leadership of their chiefs and become disorganized.

Despite the obvious danger, van der Laan chose to believe Koxinga and declared his presence was not needed. He wanted the spoils of Macao. He berated Coyett and the council for having exaggerated fears of Koxinga and departed in February, 1661 bound for Batavia, accompanied by his officers. Coyett and the council asked that the officers remain, but van der Laan refused. The soldiers, however, did remain. On his return to Batavia, the angry and disappointed admiral told his superiors that they had nothing to fear regarding Zeelandia. He depicted Coyett and the council as overly fearful and carrying out control measures harmful to trade and the colony. Disturbed by Coyett's continual alarms and the mounting cost of defense, the authorities suspended the governor and ordered him to return to Batavia to defend himself. His appointed successor, Herman Clenk van Odesse set sail for Zeelandia on June 21, 1661. Two days later, a ship from Formosa brought news of Koxinga's attack on Zeelandia; the Batavian authorities hastily dispatched a yacht to inform Clenk and to retrieve their letter to Coyett, but it failed in its objective. They also decided to send aid amounting to ten ships and 700 men under the command of Jacob Caeuw, an advocate and councillor of justice, who had no military experience. Caeuw departed on July 5 with a letter recalling Clenk, acknowledging to Coyett the mistakes of the Batavina authorities and reaffirming his leadership.

Koxinga had worked out final plans for the attack immediately after van der Laan had set sail for Batavia. He appeared in force off Zeelandia at the end of April with several hundred war junks and 25,000 men. The junks maneuvered well in the shallow waters between the isle and the mainland, and Koxinga landed troops, effectively cutting communication between Zeelandia and Fort Provintia. The initial Dutch resistance was no match on sea or land. Fort Provintia surrendered on May 4, but Zeelandia repulsed the initial attacks and forced Koxinga on June 1 to resort to the plan of putting the isle under siege.

Koxinga meanwhile rooted out the Dutch in the surrounding countryside. He made prisoners of the Dutch ministers and school teachers, charging them with secretly encouraging their native parishioners and students to kill Chinese. Several prisoners were crucified by Chinese. Koxinga sent out one Dutch minister to propose conditions of surrender to Zeelandia, using the threat of reprisals against the Dutch prisoners. However, the minister instead urged the Dutch forces to fight on, explaining that Koxinga had lost some of his best troops and was tiring of the siege. He then returned to Koxinga's camp, where he had left his wife and two of his children as hostages. Koxinga, spreading the rumor that the prisoners had incited the natives to revolt against him, ordered them put to death. Some were beheaded, and the others were also brutally killed. Five hundred Dutch were killed and buried in groups of fifty to sixty each in seperate large ditches. Women and children were not spared; most of them were massacred. The prettier and younger women were kept by the Chinese commanders and the rest sold to the soldiers.

Clenk arrived off Zeelandia on July 30, well ahead of the reinforcements and was, of course, surprised by what he found. Cautiously, he cast anchor a little to the north of Zeelandia and sent a message to Coyett informing him of his dismissal and proclaiming himself as the new governor. However, he did not seek to install himself as requested by Coyett but instead hastened to set sail for Japan, alleging he was short of food and water. The morale of the besieged on Zeelandia sank to a new low. Actually, Clenk returned to Batavia, seizing and plundering Chinese ships along the way. He was not rebuked for his conduct and continued in the service of the Company.

Caeuw and the troops under his command appeared off Zeelandia on August 12 but strong winds and ultimately a typhoon prevented them from landing and forced them out to sea. The expedition reappeared on September 8 and landed men and supplies, but the total Dutch garrison was not strong enough to break Koxinga's hold.

One last hope for the besieged Dutch came from Fukien in Early November in the form of a Manchu offer of assistance against Koxinga. The Dutch decided to accept the offer and discuss the matter with the governor of Fukien and at the same time to send as many women and children to Batavia as possible for their safety and to relieve the drain on existing supplies. Caeuw, who was regarded with suspicion by the council, offered to negotiate with the Manchus and left Zeelandia for that purpose on December 3. Once at sea, he set sail instead for Batavia with a brief visit to the Dutch colony in Siam. Later, Caeuw was punished but only lightly; he received an insignificant fine and suffered a six months' suspension from service. This comedy of errors was destined to end in tragedy.

The besieged no longer had any hope. The Company forces were beset by intrigue and irresponsibility, and some of their compatriots betrayed them. Misery and sickness took their toll. In desperation, a sergeant and twelve soldiers deserted to the enemy and helped Koxinga renew the attack. Fort Utrecht fell on January 25, 1662; Fort Zeelandia, which stood nearby on lower ground was completely exposed. Coyett decided that continued resistance was impossible and agreed on February 1 to surrender on the condition that the remaining Dutch, some 900, would be spared and free to leave with their private possessions. The defenders left, losing goods and a treasury valued at 475,000 guilders. They also left behind 1,600 dead countrymen, as many of whom died from dysentery and scurvy as died in combat. Koxinga planted his standard on Fort Zeelandia on February 12. The Dutch also gave up their bases in the north.

The comic-tragedy was not quite concluded. When the staunch defenders of Zeelandia arrived at Batavia, they were not treated as heroes but as scapegoats. "Formosa is lost" was the cry of the day. Although Coyett and his officials maintained they had been neglected by Batavia, they were given no chance to defend themselves. The higher officials at Batavia did not want to be forced to explain their actions. And some were imprisoned and had their possessions confiscated. Coyett was especially singled out for bureaucratic vengeance. He spent three years in prison in Batavia and was then condemned to life-long banishment to one of the Indies islands. Not until twelve years later, thanks to incessant petitions from his children and friends in the Netherlands and the ultimate intercession of the Prince of Orange, was he able to gain his release and return home. As a final humiliation, he was forbidden to enter the Asian service of any foreign state, and, as a guarantee to keep this commitment, he had to deposit 25,000 guilders with the Company.

The Dutch made a last unsuccessful attempt to reestablish their base on the northwest coast of Formosa. For several years, after the fall of Zeelandia, they cooperated with the Manchus against Koxinga and in 1663 landed a force of two hundred men at Keelung. However, because of the lack of trade, they departed again in 1668. Formosa had come to the end of another era of its history and for the Dutch it was the end of the dream of linking together trade with China and Japan through Formosa.

Bibliographic Notes to Chapter III

The number of works in English on the Dutch and Spanish on Formosa are very limited. Most useful is Reverend William Campbell's *Formosa Under the Dutch: Described from Contemporary Records*, London, 1903 (reprinted Taipeh, 1967). This work includes a translation of the informative *Verwaarloofde Formosa* published in 1675. There is a brief popular account of this period in W. G. Goddard, *Formosa: A Study in Chinese History*, East Lansing, Michigan, 1966 and London, 1966. Albert Hyma, *The Dutch in the Far East: A History of the Dutch Commercial and Colonial Empire*, Ann Arbor, Michigan, 1942, includes an account of the founding of the Dutch East India Company; and Bernard H. M. Vlekke, *Nusantra: A History of the East Indian Archipelago*, Cambridge, Massachusetts, 1944 is a convenient account of the Dutch administration at Batavia. Dutch relations with Japan are ably described by Charles R. Boxer, *Jan Compagnie in Japan: 1600-1850*, second revised edition, The Hague, 1950. Of useful works in European languages, the most accessible is C. Imbault-Huart, *L'ile Formose: Historie et Description*, Paris, 1893 (reprinted Taipei, 1968). This work includes a comprehensive bibliography of source materials, especially those in Dutch, compiled by Henri Cordier.

Chapter IV

Cheng Cheng-kung (Koxinga) and Chinese Nationalism in Taiwan, 1662-1683

BY PARRIS H. CHANG

In the first half of the seventeenth century, the power of the Ming empire was fast eroding as numerous calamities descended upon it from within and without. Domestically, rebellions broke out everywhere; hungry peasants, roving bandits, and other lawless elements organized into huge bands set about pillaging the countryside. Externally, the Manchus were threatening to cross the Great Wall from the north, the pirates were terrorizing the coastal provinces in the south and southeast, and the Dutch were attempting to open the China market by force and had seized Taiwan as their base in 1624. It was a time of crisis.

In 1644, the brigand leader Li Tzu-cheng marched on Peking and captured the national capital, forcing the last Emperor of the Ming dynasty to commit suicide. Wu San-kuei, the commander of the imperial forces then stationed at Shanhaikuan to hold back the Manchus, hastened to conclude an armistice with the erstwhile enemy and took a Manchu force of 100,000 to fall back on Peking. Although Peking was recaptured, the Manchus now declared the Ming House to have forfeited the "Mandate of Heaven" and proclaimed themselves new rulers of China.

North China recognized the authority of the new regime, the Ching dynasty, but the rest of China did not. In 1645 a Ming prince was proclaimed Emperor Huang-kuang in Nanking, and the whole of the south supported him; but the invading Manchus soon overwhelmed Nanking. Meanwhile under three other Ming princes the Ming adherents throughout the south continued to organize resistance.

It was within this historical context that Cheng Cheng-kung (Koxinga) emerged. This essay would try to examine three aspects of Koxinga's career. He was a great Ming patriot; to the end of his life, he sought to defend the Chinese independence from the Tartars and to restore the splendor of the Ming empire. He was a great nationalist; he waged a life and death struggle with the Western colonialists like the Portuguese, Spanish and Dutch, protected the overseas Chinese, liberated Taiwan from the Dutch colonial rule, and sought to spread Chinese influence abroad. And he was a great nation-builder; he transferred from the mainland to Taiwan a larger number of Ming supporters and poor people to begin a new life on the island where he introduced Chinese laws and customs and established the first Chinese government there.

I

The Background of Cheng Cheng-kung

Cheng Cheng-kung was born in 1624 at Hirado, Japan, near the present city of Nagasaki.[1] His mother was a Japanese woman of the Tagawa family; his father, Cheng Chih-lung, was from Nanan, Fukien, China. The early life of Cheng Chih-lung, also known as I-quan or Nicholas, was a struggle with poverty. He tried his luck in Macao, Manila and Japan, and combined piracy with trade.[2] In 1625, upon the death of Yen Ssu-ch'i, a leader of a band of pirates operating in and around Taiwan, Chih-lung took over the command and, within a few years, "amassed much shipping and men and terrorized the whole China coast, and has rendered navigation along the coast impracticable."[3]

The Ming government, already becoming hard pressed from the north by the Manchus and fearful of a Dutch invasion in the south (the Dutch occupied the Pescadores in 1622 and seized Taiwan in 1624 after they were expelled from the Pescadores by Ming forces), was unable or unwilling to divert its military power and resources to deal with the pirate bands. Therefore the government adopted a conciliatory gesture toward Cheng Chih-lung and, in 1628, succeeded in persuading him and his followers to enter the service of the Ming government.[4] By this maneuver, the Ming government hoped to utilize Chih-lung's fleet to fight other pirates as well as to deter possible Dutch attack on south China.

After joining forces with the Ming government, Chih-lung eliminated other pirate bands roving the China Seas and defeated the Dutch fleet at Amoy. His position was secure and his political career advanced steadily. He constructed a huge palace at Anping (several Western sources have rendered Anhai), only a short distance from his native village, and carried on trade with the Straits, Siam, Java, the Philippines, Japan, Macao and Taiwan. Reportedly, he was able to enforce his order that all vessels carrying on trade with the Dutch, Portuguese and Spanish settlements must pay fees to and obtain a permit from him.[5] In this way, he amassed an enormous fortune that was said to have surpassed even the Chinese emperor's. Moreover, he personally financed and commanded a fleet of 1,000 vessels (Western sources mention 3,000 vessels), as great a fleet as ever appeared in the China Seas, which now came under his domination.

In 1630, at the age of seven Cheng Cheng-kung returned to China from Japan and lived in his father's palace at Anping. He was looked upon as a prodigy of learning and passed the *hsiu-tsai* examination at fifteen; he also showed great interest in the *Art of War* attributed to the strategist Sun Tzu and spent time to achieve excellence in archery and horsemanship. In 1643, at the age of twenty, he was sent to Nanking to study at the Imperial Academy.

A few months after the fall of Nanking in 1645, Cheng Chih-lung and a few Ming officials proclaimed Chu Yu-chien, the Prince of Tang, a descendent of the Ming founder Tai-tsu, Emperor Lung-Wu, and established the Ming court at Foochow in Fukien province. It was at this juncture that Cheng Cheng-kung, now at the age of twenty-two, was presented by his father at the Imperial court of Lung-Wu. It is said that the emperor was so impressed by the young man that he exclaimed: "What a pity that I have not a daughter to give you in marriage."[6] Thereupon, the emperor appointed Cheng-kung commander of the Imperial Body Guard and conferred upon him the great honor of bearing the imperial surname. Cheng Cheng-kung then adopted his present name and because known as Kuo-hsing-yeh (rendered "Koxinga" by Europeans since that time) which means "Lord of Imperial Surname." The following year in 1646, Cheng Cheng-kung was appointed *Chao-tao Ta Chiang-Ch'un* or Grand Commander of the Punitive

Expedition, bearing an imperial sword as an insignia of extraordinary powers, and was dispatched to defend Hsienhsia Kuan,
the strategic pass between Fukien and Chekiang.

Cheng Chih-lung, although a "king-maker" and wielding
considerable power in Emperor Lung-Wu's court at Foochow, was
not unequivocal in his support for Lung-Wu. Believing the cause of
Ming doomed, he wavered when the Manchus made overtures to
him and then secretly reached an understanding with the Manchu
authorities, attempting to preserve his personal wealth and prolong
his political career.[7] He not only obstructed Emperor Lung-Wu's
war plans and withheld food supply to Cheng Cheng-kung's
troops, but also, at a critical moment, removed his troops from a
strategic point to make way for the advancing Manchu army,
resulting in the capture of Emperor Lung-Wu at the hands of
enemy forces. Subsequently, when the Manchu forces converged
on Fukien in September 1646, Cheng Chih-lung formally surrendered, and asked Cheng-kung to go along. A man of integrity and
patriotism, Cheng-kung turned down his father's request, saying
that "it is always the case for the father to teach his son loyalty;
who would have heard of the father to teach instead treason."[8]

After his capitulation, the Manchus moved Cheng Chih-lung to
Peking by guile. Although he was treated politely and given an
appointment by the Manchu government, he was kept in custody
and watched closely. He not only failed to receive the post of
Governor-General of Fukien, Kwangtung and Kwangsi, a position
which the Manchus had offered him earlier to induce his defection,
but also lost his power base in the south. His palace at Anping was
ransacked by the Manchus and his wife (mother of Cheng-kung)
committed suicide. Swearing to revenge for both the family and
the dynastic causes Cheng Cheng-kung went into the Temple of
Confucius and threw his scholar's robe into the fire, vowing to take
up arms for the rest of his life to fight the Tartar invaders.

II
A Ming Patroit

After the fall of Foochow in the autumn of 1646, Cheng
Cheng-kung made his way to Kulang Yu, an island separated from
Amoy by a narrow strait, and continued his campaign against the

Manchus from there. The Ming cause was still alive as resistance to the Manchu regime by scattered Ming forces was still active in the south and southwest China. As soon as Cheng-kung upheld the Ming standard, numerous Ming loyalists and scattered Ming forces flocked to him, and in a short time he had an army which gave hope to many who still had faith in the final restoration of Ming. Politically and psychologically, he had much on his side. Cheng-kung was close adviser to Emperor Lung-Wu, and was given the imperial surname, making him a member of the imperial family. Moreover, he distinguished himself as a true Ming patriot by refusing to follow his father to defect to the Manchus. Who then was better fitted to arouse the patriotic fervor of the people than this great patriot?

From 1646 to 1660, Cheng Cheng-kung carried on a relentless campaign against the Manchu forces in southeast China. Three major strategic objectives appeared to have underlined the battles he waged against the Manchus. The first one was to secure and enlarge his bases on the coast and to expand his military strength. In 1650, he took over Amoy and Quemoy from other Ming generals, thereby placing the Ming forces in the southeast under his unified command. He was also able to bring to his standard his father's former followers from all over the China Seas and began to possess a substantial fleet which was soon to become as formidable as that of his father before him. By 1655, he had established seventy-two military garrisons in Fukien and adjacent provinces and had, under his direct command, fifty thousand cavalry and seventy-two thousand infantry as well as the largest fleet ever assembled in Chinese waters.

The second strategic objective was to take concerted action in cooperation with the Ming forces under Prince Kuei, Chu Yu-lang, who declared himself Emperor Yung-li in 1647 and operated from bases in Kwangtung, Kwangsi and Yunnan. The forces under Cheng Cheng-kung and Emperor Yung-li had attempted on several occasions to effect a pincer movement from southeast and southwest China to restore the whole south, but military operations failed to accomplish the goal although Cheng-kung's forces did capture and hold a few cities on the coast of Kwangtung.

And the third objective was to attack and seize Nanking so as to control the vast areas south of the Yangtse River thence a massive northern expedition could be launched. In June 1658, Cheng Cheng-kung sailed north to implement this ambitious objective. His forces consisted of a squadron of eight thousand vessels, one hundred seventy thousand infantry, fifty thousand navy, five thousand cavalry, and eight thousand "iron men."[9] These "iron men" were encased in heavy armour decorated with red spots like the leopard, and were always placed in the forefront in order to cut off the feet of the horses of the enemy cavalry. Father Vittorio Ricci, an Italian Jesuit, who was an eye witness in Amoy, reported what he saw:

> Never before or since was a more powerful and mighty fleet seen in the waters of this empire than that of Koxinga's, numbering more than 3,000 junks, which he had ordered to rendezvous in the bays and rivers around Amoy. The sight of them inspired one with awe. This squadron did not include the various fleets he had scattered along the neighboring coasts.[10]

While on his way to the Yangtse in September 1658, a severe storm occurred and many of Cheng Cheng-kung's ships were sunk, drowning eight thousand of his soldiers, among them his three sons. This setback did not delay Cheng-kung long, however; for within eight months his ships were repaired and forces reorganized, and in May 1659 he led a new expedition ascending the Yangtse to attack Nanking which was the capital of the first Ming emperor, Tai-tsu. Cheng-kung's forces, conquering resistance along the way, advanced steadily and captured city after city, including Kuachow, the junction point of the south-north grain transportation route, and the heavily fortified Chenkiang, the gateway to the Yangtse River. At last, in late August 1659, Nanking was reached and encircled by Cheng-kung's troops where the retreating Manchu forces sought safety behind its walls. Victory seemed within his grasp. However, the defenders, resorting to ruse and taking advantage of Cheng-kung's over-confidence, launched a surprise attack, inflicting heavy losses on Cheng-kung's men and ships and handing him a severe setback.

Thus his first and last expedition to Nanking ended in failure, and Cheng Cheng-kung returned with his fleet to Amoy greatly crippled. To take full advantage of his discomfiture, the Manchu government dispatched a powerful squadron of eight hundred junks to Amoy in June 1660, hoping to annihilate the remnants of

Cheng-kung's forces before he had time to recover.

More accustomed to naval warfare than his enemies and being well acquainted with the tides and currents in the channels around Amoy, Cheng Cheng-kung decisively repulsed the enemy attack even though he was only able to muster some four hundred war junks. On June 17, after a bloody battle, the Manchu fleet was decimated and, as reported by the eye witness Father Ricci, "for many weeks after putrid corpse and wreckage strewed the shores of Amoy and Quemoy."[11] The Manchu general, Ta Su, blamed by Peking for the defeat, committed suicide. The defeat of the Manchu fleet seemed so thorough that for the next two years the Manchu government made no attempt to take Amoy and Quemoy by force.

Previously, the Manchu authorities had on several occasions made overtures to Cheng Cheng-kung and offered him a high position in court, hoping to induce him to give up the armed struggle. But Cheng-kung was uncompromising and repeatedly rejected the overtures. Cheng Chih-lung, a captive in Peking, was apparently pressured by his host to appeal to his son to transfer loyalty to the Manchu dynasty. In addition to letters, Cheng Chih-lung, for instance, in 1654 sent one of his sons, Cheng Tu, to Amoy to plead with Cheng-kung to have peace with the Manchu government. Realizing that the Manchus would someday harm his father and family members in Peking, Cheng-kung nonetheless sadly but resolutely replied to his father: "If something unfortunate should happen to my father, it would be what the heaven has ordained; your son will don mourning clothes and seek revenge so that I may fulfill both my loyal and filial vows."[12] To show his uncompromising attitude Cheng-kung in 1655 renamed Amoy Szuming to demonstrate his sincere commitment and absolute loyalty to the Ming cause. With the disappearance of any hope of a peaceful solution, the Manchu government put Cheng Chih-lung and his family members in irons and subsequently executed all of them.

III
A Nationalist Liberation of Taiwan

Although Cheng Cheng-kung managed to destroy the Manchu fleet in 1660, he held only Amoy and Quemoy, while other cities and territories on the mainland he once held were all recaptured by the Manchus. Meanwhile, the situation in southwest China was also deteriorating. The Ming forces under emperor Yung-li had been ousted from Kwangsi and Yunnan, and Wu San-kuei, the Ming general who defected to the Manchus in 1644, was leading his troops on a mopping-up operation forcing Yuan-li to take refuge in Burma. The Ming cause now seemed darker than ever, for after more than fifteen years of struggle since 1645, the gleam of ultimate Ming restoration seemed to be extinguishing under the steady Manchu consolidation of the mainland. It was at this dark moment that Cheng-kung made a historic decision. He would go to Taiwan and drive out the Dutch there and use Taiwan as a permanent base so that he could build up his forces for future assaults on the mainland.

Taiwan had been occupied by the Dutch since 1624.[13] The Dutch colonization of Taiwan has one major goal — to make the maximum of profits within the shortest possible time. Thus, the Dutch not only used Taiwan as a trade station which yielded considerable profits,[14] but also exploited in every possible way the local population and natural resources. They imposed a duty upon sugar and rice, two staple produce which were exported in considerable quantities by the Chinese and Japanese traders at that time. They required the local population to pay a license fee for permission to hunt and fish, and forced each male member, however young, in every Chinese family to pay a capitation tax (by the middle of the 17th century this tax totalled nearly forty thousand taels annually).[15] The Dutch treatment of the Chinese immigrants in Taiwan was often cruel and oppressive. The Dutch recorded in their own annals in 1622 the murder of 1,300 out of 1,500 Chinese settlers and soldiers in Pescadores who were forced by the Dutch to build a fort and were literally starved to death; and the shipping of Chinese to Batavia where, if they survived the cruel journey, they were sold as slaves.[16] The Chinese immigrant settlers in Taiwan, deeply dissatisfied with the exploitation and colonial tyranny of the Dutch, rose in 1652 in a major rebellion under the leadership of Kuo Huai-yi, a former associate of Cheng Chih-lung now in Taiwan, and more than 1,000 Dutch were killed.[17] But the Dutch authorities, with the assistance of 2,000 aborigines suppressed the rebellion with great force, resulting in a bloody massacre of more than 4,000 Chinese.[18]

Cheng Cheng-kung's struggle with the Dutch and the liberation of Taiwan can thus be viewed as expressions of Chinese nationalism. The ouster of the Dutch from Taiwan in 1662 was the climax of the struggle which had commenced earlier. Back in the 1630's Cheng-kung's father, Cheng Chih-lung, had on several occasions repulsed the Dutch fleet in south China when the Dutch attempted to open the China market by the threat of force. While there is no conclusive evidence that Koxinga was behind the 1652 rebellion of Chinese in Taiwan to oust the Dutch, he was apparently sympathetic to the cause of his fellow Chinese under the Dutch yoke and he subsequently instituted a punitive trade embargo on the Dutch in Taiwan. Historical records of that time showed that Cheng Cheng-kung was not favorably disposed to the Dutch who, in addition to their exploitation and repression of the Chinese in Taiwan, had often resorted to piracy against Cheng-kung's cargo ships. They also had often entertained apprehensions in Cheng-kung's intentions about Taiwan and had, prior to 1661, repeatedly requested Batavia to send reinforcement to defend Taiwan against his attack.

Cheng Cheng-kung's decision to go to Taiwan to oust the Dutch was not taken without debate in his policy council, however. Some generals argued against the Taiwan expedition from a pure military point of view; they felt that the Dutch garrisons had heavy guns which far outclassed those of the Chinese, that Dutch warships were vastly superior to the Chinese war junks, that the solid Forts Zeelandia and Provintia were impregnable, and that therefore only courage and skillful generalship on the part of the Chinese forces would not be sufficient to defeat the Dutch. Others argued that the water and soil in Taiwan were unhealthy and caused disease and that the climate there was uninhabitable. And still others, suspecting Cheng Cheng-kung was seeking a refuge in the far-away Taiwan, held that the mainland should be the focus of attention and that to leave Amoy for Taiwan would render the hope of Ming restoration further remote.

Obviously, Cheng Cheng-kung did not intend to go to Taiwan as a permanent exile, and he did not wish to leave the mainland for long. As a devoted Ming patriot, he had never forgot for a single moment his ultimate goal which was to redeem China from the Manchu scourge. As a strategist, however, he fully recognized the fact that Amoy and Quemoy by themselves were strategically

indefensible as they were extremely vulnerable to enemy blockade, and that he needed a place like Taiwan so that he may have
both a granary to draw supplies for his large forces and a secure
base thence to continue struggle against the enemy on the
mainland. Therefore, against the advice of many of his generals, he
commanded 25,000 of his best troops in 400 war junks and sailed
for Taiwan in March 1661.

As if to prove Cheng Cheng-Kung's foresight, the Manchu
government soon put forth a "scorched-earth" policy to starve his
forces by cutting all sources of supply from the villages and towns
along the coast of Kwangtung, Fukien, Chekiang, Kiangsu and
Shantung. Accordingly, in 1661, an imperial decree was issued
which ordered all the inhabitants of the coastal areas to move
thirty *li* (one *li* is equal to one third of a mile) inland and to
destroy their dwellings, fields, boats, and other properties in the
coastal belt left behind. The decree also forbid the Chinese to
engage in fishing on the seas or to trade with ports under
Koxinga's control.[19] The edict was immediately carried out, and
"to prevent the great number of destroyed villages from being
rebuilt, forts were erected at the distance of every three miles,
each one garrisoned with 100 men, who were authorized to put to
death all unfortunate beings whom they happen to find in the
immense belt."[20] The coastal dwellers, abandoning their houses,
land and property, and leaving their ancestral graves behind, were
crowded into the interior; many of them, however, put out to sea
and joined the Ming forces under Cheng Cheng-kung.

While Koxinga was engaged in active preparations for the
Taiwan expedition, the Dutch authorities in Taiwan became
greatly alarmed. They strengthened their defenses, increased
vigilance over the Chinese population there, and closely inspected
new arrivals from the mainland in the hope of gaining information
as to Koxinga's plans. The Dutch governor in Taiwan, Coyett, also
dispatched special and urgent messages to the Dutch East India
Company at Batavia requesting reinforcements.

On April 30, 1661, Cheng Cheng-kung's squadron, having
crossed the Taiwan strait without mishap, landed at Luerhmen,
the harbor entrance near Anping and out of the range of the
Dutch garrison batteries. At once, many Chinese residents flocked
to the scene to welcome their liberators and tendered the new
arrivals every assistance. On May 1, the Dutch garrison launched

an attack against Cheng Cheng-kung's forces, and the battle that ensued was both on land and water. In the first engagement, the Dutch Commander, Captain Thomas Pedel, and 118 of his 240 men were killed, and the four Dutch warships which attacked the Chinese fleet were also repulsed, with one burned by Chinese fire boats and the rest escaped from the harbor. The Chinese forces now proceeded to lay siege on the two forts and cut off all communications between the forts and the open country.

On the following day, Cheng Cheng-kung sent messengers to the two forts, summoning the Dutch to surrender. He told the Dutch: "This island was the dominion of my father and should go to none other than myself. Foreigners must leave." On May 3, Governor Coyett dispatched his envoy to Cheng-kung, offering to pay tributes annually, in addition to a war indemnity of 100,000 taels, if Cheng-kung's forces should leave Taiwan. In reply, Cheng-kung stated that Taiwan had always belonged to China and now that Chinese wanted it, the foreigners must leave the island immediately. The negotiation broke out without reaching any agreement, but Fort Provintia surrendered with all its garrison and arms the following day. On May 5, the Chinese forces mounted a fierce attack on Fort Zeelandia, which was built on an eminence enclosed with a strong wall and fortified with guns of heavy caliber. They failed to expunge the Dutch. After several engagements and indecisive assaults in the subsequent months, Cheng Cheng-kung installed a tight blockade, knowing that hunger and want would ultimately force the Dutch defenders to capitulate.

In the midst of the siege, reinforcements dispatched from Batavia in ten warships and 700 men arrived off Anping, and took the offensive against the Chinese fleet on September 16. So ineffective seemed the Dutch naval force that two of its vessels ran aground on a sandbank, thus falling an easy prey to the Chinese, leaving dead all on board except one officer and five seamen. A third ship with its crew of 118 was also captured by the Chinese. Hoping to divert Cheng-kung's strength, Governor Coyett now concluded an alliance with the Manchus on the mainland and planned to take joint action against Cheng-kung. In November 1661, the Dutch sent five warships to South China to assist the Manchus expelling Cheng-kung's forces from Amoy and its vicinity. But fate seemed against the Dutch in all their undertakings, for three of the five ships were lost in a violent storm and the other two fled to Batavia; the defensive strength of the Dutch in Taiwan was thus further diluted and weakened.

And so, on February 1, 1662, after a siege of nine months, the beleagued Dutch garrison at Fort Zeelandia, short of food, water, and ammunition, surrendered to Cheng Cheng-kung. An 18-point agreement was signed in which the Dutch agreed to leave Taiwan and hand over Zeelandia and its outworks, artillery, war materials, merchandise, treasure and other company property to Cheng-kung.[21] On the other hand, Cheng-kung was very generous in his terms; he accorded Governor Coyett all honors of war and permitted the Dutch, numbering about one thousand, including most prisoners of war, to leave Taiwan on their own vessels and to carry with them their private property. Thus, after close to forty years of cruel Dutch colonial rule, Taiwan was liberated by Cheng Cheng-kung and restored to China. In his struggle with the Dutch, Cheng-kung received substantial help from the Chinese settlers on the island who, having suffered Western colonization of its worst kind, were only too ready to cooperate with him to oust the Dutch.

Taiwan's Foreign Relations

To provide and maintain a large army as well as to bring prosperity to his people, Cheng Cheng-kung had long recognized the necessity and importance of foreign trade. Long before the Manchus enforced a trade embargo and coastal "scorched-earth" policy to cut him off from all supplies on the mainland in 1661, Cheng-kung's cargo junks had visited Japan, the Philippines, Indochina, Siam, and the East Indies. From this commerce, like his father before him, he derived substantial profits. But unlike his father, he did not accumulate a personal wealth, he used the proceeds from the foreign trade to procure supplies and materials and to finance the army and the government. After Cheng Cheng-kung's death in June 1662, his son and successor, Cheng Ching, continued the policy of fostering foreign trade. Although the mainland trade embargo was still in effect, through bribery and the connivance of Ching officials in the coastal areas, Taiwan resumed an active, albeit clandestine, trade with the mainland and were able to secure commodities from the mainland and sold them elsewhere at high profits.[22]

The Dutch colonialists were not reconciled to their expulsion from Taiwan. Not long after the surrender of Fort Zeelandia, the council at Batavia in 1662 sent twelve warships under the command of Admiral Bort with orders to take joint action with the Ching authorities against Cheng-kung. Arriving in the China Seas, the Dutch fleet anchored at the mouth of the Min River, and the Dutch commander proposed to Li Shuai-tai, the Governor-General of Fukien and Chekiang, that the Dutch fleet would assist him in expelling Cheng-kung's forces from Amoy and Quemoy, while the Ching government would aid the Dutch to recapture their former possessions in Taiwan. The negotiation failed to reach an accord, and Bort commenced a series of attacks on the fleet and garrisons of Cheng-kung at Amoy, burning and looting in a piratical manner.

In the following year, Bort was again sent back to the Far East with a stronger force consisting of sixteen ships, 1,386 sailors and 1,234 soldiers. By this time, Koxinga had passed away and his son Cheng Ching had succeeded him; therefore Fukien's Governor-General received Admiral Bort favorably and they concluded a military alliance. In November 1663, the Dutch and the Manchu ships jointly attacked Amoy and Quemoy and captured the two islands. As a reward to the Dutch for their assistance in taking the two islands the Ching authorities sent two junks to aid their Dutch ally to recover Taiwan. Now that the Ming forces were firmly trenched and had won the popular support of the Chinese in the island, Bort found it no longer possible to recover the Dutch possessions in southern Taiwan; instead, he went north and captured Keelung in 1664, and left Captain DeBitter with 200 in charge. Four years later, in 1668, the Chinese in Taiwan again drove out the Dutch with force,[23] and Dutch territorial possessions in the China Seas finally came to an end.

Cheng Cheng-kung's ouster of the Dutch restored Taiwan to the Chinese, if not to the central government of China then. He was a great Chinese nationalist both in his struggles to drive the Dutch out of Taiwan and the Manchus out of the mainland. Had he lived longer, he might be able to build a maritime empire in the China Seas and spread the influence of the Chinese even further. His plan to capture Manila from the Spaniards in 1662 underscored the great designs he cherished.

In March 1662, Cheng Cheng-kung sent the Italian missionary,

Vittorio Ricci, who had been in charge of a mission at Amoy and whom he had known intimately, to Manila as his special envoy to the Spanish governor. At that time there were many Chinese in the Philippines who held an important place in the economic life of those islands and especially in Luzon. The Chinese were there before the Spaniards who set up their colony only in 1571. But the Spanish imposed an oppressive rule on the Chinese, and rigorously enforced restrictions on Chinese migration to the Philippines. They massacred more than 47,000 Chinese in the early part of the seventeenth century.[24]

The purport of the dispatch Father Ricci brought to the Spanish governor was that the Spanish colony in the Philippines should pay tribute to the Taiwan authorities, or the Spanish colony would be attacked.[25] This demand appears to be the prelude to Cheng Cheng-kung's plan to attack the Philippines; his presence there would incite an uprising of the Chinese to expel the Spaniards from the Philippines.[26] The occupation of the Philippines by Cheng-kung would not only enable him to expand his power base and land a stronger force on the China mainland in the future but would also give him a complete control of the China Seas and a wider spread of Chinese influence.

When Ricci arrived at Manila the Chinese settlers there were elated as they had undoubtedly heard what Cheng Cheng-kung had done to the Dutch in Taiwan, and they probably anticipated him to repeat his Taiwan success in the Philippines, i.e., the expulsion of the Spaniards. On the other hand, the Spanish authorities were suspicious and hostile to the visit; they made preparations secretly and tried to provoke the Chinese settlers to action so that they could use it as a pretext to seize the initiative to eliminate the threat of a Chinese rebellion. "Two junk masters were seized, and the Chinese population was menaced; whereupon they prepared to defend themselves, ending in killing a Spaniard in the market place"[27] This was what the Spanish authorities had been waiting for; immediately they took action and, with their 8,000 infantry and 100 cavalry, slaughtered close to 10,000 Chinese in and around Manila. [28] Many Chinese were drowned "in the attempt to reach their canoes in order to get away to the sea; some few did safely arrive in Formosa and joined Koxinga's camp, while others took to the mountains." The Spanish historian, Jan de la Conception, stated that "the original intention of the Spaniards was to kill every Chinaman, but that they desisted in view of the inconvenience which would have ensued from the want of tradesmen and merchanics."[29]

Cheng Cheng-kung, on hearing of the event from the Chinese who were fortunate enough to escape to him, immediately organized a large punitive expedition towards Manila. The Spanish forces in the Philippines were not superior in strength to those that the Dutch had commanded in Taiwan, so they probably would have offered no effective resistance to Cheng-king's forces. It seems very likely that Cheng-kung would have landed his army in Manila and driven the Spaniards out of there as he had expelled the Dutch from Taiwan.

But it was not to be so. On June 16, 1662, Cheng Cheng-kung was seized with a racking cough which soon developed into a dangerous fever, and he died seven days later.[30] In subsequent years, the tensions between Manila and Taiwan relaxed, and the trade relations were restored. Actually, the Taiwan leaders had not given up the plan of the late Cheng Cheng-kung and had, on at least three occasions in 1672, 1673 and 1683, earnestly prepared to take action against the Spanish colony; however, each time the plan was put off at the last moment because of new developments on the mainland which outweighed the importance of the Manila expedition and had prevented Taiwan from diverting its military strength. Thus, Cheng Cheng-kung's plan to capture the Philippines never materialized.

IV
A Nation-Builder

Writing in 1908, Lien Heng stated in the preface to his classic work on Taiwan, *A General History of Taiwan* that: "Taiwan had not had a history. It was the Dutch who opened Taiwan, the Chengs who built it, and the Ch'ing who ruled it . . ." Cheng Cheng-kung's sponsorship of the Chinese people's migration to and settlement in Taiwan and his work in establishing a Chinese nation on Taiwan makes him a nation-builder and the maker of Taiwan.

Settling Taiwan with Chinese

One undertaking of Cheng Cheng-kung which is of great

historical significance was his transfer of Chinese settlers from the mainland to Taiwan. In addition to civilian and soldiers serving under Cheng Cheng-kung and their dependents, many Chinese who were either Ming loyals or were alienated by the Manchu rule also came to Taiwan which provided them a new hope and a safe refuge. Cheng-kung also made special efforts to encourage and help the Chinese on the mainland to migrate to and settle in Taiwan. As pointed out previously, countless Chinese inhabitants in the five coastal provinces from east to south China had been uprooted from their homesteads as a result of the Manchu government "scorched-earth" policy which forced them to abandon their dwellings and properties to resettle in the interior. In consequence, tens of thousands of refugees from Changchou, Chuanchou, Huichou and Chaochou, with the help of Cheng-kung's fleet, came to Taiwan and were resettled as farmers throughout the island.

In the words of a Western historian, Cheng Cheng-kung "started the era of great emigration of the Chinese, who today are to be found on all shores of the South Seas, from Cholon to Singapore, and from Batavia to Manila and Hawaii; it is a movement of immense importance, the ultimate consequence of which cannot yet be estimated."[31] It is probably not entirely accurate to say that Cheng-kung "started" the era of overseas emigration of the Chinese which had actually commenced long before his birth; nonetheless, he continued and promoted on a large scale the maritime venture of the Chinese people. With regard to the migration of the Chinese to Taiwan, Cheng Cheng-kung, together with his father, Cheng Chih-lung before him and his son, Cheng Ching after him, deserve all the credit.

As mentioned before, Cheng Chih-lung, prior to his entry to the service of the Ming government in 1628, was the leader of a pirate band that ravaged shipping on the China Seas, and his base of operations was in Taiwan. In 1626, Fukien had a severe famine throughout the province; thousands left for the Philippines in spite of the Spanish oppressive measures there that had resulted in occasional large-scale slaughter of Chinese migrants. Cheng Chih-lung, the Robin Hood on the China Seas, intercepted and seized government grain cargoes as well as robbed the rich in order to feed the poor; many destitute Chinese flocked to his banner and subsequently were settled in Taiwan to start a new life.

Previously, except for small settlements of Chinese in a few ports where they were engaged in trade, the island was inhabited mainly by aboriginal tribesmen. It was only since the 1620's that the Chinese, under the aegis of Cheng Chih-lung, began to settle there on a permanent basis and in increasing numbers.

In 1630, the Ming government officially promoted migration from the Chinese mainland to Taiwan. This was the first time in China's history that the government planned and sponsored such an enterprise.[32] This was the year in which the province of Fukien, after having suffered a succession of harvest failures, was threatened by peasant insurrection. The military Governor of Fukien, Hsiung Wen-ts'an, accepted the proposal of Cheng Chih-lung to provide relief by shipping the destitute people to Taiwan. Historical records inform us: "Several tens of thousands of starving people were each given three silver taels, and every three were given a cow, and shipped to Taiwan by vessels to reclaim and farm the uncultivated land."[33]

There is little doubt that it was Cheng's fleet that ferried these Chinese across to Taiwan. Cheng Chih-lung had been a pirate in his early life and had defected to the Manchus at the height of his career, so he has been condemned by Western writers for piracy and Chinese writers for treason. These writers, therefore, have failed to give him due credit when he deserved it; his undertaking of the migration of the Chinese to Taiwan is a case in point. It was a humanitarian task which sought no personal gains; it was saving people from starvation and offering them a new life.

The movement of the Chinese people to Taiwan, which Cheng Chih-lung initiated in the 1620's and his descendents, Cheng Cheng-kung and Cheng Ching, continued to promote on a larger scale, had resulted in the transfer of close to 200,000 Chinese to the island by the 1680's, according to one study.[34] The undertaking of the Chengs enabled Taiwan to be peopled by a population that considered the land its own and gradually planted its family roots deep into the Taiwan soil. These Taiwanese people were to form the nucleus from which has sprung the multitudinous and industrious population now to be found all over the island.

Nation-building at Taiwan

For centuries prior to the expulsion of the Dutch in 1662, the

Chinese government had claimed sovereignty over Taiwan, but had never actually governed the island; the Chinese government under different dynasties had stationed troops in the Pescadores from time to time but made no attempt to set up government machinery to rule over Taiwan which it regarded as its frontier possession. Due to the absence of any authority to enforce law and order, Taiwan which had been populated mainly by the aborigines became a haven for the lawless elements from China and Japan, and a secret trading post for Chinese and Japanese traders (because the Ming government forbid the Chinese to trade with the Japanese). During the period of 1624-1662 when the Dutch were in control of Taiwan, the colonial administration was concerned primarily with the extraction of resources from Taiwan and its Chinese settlers. Although the Dutch in their colonialization of Taiwan did establish a semblance of law and order and, particularly, the Dutch missionaries had done much good towards the aborigines by introducing Christianity and education, all these efforts were designed but to facilitate the Dutch control and exploitation of the island. That the Dutch in their colonial rule failed to provide a good government acceptable to the Chinese settlers there was attested by the Chinese revolt of 1652 and by Chinese popular support for Cheng Cheng-kung's efforts to expel the Dutch.

It was Cheng Cheng-kung who gave the Chinese in Taiwan their first government, the Chinese form of government which they had been accustomed to in their native lands. Accordingly, we find him introducing Chinese laws and customs and stamping out all traces of Dutch colonial rule. He divided Taiwan, according to traditional Chinese administrative system, into one prefecture, the Ch'en-t'ien-fu (later known as Taiwan-fu) and two districts, T'ienshing and Wannien, and appointed able officials to serve as prefect and magistrates there. He also set up the Ming capital at Chihkan or Sakkam and built his palace at Zeelandia which was renamed Anping to the memory of his native place on the mainland. His central administration was formed by six ministries, namely civil service, revenue, rites, war, punishment, and public works. He continued to use the title of Yen Ping Wang or Prince of Yen Ping, a rank bestowed upon him by Emperor Yung-li in 1654, even though he was *de facto* emperor of the island in every reality. He could have proclaimed himself emperor, as the heir to the Ming throne, inasmuch as he had borne the imperial surname and Emperor Yung-li had fled to Burma and fallen into the hands of the natives there. But he did not. Such was never his ambition. He was not a self-seeking man; rather, he was truly a great, selfless Ming patriot and regarded himself as the last defender of the Ming cause and the guardian of what still remained of the Ming regime. His struggles on the mainland prior to 1661 and the Taiwan afterwards were devoted entirely to one singular goal — the restoration of the Ming Empire.

To establish order in a frontier region like Taiwan, Cheng Cheng-kung applied stern criminal laws and enforced them without relent. Those who committed offenses in stealing, no matter how little, and in adultery were given the death penalty. Several of Cheng-kung's high officials were executed for either embezzlement or hoarding of grain. His critics and, at times, even his advisers considered his dispensation of justice too harsh. However, he was never partial; the death penalty which he inflicted upon offending commoner or subordinate he also sought to inflict upon his own son for his misdeeds.[35] As a result, the people in Taiwan were law-abiding and the society was peaceful and orderly, achievements even the writers of Ching dynasty spoke of favorably.

In addition to giving law and government to people in Taiwan, Cheng Cheng-kung also devoted much of his time to their welfare. He made an inspection tour of the island in 1661 which covered Sinkang, Baccalung, Soulang, Mattu and reached as far north as Tamshui and the present Taipei district. A historical account left by Cheng-kung's aide who accompanied him during the tour informs us that Cheng-kung availed himself of this extensive tour to study the nature and possibilites of the land and to meet the inhabitants and understand their problems.[36] Wherever Cheng-kung went, he treated the people with kindness and consideration and distributed tobacco and clothes among them, and he was warmly welcomed at many settlements he visited.[37] In his tour, Cheng-kung also noted long stretches of raw fertile land which could be opened for settlement and cultivation.

Upon the conclusion of the good-will and fact finding tour, Cheng Cheng-kung convened a conference attended by his civil and military officers to consider the task of building up Taiwan into a prosperous land. Addressing the assembly, Cheng-kung said:

Generally speaking, to manage a family or to govern a nation the first concern is to provide food. Without sufficient food supply, a family, inspite of ties which bind father and son and husband and wife together, will find it difficult to live happily. Without sufficient food supply a nation, notwithstanding its loyal ministers and officials, cannot be successfully governed. . . .

Now in our land not enough people are engaged in food producing while too many are consuming. If there is a shortage in food supply and the soldiers cannot be well-fed, then we will find it difficult to consolidate our nation and restore our empire. I have personally surveyed the island, investigated its conditions and found that land is available and fertile. We ought to follow the traditional policy of the "military colony," so that we will not suffer shortage in revenues and the soldiers will have abundant food, and we will mount our attack on the Manchus when opportunity presents iteslf.[38]

To carry out the "military colony," Cheng-kung decreed all the troops, with the exception of two brigades which were to garrison Anping and Ch'en-t'ien-fu, must engage in farm reclamation and cultivation, and special areas adjacent to the military posts were set aside for this purpose. Thus, the soldiers were to be both fighters and producers, "in the off-season in farming, soldiers would receive military training, in war-time, they would take up arms to fight, and in times of peace they would pull the plowshare to farm."

No efforts were spared to encourage farming and other productive pursuits for the inhabitants of the island. Native tribesmen were taught to use more advanced farming methods and implements.[39] Land was given, without payment, to those who could till, and for the first three years they were exempt from taxation, after which a land tax based on the quality of the land was imposed. It was also obligatory for all to undergo military training during the off-season in farming so they would be able to defend the island in case of enemy attack. Within two years after the expulsion of the Dutch, many farm settlements spread out along the island between the mountains of Taiwan and the waters of the Strait. From these settlements and military colonies, rural villages grew and some of them later developed into sizeable towns.[40]

When Cheng Cheng-kung passed away in June 1662, he had been in Taiwan only a little over one year. Although he had not had enough time to implement various measures required for a newly-founded nation, nevertheless he had within that brief span of time set a pattern, laid the foundation for future development, and had established the fundamental framework of Taiwan's polity. Many wise policies which he initiated were continued and worked out in detail by his son and successor, Cheng Ching. Whatever were Cheng Ching's previous shortcomings and offenses, once he was in charge, he dedicated himself with utmost vigour and unflagging zeal to his father's unfinished task — to make Taiwan a powerful and prosperous base for the eventual liberation of the mainland from the Manchus.

His first attention was to agricultural production. Like his father, Cheng Ching encouraged farming by distributing large tracts of uncultivated land to arriving immigrants from the mainland. Upon the advice of Ch'en Yung-hua, an official of considerable ability and talent, the plantation of sugar cane and manufacture of sugar were promoted, and new methods in producing salt from sea water was also introduced.[41]

Having provided for the people's material needs, Cheng Ching, acting again on the recommendations of Ch'en Yung-hua, took measures to give them educational benefits. Schools were established and maintained in every district. Civil Service Examinations were held once every three years, and those who passed the examinations were admitted to an academy of higher learning; upon graduation, the scholars were appointed officials of the government. Thus following the traditional Chinese pattern foundations of education and government of the island were laid. From 1661, when Cheng Cheng-kung came to Taiwan, to 1683 when the Ching government finally conquered Taiwan and ended the rule of the Chengs there, Taiwan had evolved from a frontier land into a viable polity that embodied consensus, community and legitimacy.

V

An Evaluation of Cheng Cheng-kung

When Cheng Cheng-kung passed away in June 1662, he was only thirty-nine years of age. He died a disappointed man; his regret was that he could not live to regain the mainland for the

Mings — the all-absorbing ambition that had led him on since 1646. On the threshold of his death, he was still holding the sacred testament of the first Ming Emperor and muttering: "The Great Ming pacified the empire and restored its ancient splendor. How can I meet him in heaven with my mission unfulfilled?"

Although described by various Western writers as an atrociously cruel and dastardly pretentious pirate, Cheng Cheng-kung was, in many ways, a great man and one of the most remarkable characters that Chinese history has produced. Unlike many vulgar pirates before, during and after his time who fought for personal gains, he was a man with a mission and a man of great vision. He was a great Ming patriot; the cause of Ming was ever present with him after 1645, and his possessions in south China and Taiwan provided a hope to all Ming adherents and a welcome refuge to the destitute Chinese alienated by Manchu rule. "Many of his nights were spent in going from one room to another or pacing up and down the corridor, planning for future conquests;" his life's work was to restore the lost empire.

The Manchus had on many occasions sent overtures to him, promising high office if he would surrender, and his father, a captive of the Manchus in Peking, had repeatedly appealed to him to come to terms with the Ching government so that the life of the elder Cheng could be spared. Knowing that it is impossible to be at once a loyal Ming official and a filial son to his father, Cheng-kung preferred loyalty to filial piety. But when he heard that the Manchus had executed his father and brothers, he was deeply grieved and many a time "at night would mourn and weep facing the north."

Although Cheng Cheng-kung did not succeed in ousting the Manchus from the mainland and in restoring the Ming dynasty, his liberation of Taiwan from the Dutch colonial yoke was nonetheless a splendid achievement and made him China's national hero. His movement of the Chinese people to Taiwan and his nation-building undertakings, which laid the foundation for Taiwan's future development, distinguished himself as the maker of Taiwan. Moreover, his restoration of Taiwan to the Chinese and transformation of Taiwan into a Chinese community produced historical consequences which were to affect international relations of East Asia in the 19th century and even to the present days; as such, he is immortal.

By way of conclusion, it is appropriate to quote non-Chinese writers' assessment of Cheng Cheng-kung's life and career. James Davidson in his historical review, *The Island of Formosa*, wrote this tribute:

> Koxinga was perhaps the most remarkable character that modern history exhibits in the Orient. Of all the bands of adventurous rovers that sailed the China Seas there was none to compare in courage, enterprise, and ability with this young chief. Born in Japan of a Japanese mother and a Chinese father we may believe he inherited courage and soldierly ability from the former and craft and diplomacy from the latter. At all events he possessed these attributes to a high degree, and was as successful in one as in the other. Holding one of the highest military commands in China at the age of twenty-two and dying while still under forty, his greatest exploits were accomplished during that period of life when others are ordinarily engaged in study and in preparation for the great deeds they hope to accomplish when they have arrived at perfect maturity. That his abilities were great is attested by his followers — a motley congregation, for all those who were oppressed or discontented found shelter under his banner, and it is a strong proof of his powers that thousands of men twice and even thrice his age were content to obey the authoritative commands of a youth who was not always gentle in his infliction of discipline.[42]

Yosaburo Takekoshi, the Japanese historian, concurred in this estimate of Cheng Cheng-kung in his *Annals of Japanese Rule in Formosa:*

> He [Koxinga] was by no means a common pirate. Inheriting tact and talent from his father and a sound judgment and daring from his mother, he was full of great ambitions roused by the tendencies of the age, and proved himself to be a hero, gifted with great governing and organizing powers. If he had been born in Nanking among high courtiers, he would assuredly have taken a prominent part in the civil war then raging in China, in connection with the coming of the Tartar dynasty. As it was, his deeds in Formosa proved him a statesman of no ordinary mould. He was indeed the leading spirit of the Government and he alone gave life and vigour to the whole institution.[43]

The French historian, René Grousset, had the following assessment of Cheng Cheng-kung's career and its impact:

Cheng Cheng-kung's destiny was not of the common run. . . . A pupil of the Spanish conquistadors who was forced by a foreign invasion to live on the outer edge of his country, his horizon was obviously wider than that of his Chinese compatriots. It was doubtless in imitation of the Spanish, Portuguese and Dutch navigators that he conceived the bold idea of building himself a maritime empire in the China seas. His attempt to do so is of great interest to the historian, being the earliest revelation of something which is by no means apparent in previous history — the maritime and colonial vocation of the Chinese people.[44]

Notes to Chapter IV

1 His original name was Shen, and another name Ta-mu; after 1645 he changed it into Cheng-kung.

2 George Phillips, "The Life of Koxinga," Part I, *The China Review* (Hongkong: China Mail Office), Vol. XIII, no. 2 (1885), p. 67. In this essay my information is based mostly on the works of Chinese writers and supplemented by various western sources. When Chinese and western sources differ on dates, names of persons and places, I have on most occasions followed the account of Chinese sources.

3 W. G. Goddard, *Formosa: A Study in Chinese History*, p. 64, quoting a report by Dutch Governor of Formosa to Batavia in 1627.

4 Lien Heng, *T'ai-wan t'ung-shih* (A General History of Taiwan), p. 729.

5 *Ibid.*, p. 730.

6 *Ibid.*, p. 26.

7 Chinese and Western accounts differ greatly on this point. All the Chinese sources including Cheng's biography compiled by the Ching government clearly and categorically state that he had compromised with the Manchus, while most western sources consulted by this author are ambiguous on Cheng's political stand during that transitional period; one writer even eulogizes Cheng as a "patriot," see Goddard, *Formosa, op.cit.*, pp. 69-70 and his *The Makers of Taiwan*, pp. 10-15.

8 Cheng I-chow, *The Biography of Cheng Cheng-kung*, p. 5.

9 *Ibid.*, p. 14 and Lien Heng. *T'ai-wan t'ung-shih, op. cit.*, p. 30. There are several other different accounts on the precise military strength of Cheng-kung's 1658 expedition; see Ch'u, *Cheng Cheng-kung*, p. 31.

10 Quoted in George Phillips, *loc. cit.*, p. 69.

11 *Ibid.*, p. 71.

12 Yang Ying, *T'sung-cheng shih-lu* (The Record of Expedition), p. 68.

13 For a detailed treatment of the Dutch rule of Taiwan, see James W. Davidson, *The Island of Formosa*, Chapters II and III. The Spaniards also founded a colony on the north coast of Taiwan in 1626, but were ousted by the Dutch in 1642.

14 In 1627 alone, for instance, the raw-silk trade with Japan yielded $240,000 (U.S. gold), and the China trade one million dollars (gold); see *Ibid.*, p. 15.

15 *Ibid.*, p. 23. A Japanese scholar estimated that in 1650 the capitation tax yielded 37,700 guilders; see Yosaburo Takekoshi, *T'ai-wan t'ung-ch'ih chih* (Annals of Japanese Rule in Taiwan), p. 109.

16 Davidson, *The Island of Formosa, op.cit.*, p. 11.

17 Lien Heng, *T'ai-wan t'ung-shih, op.cit.*, p. 20.

18 *Ibid.*; a different casualty figure, 8,000 is given by Ch'u, *Cheng cheng--kung, op.cit.*, p. 41 and Kuo Ting-yee, *T'ai-wan shih-shih kai-shuo* (A Sketch History of Taiwan), pp. 26-27.

19 Kuo, *T'ai-wan shih-shih kai-shuo, op.cit.*, p. 58.

20 George Phillips, "The Life of Koxinga," Part I, *loc. cit.*, p. 73.

21 Davidson, *The Island of Formosa, op. cit.*, p. 45.

22 Lien Heng, *T'ai-wan t'ung-shih, op. cit.*, p. 40.

23 *Ibid.*, p. 758; another source states that the Dutch abandoned the possession of Keelung in May 1668 as "no longer profitable," see Davidson, *The Island of Formosa, op. cit.*, p. 47.

24 Kuo, *T'ai-wan shih-shih kai-shuo, op. cit.*, p. 71.

25 The full text of Koxinga's message is reprinted in George Phillips, "The Life of Koxinga," Part II, *The China Review*, Vol. XIII, no 3 (1885), pp. 208-209.

26 Lien Heng, *T'ai-wan t'ung-shih, op.cit.*, p. 35.

27 Foreman, *Philippine Islands* as quoted in Davidson, *op. cit.*, p. 51.

28 *Ibid.*, and Kuo, *T'ai-wan shih-shih kai-shou, op. cit.*, p. 71.

29 Quoted in Davidson, *The Island of Formosa, op. cit.*, p. 52.

30 The nature of Cheng Cheng-kung's illness is variously given as malaria by Hsiao I-shan, *A General History of Ching*, Vol. I, p. 488, tuberculosis by Goddard, *The Makers of Taiwan*, p. 31, and flu by others. A Western writer, based on Ching sources, assert that Cheng-kung was attacked by "an appalling and fearful madness" and that "in his horrible frenzy, he tore his flesh, bit through his lips and tongue" and was "suffocated by rage;" see G. Phillips, "The Life of Koxinga," Part II, *The China Review*, Vol. XIII, no. 3 (1885), p. 211.

31 René Grousset, *The Rise and Splendor of the Chinese Empire*, p. 278.

32 Kuo, *T'ai-wan shih-shih kai-shuo, op. cit.*, p. 16. Before and after that time, the Chinese authorities for various reasons often forbid overseas emigration, millions who emigrated to Southeast Asia, the Philippines and Taiwan did so at their own risk and rarely received Chinese government protection when they were persecuted by natives or European colonialists.

33 Quoted in *Ibid.*

34 Lien Heng, *T'ai-wan t'ung-shih, op. cit.*, p. 152. It is estimated that during the Dutch rule of Taiwan, no less that 25,000 families emigrated from China to Taiwan; see Davidson, *The Island of Formosa, op.cit.*, pp. 23-24. A Japanese source set down the number of Chinese on the island before the Cheng Chih-lung sponsored migration at 25,000; see Yosaburo Takekoshi, *T'ai-wan t'ung-chih chih, op. cit.*, p. 102.

35 When Cheng Cheng-kung was informed of the birth of a child to his son, Cheng Ching, and a mistress (nurse of Ching's younger brother) in Amoy, he sent from Taiwan a messenger with orders to kill his son, for his misconduct, and his wife (Ching's mother), for her negligence in supervision; his generals there refused to execute the order, and Cheng-kung sent a second and third messenger to Amoy, but both fell into the hands of the generals there. Cheng Ching escaped the punishment only because of his father's sudden death.

36 Yang Ying, *The Record of Expeditions, op.cit.* p. 188.

37 Lien Heng, *T'ai-wan t'ung-shih, op.cit.*, p. 34.

38 This passage translated from a quote in Kuo, *T'ai-wan shih-shih kai-shuo, op.cit.*, p. 57.

39 Yang Ying, *Ts'ung-cheng shih-lu, op.cit.*, pp. 193-194.

40 Many towns and communities today can still be traced to these civil and military settlements of the 1660's. For instance, Linfengying used to be the "military colony" assigned to General Lin Feng who died in 1668 in a battle to seize the Dutch possession at Keelung; Touliu used to be the "military colony" of General Lin Su; and Hsingying and Tsoying were also "military colonies."

41 Lien Heng, *T'ai-wan t'ung-shih, op. cit.*, pp. 755-756.

42 Davidson, *The Island of Formosa, op. cit.*, pp. 52-53.

43 Yosaburo Takekoshi, *T'ai-wan t'ung-chih chih, op. cit.*, p. 106. The translation is from Goddard, *The Makers of Taiwan*, p. 32.

44 René Grousset, *The Rise and Splendor of the Chinese Empire, op. cit.*, pp. 177-278.

Bibliography

Cheng I-chou. *Cheng Cheng-kung Chuan* (Biography of Cheng Cheng-kung), (N.P., N.D.). Reprinted in *Taiwan Wen-hsien Ts'ung-k'an* (Collection of Works on Taiwan Series). Taipei: Office of Economic Research, The Bank of Taiwan, 1960, no. 67.

Ch'u Ch'i. *Cheng Cheng-kung.* (Wuhan: Hupei People's Publishing House, 1956).

Colquhoun, A.R. and J.H. Steward Lockhart. "A Sketch of Formosa." *The China Review.* (Hong Kong: "China Mail" office, Vol. XIII, no. 3, 1885).

Davidson, James W. *The Island of Formosa: Historical View from 1430 to 1900* (London, 1903).

Goddard, W.G. *The Makers of Taiwan* (Taipei: China Publishing Co., n.d.).

_____. *Formosa: A Study in Chinese History.* (London: Macmillan and Company, 1966).

Grousset, René. *The Rise and Splendor of the Chinese Empire.* Translated by Anthony Watson, et. al. (London: Geoffrey Bles, 1952).

Hsiao I-shan. *Ch'ing-tai T'ung-shih* (A General History of Ching) Vol. 1 (Taipei: Commercial Press, 1967).

Kleinwachter, G. "The History of Formosa under the Chinese Government." *The China Review*, Vol. XII, no. 4. 1884.

Kuo Ting-yee, *T'ai-wan shih-shih kan-shuo* (A Sketch History of Taiwan), 5th ed. (Taipei: Chengchung Book Company, 1970).

Lien Hung, *T'ai-wan t'ung-shih* (A General History of Taiwan). Reprinted in *T'ai-wan wen-hsien ts'ung-k'an*, no. 128. (Taipei: Office of Economic Research, Bank of Taiwan, 1962).

Phillips, George "The Life of Koxinga" Parts I & II. *The China Review*, Vol. XIII, nos. 2 & 3. 1885.

Shih Ming. *T'ai-wan-jen szu-pai-nien shih* (The Four Hundred Years of History of the Taiwanese People) (Tokyo, 1962).

Takekoshi, Yosaburo, *T'ai-wan t'ung-ch'ih chih* (Annals of Japanese Rule in Taiwan) (Tokyo: Hakubun-kan, 1905).

Yang Ying, *Ts'ung-cheng shih-lu* (Records of the Expedition). Reprinted in *Taiwan Wen-hsien Ts'ung-k'an*, no. 32 (Taipei: Office of Economic Research, The Bank of Taiwan, 1958).

Chapter V

Taiwan in China's External Relations, 1683-1874

BY CHAN LIEN

This chapter proposes to study China's early external relations with the island of Taiwan as a focus of analysis. Although it is supposed to cover a time span of almost two-hundred years — from the Manchu conquest of Taiwan in 1683 to the year 1874 when China and Japan concluded their first treaty over Taiwan — for purpose of analysis, one must confine himself to the later and perhaps the more substantial part of the story. For in terms of weight and complexity, there is no doubt that the first one and a half century of Manchu rule over Taiwan was marked with a lot more ease and tranquility. Such tranquility, to be sure, was the result not only of the official policy of isolating Taiwan from the rest of the country, but also of the situation that the Western powers were still in their pre-Industrial Revolution stage and their interest had not projected too far to the Far East. It was, in a way, a period of China's "Splendid Isolation" with the lack of external relations as its primary characteristic. The island of Taiwan, then a part of the Fukien province, shared this isolation.

This, of course, does not mean that Taiwan was entirely free from sporadic contacts imposed by the outside world. In fact, between 1683 and 1840, numerous contacts of such a nature were recorded. With its well-endowed natural resources, the island of Taiwan was never an unfamiliar place to the outside world. On the other hand, the brief occupation of certain parts of Taiwan by the Spanish and the Dutch colonists before Koxinga's (Cheng Cheng-kung) successful expedition in the early seventeenth century must have helped to perpetuate the memory of Taiwan in many Western minds.[1] It is against this background that the security of

Taiwan was frequently raised by thoughtful people during the early Ching period. For example, Lan Ting-yuan 藍 鼎 元 an early Ching official, had prophetically warned that "Taiwan holds the strategic position of the sea and is most conducive to exploration and reclamation. Such advantage will easily induce people to make encroachments there. If we do not treat the Chinese in Taiwan as our own people, they will join the aborigines or, worse still, the bandits. In case there were no threats from aborigines or bandits, external crisis might come from Japan or the Netherlands. This is why we must make preparations for it as early as possible."[2]

Lan's observation, as history shows us, was soon borne out by the unfolding of events. In fact, by early eighteenth century, Taiwan had once again stirred the imagination of many Western admirers whose picture of it was unfortunately mostly on the distorted side. In 1704, for example, a Frenchman from Avignon with the *nom de plume* of George Psalmanazaar, published his first book on Taiwan in London. The book entitled: *An Historical and Geographical Description of Formosa, An Island Subject to the Emperor of Japan, Giving an Account of the Religion, Customs, Manners etc. of the Inhabitants, Together with a Relation of What Happened to the Author in His Travels,*[3] was well received after publication. As a piece of information added to the scarce literature then existing on Taiwan, it was widely hailed and soon translated into Dutch.

In 1712 and 1716, French and German translations also appeared. But as a primer on Taiwan, it left much to be desired. Its major personalities and events of Taiwan were all fabrications, and in its omissions, even the very fact of the 1683 Manchu conquest of Taiwan was unknown to the author. Although it is recorded that Psalmanazaar, upon becoming an Anglican in his later years, confessed that the book was a "forged narrative" produced out of his "youthful vanity,"[4] but the tale had gotten around and the harm was done. For example, in 1808 the *Bibliotheque des voyages* formally included this book as one of its major authorities.[5] In 1877, the British orientalist, Terrien de Lacouperie, in his book *Formosa Notes,* also held the view that Psalmanazaar's book was by no means pure imposture but rather a polished version of the impressions of certain early European seafarers.[6] Such scholarship, based on sheer credulity, could not but be a source of misunderstanding in later years.

Another "episode" which contributed to augment early misinformation was to be found in the "adventure" of the Polish nobleman Maurice August Benyowsky. Certain historical documents described him as a commander of cavalry of the Polish confederacy who was taken prisoner by the Russians and banished to Kantschatka in 1770. In 1771, he succeeded in escaping from Russia with ninety-six others. On their way to France, it was recorded that they touched the Taiwan shore.

After a brief confrontation with the natives, it was said that they were in a position to establish a European colony. Benyowsky, however, sensed in suspicion his own insecurity facing the insubordination of his followers, soon continued his trip to Europe. Upon his arrival in France, he proposed the colonizing of the island. This proposal was subsequently submitted to Austria and Britain, and it was reported that his plan did interest many people. In any event, although he was killed in a battle in 1786 in Madagascar where he got involved in hostilities against the French, his book published in 1790 titled *Memoirs and Travels of Mauritius Augustus, Count de Benyowsky*, painted a tempting picture of Taiwan which remained vivid in the minds of many Europeans.[7] Such travelogues, whose authenticity is doubted by many historians today,[8] not only indicated once again the emerging interest of the West on the island of Taiwan in the eighteenth century, but also indicated a different angle from which Taiwan was viewed by the West during this time and in the days to come.

I
Taiwan Involvements in the Opium War

The real beginning of Taiwan's entrance into China's foreign affairs could be traced back to the Opium War in 1840 when the early straws began to bring a stormy wind. Early in the nineteenth century, prompted by the necessity of an expanded trade in the Far East, the British merchant ships had already frequently plied the Taiwan coast in the hope of establishing some trading posts. Dissatisfied with the limitation on trade imposed by the Chinese government which confined them to Canton, the British ships had unofficially frequented such ports in Taiwan as Luerhmen 鹿耳門, Keelung 鷄籠, Huwei 滬尾, and Tamshui 淡水, between 1824 and 1833, where they sold opium and bought camphor. In fact, in the summer of 1824, the British had carried out a rather detailed mission of exploring the Taiwan coast which lasted almost six months. Such activities easily drew the attention of the Chinese officials in Taiwan. For example, Yao Ying 姚瑩, then a local magistrate, had warned that once the British had "familiarized themselves with the sea routes and realized the weakness of our navy and coastal defenses they will start plotting against us".[9] To him, as well as to many others, this spelled the end of Taiwan's isolation from the outside world. Knowing, however, that the opening of Taiwan would not be voluntary, a sense of caution had permeated all their writings at this time.

The Opium War between China and Britain formally broke out in the spring of 1840 and soon led to a new page of Sino-Western diplomacy. Realizing that Canton was well fortified, the British moved to the north. On April 23rd of that year, the British attacked Amoy, and in June Tinghai was taken by them. Using it as a base of operations, the British began to extend their probings along the Chinese coast. In the meantime, Teng Ting-chen, 鄧廷楨, newly-appointed Governor-General of Fukien and Chekiang, was already casting his eyes across the Taiwan Channel. In his dispatch to the Emperor, he pleaded for a coordinated effort from other provinces.[10] He reminded the Emperor that "the most critical area of the Fukien coast lies in Amoy and Taiwan. And since Taiwan is much coveted by the (British) barbarians, its defenses should be further strengthened."[11] The Emperor readily concurred, and gave insturctions that the local officials in Taiwan, together with the former Chekiang Commander Wang Te-lu 王得祿, a Taiwanese, should jointly work out all necessary preparations for the defense of Taiwan within the shortest possible time.

In the meantime, in June 18, 1840, a British brig reached Luerhmen but soon left without engaging the local defense. Yet it signified the beginning of many similar threatening visits in the subsequent months. On July 20, the Garrison Commander of Taiwan, Ta-hung-a 達洪阿, and Yao Ying, then the Circuit Intendant, jointly submitted the emergency measures suggested for the defense of Taiwan. Among them, plans for enlarged conscription, reinforced fortifications, intensified training of naval forces, and the building of major warships were all emphasized.[12] The central government again readily concurred all these measures, and preparations were soon underway.

Between September and December of 1840, a lull was achieved in order to facilitate the initial peace talks between China and Britain. But the hostilities were soon resumed in January of 1841 when China refused to cede Hong Kong and pay the indemnity as demanded by the British. A brief truce was reached and broken again. In August, the British started their second expedition toward the north and occupied Kulang Yu, Amoy, Tinghai, Chenghai and Ningpo. Among all these developments, the loss of Amoy undoubtedly proved to be the most shocking news to the Chinese in Taiwan. To be sure, there were other sea routes that connected Taiwan with the Fukien coast, but the line between Amoy and Taiwan-fu (present day Tainan) nevertheless constituted the only major line of communications between the island and Fukien. Thus the fall of Amoy clearly implied further isolation of Taiwan from the mother country and inevitably created new problems both real and psychological.[13]

After the second attack on Amoy, a major part of the British forces moved on to the north. But a branch of it was dispatched to patrol Taiwan waters. In mid-September, British ships were sighted from various ports along the whole Taiwan coast, but still no action was taken by either side. It was not until September 30, 1841, that this eerie silence ended and the first war of Taiwan's self-defense took place. According to Yao Ying's detailed report to the Emperor, the British transport *Nerbudda* was first sighted by the Chinese forces around Keelung on September 29. In the morning of September 30, the transport suddenly entered the port and shelled the fort in Erh-sa-wan 二沙灣.

In this encounter the Chinese side suffered no casualties other than the destruction of one barrack. In return, however, the Chinese forces opened fire and hit the mast of the transport. Realizing that the coast was well-guarded, the ship attempted to withdraw. But, since it was already seriously damaged by the Chinese attack, as Yao Ying reported, it ran aground and the British were forced to abandon ship. Thus, besides some got away, ten "white barbarians" and twenty-two "black barbarians" were killed while another one hundred and thirty-two "black barbarians" were held prisoners. In addition, numerous documents and armaments were captured.[14]

In view of the repeated defeat suffered since the beginning of the war, the "victory" in Taiwan made the Chinese officials happy. When the news was reported to the capital on November 23, 1841, Emperor Tao Kuang expressed his great satisfaction and instructed that the meritorious local officals in Taiwan be rewarded and additional funds be allocated to sustain further defense measures there.[15] But the lull of peace was short. After the occupation of Chenghai and Ningpo, a British barque was dispatched to Keelung on October 19, with the acknowledged intention of securing the return of the *Nerbudda* prisoners. The British promised to pay a ransom for every prisoner held but the civilians refused to relay this demand to the local authorities. Meanwhile, the local commander, Chiu Cheng-kung 邱 鎮 功 , rapidly reinforced the defenses around Keelung and Huwei and moved the civilian population further inland.

After a silence that lasted eight days, the British, realizing that it was futile to wait any longer, finally began to take action. On the 27th of October, they started shelling the Erh-sa-wan fortifications, and at the same time landed a small contingent of men in the Pi-tou-shan area. According to the Chinese official report, while the landing was immediately repulsed, the exchange of cannon fire lasted until noon of the following day. Two Chinese barracks were destroyed and one patrol ship was lost in the encounter, but the fact that the British failed to carry out their objectives was considered a victory by the Chinese officials. The Emperor regarded the event as "successive victories within two months" and as encouragements, rewarded Ta-hung-a and Yao Ying with honorary hereditary titles. The Emperor, however, cautioned that the British "with their bestial nature will most likely plan for revenge. They may come back with even greater forces and we must be ready all the time. . . .Never underestimate the enemy and get caught unprepared."[16]

In the spring of 1842, the third Sino-British confrontation in the Taiwan area took place. On March 5th of that year, the British brig *Ann* was sighted off the Changhua coast. Following the imperial strategy of never contending with the enemy on the high seas, Ta-hung-a and Yao Ying planned to entice the ship into shallow waters so that it could easily be grounded and captured.

According to their official report, on March 11th the brig *Ann*, while making its initial thrust into the Ta-an port, was halted by local forces. Later on, however, the local official in Lukang, Wei Yin 魏 瀛 , managed to find several Cantonese fishermen and soon sent them to approach the brig. Once there, they succeeded in talking to the Cantonese aboard the ship. As a result of this contact, they further succeeded in misguiding the brig into the Tu-ti-kung port where it was grounded. Thereupon, the Chinese started to fire and the ship was destroyed.[17] This encounter, as described by the Chinese officials, was no doubt a victory. A total of eleven "barbarians" were killed, forty-nine were held prisoners, and five "Cantonese traitors" were captured. Besides, ten cannons and numerous maps and documents were seized, and certain guns and swords lost to the British during the Chenghai occupation were recovered.[18]

The news reached the capital at a time when the British were about to take Tsapu and Wusung. Small wonder that the Emperor was again greatly pleased. He pointed out that the local officials were "courageous and resourceful, and their merit contributed to national prestige." He stated that his "pleasure is beyond description."[19] Ta-hung-a and Yao Ying were once again lavished with high honors.[20] At the same time, however, a new edict was issued through the Grand Council. Since the Chinese government was unable to obtain much useful information concerning the military secrets of the enemy from the prisoners of the British transport *Nerbudda*, the Emperor now looked toward the newly captured prisoners of the brig *Ann* for such information. He thus ordered that inquiries be made to find answers to the following questions:

> Who ordered the successive invasion of Taiwan?
> What was the purpose of such an invasion?
> Were there any leaders among the eighteen "white barbarians" captured?
> Where did the brig *Ann* set sail from?
> How many barbarian ships were there along the Kwangtung, Fukien and Chekiang coast?
> How many barbarian leaders are there and who are the Chinese traitors who enjoyed the trust of the British?[21]

At the same time, he also ordered that "after the testimony was exacted, all but the barbarian leaders, together with the one-hundred and thirty-two prisoners previously captured, should be immediately executed to express our deep anger and to placate our chagrined people."[22] A short time later, in another edict, a few more questions were added to the previous ones. Here, the Emperor wanted to know:

> How large is England? How many colonies does she possess? Among these colonies, how many of them are strong enough not to be controlled by England? Are there overland routes which connect England with Chinese Turkestan? Is there a normal flow of traffic on these routes?
> Is trade carried on through these routes?
> Are they connected with Russia? Are the English officials, with the exception of Pottinger who is commissioned by the king, also commissioned by the king or sent by the military authorities?[23]

To emphasize his feelings, the Emperor here again reconfirmed his earlier conviction in this edict. He agreed with the Taiwan officials that sending the prisoners to the mainland may well expose them to the British forces. He was convinced that it would be more expeditious to carry out immediately the previous order of execution in Taiwan.

The answers to these questions were not reported until the end of that year. Meanwhile, in the latter part of July, bowing to the inevitable, the central government soon pleaded for peace. In fact, after the fall of Chenkiang, the Emperor had become increasingly aware of the futility of a prolonged Chinese resistance. To avoid further sacrifice, a final decision was reached in early summer whereby Commissioner Chi Ying 耆 英 , was ordered to seek for a peace agreement. After months of negotiations the peace treaty was finally concluded on August 29, 1842. In the meantime, reports from Taiwan kept pouring in but the Emperor showed little interest in them. To smooth the possible resumption of relations with the British in the future, he did, however, change his mind and instructed the Taiwan command in late August to withhold the execution of prisoners.[24] But his attention to the matter came too late. For the majority of the prisoners had already been executed in the early part of July. In fact, convinced of the correctness of their action toward the prisoners, the Chinese officials had never imagined the amount of complexity their action had added to the post-war settlement between China and Britain. And as such, a new issue was unexpectedly opened up.

Article 19 of the Nanking Treaty provided for the repatriation of British prisoners after the war. On October 10, 1842, the British ship *Serpent*, commanded by the military attaché W. Nevil, reached Anping for the obvious purpose of securing British prisoners. Once there, he was informed by the local magistrate Hsiung I-pen 熊 一 本 , of the disheartening news that there were only nine prisoners and two Chinese collaborators left. The Chinese government would very shortly escort them back to the mainland. The news undoubtedly strained his credulity. Unconvinced of what he had learned, Nevil sailed back to British headquarters. On October 19, a British ship was capsized by a typhoon outside the Tamshui coast. But since it had taken place after the cessation of hostilties, the twenty-five survivors were all treated as ordinary foreigners and the appropriate authorities were duly informed of the incident. On November 4th Nevil returned once again with the demand that both the British prisoners as well as the survivors of the recent shipwreck crew be turned over to him.

Yao Ying, who met Nevil on this occasion, told him that there was no problem concerning the recent survivors. But, as to the prisoners, the remaining nine were already sent back to Amoy while the rest had indeed been executed in July. To support his stand on the latter case, he further pointed out that "since we are formally at war, there is no reason to keep us from sentencing them. In fact the Chinese government has always believed in making friends from afar through virtuous conduct and was never light-headed in the use of force. Ever since August of last year and up until January of this year, all prisoners detained were unharmed. It is because of your activities in Kiangsu and Chekiang which always ended up by hurting our officials and killing our people that the Emperor was angered and the people in Taiwan grieved. That is why the prisoners were executed."[26] Nevil sailed back once again but with only the twenty-five survivors on board.

The British Plenipotentiary, Sir Henry Pottinger, arrived in Amoy on November 21, 1842. Upon learning of the execution of the British prisoners by the Taiwan officials, he immediately demanded an audience with I-liang 怡 良 , who was then Governor-General of Fukien and Chekiang. Pottinger complained

of the senseless "massacre" of British nationals and subjects who
were to him actually "unarmed laborers" and "non-combatants."
They were killed, in his opinion, purely for the purpose of
"fabricating false victories" on the part of the Taiwan officials. He
asked I-liang to convey the real situation to the Emperor so that
the local officials concerned would be seriously punished and their
property confiscated for compensation to be awarded to the
families of the victims. He warned, however, that if these
conditions remained unfulfilled, the rekindling of the Sino-British
conflict might be a distinct possibility and China, of course, would
be solely responsible for the eventuality.[27]

To add further pressure on the Chinese government, a
proclamation was subsequently issued in both English and Chinese
for general information which in part read as follows:

> Her Britannic Majesty's Plenipotentiary in China, has, on his
> arrival at Amoy, learned, with extreme horror and astonishment,
> that many more than a hundred subjects of her Britannic Majesty,
> who were wrecked in the ship *Nerbudda* and brig *Ann*, in the months
> of September, 1841 and March, 1842 along the coast of the island
> of Formosa, have been recently put to death by the Chinese
> authorities on that island, who allege they perpetrated this
> cold-blooded act in obedience to the imperial commands.

It then continued:

> Her Britannic Majesty's Plenipotentiary has already obtained
> positive official proof, that the commands issued by the Emperor
> for putting to death her Britannic Majesty's subjects were drawn
> from his Imperial Majesty by the gross and merciless misrepresen-
> tations of local authorities on Formosa, who, with the object of
> personal aggrandizement, basely and falsely reported to the
> Cabinet at Peking, that both the ship *Nerbudda*, and subsequently
> the brig *Ann*, had gone to that island with hostile intentions, an
> assertion not more lying and false, than manifestly absurd, since
> neither of those vessels were ships of war, or had, when wrecked
> any troops or other fighting men on board them.[28]

Pottinger's threat had caused immediate worry to some
Chinese officials for fear that it might prejudice China's position in
the final peace settlement. I-liang, for example, pointed out that
Pottinger was "never aware of the execution and was anxiously
waiting for the return of all prisoners. To tell him that there are

only eleven alive is something he could never lightly accept."[29] I-li-pu 伊 里 布 , then the royal Commissioner who was dispatched to Canton to meet the British, also suggested in his dispatch to Peking that:

> Since Taiwan had executed all the barbarian prisoners, it could not be avoided but used as a pretext (by the British). . . .We can no longer conceal it. We could only be honest and tell them the truth, and inform them that the execution of prisoners took place before the negotiations for peace had begun. With sweet and soft persuasion, the British may perhaps react favorably.[30]

While I-li-pu was assigned to negotiate with the British, the British clearly indicated their preference to make treaty arrangements with Chi Ying, with whom they had had some previous experience. The Emperor, fearing that complications might cause further delay, immediately transferred Chi Ying, then the Governor-General of Liang Kiang, to the south to handle the difficult problem of prisoners. Once there, Chi Ying shared the same misgivings that I-liang and I-li-pu had entertained. By this time, the Emperor had already received the report indicating that the execution of the prisoners indeed took place before the news of the cessation of hostilities reached Taiwan. Thus when Chi Ying conveyed the British demands to the Emperor that the Taiwan officials be punished and their property be used as compensation, the Emperor was indignant and retorted that:

> Before the conclusion of the commercial treaty, there were losses of soldiers and civilians on both sides; but since we are already at peace at present, it is appropriate to let bygones be bygones, for that is the way to perpetuate peace with mutual fidelity. . . Suppose there was some misrepresentation caused by Ta-hung-a's self-seeking attempts, once it is verified, it will be disposed of according to Chinese law. There is no need for the barbarians to dictate the way through which we should manage our own affairs.[31]

But Chi Ying thought differently. In his dispatch, he conceded that Ta-hung-a and Yao Ying were good officials and liked by the people in Taiwan. To dismiss them simply because the British had so demanded would be unreasonable. But, he pointed out, "If we do not concur with the British demands, I am apprehensive that

Pottinger might use it as a pretext to attack Taiwan. If Taiwan is not kept, the over-all situation will be very much adversely affected."[32]

To prepare for a possible rapprochement through appeasement, Chi Ying figured a way out by implicating the Taiwan officials through hearsay. He reported to the Emperor that he was informed by Li Ting-yu 李 廷 鈺 , the military commander in Chekiang, who had the information that the Taiwan officials did indeed frequently get involved in the indiscriminate killings of foreigners, a matter which had aroused even the anxiety of the local populace. To him, therefore, the British complaint may not be altogether groundless. In any event, in order to clarify the matter, he suggested that I-liang be sent to Taiwan to investigate the case and be invested with the authority to come up with solutions.

The story that followed was rather typical. I-liang, as suggested, was sent to Taiwan to find out if the reports were indeed true. If so, the Taiwan officials were supposed to be relieved of their official duties and brought back to Fukien. Out of jealousy and hatred of the Taiwan officials, whose report to the court always bypassed him, I-liang had found his solution before he opened the case. He enlisted the help of an opponent of the Taiwan officials, Shih Mi 史 密 , who agreed to testify against Ta-hung-a and Yao Ying whatever the case may be. At the same time, I-liang also warned Ta-hung-a and Yao Ying to confess to the charges so that the Emperor's wish for peace may be realized at an earlier date.[33] To this request, they readily complied. Thus with all needed proofs amassed, I-liang reported to the Emperor that both Ta-hung-a and Yao Ying had testified that "the foreign ships were destroyed by typhoon. Besides those who escaped, the rest came ashore and hid in houses. They were arrested by the government who gave certain rewards to the people. In actuality, there was never a military confrontation."[34]

This ended the Emperor's dilemma. In early 1843, Ta-hung-a and Yao Ying were relieved of their duties. All previous honors and positions accorded them were likewise revoked. They were even ordered to be tried by the Board of Punishment for due penalty. Looking back, it is rather clear that all these were aimed to show, as the Emperor noted, "all the people inside and outside of China my sincere wish to follow the principle of justice."[35]

Differently put, they were expediencies designed to pull the empire through the adversity. For we find that the Emperor soon made his sham anger obvious when he ordered to remove the Taiwan officials only from their official duties with no other punishments imposed. In fact, seven years later, both Ta-hung-a and Yao Ying were reinstated. But the action in 1843 was necessary. It did satisfy the British over the prisoner issue, and paved the way for peace.

Such an ending, however, did not quite smooth the sense of justice of many Western historians. Subsequent treatments of the episode have frequently characterized the Chinese action toward the prisoners as a "massacre" which was committed against "the whole civilized world."[36] For example, James W. Davidson in his major work on Taiwan had well expressed this mood when he said:

> As has often happened, however, the Chinese authorities were able to smooth over the affair by degrading and banishing the Formosan commandant and the intendant. Thus did China escape the consequences of a crime of such magnitude that had it been committed by any other nation, it would at once have been taken as a *casus belli*, and full and complete retribution exacted.[37]

But if we admit that there are always two sides in a case, a few words may perhaps be added here as a counter-weight to this prevalent one-sided point of view. To be sure, the central issue between the British and the Chinese in respect to the execution of prisoners was their difference over the question as to whether they constituted participants in time of war. The British, insisting that both the *Nerbudda* and *Ann* were ships for commerce, took the view that those on board and later captured should not be regarded as combatants. But during a time of incessant hostilities between Britain and China, this distinction between military and non-military ships is, to say the least, difficult to maintain. Between the summer of 1840 and the fall of 1841, British ships had in fact made numerous appearances and even attacks on the coast of Taiwan.[38] And as such, even had China accepted the Western legal principles, it would be highly improbable for the Chinese to believe that what they had captured were ships free from military function. Moreover, the transport *Nerbudda* did attack Chinese fortifications and barracks in Erh-sa-wan and certain armaments were found on board, while, on the other hand, loot from Chenghai were found on board of the brig *Ann*. This evidence clearly indicated that these ships had taken part in the earlier hostility. Thus, the whole issue lies in the establishment or denial of these facts. Yet this is a step which is generally glossed over not only by the opposing parties at the time of negotiation, but also by the succeeding generation of historians who wrote the story many years later.

The treatment of the prisoners, on the other hand, constituted another disagreement between the two countries. To the Chinese at this time, all persons of the belligerent country who trespassed into the territory of China were subject to the customary wartime measures irrespective of his military or civilian stature. The distinction made by international law on the combatant and non-combatant was subscribed to by China at a much later date. No one could deny that the fate of the prisoners was indeed a tragedy, but it was more appropriate to say that they were victims of a sad situation brought about by the "conflict of Western and Eastern cultures."[39] This may sound platitudinous today when much consensus on the fundamental rules of international behavior exists, but the conflict of values was no doubt the basis of serious misunderstanding at the initial stage of contact between China and the West. Thus, to characterize the prosecution of prisoners as "massacre" would tend to beg the question. For there were deeper issues involved which could not be fully grasped if we reduce the whole case to the single point of insensate brutality.

The fact that the British could come to terms with China over the prisoner issue at all is itself the most interesting point. Had the British been serious about the prisoners, they would have been demanding more than the simple dismissal of certain responsible Chinese officials, which, they know, could easily materialize. The reason for their relatively soft position must, therefore, be found elsewhere. By examining carefully the facts involved, it seems that the non-British nature of the prisoners must have played an important role in the British decision. Let us here cite one British view for illustration. Describing the "execution of Indian survivors of the *Nerbudda*," Hosea B. Morse wrote:

> In September 1841 the transport *Nerbudda* was wrecked on the coast of Formosa. The Englishmen on board, including the master,

two mates and an officer and seventeen men of H.M. 55th regiment, left the ship in the only boat available, and shamefully abandoned to their fate two-hundred and forty natives of India (one-hundred and seventy dhoolie-bearers and seventy lascars) remaining on board. Of these, two were returned to the world; of the remainder some were drowned, some died of ill-treatment, of insufficient food, and some (about one-hundred and fifty) were beheaded by the Chinese authorities in Formosa the following August. In the following March the brig *Ann* was also wrecked on the coast of Formosa. Of the fifty-seven on board, eleven were released in October, two died from privation, and the remaining forty-four were beheaded on or about August 13th.[40]

With this racial undertone understood, no other reasons would be needed, perhaps, to explain the subsequent British reticence over the whole matter. Of course the timing of the event was equally significant. The prisoner issue came up at a time when the signing of the Nanking Treaty was completed. Had it been known by the British earlier, it would no doubt have been used as a leverage against the Chinese government. But since the British had already achieved their goal in the treaty, a new beginning in Sino-British relations was about to start. Whether it is worthwhile to shed further tears, and perhaps blood, over the fate of the unfortunate Indians was a question the British probably did not fail to pose for their own discreet consideration.

II
The Opening of Taiwan

The Treaty of Nanking signified the initial opening of the Chinese Empire to the West. In China, it was hoped that by opening the five trading ports, she could limit the Western activities to certain geographical areas while at the same time make the rest of the country immune from foreign contact. But while this may be true, though briefly, to the rest of the country, it was by no means true insofar as Taiwan was concerned. The five ports, as it happened, were all on the coast of south and southeast China and two of them, Amoy and Foochow, had more than ordinary relations with Taiwan. With the ocean wide open to whoever possessed the superior naval force, the opening of the Fukien coast naturally lead to a more exposed Taiwan.

In fact, with their priviliges on the Chinese coast established, the British soon took steps to explore future trading possibilities in Taiwan. As Hsiung I-pen described in 1843, "After the pacification of the barbarians, their big ships have been frequently plying our Tamshui waters. Occasionally, they would land with small sampans and study the topography and make maps. It has caused suspicion and fear among the local people."[41] After 1847, the British interest in Taiwan had become more obvious and their visits to the island had also become more frequent.[42] By 1850, the British Governor-General of Hong Kong, Sir George Bonham, formally notified Hsu Kwang-chin 徐 廣 縉 , the Governor-General of Kwangtung and Kwangsi, of the desire to get coal for British ships in Taiwan. After Hsu declined to discuss the problem on the grounds that Taiwan was beyond his jurisdiction, Bonham soon made the same request of Liu Yun-ko 劉 韻 珂 , then Governor-General of Fukien and Chekiang. No doubt, the reply was again in the negative. As Liu pointed out, "Taiwan is not opened for commerce and the British ships should not get there arbitrarily in violation of the law."[43]

In fact, in order to make sure that the British would not get through, Liu further instructed the local officials in Taiwan to "consolidate the unity of the people and strengthen the defense of the island so as to leave them [the British] no chances."[44] At the same time, he also referred the matter to the Emperor. The latter, in his instructions, not only agreed with Liu that the British ambition over Taiwan was a matter of long standing, but also ordered his officials to guard cautiously against any possible British incursions. He pointed out that "Taiwan holds an important location in the ocean. Because of the mixed habitation between the Chinese and aborigines, it is susceptible to trouble even during normal times." Continuing, he inquired, "How could we allow the insidious barbarians to take advantage of such situations under the pretext of trade?"[45] Indeed, in the face of this kind of attitude, Bonham's failure was already a foregone conclusion.

But the British were not alone in this. The United States, though a late-comer to China, was also beginning to show avid interest in the island at this time. Encouraged, perhaps, by the British seizure of Hong Kong and the subsequent conversion of it into a base of commerce in the Far East, the American merchants in the Far East were naturally tempted to be eager for similar action. Beginning in 1847, when American officers visited Taiwan and acquired samples of coal, the interest of the United States in the island had become increasingly manifest.[46] Commissioner John W. Davis' procurement of some samples of Taiwan coal and Captain W.S. Ogden's visit on board the United States brig *Dolphine* during subsequent years were cases in point.

By the 1850's, with Japan forcibly opened by her navy, and her trade in the Far East rapidly expanding, the United States' interest in Taiwan had become even more pronounced. In fact, in 1853, after he succeeded in opening up Japan, Commodore Mathew C. Perry, by sending Captain Joel Abbot to Taiwan, had already indicated his interest in making the island "the foundation for an American commercial empire in Asia and in the Pacific."[47] In 1854, Townsend Harris, then American consul in Ningpo, in his letter to William L. Marcy, the Secretary of State during the Pierce Administration, had further suggested the purchase of the island from the Chinese government, and if they refused, then the western part of the island from the aborigines.[48]

In 1857, Gideon Nye, an American merchant in Canton, had even offered his service for the American colonization of the island.[49] But, all in all, none had perhaps been more outspoken than Peter Parker, the American Chargé d'Affaires in China at this time. In a letter to his government long before Nye had offered his services, he pointed out that:

> The subject of Formosa [Taiwan] is becoming one of great interest to a number of our enterprising fellow citizens and deserves more consideration from the great commercial nations of the West than it has yet received; and it is hoped that the government of the United States will not shrink from the action which the interest of humanity, civilization, navigation, and commerce imposed upon it in relation to Taiwan.[50]

In fairness to the United States government, however, one must point out that all these urgings and suggestions coming from the East had failed to strike a sympathetic chord. Although the Department of Navy did appear rather willing from time to time, the State Department was more practical and prudent in its views. For this was the time when the revision of the treaty between the Treaty Powers and China was very much up in the air and a concerted effort of the Powers was imperative to any meaningful bargain with China. Any individual action by the United States might well throw the whole deal overboard. Thus, Secretary Marcy, in his reply to Parker, stated quite clearly that:

> The President does not believe that our relations with China warrant the "last resort" you speak of, and if they did, the military or naval forces of the United States could only be used by the authority of Congress. The "last resort" means war, and the executive branch of this government is not the war-making power. ...For the protection and security of Americans in China and the protection of their property, it may be expedient to increase our naval force on the China station, but the President will not do it for aggressive purposes.[51]

After the inauguration of President James Buchanan, the United States government followed the same line of reasoning. To be sure, it acknowledged that a coaling-station in Taiwan would be greatly useful to United States commerce in the Far East, but it could not take any forceful measures against Taiwan in violation of the United States Constitution. On May 30, 1857, Secretary of State Lewis Cass, in his instructions to William B. Reed, the newly-appointed American Minister in China, clearly stated that the diplomat's primary responsibilites should be in the negotiation of revisions of the treaty with China. The American interest, as he pointed out, lies in the protection of American citizens and properties in the trading ports and in expanding trading opportunities through legal means, not in the acquisition of territories of establishment of new regimes. [52] This policy had, no doubt, terminated all ambitions that certain Americans might have harbored over Taiwan in the late 40's and early 50's of the nineteenth century.

But Taiwan's isolation from the Western powers, despite all these factors, proved to be short-lived. For by 1856, new opportunities were once again open to the West. As we know, ever since the opening of the five ports, the Sino-British trade had never been carried out smoothly. For China, the Treaty of Nanking was no doubt a sign of great humiliation and it was natural that she would do anything possible to sabotage it. But as far as the British were concerned, the Treaty was equally disappointing but for the exactly opposite reason. Not only were the ports opened to them confined to the southern coast, but the opium trade, the most profitable item of trade, was still prohibited. Worse still, in the five treaty ports, they were either frequently denied the right of entrance, such as happened in Canton, or were harassed and annoyed through a variety of means by the Chinese people and their government. By 1852, Yeh Ming-shen was promoted to Governor-General of Kwangtung and Kwangsi while Sir John Bowring was appointed Governor-General of Hong Kong and Harry S. Parkes was designated as the British Consul in Canton. This change of personnel on both sides soon added a new personality feature to an already explosive situation. Indeed very soon, in 1856, the tinderbox was touched off once again by two seemingly insignificant and unrelated events.

The two incidents that eventually caused a war were the *Arrow* incident and the murder of the French Catholic priest, Abbe Auguste Chapdelaine. The *Arrow* was a Chinese-owned lorcha which had been registered in Hong Kong, flew the British flag and was commanded by a British subject. On October 8, 1956, when its registration had already expired eleven days before — a fact not known to the Chinese officials then — the ship was boarded by Chinese patrolling forces and twelve of the Chinese crew were subsequently arrested on suspicion of piracy. At the same time, the British flag was also allegedly hauled down by the Chinese forces. Once these facts were out in the open, the British lost no time in exploiting the incident as a pretext to demand treaty revisions and to redress their long-term grievances.

Earlier, in the spring of that year, the French priest Father Chapdelaine was killed in Kwangsi. Realizing that the French policy in the Far East at this time was dictated very much by "national pride — pride of culture, reputation, prestige and influence,"[53] the British soon extended an invitation to the French to join in a war against China. This calculation was indeed a diplomatic coup, for Napoleon III willingly played his supporting role in turning a minor issue into a *casus belli* which soon precipitated the Anglo-French War against China.

The United States government, though reluctant to join the British invitation in a military expedition against China, nevertheless appointed William B. Reed as Plenipotentiary to accompany the British Plenipotentiary James Bruce, 8th Farl of Elgin, and the

French Plenipotentiary Baron Gros to play a diplomatic part in pressing the American claims for reparations and treaty revision.[54] Similarly, in response to Anglo-French approaches, the Russian government also made it clear that it would not join in any military measures against China but it would participate in matters relating to "questions of European interest, such as the protection of Christians, opening of Chinese ports to trade, and the establishment of permanent legations in Peking."[55] With such interests shown by the United States and Russia, the *Lorcha Arrow* War had indeed become for China, as one historian put it, "a war against four opponents in reality, but only two opponents in name."[56]

The details of the war are beyond the concern of this chapter. Suffice it here to point out that after Canton was taken, the allied expeditionary forces proceeded to the north and took Taku and Tientsin. By April 1858, negotiations were started in Taku, but they were later broken off. In May, the Plenipotentiaries of the four powers reached Tientsin. In June, Kuei-liang 桂 良 , a Grand Secretary, and Hua-sha-na 花 沙 那 , president of the Board of Civil Appointments, were sent from Peking to continue the negotiations. Through ruthless intimidations and threats, a series of treaties were finally signed in Tientsin between June 13 and June 27. Through these treaties, China had granted a series of concessions to the West, which included, among other things, the payment of indemnities, the establishment of the right of extraterritoriality, and the most-favored-nation treatment. China also agreed to a fixed rate of tariff and the stationing of permanent diplomatic representatives in Peking. At the same time, special privileges for foreign missionaries and the opening of more ports were also granted. It was on this last issue that Taiwan was directly involved. In treaties concluded with Britain, Russia, and the United States, China had agreed to open, in addition to Liuchuan, Tengchou, Chaochou, and Chiungchou, a port in Taiwan for commerce. But in the Sino-French Tientsin Treaty, China had further agreed to open Tamshui for trade. Based on the most-favored-nation clause, Tamshui was therefore also opened to the other three countries. It was further provided in all these treaties that the nationals of the four Western powers could freely move or stay in the newly-opened ports. They could bring their families to live with them, rent or build houses, and acquire land through lease for the purpose of building churches, schools or hospitals. With all these provisions sealed in formal treaties, Taiwan was for the first time formally exposed to the West.[57]

The Tientsin Treaty was concluded at a time when China was threatened by Foreign invasion from outside and the Taiping rebellion from within. The government was therefore in a terrible plight when it signed the treaty. Consequently, as soon as the foreign warships sailed out of sight after the signing of the treaties, the Emperor began to have second thoughts and hoped to disavow the whole matter. He ordered, for example, not only the restoration and strengthening of the defenses around Tientsin, but also sent an able Mongol general Senggerinchin (Tsen-ko-lin-hsin) 僧 格 林 沁 , to be in command at Tientsin. At the same time, he repeatedly ordered his officials to prepare for the worst.

On the other hand, as provided by the treaties, the newly appointed British Plenipotentiary, Frederick W.A. Bruce, and the French Plenipotentiary, Alphonse de Bourboulon, together with the American representative, John Ward, all arrived in Hong Kong between April and May 1859 for the specific purpose of exchanging the instruments of ratification. The Russian envoy, Count Ignatiev, went directly to Peking in June, 1859 for the same purpose. The British and the French envoys, in accordance with the stipulation of the Tientsin Treaty, were instructed to exchange their instruments in Peking, while the American envoy was not similarly instructed.

The Chinese officials, by now greatly influenced by the manifest wish of the court, had worked out a detailed plan to discourage the attempts of the Powers. Anticipating the arrival of the foreign envoys, Kuei-liang offered to meet them half-way in Shanghai. But Bruce and Bourboulon refused the site and proceeded directly to the north. On June 21, 1859, John Ward also followed suit. Free, however, from the specific Anglo-French instructions binding their envoys, Ward was able to reach Peking through the route which the Chinese officials had prescribed for the foreign envoys. After brief negotiations over some minor questions of protocol he finally succeeded in exchanging the instruments of ratification with the Chinese government, and thereby put the Sino-American Treaty into full force ahead of all other similar treaties.[58]

The British and the French envoys, however, had refused the

prescribed route. Resorting once again to violence, their forces soon attacked and occupied the Taku forts. In the meantime, attempts at negotiations failed, and the cities of Tientsin and Peking were soon caputred by the Anglo-French expeditionary force. The Emperor took refuge in the province of Jehol, and his brother, Prince Kung, (I-hsin, 1833-1898) was assigned the difficult task of conducting peace talks. On October 24 and 25 of the same year, after much humiliation and destruction, the Conventions of Peking were finally signed between China on the one hand and Britain and France on the other. As a result, in addition to the promise of full realization of the conditions provided by the Tientsin Treaty, Tientsin was opened for commerce, indemnity was increased, and Kowloon was ceded to Britain. Meanwhile, the Russian envoy, insisting upon the merit of his intermediary role in the last phase of the confrontation, wrested the land east to the Ussuri River from China.

After exchanging the instruments of ratification in Peking, John Ward proceeded to Shanghai in order to work out the technicalities of the treaty with Ho Kuei-chin 何 桂 清 , who was then the Imperial Commissioner in that city. On August 27, 1859, Ward notified Ho that the American treaty was already in full force and requested that local officials be notified of that fact. At the same time, he also urged Ho to instruct his subordinates to receive the American consuls appointed to the newly opened ports of Chaochou and Taiwan.[59]

At first Ho was suspicious that Ward could have been instigated by the British and the French to try this, and he therefore replied that the opening of American trade must be delayed until the treaties with Britain and France were concluded and the new commercial regulations adopted.[60] But after Ward made repeated requests on the opening of the two above-mentioned ports, Ho came up with a different interpretation. In his dispatch to the Emperor, Ho related that according to the reports from local officials in Shanghai,

> Ward was unaccustomed to the diet and accommodations (in Peking) and he felt rather isolated there. His anxiety to return to the south prevented him from making more demands, and he was deeply regretful of his failure. In Shanghai, the British and the French felt that "if they could not have their way under the new commercial regulations, there would be no reason for them to

proceed to Peking for the exchange of the instruments of
ratification. As such, (Ward) was in fact acting like a messenger
which was not befitting his ministerial rank. The United States
would still be relying on the British and the French for support."
Ward was thus under the pressure of such predicaments that he
raised the demands to revise tonnage dues and to open the two new
ports in Chaochou and Taiwan in accordance with the provisions
of the treaty, so as to vindicate his own position.[61]

The negotiation was broken off when Ward left for his mission
in Japan. Upon his return on October 17, 1859, he notified Ho
that he was dissatisfied with the delaying tactics employed by the
Chinese government. He pointed out that the Sino-American
Treaty was concluded before the British and the French treaties,
and was therefore totally unrelated to them. With regard to the
ports of Chaochou and Taiwan, he pointed out specifically that:

> Your Excellency is perhaps aware of the fact that the two ports
> opened up by the American treaty have already been and are now
> being used for ships and trade. Since the peace treaty is in full
> force in accordance with the edict of the Emperor, American
> merchants will naturally procced to trade and live there, which I
> can hardly prevent. Since Your Excellency does not wish to see
> American counsuls there, it seems that it will be difficult for
> American merchants to pay their tonnage dues and obey the terms
> of the treaty. [It will also be difficult] for American officials to
> handle other commercial matters.[62]

The fact that illicit trade had been going on in the above-
mentioned ports for more than three years must have attracted the
attention of Ho. If for no other reason whatsoever, it constituted a
serious loss of revenue to the Chinese government. Thus in his
subsequent dispatch to the Emperor, Ho pointed out the fact of
this loss and indicated that since the treaty had been ratified, the
eventual opening of the ports was only a matter of time. He
pointed out that although Ward's request for an immediate
opening of the ports was dictated by the attempt to cover up all
earlier illicit trade, the fact that he pleaded for formal opening
indicated his respect for the Chinese government. Moreover, if
Ward's request was granted, not only the American trade would
have been formally regulated, but also the future trade conducted
by the British and French will be similarly regulated. On this

ground, Ho finally recommended that the Emperor grant Ward's request.[63]

At the same time, Ho continued his negotiations with Ward. These contacts further confirmed Ho's belief that Ward was not acting as an agent of either the British or the French because Ward had never touched upon matters related to the other countries. All Ward wanted, as Ho stated later, was that after November 24, 1859, American merchants should be allowed to pay tonnage dues according to the new regulations and that within two months beginning November 3rd, American trade should be formally inaugurated at Chaochou and Taiwan.[64]Ho's report produced favorable results from Peking. On November 22, 1859, an Imperial edict which granted Ward's requests finally reached Shanghai. It instructed that the ports in Chaochou and Taiwan be opened in advance for American trade.[65]

As soon as the Imperial grant was made, local officials were ordered to draw up proposals for the implementation of the new regulations in these ports. But since Taiwan is the name of the whole island which has many ports, they had to determine, first of all, the specific port for such trade. In his dispatch to the Emperor on this matter, Ching Yueh 慶瑞 , the Governor-General of Fukien and Chekiang, pointed out that the port of Huwei, near Tamshui, appeared to be an ideal port for this purpose. For it had an excellent seaway leading to the ocean and, at the same time, was not too close to the capital. He recommended that an able official, Ou Tien-min 區天民 , be appointed with the rank of Circuit Intendant to handle the affairs of trade in the port in cooperation with the local Circuit Intendant for internal affairs. He further recommended that the port in Taiwan be subjected to the jurisdiction of the tariff officials in Fukien so as to reduce unnecessary budgeting. The Emperor concurred to all these proposals and instructed the Board of Revenue to carry out the plans as suggested.[66]

As mentioned previously, while Ward succeeded in exchanging the instrument of ratifications with China, the British and the French were refusing to take the prescribed route to Peking. This delay was construed by the Emperor as a violation of the treaty by the British and the French and could be used, in his opinion, as a pretext for retracting some of the obnoxious articles provided in the Tientsin Treaty. In particular, the Emperor wished to bring the

British and the French to agree to only seven additional ports be opened as agreed upon in the Sino-American Treaty and to leave Liuchuan, Tengchou and Tamshui out. On the last port, he specifically pointed out that "Tamshui belongs to Taiwan and since Taiwan is opened up for them, it is unnecessary to mention Tamshui."[67] But this play of words on the part of the Emperor did not help much. The delay soon led to the renewed Anglo-French attack and China's capitulation. According to the Convention of Peking, the port of Tamshui, despite its obvious contradiction, was formally and legally opened to the four countries which took part in the Tientsin Treaty.

Impressed by the privileges gained by the four powers, a number of Western powers soon began to make similar requests of the Chinese government. At a time when China was no longer in the restive mood as she was before the two wars, the answer to them was all yes. Starting form 1861, China concluded a series of treaties with foreign powers which, in chronological order, included Prussia, Portugal, Denmark, Spain, Belgium, Italy, Austria, and Japan. Patterned after the Tientsin treaties, all of them enjoyed trade rights in Taiwan. As a result of this development, Taiwan was not only opened to foreigners, but her contact with them was becoming increasingly complex and multifaceted as time went on.[68]

After the formal decree authorizing the opening of Taiwan was effected, the issue of setting up consular service on Taiwan soon emerged. Since the Americans were the first to have been granted this privilege, it was expected that they would also be the first to send their consular officials to Taiwan. Actually, as soon as John Ward was notified of the formal opening of Taiwan in December 1859, he did immediately look for a candidate who would go to Taiwan in the consular post. He was, however, unable to find a suitable candidate for the fees set for the office. He reported to Secretary Lewis Cass about his difficulty and indicated that the difficulty would persist if Congress failed to provide a salary. But the Department of State responded rather coolly. It appointed a consul to be stationed in Chaochou, but underplayed the consular issue in Taiwan by including the port in Taiwan within the consular jurisdiction of Amoy. This was due perhaps in part to the overall neglect of her Far Eastern policies from the time of the Buchanan Administration up to the time of the Civil

War.[69] But, such an attitude had nevertheless proved to be the beginning of a wane of American interest in Taiwan during the following decades.[70]

In contrast to the American attitude toward establishing consular service in Taiwan, the British were far more positive. Soon after the British treaty was completed, Robert Swinhoe, an official who had had some previous knowledge of the island, was dispatched to Taiwan as a vice consul. On July 6, 1861, he arrived at Takow (Kaohsiung) and immediately proceeded to Taiwan-fu (Tainan) where he was given accommodations in the Fungshin Temple. Once there, he was approached by Ou Tien-min who proposed that the chief port in Taiwan should be Tamshui. The validity of this proposal was soon discovered by Swinhoe himself. For, in terms of trade volume, Taiwan-fu was on the decline when compared with other ports in Taiwan. He noted that his services as consular officer would be needed more in Tamshui or Takow than in Taiwan-fu. His first mission, however, was interrupted by his ill-health which forced him to return to Amoy at the end of the year. When he came back in December of 1861, he had already firmly made up his mind on Tamshui and proceeded to that port. After living on board the British receiving ship *Adventure* for a whole year, he finally succeeded in finding a residence on shore. With the consular office thus established, he soon noticed that although the treaty port was in Tamshui, the trade of the north was conducted primarily at Banka 萬 華. Consequently, in July, 1862, George C.P. Braun, Swinhoe's assistant and acting consul during his absence in London, by further permission from the Chinese government, succeeded in obtaining Banka as a subordinate port of Tamshui. In 1863, the Imperial Chinese Maritime Customs was opened at Tamshui. The first acting commissioner was an Englishman, named John W. Howell, who was later succeeded by W.S. Schenck.[71]

By the summer of 1864, the volume of trade in Takow had far surpassed that of Tamshui. On May 5, 1864, the Maritime Customs was opened in Takow under the supervision of William Maxwell, and major British trading companies such as Jardine, Matheson and Company, Dent and Company, MacPhail and Company, and the German trading company Lessler and Hagan all had their offices opened in that city. Upon his return from England, Swinhoe soon noted that the Tamshui office was not only somewhat inconvenient for him to make contact with local officials in Taiwan-fu, but it could not even render instant help to the increasing number of foreign merchants in the south. Therefore, on November 7, 1864, he established a British consular office in Takow on board the opium receiving hulk *Ternate*, belonging to Dent and Company, and remained there until 1866 when he finally found a residence on shore.

In 1865, a British consular office was opened at Taiwan-fu under the supervision of Thomas Watters. In the meantime, Braun was left in charge of the consular office in the north. It was by then, under the personal guidance of Swinhoe, that the British consular network was finally completed. In subsequent years before his final departure from Taiwan in the spring of 1866, Swinhoe applied for, and received commissions from the legations of various other nations to represent their interests in Taiwan. He was acting concurrently at one time as vice-consul for Britain, Prussia, Denmark and Portugal.[72] In retrospect, the British establishment in Taiwan started by Swinhoe had somehow perpetuated itself as a permanent feature on the island. Neither the United States, which first obtained trade privileges in Taiwan, nor Japan, which was to take over the whole island in the future, established a consular office in Taiwan at this time. Although Germany established a consular office in Anping in 1886 and later moved to Takow under the care of Constine Morz, it was nevertheless short-lived. Thus during the entire period after the opening of the ports, Britain was the only Western country with a permanent representation in Taiwan that never closed shop.

III
Shipwrecks and Colonization

After the formal opening of Taiwan, the contact between Taiwan and the Western countries was predictably increased. More foreign ships reached Taiwan ports either for trade or for supplies. But the shores of Taiwan, notorious as it always had been, were hardly a hospitable region for the foreign mariners. While a relatively large part of the east of the island was populated by the Proto-Malay tribes which were generally referred to as the aborigines, the ocean surrounding the island was famous for typhoons as well as many other sea hazards. Thus the fight for survival for many hapless shipwreck mariners along the coast of Taiwan naturally led to a rather tragic chapter in the annals of Taiwan.

According to Davidson's survey, between 1850 and 1894, there were at least eighty-six major shipwrecks along the Taiwan coast which had involved primarily the Western countries.[74] According to another survey, the figure was even more shocking. It pointed out that between 1850 and 1869, there were at least one-hundred and fifty shipwrecks along the west coast of the island alone.[75] To be sure, the result of these shipwrecks, no matter how many, was generally a sad one. For it involved not only the loss of lives and property but frequently generated a great deal of violence and misery. More often than not, such mishaps had caused the concern of the Western countries, and official contacts for remedial measures were attempted by their representatives in China. But since this was a time when China was still more or less immersed in her isolationsist tradition *vis-a-vis* the West, such Western contacts were generally shunned. Occasionally, a token indemnity was paid to soothe the country involved. But mostly nothing was done and the issue was left to run its own course without official intervention. At times, this hands-off policy would work successfully. But at other times, it would only generate a great deal of dissatisfaction and grumbling. It was against this background that the *Rover* Incident occurred.

On the 12th of March, 1867, the American barque, *Rover*, sailing from Chaochou to Niuchuang under the command of Captain J.W. Hunt, struck rocks off Hung-tou-yu and sank immediately. Hunt and his wife together with the crew escaped by lifeboat and made shore. The aborigines who lived in this area were the Kaoluts who soon found and killed them. Only one member of the crew, a Chinese by the name of Teh Kwang, escaped and reported the story to British vice-consul Charles Carroll in Takow. Subsequently, the information reached Taiwan-fu and was later communicated by the British consul to his Mininster in Peking who in turn conveyed it to Anson Burlingame, then the American Mininster in Peking. At the same time, Carroll also requested Commander George D. Board of the British gunboat *Cormorant*, stationed in Anping, to proceed to the scene of the massacre in the hope of finding survivors. On the 26th of

March, he reached the Kaolut country and began his search. But his errand of mercy soon ended when he was attacked by the tribes. Lacking what he needed for a real encounter, he opened fire on the tribesmen briefly but soon withdrew.[76]

The American consul at Amoy, Charles W. LeGendre, was informed of the *Rover* incident on April 1, 1867. Upon receiving the news, he immediately went to Foochow to urge the Governor-General of Fukien and Chekiang to order local authorities in Taiwan to start immediate rescue of possible survivors of the *Rover* crew. The Governor-General, according to LeGendre, complied with this request and made the order accordingly. Soon afterwards, LeGendre himself sailed to Taiwan-fu on April 18 and began to negotiate with the Circuit Intendant, Wu Ta-ting 吳 大 廷 , and the Brigade General Liu Ming-teng 劉 明 登. He demanded that the Chinese General dispatch necessary forces immediately to the troubled area and investigate the matter. The local officials, however, declined to oblige on the reason that the tribes were untamed savages and action against them would be futile. In their official reply, they did acknowledge the fact that in order to pacify the area in the long run, ways must be worked out.[77] But such a reply was construed by LeGendre as deliberate equivocation. Several days later, LeGendre and his assistant, Captain John C. Febriger, proceeded independently aboard the *Ashuelot* to the scene of the tragedy and began to inquire into the matter on their own. Once there they soon found the local people quite uncooperative. They were soon forced to concede to the futility of the endeavor and returned to Amoy.

In the meantime, the American Minister in Peking, Anson Burlingame, called the attention of the *Tsungli Yamen* (Foreign Office) to the incident. The *Tsungli Yamen* replied that it would start an investigation.

Based on later official Chinese documents, the whole matter was in fact brought to the attention of the Imperial court but the implementation of the official promise was somehow delayed.[78] Meanwhile, the American consul in Hong Kong, Issac J. Allen, reported the whole incident to the Department of State and recommended "the acquisition of this great island by our government" on the basis of its increasing importance to American interest in the Far East.[79] Such an idea, however, was not quite in line with the government's thinking. Secretary of State Seward in his instructions to Burlingame pointed out specifically that the Minister's duty lies in the inquiry of the facts of the *Rover* case and in demanding appropriate indemnities where possible. But, as he emphasized, "in no case does the United States wish to seize or take possession of Formosa or any part of said island."[80] Such instructions, which were called by Davidson as "red tapeism in Washington,"[81] no doubt had the effect of cooling off the whole matter. But despite the "official dilly-dallying"[82] on both sides, the postponement did not last long.

After a three month delay, Rear Admiral H.H. Bell was finally ordered to conduct an expedition into the tribal area. The expedition, consisting of two ships, the *Hartford* and the *Wyoming*, and a force of one-hundred and eighty-one officers, sailors and marines, reached Taiwan on the 19th of June. What followed, however, was a rather ineffectual operation. As one report noted:

> The Americans experienced immense difficulties in forcing a way through the thick jungle; the intense heat rendered it almost impossible to conduct operations in the middle of the day, and many of the party suffered sunstroke. The savages, who had taken up a position in the jungle behind rocks and other places invisible to the Americans, kept up a heavy fire whenever the enemy appeared. Lieutenant-Commander A.S. McKenzie was shot dead while gallantly leading a charge up a hill, and finally, after a desperate engagement, the force was compelled to withdraw in some confusion to the ships, and soon departed from the island.[83]

But such military actions against Taiwan did cause certain misgivings on the part of the Chinese government. Fearing that if China failed to attend to her responsibilities in the matter, the foreign powers might take the whole situation into their own hand, the *Tsungli Yamen* asked the Taiwan officials to take measures toward a satisfactory solution of the matter without further delay. An imperial edict to this same effect was subsequently issued in August, and in mid-September, Liu Ming-teng began to move into the tribal area with five-hundred soldiers while, at the same time, Wu Ta-ting informed LeGendre of the action and invited him to participate as an observer. LeGendre readily agreed and arrived at Taiwan-fu on September 6, 1867. In the meantime, Liu had made some progress along the jungle roads. Wang Wen-chi 王 文 榮 , a local official, soon guided LeGendre along with William A. Pickering, a former customs officer in Taiwan, and Joseph Bernare, a French interpreter, directly to Langchiao where they joined Liu's group.[84] It seems clear to us now that the initial action taken by Liu was not primarily a military one. What he tried was more or less a policy of pacification through persuasion and gifts. Upon reaching Fangliao where the tribal country began, the Chinese officials showed much leniency toward the natives by distributing money and other daily necessities to them. Through such gestures, they were able to obtain some information. They learned, for example, that there were a total of eighteen tribes in the area, and that the Kaoluts were the most untamed. The eighteen tribes had a loose form of federation and the chief of the Kaoluts, Tooke-tok 卓 杞 篤 had a certain influence over them all.

This information led Liu to the idea that by establishing some kind of rapport with Tooke-tok, a number of the aborigines who were involved in the *Rover* incident might be caught. By giving appropriate punishment to them in front of foreign observers, it was hoped that the whole case might be closed. But the idea had proved useless for the tribal chief refused even to come out of his settlement. Realizing the uselessness of it all, Liu and Wu finally decided to apply military pressure. On October 12, details were worked out with Tseng Yuan-fu 曾元福 , a local commander, for an immediate attack.[85]

But all the time LeGendre was pursuing a different course of action. Believing that Liu Ming-teng was reluctant to use force to bring about a satisfactory solution at Langchiao, LeGendre cornered him with four demands:

1. LeGendre must meet Took-tok and other chiefs of the tribes to receive their regrets and obtain their assurance against similar happenings in the future;
2. The Chinese authorities must guarantee the cooperation of the local Chinese and the aborigines while LeGendre was on his way;
3. The Chinese authorities must require the aborigines to pay for the expenses incurred by Pickering in recovering the body of Mrs. Hunt and some personal effects of the crew of the *Rover* which he privately undertook after the *Cormorant* assault;
4. A fortified observation post must be erected at the southern bay by the Chinese authorities as a guarantee of imperial protection to shipwrecked crewmen.[86]

Liu agreed to the demands, and LeGendre immediately proceeded to the tribal territory. It is interesting to note that in this rather unique adventure, LeGendre had accomplished something that must be regarded as unprecedented. The fact that LeGendre succeeded in engaging Tooke-tok in a face-to-face confrontation may be due perhaps to the great influx of Chinese troops there, which finally alarmed the tribes and their leaders. It may be also due to the fact, that Pickering, who had had some previous experience with the tribes and was well-acquainted with the language of several tribes there, served as an intermediary, and succeeded in lessening the hostilities of the tribes. In any event, LeGendre met with Tooke-tok on October 10 of that year. LeGendre told the aborigines that he had come as a friend, not as an enemy. He was quite willing to forget the past if the future safety of mariners could be guaranteed. Tooke-tok, on his part, pointed out that the killing of the *Rover* crew was in revenge for the intrusion of foreigners some fifty years earlier when the Kaoluts were almost entirely exterminated by them. After a lengthy and dramatic exchange of opinions, the two parties finally reached an "agreement" in which the aborigines promised from then on to care for the shipwrecked and hand them over to the Chinese authorities in Langchiao. This agreement reached in 1867 was later formalized on February 28, 1869 when LeGendre visited Tooke-tok for the second time.[87]

The news of LeGendre's successful venture came at a time when Liu was about to initiate real punishment on the tribes. In order to preserve what had already been accomplished, LeGendre persuaded the Chinese officials to call off the planned attack. The officials readily agreed. Furthermore on LeGendre's pleadings, the Taiwan officials promised that a temporary fort would be erected in the Kaolut region and two big guns as well as one-hundred militia men would be stationed in the Langchiao area as a token of government authority. The *Rover* incident was thus brought to an end.[88]

Viewing it from the principles of diplomacy, the LeGendre-Tooke-tok agreement was in a way an impingement upon China's sovereign authority, for neither side possessed the authority or legal standing for such a negotiation, let alone the final conclusion of such an agreement. But since the primary concern of the local Chinese officials was a quick solution of the matter, and possible international repercussions were not comprehended by them, the dubious nature of the action was, therefore, to a great extent ignored. To what extent such a precedent encouraged the subsequent German and British attempts at establishing a foothold in Ta-nan-ao or the Japanese adventure toward the Botan tribes in 1874 was not known. But it is incontrovertible to say that certain parallels could easily be drawn from these cases.

To avoid similar involvements in the future, however, the Chinese government did take certain precautionary measures in Taiwan. The administration in the Fangliao area was strengthened by the stationing of a permanent local official; and a ready system was devised for rescuing future shipwrecked crewmen.[89] But the over-all official reticence over LeGendre's action indicated that the Chinese government did not take the whole matter too seriously. The government of the United States, on the other hand, appeared equally disinterested in LeGendre's action. During this entire operation, LeGendre had continuously reported his dealings with Tooke-tok and other tribes in southern Taiwan to the American minister in Peking. He repeatedly begged for instructions but never received any. Later on, he forwarded to the American legation in Peking the entire agreement, which he had entered into in the name of the United States, but the legation was equally reticent. Such an attitude had no doubt put the validity of LeGendre's action in discredit. But, due perhaps to the fact that the whole matter was one of such a marginal interest to both countries at this time, niether side had come out for an official clarification. It was in the midst of this ambiguity that a precedent of a contestable nature was inadvertently established.

Looking at it from its practical results, however, LeGendre's action appears useful. As one record put it, "A foreigner, unaided, negotiates a treaty of peace with the chief of a band of wild and savage head-hunters, and in a few short interviews converts them from blood-thirsty murderers of shipwrecked sailors into merciful servants who, at least so far as the chief Tokitok [sic] and his tribesmen were concerned, from that time forward gave shelter and assistance to the unfortunates cast upon their shores."[90] Though the language of this narration may sound too dramatic, it did give an interesting description of the personal triumphs of Charles W. LeGendre— a French-American who brought the frontierman's spirit to a new setting in the Far East.

At about the same time when the *Rover* incident was creating much trouble for the Chinese government in the southern part of Taiwan, another problem was shaping up in its northeast. Owing to specific geographical and historical reasons, the eastern part of Taiwan was in a relatively arrested stage of development *vis-a-vis* the rest of the island. Though this halted stage of development posed no serious problems for the Chinese government when the island remained relatively inaccessible to the outside world, the picture soon changed when the wall came down. In fact, this part of the island had figured rather prominently in the Benyowsky report as far back as 1771.[91]

During the nineteenth century and especially after the opening of the Taiwan ports, further knowledge of the island acquired through closer contact could not but further the interest of many would-be adventurers toward northeast Taiwan. For both in terms of political influence and administrative control, this part of the island must have appeared to many a no-man's land. It was, therefore, natural that many colonial designs focusing on this part of the island gradually appeared during the later part of the nineteenth century.

The particular episode that concerns us here is the joint German-British attempt at establishing a colony around Ta-nan-ao, a coastal village some thirty-four miles from Suao. The Prussian interest in Taiwan can be traced as far back as 1861 when, during the negotiation of the Sino-Prussian treaty, it demanded the opening of Keelung as a trading port. Although such a request came to no avail, it nevertheless signified the beginning of an unrelented Prussian interest on the island.[92]

During the summer of 1865, another demonstration of this interest was becoming noticeable. In July of that year, a series of articles under the title "Prussia's Colonial Policy" written by Count Eulenburg, appeared in a Berlin newspaper *Die Nord-deutsche Allgemeine Zeitung*. The author, who had led the Prussian expedition to the Far East in 1860, was then Minister of Interior in the Bismark cabinet. In his semi-official discussion, he expressed, among other things, his strong belief in the desirability for Prussia to obtain a naval depot in the China Sea. To him, this could be realized through a colonization policy patterned after the Netherland Indies colonies. Specifically, he focused on the eastern part of Taiwan as the most ideal place for this endeavor. As one record put it, Eulenburg

> deemed the eastern part of Taiwan an ideal place, for its moderate
> climate, rich soil, and commodius harbors such as Suao, would
> fulfill the basic requirements for a "Deutsch-Indiens." He thought
> that part of the island might be easily fortified and could afford
> security and shelter for Prussian ships in China seas which were
> constantly attacked by pirates in the area. . . .Before presenting
> concrete steps for the execution of the plan, the writer weighed
> the desirability of making eastern Taiwan a penal colony. But he
> soon abandoned this discussion and settled on a definite line of
> action to be taken during the Summer of that year. He proposed
> to send a couple of ships of war with a certain number of troops
> on board, to take possession of eastern Taiwan and hold it in
> military occupation. Meantime, a ship with skilled workers and
> settlers, with their families, would follow the warships. Settlers
> were to be self-sufficient in defending themselves against the
> aborigines because all Prussian male subjects would have had three
> years of military training behind them. The government would
> make liberal grants of land and funds to help the settlers get
> started.[93]

Although this plan never left the drafting board, it did raise
some interest among certain political observers in Europe. Some
dismissed it as downright impractical for it would violate Chinese
sovereignty. Others viewed it as a distinct possibility. But in
actuality, none had come closer to the meaning of the articles than
the British newspaper *London and China Express.* Its editorial
pointed out that the Eulenburg's articles must be regarded as
something representing "the feeling and the intentions of Prussia,
and foreshadow events that are on the eve of taking place."[94] It
soon proved to be true.

James Milisch was a German merchant engaged primarily in
the opium trade in Tamshui. Realizing the rather laxed state of
control over the eastern part of Taiwan by the Chinese government, he soon began to look into the situation when he arrived on
the island. Pretending to be a consul for the Hanseatic Cities of the
German Union, he enlisted the help of a British subject, James
Horn, who, as a dealer in camphor, was relatively well-informed
about the aboriginal regions in Taiwan. Thus in May of 1868,
Milisch licensed and funded Horn for an expedition into the
aboriginal territory of Ta-nan-ao with the alleged purpose of
cutting down camphor trees and the eventual establishment of a

colony there. With the help of several other westerners which included two Scots, one American, one Spanish-Mexican and one Goa-Portuguese, they first reached the Komalan district, a border area between the Chinese and the aborigines.

Once there, they were asked by the local officials, Ting Cheng-hsi 丁 承 禧 , to give up this rather daring plan. Unmoved, however, by this official discouragement, they proceeded without hesitation. They first succeeded in establishing some kind of a rapport with the plains aborigines by giving them certain articles of daily necessities. Later, Horn himself married the daughter of the Pepohoan 平 埔 蕃 chief and, by virtue of this marriage, commmanded great influence over the plains aborigines of the Suao area. Thereupon they, together with some Pepohoan helpers, proceeded further south via the sea route and finally reached Ta-nan-ao. By September, Horn had succeeded in employing more than one-hundred laborers and some twenty guards who fortified a small area in the valley and manned the fortress in Ta-nan-ao. In early 1869, more laborers and guards were added to this group. With the help of these people, Horn began to initiate a system of taxation against the aborigines around these areas. The scope and intent of his action soon drew serious objections from the local Chinese officials.[95]

When his persuasions failed to prevail, Ting Cheng-hsi tried to contact Milisch and the British consul in order to effect Horn's withdrawal from the Ta-nan-ao area. He was told that the area lies beyond the official jurisdiction of the Komalan district and nothing could be done about it. In order not to delay the issue any further, he submitted a report to the *Tsungli Yamen* through Yin Kuei, then Governor-General of Fukien and Chekiang. Prince Kung, who was in charge of the *Tsungli Yamen* at that time, soon took over the case himself. In his dispatch to the Emperor on the matter, he pointed out that "products of China should be obtained by foreigners with permission; and their contact with the aborigines may even create further trouble. (To straighten out this situation) a letter has already been addressed to the ministers of Britain and Prussia, demanding that the foreigners be withdrawn and punished."[96]

This official letter reached its destination but the responses were, at best, of a reserved nature. Sir Rutherford Alcock, the

British Minister, responded with a promise that he would detail the British consul in Tamshui to investigate the case and if the charges were proven to be true, Horn would be asked to stop. [97] Similarly, the Prussian Minister, Von Rehfus, also responded in the same way. He promised to issue a warning to Milisch, telling him that if he "keeps violating the treaty, he alone would be responsible for all the consequences."[98] He pointed out, however, that the whole matter was started by Horn, a British subject, and Milisch may be entirely innocent. He also warned at the same time that since he was not informed by his government on the official status of Milisch, he hoped that the Chinese government would do nothing to prejudice Milisch's position. To him, as he pointed out, what Milisch was doing was in perfect consonance with Chinese diplomatic practices and therefore it should not be used as a pretext in the case.[99]

Predictably, these written replies did not bring much results. To make it worse, in the spring of 1869, Milisch personally visited the Ta-nan-ao area and the colonization project was further accelerated. Horn, in the meantime, also went a step further by trying to convert some of the occupied area into a tea field. Seeing that the Germans and the British were gradually entrenching themselves in the area, Prince Kung began to press hard on the two ministers. In his letter addressed to them in the summer of 1869, he indicated his disappointment over the slow withdrawal. He warned that "the local officials in Fukien had already been instructed to arrest Milisch and Horn when necessary and hand them over to the consuls for punishment; in case of resistance, they will be summarily executed."[100] It was hoped that by putting a little muscle behind the threat, the foreigners would be brought to an early compliance.

The British Minister, in his reply, confirmed once again his earlier pledge that the Tamshui consul had been instructed to bring Horn out and promised that Horn would not be allowed to go back in the future. Von Rehfus, in his reply, however, was not as yielding as Alcock. He pointed out that Milisch should be prevented from breaking the law but his personal safety should never be endangered. In the event his arrest becomes necessary, he should be sent to Shanghai for an appropriate trial. Any mistreatment of him would no doubt create grave consequences in the relations between the two nations.[101] This seemingly adamant reply led Prince Kung to an equally strong rejoinder. In his last communication to the German Minister, he pointed out forcibly that "the territory inhabited by the aboriginal tribes falls within Chinese jurisdiction, and Ta-nan-ao is not a treaty port. Foreigners are not entitled to lease any land from the aborigines for cultivation, nor does the land belong to the aborigines that they can rent it at will."[102]

While the diplomatic correspondences were flying between the *Tsungli Yamen* and the foreign legations, the situation in Ta-nan-ao was going from bad to worse. By interpreting the attitude of their respective ministers as favorably protective, both Milisch and Horn were encouraged to start more daring projects. Milisch by now began to intervene into legal matters of the local people which gradually made him the sole authority of arrest and punishment of the whole area. At the same time, coal mines were privately mortgaged and camphor, an article of trade monopolized by the government, was being smuggled out of the island by him. Horn, on the other hand, despite Alcock's orders to the contrary, remained there as a well-established colonist. To make the whole matter more complicated, the British consul in Tamshui also formally came out in their support by alleging that there was no visible dominion from Suao down to the south cape of Taiwan, an area over which the Chinese government claims formal authority. He then pointed out that since Horn had already invested heavily in the area, in the event that his removal from the area becomes necessary, he must be compensated for his loss by the local Chinese officials.

On May 4, 1869, a British gunboat unexpectedly appeared in the Ta-nan-ao area and remained for three days. The purpose of its mission remains a dispute till this day. Some believe it was a show of force in order to intimidate the local Chinese officials.[103] Others, like Davidson, believed that it signified the British intention for retreat.[104] But given the fact that Horn had continued his project long after the visit of the gunboat, and his actual departure was not followed immediately, the peaceful purpose of the visit must be judged at best to be doubtful.

The key man who finally decided to cut the Gideon knot was the British Minister Alcock. Although he too was never fully convinced of the Chinese demand as just, he nevertheless valued more highly the over-all Anglo-Chinese relations than the individual interest of a private British citizen. Toward the end of the summer, Alcock ordered William Gregory, the vice-consul in Tamshui, to bring Horn to leave the eastern part of the island, hoping that once this order was carried out, the whole colonization attempt would naturally come to an end. The fairness of Alcock's action was criticized, as one author put it:

> After many months had passed, and much money and time had been expended, without the least hint of a possible objection being made by the British government, the good officials, as English officials are wont to do, listened to the Chinese reports, pictured a force of English adventurers driving crowds of peaceful innocent Chinese with their wives and children by fire and sword from their homes and fields, and then sent orders to China that Horn should be ordered out of the district and that the Chinese authorities should be placed in possession. Poor Horn was thus dispossessed without any compensation, and he and James Milisch, who had invested much money in the place, were obliged to declare themselves insolvent soon after.[105]

In any event, since Britain had taken the initiative by ordering Horn's removal, Prussia soon realized the futility of the whole effort and followed suit. By August, orders had reached both Milisch and Horn, but it took Horn another two months to complete his retreat. During his last trip from Ta-nan-ao to Suao, however, Horn's small schooner floundered in a fierce northern gale and was driven to the south of the island where it was wrecked. The aborigines who survived brought news to the foreigners in the south of the death of some twenty persons, among whom they counted their "white friend and protector Horn."[106] The Ta-nan-ao episode thus came to an end.

IV
The Difficulties in the Treaty Ports

The problems that Taiwan posed for China's external relations were by no means confined to such particular happenings as the *Rover* incident or the Ta-nan-ao case. Once the ports in Taiwan were opened to foreign nations, it soon became, like many other coastal areas in China, an area of confrontation and conflict. Given the difference in Chinese and Western cultural backgrounds, this was of course a natural sequence. Problems arising out of the conflict of commercial interest and religious activities had kept the entire Sino-Western relations simmering with trouble. Taiwan, as an opened-up territory of China, had its share in all these problems.

The problems arising out of the Taiwan ports usually began with the day when foreigners tried to force their way into the treaty ports under the provision of the treaties. Once there, they were confronted with the animosities of the local people which occasionally developed into physical attacks or property damages. When such situations occurred, the foreigners usually attempted to appeal to the local officials for redress. But as the presence of the foreigners in their bailiwick was to them a sign of deep humiliation, the local officials were usually unwilling to punish the offenders. By construing this as irresponsibility, it inevitably forced the foreigners to take the law into their own hands. In order to right the wrong, battleships were called in, forces were landed, and more often than not, shots were exchanged and damages were wrought. Unable to resist the superior forces of the West, the people as well as their officials were finally brought to their knees. To avoid further humiliation and destruction of their locale, new promises were made, compensations were offered, and the chaos was thus brought to an end. Ever since the opening of the Taiwan ports, most cases had started and ended along these lines.

For the purpose of analysis, the problems in the Taiwan ports can perhaps be divided into two categories: those that occurred in the north and those that occurred in the south. Among the first category, the Dent and Company case and the Bintang Anam case in Tamshui or the Madge case in Keelung were all clearly cases in point.[107] But in terms of repercussions, however, the John Dodd case in Banka was perhaps the most significant event that occurred in the north. For a better understanding of the situation in the northern ports, it is here used as an illustration.

In accordance with treaty provisions, the town of Banka, a suburban town of the port of Tamshui, was opened to foreign residence since 1862, but until 1868 no foreigners had established such residence in that town. In the summer of 1868, Crawford D. Kerr and S. Godfey Bird, two agents of Dodd and Company, attempted to move into the house of their leased property — a house known as the Lok Tow *hong* in Banka. Confronted with the opposition of the local officials who sealed its doors, they sought assistance from the British vice-consul in Tamshui, Henry P. Holt. Holt in turn sought cooperation from the Customs officials. By October 2, the Customs officials were able to inform the British merchants that they were then at liberty to enter their property in Banka. Not believing that the Chinese would oppose entrance any longer, they arrived at the gate of the *hong* on October 12. Once there, they were immediately attacked by a mob of local people and were seriously injured during the entanglement. The whole affair took place about some fifty yards from the precincts of the Tamshui *Ting's Yamen.* The official there, interpreting all these as signs of local patriotism, felt reluctant to intervene in the fight. It was not until a considerable time had elapsed that the wounded were allowed to be escorted to the river where their boats were waiting to take them back to Tamshui. The British vice-consul Holt was shocked when he received the news. In a dispatch to his superiors in Peking dated October 14, he pointed out to the effect that:

> the situation was so serious that he might be driven at any moment to haul down his flag. Remonstrances, expostulations, dispatches, letters, messages, and visits have alike failed in insuring common justice; and our very lives are threatened by people whose recent course of action has been so atrocious as to prove that the will is not wanting to murder us.[108]

Believing that force was the last resort under such a situation, Holt dispatched a letter to the British consulate in Foochow asking that a gunboat be immediately sent to Tamshui to render effective assistance to obtain quick redress. Meanwhile, the local Chinese officials in Tamshui, realizing the seriousness of the case, took the initiative by asking for a meeting with Holt for a possible solution of the matter. Smarting from early experiences, however, Holt declined this request. He decided to bide his time because he was quite aware of the fact that the local Chinese officials could become more pliable only when confronted with real military force.

To prepare for bargaining, however, a series of demands were prepared. These demands, among other things, included the relief of duty of the officials of the Tamshui *Ting Yamen* who failed to intervene in the fighting, the punishment of the clan and its headman, and compensation and indemnity for Dodd and Company and its agents.[109] The British gunboat *Janus* soon arrived on the 22nd of October. By what was called a happy coincidence, the American gunboat *Aroostook* also arrived on the same day with the American consul in Amoy, Charles LeGendre, on board. Now, with the gunboats at anchor, Holt, together with LeGendre, formally approached the Tamshui magistrate with the prepared demands. As always under such a situation, the Tamshui magistrate could do nothing but comply to every one of the nine demands submitted to him. Thus, employing actual force and without bothering the court in Peking, the whole matter, like many cases of gunboat diplomacy of the time, was once again quietly settled behind closed doors of the local official's *Yamen*.

While the cases in the north were generally solved in this rather quiescent manner, the cases in the south, which always involved the conflict of trading and religious interest, were not as easily manageable. The "Incident of Gibson" is here given as an illustration.

Of the products of Taiwan, camphor was declared a monopoly by the Chinese government as far back as 1836. But in practice, because of the serious objections raised by the early Chinese settlers in Taiwan, the monopoly was not well carried out. Upon the arrival of the first foreign traders in Taiwan after the opening of the ports, the Chinese officials claimed once again an exclusive monopoly of the camphor industry, but again, due to the high profit derived from the camphor trade, the official proclamation was always generally ignored. In 1855, an American in Hong Kong by the name of William M. Robinet sent a vessel, the American bark *Louisiana*, to Takow (Kaohsiung). The vessel returned with a profitable cargo, as did the *Santiago* which closely followed her. The success of these two voyages soon caused several other American firms to take an ardent interest in the trade. Thus, in the very beginning of the camphor trade, it had appeared to be solely an American venture.

In the years that followed an American, C.D. Williams, was given the responsibility by the American firms in Hong Kong to select a site for a permanent establishment and, if possible to enter into some agreement with the Taiwan officials for the campor trade. After calling on the Circuit Intendent in Taiwan-fu, he booked passage on the *Frolic* and visited all the ports on the West coast as far north as Keelung. His trip was a successful one for he secured an agreement from the authorities giving his company not only the monopoly of all the camphor trade but also other trading privileges, such as permission to form an establishment at Takow. In return for these concessions, the Americans agreed that their vessels should pay one hundred dollars each voyage as tonnage dues, that they would protect Takow against pirates, and that, when necessary, they would furnish the authorities there with a ship to ward off pirates.[110]

The virtual American monopoly of trade, however, soon came to an end after the opening of the ports. In the absence of positive official support, the American position was gradually replaced by the British through lease and purchase.

Upon the establishment of consular jurisdiction on the island in 1861, two British firms Jardine, Matheson and Company, and Dent and Company soon moved in as the major camphor traders while other firms such as the German firm James Milisch and Company and the American firm Field, Hastus and Company took care of the rest. To be sure, there was no little rivalry among these firms. Strenuous opposition was frequently voiced by the smaller firms against the virtual British monopoly which they regarded as an infraction of the treaty rights which guarded their equal opportunity in Taiwan commerce. And for a brief period of time, the camphor trade appeared to be a fuse that could lead to a very explosive situation.

The camphor traders, however, were soon to find out that, in the final analysis, the major stumbling block to their quick profit came from the Chinese government rather than from their own competition. In fact, soon after the ratification of the French and British treaties in 1860 and their subsequent enforcement, the Chinese government had immediately declared that the whole coast, with the exception of Taiwan-fu and Tamshui, was not open to foreign trade. This, no doubt, constituted a serious blow to the foreign firms engaged in the camphor trade. For by freely visiting the west coast and thus getting nearer to the field of production, they could avoid the incurring of additional expenses of transportation over land.

With this privilege gone and the consumer reluctant to meet the increased cost, the camphor traders had to figure out new ways to avoid this new burden. In 1868, the British firm Elles and

Company in Takow had unilaterally opened a branch in Wuchi and
soon began to purchase camphor directly from the local dealers. In
May of that year, as a result of this private purchase, some $6,000
worth of camphor was collected and readied for shipment. But it
was seized by the local officials in Lukang. The British consul
Jamieson personally protested this seizure to Liang Yuan-kwei
梁 元 桂 , then the Circuit Intendant in Taiwan. Liang, in his
reply, pointed out that camphor was an article of trade monopolized by the Chinese government which no one, without permission, could purchase or ship at random. The camphor in question
was seized, in his opinion, under the flagrant violation of the
Chinese regulation and therefore a way to return it to Elles and
Company can only be found with further deliberation.[111]

In the meantime, William A. Pickering, the firm's representative, personally intervened in the matter. He went to Wuchi to
inquire into the confiscated camphor without official permission
to do so. Once there, he resisted arrest ordered by the Circuit
Intendant, and shot his way out to escape to Tamshui. This series
of affronts commited by him had greatly angered the Circuit
Intendant who subsequently issued a proclamation offering $500
for Mr. Pickering's head. This, no doubt, contributed much
difficulty to the search for a peaceful solution to the deadlock.

While the camphor business had by now come to a standstill, a
series of attacks on foreign missionaries in the south had further
complicated the situation. Scattered assaults on the missionary
establishment had taken place as early as 1863. It happened once
again in 1865. But in terms of scope and intensity, none of them
was comparable to the 1868 eruption. Charging that the missionaries and their Chinese converts were using secret drugs to induce
the natives to become converts, a mob of natives attacked the
Roman Catholic Church in Fengshan in April of that year. Later in
the same month, based on certain trumped-up charges, the British
Presbyterian churches in both Fengshan and Takow were also
ransacked by local inhabitants. Believing in the rumors then
circulating among the people, the local officials at Fengshan put
James L. Maxwell, the head of the Presbyterian mission in Takow,
in jail when he visited Fengshan city. When this happened, the
British began to believe that what was at issue was clearly no
longer a pure economic conflict. The British consular officials in
Taiwan decided to take action.[112]

Claiming treaty rights to the protection of Christians by Chinese authorities, the acting British consul, John Gibson, requested the local officials in Taiwan-fu to intervene immediately in the case and punish the guilty. After some futile negotiations, he decided to call for help. As a result, three British gunboats were sent to Taiwan, anchored in the harbors of Anping and Takow in September of 1868. Confronted with such a show of force, the local officials in Taiwan reported the situation to Peking. Realizing that the issues in Taiwan were by now all related, a special Circuit Intendant from Fukien, Tseng Hsien-te 曾 憲 德 , was sent to Taiwan to handle the crisis. Upon arrival, Tseng took the initiative by going over to Gibson and asking for a resumption of negotiations. Gibson, by now firmly supported by the gunboats, refused to negotiate with him unless his two demands — that Liang be replaced and the assailants be punished — were met. On the basis that these demands lay clearly beyond the Sino-British treaty, Tseng refused to go along. It was then that Gibson opted for force.[113]

On November 20, 1868, the British gunboat *Algerine* and *Bustard* shelled Anping and Fort Zeelandia and subsequently took both places. During the encounter the local arsenal was destroyed, and the local commander, Chiang Kuo-chin 江 國 珍 , being wounded and feeling humiliated in defeat, committed suicide. Gibson and Lieutenant Gurdon, the British Commander, seized upon this opportunity to demand a settlement of all outstanding grievances between the foreign merchants and the local officials as well as of the immediate cause of the conflict. To make sure that their demands would prevail, they tried and succeeded in extorting $40,000 from the local merchants as a guarantee toward the eventual fulfillment of all their demands. But all these things took place at a time when official negotiations were supposedly going on. Thus, upon being informed of the British activities, Tseng protested vehemently against Gibson's use of force, and demanded an immediate return of the guarantee money.

Gibson, on the other hand, equivocated on the role he played in the hostilities but, in order not to overplay his hand, promised to return a part of the money to the local merchants when the final agreement was reached. After a series of hard bargaining sessions, a final agreement was concluded on December 1, 1868, which included the following important items:

1. The camphor monopoly was abolished and proclamations issued declaring the right of foreigners and their employees to buy freely;

2 . Passports were to be issued by the Circuit Intendant on application to foreign traders and other people to travel for business or pleasure on the island of Taiwan;

3. An indemnity of $6,000 was paid to Elles and Company for its loss of camphor;

4. An indemnity of $1,167 was paid to the Protestant mission for loss of property;

5. A payment was made to all claims of Elles and Company's agents for loss of property;

6. Liang Yuan-kwei, the Circuit Intendant, and the local officials in Fengshan and Lukang were all removed, and the various people connected with the several conflicts were punished to the satisfaction of the British consul;

7. Proclamations were issued acknowledging the injustice of the slanders hitherto circulated against the Christian Church and Christians, and injuctioning against any renewal of such;

8. The right to foreign missionaries of residence and work on the island was declared;

9. Proclamations were made calling for joint courts in dealing with mixed cases.[114]

But these results were accomplished through unauthorized and unmitigated use of force and Gibson had to pay a personal price for it.

After the incident had come to an end, Yin Kuei 英桂 , the Governor-General of Fukien and Chekiang, reported the whole matter to the throne in a series of dispatches, in which he took Gibson's action to task and warned the government of its possible repercussions. He said:

> The missionary and commercial activities of the British citizens in China are regulated by treaty, and the consular official, in dealing with a matter of this kind, should be governed by it. Even if the local officials might have mishandled such a matter, he should plead to his superior or resident minister in Peking for a solution. Why did he resort to warships for extortion and intimidation? Moreover, I have personally sent an official to Taiwan to investigate and settle the issue, and Consul Gibson expressed satisfaction with the conclusions reached by both sides. Why did he make his agents break these agreements? The money that Gibson extorted must be returned. His hostile activities toward our commander and soldiers and his burning of our government

> office buildings are even a much more serious offense. After
> Gibson's precedence, consular officials of other countries may
> very well follow his example in their dealing with our government.
> If we do not punish Gibson, foreigners of other countries will
> brew endless trouble.[115]

Upon receiving the dispatch, the Emperor instructed Prince
Kung to approach Alcock directly and demanded an investigation
of the appropriateness of Gibson's actions in Taiwan. The *Tsungli
Yamen* then formally lodged a serious protest with respect to
Gibson. In the meantime, the British government in London also
began to have second thoughts about Gibson's actions. For
example, both the Foreign Office and the Admiralty had
expressed their disapproval of the action. The Earl of Clarendon
not only strongly disapproved of Gibson's proceedings but in a
dispatch to Alcock severely condemned the consul.[116] Such
attitudes had no doubt produced an adverse effect upon Gibson's
stand. In order to reply to the charges of Prince Kung, Alcock did
officially demand an answer from Gibson. But his dissatisfaction
with Gibson's reply was only a foregone conclusion. For in an
earlier reply to Prince Kung, he had already pointed out that
although he had not been informed of the details of the whole
incident, he had never ordered Gibson to use force. The fact that
real clashes had taken place and lives had been sacrificed was to
him indeed deplorable. He promised that if what happened proved
to be as reported by the Governor-General of Chekiang and
Fukien, he would initiate appropriate punishment against Gibson.

In fact, in late spring 1868, he finally informed the Chinese
government that Gibson had been relieved of his duties and
Robert Swinhoe, the former British consul in Taiwan, had been
appointed to the post. As far as the extorted money was
concerned, he also promised that with the exception of the
portion that was paid to the British merchants as compensation,
he would see to it that the rest be returned without further delay.
At the end of the communication, he nevertheless registered a note
of complaint. According to him, "the iniquitous treatment against
the British citizens in Taiwan was by no means a spur-of-the-
moment thing. . . . Had the longstanding grievances been attended
to earlier, the present confrontation and loss of life would not have
occurred."[117] In other words, though Gibson was in the wrong, the
Chinese government was by no means totally free from fault in the

matter. He wanted to make this point as a matter of record.

The Chinese government was on the whole pleased with this reply. Despite Alcock's note of complaint to the contrary, the dismissal of Gibson was clearly a great satisfaction to the Chinese government. To make sure that Alcock would not further challenge the Chinese government on the basis of its maladministration, the Emperor immediately instructed the officials in Fukien to investigate the treatment of foreign merchants and missionaries in Taiwan and honestly report their findings to the central government. But since the British were only recently reassured of their rights and privileges, no further challenges of this sort occurred. In fact, upon Swinhoe's arrival in Taiwan in June, 1869, Gibson was immediately dismissed. He died soon after, it is said, of a broken heart. In the midst of Swinhoe's effort to improve official relations between China and Britain over the Taiwan question, the unhappy incident of Gibson gradually faded into history.

V
The Beginning of the Japanese Encroachment

While the problems discussed thus far were problems coming primarily from China's dealing with the Western powers, there were problems that soon emerged from the other direction. Because of cultural bounds and geographical propinquity, the Japanese had long indicated an avid interest in Chinese affairs. In fact, the flow of Chinese culture into Japan could be traced way back to antiquity and relationship between the two peoples was on the whole characterized by peaceful interchanges. Unfortunately, however, what was generally regarded as a beneficial relationship had gradually deteriorated when the modern history of Asia opened up its first pages.

Starting from the late Chien Lung period, China had entered into a period of internal decline, and bleeding revolts and foreign encroachments weakened it further in the nineteenth century. While Japan, on the other hand, by better adjustment to the West through effective modernization measures, was faring much better. Japan was formally opened up by the United States in 1854 and by the time of the Meiji Renovation in 1868, it had not only ended the feudal society that had existed for more than two and a half centuries, but also unleashed the forces for political, social and economic changes that gradually transformed Japan into a modern society.

The modernizing of Japan had its disruptive influences. For example, the *samurai* or warrior class, with a vested interest in the traditional society, was directly and inevitably affected by the modernizing process. Uprooted by the transformation, it was natural for them to demand new outlets for their energies when the new society took shape. To be sure, many of them had played an important and constructive role in the building of the new Japan. Others, however, tried to seek satisfaction in the ventures of foreign expansion. It was those in the latter category that became modern Japan's foremost advocates of an aggressive expansionist policy.

The conquest of Korea, for instance, was first conceived and advocated by a group of *samurai* under the leadership of Saigo Takamori 西 鄉 隆 盛 , the leader of the *samurai* of Satsuma and Choshu where feudal forces had been strongest and therefore social discontent most acute. In 1872, under his promotion the idea of the conquest of Korea had gained substantial support among government leaders. However, in 1873, due to a change of leadership, this plan failed to draw continued governmental support. This soon led not only to the resignation from government offices of expansion-minded officials like Takamori and Soyeshima Taneomi, 副 島 種 臣 , but also to local disturbances such as the one that occurred in the Saga region. To consolidate its hold as well as to pacify its more assertive elements, the Japanese government could not but shift its attention once again toward foreign horizons. It was then that Taiwan entered the picture.

Soon after the newly created Japanese Foreign Office came into being in 1870, Yanagihara Sakimitsu 柳 原 前 光 , was sent by his government to Peking to seek a commercial treaty similar to China's treaties with Western nations. Although his mission was viewed by the ultraconservative elements in the Chinese government as opportunistic and ill-timed, it was received with warmness by Li Hung-chang, then Governor-General of Chihli and the leading man to shape China's foreign policy. Li felt, as one author put it, that:

Japan, which was not a dependency of China, was totally different from Korea and Annam. That she had come to request trade without first seeking support from any Western power showed her independence and good will. If China refused her this time, her friendship would be lost and she might even seek Western intervention on her behalf, in which case it would be difficult for China to refuse again. An antagonized Japan could be an even greater source of trouble than the Western nations because of her geographical proximity. It was therefore in China's interest to treat Japan on a friendly and equal basis and send commissioners to Japan who could look after the Chinese there, watch the movements of the Japanese government, and cultivate harmonious relations between the two states.[118]

With this attitude in mind the Yanagihara mission was well received. In fact, to show Chinese good will, a Sino-Japanese commercial treaty with eighteen articles and a trade regulation of thirty-three articles were finally signed in 1871 by Li and Yanagihara. Among other things, it provided for the exchange of envoys and consuls, and the rendering of good-offices to each other should a third party intimidate or threaten either of the contracting parties. By careful negotiation, however, Li purposely excluded the most-favored-nation clause in this treaty and prohibited sword-carrying by the Japanese in the Chinese ports. By virtue of Article I of the Trade Regulations, the Japanese were for the first time granted the privilege of trading and residing in the two open ports in Taiwan: namely Taiwan-fu and Tamshui.[119]

The Japanese government was not, however, fully satisfied with this initial arrangement. It was particularly opposed to the good-offices article and the exclusion of the most-favored-nation clause. In order to reach a better position, Yanagihara was ordered to try for a revision of the treaty. To be sure, his second mission was unsuccessful and his attitude had only adversely affected the formerly sympathetic Li Hung-chang. But, while making no progress in his official mission, Yanagihara's stay in China was quite fruitful on another score. Besides his closer observation of the Chinese political situation, he also came across a piece of news that proved to be of utmost importance to coming Sino-Japanese relations.

Reading through the *Peking Gazette* of May 11, 1872, he learned of the fate of two groups of Ryukyu people who had been shipwrecked on the coast of Taiwan during the previous winter.

One group, consisting of forty-six crew members, had landed on the south-eastern coast of Taiwan when their ship was hit by strong winds and sunk. They were given food and clothing and conducted, first of all, to the Fengshan magistrate's office and subsequently to Taiwan-fu for repatriation. Around the same time, another group with sixty-nine crew members, also ran into a violent storm to the north of the island. Three members of the crew were drowned while the remaining sixty-six members were able to make shore on December 18,1871. The hapless sailors, however, landed in an area populated by the Botan tribes of the Taiwan aborigines. Upon being captured, the head-hunters soon subjugated them to a shocking slaughter. Of the sixty-six crew members, fifty-four were killed and the remaining twelve, who had managed to take refuge in the house of a local settler, succeeded in escaping the slaughter. On Janauary 1, 1872 they were escorted to the Magistrate's office in Fengshan which in turn sent them to Foochow for eventual return to Ryukyu. Upon receiving the report of these events from Taiwan, officials in Fukien and in Peking expressed their wish for a thorough investigation into the matter so as to "warn the violent and pacify the docile." Unaware of its possible repercussions, however, no other action was taken and the whole matter was soon buried in the files of the Chinese government.[120]

The news concerning the massacre of the Ryukyu sailors must have provoked the imagination of the Japanese government. At a time when a new outlet was needed to satisfy the expansionist elements in Japan, the incident of the Ryukyu sailors was undoubtedly a god-send opportunity. Exactly under what circumstances the news of the Ryukyu sailors reached the Japanese government was a point of dispute, but from the Japanese point of view, it was beyond a doubt that the rather vague and anomalous political status of the Ryukyu Islands provided a good opportunity for them to exploit.[121] Thus late in 1871, upon learning of the incident, the officials in Kagoshima, capital of the former Satsuma *han*, immediately pleaded to the Japanese government for formal action. This plea was soon echoed by the voices of many expansion-minded officials such as the Saigo brothers and Soyeshima Taneomi in the central government.

By October of 1872 the Japanese government was firmly convinced of the feasibility of such an action. Thus, taking advantage of the official visit of the Ryukyu prince to Japan on October 16,1872, the Japanese Emperor unilaterally issued an edict proclaiming the incorporation of the former kingdom of the Ryukyus into Japan as an integral part of the Empire. The former king of the Ryukyu islands was given the title of a peer in the Japanese Empire. At the same time, to make sure that it would not cause foreign objections, Japan also notified the governments of the United States, France and the Netherlands that the treaties they had concluded with the kingdom of Ryukyu would henceforth be honored by the government of Japan.

With the title over Ryukyu thus established, Japan was ready for the second step by re-opening the case of the Ryukyu sailors who were killed almost a whole year before in Taiwan. The way the Japanese went about this issue was, because of Japan's relatively recent entrance into the field of international diplomacy, highly cautious and well-planned. Realizing its lack of knowledge of the Chinese situation in general and the Taiwan situation in particular, it decided first of all to overcome this difficulty. Through the recommendations of Charles E. DeLong, the American Minister in Japan, the services of Charles LeGendre, the ex-American Consul in Amoy who was on his way home from China, was bought by the Japanese government at a high price. This purchase of LeGendre's expertise was no doubt a matter of considerable significance, for based on LeGendre's detailed planning, a series of diplomatic and military strategies were presented to the Japanese government that clearly influenced the Japanese policy during the following year.

Once the preliminary information concerning Taiwan was assured, the Emperor of Japan, on December 19, 1872, issued an edict announcing the appointment of Soyeshima as Minister Plenipotentiary and Ambassador Extraordinary to China with the alleged purpose of exchanging the ratifications of the treaty concluded during 1871 as well as to offer congratulations to the Chinese Emperor upon his accession to the throne and his marriage. In the meantime, Charles LeGendre was commissioned as an officer in the Japanese delegation to China. For further preparation LeGendre tutored the Japanese officials for several months. It was not until March 11, 1873 that Soyeshima, together with Yanagihara, LeGendre, and Cheng Yung-ning 鄭 永 寧 , finally left Yokohama for China.[122]

The mission reached Tientsin on April 20, and on April 24, they were received by Li Hung-chang. Under the spirit of cordiality, the instruments of ratification were subsequently exchanged on April 30. During this brief stay in Tientsin, Soyeshima and Li had also conferred on a wide range of topics on matters of joint concern but the problem of Taiwan was cautiously avoided by Soyeshima. On May 7, the Japanese mission finally reached Peking. After some preliminary contacts with appropriate officials, an imperial audience was granted on June 29, whereby the official purpose of the mission was completed.

In the meantime, however, the problem of Taiwan was pursued along quite different lines. In order to avoid the suspicions of the Western Powers, Soyeshima refrained from making any direct contact with the *Tsungli Yamen* on the issue. Instead, he sent Yanagihara and Cheng on his behalf. On June 21, his two deputies visited the *Yamen* where they were received by Mao Chiang-hsi 毛 昶 熙 , and Tung Hsun 董 恂 . During their conversation, the Japanese randomly touched upon a variety of issues including, for example, problems such as the status of Macao and the actual degree of independence of Korea. But, all in all, there was no denying that the major point the Japanese were driving at was the problem of Taiwan.

To proceed toward this goal, the Japanese succeeded in engaging the Chinese ministers in a rather informal conversation that eventually entrapped the entire Chinese position. This conversation, as recorded by the Japanese scholar, Nagao Agira, is no doubt worth noting in full:

> *Japanese:* Formosa had formerly been occupied by the Japanese and the Dutch, and afterwards Teiseiko (Koxinga) established his independence there. Under his descendents, however, the island became Chinese territory, but China subdued only a portion of the island, leaving the eastern portion to the aboriginal savage tribes, which your government never attempted to reduce to obedience. Now, in the winter of 1871 these barbarians attacked and murdered the Japanese subjects shipwrecked on the coast, and the Japanese government intends to send an expeditionary force to chastise them. But as the region lies adjacent to the territory under the local government of China, the Ambassador (Soyeshima) thought it better to inform you of the fact, in order to avoid a collision endangering amity between the two empires.

Chinese: We have only heard of the Formosan savages plundering and killing the people of Liukiu (Ryukyu) but never heard of their attacking Japanese. Liukiu is a Chinese territory, and Chinese officers rescued and sent home to Liukiu such of them as could escape the savages.

Japanese: Liukiu has always belonged to Japan. During the feudal ages it was a dependency of the Prince of Satsuma, and is now under the direct rule of the Imperial Government. Hence, there is not a person of Liukiu who is not a Japanese subject, entitled to the protection of the Japanese government. You say you have rescued the Liukiu people, but what have you done towards chastising the Formosan savages that have plundered and killed the rest?

Chinese: There are two sorts of aborigines in Formosa — those that have come under the Chinese rule, and are governed by the Chinese local officers, called "cultured barbarians," and those that remain beyond the influence of China, called "savage aborigines."

Japanese: The Formosan savages have molested foreign subjects more than once, and your government never chastised them. This might lead to a very serious consequence — namely the occupation of Formosa by other powers, as in the case of Cambodia, Tonquin and Annam, which is inconvenient, and a source of danger both to Japan and China. Hence the Japanese Government has decided to undertake the work of chastisement itself. But in order to avoid complications, our Ambassador, in his capacity of Minister of Foreign Affairs, caused the expedition to be postponed until he had opportunity to assure the Chinese Government that what Japan is going to do in Formosa concerns only the barbarians outside the limit of Chinese administration, and that it had no intention of interfering with the internal affairs of China. It is also to be taken into consideration that, if the Japanese Government does not act now, the Japanese public, much angered as they are at the murder of the Linkiu people, might invade the island of their own accord, and thereby give rise to a state of things incompatible with the existing treaty. The Japanese Government was orginally against the idea of informing the Chinese Government of their intention, and it is therefore on his own responsibility that the Ambassador makes the present communication, etc.

Chinese: "The savage aborigines" have not been chastised, because they are beyond the reach of our government and culture; but as we have in our hands the reports of the Governor-General of Fukien, who rescued the Liukiu people, we will consult those papers, and then answer your questions.

Japanese: (You have already stated that the savage aborigines are beyond the reach of your government and culture; and they are traditionally an independent tribe; and we shall treat them as an independent nation.) There is not a Japanese ignorant of the murder of the Liukiu people in Formosa as the incident has appeared in the Chinese journals; and as the Ambassador is preparing with all haste for his departure, he will certainly not wait for any later response.[123]

The problem concerning the so-called status of the aboriginal Taiwan was clearly an important question and the Japanese government was fully aware that it has no legal standing whatsoever to engage China in a formal discussion of the issue. Moreover, even if the Japanese government approached the Chinese government through formal diplomatic correspondence on the issue, it would have to wait a long time before it received a reply, if at all, from the Chinese government. Under such a situation, its premeditated action against China would have to be postponed indefinitely. Thus by approaching the Chinese officials informally and construing their inadvertent reply as a definite answer of the Chinese position on the status of the aboriginal territory on Taiwan, the Japanese have scored a great diplomatic success. In fact, on the very evening of the day of the conversation, Soyeshima joyfully reported to his government on the success of his mission in obtaining the desired answer of the *Tsungli Yamen* that the aboriginal territory of Taiwan was beyond the government and culture of China. With the completion of his mission, he soon packed and headed for home.[124]

History is made perhaps more frequently by coincidence beyond human intentions and what happened during the Fall of 1873 was a good example. Because of the different attitude toward the Japanese invasion of Korea as mentioned previously, it soon produced a cabinet crisis in October 1873. Expansion-minded officials like Saigo, Soyeshima and others all tended their resignation in protest and a new cabinet with Iwakura Tomomi 岩倉具視, Okubo Toshimichi 大久保利通, Okuma Shigenobu 大隈重信, and Terashima Munenori 寺島宗則, soon took over. With the removal of the war-minded members of the Japanese government like Saigo and Soyeshima, one would easily assume that for the sake of peace it was a turn for the good. But what actually happened was exactly the reverse.

In order not to make the "Great Divide" too great, the new cabinet was in fact turning its attention to the problem of Taiwan as a possible arena upon which both sides could once again close their ranks. Thus the new cabinet not only secretly dispatched an intelligence mission to Taiwan under the leadership of Fukushima Tadashige 副 島 九 成 , to spy on the island, it also began to draft detailed plans for a possible expedition based on this newly acquired information.

On February 6, 1874, Okubo and Okuma formally presented their statement on the "matter of aboriginal territory in Taiwan" to the Council of State in which a call for expeditionary action against Taiwan was made. At the same time, just as the Council was deliberating on the question of the expedition to Taiwan, the disgruntled *samurai* elements had already begun to cause disturbances in the Saga area. This was undoubtedly an uprising staged in protest against the government's stand on the Korean issue. But as the same time, it was equally a shot in the arm for the expansionists. To placate as well as to divert the attention of these rebels, the Taiwan plot began to figure even more prominently in the minds of the officials as a convenient design for appeasement. What followed was therefore a series of official acts toward the realization of this goal.

On February 25, 1874, the Council of State appointed Saigo Tsugumichi 西 鄉 從 道 , the younger brother of Saigo Takamori as the "Director of Taiwan Affairs," an act that was indubitably aimed at pleasing his frustrated brother over the Korean issue. On April 4, the Japanese government announced the establishment of the Bureau for Aboriginal Affairs of Taiwan, and Okuma, then finance minister, was appointed to head it. In the meantime, expeditionary forces were being prepared by the army and the navy and Saigo Tsugumichi was given the rank of lieutenant general and appointed commander of the expeditionary force. The sailing date was finally set for April 18, and Yangagihara, by now an old hand on China, was appointed to undertake the diplomatic front in Peking as the Japanese resident Minister there.[125]

Before the actual departure of the Japanese forces, however, foreign envoys in Tokyo such as the British Minister Sir Harry S. Parkes and the new American Minister John A. Bingham, who replaced Charles E. DeLong in the Fall of 1873, all began to express their doubt about the legitimacy of the projected Japanese action. A little later, similar reservations were also made by diplomatic representatives from Russia, Italy, and Spain. Fearful of a possible intervention from the Powers, the Japanese made a last effort to stop the forces from leaving Nagasaki. But Saigo refused to follow the cabinet order on the ground that he himself had been instructed directly by the Emperor to carry out the expedition. He advised that in case of any difficulty the Japanese government should consider him a pirate to avoid assuming officially any international responsibility. He successfully ignored the last minute decision of the Japanese government, thus set forth a precedent of disobedience that was bound to have serious repercussions in later developments of modern Japan.[126]

On April 27, Saigo reached Amoy under the pretext that his army wanted to borrow temporary drilling ground in the city. It was not until a few days before his departure for Taiwan that the Governor-General of Chekiang and Fukien, Li Ho-nien 李鶴年, was formally informed. In his letter to Li, Saigo nevertheless urged the Chinese officials and populace not to be alarmed over the expedition to Taiwan and stated his intention to punish only the aboriginal tribes who had killed some of the Ryukyu sailors two years ago. Upon receiving this letter on May 8, Li immediately refuted Saigo in a letter in which he cited several principles of international law to substantiate his argument. But it was all to no avail for Saigo had already left for Taiwan by the time Li's messenger tried to reach him.[127]

On May 7, the Japanese army landed on Langchiao and soon succeeded in threatening the local tribes into submission. On May 22, the Japanese proceeded further inland and engaged the Botans in the Shihmen area. As a result of this engagement, both sides suffered casualties. On the same day, Saigo reached Langchiao and joined his army of 3,600 men. On June 2nd, the Botan village was attacked from three directions. The Botans defended their homes and their land in a most heroic and courageous way. They fought the invaders everywhere. For a while, the Japanese suffered heavy casualties and even considered retreat. The Botans, however, were scattered too thin and their lack of coordination finally cost them the war. The Japanese, as the victorious party, soon started a campaign of annihilation. In the process many of the aborigines were killed and the entire Botan community was burned and destroyed.[128]

The news of the Japanese invasion of Taiwan reached Thomas F. Wade, the British Minister in Peking, on April 10, 1874, and he, in turn, brought the news to the *Tsungli Yamen* on April 18. On May 4, the *Tsungli Yamen* also received the news from Fukien that Japanese warships had entered the harbor of Amoy in the latter part of April.

Realizing that the invasion was by now a reality, Prince Kung began to respond officially. In his disptach to the Throne, he reported about the conversation which had taken place a year before between the *Yamen* officials and Yanagihara on the status of Taiwan and recommended that a high-ranking official, well-versed in foreign affairs, be dispatched to Taiwan to look into the real situation. On the other hand, he also notified the Japanese Foreign Ministry of his disagreement and demanded an explanation of the Japanese military action. The communication, which represented the official Chinese view on the matter at this time, read in part as follows:

> Taiwan is an island lying far off in the sea. There are some aboriginal people living there whom we have never tried to restrain by laws nor control by administrative setups. This is in line with the teaching of the *Book of Rites* which taught us never try to change the ways of a people but always let them keep their own proper one. But the territory inhabited by the aborigines is truly within the jurisdiction of China. There are many frontier regions within the Chinese empire where, just like the aborigines in Taiwan, the people are permitted to preserve their own customs. The news that you have launched military actions against Taiwan has not yet been established and to me it is highly incredible. But if it is true, why violate our prior agreement? What is the purpose of sailing your warships into the harbor of Amoy? It is my sincere wish to see your early reply to these questions.[129]

While an early reply was not forthcoming, the situation went from bad to worse. On May 29, the *Tsungli Yamen* reported to the Emperor that news from various sources indicated that the Japanese had indeed landed in the southern part of Taiwan. It warned that the Japanese might have the ambition of permanent occupation of the island and recommended that Shen Pao-chen 沈 葆 楨 , the high official in charge of shipbuilding, be sent to Taiwan as a Special Imperial Commissioner for military and diplomatic affairs, while Pan Wei 潘 霨 , the Provincial Treasurer of Fukien, be sent as his assistant. The Emperor appointed Shen to the post of Special Imperial Commissioner in charge of matters in Taiwan. At the same time, the Governor-General and other civil and military officials of Fukien were all instructed to cooperate fully with him, and Pan Wei, as recommended, was appointed as an assistant to Shen.[130]

Shen was undoubtedly one of the most capable officials of the late Ching period. Upon being appointed to the Taiwan post, he soon engaged in a thorough and detailed planning for the defense of Taiwan. The result of his thinking, embodying both long and short range measures, was presented to the Throne in a dispatch on June 3, which included four basic suggestions. First, he believed that it would be important to win moral support of the Western powers by informing their consuls in Fukien. By arousing public opinion against Japan, he felt sure that the Japanese would be discouraged or delayed. Second, he believed that China must strengthen her armaments. He pointed out that the superior armament of the Japanese forces stood in sharp contrast to the Chinese. To him, this was a matter that deserved the utmost attention without any delay. Third, he pleaded that talents be recruited for his service, particularly those who had prior experience in Taiwan. And finally, he proposed the improvement of the communications system between Taiwan and the mainland. In particular, he recommended that a cable be laid from Foochow to Amoy to Taiwan. This would render the situation in Taiwan to be more readily known to the central government.[131] To these proposals, the Emperor concurred favorably. He authorized Shen to draw funds from the Treasury of Fukien, and in case more were needed, he was instructed to make a request directly to the capital.

Paper plans notwithstanding, Shen also took up measures to strengthen the military defenses of the island. In order to guard Taiwan-fu, the capital city, he strengthened the fortification of the harbor of Anping with cannons of the latest model. For the defense of the northern part of the island, he emphasized the training of militia and replenishing the supply of arms.[132] Under his suggestion, China's most modernized divisions were dispatched to Taiwan under the command of Tang Ting-kuei 唐 定 奎 , which made the total forces under Shen well over ten thousand by

July 1874.[133] In order to prevent the Japanese from attacking other coastal provinces on the mainland, he recommended that these provinces also be put on alert.[134] These and many other measures had undoubtedly improved the military position of China *vis-a-vis* Japan.

Yet neither side took the decisive next step. Both sides seemed to have second thoughts at a time when the formal confrontation was set to begin. For China, this was a time when the revolts in Yunan and Kansu were just coming to an end and a large army was being requested for the pacification of the Sinkiang disturbances. Whether China could allow a second front in Taiwan was therefore very much in doubt.[135] Moreover, the problem in Indochina was also deteriorating. By establishing its protectorate over Indochina in 1874, France had come nearer than ever to the Chinese border. A Sino-Japanese war at this time would undoubtedly expose the vulnerability of China in such border areas. With these in mind, it was only natural that the Chinese government had opted, though secretly and gradually, for a waiting policy.

Li Hung-chang, for example, had time after time reminded Shen about the inferiority of the Chinese military forces and advised him to play it cool. In his instruction to Tang Ting-kuei, he also pointed out that "once in Taiwan, the forces should be used with great discretion. If Saigo is satisfied with what he had achieved, there is no reason why we should expel him by force."[136] The Japanese, on the other hand, were by no means altogether free from careful and hard consideration either. To be sure, the expansionist policy was in the first place never unanimously shared by all the members of the Japanese government and the inconclusiveness of the Japanese military action deepened this division. But the ever-present nightmare for the Japanese was, however, the possible intervention of the Western powers. As mentioned earlier, the Japanese action had caused the immediate concern of the British Minister in Tokyo. It was soon followed by protests and reservations from other Western countries. The attitude of the United States, in particular, must have weighed even more heavily in the minds of the Japanese policy makers.

Although Charles LeGendre and a few other American officers, such as Douglas Cassel and James Wasson, had participated in the hostile act against China, and the American steamship

New York was contracted for convey service in the preparatory stage, the United States government never approved of these acts. Not only that, but in early June, John A. Bingham, the American Minister in Japan had come out to acknowledge formally that Taiwan was a part of China and insisted on American neutrality by pressing the Japanese government to disengage all the Americans from their part in the hostility.[137] Benjamin P. Avery, the American Minister in China, also expressed his sympathy for China's toleration and similarly agreed that the entire Taiwan territory belonged to China. In his discussion with Li Hung-chang, he even promised American assistance to China in case Japan decided for permanent occupation of parts of Taiwan.[138]

In addition to all these things, the contention between Japan and Russia over the Kurile was also brewing at this time while Saigo's forces in Taiwan suffered from malaria and had lost much of its vitality. All these events forced the Japanese government to search for a way out while there was still time. It was against this background that Sino-Japanese negotiations began.

On June 6, 1874, Pan Wei, in Shanghai, made his first contact with Yanagihara, then the designated Japanese Minister with the alleged purpose of establishing a legation in China for the promotion of "friendly" relations. In their written exchanges, Pan asked Yanagihara to explain the reasons behind Japan's action regarding Taiwan. Yanagihara replied that the Japanese action was prompted by the uncivilized state of affairs to the south of its border and his government was simply following the examples of the British and the Americans in attempting to secure the safety of its sailors. He made the point that the withdrawal of Japanese troops could not be effected without some tangible results from the mission. Specifically, he proposed three conditions as the basis for further negotiation. First, the Japanese should be permitted to capture and punish those involved in the murder of the Ryukyu and other Japanese crew. Second, any person who resisted the Japanese in their punitive measures against the aborigines would be responsible for their own deed. Finally, an agreement must be concluded to prevent the recurrences of atrocities.[139] As for the immediate step, he promised to write Saigo to halt military actions for the time being so that the talks could continue.[140]

On June 17, Shen Pao-chen arrived in Taiwan in the company of Pan Wei as well as Prosper Giquel and De Segonsac, two

Frenchmen employed by Shen as military advisors. Once there, Shen immediately entrusted Pan as an emissary to engage Saigo in formal talks. In this, Pan succeeded brilliantly. Between June 22 and June 26, Saigo and Pan held five interviews in the Langchiao area. The Chinese position in these discussions was well presented in Shen's letter addressed to Saigo which read in part as follows:

> The aboriginal territory has been Chinese for more than two hundred years. Although the people living in these areas are ignorant, they are nevertheless innocent. That is why the government had never tried to impose its laws upon them hoping that they will gradually be acculturized to the principles of humanity and justice and transformed into ordinary citizens. As to the act of murder, there are laws administering justice irrespective of the origin of the criminal whether they be aborigines or Chinese. But it is the responsibility of the Chinese government to take care of the matter and does in no way involve any other country.[141]

At the same time when Shen was writing this letter to Saigo, it was reported that the Japanese might launch new attacks against the Peinans and other tribes who were never involved in the murder. This would clearly indicate that Japan had purposes other than what she had professed. Thus, in Shen's letter, he also dwelt on the inconsistency of the Japanese position by pointing out the fact that:

> With the weak and innocent tribes as the target of her army, Japan may not have fully demonstrated its superior strength. But even if Japan could score total victory, she could not avoid suffering casualties. If the lives of the aborigines are worthless, how about the lives of the Japanese?. . . In any event, China would not yield an inch of her territory. Besides, other treaty powers would not tolerate the monopoly by your country of any benefit gained in this act.[142]

In the actual negotiation, however, Pan tried to discuss with Saigo the three conditions laid down earlier in Shanghai by Yanagihara. Siago's attitude appeared at first to be arrogant. He had not only flatly denied that the aboriginal territory belonged to China but also regarded the Chinese official gazatteer, presented by Pan to prove that the aborigines had paid taxes to the Chinese officials in Taiwan, as pure "academic argument."[143] In their last interview, however, Saigo's adamant attitude was somehow softened. Alluding to the vast expenses which the Japanese government had incurred in the military action, he doubted whether further actions could be taken, and inquired whether the aborigines could be expected to pay an indemnity. As to the final solution of the conflict, he expressed the opinion that it was beyond his jurisdiction and he would withdraw from Taiwan only when negotiations between Yanagihara and the *Tsungli Yamen* had been satisfactorily carried out and his government instructed him to do so.[144]

Realizing the futility of further negotiation with Saigo, Shen and Pan returned to the mainland. On July 1, Pan tried to engage Yanagihara once again in negotiations but Yanagihara failed to respond. Yanagihara was not at all in the mood to reach any substantial agreement with the provincial officials at this time. His rather extended sojourn in Shanghai from May to July was more or less geared to Saigo's military actions in Taiwan. For what he would eventually demand and obtain from the Chinese government was, in his opinion, very much predicated on the military situation in Taiwan. Thus he played the waiting game with Pan and other officials in Shanghai through the exchange of a series of correspondence all of which tended to help him bide his time. It was not until mid-July that he was finally briefed on the military situation in Taiwan by a Japanese officer under Saigo's command. The news from Taiwan must have been gratifying to him. For it was only then, on July 17, when the situation in Taiwan was ascertained, that he soon proceeded to Tientsin without even saying goodbye to Shen and Pan.

Yanagihara arrived in Tientsin on July 24 and soon met Li Hung-chang there. In their interview, Li pointed out to him the contradictory nature of his mission at a time of military hostilities. Li accused the Japanese of adopting a policy of speaking softly yet carrying a big stick. To Li, the three conditions raised by Yanagihara in his first interview with Pan Wei had already been fulfilled. The only thing left to be attended to was, in Li's opinion, the withdrawal of the Japanese forces. If Yanagihara could not decide on the issue why, Li asked, was he calling himself Minister Plenipotentiary.

In any event, Li persuaded Yanagihara not to bring the issue to Peking and advised him to settle it then and there in Tientsin. But Yanagihara replied that Japan was only following the steps taken by the United States and Britain to secure the safety of its sailors. He had full powers only in the field of diplomatic negotiations while the final authority remained in Toyko. As to the contradictory nature of his mission of 1873 to exchange treaties at a time of war, he resorted to equivocation and gave no clear answer. Confident apparently in the somewhat entrenched position acquired by Saigo in Taiwan, he was undaunted by Li's warning of the futility of his projected trip to Peking. He left for Peking a few days later.[145]

Yanagihara arrived in Peking on July 31, and on August 13 started a discussion with the *Tsungli Yamen* on the Taiwan problem. In this initial discussion, the Chinese ministers resorted to nothing more than the earlier justifications used by Pan Wei. They pointed out that all the villages of Taiwan are Chinese territory. The official gazetteer which recorded the dates and amounts of taxes paid by the tribes must stand as an authoritative proof. Even if the aborigines were savages as the Japanese had characterized, they were Chinese savages and their crime, if there was any, must be punished by China. Moreover, if Japanese citizens had been injured by the aborigines, the Japanese government should inform the Chinese government of the time, the people involved, and the property lost, and China would handle it. Yet instead of asking China to look into the matter, Japan was blaming China for not paying heed to the case. Such actions were not only unreasonable, they also put the friendly relations of the two countries in jeopardy.[146]

On August 15, the two parties met again. During this meeting, Yanagihara denied that his statements concerning the sovereignty of China over Taiwan had been contradictory. He pointed out in a statement that the Japanese government, being independent and strong, needed no permission from any other country to take action as it pleased, especially if she undertakes an expedition of a humanitarian nature in the unclaimed aboriginal territories of Taiwan. If the aboriginal territory had been a part of Taiwan, he questioned, why had China not asked Japan to withdraw her troops when the news first reached the Chinese government? To him, the issue under discussion concerned the titles of both countries and he therefore demanded to know what China's policy was in regard to Taiwan.[147]

This strong-worded statement did not carry the discussion very far. On August 17, Yanagihara met once again with Prince Kung and other ministers at the *Tsungli Yamen*. But the *Tsungli Yamen* was unwilling to give Yanagihara a definite answer as to what it would do about Taiwan. The ministers did express on that occasion their wish that the two nations should overlook their minor differences and uphold friendly relations by speedily settling the present affair. But Yangihara, instead of pursuing the discussion in a peaceful manner, demanded that the *Tsungli Yamen* must send him within three days a written reply to his demand of August 15th. If the *Yamen* offered no reply on that day, he threatened that he would send an officer to Tokyo to report to his government that the Chinese government did not have any objection to Japan's punitive expedition in Taiwan.[148]

The *Yamen* decided to ignore this threat. On August 22, the ministers of the *Yamen* sent Yanagihara a communication indicating that the Chinese government would voluntarily undertake measures to manage the aboriginal territory as soon as the troops under Saigo had withdrawn. At the same time, they advised Yanagihara, however, to give careful thought to any action which he might propose that his government should take.[149] This official reply on the part of the Chinese government must have rendered Yanagihara more impatient, which he expressed in a letter to Prince Kung on August 24.

In this letter, beside acknowledging the receipt of the communication of August 22, he flatly declared that any further discussions of the issue would be entirely useless. He accused the Chinese officials of employing the delaying tactics which had greatly complicated the issue. He wanted to make it perfectly clear that Japan had the sovereign right and the determination to punish the aborigines on the unclaimed lands and to eventually assimilate them into Japanese culture. And, he warned, the Chinese government would not be allowed to interfere in this policy or to discuss it any further.[150]

Clearly, this arrogant communication proved to be the doom of his entire mission. For the *Tsungli Yamen*, in its reply on August 26, retorted in an equally adamant manner. It not only insisted once again of China's sovereign rights over the aboriginal territories but also warned Yanagihara to be more polite in his language.[162] Thus, with the strong positions taken and unyielding pronouncements issued by both sides, the negotiations had come to a deadlock at the end of August, 1874. Yanagihara's intention to score political gains through limited military success must by now be judged as a failure. He was, in fact, not allowed to raise any more issues and his demand for an Imperial audience to present his credentials was denied.

It was during this period when the Yanagihara mission was bogged down in the mishmash of official recriminations, that the Japanese government started to reevaluate the over-all situation once again. By this time, the Japanese government was informed in its latest report that China had stepped up its preparation for war and the Western powers had become increasingly sympathetic to the Chinese cause. Okubo, who had recommended the military action to allay the discontent of the internal dissent and who was unable to restrain Saigo when the pressure of the foreign envoys forced him to backdown, began increasingly to feel the pressure of the time.

Earlier, on May 15, he had already stated that he would take all responsibility for the consequences which would arise from his failure to halt the Saigo expedition. On July 13th, he personally appealed to the Council of State to appoint him as a negotiator to be sent to Peking. In order to meet all possible contingencies, he further proposed to the Council during the latter part of July a series of plans. Among them, in particular, were the beefing-up of Japanese military preparedness for an even larger war and the campaign to rally the moral support of international public opinion. His decision to make up the negotiations himself, though confronted with much opposition in the Council, had nevertheless prevailed in the end.

On August 2, he was finally appointed by an Imperial edict as an Ambassador Plenipotentiary and Extraordinary to supercede Yanagihara in the negotiations. By the same order, he was instructed to strive to keep peace at a price but not to avoid war if it were inevitable. In particular, he was ordered to let Japan's "righteous and humanitarian" motives in the expedition be recognized. To these ends, he was given full power to supervise all the Japanese officials and military personnel stationed in China. With such an opportunity for him to salvage a situation of his own creation, his happiness was natural and understandable. In fact, his enthusiasm for the mission was clearly evidenced by the hurriedness of his journey. His delegation soon boarded the

Japanese warship *Ryujokan* and they set sail for Tientsin via Shanghai on August 16. And, unlike Yanagihara, he made no attempt to contact Li Hung-chang while in Tientsin. Once there, he proceeded directly to the capital and arrived in Peking on September 10.[151]

Realizing the futility of engaging the Chinese government on the principle of sovereignty over the aboriginals in Taiwan, Okubo began to think of new steps to be taken to reopen the discussion with the *Tsungli Yamen*. Before long, on September 12, with the advice of Gustave Boissonade, his French adviser, Okubo came up with a new policy. In brief, his plan was to concentrate his efforts to prove the lack of Chinese jurisdiction over aboriginal Taiwan. With this in mind, talks between him and the Chinese officials were soon arranged, and beginning September 14, a series of intensive negotiation began.

In the first session, Okubo challenged the Chinese claim of jurisdiction on several counts. First of all, he pointed out that, according to international law, an effective control and administration of the territory must be enforced in order to be recognized as having property rights and sovereignty over the territory. Since China had done nothing to prove its control over the aboriginal area, he doubted its claim of jurisdiction over the region. Secondly, he produced the documentation of conversations conducted by Fukushima and the local people in the Fangliao area. In this conversation, the local settlers were quoted as claiming to the effect that they owned their land through reclamation rather than through establishing titles by governmental permission. Although China had earlier countered the view by presenting the record of the tax-collection gazetteer, Okubo insisted that the periodical collection of land taxes alone could not be accepted as evidence of a nation's indisputable control over a given land. Finally, he presented to the Chinese officials two written questions for which he demanded a reply:

> First, since your country has claimed that the aboriginal territory lies within your domain, then why do the aborigines remain uncivilized up to this very date? The claims of jurisdiction implies that an administrative and educational system must be established there. To what extent have you tried to administer and educate the aborigines?

Second, at the present time when international contact and travel
have become a reality, every country has taken steps to insure the
safety of mariners on its shores. Your country is well-regarded
throughout the world for its high morality and its principles of
humanity and righteousness. To expect from you a generous
treatment of shipwrecked foreigners is therefore only natural. But
the murder of the foreigners by the aborigines has never received
your attention. It shows not only your disregard of the life and
property of other countries, but also your encouragement of the
cruel undertakings of the aborigines. Is this reasonable?[152]

On September 16, Okubo and the *Yamen* officials met for the
second time. During this session, the Chinese officials undertook
to answer some of the issues raised by Okubo in the first session.
As far as the Fukushima conversation was concerned, they pointed
out that it could not be used as a proof to dispute China's
jurisdiction over the area. Although the local people may acquire
their land through reclamation or any other means, it was by no
means disputable that their land laid within the domain of China.
Futhermore, many of the local people were educated at the
expense of the Chinese government upon the recommendation of
local officials. It therefore served as additional proof that Chinese
jurisdiction reached into that eastern region of Taiwan. For it is
simply unreasonable to say that they lived on a piece of unclaimed
land while going to Chinese schools.[153]

As to the specific questions raised by Okubo, the *Yamen*
replied as follows:

To the first question: In the aboriginal territories of Taiwan, the
Chinese Government adopts the policy of letting them keep their
customs. Let those who are able to pay taxes pay it, and let those
who are talented enough to go to school go to school. A generous
and lenient policy to bring them up to a high level of culture is
entrusted to the officials of nearby districts. The Chinese
government and its educational policy do not believe in forceful
subjugation or rapid assimiliation but would rather emphasize
gradualism. The aborigines in the island of Hainan are treated in
the same manner. In fact China has many regions with similar
conditions. It is by no means confined to Taiwan and Hainan.
Every province has its own practices. This is the condition of
varying political setups such as referred to in the treaties.

> To the second question: In China's relations with various countries, no matter what the case may be, they are always handled by the government once the *Tsungli Yamen* is notified. There are some cases which are more difficult to handle or slower to solve than others. But there was never a case which was completely ignored. Take the case of the aborigines for example. If your government had notified the Chinese government, this *Yamen* would never have failed to investigate the matter. . . .[154]

In the next meeting on September 19, Okubo took the offensive again. Based on the Chinese reply, he raised seven more points of objection. Among them, he pointed out particularly that China's policy of keeping customs of the aborigines was incompatible with China's claim of jurisdiction. At a time when law was obeyed, such a policy may be construed as leniency; but at a time when crimes were committed and remained unpunished, it meant there was no law. And when there was no law, there was no jurisdiction. He then took China's policy of gradualism to severe task. He restated his conviction that an effective control through proper administration must be established as an evidence of sovereignty over certain territory. Yet in Taiwan, he failed to see such evidence. He taunted that gradualism could sometimes be acceptable, but it was a bit too much when nothing was done after two hundred years. He asked why China was so patient. Finally, he disputed the relevance of the "token" representation of China's control presented by the Chinese officials. To him a system of taxation should be applied uniformly upon every citizen or subject within the domain and should not be used to discriminate against only those who were found capable of paying. Similarly, the system of education should also be applied universally to each and every citizen. If it was limited to a small minority of the tribe, it could not be regarded as a civilizing effort. In any event, these and other objections lead him once again to the conclusion that Japan could not regard the aboriginal territories in Taiwan as Chinese because there was no evidence acceptable under international law to prove it.[155]

Wen Hsiang, 文 祥 a Grand Secretary, refuted all these observations. In particular, he took pains to explain the relevance of international law in this case. As he related, international law was a new innovation of Western origin and that the provision within that law could not be applied directly to a Chinese system which existed long before the Western system came into being. To him, therefore, the proper way to seek redress should be through the Chinese government and not through the mockeries of the so-called international law.[156] But Okubo refused to budge. Before the meeting was adjourned, he insisted once more that the Chinese government should produce conclusive evidence within the shortest possible time. Failure to do so would lead Japan to consider it as evidence of lack of Chinese control over the whole disputed area. The meeting was thus drawing once again to an inconclusive ending.

Three days after this meeting was held, the Chinese government formally replied to the seven points raised by Okubo. As expected, the Chinese government refuted each and every point as untenable. To make its position better known, perhaps, the Chinese government took the opportunity to reaffirm, once again, its stand on the issue. In the preface of the communication, the *Tsungli Yamen* pointed out that:

> During our first meeting, you (Okubo) have pointed out your familiarity with early discussions (on the Taiwan problem) and stated that the purpose of your mission was to restore friendly relations (between China and Japan). Thus when you asked us two questions, we have tried to answer them as truthfully as possible, with the understanding that it will lead to a sincere negotiation. But your recent communications have raised new questions on our jurisdiction (over the aboriginal territory). This *Yamen* has examined the Sino-Japanese Treaty which stipulates in Article 3 that each nation has a different system of government from the other and that administrative matters lie solely within the confines of domestic jurisdiction of each country. If we undertake to explain to you every system of government, it will be endless and impossible. If we do not, you would construe it as our lacking jurisdiction over the area. That is why we answered you at all. As for the case of Taiwan, although you have sent troops to our territory, we have not returned fire. The fact that the aboriginal territory belongs to China is well known everywhere. The reason that we did not refuse to answer your inquiry concerning Taiwan lies in the hope that it will lead to compromise and peace. What you have responded, on the other hand, was a series of questions that contend our sovereign right. It not only put us on trial but also violated the principle of domestic jurisdiction. What would you feel if you were in our position? If you shall continue this

endless questioning, this *Yamen* would not oblige again. For that will lead only to futile argument and even to jeopardizing our friendly relations. If you should feel a sense of obligation to the general welfare of international navigation, you could so indicate to us. After all, the territory has been a Chinese territory and we would certainly want to discharge our responsibility as its owner.[157]

The rather uncompromising tone of the letter had undoubtedly irritated Okubo. What followed was a series of similarly reproachful letters dispatched by him on September 27. In his first letter written to refute the *Yamen's* charges, he pointed out that his attitude in the negotiations was dictated by the principle of frankness. He did not believe that the whole issue could be settled by a policy of muddling through. In fact, the Chinese government would, in his opinion, save a great deal of effort if it could prove in a clear-cut fashion its jurisdiction over a territory where it did not establish law and administration.[158]

In his second letter, he remarked that China was trying to sidestep the whole issue by hiding behind the principle of domestic jurisdiction. What he intended to know was whether China had managed the area in question rather than how it was managed. He revealed that he was tired of repeating all the arguments over and over again and hoped that the Chinese officials would re-read them and reconsider them without his repeating them.[159] In the last of the three letters, Okubo, apparently with the help of Boissonade, took the opportunity to demonstrate his newly acquired erudition. He had all the pertinent passages from several books on international law written by such authors as Vattel, Martens, Heffter, and Bluntschli copied out to either support his argument or justify the Japanese action.[160]

This resort to Western legal works was, in retrospect, clearly an attempt to put China in the wrong in the eyes of Western countries. It was equally clear that through this gesture, he hoped to enlist further support from the Western countries at a time when the whole mission was getting nowhere since it started in early September. But, as always, the Chinese ministers were unimpressed. In their reply to Okubo on September 30, they pointed out that the relationship between China and Japan should be guided by the Sino-Japanese treaty which was negotiated and signed by both parties and the instruments of ratification duly exchanged. To them, the territorial question of China should not be determined by surmises nor challenged by any casual bystanders. The cited passages from Western legal treatments were therefore to them totally irrelevant.[161]

The Okubo mission, which started in early September had lasted almost a month up to the time of this transmittal, and no concrete result was in sight. To a man who had pledged his responsibility to finding a solution, this seemingly endless exchanges of notes must have been frustrating. Thus, upon receiving the latest reply from the *Tsungli Yamen*, Okubo decided to add a little pressure in his dealing with the rather unpliable Chinese ministers and hopefully to accelerate the pace of the negotiation. To proceed along these lines, he demanded an appointment with the *Yamen* ministers to discuss the matter in person and October 5 was subsequently agreed upon for this purpose.

On that date, Okubo, accompanied by Yanagihara and others, arrived at the *Yamen* for a face-to-face confrontation with the Chinese ministers. From what was recorded, this confrontation was no doubt an explosive and most trying one. It started at one o'clock in the afternoon and continued until dark. During this extended session, Okubo repeatedly accused the Chinese ministers of subterfuge and evasiveness. Citing the *Rover* case, he also accused China of having treated Japan differently from other foreign nations. After reiterating many of his earlier arguments, he finally announced that since no progress was made thus far, he was prepared to leave Peking and cut off further negotiations entirely.[162]

A strong threat notwithstanding, the Chinese ministers remained undaunted. For students of Sino-Japanese relations of this period, it is both interesting and pertinent to ask what had sustained China in adopting this seemingly hard line *vis-a-vis* Japan that contributed to this long drawn out negotiation. Several reasons could, perhaps, be ventured here as explanations. First of all, it may perhaps be pointed out that the conviction of the Chinese government in its claims over the aboriginal territory was under no circumstances ever doubted. For in terms of history, geography, and legality, Taiwan was always a part of China. The attempt to draw an artificial demarcation between what was Chinese and what was un-Chinese in Taiwan was not new to China as we have seen in the preceding pages. But no matter how the problem was posed, it was always a problem fabricated out of something that was entirely groundlesss. The British had tried it. The Germans, also, had tried it. But none of them had succeeded.

To China, what Japan was trying to do was in essence not entirely different from those earlier attempts which, experiences told her could be dissolved only through firmness, perseverance, and the gradual passage of time. Thus, what China had played vis-a-vis the Japanese may perhaps be characterized as a waiting game, a game that had invariably succeeded in the past.

Secondly, China knew that the international situation would not allow Japan to have her way, with Western powers having extended and vested interests in this part of the world. Both Li Hung-chang and Shen Pao-chen had called the attention of the Chinese government to this fact. Li's active and wide diplomatic contacts in Tientsin during the time of negotiations, for example, had indeed generated much enthusiasm from men such as Benjamin Avery, the American Minister in China, and many others. It was clearly believed by the Chinese officials that a prolonged negotiation could only strengthen China's international position and bring added pressure on the Japanese.[163]

Last, but not least, the domestic scene of Japan had also played an important role in the minds of the Chinese decision makers. The Japanese government, as mentioned earlier, was divided over the Taiwan action in the very beginning. An extended and unfruitful negotiation, such as the one going on at this time, could only deepen this division. To abandon diplomatic effort entirely would most likely lead to an expanded military confrontation with China with a result that was very much in the unknown. But to continue this negotiation in any meaningful way, Japan must retreat substantially from its early demanding position. This is a point the Chinese officials had firmly grasped.

In Shen Pao-chen's letter to Li Hung-chang, he pointed out that Okubo was obviously under pressure from Tokyo to strike a quick bargain with China. For this reason, he advised the government to play it cool and bide its time. In Li Hung-chang's communication to the Tsungli Yamen, he, too, characterized the Japanese attitude as "intimidation" which should not, in his view, disrupt China's effort to bide for her time.[164] All in all, they believed that China could wait while Japan could not, and it was all to the good for China if she could stick it out.

To be sure, this concealed optimism on the part of the Chinese government was not equally shared by all the foreign representatives in China. For example, the British Minister Thomas Wade and the French Minister Louis de Geogroy had approached the matter quite differently. Thinking from their own interest, the deadlock could develop into a war between China and Japan and to them Japan was something to be feared. Should a war end with a Japanese victory, their interest in Taiwan and other parts of China would inevitably be prejudiced by an expanded Japanese power. In case of a Chinese victory, the pride of a victorious China would be so inflated as to create many problems for the West. Caught by the horns of such a dilemma, they tried to play both ends against the middle. What followed, therefore, was a series of unsolicited offers rendered by Wade and De Geogroy to both of the feuding parties in the Taiwan crisis.

As early as September 16, Wade had informally tried to sound Okubo out on the probable conditions under which the Japanese would be willing to settle the whole case. But Okubo flatly denied that there was such a possibility. On September 26, he visited Okubo again and suggested that Japan should withdraw her forces in return for some compensation. But Okubo declined once again. Around the same time, Wade also tried to approach the Chinese government with the same idea. Based on the report of Charles Shadwell, the British Naval Commander in Japan, which indicated that Japan had been preparing for a military showdown, he tried to persuade the Chinese government to accept a possible mediation. The *Yamen* ministers, however, were not entirely convinced with either the usefulness of such an effort or the sincerity of Wade himeslf.[165]

On September 29, De Geogroy approached Li Hung-chang with the same idea but had the same negative answer.[166] The official position of the Chinese government towards mediation at this time was well summarized in the dispatch submitted by Prince Kung to the Emperor. As he pointed out:

> At present, the willingness of the British and the French ministers to mediate is dictated by their wish to help others as well as their own selfish considerations. Against this background, we could only

> pretend to be interested in their offer so as to avoid their distorting the truth. (But at the same time), we must show them the true principle of justice in the case and let them know that we would not be intimidated by threats or treachery.[167]

After the negotiations reached a deadlock on October 5, Wade tried once again to bring both sides together. To his surprise, perhaps, he found much had been changed during the intervening period. It is clear to us that much of this change came from the Japanese side. Although the impasse was a creation out of his own attitude, Okubo soon realized that it must be treated at best as a tactical arrangement. Fearful that it might lead to serious deterioration of the Sino-Japanese negotiation, he sought to give his intimidating effort one last try. On October 10, he addressed the *Tsungli Yamen* with a long and strong-worded communication.

In it he accused the Chinese ministers of bad faith and violation of treaties. He denied the gazetteer of Taiwan as a valid evidence of Chinese jurisdiction and pointed to the *Rover* case as a proof that China did relinquish her rights over the aboriginal territories in Taiwan. He implied that although Japan had spent a great deal of money in the expedition, the over-all purpose was still the protection of its citizens abroad. For this purpose, he proposed a solution which would be convenient to both parties, namely, China should redefine its state boundary line and leave the aboriginal territories outside of this line. He allowed five days for the *Yamen* to give a definite answer to this request and threatened to leave Peking if the Chinese government failed to respond.[168]

At the same time, however, making sure this threat would not overstep his purpose, Okubo also began to pursue an entirely different course of action. Fearful that the Chinese ministers might still remain tenacious in regard to his new threat, he decided to give himself a little flexibility. On October 14, three days after the last request was lodged, he voluntarily visited Wade and De Geogroy and explained to them the honorable and humane nature of the entire Japanese action. In his converstation with De Geogroy, he specifically pointed out that it was the obstinacy of the *Yamen* ministers that made an early solution impossible. But to him, there was still a possible way out. He told De Geogroy that Japan had incurred vast expenses in sustaining its military actions in Taiwan. In order to search for peace, a possible solution should not be ruled out if this fact is taken into proper consideration.[169] Though he would not guarantee it would work, he nevertheless indicated that it would be worth exploring.

In the meantime, as expected, the reply from the *Tsungli Yamen* on October 16, in regard to Okubo's threatening notes of October 10, was firmly negative. But his need not mean the end of the negotiations. For Okubo's interest in finding a solution through compensation — a fact well known to the Chinese officials for a long time — had finally been acknowledged by the *Tsungli Yamen* through the message of an intermediary. On the same day that the *Yamen's* reply was forwarded to him, he also received a note from Wen Hsiang, indicating that a meeting could be arranged to search for solutions which would be convenient to both parties. Well aware of the meaning of this invitation, Okubo replied favorably.

On October 18, Okubo and the ministers from the *Tsungli Yamen* met for the first time under the new understanding. After many hours of heated arguments, they finally decided that a possible Japanese withdrawal should be hinged upon sufficient Chinese compensation. To further explore this possibility, they agreed that a meeting be scheduled for the next day. The second meeting, however, was not held until October 20. During this meeting, Okubo was presented with a statement by Wen Hsiang in which the Chinese position was clearly stated as follows:

1. Japan dispatched its troops to aboriginal Taiwan for it considered aborigines as unsubjected barbarians. It did not know that the territory belongs to China. There is a difference between dispatching troops knowing the region to be Chinese and not knowing it. For this reason, China would not blame Japan for its action.
2. Now that the fact has been made clear and it is recognized that the territory in question is Chinese, the Chinese Government would not bring up the case — of the expedition — against Japan once Japanese troops are withdrawn. Japan is not to say that it did China a favor by giving the territory to her.
3. Since the dispute arose from the murder of shipwrecked people by aborigines, once the troops are withdrawn it would be for China to handle the case in Taiwan.
4. The Chinese Emperor would pay compensation to those Japanese who had suffered at the hands of the aborigines.[170]

To consider these terms carefully, Okubo did not commit himself immediately to the specifics, and another meeting was scheduled for the following day. Between October 21, and 23, three meetings were held by the two parties and differences arose on the amount of the compensation and the form under which it was to be paid. Okubo demanded 5,000,000 taels as an "indemnity" and dictated that it should be written into a formal contract. For the ministers of the *Tsungli Yamen*, the money would be given to the sufferers only as a sign of the good will of the Chinese Emperor, and as such, no formal stipulation would be needed. Moreover, as consolation money, it should be considerably smaller than what the Japanese had demanded, perhaps somewhere in the neighborhood of 500,000 taels.

During the last session on October 23, intensive bargaining took place and furious words were exchanged but it was all to no avail. Knowing that it was not easy to bring the Chinese ministers down to their size, Okubo resorted once again to his old stock-in-trade. He informed them that he had resolved to break off the negotiations and arrange for the mission to depart from Peking on October 26. But at the same time, on October 24, he visited Wade once again. Ostensibly to bid Wade farewell, Okubo took the opportunity to inform Wade of the two thorny issues involved in the negotiations. Realizing the true intention of this visit, Wade counselled patience and advised Okubo that if the real question was the fulfillment of a promise and Japan was willing to compromise on the total sum of the compensation, then he could intervene in the matter once again. It was then that Okubo "reluctantly" expressed his willingness to go along.[171]

On October 25, Wade visited the *Tsungli Yamen* and told the Chinese ministers that Japan was demanding 2,000,000 taels, which, in his opinion, was not too high. The minister, after careful evaluation of the whole situation so as not "to force the Japanese to take the risky route or to push the British to the Japanese side," finally revealed that China would not offer more than a total of 500,000 taels, 400,000 for the families of the murdered sailors. When this condition was brought to Okubo, Okubo pointed out that it would be accepted only when three further conditions were met. First, China must recognize Japan's action in Taiwan as righteous. Second, all evidence concerning the case must be obliterated. And third, a total sum of half a million taels must be paid over to Japan before Japan would agree to withdraw her troops from Taiwan.

On the following morning, Wade solicited the opinion of the Chinese ministers on these conditions and found the reaction was favorable. He soon urged the ministers to prepare the text for the final agreement, and the light at the end of the long tunnel seemed finally visible. One situation remained to block the final rapproachement. Okubo, for fear of a possible breach of the terms, insisted on incorporating the precise sum of the compensation into the text of the agreement. But the *Tsungli Yamen* held fast to its original position and declined. In the end, Wade was again instrumental in ironing out a solution. By proposing to incorporate the precise sum of compensation in a separate instrument entitled "guarantee" to the main agreement, he succeeded in bridging the gap once again between the two sides. By October 28, Okubo finally gave his concurrence of this arrangement. Thereupon, the final agreement, including a short preamble, three articles and one guarantee was formally signed on October 31, 1874 by Okubo and the ministers of the *Tsungli Yamen* in Peking, whereby the five months' hostilities and negotiations between China and Japan over Taiwan came to an end.[172]

In terms of its over-all impact, the Sino-Japanese confrontation of 1874 must be judged, it seems, as a serious setback for China. The Chinese government's consciousness over China's rights and privileges was something less than complete. China's reaction to Japan's resort to force had revealed nothing but her military weaknessess and administrative inefficiency. In diplomacy, the passive stance assumed by a country is not a sign of tenacity but a sign of weakness. By appeasing the aggressor in the very outset, it has only whetted its appetite for the future. In fact, what had happened following this initial confrontation could easily bear out this point.[173]

Insofar as the eventual signing of the Sino-Japanese agreement was concerned, it appeared to be equally defective technically and politically. The agreement had not only rendered the historical relationship between China and Ryukyu obscure, it also exposed unreservedly the poor understanding of the Chinese officials towards international affairs. Specifically, by signing this agreement as a means to ending the troubles in Taiwan, Japan had successfully challenged China's traditional system by asserting the principles of a modern state system as outlined by Western international law. As a result of this agreement, China had theoretically opened not only the doors of Taiwan but also the doors of many areas within her domain to the outside world. Moreover, the fact that Japanese withdrawal was effected only after China paid a handsome sum of compensation could not but encourage the ever-increasing avarice of other would-be emulators.

To be sure, the episode taught China a lesson. She was compelled to realize that power, responsiblity, and the right of sovereignty must go hand in hand with each other. To increase China's position *vis-a-vis* foreign powers, new methods, as recommended by Shen Pao-chen and others, have all been gradually adopted by the government. Under Shen's recommendation, for example, Taiwan was subsequently given province status which had in many ways contributed to the political progress and the social and economic welfare of the island. The ministers of the *Tsungli Yamen*, for another example, realizing from their experience in dealing with the Japanese that diplomacy must be backed by military strength, also recommended new ways and means to strengthen national defense. The new army and navy started around this time must be considered as the direct products of this conscientiously designed self-strengthening movement, although they were still too little and too late compared to the immensity of the situation. With the vulnerability of the island exposed to the Powers, they were naturally led to explore their future possibilities in Taiwan once new opportunities arose.

Numerous incidents befell Taiwan after 1874, among which the French attack of 1884 stood out as ominous and the Japanese landing in 1895 fatal. The eventual fall of Taiwan in 1895 could not fail but generate repercussions of the most serious kind from the mother country. The fact that the first spark of modern Chinese revoluton was ignited by Dr. Sun Yat-sen in Canton in 1895 — the very year when Taiwan was ceded to Japan — was by no means a coincidence when it is viewed with the concomitant national mood in mind.

Notes to Chapter V

1 William Campbell, *Formosa Under the Dutch* (London: Kegan Paul, Trench, Trubner & Co., 1903), pp. vii ff.

2 *T'ai-wan-sheng tung-chih-kao* (台 灣 省 通 志 稿) Vo. III (Taipei: Tai-wan-sheng wen-hsien wei-yuan-hui, 1960), p. 45. Hereafter known as *Tung-chih-kao*.

3 Frederic L. Foley, S. J., *The Great Formosan Imposter* (St. Louis: St. Louis University Press, 1968), p. 81.

4 *Ibid.*, pp. 10, 55.

5 *Ibid.*, p. 76.

6 *Tung-chih-kao*, p. 47.

7 *Ibid.*, pp. 48-53. Also see James W. Davidson, *The Island of Formosa: Historical View from 1430 to 1900* (Taipei: Publisher unspecified, 1903), pp. 83-84.

8 Kuo Ting-yee, *T'ai-wan shih-shih kai-shuo* (台 灣 史 事 概 說) (Taipei: Chengchung Book Co., 1969), p. 138.

9 *Ibid.*

10 *Ch'ou pan i-wu shih-mo hsuan-chi* (籌 辦 夷 務 始 末 選 集) Vol. I (Taipei: Bank of Taiwan, 1964), p. 3. Hereafter known as *CPIWSM*.

11 *Ibid.* p. 15.

12 *T'ai-wan-sheng tung-chih* (台 灣 省 通 志) Vol. I (Taipei: Tai-wan-sheng wen-hsien wei-yuan-hui, 1968), p. 81. Hereafter known as *Tung-chih*.

13 *Ibid.* p. 82

14 *CPIWSM*, Vol. I, pp. 46-48.

15 *Ibid.*, pp. 48-51.

16 *Ibid.*, pp. 64-65.

17 *Ibid.*, p. 68.

18 *Ibid.*

19 *Ibid.*, p. 70.

20 Ta-hung-a received *Tai-tzu-tai-pao* (太 子 太 保) which ranks ninth in the twelve ranks of honors conferred to the members of the metropolitan administration. Yao Ying received the title of *Erh-pin-ting-tai* (二 品 頂 戴) which ranks second in the nine ranks conferred to civilian magistrates.

21 *Ibid.*, p. 71.

22 *Ibid.*

23 *Ibid.*, p. 75.

24 *Ibid.*, p. 82.

25 *Tung-chih-kao*, p. 68.

26 *Ibid.*, p. 69.

27 *Chinese Repository*, Vol. XI (1842), p. 682.

28 *Ibid.*, p. 683.

29 *CPIWSM*, Vol. I, p. 92.

30 *Ibid.*, p. 94.

31 *Ibid.*, p. 107.

32 *Ibid.*, p. 106.

33 *Tung-chih-kao*, p. 73.

34 *Ibid.*

35 *CPIWSM*, Vol. I, p. 146.

36 Davison, *The Island of Formosa: Historical View from 1430 to 1900, op. cit.*, p. 108.

37 *Ibid.*

38 Lien Heng, *T'ai-wan tung-shih* (台 灣 通 史) (Taipei: Chung-hua Tsung-shu, 1955), p. 313.

39 Sophia Su-fei Yen, *Taiwan in China's Foreign Relations — 1836-1874* (Hamden: The Shoe String Press, 1965), p. 43.

40 Hosea B. Morse, *The International Relations of the Chinese Empire*, Vol. I (London: Longmans, 1910), p. 293.

41 *Tung-chih-kao*, p. 75.

42 For example, in 1847, the British ship *Royalist* reached Keelung under the command of R. N. Gordon who personally conducted survey on the quality of the coal mine there and reported to the Royal Geographical Society in London. The Peninsula and Oriental Steam Navigation Co. also ordered 700 tons of the Keelung coal in the same year but was refused by the Chinese government. See *Ibid.*, pp. 76-77.

43 *CIPWSM*, Vol. II, pp. 152-153.

44 *Ibid.*

45 *Ibid.*, p. 156.

46 Tyler Dennett, *American in Eastern Asia: A critical Study of the Policy of the United States with reference to China, Japan and Korea in the 19th Century* (New York: Macmillan Co., 1922), p. 284.

47 *Ibid.*, p. 270.

48 *Ibid.* Also see Lai Yung-hsiang, *The Study of the History of Taiwan* (Taipei: Shan Ming Book Co., 1970), p. 186.

49 Yen, *Taiwan in China's Foreign Relations — 1834-1874, op cit.*, p. 60.

50 *Ibid.*

51 *Ibid.*, p. 67.

52 Dennett, *American in Eastern Asia, op. cit.*, pp. 290-291.

53 John F. Cady, *The Root of French Imperialism in Eastern Asia* (Ithaca: Cornell University Press, 1954), p. 294.

54 Dennett, *American in Eastern Asia, op. cit.*, p. 298.

55 Masataka Banno, *China and the West 1858-1861* (Cambridge: Harvard University Press, 1964), p. 12.

56 Kuo, *T'ai-wan shih-shih kai-shuo, op.cit.*, pp. 149-150.

57 *Tung-chih-kao*, pp. 86-87.

58 *CPIWSM*, Vol. II, pp.

59 *Ibid.*, p. 231.

60 *Ibid.*

61 *Ibid.*, p. 234.

62 Huang Chia-mo, *Mei-kuo yu Tai-wan: 1784-1895* (美 國 與 台 灣) (Nankang: Academia Sinica, 1966), p. 176.

63 *CPIWSM*, Vol. II, p. 237.

64 *Ibid.*, p. 240.

65 *Ibid.*, p. 241.

66 *Ibid.*, p. 244.

67 *Ibid.*, p. 230.

68 *Tung-chih-kao*, p. 90.

69 Leonard Gordon, "Early American Relations with Formosa, 1847-1870," *The Historian*, XIX, No. III (1956), p. 278.

70 Huang, *Mei-kuo yu Tai-wwan, op.cit.*, p. 194.

71 Davison, *The Island of Formosa: Historical View from 1430 to 1900, op.cit.*, pp. 175-176; *Tai-wan tung-shih, op.cit.*, pp. 190-192.

72 Yen, *Taiwan in China's Foreign Relations—1836-1874, op.cit.*, p. 102.

73 *Tung-chih-kao*, pp. 110-111.

74 *Davison*, The Island of Formosa: Historical View form 1430 to 1900, op.cit., Index pp. 35-36. Also see *Tung-chih-kao*, pp. 114-118.

75 Lien, *T'ai-wan tung-shih, op.cit.*, p. 199.

76 *Tung-chih-kao*, pp. 118-119.

77 *Ibid.*, p. 119. Also see *CPIWSM*, Vol. III, pp. 362-363.

78 *Ibid.*

79 Yen, *Taiwan in China's Foreign Relations—1836-1874, op.cit.*, p. 129.

80 Dennett,, *American in Eastern Asia, op.cit.*, p. 411.

81 Davison, *The Island of Formosa: Historical View from 1430-1900, op.cit.*, p. 116.

82 *Ibid.*

83 *Ibid.*

84 *Tung-chih-kao*, p. 121.

85 *Ibid.*, p 122.

86 *Ibid.*

87 For full text, see *Ibid.*, pp. 124-125.

88 *Ibid.*, p. 123.

89 *Ibid.*. p. 124.

90 Davison, *The Island of Formosa: Historical View from 1430 to 1900, op.cit.*, p. 117.

91 Kuo, *T'ai-wan shih-shih kai-shuo, op.cit.*, p. 152.

92 *Ibid.*

93 Yen, *Taiwan in China's Foreign Relations—1836-1874, op.cit.*, p. 103.

94 *Ibid.*, p. 104

95 *Tung-chih-kao*, p. 138.

96 *CPIWSM*, Vol. III, pp. 343-344.

97 *Ibid.*, p. 348.

98 *Ibid.*, p. 351.

99 *Ibid.*

100 *Ibid.*, pp. 352-354.

101 *Ibid.*, pp. 354-355.

102 *Ibid.*, p. 358.

103 *Tung-chih-kao*, p. 140.

104 Davison, *The Island of Formosa: Historical View from 1430 to 1900, op.cit.*, p. 187.

105 *Ibid.*, p. 186.

106 *Ibid.*, p. 187.

107 *Ibid.*, p. 188.

108 *Ibid.*, p. 199.

109 *Tung-chih-kao*, p. 137

110 Davison, *The Island of Formosa; Historical View from 1430 to 1900*, *op.cit.*, pp. 401-402.

111 *Tung-chih-kao*, pp. 126-127.

112 *Ibid.*, pp. 152-153.

113 *Ibid.*, p. 128.

114 *Ibid.*, pp. 129-130. The rules governing the camphor trade were further formalized in the Camphor Regulations concluded by Alcock and the *Tsungli Yamen* in 1869. See *Ibid.*, pp. 130-132.

115 *CIPWSM*, Vol. III, p. 341.

116 Davison, *The Island of Formosa: Historical View from 1430 to 1900*, *op.cit.*, p. 198.

117 *Ibid.*, p. 336.

118 Immanuel C. Y. Hsu, *China's Entrance into the Family of Nations: The Diplomatic Phase 1858-1880* (Cambridge: Harvard University Press, 1960), pp. 172-173.

119 *Tung-chih-kao*, p. 176.

120 *Ibid.*, pp. 171-174.

121 The island group had been a Chinese tributary ever since the fourteenth century and it had continued to send tributary missions to pay homage to the succeeding Chinese emperors to 1872, the year when it was formally incorporated by the Japanese government. But according to the Japanese record, the islands had been conquered and reconquered by the forces of the daimyo of Satsuma in 1185 and 1609. The fact that Ryukyu was allowed to continue its tributary relations with China was because during the period of isolation under the Shogunate, the trade between China and Ryukyu through the tributary system was immensely profitable. Thus, according to the Japanese view, for two hundred and fifty years the Ryukyus had been under the dual suzerainty of both the Chinese and the Japanese.

122 *Tung-chih-kao*, pp. 176-177.

123 Alfred Stead (ed.), *Japan and the Japanese* (New York, 1904), pp. 142-218. The sentence quoted in parenthesis did not appear in Agira's text. It appeared in the *Japanese Foreign Affairs Documents* and were added to the Agira text by Sophia Yen in her book. See Yen, p. 189.

124 Li Hung-chang, *Li-wen-chung-kung chuan-chi*, (李 文 忠 公 全 集) Vol. V (Taipei: Wen-hai Book Co., 1962), p. 57.

125 *Tung-chih-kao*, pp. 178-180.

126 *Ibid.*, pp. 181-182.

127 *Tung-chih chia-hsu jih-ping ch'ing-tai shih-mo*, (同 治 甲 戌 日 兵 侵 台 始 末) Vol. I (Taipei: Bank of Taiwan, 1959), p. 9. Hereafter known as *CTSM*.

128 *Tung-chih-kao*, pp. 182-187.

129 *CTSM*, pp. 4-5.

130 *Ibid.*, pp. 6-8.

131 *Ibid.*, pp. 16-18.

132 *Ibid.*, p. 28.

133 *Ibid.*, p. 53.

134 *Ibid.*, p. 36.

135 This leads to the famous debates between Sai-fang (Land Defense) and Hai-fang (Sea Defense) within the Central government at this time. On the

one hand there were Li Hung-chang, Ting Jih-chang, Li Ho-nien and Shen Pao-chen who advocated the importance and imminence of the sea defense and advised concession in Sinkiang. But, on the other hand, there were Tso Tsung-tang, Ting Pao-chen and others who regarded the former position as impractical and demanded the continuation of the early effort in pacifying Sinkiang. With the help of the *Tsungli Yamen*, the latter position finally prevailed. See *Li-wen-chung-kung chuan-chi*, Vol. II, pp. 91-92 and *Tso-wen-hsiang-kung chuan-chi* (左 文 襄 公 全 集) Vol. III (Taipei: Wen-hai Book Co., 1964), pp. 18.

136 *Li-wen-chung-kung chuan-chi*, Vol. V, p. 51.

137 *Tung-chih-kao*, p. 181.

138 *Li-wen-chung-kung chuan-chi*, Vol. V, p. 58.

139 Yen, *Taiwan in China's Foreign Relations—1836-1874, op.cit.*, pp. 222-223.

140 *CTSM*, Vol. I, p. 26.

141 *Ibid.*, p. 31.

142 *Ibid.*, p. 43.

143 Yen, *Taiwan in China's Foreign Relations—1834-1874, op.cit.*, p. 226.

144 *CTSM*, pp. 45-46.

145 *Li-wen-chung-kung chuan-chi*, Vol. V, pp. 48-49.

146 *CTSM*, pp. 106-107.

147 *Ibid.*, pp. 108-109.

148 *Ibid.*, p. 111.

149 *Ibid.*, p. 112.

150 *Ibid.*, p. 113.

151 Yen, *Taiwan in China's Foreign Relations—1836-1874, op.cit.*, pp. 244-252.

152 *CTSM*, Vol. II, pp. 142-144.

153 *Ibid.*, p. 143.

154 *Ibid.*, pp. 144-145.

155 *Ibid.*, pp. 145-146, 150.

156 Yen, *Taiwan in China's Foreign Relations—1834-1874, op.cit.*, p. 257

157 *CTSM*, Vol. II, pp. 146-147.

158 *Ibid.*, pp. 150-151.

159 *Ibid.*, pp. 152-153.

160 *Ibid.*, pp. 153-154.

161 *Ibid.*, pp. 154-155.

162 *Ibid.*, pp. 159-160.

163 *Li-wen-chung-kung chuan-chi*, Vol. V, pp. 52-53.

164 *Ibid.*, p. 53.

165 *CTSM*, Vol. II, p. 141.

166 *Li-wen-chung-kung chuan-chi*, Vol. V, pp. 53-54.

167 *CTSM*, Vol. II, p. 141.

168 *Ibid.*, pp. 159-160.

169 Yen, *Taiwan in China's Foreigh Relations—1836-1874, op.cit.*, p. 272.

170 *Ibid.*, pp. 275-276.

171 *Ibid.*, p. 278.

172 For full text, see *CTSM*, Vol. II, pp. 178-179.

173 Tsiang Ting-fu, *Ching-tai chung-kuo wai-chiao-shih chih-yao* (近代中國 外交史資料輯要) Vol. II (Taipei: The Commercial Press, 1959), pp. 106-107.

Chapter VI

The Internal Development and Modernization of Taiwan, 1863-1891

BY TING-YEE KUO

I
The Maturity of Sinicization (1683-1874)

In 1683 China regained its complete unification, as Taiwan returned to the fold of the mainland to become again one Empire and one state, in form and in substance. Thus the history of Taiwan has entered its second phase. At the beginning, the Manchu government was ignorant of the importance of Taiwan, especially at the time when the policy of continental embargo or closing the coast was in force. There were even talks of "move the people and abandon the land," which might have been materialized were it not for the consideration that "though keeping it would be of no advantage, but giving it up might cause trouble."

Shih Lang, the Admiral in Command of Naval Forces in Fukien, who was well oriented in overseas affairs and who had been to Taiwan, was the one voice arguing persistently against the abandonment of Taiwan. He says that, considering the economic aspects,

> Taiwan is fertile in soil and rich in its variety of products. Its land is fit for both farming and sericulture; and its waters supply unlimited quantities of fish and salt. Its mountains are densely covered with full grown forests; and bamboo groves are seen everywhere. Products such as sulphur, rattan, sugar cane, deer skin, and innumerable others that are indispensable to the daily life of the people, are all produced there. Formerly it was short of cotton cloth, but today cotton is richly grown there and ample

supply is provided for local textile. It is indeed a land of rare riches and natural defensibility.

In consideration of the people, he says that:

the natives and Chinese are both innocent subjects. Any policy or plan to be adopted must include detailed and comprehensive reckoning of their well-being as a part of the plan's entailed consequence. . . .The population of Taiwan is now quite dense, and propagating rate high. The long time settlers all have their definite walks of life, as farmer, craftman, trader, or shopkeeper. Once a fateful policy is decided upon, should it be either to move or to abandon them, they would either be left to languish in a deserted land should their attachment for that land persuade them to stay, or be deprived of their means of livelihood and left to the hardships of drifting along on the verge of starvation should they choose to move. Such a situation would indeed be a headache to the government that cannot be left unattended to.

In consideration of geographical factors Shih Lang says that,

the island of Taiwan stretches thousands of li parallel to the mainland coast, in the north reaching to the land of Wu or Kiangsu-Chekiang and in the south bordering the land of Yeuh or Kwangtung. Its mountains ranges rise high to form impassable barriers and its coast line twists and turns to form useful bays and harbors for shipping shelter and strategic positions. Thus it forms a defensive fortress covering the flank of our coastal provinces of Kiangsu, Chekiang, Fukien, and Kwangtung. . . .It is indeed a miracle of cosmogony that nature should provide our country with this island mass for the protection of our southeast shores. The possession of this island barrier will enable us forever to be free from attacks from that direction. Considering maritime defense under current and foreseen exigencies, Taiwan was for a time the base of the Dutch, and its recovery has always been their craving desire. They have been waiting for a chance, and once they laid their hands on it again, the consequences would be unthinkable. The Dutch are a wily and artful people and are good at influencing man to serve their interest. Their double deck seagoing ships are strong and exquisitely built, long unrivaled over the highseas of the world. . . . If in case this rich island of several thousand li fell into their hands, so that their ships and men would have a base for operations, they would be in a position to rally allies and supporters from all sides, in order to peep at our shores from the advantageous position of a nearby base. It would be then the cast of the ominous dice for our future, and our coastal provinces would from that day on enjoy not another moment of peace.

Finally, he says in conclusion that

Taiwan, although only an island on the highseas, is intimately related to the security of our four coastal provinces. Not to say that farm production there is capable of supplying a garrison force to some extent, and for this reason alone we should decide on its keeping. Even if in case it were barren land incapable of farming, our policy should still be grain transportation from the mainland for its support and entertain not for a single moment its abandonment . . . .To abandon Taiwan would mean to create a catastrophe for the future; to keep it in possession means to seal permanently the defense perimeter of our southeast.[1]

The sagacious Emperor Kang-hsi took his advice, and in May 27, 1684 (Kang-hsi yr. 23, 4/14) officially promulgated the establishment, in accordance with the divisions set by the Cheng administration, of the prefecture of Taiwan (Taiwan-fu, formerly Ch'en-t'ien-fu) on the island of Taiwan, to be consisted of the three districts of Tai-wan, Fengshan (formerly Wan-nien-chou) and Chu-lo (formerly T'ienhsing-chou), together with the sub-district of Penghu (administered by the sub-district magistrate or hsun-chien). A Circuit Intendant of Defense and Petrol Affairs was created to have jurisdiction over Taiwan and the off shore island of Amoy of Fukien *(T'ai-hsia-ping-pei-tao)*, and also created was a General in Command of Taiwan Garrison Forces *(T'ai-wan-tsung-ping)*, both under the Fukien Provincial Government, to strengthen the link between the mainland and Taiwan.

Shih Lang was of the opinion that Taiwan is of primary importance to the maritime defense of China, and its economic importance is only secondary. In the first place, he thought that Taiwan stands as a strategic key position along the southeast coast and should not be allowed to fall again into the hands of a foreign power; secondly, Taiwan's steep hills and secluded valleys provide natural haven for unlawful groups prone to take to piratical activities and seditious course. Both situations were intimately related to the security of the four coastal provinces. This was the main reason that Taiwan should not be abandoned. That taxes and revenues could be raised was not considered as a relevant factor. The policies and measures adopted by the Manchu government during its early period of Taiwan administration was based upon this line of thinking.

In other words, the aim of government was limited to the maintenance of *status quo*, or the safeguard of peace and order. It was only a passive or conservation policy and there were no ambitions whatsoever at development or growth. Right after the taking over of Taiwan, the Manchu government transferred all civil and military personnel of the government, and officers and men of the army, of the former Cheng administration, to the mainland. All people formerly migrated to Taiwan from all provinces of the mainland during the continental embargo period were also ordered to move back to the mainland. Thus the first years experienced the sad situation of fields and trade being abandoned and population and production on the wane. Furthermore, the districts of Chaochou and Huichou of the province of Kwangtung, since they were once the sanctuary of pirates, were therefore ordered that people of these two prefectures were prohibited from migrating to Taiwan.

Yet, in spite of all these, in the long run the authority and power of political decisions were not able to hamper activities dictated by economic forces. Fukien and Kwangtung were both lands crowded with population but poor in resources, which made life difficult. For centuries, people from these two provinces have risked the highseas to migrate far to the South Seas for a better living. Now that Taiwan is so near at hand, the land being rich and habitants scanty, which they had either seen or heard of, how could they then be stopped from contemplating moving over.

Although the people from Chaochou and Huichou were prohibited from migrating to Taiwan, those from southern Fukien still could go under specified conditions. One was to obtain a migration certificate from the office of the Maritime Defense Sub-Magistrate *(hai-fang-t'ung-chih)* at Amoy at the time of their embarkation, which they would then submit for checking when they pass the port of Luerhmen in Taiwan, after which they would be allowed to disembark. This was intended to prevent all unlawful passage. Another way was to assume the status of the non-settling farmer who would move to Taiwan each year for the spring farming, only to return to his mainland home after the harvest, avowing in advance not to settle permanently in Taiwan.

A third way was to leave his family behind, under which condition he would be allowed to go to Taiwan, guaranteed to return by his family members being left at home virtually as hostages. This would hold him from committing serious offenses while in Taiwan, nor to have any extra-marital children. Such practices were of course against practical sense and human nature, and the effectiveness of their enforcement was indeed open to question.

Besides bribery and leniency which did work to let go many cases of violation unquestioned there was the fact that there were other ports of departure than Amoy, and other places of landing besides Luerhmen. Thus, during the course of the 17th and 18th centuries, the migration of mainland Chinese to Taiwan was still numerous.

Under the Manchu government, the first Prefect of Taiwanfu, by the name of Chiang Yu-yin, was known to be well versed in the principles of government and a good administrator. He looked after the well-being of the natives, brought the drifting to settle down, and did a lot for the people's guidance and comfort. He scaled the tax rate into graduations in accordance with the soil quality and other conditions of the land, in order to encourage the extension of farming. In cooperation with Chou Ch'ang, the Intendent of the Taiwan-Amoy Circuit *(Tai-hsia-tao)*, they "promoted culture and education, founded local free schools" to instruct the young and propagate the ethical principles of filial piety and brotherly care and the social and economic value of devotion to farming.[2]

Chi Ch'i-hsien, Magistrate of the district of Chu-lo, was well known in his sympathetic attitude toward the livelihood of the people and his overall understanding of the strength and weaknesses of the current military and civil measures of the government. He did a lot to lessen the burdens of the people and contributed to the promotion of education.[3] Chang Yin, another Magistrate of Chu-lo, enlisted people to settle and farm idle lands and paid great attention in giving people encouragement in their hardships and care for their needs. Many drifters came to settle under him and farm land acreage was greatly expanded and people thrived under his patronage.[4]

Ch'en Pin, at first Magistrate of the district of Taiwan and then promoted to Intendant of the Taiwan-Amoy Circuit, was known for his simple living and hard work, his kindness to the people, and especially his promotion of culture and education. He personally attended to the periodic examination of the students of the district academy to check their progress. He founded a school fund in land estate to provide for subsidies for the students. Under his care many talents were successfully developed and the academic and literary standing of Taiwan scholars greatly lifted.[5]

Sung Yung-ch'ing, Magistrate of the district of Fengshan, was known for his personal integrity. He founded local free schools. He built several *li* of dikes for flood prevention and irrigation and thus brought assured rich harvests to the area.[6] Chou Chung-hsuan, Magistrate of Chu-lo, encouraged the building of irrigation ditches by raising funds for the work, ending in the completion of several *li* of ditches. He took records of all available land capable of opening up and developing into farms from Chu-lo northward as far as Keelung. He was indeed a government man of farsight and good intentions.[7]

Besides the above, others like Chin Chih-yang and Shen Ch'ao-p'ing, both Prefects of Taiwan-fu; Sun Yuan-heng, Sub-Prefect of Taiwan; and Huang Shu-ching, the first appointed to the office, created in 1722, of Circuit Censor of Taiwan *(hsun-t'ai-yu-shih)*, all were known for having made contributions to the development of education and economy in Taiwan. All the above were records of good government throughout the years of the reign of Emperor Kang-hsi.

During the period of the Cheng's, although the military farm system was practiced in order to encourage farming, but man power was limited and large scale opening up was really limited to the plains of southern Taiwan, spreading north to what is present day Chia-i and south to what is present day Kaohsiung, with a population of three to four hundred thousand. In this early period of Taiwan's incorporation with the mainland, the area covered by the newly created local units of *fu* and *hsien* (prefecture and district) extended north-southwise to only more than hundred *li*. After less than a score years, the picture changed a great deal.

From the north of Chia-I extending to what is today Taichung, Chinese settlers there had increased by leaps and bounds. In another more than ten years, the northward expansion had crossed the river Ta-chia-hsi of central Taiwan, and the southern vanguard had reached Lang-chiao (present day Hengchun). The Tamshui and Keelung area in the northern tip of Taiwan, and areas in the southern tip, were also settled by mainlanders, turning virgin soil into happy abodes. The land opened up and inhabited by settlers spread lengthwise to more than a thousand *li*, with its rich production of sugar and rice unmatched anywhere. Moving eastward, settlers would advance into hill lands, open up and farm fields close to native tribal possessions, unhindered by cases of slaughter by the natives. On the east coast, "Native tribal centers like Ha-tzu-lan (present day Ilan), Ts'ung-hsiao (present day Haulien) and Pei-nan-mi (present day Taitung) had all been visited by Chinese traders, for as the number of settlers grew and population procreated fast, their spread and expansion came to reach far off areas, unable to be checked even by the strictest prohibitions."[8]

Thus within the span of more than thirty years (1684-1720), the spread and development of Chinese settlers in Taiwan had indeed been extremely rapid, a result of the pressure of economic forces in operation. In this period, the production of grain had a marked increase, and the production of sugar had reached the annual rate of over one hundred thousand catties, regularly exported to the mainland ports of Amoy, Ningpo, Shanghai, Suchow and Tientsin. "Usually the sugar was sold to orders before it was produced, and on delivery it was immediately packed and shipped."[9] Commodities for consumption at Taiwan were imported from the mainland, such as silk textiles from Kiangsu and Chekiang, and cotton and cotton textiles from Fukien and Shanghai. This indicated the exchange of products and the mutual gaining economy between Taiwan and the mainland.

Ch'en Meng-lin, who had been in Taiwan in 1711 for directing the compilation of the *District Gazetteer of Chu-lo*, was one who had a very good overall comprehension of the situation of Taiwan at that time. He mentioned that the area north of what is present day Changhua is fertile in soil and plenty of sources for irrigation, that Keelung is the key to the northgate of all Taiwan, that Tamshui is another strategic key south of Keelung, that together with points like Tachia, they are all defendable and of strategic value, and should be created districts with districts towns as regular local government units. Thus he was the earliest to come out for the development of northern Taiwan.

In the year 1721, an insurrection broke out in Taiwan. After the suppression, Man Pao, the Governor-General of Fukien and

Chekiang, thought that the region along the foot of the mountain range was usually where the undesirables took refuge to, thus planned to order all inhabitants within a ten *li* of the mountain range move away, after which a wall and a moat flanking it were to be built with the proscription that no crossing be allowed. Lan Ting-yuan, who took part in the suppression, argued strongly against it. His propositon was that "once an area is opened up, it will only be opened the more, never the less." He suggested that what should be done was "to increase the patrol force, and to attract more settling farmers to further open up the area. When the resources of the land are fully utilized, and manpower fully congregated for the task, not a single spot is going to be a refuge for undesirables even if there were still men living on robbing and stealing. What is then the need to stop all eating because of a little chocking?" He also suggested that garrison forces should be stationed in the north and south, to operate military farms on the spot; that a district be created in the north; that important ports like Pa-li-ch'a (opposite what is now Tamshui) and Pei-kang be made posts each to be stationed with a sub-magistrate *(hsun-chien)*; and that the promotion of education and culture should be attended to be "establishing schools and honoring scholarship."[10]

Man Pao also advanced the opinion that "Taiwan, with its high mountains and rich soil, is best suited for reclamation and farming. When and where there is profit, there will be people after it. If this profit is not allowed to be held by the settlers, it is to be left to the natives, or to be fed to the thieves and robbers. Even if such undesirables did not appear from among the immigrants, nor savage natives from the mountains, to disturb the peace and order, there is always the possibility that trouble will come from without, of which the Japanese and the Dutch were good precedents."[11]

The Manchu government finally took Man Pao's advice, and in 1723, the first year of the region of Yungcheng, a new district, Changhua, was created north of Chu-lo, and further north a sub-district, Tan-fang-t'ing, was created. These new local administrative units indicated that political authority was extending northward following the footsteps of the settlers. The office of the Defense and Petrol Intendent of the Taiwan-Amoy Circuit, scheduled to station alternately in Taiwan and Amoy in semi-annual turns, was changed in 1728 into the Defense and Petrol

Intendant of the Taiwan Division Circuit *(Tai-wan-fen-hsun-tao)*, to be stationed in Taiwan all year round, with Taiwan as his specified area of jurisdiction and responsibility.

Another important suggestion on the development of Taiwan offered by Lan Ting-yuan was to abolish the proscription on mainland emigrants' bringing families, so as to leave the emigration to Taiwan completely open and free. He argued that one of the causes of the insurrection of 1721 in Taiwan was that many settlers did not have the natural human desire of having their families with them satisfied. Thus frustration and search for a release led them into dangerous involvements. This he considered especially true of the so called *"ke tzu,"* who were more commonly known as the Hakka. They emigrated to Taiwan from the eastern part of Kwangtung to hire themselves out as tenant farmer or farm hands in Taiwan. They never had families, and "when they were not inhibited by family and clan ties, they were more prone to deviate from the lawful path."

Thus Lan Ting-yuan suggested it be ordered that "those who wish to emigrate and settle in Taiwan as farmers must bring their families with them. And those settlers in Taiwan who left their families on the mainland, if they intended to move their families to Taiwan, can send in an application for such, and upon examination of the case, an emigration permit be issued the family."[12] The provincial authorities of Fukien considered the suggestion practicable, and upon consulting the central government in 1732 (Yung-cheng yr. 10), and with due approval, it proclaimed that all propertied and law abiding settlers in Taiwan who wish to have their families moved from the mainland to Taiwan, are permitted to do so as desired. This act of grace, although its beneficiaries were limited to those who had established themselves in Taiwan, had a favorable influence of incalculable magnitude on the settling and development of Taiwan. It was indeed an enlightened policy.

In the first years of the reign of Emperor Chien-lung, policy towards Taiwan once more returned to the passive. In 1736, the first year of Chien-lung, the order prohibiting emigration to Taiwan without official approval, being rescinded, was revalidated. Four years later, the order allowing settlers in Taiwan wishing to move their grandparents or their wives from the mainland can do so upon approval of their application. The allowance was again rescinded in 1748. But, after all, such insensible proscriptions were hard to enforce.

Mainland Chinese settling in Taiwan at the time numbered hundreds of thousands. They had, as the fruit of their labor, property in fields and houses which they did not want to abandon to return to the mainland. Many of them did have their parents or wife on the mainland, whom they were eager to be united and together with, for which they would not refrain from recourse to unlawful ways. In a period of seven months in the year 1759, those on their way to Taiwan being detained upon   inspection by authorities numbered one thousand. Those who fortunately got through, and others who on being smuggled confronted hazards and met their end in one way or another on their way, must have been numerous.

In 1760, Wu Shih-kung, the Governor of Fukien, strongly remonstrated that the moving of families from the mainland by Taiwan settlers is all to the good and without a single disadvantage. He memorialized the throne that

> those who turned outlaws in the insurrection in Taiwan were all unmarried vagabonds of villainous character. As for the law-abiding good subjects, as far as they had registered as settlers and established themselves as property owners, and had furthermore parents and wives forming intimate ties, there is no doubt that they would look upon their family and person with much more attachment and care. . . . Now that the desire of moving their families by the law abiding settlers had caused the government to deal them the same prohibition that was applicable only to the prevention of the emigration of undesirables. . . the result is that many people, men and women, old and young, being eager to move to Taiwan to effect their family reunion, were forced to take to the many precarious ways of passage, causing a great number of innocent lives to perish in the rolling waves of the sea.

Wu's memorial met with approval and the subsequent new regulation was that all propertied and law abiding Taiwan settlers, who wish to move to Taiwan from the mainland their grand-parents, wife, concubine, sons and daughters, daughters-in-law, grandsons and granddaughters, or brothers, should send their applications to their respective local governments in Taiwan, upon having their applications transferred to the mainland, and being checked and confirmed by the respective local government offices there, transport permits will be issued for due emigration. In case the procedure moves the other way round, should the family members, the grandparents, etc., wish to emigrate to Taiwan to effect a family reunion, they should send their applications to their local governments to be transferred to Taiwan for checking and confirmation, upon which permits will be issued for their emigration.[13] This regulation was still limited to the moving of family members by Taiwan settlers, and was not extended to letting people freely emigrate with their families to Taiwan. The proscription forbidding free crossing was still in force.

But the proscription against free crossing was never effectively enforced. Considering Fukien alone, emigrants stealing over numbered tens of thousands each year. The 1760 regulation for the emigration of family members provided those who wish to go to Taiwan with convenient loopholes, for the term "family members" was given broad inclusiveness. Under such circumstances, the emigration of mainlanders from Fukien and Kwangtung to Taiwan increased greatly in number, and the area of settlement in Taiwan expanded rapidly.

In the beginning of the 18th century, the population of Chinese settlers in Taiwan was about 600,000, and their settlements, though reaching the central part of Taiwan and some areas in the north, still had its political, economic, and cultural center in the south. The creation of the district of Changhua indicated the maturity of the opening up of the central part, and served as a milestone in the advance towards the north.

In the early days, the port of Luerhmen in the south was the gate of entrance for crossing from the mainland to south Taiwan. Next came the port of Lukang, which served as the shorter passage from the mainland to the central part of Taiwan. It was especially the port used by the emigrants stealing across from Chuanchou, for at this port there were no officials inspecting the immigrants. Furthermore the crossing took only half a day with favorable wind. Before long, the port became the concourse of traders in northern Taiwan, with ships swarming the harbor and townsmen numbering several thousand households.

In 1784, the office of Maritime Defense Sub-Magistrate of Lukang *(Lu-kang-hai-fang-t'ung-chih)* was created, and the town was officially declared a seaport, open to free entrance and

departure for all. Grain transport ships sailed from there southward to Fukien and Kwangtung and northward to Ningpo and
Shanghai, and towards the beginning of the 19th century rice ships
further reached Tientsin, and on to the Liaotung Peninsula and
Chinchou of the Northeast. The opening up of Changhua and the
construction of irrigation works there were in an advanced stage in
the 1820's, and reached consummation in the 1860's.

The development of the North began with the region of what
is present day Hsinchou. At the beginning of the 18th century,
that area already boasted of several thousand *chia* (a *chia* is equal
to eleven *mou*) of fertile fields. In 1733, the Sub-Prefecture
(t'ung-chih) of Tamshui-*t'ing* was moved to station here. What is
present day Taipei was also opened up to the beginning of the
18th century. The port of disembarkation for ships sailing from
the mainland to north Taiwan was Pa-li-ch'a, and in the 1730's a
sub-district magistrate *(hsun-chien)* was created to station there. In
1759, a military officer was created to station at Mengchia (present
day Wanhua) with the title of captain *(tu-ssu)* of Tamshui.

In 1788, an assistant magistrate *(hsien-ch'eng)* was created to
station at Hsinchuang. Four years later, Pa-li-ch'a was formally
proclaimed a seaport, but Mengchia was the most prosperous of
all. The assistant magistrate at Hsinchuang was moved to station at
Mengchia, which, together with Taiwan-fu and Lukang, were at
that time called the three big cities of Taiwan, colloquially
expressed as *"fu* first, *t'ing* second and Mengchia the third" *(i fu er
t'ing san meng chia).* The rise of Ko-ma-lan (present day Ilan) in
the northeast began after the year 1768, and was mainly due to
the effort of Wu Sha, a native of Changchou of Fukien. He was on
good terms with the native tribes, he practiced medicine among
them and gave them drugs both without charge, which won their
deep gratitude and they promised him to let settlers share their
land. Thus he summoned a large number of immigrants from
Fukien and Kwangtung to settle and farm there, keeping up a
good relationship with the natives.

Towards the end of the 18th century, the congregation and
settlement was formally recognized by the government as a local
unit. An agreement stipulating rules or terms governing local
public affairs was proclaimed, roads were built, a militia was
organized, and more and more land was opened up. In 1812, the
sub-district *(t'ing)* of Ko-ma-lan was created, with a population of

over a hundred thousand.

The opening up of the extreme south (present day Pingtung area) began at the turn of the 17-18th century, settlers there were mostly Hakkas from Chaochou of Kwangtung, who came to Taiwan at a late date. In 1731, a sub-magistrate was created to station at Wanton, and later moved to A-li-kang. Then there was Lang-chiao, spacious and fertile, where settlers went for land and farming and many others for timber and hunting, while trading was also brisk. Fangliao, where a sub-magistrate *(hsun-chien)* was stationed, was a prosperous center in which traders and craftsmen converged.

In the case of east Taiwan, although it was barred from easy reach from the west by the north-south mountain range, but during the end of the 17th century, the footsteps of the immigrant Chinese had reached Chi-lai (present day Hualien) and Pei-nan-mi (present day Taitung), first as traders, then as settlers taking to farming. In 1725, the government pacified the native tribe at Pei-nan-mi, thus attracting more Chinese settlers, brought more land into cultivation and increased farm production, while the natives were being taught to use advanced farming methods.

If we look back at the period from the end of the 17th century to the middle of the 19th, we see that the mainlander population in Taiwan had increased from several hundred thousand to more than three million, and that all parts of the island had been more or less opened up. A marked point that will not evade our notice is that all this achievement was none but the result of years and years of adventure and hardships, struggling and toiling, sometimes with blood and always with sweat, of these millions of Chinese people.

We can see that the government never did support or help them, instead only imposed upon them harassment and restriction. We can see that the initiative for reclamation and settlement was always taken by the people and never by the government, and when the work was accomplished without any aid whatsoever from the government, the latter would still hesitate and linger in giving the official recognition. It was not until the very last moment, when the step became unavoidable, that the local administrative unit was created and an official appointed.

In a word, the early development of Taiwan was totally an accomplishment of the Chinese people, and it was their effort that

laid the irrevocable foundation that developed into the inclusion
of Taiwan into the Chinese nation and Chinese state. This
achievement was not easily won, for it was not won through
political power and military might, but by the toiling hands of
millions of Chinese people throughout a long period of time.

II
The Beginnings of Modernization (1874-1883)

At the time Chinese settlers were busy in the internal
development of Taiwan, Western Powers were moving steadily
eastward. China was confronted with changing circumstances, and
the external situation of Taiwan underwent the same sequence of
change. Since the 19th century, Western Powers had long been
entertaining ambitions in Taiwan. Some thought of having ports in
Taiwan opened to trade, and others thought of occupying it in
total or in part as a base for their activities towards the Chinese
mainland. Competition and plotting led to unending conflicts and
crises, and the safety of Taiwan was complicatedly and dangerous-
ly involved.

Open military attack in the form of an undeclared war finally
came in 1874, the 13th year of the reign of Tung-chih, not from
the West, but from the east, from Japan which had lately joined
the ranks of the expanding Powers. The Chinese government, for
defending her territory and protecting her nationals, appointed
Shen Pao-chen Imperial Commissioner in charge of the maritime
defense of Taiwan and related areas, and started diplomatic
negotiations while planning war. It came to a peaceful solution
with Peking yielding to Japanese demands.

Wen Hsiang, Grand Councilor *(chun-chi-ta-ch'en)*, who took
part in handling the affair, came out of it with great resentment
and pent up indignation. Li Hung-chang acknowledged that the
handling was "a little bit too yielding, unbefitting the dignity of a
great nation, and tending to whet the appetite of the aggressor."[14]
Naturally, the reason for this was that at the time China's military
power was inadequate, her maritime defense non-existent, and the
authorities were quite aware of the fact that China was no match
for Japan on the high seas.

It was due to the blows suffered from superior military forces from without that China in the 19th century began to turn to policies of national self-strengthening and took her first steps on the way to modernization. By the time nearing the end of the third quarter of the century, China was already far more than ten years on the path of building ships and making guns, intended for suppression internal rebellion and repelling foreign aggression. By foreign aggression it was meant to be from Western Powers. Yet now that even Japan, a state hither to belittled by China, would dare to raise trouble to take advantage of China, this indeed was an unsurpassed humiliation to China to serve as a sharp stimulus to the policy shapers of the time, Prince Kung, Wen Hsiang, and Li Hung-chang.

Wen Hsiang was of opinion that the most urgent matter confronting China was the defense against Japan, because there was no guarantee that Japan would not strike again. If steps were not taken right away, any further unpreparedness would make future occasions that much more difficult to handle, because no yielding compromise will ever work again. He thought that for the time being, the most pressing business was the procuring of warships, for no relaxation should come from the withdrawal of the Japanese forces. Li Hung-chang declared that: The Japanese are very ambitious. What made them dare to encroach upon China was their modern warships. China must hurry up to overtake them by strengthening our naval force. Ting Jih-chang, Finance Commissioner of Kiangsu province, had already proposed the creation of a naval force with modern ships. The plan was not expanded into the founding of three fleets, the North Sea, East Sea and South Sea fleets, with the last one intended for the defense of Taiwan.

At this junction the Manchu government was planning to launch an expedition under Tso Tsung-tang for the suppression of the insurrection in Sinkiang. Li Hung-chang argued that the maritime defense of the southeast was more important than the frontier defense of the northwest, or that Taiwan was more important than Sinkiang. Thus he suggested a temporary halt to the northwest expedition and concentration of all resources to the building of maritime defense. The final decision taken was simultaneous action on both. Thus orders were placed for purchasing warships from the West for the building of a modern naval force, a step definitely prompted by the crisis of Taiwan, a situation foremost in the minds of all who worried about China's future.

Shen Pao-chen (1820-1879), a native of Houkuan of Fukien, began his career by passing the Metropolitan Examination and graduating from the Han-lin Academy. His father-in-law was no other than Lin Tse-hsu, a statesman of integrity, sagacity and aptness, and experienced and knowledgable in external affairs of the time. Lin studied the West and understood the world situation, and set his mind on calling to the attention of all the importance of maritime defense. He was the first to emphasize "ships and guns" by saying: Ships — make them strong; and guns — make them powerful. Shen, being related, must have learned a lot from him. Shen's civil service career brought him to local appointments in Kiangsi, to the position of Provincial Governor, and was rated among the ranks of Tseng Kuo-fan, Tso Tsung-tang and Li Hung-chang as one of the eminent statesmen who led the Manchu government to its revival following the middle of the 19th century.

In 1866, Shen was appointed to the post of Director of the Foochow Shipyard. He founded the Naval School, built more than a dozen ships, and sent China's first batch of navy students to England and France. When he was appointed Imperial Commissioner to Taiwan, and was about to go there to take up the assignment, he memorialized the throne suggesting four exigent steps to take. Beside the one on diplomatic maneuvers to mobilize international public opinion to put pressure on Japan, the rest were all internal measures such as the procuring of ironclad warships, mines, and rifles, and the construction of a cable line between Taiwan and Fukien. On his arrival at Taiwan, he immediately ordered the construction of the fort at the port of Anping with cement gun placements for mounting five large and four small Western artillery pieces, to strengthen the defense of the city of Taiwan-fu. He also started enlisting and drilling a militia, and took measures to win the allegiance of the natives.

The peaceful settlement of the current Sino-Japanese crisis was of course what Shen had wished for, but what he was more worried about was that a plan should be evolved for the future of Taiwan after the settlement of the crisis, for he figured that "when the Japanese withdraw and we keep our defenses ready, they would quietly leave; but if they withdraw and our defenses lapse, they would certainly come again at the earliest opportunity."[15] When the negotiations at Peking were about to come to a conclusion, he wrote that

> Taiwan is a fertile land and has long been the object of envy of other peoples. At present although the encroachment from without is for the time being taken care of, but the coveteous eyes are still staring at it. It is now the time for us to make preparations for that eventuality. . . . Reforms should be effected, initiatives should be taken, it would take more than ten years to get results. . . . Currently the pressure of external affairs has been mounting, and the focal point is in the southeast. Taiwan, although an island on the high seas, is the gate to seven provinces. Its relevance and importance cannot be overrated.[16]

Shen's intention was to change the passive policy of the past into an active policy. By seven provinces he meant all of China's coastal provinces: Kwangtung, Fukien, Chekiang, Kiangsu, Shantung, Chihli (now Hopei), and Fengtien (now Liaoning). By the gateway to seven provinces he meant to say the key to the total maritime defense of China. He considered the post-crisis reconstruction work in Taiwan different in nature compared to other reconstruction works in the past. "In Taiwan, what is reconstruction is actually initiating something new. Any post-war or post-crisis reconstruction is difficult, but it is much more so when reconstruction amounts to initiation."[17] What he meant was that the reconstruction should not be limited to the passive restoration of what was. It should be the active creation of a new phase. It should be constructive and progressive in nature.

Li Hung-chang, who was in charge of supreme military and diplomatic policy at the time, also claimed that the central government, in compromising with Japan, had in mind the more farsighted view of a speedy build-up of maritime defense to be ready for a future round. And that it is expected that all Chinese, high and low, "from this day on by 'sleeping on fagots and mouthing bile,' struggle for the nation's self-strengthening," and strictly refrain themselves from "letting things lapse and when crisis comes to face it with nothing more than emergency measures, and when it is over to relax and have a good time again."[18]

Shen's mission to Taiwan was a temporary one, and the post-crisis reconstruction, being a time consuming job, got to be the responsibility of the high local authorities, the Governor-General of Fukien and Chekiang and Governor of Fukien. Wang K'ai-t'ai, the current Governor of Fukien, was for a time under Li Hung-chang's employment as a member of his private advisory-staff. Li addressed a special letter to him, stating that the post-crisis reconstruction of Taiwan is an all encompassing complicated job involving tremendous responsibilities, and asked him to cooperate with the Governor-General of Fukien and Chekiang and Shen to "carefully deliberate and arrive at sound policies and effective measures to forestall any future abrupt or creeping attempts from without, and most important of all, the defense of the coastal areas should be seriously and substantially reorganized, to be effectively carried out step by step to the full."[19] All in all, Shen's Taiwan policy was a policy centered in national defense.

According the Shen, the post-crisis reconstruction of Taiwan, though variegated and diverse, yet the starting point or basis for all was administrative reform. In other words, the political apparatus must be reformed and improved, and administrative efficiency raised. Based upon the plan formulated in 1787, it was scheduled that the Governor-General of Fukien and Chekiang, the Governor of Fukien, and the Commanders (t'i-tu) of Naval and Land Forces of the area are to alternate in turn for annual inspection tours in Taiwan. Such short term inspections usually not only did no practical good to the political and military affairs of Taiwan, but would impose duties on local officials of the respective areas in their having to arrange for the itineraries, supplies, and attendance for such tours, and also would put extra burden on the people.

Shen, after a thorough on-spot examination of the local conditions of Taiwan, was of opinion that local administrative units, both prefecture and district, or fu and hsien, should increase in number; that the responsibilites of post-crisis reconstruction should be vested in one higher official appointed with the authority of an overall director; that the suggestion of creating a separate province of Taiwan seemed to be premature, considering many developments there not yet measuring up to provincial-level status, and above all, the fact that the interdependance between Taiwan and Fukien on the latter subsidizing the former's military pay and the former exporting rice to the latter, making their separation inconvenient; that the appointment of an Imperial

Commissioner was an emergency, but not standing measure, for a permanent Commissioner would make local subordinate officials having difficulty in serving two sets of equal ranked superiors, the Commissioner on the one hand and the Governor-General on the other; and that the best solution would be to station the office of Governor of Fukien permanently in Taiwan.

In case such a step was taken, the Taiwan local officials would enjoy immediate accessibility to the Governor for matters requiring his personal consideration and approval; the Governor would enjoy the efficiency of awarding prompt decisions on matters requiring expedition; and the responsibility and authority would be vested in one source which would make the inspection and checking of progress and examination and evaluation of results more effectively done, the carrying out of orders more thorough and without evasion, and the wiping out of piled up practices of corruption and inefficiency would get a chance to get started and done.

In Shen's own words:

> In order that the defense value of the land could be made full use of, the pre-requisite is to win over the people of the land; in order to win over the people, the pre-requisite is to perfect the administrative efficiency and military discipline. And the authority for reforming and improving the administrative and military set up lies in the hands of the Governor-General and Governor." Other reasons he advanced for recommending the permanent stationing of the Governor of Fukien in Taiwan were: First, Taiwan is still in its initial stages of development, its local conditions vary with the mainland, and traditional ways there may not apply with good results here, and the Governor if stationed here can make the necessary adjustments as he sees fit. Secondly, areas for which new administrative units should be created or old ones promoted can be promptly dealt with by the Governor as expediency requires. Thirdly, the opening up of coal mines and iron works, though some could be done through local efforts of the people, others might require modern methods and machinery, and the Governor can take on site investigation and make appropriate decisions as to the location and process best for suited development. [20]

Li Hung-chang gave his full support to Shen's suggestions, praising it as a plan of long time usefulness and lasting value. The Fukien authorities maintained that the Governor should be responsible for the whole province and therefore not proper to be stationed in Taiwan all the time. Peking agreed with Shen and Li that the development of Taiwan was a key step in future maritime defense which has to do with the whole of China, north as well as the south, and therefore the Governor should be responsible for both Fukien and Taiwan. In November 1875 (Kuang-hsu yr. 1, mon. 10) the final decision was made that the Governor of Fukien was to station in Taiwan and Foochow alternately every year with the winter and spring in Taiwan and summer and fall in Foochow. This was the initial step taken towards the creation of the province of Taiwan.

At the time of Shen Pao-chen's arrival at Taiwan, the administrative units of Taiwan were one prefecture, the Taiwan-fu, administering four districts: Tai-wan, Fengshan, Chia-i (name changed from Chu-lo) and Changhua; and two sub-prefecture (t'ing): Tamshui and Ko-ma-lan. The political and military, cultural and educational, center was still in the south. In the south, the importance of Lang-chiao was evidenced by its attack by the United States naval forces in 1867 and by the landing of Japanese forces there during the late crisis. Shen therefore paid it a personal inspection and decided to found a city there and create it into a district, with the name of Hengchun, to be under Taiwan-fu. In the north, the Tamshui sub-prefecture (t'ing) had become too vast, stretching north-south to about 300 li, (about one- third of a mile), with a population of more than 400,000. Within its jurisdiction, Huwei (present day Tamshui) and Keelung had been ports for more than ten years in which Chinese and foreigners lived side by side; Mengchia (present day Wanhua of the Metropolitan area of Taipei) was even more prosperous.

This raised problems of law enforcement and security difficulties, cultural and educational unevenness, administrative and judicial complications, and domestic-foreign relationship entanglements. The suggestion was of longstanding that the adminstrative set-up should be up-dated. In August 1875, based upon Shen's recommendation, the following revamping was made: The Tamshui sub-prefecture was made into the district of Hsinchou; the Ko-ma-lan sub-prefecture was made into the district of Ilan; Meng-chia was created into the district of Tamshui; and Keelung was assigned an office of the assistant-to-the-prefect (t'ung-p'an). All above were to be under a new prefecture, the Taipei-fu, with the prefect stationed in the district of Tamshui.

In the next year, the Southern Sub-Prefect in Charge of Native Affairs *(nan-lu-li-fan-t'ung-chih)* stationed at Pei-nan-mi was re-titled Sub-Prefect in Charge of Settlers and Native Affairs *(fu-min-li-fan-t'ung-chih)* to be stationed at the same site which was made into a sub-prefecture with the title Pei-nan-t'ing; and the Northern Sub-Prefect in Charge of Native Affairs stationed at Lukang was re-titled Central Area Sub-Prefect in Charge of Settlers and Native Affairs *(fu-min-li-fan-chung-lu-t'ung-chih)*, to be stationed in the newly created sub-prefecture of P'u-li-t'ing. It was Shen's original design to organize Taiwan into three prefectures governing altogther more than ten districts. The eventual set up, as we see, was two prefectures administering eight districts and four sub-prefecture. The administrative apparatus was now much more adequate, and administrative efficiency improved.

The natives constituted a difficult problem to Taiwan's security and order. During the period of the rule of the Cheng's, the efforts made in pacifying and civilizing the natives were limited to the southern plains, while the natives of the mountain areas maintained their primitive life and customs, and because of which they were called primitive natives *(sheng fan)*. For the ensuing more than two hundred years, the government adopted a policy of separation of natives and Chinese, forbidding the Chinese from going into native lands, and dealing the offenders with heavy punishment. The American naval attack and the Japanese landing were both because of trouble caused by primitive natives.

Shen Pao-chen, on his appointment to the Taiwan Commis-sionership, had deliberated on a plan for the pacification and control of the natives, which, on being reviewed by Li Hung-chang, was praised as a promising design for achieving durable peace and lasting order. According to Shen, the pacification of natives should be undertaken simultaneously with the opening up of the mountains. "If you try opening mountains before pacifica-tion, you have no way to get to the mountains; if you do pacification without opening the mountains, the few you did pacify won't remain so for long."[21] What he meant by the opening up of the mountains was the opening up and maintenance of communication lines. Beginning in December 1874, he abolished the law forbidding Chinese from going into native lands, and ordered the opening of mountains from three routes, the southern,

the northern and the central. The southern route was again divided
into two, both leading from the Fengshan   area eastward to
Pei-nan, altogether about 400 *li*. The northern route led from the
Ilan area southward to Chi-lai, about 200 *li*. The central route led
from the Changhua area eastward to P'u-shih-ko, about 260 *li*. It
was planned that the central route would lead further eastward to
Chi-lai, to form a east-west through route. The road was to be ten
ch'ih (traditional *ch'ih* is .3581 metre) wide on plain ground and
six *ch'ih* in steep or streamside terrain. The three routes were all
completed in 1875. Along the routes stone forts were constructed
and garrison and patrol forces were stationed. Pacification and
reclamation commissioners were created.

The pacification program included items such as: the selection
and authorization of native leaders, the census taking of native
households, the ascertainment and recognition of native engagements in farming and trades, the study of languages for communication, the forbidding of killing for vengeance, the teaching of farm
methods to the natives, the free supply of salt and tea to the
natives, the persuasion of the natives to adopt Chinese clothing,
the founding of schools for the natives, the persuasion to change
some of the native customs, etc.

The reclamation program included items such as: the evaluation of soil and the standardization of its grading, the opening
of irrigation waterways, the utilization and protection of forests,
the building of village forts, the encouragement to craftsmen and
tradesmen to make them available to the natives, etc. The result
was that "pacification and reclamation moved on simultaneously
and natives administration turned on a new page."

During the process of opening up the mountains, attacks and
violent resistance from recalcitrant natives were unavoidable. Cases
such as those of Chi-lai and Ta-nan-ao of the north route were
exemplary, but it was in the south that the most serious case of
the Lion Head Tribe *(shih-t'ou she)* took place, in which the
natives repeatedly killed innocent Chinese and attacked government forces. Eventually pacification had to be abandoned and
suppression took its place, and the restoration of peace came in
several months time. The natives accepted pacification through
force, were given supplies of food and clothing, an office for
pacification affairs was created, and regulations agreed upon and
accepted by the natives were instituted for their guidance.

Before the execution of Shen's program, the development of Taiwan was limited to the plains of the west. Shen's opening up of the mountains and pacification of the natives were intended for the development of the east, so that the east could be included into areas where government orders could reach and resources of the land could be available to the people, and that the area be not any more considered untamed and inaccessible. As soon as the routes through the mountains were opened up, it was urgent to have settlers to work on the reclamation and farming of the adjacent lands, for otherwise the opened roads would remain in disuse, with minimized service and costly maintenance.

In order to encourage settlers, it was necessary to announce first the termination of the law forbidding the free emigration of Chinese, for otherwise no people would be looking to settle there. The fact was that in west Taiwan, people had all settled down, and there was no surplus population, and therefore few answered the call to reclamation in the east. The only way open was to enlist emigrants from the mainland. Thus in February 1875, the prohibition of emigration to Taiwan was dropped, and all of Taiwan was officially opened to immigration of farming people.

Shen then set up farming emigrants recruiting office in Amoy, Swatow and Hong Kong, had his attractive terms and program for reclamation and settlement in Taiwan proclaimed, declared government protection for emigrating settlers, and guaranteed government provisioning of all necessities and conveniences. It was announced that all farming emigrants would be provided with the transportation fare, seeds for initial sowing, costs for building a house, and one and a half years' supply of food. Each settler would be given one *chia* (eleven *Mou*) of watered rice paddy and one *chia* of arid grazing land. Every ten settlers would share four farm draft cows, and four sets of farming implements. The first three years of settlement would be exempted from all taxes.

The modernization items of Shen's reconstruction work were telegraph service and coal mining. Concerning the former, his plan was to construct the line connecting Taiwan to Amoy and Foochow, and the Danish Great Northern Company was commissioned for the installation, but work was not commenced. Concerning the latter, the best prospect was the Keelung coal mine, which had long been an object of envy to some foreign Powers. When the Foochow shipyard started operations, the need for coal was urgent, and Shen had, in 1868, sent a Frenchman, Dupont, an employee of the shipyard, to survey the site.

When Shen came to Taiwan, he realized further the importance of the mine, and began to understand that the overall opening up of the resources of Taiwan would depend upon the coal mine as primary basis, and that the mine must be worked by modern Western methods. Li Hung-chang, in a letter to Shen, expressed his enthusiastic approval:

> To open our own mines is a primary step in the development of our resources. . . . It is to my knowledge that this enterprise would require a huge sum for initial expenses, because it requires the employment of Western technicians, the procurement of Western machinery, and the use of Western methods, to guarantee a profitable and rewarding success. . . . Taiwan is rich in natural resources, ten times that of the mainland. Now that you are there to set the example and initiate this spirit of developing our own resources, what you have done for our country is indeed surpassing that of crushing a Japanese army of a hundred thousand.[22]

In 1875, Sir Robert Hart, the Inspector-General of the Chinese Maritime Customs, employed for Shen an English mining engineer, David Jyzack, to survey the mine ores from Huwei, Pa-li-ch'a, to Keelung. It was found that the Keelung ore was of higher quality, and Shen therefore ordered him to plan to carry out the purchasing of machinery and the employment of personnel. Peking gave the approval to raise a loan of 2,000,000 taels for the initial expenses, and the mine started to operate in 1876. Besides the coal mine, Shen also requested to start iron mining and refinery and the mining of petroleum.

Concerning defense installations and military reorganization, beside having the Anping fortress and artillery positions designed and constructed by a Western engineer, he also ordered the building of the Chihou (present day Kaohsiung) and Tungkang forts, and the installation of ordnance and munitions factories. For the reogranization of ground forces, he ordered the refitting of all units into shape, the cutting of superfluous posts, the joint drilling of units, the cutting of the old and weak to be replenished with able-bodied enlistments, and the division of garrison duties into the south, central, and north routes. Concerning the naval forces, he ordered the termination of the high seas patrol and the transfer of ships built by the Foochow shipyard to Taiwan for active service.[23] It was planned that the Command of the South Sea Navy, when organized would be stationed in Taiwan.

Concerning the building of morale, in order to comply with popular desire, to preserve good traditions, and to encourage patriotic spirit, a shrine in Taiwan-fu was built for Cheng Cheng-kung, [24] a historic figure of real greatness, both in the sense of man of virtue and courage and a leader who had done the most for the people of Taiwan. This is the shrine of the King of Yen Ping that now stands in Tainan, a monument that has tremendous influence in the strengthening of the national spirit of the people of Taiwan.

Shen Pao-chen was in Taiwan twice, the first time from June 1874 to January 1875 and the second time from March to August 1875. In this period of one year's time he had formulated a general plan for the present and future development of Taiwan, and had personally materialized a part of this plan. Still more important, he had made the central authorities and the public understand the important position of Taiwan; he had completely changed their view, and completely reversed the policy.

In the middle decades of the 19th century, among the Chinese leaders who understood foreign affairs and knew the principles of government, besides Shen Pao-chen and Li Hung-chang, another was their good friend, Kuo Sung-tao (the three passed the Metropolitan Examination in the same year). Kuo was for a time the Governor of Kwangtung. When the Sino-Japanese Taiwan crisis arose, Kuo was summoned to Peking and appointed the Judicial Commissioner *(an-ch'a-shih)* of Fukien. The post was below his ranking, but the appointment could be interpreted as the fittest selection for the occasion, expecting his eminence and ability to render due service for the handling of the affairs of Taiwan.

In the beginning of 1875, Peking had reached the decision to transfer Shen to the post of the Governor-General of Liangkiang, to share with Li Hung-chang the responsibilities of putting into shape the maritime defense of the North and South Seas. Thus the Fukien shipbuilding and Taiwan affairs responsibilities left by Shen needed a proper successor, and Li considered Kuo the best choice.[25] In May 1875, the appointment of Shen to the Governor-General of Liangkiang was announced, and the Taiwan affairs job was handed over to Wang K'ai-t'ai, the Governor of

Fukien. Wang was also a Metropolitan Examination-made scholar-official, open minded and careful, honest and dispassionate. He consulted Kuo on the handling of Taiwan and Kuo advised a step by step honest carrying out of the reconstruction plan.[26] After Wang returned from his inspection tour in Taiwan, he soon died of illness. The central authorities and Li Hung-chang gave the affairs of Taiwan top priority, and had it in mind to have Kuo succeed Wang. It was because of Kuo's appointment to be the first Envoy to represent China at London that the Taiwan task fell on the shoulders of Ting Jih-chang.

Ting Jih-chang (1823-1882) was a native of Feng-hsun, Kwangtung. He was in the early days of his career recognized by Tseng Kuo-fan as outstanding, and had been in the service of Li Hung-chang assisting him in working the Shanghai Arsenal. His tour of office included the following: Intendent of the Shanghai Circuit, Finance Commissioner of Kiangsu, and Governor of Kiangsu. He was the one whose effort was mainly responsible for the sending of the first batch of students to study in the United States. He became a good friend of Yung Wing, the most well known of these students. He had prepared a comprehensive overall program on the policies and measures of national self-strengthening and maritime defense. Many of the points he presented were points which Li Hung-chang had very much on his mind but held up at the tip of his tongue. Thus Li, upon reading Ting's program, praised it highly as "bold and vigorous presentation giving vent to all the things that had to be said," and that "anyone who undertands anything about our foreign affairs cannot but give it heartfelt praise and loud acclaim."[27] Li also spoke of him as "his unmatched excellence and dexterity in foreign and administrative affairs made his service of great need to the nation at this hour of crisis and pressure."[28] Kuo Sung-tao spoke of him, together with Li Hung-chang and Shen Pao-chen, as the topmost three in the field of foreign affairs.

In September 1875, Ting was appointed Director of Shipbuilding Affairs, and soon later, concurrently Governor of Fukien. Public opinion was exceedingly favorable to the appointments, and praised him as of broad vision but meticulous planning, of penetrating mind and far-reaching sight; that whatever he planned and decided upon, his comprehension usually wrapped up all corners and every point; that he was well versed in modern

Western knowledge; and that in government he always put sincere intention and solid effort behind honest measures.[29] Ting was aware that the bureaucratic members of the Fukien government were known to be antagonistic towards each other, so he repeatedly desisted from accepting his appointments. It was of no avail; and he retreated to ask for a separate appointment of someone to take over the shipbuilding affairs, and an eventual appointment of another to take over the Governorship of Fukien, so that he could concentrate on the affairs of Taiwan. Peking agreed only to appointing Wu Tsan-ch'eng to take over the shipbuilding affairs.

In May 1876, Ting began to attend to his new assignment, started to carry out administrative reforms in Fukien and to plan for things to be done in Taiwan. He memorialized Peking on his overall plan for Taiwan. The first point he raised was the suggestion that a special high official of great prestige and military competence be appointed to Taiwan to take charge of things there for a few years, and after that time, if things had gone well, then consider the arrangement of having the Governor-General and Governor stationed separately in Fukien and Taiwan respectively. The second point was the proposal of a series of things to be done in Taiwan: procuring of ironclad warships, organizing mine-laying forces, drilling of rifle and artillery units, construction of artillery forts, building railroads and telegraph lines, and increasing reclamation activities and farm settlements. He reported that the Keelung coal mine was on its way to a good start, but other mining and manufacturing enterprises, such as sulphur, petroleum, camphor, tea and iron, should also be undertaken, by organizing private management, to be provided with government loans or with private capital raised by business companies; and in his opinion all investments would be capable of being refunded in ten years, and with good prospects of providing rich revenues for the government in thirty years.

Ting also advanced the opinion that railroads and telegraph lines are complementary to each other, that their services to business in peace time and for military transport and rapid communication in war are of immense importance, and that they formed the basis of all other developments which in turn laid the foundation for the power and wealth of the modern states of the East and West. Later when Ting had surveyed the situation in

Taiwan in person, he wrote several letters to Li Hung-chang emphasizing the fact that Taiwan, with its long coast line and numerous ports, would be extremely difficult for effective defense if railroads and telegraph lines were not constructed to provide for ready communication and emergency defense plugging.

Back to the memorial, Ting suggested also that the defense industries undertaken in China, such as arsenals and shipyards which were all government managed, came out with doubtful results and were plagued by abusive practices and irregularities. He thought that the recent new enterprise, the Mercantile Steamship Company *(chao shang chu)*, with government supervised private management, was not a commendable way of handling enterprise either. He strongly advised that the constructions and developments to be taken up in Taiwan be managed by private businessmen, aided by appropriate government loans if necessary. This indicated that he held advanced views of modern business management.

The central government referred all his proposals to Li Hung-chang for review and consideration. Li's decision was as follows: On the matter of raising the necessary funds for Taiwan development, the reply was negative. Ting expected that Chekiang, Fukien and Kwangtung should together be responsible for half of the required funds. Li maintained that available funds were to be appropriated to provide for Tso Tsung-tang's expedition in Sinkiang, the procuring of warships for maritime defense, and the construction of forts, which were all of top priority and in great urgency, and therefore hardly anything could be spared for Taiwan. He advised Ting to concentrate his efforts in mining, reclamation, railroad, and telegraph.

Furthermore, in Li's final memorial to Peking reporting his considerations, he limited his range of priorities for Taiwan still further to only mining and reclamation, mentioning only these two as the most advantageous developments that should be undertaken right away as far as funds would permit. And as for railroads, the construction cost would be too high, and it would be more economical to wait until the operation of the coal mine to bring in profits to finance railway building. And as for telegraph lines for land communication, there were equipment and materials at Foochow and Amoy (those purchased by Shen Pao-chen for building the planned Foochow-Amoy line) which could be transferred to Taiwan. As for ironclad warships and mines, they were indeed needed items, but as even the North Sea and South Sea Naval Commands had not yet made the decision for prompt procurement, it would be proper for the case of Taiwan to use more discretion. As for the appointment of a prestigious high official to direct the affairs of Taiwan and then later on to station the Governor-General and Governor separately in Fuchow and Taiwan, it was considered that since the decision to station the Fukien Governor in Fuchow and Taiwan alternately every half year was only recently made, it would be too soon to make a change. It would be better to leave everything in the hands of Ting alone, so that Fukien and Taiwan would be under one overall guidance and control, which would render them more prompt and ready in their mutual assistance in peacetime and succor in crisis. Only after Ting had made real progress in Taiwan could the matter of the jurisdiction of the Governor-General and Governor over Fukien and Taiwan be reconsidered.[30]

In a word, Li agreed in principle that what Ting suggested were all necessary projects, but in practice, to undertake them all at once would require three or four million teals, for which there were hardly any sources to lean on. The usual source, the maritime tariff customs, was already over committed to government drafts.[31] Li was therefore making his own position clear that he was not belittling the importance of Taiwan or against plans aiming at the wealth and power of the nation, but it was on the practical difficulty of being unable to procure the required funds that he could not commit himself to actually supporting these projects for Taiwan development. He also claimed that considering the limited and undeveloped nature of the resources and population of Taiwan, it was not yet in a position to talk about or carry out any large scale or multiple purpose development plan projecting far into the future; any adventure along this line would drag the central government into the red and therefore the undertaking itself would not be able to go ahead for long.[32] All in all, Ting was eager to get results and Li insisted on walking on firm grounds. Both had good reasons.

In December 1876, Ting Jih-chang went to Taiwan to assume office, on the one hand to direct the development and reform, and on the other to face the confrontation against Spanish demands and threats. It was in 1864 that a Spanish merchant-man was pillaged while encountering rough seas near Taiwan. In 1874, the Chinese government, on account of Chinese laborers being ill treated in Latin American Spanish Colonies, declared the prohibition of further exportation of Chinese laborers from Macao (actually indentured labor, some pressed for work overseas, under the then popular term "piglings" or *(chu-tzu)*. Thus came the Sino-Spanish controversy.

In 1876 the dispute between England and China over the Margary case developed almost into open conflict, and the Spanish government took the chance to press her demands for indemnities for the ships and for a reconsideration of the labor export injunction. The *Tsungli Yamen* turned down the demands and the Spanish delegate declared that his government was going to back up the demands with force and that warships would be on their way. Ting Jih-chang therefore ordered the forces under Land Force Commander Sun Kai-hua in Fukien to move into Taiwan, while at the same time requested Li Hung-chang and Shen Pao-chen to send ships and guns from their commands. Li immediately sent over the two gunboats, *"Lung hsiang"* and *"Hu wei"*, recently bought from England. Ting himself also started to take action in purchasing warships and training new forces. But Spain was only threatening the use of force, and the case was closed with China paying an indemnity.

The first business Ting undertook on his arrival in Taiwan was to take stern measures in restoring administrative integrity and military discipline. For offenses such as dereliction of duty, tyrannies over the people, delinquency in the apprehension of criminals, and graft in public funds or military provisions, the offender, civil or military, high ranking or low, was always accorded due punishment in certain cases as severe as the death penalty or dismissal from office. He ordered the abolition of all surtaxes to lighten the burden of the people.[33] He sent men to Amoy and Swatow to recruit emigrants for Taiwan, offering them rewarding prospects in a detailed plan of reclamation and settlement, guaranteeing government provision of farm draft cows and implements, and transport to Taiwan by steamships provided by the Intendant of the Taiwan Circuit. He enlisted natives from the west of Taiwan to settle and farm in mountain areas like Chi-lai.[34] He inspected in person the native tribes in southern, central and northern areas, braving the rugged hills and shady forests over trails crossed by few Chinese and alleged to be enveloped by pestilence-carrying vapors.

There were still two or three tribes in the south who refused to declare alligiance, but once his persuasion won them over, they were promptly rewarded with silver and cloth, a code of articles mutually agreed upon to regulate the relationship between them and the Chinese, and the founding of native schools. For some of the natives of the central area who were still alien to agriculture, the government provided them with money and rice, and employed Chinese to farm their land for them as an initial step. Strict injunction was imposed upon the Chinese for the protection of law abiding and peaceful natives, so that no Chinese should oppress, cheat or take advantage of them in any way, or that no translators should take advantage of their position to monopolize native affairs to cause any damage, loss or inconvenience to the natives. He laid boundary marks to protect land used or farmed by the natives. He authorized a head for each tribe and gave recognition to his position by requiring due treatment for the Chinese. In Ting's own words, it was

> to let the natives who declared allegiance to enjoy all advantages without any inconvenience, thus making their acceptance of the Chinese all the firmer; and to make the natives who refused allegiance suffer from all inconveniences without any advantage, thus inducing their change of mind to come all the sooner."[35] He paid all his expenses, although travelling on official duty, from his own pocket, without letting it be defrayed by government coverage or be provided for in material or in service by the involved local offices.[36] He won the wholehearted support of the people of Taiwan and was praised as having loved the people with all sincerity and protected the land with all care. He was loved by all the people of Taiwan and his image stayed unforgettable in their memory.[37]

Among Ting's modern construction projects, some were just keeping up what Shen Pao-chen had started, pushing them forward on their way to development and growth, such as mining. The Keelung coal mine had operated well, and had reached the deep levels. The quality of coal produced was good, just right for use on the steam vessels, and the production had later on maintained the rate of more than 50,000 tons per year. In the year 1881 alone, foreign steam and sail ships to the number of sixty to seventy came for coal, not counting the warships.[38] There were other items that were planned by Shen but not carried out, such as the telegraph. The original plan was to construct the Keelung-Taiwanfu line of which the surverying was done and construction was about to start. Then Ho Ching, the Governor-General, opposed the plan, with the result that only the two lines from Taiwan-fu to Anping and to Chihou were constructed. Although it was altogether only ninety *li*, this was the earliest land telegraph line in China and quite an accomplishment.

Shen's originally planned line was the Foochow-Amoy line which was suspended. Ting then moved all the equipment and materials to Taiwan for the line in Taiwan, and had a Chinese engineer in charge of the construction.[39] Some of Ting's projects were new ones, planned by himself and undertaken as a new enterprise, such as railways. The first section constructed was the railroad line from the Keelung coal mine to the coast, to be used for transporting machinery to the mine and coal from the mine to the ships at sea. His ambition was to build the north-south trunk line to link up the southern and northern parts of Taiwan.

In 1876, the English-built Shanghai-Wusung railway line was torn down, because of strong opposition from Chinese public opinion. Ting requested that the equipment and materials saved from the Shanghai-Wusung line be moved to Taiwan. However, what could be salvaged was not much and its transportation had to wait for another year. Ting therefore decided to start with purchased materials to construct the Taiwan-fu-Chihou section and requested the service of Inspector-General Sir Robert Hart to raise a loan of 600,000 taels from an English bank. The negotiations failed because of the interest rate charged being too high. Soon afterwards Ting left office because of failing health and the rails moved from the Shanghai-Wusung line were left to rot in Taiwan without being made use of.

As for military developments, in the case of warships, Li Hung-chang had ordered four gunboats purchased from England to be kept at Taiwan for defense duties there. Ting tried at first to employ English officers to command them, but as the English officers approached insisted that if they be the commanding officer, they might be given the authority of control over personnel and decision in the promotion and demotion of the personnel. Ting did not want such powers to get to their hands, so he agreed only to employ them as training officers; while at the same time Li Hung-chang refused to take possession of two of the gunboats because of a dispute in price.[40] In the case of rifle units, they were being organized and trained in the land forces but the number was not high.

In June 1877, Ting left Taiwan and went back to Foochow to treat his illness. Soon it got worse and worse and he had to ask for sick leave to go back to his native home for care. His departure was very much regretted by contemporary opinion, which credited him with

> knowing thoroughly what was good for Taiwan and what was wrong, he took over the direction of the affairs of Taiwan with great dedication, conquering all kinds of difficulties with patience and application, and gave Taiwan a new look in its features and a new page in its life, amounting to have led the revival of Taiwan singlehanded. Because of this the people of Taiwan had expected his return as earnestly as their expectation of a bountiful harvest after long scarcity. Ever since his presence in Taiwan, in all his reforms and re-construction, in whatever he did he had loved the people with all sincerity and protected the land with all care. He was loved by all the people of Taiwan and his image stayed unforgettable in their memory. A successor might be found to take over what he had left in Taiwan, but to expect one who would win so much love and praise from the people, indeed, would not be easy.[41]

Li Hung-chang had on many occasions praised his talents and vision, but criticism was not always withheld. Li said to Wu Tsan-ch'eng that Ting was sharp in his observation and fast in sizing up a situation. In Li's own words,

> His plans are embracing and far-reaching; his work is careful, precise, and decisive. He is pre-eminent among today's leaders, and indispensable to both Fukien and Taiwan. In a memorial to Peking, Li said that Ting "takes things seriously in his work, and to get things done he would not shrink from heavy burden and adverse criticism. But on account of being afflicted with an unhealthy liver, he tended to be over hasty and over anxious in getting results. If all the projects were to be undertaken at once, our financial competence is definitely not up to the task; but if we consider their relative importance and give them a choice of priority, in a few years we will be able to see results.[42]

If we look back at the situation and observe from hindsight, we can see that Ting's failure to stay for a longer time on his job in Taiwan was undoubtedly due partly to his ill health, his over anxiety, and his conflicts with Ho Ching, the Governor-General, who was a narrow-minded man; but the main cause was rather the paucity of funds. Taiwan at the time was incapable of having revenues to support its own development. Fukien was not a rich province and was currently committed to contribute its quota to finance the expedition to the Northwest, thus the authorities in Peking, though all knew the pre-eminence of Ting, were not able to keep him longer at the job.

Li Hung-chang at the time was hardly well provided for in his own undertakings. Understanding that the European Powers had just been involved in a war in the Near East, and that Japan was having internecine disturbances in its southwest, he saw no prospect of any troubles confronting Taiwan in sight, and therefore considered the construction of railroads and telegraph lines there not the most urgent business of the day. Although Li criticized Ting for too many suggestions and too few achievements, he acknowledged that "his efforts in the opening of mines and pacification of natives were two achievements of enduring and far reaching effect," and he was therefore worried that once gone Ting would never be back.[43]

That Ting was a man of serious-mindedness and sincerity can be seen from his raising funds while in Taiwan for famine relief in Shansi and Honan provinces. The people of Taiwan had made generous contributions, among which was the single donation of $520,000 made by the local wealthy – the Lin Wei-yuan brothers. Ting also led an effort in raising contributions from overseas Chinese elsewhere. He continued to carry on the fund raising without let-up while he was taking care of his health at home, and the sum he raised exceeded one million dollars.[44] While at home, he gave encouragement and assistance to people of his native areas to emigrate to Taiwan for reclamation and settlement. In 1879 an Imperial edict commissioned him to take charge of South Sea maritime defense affairs. Ting declined pleading ill health. He died in 1882.

As Ting left Fukien, Wu Tsan-ch'eng, Director of Shipbuilding Affiars, took over the duties of Taiwan. He worked as hard as Ting did. On his first arrival in Taiwan, he undertook inspection tours to Penghu (the Pescadores), the Anping fort, and the quarters of garrison forces, passing through Hengchun to Pei-nan-t'ing. In the native areas of Pei-nan local free schools thrived. In one area alone there were sixteen. He found that native boys could read, and could recite Wang K'ai-t'ai's *Primer for the Instruction of Natives,* and some native girls had finished the Four Books and the Book of Poetry. He gave the teachers and students awards for encouragement, and founded a few more free schools. He also found that the natives had learned to farm rice paddies. He encouraged them to go on with the reclamation of more lands, and ordered the recruiting or natives from the western areas to come over for farm settlement. He also undertook the dredging of harbors to make them more open to shipping.[45]

On his inspection trips, Wu travelled in hot summer days, and passed nights in thatched roof houses which were hot and humid, which made him suffer from illness. In 1878, he was appointed Governor of Fukien and was in Taiwan for a second time. He went to east Taiwan to inspect the native tribes in Hualien. He installed an office of pacification affairs there, and opened up a steamhip line between Keelung and Hualien.[46] Soon after that his illness became acute and he died the next year.

In the years subsequent to 1879, the atmosphere of crisis once more seized upon Taiwan. One war scare was caused by Russian menace and another Japanese. As Tso Tsung-tang's expedition succeeded in suppressing the insurrection in Sinkiang, the Russian forces which advanced into the city of Ili during the disturbance refused to withdraw. China sent a delegation headed by Ts'ung-hou to Russia to negotiate. He agreed to a preliminary treaty relinquishing a lot more of China's rights. Peking denied recognition of Ts'ung-hou's treaty and public opinion was inflamed with talks of recoving Ili by force. The Russian government also began preparations for war.

In 1880, the Russian fleet moved east, no doubt to pose a threat to the Chinese coast. Before this it was maritime Powers which had threatened Taiwan, now it was a land super Power. Peking ordered the speedy strengthening of the defense of Taiwan, and as the Russian menace subsided in favor of diplomatic negotiations, the Japanese confrontation rose in its stead.

Japan, after wresting favorable terms from China by landing on Taiwan, moved on and took possession of Ryukyu. These islands were annexed in 1879. A confrontation arose when China refused recognition to the claim. When the Sino-Russian crisis brought the imminence of an outbreak of war, Japan found it high time to force on Peking the demand for a solution to the Ryukyu problem. It was reported that a Japanese ultimatum was delivered. Rumor had it that the Japanese and Russians were joining forces. Le Fang-ch'i, Governor of Fukien, moved to Taiwan to direct the strengthening of defenses. He added more forts and replaced some with heavier artillery, such as Keelung fort with five and Takow (present day Kaohsiung) with six longer range and bigger calibre heavy guns from the famous Krupp manufacturers. Besides, Li Hung-chang also pressed his negotiations for purchasing ironclad warships from England and Germany.

In 1881, when the Sino-Russian conflict was settled while the Japanese were still pressing, the Chinese government appointed Tseng Yu-ying, long in military service with proven military competence, the Governor of Fukien, and Liu Ao, a general serving in Tso Tsung-tang's army, the Intendant of the Taiwan Circuit. The two proved capable and dedicated to their duties in their new assignment. Tseng was in Taiwan repeatedly, inspecting southern and northern areas, mending weak spots in the defense structure and repairing roads and bridges. Soon afterwards Japan shifted her target of expansion to Korea, and feeling assured that Ryukyu was firmly in her possession, she bothered no more about forcing China's recognition. Thus the false alarm was again over and Taiwan once more breathed easier.

Liu Ao was very attentive to Taiwan's reform and construction. Besides efforts in the fields of administrative discipline, native pacification, and cultural and education works, he emphasized also the reorganization and reform of the coal mine. In current years the mine had been drifting towards loose spending and no gain in marketing. They were faced with constant deficits and no profits.[47] The artillery units equipped with Krupp guns and the rifle units of the Anping and Chihou forts, organized under Ting Jih-chang, were also founded to be languishing in discipline and morale and had to be disbanded and reorganized. He also planned to build a munitions factory and magazine, to purchase mines and gunboats, and to dredge the harbor of Chihou.[48] Although not all of these were accomplished, at least there was initiation of new ideas. What he did complete was the construction of sewage ditches for Taiwan-fu and a road leading from Taiwan-fu to Anping.

III
The Defense of Taiwan (1884-1885)

Since the Opium War China hardly had any peaceful time, and the same was true with Taiwan. The foreign war of China that had affected Taiwan the most was the Sino-French War, in which Taiwan was not only attacked by the land and naval forces of a Western Power, and had become actually a part of the battle-grounds, but also had almost suffered the fate of annexation and being severed from China. It was only at the painful sacrifice of giving up her suzerainty over Indochina that China was able to save Taiwan from such consequences and bring it back to her fold.

The Sino-French controversy over Indochina had lasted almost ten years, reaching the crisis stage in 1883. France intended to annex the whole of Indochina, including the Tokin area *(Pei-ch'i* in Chinese) which borders on the Chinese frontier, thus posing a problem of national security for China. After a period of preparations the war broke out in November 1883. In December 1883 and March 1884, Chinese forces in Pei-ch'i suffered reverses. Apprehending the attack of French naval forces to the north the Chinese government alerted all coastal defenses and reinforced the garrison force in Taiwan.

In May 1884, Li Hung-chang negotiated successfully with France and an agreement was reached which could have settled everything. After the lapse of more than a month, however, the French resumed their military action. Hostilities broke out again and this time the French suffered losses. The thing that hindered the agreement from consummation was the French insistence on indemnities which met with firm Chinese refusal. The war up to this stage was local in nature, the battleground being limited to the Sino-Indochinese border. Now it was turned into an all-out war, fought by land and sea forces on all fronts.

The French naval authorities at first envisaged an attack to the north on Wusung, Nanking, Chefoo, Wei-hai-wei and Port Arthur, to effect landings and to hold territories for ransom. And then to blockade the Yangtse and the Gulf of Pei-ch'i to force China to terms. Subsequent considerations of the   plan's having over-reached their commitment of forces and over-stretched their supply lines reduced their targets to Foochow and Keelung in the south, thus making the Fukien area the chief battleground. In the middle of July the French fleet appeared closing in on the two targets.

On the Chinese side, Li Hung-chang was in charge of the overall direction of military measures of the war, and Liu Ming-chuan (1836-1896), a general experienced in and with an understanding of modern warfare and new military techniques, was the ablest field commander under Li Liu, a native of Hofei, Anhwei, had shown his born leadership when he was only eighteen by organizing a militia for the defense of his native area. Since then he was well known for his daring tactics and awe-inspiring display of authority. At the age of 27 he joined the Huai (or Anhwei) Forces organized by Li Hung-chang and took part in the campaigns in the Lower Yangtse area during the Taiping Rebellion. He was part of a force sent to reinforce Shanghai. His units were called the "Ming Army" (ming-chun). They fought side by side with Anglo-French forces and the rifle units under the American officer, Frederick Ward which became the famed "Ever-Victorious Army," noted for their effective defense of Shanghai.

Li was very much impressed by the Anglo-French and the "Ever Victorious" forces, and considered their fire arms, training, and discipline far superior to the Chinese units. He therefore purchased rifles and employed foreign officers for training, and ordered his officers and men be trainees. Liu, among the officers, was the one most susceptible to modern ideas and technology and his "Ming Army" came out of the training with the best results. In the subsequent campaigns in the suppression of the Taipings in the south and the Nien Rebellion in the north, the "Ming Army" was rated highest in accredited merits, and its fame was unmatched by all.

In 1871, the central government made special mention of the "Ming Army" in the effectiveness of the training and discipline of its rifle and artillery units, and ordered that the training of modern units in all the provinces be modelled after the method of the "Ming Army."[49] He was thus made the sergeant trainer of all armed forces of China.

Liu was not a man taking too much to mind his personal

success. He resigned from his command when he was only thirty-six, and went back to his native home a private subject. But whenever a national crisis made the government need his service, he zealously took up the challenge.

Thus in 1883, Liu was ordered to report to Tientsin to consult with Li Hung-chang in defense matters concerning the Sino-French crisis. In June 1884, he memorialized Peking his ideas of strengthening maritime defenses to face the present crisis and developing military power as the cornerstone for national self-perservation. In June 26, he was conferred the title of Provincial Governor and commissioned Director of Military Affairs in Taiwan.

The French war plan at the Taiwan front was to attack and take Keelung and other Taiwan ports, and if possible to effect the occupation of all of Taiwan. The one who was in charge of Taiwan defenses before Liu Ming-chuan was Liu Ao, the Intendant of the Taiwan Circuit. He reported that in peace time Taiwan emphasized mountain region defense more than maritime defense, and in crisis maritime defense took precedence over mountain defense. "But the security against the mountains must be secured before the defense against the sea can feel safety behind its back. Otherwise if attacks come at the same time from both the sea and the mountain, the defense would be at a loss to deal with the situation." Thus the defenses against the sea and the mountain must be planned for at the same time. In Liu's own words:

> But what was done in recent years has not yet been proven fruitful, and in case Taiwan be taken by the French, all China's coast line, north as well as south, will not feel a moment of safety. Thus the failure of Taiwan defense is tantamount to the failure of national defense. The Taiwan coast line is too long, enemy landing could come at any point. Garrison forces are less than 20,000, not enough to cover all points. There are no warships for defense use. Thus the idea of fighting the enemy on the high seas must be given up, and bet our chances on beating them on land.

It is therefore his plan that the defense be divided into five zones: south, central, north, front and rear.[50] But the overall command must be vested in the hands of one authority, thus he requested at first that the Governor-General at Fukien be stationed in Taiwan to take charge and then requested the appointment of a high ranking official of military competence to assume the overall direction. It was not until the threat of war was close at Taiwan's threshold that the central government appointed Liu Ming-chuan to Taiwan.

Liu Ming-chuan arrived at Keelung on July 16, 1884, and at Taipei-fu four days later. Soldiers of his old command stationed or to come to Taiwan were: 500 under General Chang Kao-yuan, 130 who came with Liu, and 1,300 more to arrive subsequently. Besides these there were 3,000 Hsiang (or Hunan) Forces under the commands of Sun Kai-hua and Tsao Chih-chung stationed at Taiwan. Garrison forces in Taiwan were habitually not kept up in training and discipline, and their number was only 4,000 to 5,000, with poor firearms and inadequate ammunition.

Li Hung-chang had just sent over 3,000 rifles, and Tseng Kuo-chuan, Governor-General of Liangkiang, had sent ten muzzle-loading guns, twenty breech-loading smaller size guns, and several dozen small mines, hardly adequate for the single port of Keelung. Liu planned the purchase of more heavy artillery, more rifles, and the reshaping of the forts. This would come to 400,000 taels. Peking ordered the Fukien government to speedily provide for that sum but it would be too late for the emergency.

There were four steam warships in Taiwan, two were commissioned for the transport of coal and other things, and two stationed at Tainan. Furthermore, they were old and could sail only at low speed. Liu requested that the four warships originally assigned to Taiwan, but remained at Kiangnan, be sent back. This was not complied with. Thus the control of the sea was completely in the hands of the French, and ships transporting troops and arms from Shanghai were often blocked by French warships. Besides, it was summer and disease spread among officers and men, taking heavy toll and adding to his many difficulties.

On the second day after Liu Ming-chuan's arrival at Keelung, the French fleet was on his heels. On August 4, Vice Admiral Lespés of the French Navy was there with five French warships and demanded the surrender of the fort within twenty-four hours. On the 5th, the French opened fire. The Keelung fort had only five guns of western type and after four hours of gun dueling, the fort was completely smashed. Four hundred plus French marines landed.

On that very day Liu rushed from Taipei-fu to Keelung to take command of things and boost the morale of the troops. The next day, he took the generals Tsao Chih-chung and Chang Kao-yuan with their forces of over 1,000 to face the French advance. They beat back this advance and captured several dozen French rifles. This was the prelude to the war for the protection of Taiwan and the first Chinese victory ever since the Sino-French conflict started. Liu figured the French would counterattack with re-inforcements and knowing that his weak forces, with poor weapons and fighting without the support of warships, would suffer from the artillery fire of enemy ships if they were deployed within artillery range, he thus ordered Tsao and Chang to move the forces back to the hills to be out of the range of naval guns. Liu then scuttled some ships to block the entrance to the harbor and ordered the demolition of the coal mine lest it be available to the enemy.

At this juncture, Sino-French negotiations were still going on and not suspended. The French attack on Keelung was therefore an unwarranted sneak attack. The *Tsungli Yamen* appealed to the envoys of the Powers, stating that the French were "negotiating on the one hand and taking possession of lands on the other," and asked them to award an impartial opinion.[51] Liu Ming-chuan was also expecting that Li Hung-chang would be able to reach an agreement and save the situation.[52] All went to naught, however, and instead, the French expanded their war efforts.

The French force that converged on Foochow consisted of ten warships (two of which were ironclad), with a total tonnage of about 24,000, a force of about 1,800 officers and men, and seventy-seven guns. The Chinese had eleven warships of varying size of which nine were of wooden hull-frame, with a total tonnage of 6,5000, a force of 1,400 officers and men, and forty-five guns. On August 23, the French fleet, under the command of Admiral Courbet, attacked and destroyed the Chinese Fukien fleet. They then withdrew and moored at Matsu. Courbet favored advancing to the north, but the French government apprehended that expansion of the war to other areas might incur the intervention of other Powers, or adversely influence the position of Li Hung-chang, who stood for peace. Thus it ordered Courbet to attack and take Keelung.

On September 29, Courbet ordered Lespés to sail from Matsu

to attack Huwei with three ships, and himself took the rest of the fleet sailing towards Keelung. The Chinese forces garrisoning Huwei were the 1,000 Hsiang (Hunan) forces under Sun Kai-hua and the 600 Huai (Anhwei) forces recently sent from Kiangsu. On October 11, a fleet of eleven ships made the second French attack on Keelung. A landing force of about 1,000 got ashore supported by guns from the ships. Liu Ming-chuan personally led the Hsiang and Huai forces of about 2,000 with their commanders, Tsao Chih-chung, Su Te-sheng and Chang Kao-yuan, to face the French assault.

It was a combat at close range, with repeated charges and counter-charges from both sides. The combat lasted ten hours, from morning till night, and remained at a draw. At this critical moment, the French attack on Huwei was reported. The fort at Huwei was recently built, yet incomplete. There were only three pieces of artillery, easily overpowered by the French guns. Liu considered it impractical to send a part of the actively engaged Keelung forces to reinforce Huwei. Huwei, however, was at the rear of Keelung, and between Huwei and Taipei-fu there were only sixty *li* of open, plain road unprotected by any defendable positions and with a navigable fresh-water river. The loss of Huwei, therefore, would pose an immediate threat to Taipei-fu.

Taipei was where the headquarters was located and where the stores of provisions and arms were kept. The loss of Taipei would therefore be disastrous, for it would definitely lead to the collapse of the whole defense set-up. Liu therefore immediately made the decision to withdraw from Keelung. He ordered a general retreat; deployed a part of his forces to move into the hills close to Keelung to avoid enemy artillery and to guard the strategic position between Keelung and Taipei. He sent Chang Kao-yuan with several hundred men to rush to reinforce Huwei.[53] Chang was against the retreat and remonstrated in tears. Liu therefore said firmly to his generals, "we will not be able to hold Taipei if we don't give up Keelung. I have made up mind. I will be responsible for any eventuality. Anyone who disobeys my orders is to face the executioner right here and now."[54]

On October 8, 800 French marines, under the protection barrage of their ships, landed at Huwei, intended for effective occupation. The Hsiang and Huai forces under Sun Kai-hua, Chang Kao-yuan and Liu Chao-hu, and Taiwan local units under Chang

Li-cheng stood their ground, and in a six hour fierce battle routed the French. The French then withdrew to their ships, leaving twenty some captives and a piece of field artillery. The Hsiang-Huai forces, without any artillery, relied solely on close range combat. The French fire power was formidable, coming at them like rainfall, inflicting casualties to over two hundred, but they unflinchingly held their line.

Sun Kai-hua and his men showed especial bravery and was the mainstay of the battle. Some English employees of the Huwei maritime customs, watching the fight from the sidelines, were greatly impressed, and voiced their admiration and praise.[55] Liu's memorial reporting the battle was simple and factual, without the slightest overstatement or exaggeration. This was the second act of the war for the protection of Taiwan, and the second Chinese victory in the Sino-French conflict.

Courbet, fresh from his victory at Foochow, was counting on the landings at Keelung and Huwei, hoping they would readily place these two places in French hands. It was a surprise to him to run into stubborn resistance and to suffer losses, and because he had only limited men and resources at his disposal, he gave up the idea of further attacks and deployed his ships for a blockade. Before this, transports from the mainland were often blocked by French warships, causing a decrease of supplies to Taiwn. The blockade almost totally cut the sailing to and from of merchant marine between the mainland and Taiwan, stopping the exchange of goods and information, and bringing a rise of price in all commodities.

At the same time the Hsiang-Huai forces were depleted in number because of casualties suffered on the battleground and from illness, and the latter cause brought continuous depletion, reducing the war-worthy to less than 3,000. The situation was indeed critical. Under the pressure of all these difficulties, Taiwan stood firm against the French siege. There were many reasons that this could be achieved. Above all, the most important reason was the wise, courageous and convincing leadership provided by Liu Ming-chuan. He had the knack of making his subordinates each to contribute his best.

The Hsiang-Huai forces had a long history of being at variance with each other, especially between the Ting Army, which was Hsiang and Liu's "Ming Army," which was Huai. The generals Sun

Kai-hua and Tsao Chih-chung, now serving under Liu in Taiwan, were officers from the Ting Army. Liu tried to remind them of the national war they were in together, to move them with the feelings of a compatriot, to convince them of his sincerity, and to win them over by constant courtesies, such as praises or even deferences. The result was that Sun and Tsao exerted themselves in the war beyond the call of duty.

Liu put into practice the traditional Chinese mottoes for a military commander: Be with your officers and men through thick and thin, in life and death. In an informal jacket and ordinary straw footwear, he would go among the soldiers to talk to them, visit the sick and mourn the dead, and share the same food and drink with them. In battle, he was at the front, personally taking charge, and his presence made every soldier glad to die for him. He had the eye for talent and would value their service. Shen Ying-kuei, an official on probation due to some former offense, had one single interview with Liu and was immediately recognized as a man of exceptional aptitude and talent. He was entrusted with the work of handling the military provisions and pay of all Taiwan and was given official commendation repeatedly.

The second reason was the cooperation of the local leaders of Taiwan with Liu's leadership. The Taiwanese were generous, public-minded and patriotic. Liu paid them high tribute and approached them for help and advice. The local leaders responded by contributing funds to raise local militia forces. There were Lin Chao-tung and Wang Ting-li leading militia to help the defense of Keelung. Lin Ju-wei in the defense of Hsinchou, and Chang Li-cheng who contributed to the victory at Huwei as related above. Altogether there were 5,000 local militia forces, which indicated that the government and people were certainly in unison. The well-known Lin Wei-yuan, who in the past repeatedly contributed large sums for the cause of famine relief, construction of dikes for flood prevention, and the building of city walls, this time again made a great effort to contribute $200,000.

The third reason for the success of the defense of Taiwan was the support of the whole nation throughout the mainland. The central government appointed Tso Tsung-tang as Imperial Commissioner and Director of Military Affairs in Fukien, and Yang Yueh-pin, former commander in the Hsiang Forces, as Assistant Director, and Yang Chang-chun as Governor-General of Fukien and Chekiang. It ordered all coastal provinces to send quotas of troops and funds. It ordered the Chinese forces in Yunnan and Kwangsi to advance to attack Pei-ch'i (Tonkin) in order to divide the French effort and lessen the pressure on Taiwan. Li Hung-chang naturally did his part best as he could, but other provincial authorities also made valuable contributions. Ever since the commencement of hostilities, Li had by means of heavy commissions hired both foreign merchant marines and Chinese sail boats to transport supplies to Taiwan. Within the space of several months they had made ten trips, usually sailing at night and laying low at daytime, and had sent to Taiwan more than 3,000 Haui troops, more than sixty pieces of steel artillery of various size, 9,000 rifles, 2,000,000 rounds of artillery and rifle ammunition, forty pieces of mine, and more than 100,000 taels of military pay. That the defense of Taipei-fu could be sustained for the duration was to a large extent due to these supplies.[56]

The center for the collection of supplies for Taiwan was Shanghai, and a "Center for Contributions for Taiwan" was installed there to mobilize financial assistance from among the people. Thus Li said that "the foundation upon which Taiwan could make its stand is in Shanghai."[57] Besides the above, Li also sent Huai forces from North China to Taiwan for reinforcement.

In August, besides Li Hung-chang, Tseng Kuo-chuan, Governor-General of Liangkiang, repeatedly commissioned British steamships to transport guns, ammunition, and the "Ming Army" under Liu Chao-hu, (which at that time was the garrison force of the Kiangyin fort in Kiangsu) to Taiwan.[58] Ting Pao-chen, Governor-General of Szechuan, offered to organize ten battalions (ying) for the reinforcement of Taiwan and I Pei-sheng, Finance Commissioner of the province, offered to take them there.[59] Chang Chih-tung, recently appointed Governor-General of Liang-kwang, had made special and repeated efforts to send over 3,000 rifles, more than a million rounds of ammunition, funds to the amount of 80-90,000 taels, Kwangtung troop reinforcements and also much more that was procured but was not shipped.[60]

Tso Tsung-tang and Yang Chang-chun, both now in Fukien, were directly in charge of organizing the transport of the supplies and reinforcements to Taiwan. These were shipped, under extremely difficult conditions and many risks, to the southern tip or eastern shores of Taiwan and then by land route to the front in the north, taking often three to four months.

At the end of 1884, Li Hung-chang and Tseng Kuo-chuan, in separate but concerted action, sent warships of the North Sea and South Sea Commands southward, intending to break the French blockade. However the Korean crisis, instigated by Japan, broke out just at this time and the North Sea Fleet, the stronger of the two, had to shift direction mid-course to sail to Korea. The five ships of the South Sea Fleet, sailing past the east of Chekiang in February 1885, were intercepted by the French fleet on the high seas, suffered two ships sunk in the ensuing battle and the rest returned to their base, Shanghai. The attempt was frustrated but at least it served to divert or distract the attention of the French blockading fleet. The occasion enabled part of the troop reinforcements sent by Tso Tsung-tang successfully transported from Amoy to Tainan at this time while the other part landed at Pei-nan. [61]

In January 1885, the French forces at Keelung, being reinforced, began to advance westward. The forces under Tsao Chih-chung and Lin Chao-tung offered stiff resistance and there were casualties of more than 300 on each side. On March 4, the French forces, numbering about 4,000 renewed their offensive in a massive attack and the Chinese forces, although also numbering 4,000, were forced to retreat after a good fight leaving only Liu Chao-tung's troops to keep up the resistance. Lin Ming-chuan then threw in the newly arrived Hsiang-Huai forces for a counteroffensive. This was without much success. Many higher officers were killed and the French advanced to a point about forty *li* from Taipei.

Liu's forces then formed a defensive line on the Keelung River. In the ensuing battle, Liu's forces suffered more than 1,000 casualties while the French only about 200. Liu still had about 10,000 men while the French only 3,000 and viewing the persistant and courageous resistance put up by the Chinese, the French chose to withhold further advance and limited themselves to holding their line. Thus it ended in a draw. This was the third and main scene of the war for the protection of Taiwan and the major battle fought.

On March 31, Courbet took Penghu, or the Pescadores, intending to turn it into a permanent French naval base. But a few days later, peace terms were arranged and the withdrawal of all forces was agreed upon. The blockade of Taiwan was soon lifted, and Courbet, his ambition thwarted, died in the Pescadores.

In the two year period of the Sino-French conflict, negotiations and armed conflicts intertwined with each other because of the delicate considerations on both sides. France was not free to act as she desired because of probable international interference, of her own inadequacy to finance the war for too long a period, and of the fact that her military superiority, though established somewhat, was never enough to impose terms. The Chinese side was even less inclined to keep the war going. It was through the intermediation of Inspectorate-General Sir Robert Hart that a preliminary agreement was reached in March 1885.

No cessation of hostilities, however, was immediately effected. At the end of March, the Chinese forces on the Indochina front launched a counteroffensive. In the battle of Langson, the Kwangsi forces under Feng Tzu-tsai scored a victory and the Yunnan forces under Tseng Yu-ying, advanced eastward. At this juncture of Chinese success, the final peace terms were signed. This caused a flurry of public disapproval. Li Hung-chang became the most misunderstood man at the time, but Li and the Peking authorities had insurmountable difficulties.

In the first place, in terms of national strength, China was not yet the equal of France and the relative naval strength was clearly inadequate. In case the French Fleet sailed north and started activities there, the consequences might bring down the roof. In the second place, Japan had taken advantage of the Sino-French conflict to create situations in Korea to her advantage. The incident at Seoul in December 1884 was especially serious. Li considered that the Japanese ambition was more ominous than the French intention and Korea more important than Indochina. To him it was therefore urgent to have the French affair settled as soon as possible, lest China be sandwiched between a Franco-Japanese pincer attack. In the third place, the most realistic consideration they had in mind was the safekeeping of Taiwan. Since the blockade, Taiwan was guarded by forces limited in number, poor in arms, with uncertain supplies and long days ahead. The prospect was indeed grim. In case anything happened to Taiwan, once lost there would be little probability of recovery. Taking the land victory into consideration would not brighten the picture because after Feng's victory at Langson, Courbet balanced it by taking Penghu. Having gained the upper hand, it was nice to take advantage of this balance and count the gives and takes, for at the moment China at least could come out without a heavy loss. Otherwise the whole balance might be upset.

The offensive in Indochina was marching an unsupported army into an alien land, a gamble from the very inception of the idea. Futhermore France had effectively taken hold of all Indochina. Any limited success in the offensive would not be able to break it up. To China, Indochina was but a vassal state while Taiwan was a Chinese administrative unit and territory, an integral part, intimately related to China's maritime defense.

Now, while Taiwan was still whole and unimpaired, weighing the pros and cons, it was indeed to China's interest to sacrifice her rights to Indochina for the sake of keeping Taiwan. Under the circumstances, the step was probably the only way out and any adverse ciritical view could only be an emotional one. That this was the policy finally adopted by Peking indicated how much Taiwan meant to China.

IV
The Rapid Advancement of Modernization (1885-1891)

The landing of Japanese forces in Taiwan pushed forward the national self-strengthening movement or national defense building in China, and started Taiwan on its way to modernization. The Sino-French conflict stirred up further awakening in China, making her realize that the development of resources and the self-strengthening must go hand in hand and that national wealth and military power must grow simultaneously. This awareness had most distinctly served as the driving force in the development of Taiwan which had exemplary success in the post Sino-French War Period.

The basic step taken in anticipation of this development was the promotion of the political status of Taiwan. It was made a province, the highest local administrative unit in China's government structure, in order to increase local government prestige and policy effectiveness. The preparatory work for this step was done under Shen Pao-chen, when the regulation was decreed that the Governor of Fukien should station in Taiwan every other half year. Yuan Pao-heng, the Deputy Minister of the Board of

Punishment, advised Peking that the Governor's alternating residence in Foochow and Taiwan made the two areas under his jurisdiction alternately remote to him and therefore making his supervision ineffective. This was especially the case in Taiwan, where administrative apparatus and construction works were just getting under way and the lapse of supervision would prove detrimental. It would therefore be better, Yuan advised, to change the Governor of Fukien into the Governor of Taiwan, and let the Governor-General of Chekiang and Fukien take over the affairs of Fukien.[62]

A few years leter, a further step towards the plan was taken by Tseng Yu-ying, who planned to place the provincial capital and administrative center in central Taiwan, somewhere in the area northeast of Changhua. In December 1884, on the threat of French naval attacks on Taiwan, Peking appointed Liu Ming-chuan the Governor of Fukien to be stationed in Taiwan to direct military affairs there. This was tantamount to changing the Governor of Fukien into the Governor of Taiwan, except that no explicit administrative organization was proclaimed during the pressured hours of the war.

At the end of the conflict, a painful retrospect of what had happened brought the central and local authorities to acknowledge that the blow that crushed and humiliated China was the defeat suffered on the high seas and that what must be done was to greatly strengthen the maritime defense and organize a strong fleet. Taiwan, being the key to the defense of the South Sea and a defensive barrier protecting the coast, should be paid special attention and taken special care of in its post-war redevelopment.

The man naturally suited for this job was Liu Ming-chuan, who had been there for more than a year. His on the spot experience from inspecting the land and talking to the people made him more aware of the conditions there and gave him the realization that the situation was capable of being successfully handled. The reason it had failed was due lamentably to the laspe of human effort. This realization strengthened his long cherished ambition of playing a role on the high seas. He well understood that the Powers all had their eyes on Taiwan and

> were waiting for a chance to annex it for a naval base. Now that peace is achieved and breathing space is gained, but reflecting on

> what had happened and thinking of what is going to befall us in
> the future, we must not spare a single moment to go right ahead to
> tackle one by one such main problems as defense construction,
> armed forces training, native pacification, and land survey and tax
> reassessment. Even if our dedication is in earnest and our effort is
> concentrated, ten years might not be enough for us to get results.[63]

Liu offered to dedicate his whole effort to the job, and
requested to be relieved of his duties as Governor of Fukien lest
his concentration in one place might lead to the neglect of things
in the other. "If the stationing in Taiwan is not held constant,
then working for one day and laying off for ten, what use would
that be to Taiwan."

To compare the responsibilities in Fukien and Taiwan, the
office of the Governor of Fukien was safe and the duties of
Taiwan defense dangerous, the Governor of Fukien easy and
Taiwan defense burdensome.

> To be concurrently the Governor of Fukien, the jurisdiction is
> broader and authority higher. To concentrate on duties in Taiwan,
> it would be no more than the showy title of an Imperial
> Commissioner. In peace time his funds for defense and develop-
> ment projects hang on the grace of other high local authorities;
> once there is a crisis on the horizon, he is the one at the forefront
> to shoulder all responsibilities.[64]

But Liu was willing to give up Fukien to concentrate on Taiwan,
to take up the challenge all by himself, to lay the foundations of
development, and put Taiwan on a firm basis.

Taiwan was an essential link in the maritime defense ring of
China. Peking naturally accepted his request when the veteran Liu
Ming-chuan offered to take charge of the defense affairs of
Taiwan. At the same time, Li Hung-chang was ordered to
negotiate for the purchase of four high speed ironclad warships for
service at Taiwan and Penghu. It was intended that this area soon
be made a separate and additional naval base. In June 1884, Liu
memorialized Peking requesting the establishment of Peking Office
of Naval Affairs.[65] On November 12, 1885, this was officially
instituted under the title *tsung-li-hai-chun-shih-wu ya-men*. This
was the fifth day of the ninth month of the eleventh year of the
reign of Kuang-hsu.

It was on this same day that an edict was issued proclaiming

Taiwan a province. Liu Ming-chuan was appointed the first Governor of Taiwan. Before this, China had eighteen provinces (under the Manchu government, the Northeast was under the status of "special regions," differing from "provinces") with the addition of Sinkiang which was made into a province in 1884. Taiwan had thus become the 20th province of China. That Sinkiang was made a province was due to the effort of Tso Tsung-tang. Tso also made a contribution to Taiwan. Before his death in September 1885, he memorialized Peking saying that considering its economic potential, Taiwan was well qualified to become a province; considering its strategic importance, it was urgently necessary for Taiwan to become a province.

In July 1886, Liu Ming-chuan and Yang Chang-chun, Governor-General of Chekiang and Fukien, jointly memorialized Peking on the plan and measures for promoting Taiwan into a province. Firstly they suggested maintaining the existing relationships between Taiwan and Fukien. The Governor would not be titled Governor of Taiwan but of Fukien-Taiwan, to remain jointly with Fukien, under the jurisdiction of the Governor-General of Chekiang and Fukien, so that the mainland-island mutual assistance relationship be maintained. The civil service examinations, both civil and military, would be held in Fukien. The salt gabelle of the two areas would remain administered by Fukien and the periodical reports would be made by the Salt Intendant of Fukien for both areas. Secondly, they suggested setting up a provincial capital, and subdivide the districts of which the jurisdiction had been governing too broad an area, into new units with additional administrative officials.[66]

In 1887, a formal and definite plan for the reorganization of local administrative units was made. The district of Changhua was to be divided. Its northeast area was to be created into a District of Taiwan (present day Taichung), and its southern area to be created into a District of Yunlin. Hsinchou was also to be divided. Its southwest area was to be created into a District of Miaoli. The above, plus the sub-prefecture *(t'ing)* of P'uli, would together form the Taiwan-fu. The original Taiwan-fu will be renamed Tainan-fu, and the original Taiwan district *(hsien)* would be renamed Anping district. The new Tainan-fu would have under its jurisdiction the districts of Anping, Chia-i, Fengshan, Hengchun and the sub-prefectures *(t'ing)* of Penghu (Pescadores). In the north, the Taipei-fu would have the districts of Tamshui (Taipei), Hsinchou, Ilan, and the sub-prefecture (t'ing) of Keelung (and later another sub-prefecture of Nan-ya-t'ing was added). in the east, there would be Tai-tung, a special chou or district level unit directly under provincial government jurisdiction without the intermediary fu (prefecture).

Then there is the sub-prefecture (t'ing) of Pei-nan, and later the sub-prefecture of Hualien was added. Altogether the province would consist of three fu (prefectures), one chou (special district), six t'ing (sub-prefecture) and eleven hsien (district). This was very much the same as the administrative units Taiwan has today. The provincial capital would be at the prefectural city of the new Taiwan-fu, but the Governor would be for the time being stationed at the prefectural city of Taipei-fu (which was the district city of Tamshui).

Liu Ming-chuan was more than a man of military competence. He was also a statesman of progressive ideas and noble dedication. He said:

> Since the Western Powers, relying on their strong ships and powerful guns, took control of the seas, China had her doors thrown open and the multi-millenia strategic seclusion was lost. At no time in her history had China been confronted by so many and so powerful contenders from without. It is now our urgent task to develop technology and manufactures, agriculture and commerce, shipping and forts, telegraph and firearms. The West was making technological improvements and progress by the day and by the hour. China, even if she could follow close at their heels, is still behind. If instead we linger and procrastinate, our backwardness will make us too frail to stand up as a nation at all.[67]

Taiwan, being closely related to national security, would have to be developed with utmost haste, so that on the one hand national maritime defense could be strengthened, and on the other the developments in Taiwan could ripen in time to serve as the cornerstone of national wealth and power and the model for national development.

Liu's three pronged policy for the development of Taiwan was: solidify its internal security, reorganize its finance, and strengthen its defenses. In its actual measures the emphasis was centered on defense. We can best summarize his main achievements as follows.

His first achievement was the strengthening of the natives'

pacification program for the safeguarding of internal security and order in Taiwan. The opening of the mountain areas was the most difficult part of the construction work in Taiwan. In the past decade, no marked results had been achieved. The mountain roads opened were not kept in use and many native tribes, pacified one day, rebelled the next. There were all together about 800 tribes of about 200,000 in population, and the cases of manslaughter each year numbered around 1,000. The Chinese who mistreated the natives and took their land or money were mostly good-for-nothing law breakers and those who were killed when the natives took revenge were mostly law-abiding people. With regard to internal order, this was harmful to both Chinese and natives; and with regard to external defense, the trouble from without. If the allegiance of all the natives could be won and internal peace guaranteed, then in case of external war, the natives would fight on the national side. In this way military and other expenses spent on internal defense could be spared and timber from the mountains could replenish government revenue.[68] Furthermore, reclamation in the mountain areas could be encouraged to increase production and improve the livelihood of Chinese and natives alike.

The measures Liu took to achieve his goal were simple; grace before force and peaceful persuasion supplemented by forceful suppression. When persuasion failed, suppression followed: when use of force succeeded, graceful embrace was accorded. Before the government, Chinese and natives were one and the same, no discrimination in treatment was allowed.

In November 1885, natives in the southeast of Taipei caused trouble. Liu sent men to persuade them to keep peace and all accepted his offer. Liu therefore reached agreements with them and had regulations set up, appointed the head of each tribe to be the official tribe leader *(she ting)*, gave them monthly stipends of grain and silver, bid them all live peacefully and everyone to pursue a trade or farming, aided them to send their young to school in town, and built for them more bridges and roads. Liu stationed himself in Hsinchou and Lin Chao-tung in Changhua to direct the work on the natives. In a period of several months, they persuaded more than 400 native tribes to claim allegiance, with a population of 70,000.

In 1886, many native tribes in the central section complained bitterly of Chinese oppression. Liu dismissed the local pacification and reclamation commissioner, and hoped to clear up the troublesome relationship of loans and indebtedness between the Chinese and the natives. In 1887, more than 260 native tribes in the central section of Taiwan claimed allegiance with a population of more than 30,000, and so did 220 tribes in east Taiwan with a population of 50,000.

The road from Taipei to Ilan was opened in 1885. The east-west cross Taiwan road was technically the most difficult to open but it was also the most important road. It was opened up from both ends, one from Changhua eastward and one from Hualien westward. It was completed in 1887, and the communication between the east and west was established, more natives claimed allegiance, tribal regulations were proclaimed, tribal leaders appointed, and the foundation for what is today the cross island highway was laid, In the South, the opening up spread from Chia-I to Taitung. In 1889, serious natives insurrection occurred in the east, Pei-nan (Taitung) was beseiged, and peace was restored only two months later. In 1890, natives disturbance appeared between Ilan and Hualien, which was soon suppressed.

Liu then vigorously encouraged and recruited people for reclamation and settlement, made the settlements more and more of an ethnically amalgamated kind, to let Chinese and natives get used to each other by living side by side and share things together, thus sinicizing or culturizing the natives naturally and effortlessly. Offices of reclamation and settlement were instituted in all important native areas, teaching the natives how to farm, weave and trade, encouraging the cultivation of tea and camphor, giving free medical service and drugs, operating native market places, and starting more local free schools. A native school was founded in Taipei, subsidizing the students' meals and clothing, teaching them Chinese, arithmetic, mandarin, Taiwan dialect, and decorums of daily life. The students were made to have constant contacts with the Chinese, so that their disposition and temperament be changed, their suspicion and apprehension mitigated, and gradually would cease to consider themselves different.[69] Such economic and cultural-educational measures were indeed the enlightened and proper policy toward the natives.

The second achievement under Liu was the reorganization of provincial finance. Reconstruction needs financing and the failure of Ting Jih-chang's ambition in Taiwan was mainly due to the lack of funds. In the past, it was scheduled that Fukien should subsidize Taiwan 800,000 taels every year, but it was usually not fulfilled. Liu Ming-chuan was of the opinion that Taiwan was a rich land, and that if the revenues were thoroughly reorganized, Taiwan would not only be self-sufficient, but also be with surplus instead of deficits. But in the initial period, his new measures such as pacification, road building, city and office construction, and other developmental projects will all be under way, the expenditures definitely would exceed the revenues. He therefore reached an understanding with Yang Chang-chun, the Governor-General, to reduce the annual subsidy from Fukien to 440,000 taels per year, to be paid in time and in full for a period of five years, after which Taiwan will be able to defray its own regular expenditures by its own revenues. Thus he had committed himself to a thorough reform and reorganization of provincial finance within the five year period. He would have to check all revenues at their source, reduce abusive practices in financial administration, and above all, undertake the resurveying of land and re-assessment of land tax.

Taiwan had land and climate perfect for farming, the central and southern sections yield three harvests a year. But the rice paddies and arid lands were never re-surveyed, thus reclamation and settlement increased day after day without any increment in taxation. This lapse in tax charges did not lessen the burden of the little people, for landownership usually went to the big families and influential gentry, who had only to file registration papers with the government to acquire land, which they then enlisted tenants for its reclamation and farming, charging rent on the tenants but paying no taxes to the government.

After gaining a general view and clear understanding of the situation, Liu began his reform work. In 1886, he ordered the check up of the rural *Pao* and *Chia* organization which had in part tax collection functions, and based upon that to register the current tax figure at every household; then he had the fields all re-surveyed, and based upon that to register the tax figure each field should be charged. An office for land tax re-assessment was instituted in each of the two areas of north and south Taiwan, and all private charged rents were to be transferred to the government.[70] The experience of land surveying on the mainland was that the survey of one district usually takes several years. Taiwan finished the whole province in two years, and in the third year the new tax form was issued by the provincial Finance Commissioner.

Land in excess of original registration amounted to about 4,000,000 *mou*, several times as high as the originally registered acreage. "All hidden lands were brought out; newly opened lands were promoted to the taxable land category. Land tax in excess of the original registration came to as much as 400,000 taels (the original tax total was 180,000 taels). As the people who did the paying are now paying to the government, they are paying less than they used to." "This is indeed beneficial to the people's livelihood, and resuscitating to government finance."[71]

The officials who contributed the most to the carrying out of this project were Shen Ying-teng and others; while among the local gentry, Lin Wei-yuan was the biggest landowner with the most rice paddies and arid lands, and he took the lead in offering cooperation to the government. As to the rate of taxation, formerly it was heavier in the south than in the north. Now it was brought under the same rate, and tax gatherers were forbidden to deviate from and collect anything above the rate.

The old measurement unit of *chia* was discontinued, and all registration made in or transformed into the *mou* unit. Thus simplicity was brought out of complexity and it became much easier for the people to understand and to follow, and harder for collectors to dupe or victimize the people. There were of course cases of resistance in the reform measures, but Lui was persistent in the strict carrying out of the project, saying that he would "rather be resented by the mighty than be unfair to the little people."[72] All in all the reform brought the revenue from land taxes up to an annual 700,000 taels.

The loss of tax revenue from squeezing or other corruptive abuses is common to governments but Taiwan suffered from this more than usual. Taxes charged on tea, camphor, and opium (under the denominator *yang yao* or imported medicine), and transit dues *(likin)* charged on commodities, after the operation of all kinds of abuses, such as the smuggling of traders, the squeeze by collectors, or the deny of payment by foreign companies, the annual revenues derived from the tariff customs and the salt gabelle amounted to only a scanty 900,000 taels. After Liu's reform measures, collection from tea increased to annually 130,000 taels, salt 120,000 taels, and camphor and sulphur, brought under governement monopoly, contributed an annual income of 300,000. But the most notable item was the charge of transit dues *(likin)* on opium and other import and export commodities.

According to the treaties of commerce China entered into with foreign countries, foreign traders, on all import and export commodities they handle, besides paying the customs tariff dues, were to pay an extra 2.5% *ad valorum* of transit dues, in order that the commodities be freed from any further inland collection of *li kin;* with the exception that commodities intended for a treaty port or concession will be exempted from the transit dues. There were no concessions in Taiwan, but foreign traders insisted that Taiwan-fu was a treaty port, and they therefore claimed, and were improperly granted, the exemption from paying transit dues.

In 1886, Liu found a way of giving the situation some remedy. He charged Taiwan goods intended for export an export *likin*, and installed a *likin* collecting office outside of the Taiwan-fu city to charge and collect an import *likin* on all imported foreign merchandise.[73] In this way revenues from tariff and *likin* due charged on opium yielded an annual increase of more than 400,000 taels, and the same from other commodities more than 70,000 taels. The total revenue from all taxes in Taiwan increased to an annual 3,000,000 taels which ultimately went to as high as 4,500,000 taels.

Liu also founded a government mint, purchased minting machinery and produced hundreds of thousands of silver coins every year. The military pay and provisions of Taiwan, about 1,500,000 taels per year, and other expenditures on road building, pacification, city and office construction, etc., for the first time all could be paid from Taiwan's own revenues without depending on subsidies from Fukien anymore, and modernization projects were also gradually under way as more funds were ready to finance them.

The third achievement under Liu was the build up of land and maritime defeneses of Taiwan. Taiwan's regular military force numbered about 20,000 which was increased to more than 30,000 during the Sino-French War. After the war, a total of 35 battalions, numbering about 17,000 men were kept. Beside the regular forces there were also the natives militia of 4,000, called the military settlement forces *(t'un chun)*, supported by the grain collected from 100,000 *mou* of native tribe lands and Chinese settlements. Liu thought the natives militia better trained than regular government forces, he therefore doubled their pay from four to eight dollars per month per man, and turned the 100,000 *mou* of land back to the people. All the forces were equipped with modern fire arms, and trained and drilled in the modern way by employed foreign training officers.

In 1885, Liu founded the Taipei Arsenal, a small factory for the manufacturing of rifle bullets and a large one for artillery shells, under the direction of foreign technicians. Thus a self-supply of ammunitions was intended for, lest wartime supplies be cut by blockade. A powder magazine was also built for storage of ammunitions. In the case of forts, he estimated that to rebuild the forts along the coast with added gun placements would require 800,000 taels, which Peking told him to try to finance himself. He managed to add two concrete gun placements at Keelung, two at Huwei, two at Anping, four at Chihou, and three at Penghu, with a Peking subsidy of 640,000 taels. The guns, thirty-one of them, were bought from Armstrong, the English firm. Also eighty mines were bought, and a mine laying battalion was formed at Keelung and Huwei.

Since Penghu was the entrance gate to all Taiwan, and a key point in the South and North Sea defenses, a force of 3,000 was stationed under a commanding officer, formerly a lieutenant general *(fu chiang)*, now a general *(tsung ping)*. The appointment was made to Wu Hung-lo, who was a general with military competence, a disciplinarian who had faith in training, and an officer knowledgeable in modern fire arms.[74] The most urgent need for the defense of Taiwan was warships, a modern fleet would be the best. In July 1885, Liu, together with Yang Chang-chun, tried to revive Ting Jih-chang's "Three Navy Plan" for the founding of a Taiwan-Penghu Navy which was to be one of the three.

Peking agreed to the principle, but was in no position to have the financial ability to build three fleets at the same time, and was forced to concentrate on the North Sea Fleet. Thus came the order that the four ironclad warships, being purchased for the use of Taiwan and Penghu, be transferred to the North Sea Fleet.[75] In August 1888, Liu requested that two high speed warships be transferred to Taiwan, so that, with several torpedo boats which

Taiwan would purchase on her own, they would be ready for patrol service at Taiwan and Penghu. The Office of Naval Affairs did not comply with this request either.

The fourth item of Liu's achievements was communications and transportation construction. On his arrival in Taiwan, he ordered the purchase from Hong Kong four small steam ships for service. In 1887 two German steamships were bought, together with another two high speed steamships purchased by enlisted investments from Fukienese businessmen among the Overseas Chinese in Southeast Asia. A lighter, for transhipment use, was turned over from the Fukien shipyard; and a dredger was ordered.[76] The two high speed steamships were used for routes from Taiwan to Shanghai and Hong Kong, and further to Manila, Saigon and Singapore. The harbor at Keelung was under construction, and the two ports at Chihou were in the planning state. The dredger was for such works.

Liu's voice had been one of the strongest in urging the building of railroads, but his earlier pre-Taiwan plan did not have any change of materialization. At the outset of the Sino-French conflict, Li Hung-chang had it said that if China had had railroads and ironclad warships to bolster her power and prestige, foreign countries would think twice before they dare to raise trouble. In 1886, Peking agreed to Li's request in extending the railroad of the Kaiping Mine; and later, a decision was reached to further extend the line west to Tientsin and east to Shanhaikuan.

Thus the building of railroads was no longer a taboo. The north-south railway line in Taiwan was one of Ting Jih-chang's projects; Liu thought the time had come for its realization. He therefore persuaded the Fukien businessmen in Singapore and Saigon who had invested in the two steamships to expand their enterprise to the building of the railroad, so that products of the mountain regions could be shipped to ports for export, in coordination with the service of the steamships, all to contribute to the business prosperity of Taiwan. The cost was estimated to be 1,000,000 taels, which was to be raised by private businessmen. Expenses for land buying will be provided by the government, army men will be provided by the government for the constuction work, ships will be provided by the government for the transporting of wood for sleepers, all in all to be a private enterprise under government supervision.

In April 1887, Liu was able to formally memorialize Peking of the plan. He expostulated the many advantages of the railroad, stressing that is the key to national wealth and power, not only good for trade and transportation, but also indispensable to military mobilization; that it would work for the prosperity of the land, to increase its revenues, so that more funds will be available for maritime defense. It was decreed be it done as planned.[77] The engineers employed were the German Becker and the Englishman Matheson. From England and Germany were ordered 330 *li* of rails and seventy passenger cars, and the construction was to begin with the Taipei-Keelung section.

The section consisted of more than ninety *chang* (one *chang* is 10 chih or 3.58 metres) of tunnels and more than 120 bridges of various size, the construction was therefore quite involved and progress was slow. The fund provided by business investments was inadequate and loans were advanced by the government. When the rails were half laid, Li En-tung, the leader responsible for and in charge of the work, died of illness, which made the business partners hesitate, and the enterprise had to be turned over to the government.[78] In 1891, the Keelung to Taipei section was completed and through train scheduled. In another two years, the Taipei to Hsinchou line was completed, all together about 180 *li*, forming the basis for the north-south trunk line in northern Taiwan. Thus Taiwan was the second province in China that could boast of railways besides Chihli, present day Hopei, which was the first.

In the case of telegraph lines, those constructed by Ting Jih-chang were in Taiwan. Liu Ming-chuan followed the plan conceived by Shen Pao-chen, with a land line from both Keelung and Huwei joining at Taipei and from there to Tainan; and two cable lines one from Huwei to Foochow and one from Anping to Penghu. The construction was contracted by the Jardine Matheson Company and completed in March 1888. The whole length of the land and cable lines came to more than 1,400 *li*, with nine telegraph offices. This brought the modernized communications system servicing rapid transmission of information between north and south; and the system that rendered the communication between Taiwan and the mainland always open, no longer suffering from wartime interference. Furtheremore, the relay express system could be dismantled and operation expenses cut.

The postal service was also installed, with a post office in Taipei and branch offices in other cities. Government messages were delivered free; private mail was charged according to the number of stations the delivery would cover, such as from Taipei to Tainan were thirteen stations. There were two mail ships for the delivery of overseas mail, making scheduled runs between the port of Taiwan and between Taiwan and Foochow and Shanghai.[79] This was ten years ahead of the postal service on the mainland. Liu also planned to start a telephone service, which failed to materialize.

The fifth item of Liu's accomplishments was economic construction. The Keelung coal mine was not under competent management in its initial years and a deficit resulted, followed by the self-inflicted demolition during the Sino-French War. After the war it was turned over to private management, but the deficit kept on. Liu Ming-chuan, viewing that local produced coal was indispensable to the shipyards, arsenals and steamships, therefore persuaded the Governor-General of Liangkiang and the Fukien Shipyard to jointly provide funds, to be matched by an equal amount of funds raised from private business, to finance the purchase of mining machinery and the employement of foreign technicians.

Thus in 1887 he was able to start operating the mine by a government-private Coal Mining Management. The yield was one hundred tons per day. Although this made both ends meet, but the lack of profit caused the private businessmen to demand their withdrawal, and forced the mine's return to government management. Then the Englishman Matheson was employed as supervisor to take charge of technical operations, and a railway was constructed from the mine to the Keelung wharf to expedite sales. It was intended that once marketing improved and profits grew, the mine was to be returned to private management, which was, according to his conviction, always better than government management.

In 1889, it was considered that the old pits were about to be exhausted, thus production became lower and lower, and it had become necessary to put in new investments to open up new pits. The government was not in a position to provide it, and private businessmen were reluctant to respond. An English business group offered to raise adequate funds to take over the operation, to repay by installments all government investments made thus far. Liu accepted the offer and a draft contract was signed. But it was rebuffed by Peking, which ordered that it be nullified, and that Liu be responsible to plan for the mine's improvement by employing proper personnel for its direction on the one hand while trying to enlist private business taking over on the other.

In 1890, the operation was improving, and Liu was able to change it to government-business joint management, under a new contractual basis to be run for a period of twenty years. Then there were conditions in the agreement such as that all operations be managed by the business side without interference from the government side, and that the technical operations of the mine be under the direction of a foreign technician. The agreement met with the disapproval of the central government, and orders came that government management be restored.

On his signing the contract with the English business group, Liu had been officially reprimanded; this time, he was to be referred to the Board of Punishment for proper censure.[80] He was, accordingly, punished by deprivation of office but to remain on probation. Thus the joint operation project failed and new pits were not to be opened. He was frustrated and discouraged, and this was one of the main reasons for his determined resignation later on. This indicated the difficulty of getting things done, especially in pushing through measures of modernization for national wealth and power. At this juncture, the annual export of coal had reached 77,000 tons.

The petroleum mine at Miaoli, Taiwan, had been discovered some twenty years back, and in 1877 Shen Pao-chen had employed an American engineer to do some surveying. Ting Jih-chang tried to operate it, but gave up after suffering losses. In 1887, Liu Ming-chuan revived the endeavor, founded the Petroleum Mining Management and assigned Lin Chao-tung to take charge, with unsatisfactory results. In 1889, Liu signed a draft contract with the same English business group who agreed to take over the coal mine, to let them operate the petroleum mine.[81] It was also rebuked by the central government.

Sulphur and camphor were both famed products of Taiwan. In 1887, the Camphor and Sulphur Production Management was established. Sulphur was used in China for making gunpowder, and camphor was demanded by the English who exchanged it with opium. Private traders usually engaged in the making and selling of camphor on their own, and the rivalry and competition between them often resulted in lawlessness. The price of camphor from the private sellers was eight dollars per hundred catties (one *tan* or *shih* of 133 lb.). In 1855, government authorities reached an agreement with the English traders, making the price sixteen dollars per *tan*. Later when the export amount increased, the government claimed a monopoly by installing an office for government buying of camphor. The English traders, finding it not to their benefit, demanded the repeal of the monopoly. In 1869, the monopoly was withdrawn and foreign traders did their own buying from private suppliers. During Shen Pao-chen's administration, he declared sulphur government property and prohibited its export. A large quantity was accumulated to no purpose. In 1887, Liu Ming-chuan made both commodities government monopoly for the explicit purpose of exporting, to be managed by the Camphor and Sulphur Production Management. In camphor alone, the annual profit was close to 200,000 taels.[82]

In agriculture, irrigation work was planned. In Hsinchou, there was an area by the name of Ta-k'o-kan (present day Tahsi), which had excellent soil but not enough rainfall. In 1887, Liu employed a German engineer to study the water sources of the area, so that an irrigation canal could be dug. The work was not able to get started before Liu left office, but it was the earliest plan of what is today the Shih-men Dam.

Rice was the stable produce in Taiwan, Liu used to bring his staff along with him to visit the rice farmers, asking about their harvest, telling them to have their young go to school or learn to work hard in the farm, and encouraging them by giving awards to the industrious and frugal.

The second came sugar, which had been an export marketed to Shanghai and Tientsin, and brought to Japan, Hong Kong and London by English, American and German traders. Its production was further encouraged and developed under Liu. At his time, the annual production of rice was 7-8,000,000 *tan*, (traditional picul of 100 catties or 133 lb.), and sugar 7-8,000,000 *tan* of which 80% was exported.

Tea was another profitable produce which was beginning to be exported, the most demanded was the oolang tea for the United States, for which many Fukien and Cantonese traders came to

Taiwan to operate exporting companies. Liu gave more impetus to tea growing, and planters and production grew very fast, each year to come to worth several million taels.

Liu also tried to encourage cotton growing and sericulture. He bought cotton seeds and distributed them among the farmers, together with instructions for planting. Since the climate in Taiwan does not fit cotton growing too well, emphasis was put on sericulture. In 1889 he sent men to Kiangsu, Chekiang and Anhwei to collect silkworm eggs and methods for growing mulberry trees and rearing silkworm, had them complied into pamphlets and distributed among the people, causing a flurry at the time.[83]

In commercial developments, Taiwan had its staple exports in sugar, tea and camphor. In 1886, a Taiwan Trade and Investment House (chao-shang-chu) was operated in Singapore, men were sent there to study trade situations, to get overseas Fukienese there interested in Taiwan, and to increase the demand for Taiwan exports. The two steamships bought partly by investments from there were meant for passenger and freight transport for South Sea ports and the Chinese mainland southeast coast.

For the development of Taipei as a trading center, the area along the Tamshui River was zoned as the commercial section, and wealthy Taiwan merchants shared the responsibility for building the streets and other public utilities there, and it became the port center where Chinese and foreign traders converged. A General Trade and Investment Center (t'ung-shang-tsung-chu) was established in Taipei in 1887, in which year the annual foreign trade of Taiwan reached 9,000,000 taels. A Metropolitan Development Company (Hsing-shih-kung-ssu) was formed by investments made by Chekiang businessmen, and projects like street construction, a city water supply system, and a hospital were undertaken.

In 1888, electric lighting was installed and all main streets, offices like the Governor's and the Financial Commissioner's, and factories like the arsenal, all had electric lights. The metal bridge across the Tamshiu River was also completed in that year. The engineer was Chang Chia-tek, a Cantonese. It was a drawbridge operated by machinery, which opens the bridge to let pass ships in the river. Thus at that time Taipei was already a modern city.[84]

The sixth item of Liu Ming-chuan's achievements in Taiwan was the development of education in science and technology. In Liu's modernization measures, the erection of modern schools was the most purposeful and farsighted, and most fundamental to the attainment of national wealth and power. The opening of Taiwan had been by then more than twenty years, and its public affairs, such as foreign trade and maritime defense, often would involve dealings with foreigners. For the handling of such, not only were there no Chinese specialists, but even foreign languages were not taken up as subjects of serious study. When Liu first came to Taiwan, he had to employ translators from places like Shanghai, those who imposed exorbitant terms, but with none too high qualifications even in languages, not to say special knowledge in technical subjects.

Taiwan was one of the first to have telegraph lines, and Liu was also the first to found in 1886 a school for telegraph work instructions, to train personnel for service. Soon after modernization projects were under way, the requirement for special personnel was met on the one hand by the employment of foreign specialists, and on the other by employing instructors for on the spot training. He tried as an initial step to raise funds from contributions from local officials and gentry to finance classes for training technicians for needed services.

In the past four decades, the cultural climate of Taiwan had risen to quite a high level. There were more than a dozen private academies *(shu yuan)* with several thousand students, and all talented young men were attracted to schools. Liu therefore started a school of Western studies *(hsi-hsueh-t'ang)* in 1887, employed English and Danish instructors, and had students all provided with government grants. The curriculum was Western studies in the forenoon and afternoons, and Chinese classics and history and Chinese language in the morning and evenings by Chinese instructors, so that the students would be knowledgeable in both Chinese and foreign subjects, and well versed in Confucian traditions and decorum so that there would not be any danger of their falling into foreign ways.

Western studies consisted of English and French; history and geography; mathematics, physics and chemistry; and surveying, designing and mechanical engineering. It was intended to give students basic training and basic knowledge to lay a foundation for developing their talents to become specialists in the future, so that in all fields such as mining, railroads, machinery, and manufacturing there will be plentiful of service personnel and potential leadership.[85]

Liu once strenuously asserted that "If China does not take to Westernization, suspend the civil service examinations, burn the bureaucratic established procedures and precedents of the Six Boards, open schools of Western studies, translate Western texts on various subjects, in order to develop potential talents and create new leadership, the situation would be beyond help in another ten years![86] The establishment of schools for Western studies and the emphasis of science in education had been persistently advocated by him. Among the Chinese provinces, only a very few had public modern schools at that time. Taiwan, the youngest member, was one of them.

Liu Ming-chuan took charge of Taiwan province for six years (1885-1891), during which time he exerted his utmost to push Taiwan unto the main road of modernization. Under the difficulties of insufficiency of human and material resources, under the harassment imposed upon him by bureaucratic practices of conservative policies, he fought his way through thick and thin, with results hardly ideal, yet quite remarkable.

In the case of communications and transportation, the mainland provinces, though most of them had the telegraph service, but only one, Chihli (present day Hopei), had railways, and none had yet formally started the postal service. In modern industries, the only provinces that knew of manufacturing by machinery were Kiangsu, Fukien, Chihli, Kwangtung, Kansu, Shensi, Shantung, Hupei, Hunan, Szechuan, Chilin, Chekiang, and Yunnan, altogether thirteen. In mining, those which had mining by machinery were Chihli, Hupei, Shantung, Kiangsu, Kueichow, Yunnan, Chilin, and Heilungkiang, a total of eight. In modern education, only four had public schools: Chihli, Fukien, Kiangsu and Kwangtung. Yet the above array of accomplishments was achieved throughout a period of thirty years.

Taiwan alone, in the span of a few years, had all of them. Only the province of Chihli could boast of the same broad coverage. Yet Chihli was the province beheld by all as the site of the national capital, patronized with special favors by the central government, and presided over by none other than the arch promotor of modernization, Li Hung-chang, and that by then for no less than a period of twenty years. What had Taiwan to match Chihli? But here was the one balancing factor, the leadership and effort of Liu.

Liu Ming-chuan's accomplishment was unique and outstanding in that he promoted Taiwan to the most advanced province of China. It was said that Liu, in "forging the Huai Forces, Westernizing the army, championing railroad construction, and building up the province of Taiwan, had created Four Wonders in China."[87]

The scourge of modern China came from over the high seas. After 1874, Japan gradually became the chief menace. Liu Ming-chuan had a clear vision of this, and used to say that should China not speedily strengthen herself, that menace would be the calamity to overwhelm her. Taiwan, being the key to the whole of China's defenses, should not stay idle and be contented; with its primitive conditions, lest when the time comes she would be the first to go. Thus the way that he applied himself to the building up of Taiwan, with every ounce of his energy, eschewing no hardships and taking all the blame, was indeed but to try to realize his hope that Taiwan be made rich and strong to become a model modernized province of China and therefore the foundation of national wealth and power, so that the central government could follow up with larger scale and farther reaching nationwide plans.

But how could the central government, under such a ruler as the Empress Dowager, with no knowledge and understanding, reaching only for power and indulging only her lust, be able to comprehend such statesman-leadership? Thus came the end of Liu Ming-chuan, who resigned from his post in May 1891. Chang Yao, Governor of Shantung, a contemporary of Liu and an outstanding, leader upon Liu's resignation requested his own transfer to Taiwan to take up what Liu had left unfinished. In his memorial he wrote that "although Shantung is broader in territory, Taiwan is a much heavier responsibility."[88] His patriotic dedication, courage under challenge, and loyalty to duty was of Liu's caliber, and would be a perfect successor.

But unfortunately, as it was to be expected, the government turned down his request, and Liu's successor turned out to be just another bureaucrat of habitual indolence and characteristic irresponsibility, who reversed all of Liu's ways and doings. In another three years, the Sino-Japanese War came, the Chinese land and sea forces were crushed, and Taiwan fell into the hands of the conqueror. And as Taiwan fell, so did Liu Ming-chuan, who soon died with a broken heart full of sorrow, bitterness, and frustration.

Notes to Chapter V

(For convenience sake, the editions used are as many as available from the Bank of Taiwan's *Taiwan Historical Literature Series*, Taipei, Taiwan, 1957-1972 (Tai-wan yin-hang, *T'ai-wan wen-hsien ts'ung-k'an* — shown here as TWT.)

1 Yu, wen-i, *Hsu-hsiu t'ai-wan fu-chih* (Prefecture Gazetteer of Taiwan-fu, Supplemented Edition) ch. 20, pp. 22; 712-714, TWT ed.

2 *Ibid.*, Vol. 3, p. 179; Lien, *T'ai wan t'ung shih*, Vol. 34, pp. 937-938.

3 Lien Heng, *T'ai-wan t'ung-shih*, Vol. 34, pp. 935-937.

4 *Ibid.*, Vol. 34, p. 938; Yu, *Hsu-hsiu t'ai-wan fu-chih, op.cit.*, ch. 3, p. 180.

5 Yu, *Hsu-hsiu t'ai-wan fu-chih, op.cit.*, ch. 3, p. 178; Lien, *T'ai-wan t'ung-shih, op.cit.*, ch. 34, p. 933.

6 Yu, *Hsu-hsiu t'ai-wan fu-chih, op. cit.*, ch. 3, p. 188; Lien, *T'ai-wan t'ung-shih*, ch. 34, p. 939.

7 Lien, *T'ai-wan t'ung-shih, op.cit.*, ch. 34. p. 940.

8 Lan Ting-yuan, *P'ing-t'ai chi-lueh* (The Suppression of the Taiwan Insurection), p. 30, TWT ed.

9 Huang Shu-ching, *T'ai-hai shih ch'a-lu* (Taiwan, Its Land and Natives), Vol. 1, p. 21, TWT ed.

10 Lan Ting-yuan, *Tung cheng chi* (Campaign in Taiwan), Vol. 3, pp. 34-40, TWT ed.

11 Lan, *P'ing-t'ai chi-lueh, op.cit.*, p. 32.

12 *Ibid.*, pp. 51-52.

13 Yu, *Hsu-hsiu t'ai-wan fu-chih, op.cit.*, ch. 20, pp. 725-728.

14 Li Hung-chang, *Li-wen-chung-kung hsuan-chi* (Selected Writings of Li Hung-chang), p. 91, TWT ed.

15 *Ibid.*, p. 34.

16 Shen Pao-chen, *Fu-kien t'ai-wan tsou-che* (Memorials of the Fukien and Taiwan Period), p. 4, TWT ed.

17 *Ibid.*, p. 1.

18 Li, *Li-wen-chung-kung hsuan-chi, op. cit.*, p. 91.

19 *Ibid.*, p. 90.

20 Shen, *Fu-kien t'ai-wan tsou-che, op.cit.*, p. 3-4.

21 *Ibid.*, p. 2.

22 Li, *Li-wen-chung-kung hsuan-chi, op.cit.*, p. 92.

23 Shen, *Fu-kien t'ai-wan tsou-che, op.cit.*, pp. 62-64.

24 *Ibid.*, p. 17.

25 Li, *Li-wen-chung-kung hsuan-chi, op.cit.*, p. 27.

26 *Ibid.*, p. 137.

27 *Ibid.*, p. 120.

28 *Ibid.*, p. 129.

29 Shen-pao Kuan, *Ching-chi shen-pao t'ai-wan chi-shih chi-lu* (Collection of Reports on Taiwan from the *Shen Pao* of the Late Ching Period), p. 558, TWT ed.

30 Li, *Li-wen-chung-kung hsuan-chi, op.cit.*, pp. 199-200.

31 *Ibid.*, P. 19.

32 *Ibid.*, p. 137.

33 Shen-pao Kuan, *Ching-chi shen-pao t'ai-wan chi-shih chi-lu*, pp. 681-685.

34 Wu Tsan-ch'eng, *Wu-kuang-lu shih-min tsou-kao hsuan-lu* (Selections from the Memorials of Wu Tsan-ch'eng during His Mission in Fukien), p. 11, TWT ed.

35 *Kuang-hsu ch'ao-chung jih-wai chiao-shih-liao* (Documents on Sino-Japanese Relations of the Reign of Kuang-hsu), Peiping, Ku-kung po-wu-yuan (Palace Museum), ch. 1, p. 17.

36 Shen-pao Kuan, *Ching-chi shen-pao t'ai-wan chi-shih-chi yao, op.cit.*, p. 710.

37 *Ibid.*, p. 734.

38 *Ibid.*, p. 1025.

39 Wang Yen-wei and others, eds., *Ching-chi wai-chiao shih-liao* (Foreign Relations Documents of the Late Ching Period), ch. 10.

40 Li, *Li-wen-chung-kung hsuan-chi, op.cit.*, pp. 230-231.

41 Chu Shou-peng, *Kuang-hsu ch'ao-tung hua-hsu-lu hsuan-chi* (Selections from the Tung-hua Documents of the Kuang-hsu Reign), pp. 23-30, TWT ed; Shen-pao Kuan, *Ching-chi shen-pao t'ai-wan chi-shih chi-lu, op.cit.*, pp. 722-724.

42 Li, *Li-wen-chung-kung-hsuan-chi, op.cit.*, pp. 21; 200.

43 *Ibid.*, pp. 275; 256.

44 Chu, *Kuang-hsu ch'ao-tung hua-hsu-lu hsuan-chi, op.cit.*, p. 32.

45 Wu, *Wu-kuang-lu shih-min tsou-kao hsuan-chi, op.cit.*, pp. 10-11.

46 *Ibid.*, pp. 27-28.

47 Liu Ao, *Hsun-t'ai-t'ui ssu-lu* (Documents from the Taiwan Intendant's Office). pp. 16; 20, TWT ed.

48 *Ibid.*, pp. 81-83, 94, 103, 179, 228, 241.

49 Kuo Ting-yee, *Ching-tai chung-kuo shih-shih jih-chih* (Daily Chronicles of Major Historical Events of Modern China), Taipei, Academia Sinica, 1963, Vol. l, p. 550.

50 Liu, *Hsun-t'ai t'ui-ssu-lu, op.cit.*, p. 219; Lien, *T'ai-wan t'ung-shih, op.cit.*, pp. 922-924.

51 Wang, *Ching-chi wai-chiao shih-liao, op.cit.*, ch. 43.

52 Li, *Li-wen-chung-kung hsuan-chi, op.cit.*, p. 414.

53 Liu Ming-chuan, *Liu chuang-su-kung tsou-i* (Memorials of Liu Ming-chuan), ch. 3, pp. 174-175, TWT ed.

54 *Ibid.*, ch. pre-1, pp. 15-75.

55 *Ibid.*, ch. 3, pp. 176-178.

56 Li, *Li-wen-chung-kung hsuan-chi, op.cit.*, p. 484.

57 *Ibid.*, pp. 475-477.

58 TWT ed., *Fa-chun ch'in-t'ai-tang* (Documents on the French Military Attack on Taiwan), pp. 139-140; TWT ed., *Fa-chun ch'in-t'ai-tank hsu-pien* (Documents on the French Military Attack on Taiwan, Supplementary Volume), pp. 64, 194.

59 TWT ed., *Ching tsau-shu hsuan-huei* (Selections from Ching Dynasty Memorials), pp. 87. 89.

60 Chang Chih-tung, *Chang-wen-hsien-kung* hsuan-chi (Selections from the Writings of Chang Chih-tung), p. 12, TWT ed; TWT ed., *Ching-chi wai-chiao shih-liao hsuan-chi* (Selections from Foreign Relations Documents of the Late Ching Period) pp. 105, 103.

61 Tso Tsung-tang , *Tso-wen-hsiang-kung tsou-tu* (Memorials of Tso Tsung-tang), pp. 60-61, TWT ed.

62 TWT ed., *Ching-shih lieh-chuan hsuan-chih* (Selections from Biographies of the Ching Dynasty History), p. 361.

63 Liu, *Liu-chuang-su-kung tsou-i, op.cit.*, ch. 1, pp. 106-107.

64 *Ibid.*, ch. 1, pp. 107-108.

65 *Ibid.*, ch. 2, p. 131.

66 *Ibid.*, ch. 6, pp. 281-283.

67 *Ibid.*, ch. 1, p. 111; Vol. 2, p. 127.

68 *Ibid.*, ch. 2, p. 148.

69 Lien, *T'ai-wan t'ung-shih, op.cit.*, ch. 11, p. 276.

70 *Ibid.*, Ch. 7, p. 304.

71 *Ibid.*, ch. 7, p. 311.

72 *Ibid.*, ch. 7, p. 310.

73 Li, *Li-wen-chung-kung hsuan-chi, op.cit.*, pp. 535-539; 584; TWT ed., *Ching-chi wai-chiao shih-liao hsuan-chi, op.cit.*, pp. 201-203.

74 Liu, *Liu-chuang-su-kung tsou-i, op.cit.*, ch. 5, pp. 243-245.

75 Li, *Li-wen-chung-kung hsuan-chi, op.cit.*, p. 549.

76 Liu, *Liu-chuang-su-kung tsou-i, op.cit.*, ch. 5, pp. 255-256.

77 *Ibid.*, ch. 5, pp. 268-273; TWT ed. *T'ai-wan hai-fang-tang* (Documents on Taiwan Maritime Defense), pp. 115-123.

78 Liu, *Liu-chuang-su-kung tsou-i, op.cit.*, ch. 5, pp. 273-275.

79 Lien, *T'ai-wan t'ung-shih, op.cit.*, ch. 19, pp. 534-535, TWT ed.; *Liu Ming-chuan, fu-t'ai ch'ien-hou tang-an* (Documents Related to Liu Ming-chuan's Military and Administrative Measures in Taiwan), pp. 183-186, TWT ed.

80 Liu, *Liu-chuang-su-kung tsou-i, op.cit.*, ch. 8, pp. 351; 356-360; 366-368.

81 *Ibid.*, ch. 8, pp. 357; 361-363. Lien, *T'ai-wan t'ung-shih, op.cit.*, ch. 18, p. 503.

82 Lien, *T'ai-wan t'ung-shih, op.cit.*, ch. 18, pp. 499; 504-506.

83 *Ibid.*, ch. 26, pp. 641; 645-655.

84 *Ibid.*, ch. 25, pp. 629-630.

85 Liu, *Liu-chuang-su-kung tsou-i, op.cit.*, ch. 6, pp. 297-298.

86 *Ibid.*, ch. pre-1, p. 13.

87 *Ibid.*, ch. pre-1, p. 8 (These were the words of the editor Ch'en Tan-jan.)

88 Kuo Ting-yee, *T'ai-wan shih-shih kai-shuo* (A Sketch History of Taiwan), p. 207., Taiwan, 1954.

Chapter VII

A Short-lived Republic and War, 1895:
Taiwan's Resistance Against Japan

BY HARRY J. LAMLEY

The year 1895 proved most crucial in Taiwan's historical development. At that time China was forced to cede Taiwan and the Pescadores as an outcome of the first Sino-Japanese War (1894-1895). As a result, the entire territory of China's only insular province was transferred from Ching to Meji rule and the inhabitants transformed into the inferior status of colonial subjects. The fate of the Pescadores was determined relatively early, for Japan seized that island-group late in March while the war was still in progress. However, the Japanese occupation of Taiwan did not begin until near the end of May, three weeks after the ratification of the Treaty of Shimoneski (May 8). By then there had emerged a resistance movement, headed by local leaders who proclaimed a republic and sought to keep Taiwan from falling to Japan. This effort engendered a five-month war before organized resistance was brought to an end and Taiwan and its inhabitants were brought under permanent Japanese rule.

The rise of the Taiwan Republic and the ensuing war of resistance were extraordinary episodes since they came to pass without the sanction of the Ching court and in defiance of both the Japanese military power and the terms of the peace treaty. The republic, inaugurated in Taipei on May 25, turned out to be a short-lived affair lasting only twelve days. Nevertheless, it represented the spirit of resistance which was aroused throughout Taiwan. Subsequently, vestiges of the republic flourished to the south under Liu Yung-fu 劉 永 福 until the end of the war.

Meanwhile, the five-month war of resistance remained a self-contained conflict distinct from the Sino-Japanese War which

had terminated in April with the signing of the peace treaty.¹ The
fighting was limited solely to the terrain of Taiwan, and no direct
confrontation between the Ching and Meiji governments developed.
By the time hostilities broke out after the initial Japanese landings
on May 29, the Ching court appeared determined to abide by the
treaty to cede Taiwan so that Japan might be placated and made
to retrocede the Liaotung Peninsula. Already in mid May the
court had instructed that no more troops and supplies be sent to
Taiwan from mainland ports.² Next, on May 20, an imperial
edict ordered the acting Taiwan governor, Tang Ching-sung
唐 景 崧 , to send the island's civil and military government
personnel back to the mainland and then to appear in Peking for
an audience with the emperor.³ Finally, on June 2, a Chinese
commissioner, Li Hung-chang's nephew and adopted son, Li
Ching-fang 李 經 方 , formally turned Taiwan over to Japan
amid ceremonies conducted on shipboard off the island port of
Keelung.⁴ At this point China officially relieved herself of all
further responsibility for the affairs of her former island province,
and the struggle for Taiwan, which had commenced five days
previously, remained a separate, undeclared war.

Generally, the Taiwan Republic and the 1895 war of resistance
have been treated with in a defamatory vein by Chinese and
foreigners alike. Due to the republic's brief existence and the fact
that its key supporters chose to flee to the mainland rather than
face oncoming Japanese forces, Chinese have usually stressed the
weakness of the Taiwan Republic as well as the inadequacies of
the resistance movement and war effort. In a more disdainful
manner, most Westerners at the time simply dismissed the
republic as a hoax fabricated by the Ching court or by one of the
foreign powers. ⁵ Moreover, Japan took pains to play down the
republic and the resistance. The Meiji government refused to
admit that the occupation of Taiwan had embroiled Japan in
another war, while Japanese authorities maintained that military
operations on the island were merely actions to pacify local unruly
elements whom they termed "local brigands and insurgents."
(doki sōzoku 土匪草賊)⁶

Such negative views are misleading and in part highly
inaccurate. A more objective approach to the limited historical
sources available reveals that the Taiwan Republic was formed by
desperate local leaders who hastily made use of Western political

concepts which seemed practicable for their resistance purposes with little regard for the alien principles and usages involved. The notion of a republic appealed to these founders for several reasons. By representing Taiwan as a new republic about to be overrun by an aggressive Asian foe, they hoped to gain sympathy and enlist support from one or another of the Western powers. In particular, the key leaders wished Taiwan to gain formal international recognition as a separate state distinct from imperial China so that they might directly negotiate with the various powers through regular diplomatic channels. They reasoned that in this way foreign backing could be enlisted and resistance to the Japanese sustained on the island without further embroiling the Ching court with Japan. Again, the founders and supporters apparently believed that the inauguration of a new island government in Taipei would bolster the morale of the island's inhabitants and defense forces as well as present the appearance of a unified resistance effort. Finally, personal ambition and rivalries among several of the chief resistance leaders had an important bearing on the adoption of a republican facade for Taiwan by mid May, 1895. A study of the hasty manner in which the new island government was established in Taipei reveals that the Taiwan Republic was indeed a facade hardly worthy of its republican label. Yet this alleged republic played an important role in that it did initiate armed resistance against Japanese occupation forces.

On the other hand, the war of resistance was not a sham affair, nor was it merely an uprising or rebellion, as Japanese accounts indicate. Rather, this war constituted a sustained struggle between the Japanese occupation forces and various Chinese regular and irregular defensive units for control of Taiwan. Those who engaged in defense refused to acknowledge Japan's claim to the island, and attempted to save Taiwan for China or protect their native land from a hated foreign foe still commonly referred to as "dwarf bandits." What the Japanese had to subdue were not so much lawless elements intent on pillaging or seizing power, but defensive efforts organized by responsible resistance leaders who worked within the local Chinese administrative framework established under Ching rule.

Viewed in this positive light, the advent of the Taiwan Republic and war of resistance may be regarded as one of those desperate Chinese reactions to the outcome of the first Sino-

Japanese War. These episodes call to mind other remarkable developments on the mainland during 1895: the hundreds of spirited protest petitions addressed to the throne during April and early May, after the terms of the peace treaty became known; the study societies which began to spring up in cities later in the year; and the Canton Revolt staged by the *Hsing Chung hui* 興 中 會 , in October. In Taiwan, "Asia's first republic" and the separate war against Japan arose under even more distressful conditions as an aftermath of the Sino-Japanese War. Examined in reference to the local scene, these two extraordinary episodes shed light on Taiwan's unstable situation during the fateful year of 1895 when the island was lost to imperial China.

I

The Local Setting and Political Background

The setting in which the republic and war of resistance occurred is important   to   assess. These episodes were not manifestations resulting from a well integrated provincial society and government, nor were they products of the frontier, as has often been alleged. In 1895, the new and relatively prosperous offshore province of Taiwan was still undergoing change in keeping with traditional Chinese modes of development. By then, Taiwan's frontier settlements were mainly limited to mountainous areas contiguous to the lofty central range, extending north to south in the interior, and to sparsely settled localities situated along the east coast and at the southernmost end of the island. In contrast, the bulk of the Chinese inhabitants, numbering well over two and a half million, dwelt in the Taipei Basin and Keelung vicinity in the north and throughout the lowland areas along Taiwan's west coast. Almost the entire five-month war was staged in these more densely populated areas where villages, towns and walled administrative centers came under attack. Meanwhile, the republic flourished in urban environments: first in Taipei, the provincial capital; then in Tainan, the island's oldest prefectural center. Only after the war ended in October, upon the surrender of Tainan, did the Japanese begin to occupy the main frontier settlements located in Hengchun areas to the extreme south, the

P'u-li district in the central highlands and, finally, the Hualien and
Taitung areas on the east coast.[7]

Actually, the frontier contributed little to the resistance
effort. Frontier areas were lightly defended for the most part, and
elements of the frontier population used sparingly by most
Chinese leaders. Reputedly courageous Hakka frontiersmen were
only occasionally recruited. Again, Liu Yung-fu made several
attempts to arm aborigine bands and set them against the
Japanese, but to no avail.[8] On the whole, the republic and the war
received support from the more developed regions of Taiwan
which had come to resemble the much older mainland areas in
southern Fukien and eastern Kwangtung from whence the island's
Chinese inhabitants stemmed.

Although neither the republic nor the war were products of
the frontier, these episodes nevertheless took place in a transitional society where discord and acts of violence had been
common. During the entire 212 years Taiwan was under Ching
rule, the island experienced some seventy major disturbances, an
average of one severe outbreak approximately every three years.[9]
Such organized strife sometimes lasted for months and affected
whole *hsien*, subprefectures or prefectures, and occasionally the
entire island territory under permanent Chinese settlement. The
major disturbances assumed two main forms: uprisings or rebellions in which the government came under attack; and armed
conflicts *(hsieh-tou* 械　　鬥) either between groups of local
Hakka and Hoklo (Fukien) inhabitants or among disparate Hoklo
communities whose members emanated from different southern
Fukien areas, principally those of Chuanchou and Changchou.
Massive pitched battles, generated by such sub-ethnic strife, grew
more prevalent in the 1780's, but finally died down by the last
quarter of the nineteenth century. Large-scale uprisings also
became less frequent during this late period. By the time the
Sino-Japanese War began, most established Chinese communities
in Taiwan enjoyed a more peaceful environment even though
sub-ethnic tensions still prevailed, as did troublesome bandit and
vagrant bands of the type that had long infested the island.

However, once rumors concerning a Japanese takeover of
Taiwan started to circulate early in 1895, social problems that had
continually beset the strife-ridden island again became acute. Long
existing cleavages among Taiwan's disparate sub-ethnic groups

deepened, while banditry grew rampant. Moreover, the local Chinese population, Hoklos and Hakkas alike, came to resent the presence of unruly mainland forces stationed about the island. Even before the appearance of Japanese troops upon the scene, turbulent conditions suggestive of the old Taiwan adage, "an uprising every three years, a rebellion every five," had set in once more.[10] Subsequently, two of the most bloody battles waged by local defense units during the five-month war were not encounters with the Japanese, but rather actions taken against marauding Kwangtung troops near the city of Hsinchu, (Chu-ch'ien 竹 塹) then later, belligerent Hakka villagers in the Tainan prefecture.[11]

The political background in Taiwan also had a profound influence on the entire resistance effort. From the outset, as steps were initiated to build up Taiwan's defenses during the latter part of 1894, the need for stronger central government on the island became apparent. The lack of centralized authority already had emerged as a critical problem in 1884-1885 when Taiwan came under French attack. Then the rivalry between the Taiwan intendant in the south and Liu Ming-chuan, who commanded the northern defenses, had jeopardized the security of the island.[12] This bifurcation of authority between north and south continued after Taiwan was administered as a separate province, beginning in 1887, for the ranking official posts remained divided between Taipei, the new provincial capital in the north,[13] and Tainan, the old sourthern prefectural center. Thus, while the governor and provincial finance commissioner (pu-cheng-shih 布 政 使), stationed in Taipei, exerted strong control over the northern portion of the island, their authority tended to be balanced off in the southern and mid-island regions by long established posts in Tainan: those of the intendant (who served concurrently as the provincial judge or an-ch'-a-shih 按 察 使) and the Taiwan brigade-general. Partly in response to this problem, Tang Ching-sung, upon becoming governor in October, proceeded to build up the defenses in northern Taiwan at the expense of most areas to the south.

Later on, the resistance movement that arose in the spring of 1895 reflected another aspect of regional politics in Taiwan. This involved leadership at the prefectural level. When Taiwan became a province, a third prefecture was established in the mid-island region and Changhua, an old hsien seat, served as the prefectural center as well. With the support of powerful mid-island gentry and wealthy merchants of the nearby port town of Lukang, Changhua emerged as a major seat of government almost on a par with Taipei and Tainan as far as regional influence was concerned. The rival influence of Changhua and the mid-island region, vis-a-vis Taipei, grew apparent during April and May. Then local resistance leaders staged demonstrations in Changhua and supported the mid-island gentry figure, Chiu Feng-chia 邱 逢 甲 , when he challenged Governor Tang for leadership of the resistance movement. Meanwhile, influential Tainan officials and gentry appear to have remained aloof from this northern and mid-island movement which culminated in the establishment of the republic.

Subsequently, the major defense forces that waged war against the Japanese depended heavily on Taiwan's three key administrative centers: Taipei, Changhua and Tainan. These centers operated as separate wartime capitals within regions analogous to their respective prefectural bounds. As the fighting shifted southward, each center in turn bore the brunt of the war and drew upon the available resources and manpower of that particular region. From the local Chinese standpoint, the five-month war underwent three distinct phases corresponding to the period in which support for the active defensive units stemmed mainly from one or another of these centers. Thus the war effort, like the resistance movement that preceded it, came to depend on leadership and organization emanating from official and gentry-merchant involvement within nearly discrete prefectural regions.

In all, the setting and political background indicate that, by 1895, conditions in Taiwan still tended to inhibit the development of island-wide allegiances on the part of the inhabitants. The frontier had receded to less productive areas, yet in the settled portion of Taiwan the Chinese population, for the most part, continued to live in disparate communities where strong sub-ethnic ties prevailed. Only members of the gentry and merchant classes residing in the walled cities and their environs or the larger port towns seem to have transcended such localized attachments. However, these privileged and wealthy inhabitants generally formed few alliances outside of their respective *hsien* or prefecture, and tended to become committed to regional prejudices and rivalries. This divisive tendency was also fostered by Taiwan officials who served under the bifurcated form of island government. Clearly, by 1895, an island-wide, provincial spirit had not evolved among the inhabitants, nor had an equivalent sentiment developed among most government functionaries assigned to Taiwan.

For a time during the troubled spring of 1895, the resistance movement managed to evoke a degree of island-wide sentiment akin to a provincial spirit among a number of anxious inhabitants. Chiu Feng-chia and his gentry supporters proved particularly effective in stimulating such sentiment when they urged that Taiwan self-rule be implemented since the island had been "abandoned" by the Ching court.[14] The short-lived republic also briefly aroused some expression of island patriotism. On the other hand, the general breakdown of local order, continuous setbacks suffered by the defenders, and the many hardships experienced by the general population served rather to retard the development of any widespread provincial spirit. The chaotic conditions also disrupted many alliances and ties already formed among local elements of the population. Consequently, families and communities responded in diverse ways to the resistance and takeover. Only a minority of the inhabitants actively supported the war effort. The majority remained in seclusion, while a few collaborated with the Japanese. Several thousand others managed to secure passage to the mainland, and made hasty departures from Taiwan bearing with them what wealth they could carry, as did eventually most of the Ching officials stationed on the island. Even those inhabitants who volunteered to bear arms exhibited more interest in protecting their own communities than in defending other areas or the island as a whole.[15]

Naturally, such responses adversely affected the war effort. A considerable amount of local resources and manpower could not be tapped by the leaders and organizers who staged defensive operations. Armed resistance against the Japanese was sustained through ad hoc leadership, limited recruitment of additional volunteers during the second and third phases of the war, and reliance on military units and weapons left over from the defense buildup undertaken prior to the conflict.

II
The Defense Buildup

The effort to strengthen Taiwan's defenses began during the summer of 1894 shortly before August 1, when war between China and Japan was declared. This military buildup was carried on in conjunction with war preparations in the coastal provinces, but proved longer lasting and relatively more massive in scale than other provincial defense efforts undertaken in southeastern China. The Taiwan buildup continued even after the Sino-Japanese War came to an end, terminating only a few days prior to the first Japanese landings. By then, a large standing force totaling well over two hundred battalions had been amassed on the island.[16] This sizable force amounted to more than a tenfold increase in troop strength over the eleven-month period of defensive preparation.

Such a large-scale military buildup affected defense strategy as well as local and regional politics in Taiwan. Ultimately, the deployment of additional battalions about the island influenced the manner in which armed resistance was carried on against the Japanese. This influence turned out to be especially noteworthy during the first and third phases of the war even though a number of units had been withdrawn or else temporarily retained in Taiwan on an inactive basis. Previous to the outbreak of war, the defense buildup had an appreciable effect on the resistance movement. The regional power acquired by several key leaders as a result of their expanded military roles enabled them to strengthen their control over the movement. This was evident in the case of Tang Ching-sung who emerged as the most prominent resistance leader due in part to his continuous efforts to bolster Taiwan's defenses as acting governor.

At the outset in 1894, however, Shao Yu-lien　邵　友　濂 was governor and Tang the provincial finance commissioner. Shao was known as a cautious and frugal official who had greatly curtailed Liu Ming-chuan's costly reform program and self-strengthening measures. When faced with the responsibility of undertaking a military buildup in Taiwan, Shao acted in keeping with his reputation. He endeavored to purchase old weapons at reduced prices, and requested assistance in reorganizing the island's defenses.[17] In response to his requests the Ching court, in July, ordered the Fukien admiral, Yang Chi-chen 楊 岐 珍 , and the renowned Black Flag commander, Liu Yung-fu, to proceed to Taiwan with assigned forces to assist Governor Shao in military matters. Under this arrangement Yang divided his Huai (Anhwei) troops between the northern ports of Tamshui (Hobe) and Keelung, the two ports guarding the approaches to the Taipei Basin and the provincial capital. Liu, on the other hand, was sent to Tainan to deliberate with the Taiwan intendant and brigade-general as to the deployment of his Black Flag battalions in the southern part of the island.[18] Towards the end of July, Governor Shao also attended to the matter of local security by commis-sioning Lin Wei-yuan 林 維 源 , a prominent and wealthy gentry of northern Taiwan, to direct the island's *tuan*團or militia forces.[19]

This setup did not suit the ambitious and resourceful Tang Ching-sung. Tang's influence over Taiwan's military affairs, as finance commissioner, had been overshadowed by the new appointments from the mainland, while even in matters pertaining to local enlistments he wielded less authority than Lin Wei-yuan. Accordingly, Tang arranged that he too would receive orders from the throne to assist Governor Shao in defense matters. On August 6, such an order was duly cabled from Peking, and over the next two months Tang and Shao wrangled over problems related to Taiwan's defense.[20] Finally, in October, Tang was appointed acting governor of Taiwan, and Shao was transferred to Hunan.[21]

Approval of Tang's appointment at this time hinged on the experience and reputation he had gained previously in northern Indochina prior to the Sino-French War. In 1883, he successfully urged Liu Yung-fu, then a renegade in Indochina, to cooperate with Chinese authorities and deploy his Black Flag force to forestall the French advance towards China's border.[22] As a result of this timely action, Tang won honors and the lasting admiration of the powerful regional official, Chang Chih-tung. Now Tang was made responsible for the defense of Taiwan on the basis of his alleged military ability. Nonetheless, he was instructed to deli-berate with Yang and Liu in regard to the deployment of troops and cautioned not to act without due consideration, for undoubt-edly the Peking authorities considered him rather impetuous, judging from his harsh criticism of Governor Shao.[23]

Despite these instructions, Governor Tang carried on a defense buildup at his own discretion, and failed to solicit the advice of either Yang or Liu. Admiral Yang continued to maintain his military headquarters in the Taipei examination hall nearby the governor's *yamen*. Tang, however, assumed full control over matters concerning conscription and supplies. He also proceeded to station Kwangtung forces with independent commanders in the Tamshui and Keelung vicinities. By the spring of 1895, Yang's troops were far outnumbered in both port areas, and the admiral came to exert little influence over military affairs in northern Taiwan.[24]

Tang treated his old partner in Indochina, Liu Yung-fu, as even more of a rival. The two met briefly in Taipei soon after Tang became acting governor. Liu, in his usual forthright manner, recommended that Tang attend to civil administration and leave all military matters to his own experienced hands. Such a division of authority obviously was not suitable to Tang's designs. Thereafter, Tang kept Liu and his force confined to southern Taiwan where Liu's military authority remained balanced off with that of the Taiwan brigade-general, an officer of equal rank.[25] In this manner Tang Ching-sung sought to rid himself of Liu Yung-fu and offset the charismatic appeal this hero of the Sino-French War tended to have on many insecure island inhabitants.

Lacking expert military advice, Governor Tang carried on a makeshift defense buildup in his province. He arranged for two thousand Hsiang (Hunan) braves to be sent to the Pescadores to reinforce the defense of that island group. He also requested that an expectant Fukien intendant, Yang Ju-i 楊 汝 翼 , be permitted to recruit nearly as large a Hsiang force for deployment in mid Taiwan, a region that had been neglected by Governor Shao.[26] Otherwise, Tang held the troop strength of the standing forces stationed in the regions to the south at about the same level, and attended mainly to the defenses in northern Taiwan. There he fostered a large buildup of Kwangtung units consisting mostly of raw recruits and led in part by known bandits and pirates from that coastal province. These forces he concentrated not only at Tamshui and Keelung but also in the vicinity of Hsinchu at the southern terminus of the railroad line serving Taipei and Keelung. Not content with concentrations of troops at these three points, Tang brought in more Kwangtung recruits to man small outposts scattered about in the mountainous coastal areas of the north.[27] In addition, he assigned Lin Chao-tung 林 朝 棟 , a powerful mid-island gentry leader, to defend the strategically important mountain range, called Shih-ch'iu-ling 獅 球 嶺 , which rises behind Keelung and shields the eastern approach to the Taipei Basin. Lin and his Taiwan braves had successfully withstood French attacks in that rugged terrain ten years before.[28]

By the latter part of May, Tang had enlarged Taiwan's standing defensive force to around 70,000 troops.[29] Altogether, he spread about three-fifths of these troops over the Taipei prefectural region, neglecting only Ilan, the rather isolated *hsien* south of Keelung on the east coast, and portions of Hsinchu lying to the south of the *hsien* seat at Chu-chien. Tang also kept the Taipei arsenal, powder mill and rifle repair shops operating at full capacity to provide mainly for the numerous defense units he had stationed in the north. Despite criticism and pleas from commanders to the south for more troops, funds and supplies, Tang stubbornly adhered to the plan of achieving a rapid buildup in the north where the capital was located and his authority stronger. In retrospect, Tang, as well as many contemporaries, correctly estimated that the Japanese would initially concentrate their attack in that portion of the island much as the French had done previously.

In order to protect areas not covered by regular defense units, and thus help compensate for the preponderance of troop strength in the north, Tang endeavored to form an island-wide reserve force. In November, 1894, he deputed the young Hakka scholar, Chiu Feng-chia, to recruit local "volunteer braves" (*i-yung* 義 勇) from among the inhabitants.[30] Chiu was Tang's protege and one of the few Taiwan gentry to have attained the civil *chin-shih* degree. A native of Changhua and Miaoli in mid Taiwan, Chiu traveled about all three major regions of the island in an effort to raise new battalions of volunteers. The *i-yung* battalions resembled the *tuan-lien* 團 練 units then being mobilized by Lin Wei-yuan and other influential inhabitants since these battalions consisted of enlisted men trained and led by local gentry. Such *i-yung* units were expected to be more mobile, however, and to fight in other areas besides their own locales. In this respect Chiu's reserve force operated more like the regular Hsiang and Huai units and such "local-brave" (*tu-yung* 土 勇) outfits as

the one commanded by Lin Chao-tung. Again, though, the *i-yung*
battalions were different, for this reserve force had no permanent
base of operations; the officers and enlisted men were to be
mustered in times of emergency and sent to specified areas.[31]

For several months Chiu received funds and rations from the
governor for use in building up *i-yung* units. By the end of the
year Chiu reportedly had created from fifty to sixty battalions.
During the following spring he is said to have more than doubled
the size of this force.[32] Such reports were undoubtedly exaggerated, judging from the smaller number of *i-yung* battalions known to
have been mobilized against the Japanese. Chiu nevertheless was
instrumental in organizing a ready reserve force, one that he
eventually designated by the term "*i-chun*" 義 軍 or volunteer army.[33]

There is evidence that Chiu sought to assume command over
this volunteer force and organize it on a formal island-wide basis.
Realizing that Chiu was emerging as a formidable rival, Governor
Tang withheld funds and supplies from Chiu, and apparently
prevented his erstwhile protege from regaining authority in
northern Taiwan. By March, Chiu had confined his activities to
mid-island districts where he personally led Hakka battalions in
defense preparations.[34]

With both reserve battalions and a large standing force at hand,
Governor Tang managed to provide some means of defense for
most major areas of the island. Moreover, he saw to it that
Taiwan's defense forces were more numerous and somewhat better
deployed than during the French war. Yet a number of shortcomings were evident in the defense buildup he staged. There
continued to be a shortage of modern fire-arms in Taiwan, for
example. Although many of the regular troops assigned to Taiwan
were well equipped, other units were furnished with old and
worn-out arms of little use.[35] The *i-yung* battalions suffered from
a shortage of firearms, dependent as they usually were on poorly
stocked *hsien* or local communities for equipment. Governor Tang
attempted to remedy the arms problem by arranging for weapon
purchases in Shanghai. He also requested additional arms and
supplies from various mainland authorities. Apparently, only those
in Foochow, Canton and Nanking responded, sending gunpowder,
ammunition and several thousand used rifles.[36]

Another serious shortcoming that confronted Tang was the

lack of a protective naval force. Again, he appealed to the court and
regional authorities for help, but not a single armed vessel for use
in Taiwan waters was forthcoming from China's northern and
southern fleets or the Kwangtung water force.[37] The lack of ships
to protect the insular Taiwan province became apparent when
Japan easily seized the Pescadores in four days (March 23-26).
During the course of action Governor Tang was unable to send
relief forces, and could only stand by and wait for news of the
developments as this nearby island group, so vital to Taiwan's
defense, fell to the enemy.[38]

The loss of the Pescadores was followed shortly by another
ominous development, the announcement on March 30 of a truce
agreement between China and Japan that did not extend to
Taiwan or South China. These developments caused widespread
alarm in Taiwan, and led to the belief that a Japanese invasion was
imminent. Under more tense conditions further weaknesses of
Taiwan's defense buildup became evident. One obvious problem
was the poor discipline of the newly recruited troops sent from
the mainland. The behavior of rowdy Kwangtung units and their
bandit-like leaders in northern Taiwan proved especially disturbing at this time. These raw troops annoyed the inhabitants,
lowered the morale of other military units in their respective areas,
and accounted largely for the poor showing of the defense forces
in the north during the initial phase of the war.[39]

The trouble fomented by these Kwangtung troops, in turn,
revealed Governor Tang's deficiencies as a military leader. Tang
had failed to install any unified chain of command among the
different defense units he had stationed in the north. Following the practice of his predecessor, Governor Shao, Tang uniformly commissioned those military officers having several bat-
alions at their disposal as "commanders" (t'ung-ling 統領).[40]
They were of equal rank and therefore tended to act
independently in their assigned areas. Tang's authority as governor
was further undermined by the animosity and antagonism he
incurred in his unceremonious handling of military affairs. By
April, not only were Admiral Yang and Liu Yung-fu at odds with
Tang, but influential Taiwan gentry such as Chiu Feng-chia and
Lin Wei-yuan were provoked by him as well. Thereafter, many
defense units stationed in Taiwan, including battalions of Hsiang,
Huai, Black Flag and local Taiwan braves, were gradually estranged

from Tang and his authority.

The steady deterioration of Tang's authority on the local scene reached a low point on April 22 when a bloody incident occurred within the very gates of the governor's *yamen*. This involved the departure of Tang's aged mother from the island. As the military escort and troops carrying her belongings approached the Taipei city-gate, a crowd of soldiers and commoners raised a cry that she was leaving with concealed treasure. Discord ensued and a mob pursued the military escort back to the governor's *yamen*. Li Wen-kuei 李 文 奎, a brigand from North China, took advantage of the turmoil to seek vengeance on an officer in command of the *yamen* guards. The outer gates to the governor's quarters were forced open and some forty soldiers and commoners were killed or wounded before the mob was dispersed. Li had come to Taiwan with some Huai units. He now involved a few of these troops serving under Admiral Yang in the attack on the *yamen*. Instead of punishing this notorious figure at a time of mounting disorder, Tang assigned Li and his gang to an outpost in the Keelung area. This act branded the governor as weak and cowardly in the eyes of the local troops and populace.[41] Moreover, the participation of some of Yang's soldiers in the *yamen* attack implied serious friction between the admiral and the governor.[42]

Tang reacted to this incident by relying even more heavily on Kwangtung forces, particularly those units commanded by officers from Kwangsi, his native province. Tang quickly transferred five Kwangtung battalions to the capital so as to bolster his guard units. Soon afterwards, he also shifted other Kwangtung battalions under a Kwangsi commander to the important Shih-ch'iu-ling post, and transferred Lin Chao-tung and his Taiwan braves back to Changhua. Tang might have reassigned Lin to his home area at the urgent request of the newly appointed mid-island prefect, as shown in some accounts.[43] All the same, local opinion was again aroused by a seemingly imprudent act on the part of the governor, that he had replaced seasoned Taiwan troops with raw Kwangtung recruits in a highly strategic area. Meanwhile, during the several weeks following the Li Wen-kuei affair, Governor Tang appeared virtually a prisoner within his own *yamen* amid an increasingly more turbulent environment.[44]

Despite his evident weakness and deficiencies, Tang remained indispensable to Taiwan's defense buildup. Still essentially a wartime governor, he continued personally to supervise matters pertaining to defense, and retained direct charge of the native customs impost. He also exercised full control over appointments to civil as well as military posts throughout the island. Moreover, his influence on the mainland increased as official concern over the loss of Taiwan grew following Japan's seizure of the Pescadores. Tang maintained contact with ranking provincial and regional authorities, and gained recognition among key officials at the imperial capital through the frequent memorials he cabled. At the same time, the continuous support he received from Chang Chih-tung, then the acting governor-general at Nanking and concurrently the Superintendant of Trade for the Southern Ports, served to enhance Tang's reputation among officials in South China and lend weight to the memorials he dispatched to Peking. Chang's support was especially valuable to Tang in his efforts to purchase military provisions and supplies. In Taiwan, this backing made Governor Tang seem an even more indispensable head of the island's defenses.

Fund raising continued to be most crucial to Tang's role as defense chief. Taiwan's military buildup turned out to be a costly effort; from the outset expenditures soared beyond the limited revenues committed to defense. Governor Shao had initially proposed to borrow from foreign merchants in Shanghai. But his proposal was rejected by Peking and he was instructed to make use of funds allocated by the Board of Revenue.[45] Tang had to use more ingenuity after he took over as acting governor. In December, he attempted to borrow two million taels from the Hong Kong and Shanghai Bank, but discovered that Western businessmen were reluctant to extend provincial loans without the security of imperial maritime customs duties (over which Tang had no control).[46] He then considered local fund-raising schemes, including two-year advance payments of the land tax, the issuance of paper money, and a bond subscription campaign among the local merchants. All of these schemes he abandoned during January. Even among the Taiwan inhabitants, Tang learned, substantial financial support for defense measures would only be forthcoming if certain reliable, but unattainable, forms of security were offered: pledges made on the maritime customs or warrants backed by tangible mainland assets.[47]

In desperation, Tang endeavored to negotiate with Lin

Wei-yuan, a member of Taiwan's wealthiest family. Again, evidently, Tang had little success in borrowing until he was permitted by Peking to extract a forced loan of one million silver taels from this gentry leader. After having settled the terms of this loan in March, the Board of Revenue arranged for Taiwan war materials to be supplied through the auspices of Chang Chih-tung in Nanking with the assistance of the Shanghai Intendant.[48] Under these provisions, Chang was able to juggle accounts and allocate Taiwan considerable supplies of provisions worth far more than the 400,000 taels Lin advanced as the first installment of his loan.[49]

Ironically, Tang became more successful in raising funds as his authority on the local scene declined and his ineptitude in military affairs grew more apparent. When the Pescadores came under attack, Tang received authorization to borrow three million taels from a foreign bank in Shanghai. Proceeds from this loan were to be administered in Peking by the Board of Revenue and the *Tsungli Yamen*, but allocations came to be handled by Chang Chih-tung as in the case of the previous loan.[50] Thereafter, large sums of money were more readily available to Tang. Early in May the Board of Revenue ordered Chang to prepare half a million taels for Taiwan's use.[51] Again, on May 26, the day after Taiwan was proclaimed a republic, Chang advanced another 300,000 taels at Tang's disposal.[52] Although Tang seems never to have drawn upon this sum, such a sizable allocation at this late date indicates the essential fund raising role that he continued to perform in Taiwan. Tang proved indispensable not only to Taiwan's defense buildup but also to the resistance movement and the republic that had emerged on the island. No other Taiwan official or resistance leader was able to secure such substantial support from sources on the mainland.

III
The Resistance Movement

Following the loss of the Pescadores, local defense became of more popular concern in Taiwan as anxious inhabitants sought ways and means to ward off an impending Japanese invasion. Then a greater number of influential gentry assumed the initiative in their regions, and were instrumental in fomenting a widespread spirit of resistance. In mid April, after news of the peace treaty and the terms by which Taiwan was to be ceded reached the island, this resistance sentiment was manifested in patriotic outbursts. Gentry petitions and placards appeared in protest to the terms of the treaty. Public meetings also were held, and demonstrations staged in cities and towns. Soon outstanding local figures emerged as resistance leaders, heading what amounted to an island-wide movement. Although this Taiwan resistance movement remained loosely organized, the defiant attitude assumed by the key leaders made it a potent force in support of local armed opposition against the Japanese.

Serious efforts to foment such organized resistance were made after the peace treaty was signed on April 17. Official word of that event did not reach Taiwan until two days afterwards. However, members of the gentry learned of the signing on the previous day, probably from resident western merchants. Aroused by the news that Taiwan was actually to be ceded, one group drafted a petition in protest on the same day. This petition was transmitted to Peking by Governor Tang in a subsequent memorial where it bore only the name of Chiu Feng-chia.[53]   Yet this particular petition claimed to represent "the entire Taiwan gentry and people," and undoubtedly expressed the wrought up feelings of many gentry and commoners over the cession terms of the treaty. This petition was the first of a number of Taiwan gentry protests addressed to the Ching court.

The petition stated the intent of these gentry spokesmen to resist Japan by force if need be. It also complained that the inhabitants of Taiwan had been abandoned by the Ching emperor after they had received the great benevolence and beneficence of his imperial ancestors for over two hundred years. Claiming that the inhabitants of Taiwan would rather die righteously in defense of their island homeland, these petitioners addressed a moving appeal to the throne: "Should a war be waged without success, please wait until after we subjects have died before any more talks of ceding territory. The Emperor may then face his ancestors on high as well as the common people below." Thereupon their petition closed abruptly with the prophetic remark: "If the Dwarf Chieftains come to take over Taiwan, the Taiwan people must initiate a struggle."[54]

On the following day (April 19) official word of the cession of

Taiwan finally was sent to Governor Tang in the form of a cable from the *Tsungli Yamen.* This message contained an explanation of why Taiwan was to be ceded, and announced that according to the treaty the island was to be turned over to Japan within two months' time. It also specified that the people of Taiwan would be allowed to cross over to the mainland within the two-year period stipulated in the treaty provisions if they so desired. Those remaining in Taiwan were to become Japanese subjects and would have to adjust to the new rule. This cable directed Governor Tang to issue a proclamation to make these facts public, and further enjoined him at the time of the island's transference to take extreme measures of precaution and admonish the people not to cause any incidents.[55]

This message added insult to injury in the opinion of many Taiwan inhabitants. In effect, it offered no hope or positive instructions, but merely advised them to flee or else become good subjects of Meiji Japan. Moreover, it warned them not to resist the Japanese occupation of Taiwan. To the gentry this rather callous cable was particularly disturbing. As the privileged group in local Chinese society, they expected special consideration from the emperor and court. Yet no specific instructions were forthcoming, nor was notice taken of their plight, either in this message or in any of the subsequent orders issued to the governor. The Ching ruler "did not have a single word for the gentry," complained one member when recalling this period.[56]

Thereafter, until the treaty was ratified on May 8, a number of Taiwan gentry busied themselves preparing petitions and placards. Most of their placards, as announcements displayed in public places, attempted to inspire the local inhabitants to resist the Japanese. Some also sought to arouse popular indignation by heaping blame on Li Hung-chang, who had negotiated and signed the treaty, and maligning the high officials who urged its ratification.[57] The petitions drafted by the gentry further display-ed a variety of inspired arguments and strong protests. Governor Tang, who was apparently besieged by such petitions circulated by local resistance leaders, noted in one memorial that to have submitted them all would have been inconvenient.[58]

During this period the petitions and placards produced by the Taiwan gentry formed part of the larger outpouring of written protests from all parts of China in reaction to the outcome of the war and the humiliating terms of the peace treaty. The cession provisions especially aroused the wrath of Chinese literati everywhere. One of the most significant Taiwan petitions representative of this mood originated in Peking. Dated April 28, it expressed the resentment of five of Taiwan's higher degree holders then residing at the capital.[59]

Their petition consisted mainly of a rebuttal to the *Tsungli Yamen* cable of April 19, although that communication was not directly cited. The *Tsungli Yamen* message had presented two essential reasons which, it alleged, necessitated the cession of Taiwan. First, any resistance offered in Taiwan after the signing of the treaty would place Peking in danger of a Japanese retaliatory attack. Secondly, Taiwan was a remote place overseas which could never be defended; to try to do so would only entail a waste of lives and resources. In reply, these petitioners argued that China's sea frontier, including the island of Taiwan, was also vital. The defense of the empire did not end with the capital area. Again, they described the defenses of Taiwan, and claimed that whether Japan could extend her sway over the island was highly uncertain. To prove their point, they stressed the courage and loyalty of the Taiwan people, and emphasized that these inhabitants were willing to sacrifice their lives in defense of their island rather than either surrender to the Japanese or move to the mainland (as the *Tsungli Yamen* cable had instructed). These petitioners also expressed concern for their fellow gentrymen in Taiwan. Cautioning the throne not to abandon the island's gentry-scholars, they stated: "Suddenly to give up and abandon them today is to drive the loyal and righteous literati to serve the cruel enemy."[60]

The widespread display of public indignation by the literati, as exemplified by this petition, proved rather transitory on the mainland. When the treaty was ratified and it appeared that Japan would be forced to retrocede the Liaotung Peninsula, the large outpouring of protests abated. In Taiwan the situation was different. There aroused resistance leaders continued to inveigh against a Japanese takeover and circulate petitions that grew more outspoken against the peace treaty and the instructions sent down from Peking. The defiant spirit apparent in the pronouncements of Chiu Feng-chia and his mid-island supporters reflected this resentful and increasingly desperate attitude. Since Chiu turned out to be a most active and influential resistance leader, this more defiant spirit eventually permeated the entire movement.

Chiu set out to organize a resistance effort as soon as news of the cession terms reached Taiwan. After delivering the above-mentioned petition to Governor Tang, Chiu and his group communicated with one another as well as with other gentry throughout the island to spread resistance sentiment. Over the next week or so, Chiu also staged meetings in Hsinchu and Changhua. On these occasions he circulated a pledge which lent a sense of unity and determination to the movement. Portions of this pledge were incorporated in the outspoken "petition written in blood" *(hsieh-shu ch'eng* 血 書 呈 *)*, cited by Tang in a memorial dated April 28.[61]

This petition, signed by Chiu and other island gentry, urged the authorities in Peking to take immediate steps to annul the cession terms and abrogate the treaty. It was composed in a direct and forceful style revealing the desperation of the petitioners. Chiu and his group began in a matter-of-fact way by stating that the "myriad people pledge not to submit to the cession to the 'Dwarfs'!"[62] They then sought to underscore their own frustration as loyal subjects who had been abandoned by the throne. They faced not only the prospects of resisting the Japanese, but the more immediate problem of quelling local disturbances in their home areas as well. Death seemed inevitable, their petition alleged, no matter whether they attempted to withstand the impending attack from without or the forces of anarchy from within.

Finally, these petitioners registered an urgent plea. With the possibility of Western intervention there was still a chance that the cession terms could be annulled. They urged the throne and court officials to seize this opportunity. Otherwise, they warned, if Taiwan and its inhabitants were abandoned, the dynasty stood to lose the affection of its subjects and then control over the empire. As a basis for nullifying the cession terms of the treaty, the petitioners cited several short passages from an international law reference alluding to a plebiscite arrangement for the inhabitants of a ceded territory. According to this reference, such inhabitants had to be consulted and then acquiesce to a change of rule before the territory could be transferred.[63]

The idea of a plebiscite was new to Chiu and his group. Their allusion to such an unfamiliar Western concept at this time suggests that they were in close touch with the governor. Tang had only recently learned of this international law principle from Chang Chih-tung, and apparently passed on the information to these resistance leaders.[64] The related idea of "self-rule" *(tzu-chu* 自 主), which Chiu began to espouse afterwards, may also have been proposed by Tang. The governor later mentioned this term in connection with his design to appear as a popular ruler and dominate the resistance movement.[65]

The likelihood that Chiu might gain control of the movement and supersede Tang as Taiwan's preeminent leader prompted the ambitious governor to resort to this scheme. While his own authority waned on the local scene during the latter part of April, Tang tolerated the rapid rise of his protégé as a resistance leader until Chiu again seemed a formidable rival. Chiu already commanded battalions of Hakka braves from his native area of Miaoli. Moreover, he had won acclaim as a talented poet and scholar, and was widely respected by Taiwan gentry of both Hoklo and Hakka descent. Chiu also gained renown when he was deputed to raise *i-yung* units about the island. Now, at the head of his Hakka force, Chiu was emerging as a powerful figure in mid Taiwan. He even claimed to shelter various local officials, together with their secretaries and household members, at his Miaoli estate.[66] By May, rumors stated that Chiu was being hailed as "King" in Changhua.[67] Whether true or not, these rumors further reminded Tang that Chiu could well become Taiwan's foremost resistance leader.

Under the circumstances Tang at first cooperated with Chiu and his supporters. The governor passed on news he received from the mainland and obligingly included portions of Chiu's petitions in his memorials to the throne, alleging that these appeals represented the heartfelt sentiment of the "Taiwan gentry and people." Meanwhile, Tang strove to assume the guise of a popular leader in northern Taiwan and attract a following of his own from among the inhabitants. For a time he may have succeeded. After the contents of the *Tsungli Yamen* cable were divulged, the gentry and people of the Taipei area, men and women alike, flocked to his office to grieve over their fate and solicit help, Tang reported.[68] Soon, however, he suffered considerable loss of prestige due to the Li Wen-kuei incident and his inept handling of military affairs. Nevertheless, late in April Tang claimed that wires were sent (presumably by his supporters in Taipei) to gentry members in the regions to the south urging that he be retained to head Taiwan's defenses.[69]

Such gentry support was essential to Tang in his bid for popular support. In the Taipei area he managed to secure the backing of various influential gentry, as well as merchants, who later on assisted him to become president of the republic. Tang also appears to have had some success in working with mid-island gentry representatives, particularly when he endeavored to attract foreign assistance through local channels. Thus, late in April, he was able to stage an impressive meeting between the English consul and a body of northern and mid-island gentry figures. At Tang's bidding, this representative body proposed a plan whereby England would be granted the proceeds from the native customs impost, as well as control over the island's coal and gold mines and the tea, camphor and sulphur industries, in return for British protection and assistance against the Japanese.[70]

Besides gentry and other commoner support, the resistance movement gained a following among certain turbulent elements about the island. In mid April, local gangs and malcontents among the populace, along with idle and troublesome soldiers, took advantage of the chaotic situation and imposed mob rule as a patriotic gesture. Exhibiting resentment and defiance, as did resistance leaders who may sometimes have incited mob action, these elements charged that neither government funds and revenues nor personal valuables were to be removed from the island. Instead, all such wealth was to be retained, and confiscated if need be, to help finance the resistance effort. Under this pretense mobs looted the *likin* and salt offices at Changhua, Ilan and other centers, and temporarily halted *likin* collections in Ta-tao-ch'eng 大 稻 埕 , a thriving port town serving Taipei. Threats of further attacks of this sort were made against foreign merchant establishments, especially those that held government funds on deposit.[71]

The mob rule that ensued also served to intimidate those officials and wealthy inhabitants who sought to flee to the mainland during April and May. Unless well protected, these refugees were invariably searched and their belongings seized on the pretext that they sought to carry valuables and ill-gotten gains from the island. These acts were accompanied by warnings that officials and their families were to remain and participate in the resistance against the Japanese, or else forfeit their lives.[72]

Governor Tang's mother was said to have obtained special permission to leave, yet her belongings were also searched and looted by a surly mob which flaunted all authority, including that of the governor.

Tang had to contend with this mob action connected with the resistance movement in his endeavor to emerge as a popular leader and ruler. As governor, he bade those in charge of the *likin* and salt stations to enforce collections at all costs in order to evidence stable government.[73] Otherwise, he made little effort to try and restore order. Instead, he cleverly used the threat of mob rule and violence to gain sympathy and support for Taiwan and call attention to his own precarious situation there. In this respect his memorials and reports resembled Chiu Feng-chia's petitions. Chiu launched spirited protests, however, while Tang tended to dramatize his personal role as the protector of Taiwan. Evidently, Tang expected to reap further glory and rewards as a loyal Ching servitor in another timely act suggestive of the one he had performed in Indochina against the French.

Tang was encouraged by Chang Chih-tung to continue reporting local strife and mob action in his memorials so as to evoke sympathetic responses from the court and throne. Chang also reminded Tang that such reports would serve to attract the attention of Western powers as well.[74] Chang saw to it that China's several envoys in Europe received news of Taiwan's turbulent conditions so that negotiations favorable to the island and its inhabitants might be stimulated. Meanwhile, Tang tried to solicit foreign assistance by confiding to the Western merchants and consuls at hand the dire prospects of revolt and widespread violence in Taiwan. The governor made a special effort to warn the foreign residents soon after the Li Wen-kuei incident occurred. Then Tang invited local consular representatives to a conference where he solemnly admitted his inability to control the troops and people or to protect foreign lives and property, much less his own person, should the peace treaty be ratified.[75] In this rather melodramatic manner Tang endeavored not only to enlist Western support against the cession terms, but also to intimate that Western gunboats and troops were needed to protect the foreign merchants and their investments in Taiwan. Should the foreign consuls and their governments become more involved in Taiwan's affairs, he reasoned, one or another of the Western powers would eventually be led to help defend the island against the Japanese.

Acknowledging his weak position and lack of control at this critical period late in April, Tang came to rely more on diplomacy than on force of arms as a means of resistance. Already he had tried to gain the support of England through the gentry proposal made to the English consul in Taipei. Meanwhile in his messages to Chang Chih-tung he frequently referred to a "turning point" in diplomacy that would enable China to retain Taiwan and perhaps lead to the abrogation of the peace treaty as well.

As he ventured into the field of foreign relations, Tang depended on the advice and assistance of Chang Chih-tung. In turn, he supported Chang in the latter's efforts to nullify the peace treaty and humiliate Li Hung-chang. Before the treaty was ratified, Tang and Chang had worked on different levels. Chang strove to "overthrow the entire treaty," as he put it, while Tang sought primarily to have the Taiwan provisions annulled.[76] In their mutual efforts, however, both thought it feasible to lease Taiwan or mortgage the island's resources in order to "bribe" the Western powers to intervene on China's behalf.[77] Since France and England seemed apt to be the most responsive to such proposals, Tang and Chang made concerted efforts to interest French and English officials in secret agreements involving the use of Taiwan as a pawn.

After the ratification of the treaty early in May, Tang and Chang continued their attempts to attract Western support for Taiwan. The news that France, Germany and Russia objected to the cession of the Liaotung Peninsula kept them hopeful that through negotiations a "turning point" might be reached whereby Japan would also stand to lose Taiwan. They continued to regard France and England as the most promising sources of foreign backing. By mid May, though, both began anxiously to consider other countries as well. First, they attempted to ascertain what interest either Germany or Russia might have in Taiwan. Eventually, through their constant exchange of telegrams, they also came to consider the United States as a nation that might be induced to offer Taiwan protection on the basis of a mortgage agreement. Finally, early in June after war had set in and Tang was preparing to flee the island, Chang proposed Spain as a possible protector for Taiwan.[78]

In the meantime, following the ratification of the treaty,

conditions worsened in Taiwan. Outbreaks of disorder became more frequent, while larger numbers of officials and wealthy inhabitants departed for the mainland. Consequently, Tang was forced to depend even more heavily on the possibility of Western assistance to stave off a Japanese takeover and to guard against internal upheaval. Caught up in a difficult situation, he determined to stay on and negotiate with Western representatives in the guise of a popular ruler and resistance leader. Yet Tang still had to contend with his powerful rival, Chiu Feng-chia, with whom he found it increasingly difficult to maintain an agreeable working relationship. Eventually, a confrontation between Tang and Chiu took place when Chiu and a delegation of mid-island gentry appeared with demands at the governor's *yamen* on May 16. According to Tang's account, Chiu's group urged him to become the temporary head of a separate "island-state" *(tao-kuo* 島　國), but he strongly refused to take such a step at the time.[79] In contrast, other contemporary sources disclose that this delegation was not as submissive as Tang alleged. Chiu and his followers reportedly explained their plans in detail, demanded arms and money, and after the meeting issued a declaration stating their determination to resist the Japanese.[80]

Their formal declaration consisted of a short, sixteen-character message expressing their vow to form an island-state as well as "to uphold forever the sacred Ching."[81] Obviously, Chiu and his followers in their bid for self-rule wished to stop short of appearing to rebel against Ching authority. After Chiu wired this terse declaration to Peking, his group made further use of the telegraph office located in the governor's *yamen* to dispatch a strongly worded statement to Chang Chih-tung in Nanking. This longer message reiterated their intention to establish an island-state, and declared that by popular acclaim Tang had been "retained" temporarily to oversee the affairs of Taiwan and Liu Yung-fu to defend the southern portion of the island.[82]

At this juncture Tang was not so adverse to the idea of heading a separate island-state as his refusal implied, for he aspired to exercise more autonomous rule. What bothered him was the necessity of working with Chiu under such an arrangement. The statement dispatched to Chang Chih-tung suggested that Tang was to be "detained" more like a hostage by Chiu and his group, rather than "retained" as an active leader. Tang's presence as a nominal head of state would insure the continued support of Chang, and give the impression that the resistance movement was a unified effort on the part of Tang in the north, Chiu in the mid-island region, and Liu Yung-fu in the southern part of Taiwan. On the other hand, under this arrangement Tang stood to lose much of the authority he still commanded as governor and all hope of overcoming his rival, Chiu Feng-chia, to personally dominate the movement.

Tang's predicament soon grew worse as additional pressure was brought to bear on him from Peking. The statement that Chiu and his group had wired to Nanking was circulated by Chang Chih-tung at the time that China seemed likely to recover the Liaotung Peninsula from Japan. Li Hung-chang, taking advantage of this turn of fortune, used the statement as a means to strike back at Chang Chih-tung and attack the resistance effort in Taiwan. Li named Chang and Tang as leaders of "rebellious people" on the island, and cautioned the court to avoid becoming involved in an unwarranted affair that might furnish Japan an excuse for not relinquishing the Liaotung Peninsula.[83]

The court heeded Li Hung-chang's warning and responded to the situation in Taiwan with unusual promptness. On May 18, Li Ching-fang was ordered to proceed to Taiwan and formally turn the island over to Japan in strict accordance with the terms of the peace treaty.[84] Then two days later the imperial edict, which directed Tang to order all civil and military personnel to leave Taiwan and proceed to Peking himself, was sent. Thus within only four days from the time Chiu and his group had appeared at his *yamen*, Tang found his tenure as acting governor about to end and the dreaded Japanese occupation of Taiwan soon to commence. As yet, though, Tang had not assumed the guise of a popular ruler, nor had he been able to gain full control of the resistance movement. Still determined to remain in Taipei and lead the resistance, Tang at this crucial juncture began to consider a more radical plan, that of creating an island republic which he could head.

IV
The Rise of the Republic

There has been much speculation concerning the rise of the

Taiwan Republic. At the time many foreign observers believed that Westerners must have had a direct hand in the event, so novel were republican concepts to the Chinese. In Peking, diplomats blamed rival European powers for having instigated this unheralded development in Taiwan. The English minister, for example, charged that the creation of the distant island republic was a "French plot."[85] Still other observers claimed that the Taiwan Republic had been conceived surreptitiously by Ching authorities in Peking, or that the initiative behind its rise emanated from the court and provinces.[86] Tang Ching-sung helped spread these latter notions among Westerners with whom he had contact in Taipei, for he was anxious to create a favorable impression of the republic and make the island regime over which he came to preside appear legitimate to the outside world.[87]

On the other hand, ample evidence indicates that the rise of the republic can be directly attributed to the efforts of Chinese residing in Taiwan. The idea of a republic was originally proposed by Tang or his close adviser, Chen Chi-tung 陳 季 同 . Shortly thereafter, plans for the new form of government were worked out at secretive sessions held in Taipei. Tang remained the key figure behind these arrangments which led to the establishment of the republic and his own inauguration as president. Available sources also disclose that rivalry between Tang and Chiu Feng-chia and the hope that a republican label would attract foreign support — rather than any alleged plots by the Western powers or surreptitious activities on the part of Ching authorities on the mainland — provided the main impetus behind the adoption of a republican facade for Taiwan.

Tang had confided to Chang Chih-tung the advantages that might be gained from a republican facade the day after his confrontation wtih Chiu and the mid-island delegation. Still casting about for a semblance of popular support, Tang explained: "Likely the more suitable [plan] is first to create a veneer of Taiwan self-rule; then next be chosen as ruler by the Taiwan people themselves."[88] At this point he proposed "popular rule" (min - chu 民 主) as a means to augment his own power and influence on the island. However, in this wire and his subsequent communications with Chang, Tang tended to emphasize more the positive role that a republic would play in their negotiations with Western nations. He evidently believed that Chang would not fail to render him support as the head of a singular new state if attractive enough conditions for diplomatic maneuvering seemed in the offing. In this respect Tang judged correctly. He continued to receive the backing of Chang Chih-tung even though the latter grew alarmed over Li Hung-chang's accusations and became upset whenever Tang mentioned such radical designations as "popular rule" and "president" in his messages.[89]

Tang began to espouse ideas of popular rule and a republic soon after Chen Chi-tung arrived in Taiwan around the middle of May. Quite possibly, Chen may have been the first to propose the use of these Western political concepts at a time when Tang was desperately seeking to offset the influence of Chiu and his stirring self-rule pronouncements. Chen was well acquainted with the republican form of government, for he had resided in Europe for over sixteen years, mostly in Paris where he served on the staff of the Chinese legation. He had studied law in Paris not long after his graduation from the naval school at the Foochow Arsenal.[90] Holding the title of an expectant colonel, Chen was summoned from Shanghai by Governor Tang to serve as a personal adviser due to his knowledge of European diplomacy and his French contacts.

Under the influence of Chen Chi-tung, Tang grew more aware of the fact that a republic in Taiwan could strengthen his own position and enhance his chance of gaining Western support from abroad. By May 20, the day the imperial edict ordering Tang and all government officials to quit the island was sent from Peking, he had resolved to become president of a separate island republic.[91] Tang now sought desperately to retain control over the civil government and defense forces in Taiwan, to exercise complete authority on behalf of the resistance effort without implicating the Ching court or abiding by its dictates, and at the same time to curtail Chiu's bid for power and popular support on the island.

With these motives in mind Tang set about to improve his own image as a popular leader and form a new government in Taiwan. In his pronouncements, he tried to make it appear that the entire Taiwan population had retained him in order that he might head a separate island-state. His meeting with Chiu and the mid-island delegation, according to Tang, had been merely the first outburst of such public sentiment.[92] Subsequently, sessions of a secretive nature were held in Taipei on or about May 21, and for several days thereafter. From such "councils of the Taiwan people," as

they were referred to in public, a plan to establish a republic was
devised which closely corresponded to Tang's aspirations.

The plan was divulged bit by bit to the island inhabitants in a
manner that made Tang seem to have the full confidence and
support of the people. First, on May 21, a group of local gentry
and merchants called upon Tang at the governor's *yamen* to urge
him once more to become the temporary ruler of a new island
government. Again Tang declined.[93] Then two days later an
announcement, allegedly endorsed "by the whole of Taiwan,"
declared that the people in council had determined to establish a
republican state over the entire island and raise Governor Tang to
the position of president. Tang, the announcement explained, was
to be in charge of both the resistance against the Japanese and the
organization of the new government.[94] This apparently was the
authority which he sought. On May 25, as the announcement had
specified, Tang was duly inaugurated as president amid ceremonies
marking the formal establishment of the Taiwan Republic.[95] Outwardly, at least, Tang's bid for power and popular support appears
to have been successful.

Yet this is not the full story behind the rise of the republic. Its
creation amounted almost to a separate drama which unfolded
behind the scenes at the secretive sessions held in Taipei.
Unfortunately, records of the discussions and actions taken by the
select group of founders in attendance are lacking. Evidence
indicates that these so-called "council meetings" were held at the
defense bureau *(ch'ou-fang chu* 籌　防　局 *)* instead of at the
governor's *yamen*. Among the members present, those who
apparently proved most adept at applying Western notions to the
particular needs of the time turned out to be Tang's close adviser,
Chen Chi-tung, and the strong advocate of self-rule, Chiu
Feng-chia.[96]

Contemporary accounts, as well as later works dealing with the
republic, tend to credit either Chen or Chiu as the founder. Both
versions are plausible. Chen undoubtedly was better versed in the
theory and practice of republican government due to his training
and long sojourn in Paris. Chiu, in contrast, had neither experience
in foreign affairs nor direct contact with Westerners. Nevertheless,
he displayed a keen interest in Western ways, and was regarded as
a progressive-minded scholar. Those who credit Chiu with the
founding of the republic claim that it was he who devised the new

institutions of government, including a parliament *(i-yuan* 議院 *)*.
Some even assert that Chiu wrote a draft constitution for
the republic.[97] Since records are lacking, one can only surmise that
while Chen vigorously promoted the idea of a republic, Chiu must
have advanced a version of representative government based on his
own strong predilection for self-rule in Taiwan.

This controversy over the identity of the founder of the
republic is misleading, however, for it has diverted attention from
the whole episode which led to the creation of the republic. Chen
and Chiu, after all, were only two among the select group which
gathered for the purpose of establishing a separate island-state to
carry on the resistance effort. Tang Ching-sung, the prime mover
behind the republic's rise, undoubtedly attended these sessions. A
few of Tang's *yamen* associates, some influential merchants and
gentry of the Taipei area, and other gentry from the mid-island
region are said to have also been in attendance.[98] These members
all would seem to qualify as founders, along with Chen and Chiu.
At least, we may be sure that there was a group involved, and not
just a single individual who created the republic on his own
accord.

The tendency to name one particular individual as the founder
also has obscured the fact that the republic emerged in the form
that it did as a result of the contest for leadership between Tang
and Chiu. We can infer that those present at the secretive sessions
were divided in respect to their support of the two rivals, and that
most likely Chen and Chiu expressed views representing their
respective sides. Chen seems to have had an advantage at the time,
for he was able to make a convincing argument that an island
republic, headed by Tang, would soon attract French support.

Chen had appeared on the scene at a time when Tang once
again began to consider that France might be persuaded to
intercede on behalf of Taiwan. With his diplomatic experience and
command of the French language, Chen became especially useful
to Tang in attempts to establish contact with authorities in Paris
and other French officials nearer at hand. While the series of
secretive sessions were in progress, Chen worked closely with Tang
to spread the notion that French help would be forthcoming after
an island republic had been established. On May 21, Chen paid a
visit to the commander of a visiting French warship anchored at
Tamshui, and delivered a letter from the governor. In turn, French

naval officers called at the governor's *yamen*, and allegedly urged that Taiwan be turned into an autonomous state so as to attract help from their country.[99] Following their visit, Chen circulated news that Taiwan was to declare self-rule and French protection was to be expected.[100]

Chiu Feng-chia reportedly was swayed by the hopeful tidings spread by Chen. Ultimately, Chiu came to support the republic and concede control of the new government to Tang and his advisers due to the expectation of French help.[101] Thus we may conclude that Chiu conceded the most at the secretive sessions, and conjecture that the influence exerted by Chen was the main reason why Tang was able to prevail over his powerful mid-island rival. The other founders must also have relied heavily on the ability of the suave and experienced Chen Chi-tung. The fact that Chen was appointed foreign minister of the new republic indicates the confidence which was placed in him at the time.

V

The Republic and its Vestiges

It is clear that the rise of the Taiwan Republic represented a victory for Tang Ching-sung over his chief rivals. Upon his inauguration as president, Tang placed his close associates in positions of authority, and prevented his rivals from gaining appreciable power under the new regime. Chiu was not appointed to high office as has often been claimed.[102] Meanwhile, Liu Yung-fu, who had not participated in the founding, was made commander-in-chief of the republic, a position which in effect amounted to an empty title. Liu remained stationed in the south where he continued to share military authority with the Taiwan brigade-general until early June when the republic in Taipei was on the verge of collapse.[103]

The emergence of the republic also signified a personal triumph for Tang in that it allowed him to govern Taiwan in accordance with his professed roles as a popular ruler and loyal Ching servitor. He proceeded to fashion the new republic and its government in such a manner as to make it seem he represented the will of the Taiwan people yet acted in the best interests of Ching rule.

Tang's efforts to represent himself and the Taiwan people as loyal Ching subjects led him to shy away from claims of independence and sovereignty for the new republic. He merely proclaimed that the Taiwan Republic was "self-sustaining" (tzu-li 自立).[104] To be self-sustaining and autonomous under self-rule (tzu-chu) did not mean that Taiwan was fully independent, according to Tang's use of these terms. Tang, after all, headed a resistance effort to save Taiwan for China rather than an independent movement to sever the political ties between the island and the mainland. Hence, he was careful in his public statements and official correspondence to avoid suggesting a complete break with Ching authority. In this respect Tang followed the practice of other key resistance leaders. Both Liu Yung-fu and Chiu Feng-chia exercised similar caution and professed loyalty to the Ching throne whenever they expressed support for the republic or an autonomous island-state.

Tang took further precautions to stress his own loyalty and indicate the subordinate position of the Taiwan Republic to the Ching state. He announced that the period name for his term as president would be styled "Forever Ching" (Yung Ch'ing 永清).[105] He also authorized the use of a republican flag bearing the image of a rather docile looking tiger clearly inferior to the awesome dragon that symbolized imperial rule in China.[106] Furthermore, Tang made a deliberate effort to reveal to the Ching authorities the dual nature of his presidential office. He reported that he would continue to function as the acting governor of Taiwan, and promised to use his regular titles of office in his dispatches and memorials.[107] Only in his representations to Westerners did Tang make use of his title as president. In order to carry on in such a manner, Tang devised a double set of office seals, and behaved like a "governor-president," as Hosea B. Morse once described his conduct.[108]

Tang's dual role as a "governor-president" seems farcical. Yet at the time he was playing a deadly serious game. Tang had committed a grave breach of conduct by neglecting to appear for an audience with the emperor. His continued presence in Taiwan at the head of a government set up to resist the impending Japanese takeover also meant that he was acting contrary to the cautious policy which the Ching court had adopted to avoid becoming embroiled in a possible Taiwan incident. Tang realized that he could be executed or otherwise severely punished for his actions. While carrying on in his dual role, he reiterated a vow to return and receive his due punishment whenever a suitable opportunity arose.[109] Privately, however, Tang held out hope that he could remain in power and ward off the Japanese until a "turning point" in Taiwan's favor ensued. Then, he realized, his return would be marked by honor and rewards instead of dishonor and punishment.

Tang, of course, might have attempted to establish permanent rule in Taiwan. At times he did imply that the republic, though not his own regime, would be of an enduring nature. In one communication, for example, Tang indicated that he was only a provisional president; those who were to succeed him would be "elected" to office.[110] Meanwhile, rumors circulated charging that Tang planned to become a Taiwan king or emperor.[111] These charges seem totally false. As his actions and pronouncements indicate, Tang was basically a cautious person, albeit an ambitious one. Under the prevailing tense conditions in Taiwan he did not entertain bold, long-range plans of founding a dynasty or nation-state. Rather, Tang risked clinging to power in Taipei and posing as a popular ruler only so long as it appeared possible that Taiwan in some way could be saved for China and he, in turn, would be accorded full credit for the accomplishment.

With this mission in mind, Tang set about to create a new regime over which he could exert firm control. After his inauguration as president, he formed a central government consisting of three ministries to deal with civil, military and foreign affairs. In order to assure that he would be able to exercise personal supervision over these new offices. Tang appointed three of his close aides to head each one. He also assigned the three appointees concurrent vice ministerial positions in each of the other two ministries.[112] Under this arrangement they carried on overlapping duties, and were expected to submit all matters to Tang for final approval. Tang thus governed through a highly centralized apparatus which he completely dominated.

That Tang was able to initiate such tight central authority was due in part to the power vacuum that came to exist in Taipei following the establishment of the republic. Over the next day or so the other ranking civil officials stationed in the provincial capital all departed for the mainland. These included the finance commissioner, Taipei prefect and the Tamshui magistrate. Admiral

Yang also left, accompanied by his Huai troops, while another important figure who had become critical of Tang's leadership, Lin Wei-yuan, slipped away as well.[113] Therefore, Tang had a relatively free hand to create a regime which represented control emanating from his own *yamen*. He did not have to maintain the customary balance of power on the provincial level that prevailed elsewhere in China under Ching rule, nor did he seek to initiate popular rule representing the will of the governed.

The republic in Taipei, nevertheless, did feature one representative body — a parliament. Since no records of this body nor copies of any constitutional provisions appear to exist, little is known about this parliamentary body. Apparently, the short-lived Taipei parliament was convened at least once.[114] Moreover, the members reportedly received daily pay when in session. Lin Wei-yuan had originally been named to head this body. He declined to accept this position, and is said to have refused to support the republic prior to his abrupt departure.[115] Yet Lin is mentioned as the presiding officer in most accounts. Since only one officer has been identified, even by contemporary writers, it may be conjectured that the Taipei parliament was a unicameral body, despite claims that it was organized as a bicameral type.[116] Undoubtedly, this parliament was devised to serve as the center of gentry and merchant influence in the new republic. Besides Lin, a number of other Taipei inhabitants of eminence and wealth are know to have been named as members.[117] These prominent local figures were selected in a manner Chen Chi-tung once described as "representation without election." Such a method enabled the "learned and literary" to become the "natural advocates of the people," Chen believed,[118] as did probably the gentry members of the Taipei parliament.

This parliament, the presidency and the three ministries constituted the only new institutions of government created for the republic. Government on the prefectural and low levels remained the same as under Ching rule, and those who held civil and military posts on the island continued to use the old titles and seals of office.[119] However, the office holders about the island changed, as in the case of Taipei. Even before the advent of the republic, Governor Tang had made a number of temporary appointments to vacancies left by departing officials. This exodus of Ching functionaries continued after he became president, and allowed Tang further leeway in extending his influence through his power of appointment. Altogether, Tang appointed all but five of the twenty ranking civil authorities holding office in Taiwan at the outset of the war of resistance.[120]

Since the republic lasted in Taipei for only twelve days, it is difficult to assess the effect Tang and his regime had on the situation in Taiwan. Westerners noted that more orderly conditions prevailed in the north for a few days after the rise of the republic. Yet they also reported that even in the Taipei area most people seemed apathetic and the soldiers indicated little desire to fight.[121] On the other hand, judging from the gentry and merchant participants in the inaugural ceremonies, a number of the local elite representing various Chuanchou communities in the nearby port towns at least outwardly professed allegiance to Tang and the new government. Such overt manifestations of devotion were most evident among certain Mengchia 艋 舺 gentry and merchants.[122] Tang, meanwhile, carried on much as before. He remained confined to the governor's *yamen*, which now also served as the presidential office, and continued to depend on Kwangtung forces for his own protection and for the defense of northern Taiwan. Tang was inspired to send one of his aides to Peking as a representative of the Taiwan Republic.[123] Otherwise, he relied on telegraphed messages and personal contacts with Westerners to carry on his quest for outside support.

During his short term at the head of the republic, Tang does not seem to have devised any new policies of government. His few pronouncements, suggesting what might have been long-range policies, were based on familiar self-strengthening precedents set by Liu Ming-chuan under whom he had served. Tang, for instance, alluded to railroads, ships and mines as a means to increase Taiwan's power and standing under the republic.[124] Previously, Tang also had hopefully explained to Chang Chih-tung that under an autonomous arrangement in which they could negotiate directly with Western nations, opportunities to strengthen Taiwan would arise. Funds could be borrowed, mines opened, shipping established and arms purchased.[125] Then, however, as later on during his tenure as "governor-president," Tang appeared more preoccupied in making Taiwan an attractive pawn to the Western powers than in enriching the island for the sake of the people. In all, Tang proved neither a revolutionary nor even a radical reformer in his guise as a popular ruler, while the republic turned out to be a transitory device for one-man rule, quite as he had intended.

The Taiwan Republic collapsed in Taipei with the sudden departure of Tang and his aides, along with the outbreak of uncontrolled looting that followed. However, vestiges of the republic soon emerged in Tainan after Liu Yung-fu assumed control of the resistance effort in southern Taiwan. These vestiges are important to note, for they disclose more about the nature of the republic, as well as indicate how the notion of popular rule was used by still another resistance leader to maintain himself in power.

Unstable conditions in southern Taiwan led to Liu Yung-fu's assumption of power there. Late in 1894, Liu and the Taiwan brigade-general had worked out an agreement for the deployment of their respective forces. Concentrating mainly on coastal defense, the brigade-general kept his troops in the strategic area between Anping and Chihou (Kaohsiung), while Liu assigned his battalions to coastal areas in Fengshan and Hengchun *hsien* to the south of Chihou.[126] In March when the Pescadores came under Japanese attack, Liu was ordered to redeploy most of his Black Flag force to the vital Chihou and Fengshan area.[127] Liu and his forces remained in that area until early in June when the republic collapsed and Tang fled to the mainland. Then apparently acting on his own initiative, rather then following the last-minute instructions allegedly sent by Tang, Liu shifted his troops to the strategic coastal positions extending from Chihou north to Anping previously allotted to the brigade-general. [128]

At this time a power vacuum was created in Tainan, the old capital, as had happened in Taipei with the advent of the republic. During the month of June the ranking officials stationed there — the intendant, brigade-general, Tainan prefect and Anping magistrate — all crossed over to the mainland.[129] The inhabitants grew alarmed, and local gentry representatives prevailed upon Liu Yung-fu to re-establish his headquarters in Tainan. These anxious gentry also urged Liu to head another resistance government as a "popular ruler." Subsequently, they encouraged him to succeed Tang as president of the republic, and offered him a silver seal of office similar to the one presented to Tang in the north.[130]

Evidently, Liu was impressed by such public acclaim, though not by the offer to become president. He moved to Tainan city and established his headquarters at the vacated office of the brigade-general. Soon thereafter he came into possession of the intendant's seal of office.[131] By these actions he not only gained recognition as the supreme military commander in Taiwan (a position he nominally held already as commander-in-chief of the republic), but by default also became the chief civil authority. Liu then took advantage of his reputation as a military hero and the vacant offices at hand to set up an ad hoc government in Tainan.

Thereafter, Liu paid lip service to the idea of popular rule, and arranged that prominent gentry and wealthy merchants of the Tainan vicinity be selected for membership in a parliament. Unlike the one created in Taipei, this Tainan parliament, or at least a standing committee of its members, met regularly and acted upon matters pertaining to the resistance effort and the security of their community.[132] In August, this body approved the use of postage stamps and paper currency in the form of government notes to relieve the critical fiscal and monetary problems that continually plagued Liu and the population in general. The paper notes bore the name "Taiwan Republic" (T'ai-wan min-chu-kuo 台 灣 民 主 國), while the stamps featured an imprint of the tiger emblem as well.[133] Both serve as reminders that the republic played a role in the Tainan resistance effort.

Yet Tainan's version of the republic remained but a vestige of the original, for it lacked a formal head of state and central administrative apparatus. Liu on three separate occasions bluntly refused to become president after delegations of local spokesmen appeared before him and urged that he accept the seal of that office.[134] Unlike Tang Ching-sung in the north, Liu saw no need to inaugurate a formal state government and install himself as president. He did not have any immediate rivals to contest his power and leadership in Tainan. Neither did he seek to attract Western help by posing as a ruler of a separate state, although he too held out hope that one or another of the powers might bring about a "turning point" and relieve his desperate situation in Tainan. In his pronouncements Liu consistently stated that his sole function in Taiwan was to command the defense against Japanese attack, as he had originally been ordered to do by imperial decree.[135] To indicate his loyalty to Ching rule, he used only his regular military title. He also preferred to be addressed as "Ch'in Shuai" 欽   帥 (literally, Imperial Commissioned Commander), a title befitting a trusted Ch'ing servitor.[136] Due to these considerations, Liu felt under no obligation to succeed Tang as president. Instead, he chose to impose his authority in Tainan along lines suggesting a makeshift military dictatorship.

Liu's dictatorial rule was evidenced in the manner he handled the Tainan parliament. Liu depended on the parliament to provide for the resistance effort. Gentry and merchant members of that body subsidized the bulk of Liu's military expenditures. Moreover, they passed upon other measures, such as appointments to official posts in Tainan and the *hsien* seats of government within the southern prefecture. Nevertheless, the Tainan parliament hardly suggested a representative form of government, for Liu exacted heavy contributions and services from the members almost as if they were directly under his military command. Under Liu's coercive rule this parliament reportedly proved ineffective as a legislative body while its members grew corrupt.[137]

Liu based his dictatorial rule on a blood-pledge he administered to representatives of the local gentry and *tuan-lien* units soon after he had established himself in Tainan. Under oath, Liu and those in attendance swore to be "comrades" *(t'ung-jen* 同 人 *)* and cooperate with one another on behalf of the resistance against the Japanese. More specifically, Liu had his audience promise to share their wealth and property for the war effort. Through this blood-pledge those in attendance, as well as the inhabitants and *tuan-lien* units they represented, became bound, as it were, by a solemn convenant to support whatever measures Liu authorized. Liu, on his part, pledged to carry on the resistance and share the dangers and personal sacrifices that war entailed.[138]

The contents of this blood-pledge reveal Liu's position in regard to the Taiwan Republic. In May, when the republic was proclaimed in Taipei, he had indicated his staunch support.[139] Now Liu declared that the republic was to be preserved by the people themselves as part of the resistance effort. Taiwan had been transformed from a province into a state, and the people had become self-ruled, he claimed. This development Liu considered legitimate. Even though the status of Taiwan as a republic appeared outwardly to defy the emperor's instructions, he explained, covertly the situation remained in accordance with the imperial intent.[140] Liu thus sought to uphold the Taiwan Republic and appeal to the spirit of resistance it epitomized, even though he neglected to resurrect the republic in its complete form.

Ultimately, Liu and his Black Flag forces were unable to hold out against the Japanese. On October 18, when a concerted attack was about to be launched on Tainan city, Liu secretly crossed over to the mainland, much as Tang Ching-sung had done some four months previously.[141]   Liu, however, had helped to prolong the war and, unlike Tang, remained a popular figure to most Chinese even after he fled the island. Nevertheless, the severe measures and harsh discipline Liu imposed in southern Taiwan tarnished his image as a ruler. Under his sway the reputation of the Taiwan Republic also suffered further decline, at least in the Tainan area, for Liu used republican vestiges to keep the local inhabitants submissive to his wartime leadership.[142]   To Liu, with his background as a bandit leader and soldier of fortune, popular rule was tantamount to personal command on his part, while republican usages meant only a semblance of representation by the people. He had assembled local representatives who made solemn vows to assume wartime duties and obligations. Thereafter, the most striking republican vestige, the Tainan parliament, amounted to an assembly where local delegates were expected to fulfill these vows as Liu desired. Constantly beset by shortages and other pressing problems, this body lost even the image of select representation by the "learned and literary" as Liu forced its standing committee to comply with his demands arising from the grim realities of war.

VI
The Nature of the War

Judging from more reliable accounts, the Taiwan war of resistance was indeed a grim affair. This five-month conflict featured the usual hardships and suffering of warfare, yet yielded little glory for either side. The number of combatants involved became quite large considering the relatively narrow coastal and hill areas where the action mainly took place. The Japanese occupation forces consisted of two and a half divisions totaling about 50,000 troops. These forces were accompanied by some 26,000 coolies from Japan, and were supported at times by Japanese naval units.[143] The local defense forces that saw action during various phases of the war totaled well over one hundred thousand. These Chinese units included Hsiang and Huai battalions, troops from Fukien, Black Flag and volunteer units from Kwangtung, and a diverse assortment of local Hoklo and Hakka forces.[144]

Altogether, the casualty count of the war was fairly high. The Japanese may have lost as many as 7,000 troops, largely through disease. The losses incurred by the defenders due to battle casualties and epidemics undoubtedly were much greater. Even though few large-scale battles were fought, fatalities from sickness and infections contracted during the war made the casualty figures soar on both sides.[145]

The scene in Taiwan was made even more grim due to the untold number of noncombatants who suffered during the war and for long periods thereafter. Epidemics of cholera and typhus raged in war-torn localities as well as among the fighting forces of both sides. Moreover, Japanese officials and coolies, who accompanied the occupation troops to Taiwan, also were affected by endemic diseases such as malaria. Then as the war extended into the autumn months, Chinese inhabitants of the mid-island and southern regions experienced floods as well as prolonged famine in some areas, resulting in numerous casualties among the local population. Meanwhile, other inhabitants were wounded and killed when fighting took place in densely populated urban areas, as during the bloody battles for the walled cities of Changhua and Chia-i. Rural dwellers also experienced grief when Japanese units attacked and sometimes razed whole villages in order to disperse local resistance forces in the line of march or quell partisan bands operating in rear areas already under military occupation.[146]

Even before war broke out in Taiwan, the local population had begun to suffer from increased banditry and local strife. As internal disorder spread, the inhabitants experienced further hardships and uncertainties. Chinese in some localities became fearful of attacks by dreaded indigenous tribesmen dwelling in nearby mountainous areas. Hoklo inhabitants also grew alarmed over weapons and training being received by their habitual foes, the local Hakkas. In addition, as mentioned above, the Hoklos and Hakkas both came to resent the presence of troublesome mainland troops scattered about the island. The long expected arrival of Japanese forces merely compounded the panic and turmoil in

Taiwan for many inhabitants, while the Japanese, in turn, were troubled by bandit groups and local disturbances in areas they occupied, as were the resistance forces in the unoccupied portions of the island.

It was against this dismal background that the chief resistance leaders in each of Taiwan's three prefectural regions attemped to carry on the war. Although in their stirring pronouncements they continually alluded to the aroused inhabitants and local fighting spirit, their intent was usually to impress the authorities on the mainland or to incite the populace to action. In reality, the grim wartime conditions, along with the diverse background and localized outlook of the inhabitants and other unfavorable circumstances, made armed resistance against the Japanese difficult to sustain. Not surprising, after each region was overrun by the occupation forces or the key administrative center came under attack, some resistance leaders became disillusioned and fled to the mainland.

Tang Ching-sung set an example early in June as Japanese forces began to advance from Keelung towards Taipei. Tang at the time refused to leave his *yamen* to lead a counterattack. Neither could he be persuaded to move southward to Hsinchu. Instead, Tang, together with his ministers and close advisers, secretly fled to Tamshui where they secured ship passages to the mainland. [147] Tang's departure and the rapid takeover of northern Taiwan discouraged other leaders in the south. Lin Chao-tung and the Fukien authority, Yang Ju-i, both decided to quit the island rather than proceed north with their forces to rescue Taipei, as Tang had ordered.[148] Chiu Feng-chia also abandoned his forces and fled to the mainland soon afterwards.

The departure of these important mid-island leaders left the prefect at Changhua, Li Ching-sung 黎 景 嵩 , in full charge of the resistance effort in areas to the south of Hsin-chu. Li, an expectant prefect, was appointed to the office by Tang and authorized to deal with military as well as civil affairs in mid Taiwan as Lin and Yang were ordered north.[149] Li evidently was an ambitious official who strove to increase his authority in the mid-island region. He assumed the role of a popular leader by seeking gentry support, and endeavored to rival rather than to cooperate with Liu Yung-fu in Tainan.[150] As Japanese units began to move southward from Taipei late in June, Li Ching-sung strove hard to rally the inhabitants and troops in his prefecture. Moreover, he organized a separate Hsin Chu Army *(Hsin Ch'u chun* 新 楚 軍 *)* composed of various defensive units, including Hoklo, Hsiang and Hakka battalions that had previously been under the command of Lin, Yang and Chiu, respectively. Prefect Li succeeded in organizing sustained resistance against the Japanese until Changhua fell late in August. He then withdrew from that administrative center and made his way back to the mainland.[151]

In the end Liu Yung-fu turned out to be Taiwan's foremost resistance leader. Not only did he hold out the longest, but his mere presence on the island helped to prolong the war. This was because Liu and his Black Flag battalions had become so celebrated as dauntless warriors that the Japanese hesitated to attack Tainan before gradually amassing a considerable striking force in that area.[152] Liu, like Tang Ching-sung, did not live up to the military reputation he had gained against the French in Indochina. Liu was older and less vigorous, while his Black Flag troops contained many raw recruits as well as a number of veterans well past their prime. Nevertheless, until near the end of the war he maintained effective control over his troops and the other units he commanded in southern Taiwan by means of strong discipline and close surveillance over the coastal defenses.

None of these chief resistance leaders emerged as heroes from the Taiwan war. They did not directly engage the enemy in battle, nor did they linger on the island and attempt to recover lost territory. The defenders who gained glory for their heroic exploits were more often the commanding officers who died in action. These martyrs, or at least the ones best remembered, were secondary figures in the resistance effort who generally had served one or another of the chief leaders. Some were scholars from the mainland, but most were local gentry. Wu Peng-nien 吳 彭 年 , a trusted aide of Liu Yung-fu from Chekiang province, was possibly the most celebrated Chinese war hero. In the latter part of July, Wu had led two Black Flag battalions north to the mid-island region to help bolster the Hsin Chu Army. In spite of Prefect Li's jealous actions, Wu proved an outstanding military leader, and was appointed the Hsin Chu commander shortly before he was killed in the battle for Pa-kua Mountain, the stronghold guarding the northern approaches to Chunghua city.[153]

Another renowned martyr was Wu Tang-hsing 吳 湯 興 ,

a Hakka leader from Miaoli. This gentry figure, who had been a close confidant of Chiu Feng-chia, also met his end during the fateful Pa-kua Mountain battle late in August.[154] Several other young Hakka gentry, previously enlisted in Chiu's *i-chun* force, proved valiant *i-yung* commanders before suffering death at the hands of the Japanese. These included Chiang Shao-tsu 姜紹祖, a Hsinchu scholar adept at guerrilla warfare in his native area, and Hsu Hsiang 徐驤, of Miaoli, who saw action during almost the entire second and third phases of the war prior to his untimely death in mid October when defending the northern reaches of Tainan.[155] Some local efforts also produced martyrs during the course of the war. The gentry figure Lin Kun-kang 林崑岡 and his son, for example, were honored as local heroes when they died the same day as Hsu Hsiang at the head of villagers they had assembled to defend their Chia-i community.[156]

All these martyrs proved exceptional in their bravery and fighting zeal. Their numbers, however, were few in relation to the total defensive force or the Taiwan population at large. Their actions seemed so extraordinary, in fact, that one contemporary Taiwan scholar was led to wonder what had impelled these heroes to fight to the death they way they did.[157]

Since heroes among the defenders of Taiwan proved relatively few, as did the number of capable commanders, the sustained effort at armed resistance which occurred on the island depended on factors other than sheer courage or military aptitude. In the long run, it was primarily the leadership and support forthcoming from the island's three key administrative centers that sustained the continuous war effort. At each center, the chief resistance leader managed to exert decisive influence over the major defensive operations in that region. In doing so, these leaders wielded supreme civil and military authority over organized efforts on the part of their aides and the gentry managers employed at the administrative centers and the *hsien* magistrates and reliable commanders stationed within the prefectural boundaries. Thus, despite the difficulties they encountered and their decisions to flee rather than personally encounter the enemy, Tang Ching-sung in Taipei, Li Ching-sung in Changhua, and Liu Yung-fu in Tainan all attempted to carry on armed resistance in their respective regions to the extent that the limited resources and available manpower permitted.

The responsibility of supplying arms, provisions and funds to their armed forces remained a vital task for these chief leaders and their subordinates at each center during the war. Since Taipei contained the provincial treasury, as well as the arsenal and powder mill, the units stationed in northern Taiwan tended to be better equipped and provisioned at the outset. In Changhua and Tainan, the local gentry who managed the finances and supplies for the war effort had a more difficult task. The treasuries located in these two prefectural centers were soon depleted of funds. Accounts indicate that the gentry managers relied heavily on salt, *likin* and native custom imposts when possible.[158] They also had to devise more extraordinary ways to gain revenue and provisions. The Changhua managers, for instance, sometimes confiscated the properties of wealthy families that had crossed over to the mainland. In Tainan, the managers also confiscated property and resorted to other devices such as selling lottery tickets.[159] Meanwhile, the gentry and merchant delegates to the Tainan parliament supported the issuance of postage stamps and paper currency, partly as a means to offset the harsh commandeering methods employed by Liu and his aides to collect funds and supplies.

As the leaders, along with their aides and managers, undertook to carry on resistance efforts in their respective regions, they established separate wartime agencies at each center. Li Ching-sung and Liu Yung-fu set up defense bureaus *(ch'ou-fang chu)* near their headquarters in Changhua and Tainan. Both modeled their bureaus after the Taipei office, bearing the same name, that had existed under Tang Ching-sung.[160] Each bureau functioned as a vital procurement and supply center, and operated under local gentry management.

These defense bureaus also served as meeting places where the leaders and their aides consulted with prominent gentry and wealthy merchants of the area. Important matters pertaining to the resistance effort were resolved at such gatherings. The secretive sessions which led to the formation of the Taiwan Republic in late May were held at the Taipei *ch'ou-fang chu.* Again, Prefect Li conferred with the gentry managers of the Changhua bureau and discussed ways and means of raising funds and provisioning troops in that region.[161]

In Tainan, a commissariat *(liang-t'ai* 糧 台 *)* had been

created to operate in conjuntion with that center's defense bureau. Its main function was to distribute rations and funds to the military units under Liu's command. The commissariat was headed by the same wealthy Tainan figure who later on was placed in charge of the defense bureau.[162] On the whole, these two agencies seem to have played a somewhat less significant role as places of contact between Liu Yung-fu and the southern gentry and merchants, for Liu and his aides maintained close ties with local delegates of the Tainan parliament. Nevertheless, Liu undoubtedly consulted with the defense bureau managers as well. At least the prominent gentry figure who at first presided over that bureau could hardly have been ignored, so active was he in local defense matters.[163]

Other bureaus, similarly managed by island gentry and headquartered in each of Taiwan's three key centers, also helped support regional resistance efforts both before and during the war. Two such types were the *pao-chia* 保 甲 and *tuan-lien* bureaus. Unlike the defense offices, these bureaus had functioned intermittently on the island over the previous decades when need arose for organized local control and defense.

In 1894, *tuan-lien* bureaus had been reactivated after Lin Wei-yuan was commissioned to direct Taiwan's *tuan* defense units. At first this action was undertaken in conjunction with the island-wide defense buildup in preparation for a possible Japanese attack. Accordingly, some effort was made to organize *yu-tuan* 漁 團 units composed of coastal fishermen and their craft, along with the regular *tuan-lien* militia force.[164] However, when conditions grew chaotic in Taiwan during the spring of 1895, local authorities paid more attention to providing protection from internal strife. Then *tuan-lien* bureaus and branches proliferated about the island as wealthy gentry set about organizing and financing local battalions of "drilled braves" *(lien-yung* 練 勇*)* to safeguard their communities, or in some cases merely their own properties. Although Lin was supposed to have directed the *tuan* defense, no effective overall chain of command was devised to weld the *tuan-lien* bureaus and battalions throughout Taiwan into an integrated local defense system.

Eventually, the *tuan-lien* bureaus in the mid-island and southern regions did contribute something to the resistance effort in their respective areas.

In Chang-hua the operations of the *tuan-lien* and *pao-chia* bureaus were merged. Thereafter, local gentry more responsive to the dictates of the regional bureau managers were assigned to *tuan* battalions in their respective localities. As a result, the revamped bureau in Changhua soon had better organized and more mobile units at its disposal to offer protection against banditry in the mid-island region. Like other *tuan* units about the island, such forces were not used against the Japanese. Yet they enabled the government's administrative and vital wartime activities to proceed in a more orderly manner.[165] Elsewhere, the Tainan *tuan-lien* bureau molded the battalions of local troops in and around the city into an effective protective force. These units proved able to quell insurgent elements in the surrounding countryside as well as maintain order in Tainan city.[166]

In the spring of 1895, *pao-chia* offices were established or reactivated in Taiwan in an even more disjointed manner than were the *tuan-lien* bureaus and branches. Most of these offices commenced to function when the authorities became alarmed over the increase of banditry and disorder. Then *pao-chia* bureaus or units mushroomed in *hsien* seats and market towns about the island. Villages also cooperated to form "united village offices" *(lien-chuang chu* 聯　庄　局) comparable to *pao-chia* bureaus.[167] Early in April, efforts were made by the mid-island prefect to establish a *pao-chia* headquarters in Changhua. This office was named the "united *chia* bureau" *(lien-chia chu* 聯　甲　局). At first, it attempted to set up a system of mutual protection in the city of Changhua and its environs, bolstered by a small standing force of trained militia. Several months later, when this office was merged with the regional *tuan-lien* bureau, its protective services were augmented and extended over a much wider area.[168]

In September, several aides of Liu Yung-fu proposed a further use for a similar type of *pao-chia* network. They advocated that the local "braves" throughout the island be enrolled in a united village *pao-chia* system with headquarters in Tainan. According to their reasoning, a large resistance force stretching from Tainan all the way north to Taipei would thus be formed to combat the Japanese in the south as well as elsewhere in the occupied areas of Taiwan. Liu Yung-fu endorsed this plan but was never able to put it into effect.[169]

That Liu and his aides proposed to direct such an extensive *pao-chia* network from their headquarters in Tainan indicates their continued concern about developments elsewhere on the island. All three chief leaders, in fact, thought in terms of an inclusive resistance effort embracing the whole of Taiwan. Moreover, during various stages of the war they each engaged in activities which transcended their respective regions. Tang Ching-sung, as "governor-president", issued orders to various commanders and officials throughout Taiwan even though his actual wartime power was limited to the Taipei area. Later on, after the loss of Taipei, both Li Ching-sung and Liu Yung-fu extended the scope of their operations farther to the north beyond their own regions in attempts to curb the Japanese advance southward and retake occupied territory. Prefect Li launched a series of counterattacks in rescue of the beleaguered city of Hsinchu in July. Liu, meanwhile, sent Wu Peng-nien to lead Black Flag reinforcements to the mid-island region. Thereafter, Liu dispatched other bodies of troops, as well as funds, to the Changhua, Yunlin and Chia-i areas north of Tainan.

In their capacity as Taiwan's ranking wartime authorities, Li and Liu also saw fit to request aid from provincial and regional officials on the mainland. Both leaders sent urgent telegrams and ordered trusted aides to cross over and personally contact key functionaries. Following Tang's example, they seem to have counted most on support from Chang Chih-tung, but received only negative replies to their pleas.[170]

Gentry managers of Taiwan's wartime bureaus sometimes also engaged in inter-regional activities within unoccupied areas of the island. In mid July, for example, the anxious managers of the Changhua defense bureau petitioned Liu Yung-fu to send troops to their area. A month later, managers of that center's united *chia* bureau requested relief rations from the Tainan *pao-chia* bureau. In both instances, the pleas of these Changhua gentry were heeded, and troops as well as supplies were duly sent north from Tainan.[171]

Besides the resistance efforts emanating from the three regional centers, other defensive activities of an intra-regional nature were carried on among or entirely within various *hsien*. Some *hsien* seats developed into minor wartime centers. There acting magistrates supported military operations staged within their areas as best they could. The Miaoli magistrate supplied local units in his *hsien*, as did the magistrates of Changhua and Yunlin during the second stage of the war. In the south, the magistrates of Anping and Fengshan *hsien* seem to have been active in support of southern coastal defenses for a time after Liu Yung-fu assumed power in Tainan. The *hsien* seat of Chia-i proved a more active center of local defense preparations due in part to its remoteness in location, as it is about midway between the Changhua and Tainan prefectural centers.[172]

These centers and *hsien* seats, however, were not able to exercise full control over the war efforts in their particular regions and areas. The resistance leaders and other authorities operated under adverse conditions which severely hampered their activities. Poor transporation facilities, a lack of funds and provisions, the prevailing banditry, and varying responses to the war and occupation on the part of the local inhabitants proved to be among the chief impediments. Again, not all the numerous defensive units which offered opposition to the Japanese at one time or another during the war were supported or recognized by the resistance leaders and authorities. Many irregular forces were entirely dependent on the backing of particular rural districts, towns, villages, or even powerful lineages and families.

Yet, on the whole, the three regional centers, rather than the *hsien* seats or separate localities, played the major roles in waging organized resistance against the Japanese. Without the efforts of the chief resistance leaders, their aides, and the gentry managers at these key administrative centers, it is doubtful whether more than sporadic actions by local armed bodies in the more densely settled areas of Taiwan would have been forthcoming during the 1895 takeover.

VII
High Lights of the War

High lights of the war in each of its three phases reveal more clearly the vital roles of these regional centers as well as the composition of the active resistance forces. The war commenced on May 29, when units of Japan's Imperial Guard division landed at the secluded area of Ao-ti, some twenty miles southeast of

Keelung. This landing force encountered only light resistance, and by June 3 was able to occupy the port town of Keelung. The defense units assigned to guard Keelung and the strategic mountainous terrain to the west consisted mainly of ill-trained Kwangtung troops. Their meager resistance proved futile, and four days later a small Japanese force, guided by an inhabitant and several foreign residents of the Taipei area, was able to enter and gain control of the capital. During this period Tang's aides had been unable to restore order among the defenders in Keelung and the Taipei area. By the time Tamshui harbor fell to the Japanese on June 9, resistance in the north had collapsed. The chaos that resulted in Taipei city and its environs before the occupation forces arrived reveals the faulty military leadership and the ill-organized systems of defense and security that prevailed in northern Taiwan during this brief first phase of the war.[173]

The loss of northern Taiwan amounted to a severe setback for the resistance effort. The best-equipped defense units in Taiwan, including most of the Chinese mainland troops, surrendered with the fall of Keelung, Taipei and Tamshui. The bulk of government funds on hand also was lost to the war effort when the provincial treasury in Taipei was looted by a frenzied mob. In addition, the island's only arsenal and powder mill were destroyed by vandals. Consequently, the resistance leaders and defense forces to the south were left to their own devices in amassing troops, funds and supplies to continue the war.

In contrast, the Japanese were delighted with their quick and easy takeover of northern Taiwan. Confident that organized resistance would soon subside throughout the island once the capital had been taken, Governor-General Kabayama Sukenori inaugurated his new government in Taipei (Taihoku) amid festivities on June 17.[174] Immediate preparations were then made to occupy areas to the south. Two days later, Imperial Guard units marched from the capital and in three days took their first objective, the *hsien* seat of Hsinchu.[175] Meanwhile, on the east coast an auxiliary force composed of Osaka Fourth Division reserves staged landings in the Ilan area on June 21, and in only two days had peacefully entered the main towns of Lotung and Ilan in that isolated *hsien*.[176]

Before long, however, the Japanese military authorities grew concerned that the occupation of Taiwan might prove longer

lasting and more costly than anticipated. There had been a delay
in the arrival of war equipment that would have permitted a major
landing in the Tainan vicinity early in June. Already the
monsoon season was at hand, a factor which made operations in
the Taiwan Strait extremely hazardous during the summer
months. Hence, the Imperial Guards were ordered to proceed
orverland along the western coast towards their main objective,
Tainan city.[177] Soon after the Imperial Guard forces set out from
the Taipei vicinity, a more spirited type of resistance was
encountered. Along the routes to the south their rear supply
columns came under the attack of local guerrilla bands. Then,
when the *hsien* seat of Hsinchu was taken, the troops occupying
that city were bottled up by newly formed resistance forces.
Subsequently, the Japanese advance southward was stalled for
over a month and a half in the Hsinchu area.

The resistance forces that entered the war at the start of its
second phase differed markedly from the Kwangtung units which
had offered only token resistance in northern Taiwan. Most
consisted of local mid-island units under Taiwan gentry commanders. Some were seasoned Hoklo "local-brave" units that had
served under Lin Chao-tung and remained in the Hsinchu area
after Lin's departure. Others were Hakka *i-yung* battalions which
had once formed a part of Chiu Feng-chia's *i-chun* force. These
Hakka battalions hailed from the southern Hsinchu and Miaoli
areas, and proved most effective in carrying on guerrilla warfare
under inspired leaders like Chiang Sho-tsu and Hsu Hsiang. Still
other battalions of Hoklo and Hakka "volunteer braves" were
recruited by the magistrates of mid-island *hsien* extending from
Miaoli south to Yunlin. Besides these local units, the thousand or
so mainland Hsiang troops abandoned in mid Taiwan by Yang Ju-i
were reassembled for action.[178]

Late in June, Li Ching-sung succeeded in forming these various
units into a more tight-knit force, the Hsin Chu Army. To
accomplish this rapid military buildup, he placed veteran Hsiang
officers in positions of top command. They, in turn, reorganized
this force in accordance with the old regulations of the Hsiang and
Chu 楚 mainland regional armies that had been created during
the Taiping Rebellion. Altogether, the Hsin Chu Army came to
comprise some fourteen battalions and number over 7,000 braves,
exclusive of the Hsiang troops.[179] In order to secure initial

support for this sizeable force, Prefect Li called a meeting of local gentry and wealthy inhabitants of the four mid-island *hsien* under his jurisdiction.[180]

With this army, Li attempted to drive the Japanese from the Hsinchu vicinity. Without consulting Liu Yung-fu or heeding the cautious advice of the Changhua gentry managers, he rashly ordered a series of counterattacks against the besieged *hsien* seat between July 9 and 24. These desperate attacks proved futile and only served to weaken the Hsin Chu Army and deplete the meagre funds and supplies in the mid-island prefecture, as the gentry managers had forewarned.[181]

Besides the Hsin Chu Army, other local forces of a lesser size came into existence as the second phase of the war began. These forces were primarily *i-min* 義 民 , or partisan bands, which carried on intermittent attacks against the Japanese. Such partisan bands generally fought under their own leaders and apart from the regular Hsin Chu units. These bands did not fit well into the prefectural or *hsien* defensive operations, nor did their leaders always heed the orders of local authorities. Yet, when activated, the partisans demanded pay and rations, and thus tended to compete for the slender resources available to the regular forces in each area. During the third phase of the war such *i-min* bands grew more numerous, and posed a problem to both the inhabitants and authorities when bandit chieftains and their gangs were enrolled as armed partisans. Prior to that time, the active *i-min* bands apparently were composed of aroused villagers and functioned as rural militia, as similar village units bearing the same designation had done in Taiwan for well over a century when large-scale uprisings occurred.[182]

This type of partisan force gained notoriety during the siege of Hsinchu due to the spirited actions of Wu Tang-hsing and his *i-min* force. This gentry figure recruited fellow Hakkas from among the villagers of his native locality in southern Miaoli by warning them of the dreadful consequences of becoming "slaves of the Dwarfs. "[183] Under Wu's leadership his force operated against the Imperial Guards from July until his death at Changhua late in August. Yet problems arose from Wu's escapades. The inhabitants of Hsinchu city did not trust his band of Hakkas when Wu attempted to gain local help in driving the Japanese from that *hsien* seat. Eventually, Wu also quarreled with the Miaoli magistrate over pay for his men.[184]

During his career as a partisan leader, Wu Tang-hsing claimed to be the authorized commander of an island-wide partisan force. His claim was based on the title, "Commander of the Taiwan *I-min*", that Tang Ching-sung allegedly had bestowed on him before the war. Wu used a seal bearing this title.[185] Yet no such extensive command was ever organized, nor did the other partisan bands that emerged later during the war acknowledge Wu as their leader.

Despite the problems that arose from the insatiable demands of partisan bands and Prefect Li's rash use of the Hsin Chu Army, these mid-island resistance forces were able to launch counter-attacks against the Imperial Guards occupying Hsinchu city. At that *hsien* seat, some 2,000 Japanese troops fought off local forces five times as numerous. To the north, other Japanese units engaged local guerrilla bands in an effort to pacify the area and maintain communications between Taipei and the besieged city of Hsinchu. Outwardly, at least, this was the most impressive period of the war from the standpoint of the resistance. Nevertheless, by the end of July, as sizeable Japanese reinforcements and supplies reached Hsinchu, the tide of battle turned heavily in favor of the Imperial Guards. Areas in the northern part of the *hsien* were secured, and the main Imperial Guard force began to make a wide, multi-pronged sweep southward during the first week in August.[186]

Thereafter, the Japanese enjoyed a heavy preponderance in weapons and fire power. Meanwhile, the resistance efforts in Hsinchu had seriously depleted the local resources available for the defense of the mid-island prefectural region. Even though several Black Flag battalions joined the Hsin Chu Army and Wu Peng-nien eventually assumed command of that force, little could be done to replenish the regional defenses. Consequently, the Japanese were able to take over most of the mid Taiwan prefecture during the month of August. On the Fourteenth, the *hsien* seat of Miaoli was captured without resistance.[187] To the south, the remains of the Hsin Chu Army attempted to make a last-ditch stand at the Changhua prefectural center. Strong positions were taken on Pa-kua Mountain. Nevertheless, in a single battle on August 28, the Japanese, by means of a well-executed stratagem, managed, to drive the defenders from the mountain and seize Changhua city along with the nearby port town of Lukang.[188]

The celebrated battle of Pa-kua Mountain marked the climax of the second phase of the war. The main mid-island resistance force, the Hsin Chu Army, had been shattered and some of the most spirited commanders killed. Furthermore, the chief leader, Li Ching-sung, had left the scene as had the magistrates of Changhua and the other *hsien* to the north. In the mid Taiwan prefectural region only Yunlin, the southernmost *hsien*, remained unoccupied.

In the meantime, the Imperial Guards had turned the Changhua administrative center into a military headquarters. From there Japanese forces were sent south to pacify the rest of the Changhua area and occupy Yunlin. On September 1, Imperial Guard units advanced into the latter area and seized Touliu, the *hsien* seat, and the market town of T'a-li-wu (Tou-nan) to the west. In these localities they met sharp resistance from the local defenders, and were forced to retreat north. These setbacks were followed by heavy rains and severe floods, causing the Japanese to delay their southern advance for nearly a month. During this period of inactivity the Imperial Guards suffered from a malaria epidemic and other diseases rampant in Changhua.[189]

The setbacks which the Japanese experienced early in September heralded another defensive buildup, this time in Yunlin and the neighboring *hsien* of Chia-i to the south. Over seven Black Flag battalions had taken up positions there. Liu Yung-fu also dispatched other southern defensive units, together with funds and supplies, to areas north of Chia-i city. Again, local volunteer units supported by the Yunlin and Chia-i *hsien* authorities were active in their respective areas. Unlike the previous mid-island buildup, however, these various units were not reorganized into a single force comparable to the Hsin Chu Army.[190]

During the first brief Imperial Guard actions in Yunlin, the brutal conduct of their troops aroused the wrath of several powerful bandit chieftains. These chieftains and their gangs were instrumental in forcing the Japanese to retreat. Subsequently, Liu Yung-fu enrolled these local bandit gangs as *i-min* bands, even though he had to reward the chieftains with exorbitant gifts of silver from his dwindling Tainan funds.[191] These and other bandit-led partisan bands that Liu and his aides mobilized in southern Taiwan sometimes made brief, spirited stands in their own localities. Yet in the long run such *i-min* bands proved of little lasting benefit to the war effort. They merely helped deplete the slender resources available to the estimated sixty odd battalions (or some 26,000 men) which comprised the total resistance force along Taiwan's west coast extending from Yunlin southward when the third phase of the war began.

Not until the very end of September did the forces of the Imperial Guards commence to push south once again. By then, the Japanese had devised plans to converge on Tainan by sea as well as by land. The monsoon period had passed, and Japan's Second Division was assembling at the Pescadores in preparation for landings to be staged at points to the north and south of the Tainan and Anping area. The advance of the Imperial Guards overland was planned in conjunction with these landings.[192]

Against such superior forces, the beleaguered defenders in the southern portion of Taiwan were relatively helpless. The Imperial Guards met with occasional stubborn resistance on the part of local forces, supported by Black Flag detachments, as they drove southward through the Yunlin and Chia-i areas early in October. Nonetheless their advance was rapid. The *hsien* seat of Yunlin (Touliu) fell on October 7, and the important seat of Chia-i two days later after a heavy battle. Following a brief rest, the Imperial Guards pushed to within ten miles of Tainan city on the Twentieth.[193]

By that time, units of the Second Division already had staged landings along the southwest coast and made rapid advances against areas under Liu Yung-fu's command. On October 10, that division's Fourth Mixed Brigade landed about twenty-eight miles north of Tainan city near Pu-tai, then proceeded to far south. By the Sixteenth this force had marched to within easy striking distance of the Tainan and Anping area from the north. Meanwhile, on October 11, the rest of the Second Division landed unopposed near Fangliao some twenty-five miles south of Chihou. This force proceeded north, occupying the town of Tungkang on the Twelfth and the *hsien* seat of Fengshan on the Fifteenth. Altogether, about 12,000 Japanese troops engaged in these two landings, while Liu Yung-fu's forces that had once totaled around 30,000 now comprised mainly the 4,000 Black Flag troops still on hand.[194]

Initially, the Japanese appeared cautious on their southern campaign. Both landings were made at spots beyond the areas where Liu's Black Flag units were known to be stationed.

Actually, as it turned out, the Japanese commanders had overestimated the Black Flags as a fighting force. When the occupation troops converged on well-fortified coastal areas manned by Black Flag units, the lack of fighting zeal among Liu's men became evident. On October 15, Japanese naval units easily seized Chihou (renamed Takow) and its fortifications where a sizeable Black Flag detachment was stationed. The defenders fled to Tainan city, as happened in other instances when Japanese forces approached Black Flag installations.[195] The sporadic opposition encountered by the various Japanese forces as they converged on the Tainan area came mainly from local volunteer units and partisan bands, as well as possibly a few prefectural and *hsien* defense units remaining in the region. Finally, during the last several days before Tainan fell, the local *tuan-lien* battalions maintained order in the city. On October 21, three days after Liu Yung-fu escaped, these battalions helped to hand the city over to the Japanese without major incident.[196]

Following the surrender of Tainan, Governor-General Kabayama declared that Taiwan had been pacified.[197] His proclamation was premature, for areas to the south of Chihou, as well as regions in the central highlands and along the east coast had not yet been taken. Subsequently, the Japanese were to encounter further armed resistance from Hakka bands in the southernmost *hsien* of Hengchun, then soon afterwards experience desperate partisan attacks in Taipei near the end of the year and Ilan during the first part of 1896. Thereafter, bandit-like partisan bands continued to plague the Japanese authorities in all three major regions of the island for five or six more years.[198] Nonetheless, Kabayama was correct in assuming that the main work of pacification had been completed with the surrender of Tainan. The takeover of Taiwan's last key administrative center meant that organized resistance, carried on mainly through the administrative framework left over by the Ching government, was no longer present on the island.

VIII
The Republic and the War in Retrospect

Viewed in retrospect, the Taiwan Republic and the war of

resistance illustrate how crucial the year 1895 proved to be for the island and its troubled inhabitants. Taiwan was becoming a more integral part of imperial China, and had acquired provincial status only eight years previously. To guard against the possible loss of this rich and strategically located island province, the Ching court had initiated a buildup of Taiwan's defenses prior to the outbreak of the Sino-Japanese War in August, 1894. Subsequently, the news that the Peking government had reversed itself and agreed to cede Taiwan to Japan caused widespread consternation throughout China when announced in April, 1895. The cession of Taiwan, as stipulated in the peace treaty, was particularly disheartening to the island's inhabitants. Suddenly their future seemed bleak as they faced the uncertainties of a Japanese takeover and life under foreign rule.

With the fate of Taiwan and its Chinese inhabitants in jeopardy, anxious island leaders had launched their resistance movement in a desperate effort to forestall the loss of Taiwan to Japan. In May, after the vacillating court in Peking was persuaded to abide by the cession terms of the peace treaty, key resistance leaders on the island assumed full responsibility for the defense of Taiwan. Soon their movement gave rise to the republic which was inaugurated in defiance of the Ching government, the ratified treaty, and the impending Japanese takeover. Caught in a tight situation, Tang Ching-sung was forced to wage war when Japanese forces staged their initial landings in northern Taiwan, with no foreign aid or intervention in sight. During the five-month conflict that ensued, the island's inhabitants suffered severely from the disorder, epidemics and famine that accompanied the struggle as well as from the destructive warfare itself.

Since organized resistance against the Japanese proved unsuccessful and brought about widespread misery in Taiwan, neither the republic nor the war created a very favorable impression in the long run. The Taiwan Republic and its vestiges failed even to impress distraught Chinese who were turning to radical political solutions for China. Sun Yat-sen, who began his revolutionary career at this time, seems not to have noticed the republican precedents set in Taiwan. Mainland reformers urging representative government under a constitutional monarchy apparently were not influenced by the short-lived republic either. Liang Chi-chao, when visiting Taiwan early in 1911, recalled in a poem that the 1895 republic "had really been like a joke."[199]

On the other hand, as an aftermath of war, the republican image did help to perpetuate resistance spirit among certain Taiwan partisan elements which plagued the Japanese in occupied portions of the island. At least two *i-min* bands, operating from mountainous strongholds, endeavored to pose as defenders of the republic in attempts to revive popular resistance in their respective areas.[200] The 1895 war also served to intensify subsequent partisan attacks against the new colonial authorities. The conflict had enabled villagers and bandits to secure weapons and gain experience in guerrilla-type combat. This mode of warfare had shown that Japanese occupation forces were not invincible when ambushed or encountered in lesser numbers. Thereafter, Taiwan partisan elements continued to bear arms against the new authorities. As a result, the Japanese encountered such widespread armed opposition during their first several years of rule on the island that government heads in Tokyo came to feel Taiwan was not worth keeping. Their pessimism ceased as order was gradually restored and Taiwan's resources profitably exploited, but not before the wealthy Taiwanese refugee, Lin Wei-yuan, had proposed to buy back the island for China.[201]

Despite the lack of more lasting effects accruing from the republic and war, these extraordinary episodes are worthy of study. Both reflect something of Taiwan and its development over the last decades of Ching rule there. By that time Taiwan was no longer an isolated area of China, for the island had been more closely linked with the mainland by telegraph and steamship. These modern services allowed for the rapid transmission of news and official dispatches as well as expeditious movements of supplies and troops to the island. Such facilities also enabled unfamiliar Western concepts to reach Taiwan more readily. The manner in which the idea of a plebiscite arrangement was telegraphed to Governor Tang in Taipei illustrates the influence of modern communications. The fact that a republic, boasting of a parliament and some form of constitutional draft, could appear on the island is likewise indicative of Taiwan's contact with the outside world.

Again, a study of the war of resistance reveals that conditions in the settled regions of the island did not differ markedly from those prevailing in the provinces of southeast China. The war took place in an area which retained the semblance of a province of imperial China, and involved resistance on the part of Chinese who still professed to be loyal Ching subjects. Moreover, the struggle was waged in a setting similar to that of Fukien and Kwangtung, the ancestral homeland of the island's Chinese inhabitants. In these two coastal provinces tension also prevailed between local Hakkas and indigenous Chinese groups. There, too, dissimilarities in customs and speech existed as did natural boundaries formed by mountainous terrain.

By 1895, Taiwan had become prosperous enough to foster organized resistance against a Japanese takeover. The resistance movement and republic were led by protagonists who were key figures on the island. The Taiwan war also proved to be an independent effort on the part of local resistance leaders. That conflict remained detached from China proper even though Ching functionaries and troops from the mainland were involved and the costly defense buildup staged in Taiwan during the previous eleven months was conducted by the Peking government.

This defense buildup amounted to an extension of earlier self-strengthening efforts on the island. Reforms related to Taiwan's defenses had begun in the 1870's when modern Armstrong and Krupp artillery pieces were first installed in coastal locations.[202] Later on, Liu Ming-chuan had launched other major undertakings. These included the construction of the Taipei arsenal, powder mill and railroad which figured heavily in the military preparations carried out by Tang Ching-sung in his capacity as acting governor. Tang relied on policies and strategy adopted by Liu, and voiced similar self-strengthening sentiments. Moreover, Tang concentrated on the defenses in northern Taiwan, as Liu had been forced to do ten years before. Consequently, the military situation in Taiwan at the outset of the 1895 war somewhat resembled that of 1884-1885 when the French launched attacks on Keelung and Tamshui.

Previous self-strengthening efforts in Taiwan had also resulted in the gradual introduction of semi-modern military forces, trained in the use of Western firearms, to supplement the old-style units stationed there. In the 1880's Hsiang and Huai battalions had permanently replaced Green Standard units as Taiwan's regular defense force.[203] During the 1894-1895 defense buildup more Hsiang and Huai units were brought over to Taiwan, along with

other mainland forces equipped with modern firearms and organized along similar battalion formations. Yet old-style defense units
still prevailed, especially among the local volunteer forces. The
i-yung reserve battalions, organized in 1894-1895, received little
modern training and few Western arms. Other local forces enlisted
before and during the war — the *tuan-lien* militia, *pao-chia* security
units, and *i-min* partisan bands — were old-fashioned in terms of
their arms and make-up. These types of irregular forces had long
been recruited for temporary duty in times of war or internal
upheaval on both the island and the mainland. In Taiwan they
continued to be equipped with obsolete weapons, such as pikes,
spears and gingals, and to reflect customary patterns of local
leadership.[204]

Self-strengthening policies and defensive buildups had been
carried out in other threatened areas of China as well over
the latter decades of the nineteenth century. Hence, the military
preparations which preceded the Taiwan war of resistance lent a
familiar cast to that conflict. The Taiwan war, in fact, turned out
to be still another unsuccessful effort on the part of Chinese forces
to ward off the incursions of formidable foreign powers during
that century. All such defensive wars that China had previously
waged, beginning with the Opium War of 1839-1842, had
amounted to regional conflicts rather than nation-wide struggles
involving the whole of China and her resources. The Taiwan war
fits well within this category of limited defensive actions, except
that in this case an island province was directly involved instead of
one or several mainland regions. The Taiwan war was also unique
in that the Ching government did not become embroiled in the
conflict, for the apprehensive court had succeeded in keeping the
struggle in Taiwan from spreading to the mainland. After the
outbreak of hostilties on the island, few supplies and apparently
no troop reinforcements reached Taiwan. Meanwhile, the Peking
authorities officially ignored the war, refused to recognize the
Taiwan Republic, and declined to acknowledge either the memorials submitted by Tang Ching-sung or the urgent pleas Li
Ching-sung and Liu Yung-fu directed to mainland functionaries.

The Taiwan conflict could be described as a separate provincial
war against a foreign power if the term "provincial" were not
misleading in this context. Taiwan had become a province of
China, but few inhabitants had acquired an island-wide provincial

spirit as yet. Consequently, the war effort did not attract as much popular support as it might have from the island's diverse sub-ethnic groups. The bifurcation of governmental authority between Taipei and Tainan also worked against a more integrated resistance effort on the island. On the other hand, the relatively decentralized system of administration enabled separate wartime capitals to operate in each of Taiwan's three prefectural regions. Ironically, the existence of these separate centers allowed organized resistance to continue much longer than would otherwise have been the case had the war effort depended solely on central rule stemming from Taipei in the north.

Considering the lack of centralized authority and the disparate social groupings among the local Chinese, the prolonged resistance carried on in Taiwan was a remarkable feat. This defensive action undoubtedly would have been adequate to quell any of the extensive rebellions that had ravaged Taiwan in the past. Against the superior power of a nation like Japan such localized action was bound to fail. The defenders of Taiwan lacked a navy and a modern army. Moreover, they were constantly beset by banditry, fear and apathy on the part of the majority of the inhabitants, misery and disease bred by warfare, and the ever present dangers of widespread disorder and mob rule. Nevertheless, sustained resistance was waged against Japanese occupation forces although no outside help was forthcoming, even from China, and the defenders had to depend on the dwindling resources available in Taiwan itself.

While the defense buildup and Taiwan war involved familar practices, the resistance movement and republic proved unique to the Taiwan scene. Government under a republican label, of course, was something new to imperial China. The rise of the republic in Taipei marked the first time a Ching servitor attempted to perpetuate himself in power under the guise of a Western-derived political system. For a short twelve-day period the ambitious Governor Tang posed as a republican president in a vain effort to mobilize popular resistance under his lead and attract Western recognition and support. Later, Liu Yung-fu made use of unfamiliar republican vestiges in Tainan to help secure local backing for the war effort.

The resistance movement that gave rise to the republic also was unprecedented in Taiwan. It is true that the defiant spirit which characterized the movement did suggest the rebellious tendencies apparent among the island population over much of the Ching period. In 1895, even pro-Ming sentiments, stemming from the period Cheng Cheng-kung (Koxinga) and his family had controlled the island, were manifested in the Tainan area.[205] Yet the resistance movement differed from Taiwan's past uprisings and rebellions. The chief leaders of the movement turned out to be Governor Tang and his protégé, Chiu Feng-chia, while their supporters were respectable gentry and wealthy merchants. Previously, under Ching rule neither ranking island officials nor such eminent gentry and merchant figures had openly defied the pronouncements of the Peking court. The 1895 resistance movement represented a new departure for these elite island elements at a time when it appeared that Taiwan had been abandoned by the Ching government.

During 1895, outspoken resistance leaders differed not only in mood but also behavior from the indignant mainland literati and officials who merely submitted strong protests against the cession of Chinese territory. The Taiwan leaders proceeded to take action as well, and brought about self-rule on the island. Notwithstanding their defiant behavior, those leaders who became founders and defenders of the republic professed loyalty to the Ching rule. On the whole, they appear to have been sincere in their allegiance, for they still linked their fate to that of China and the Ching dynasty. Thus, Tang Ching-sung in his memorials and proclamations, and both Chiu Feng-chia and Liu Yung-fu in their petitions and oaths, constantly made it clear that they did not wish to sever their ties with the mainland no matter how much the weak and vacillating Ching court had disappointed them.

This combination of defiance and loyalty to Ching rule, as displayed by the resistance leaders, made their utterances and actions appear incongruous. The effort of Tang Ching-sung to function as both Ching governor and republican president best exemplify this tendency. Furthermore, the foreign concepts and radical terms they employed led to further inconsistencies on their part, and alarmed many contemporaries who abided by traditional political usages. The term "popular rule" *(min-chu)* and the related idea of a republic *(min-chu-kuo)*, as well as the alien title of "president," especially disturbed Ching subjects and servitors, including Tang's chief benefactor, Chang Chih-tung. To Tang and other key leaders of the resistance, however, the movement and republic were only temporary devices and the strange terms and foreign concepts they used merely handy labels. In their desperate situation it did not matter to them whether they had resorted to incompatible usages or not, as long as the resistance effort might serve its purpose as a "turning point" whereby Taiwan could be restored to China. Thus, Liu Yung-fu freely made use of traditional and republican designations to rally popular support during his blood-pledge ceremony. As one witness recalled, those in attendance hardly knew what a "president" (pronounced *pai-erh-hsi-t'ien-te*) was, yet they cheered the Taiwan Republic and its president just as they did the Ching state and emperor.[206]

The resistance leaders and supporters of the republic might have gained more widespread support and sympathy, and have acted in a more congruous manner, had modern nationalism been current in China at the time. Quite possibly, the leaders would have expressed anti-Manchu sentiment and claimed independence from Ching authority, the way provincial spokesmen on the mainland did later during the 1911 Revolution. Moreover, Tang and members of the local gentry might have refrained from attempts to lease Taiwan or mortgage its resources to one or another Western nation. The leaders and founders of the republic, however, were not revolutionaries nor even radical, nationalistic reformers although they were the first Chinese to experiment with limited forms of popular rule and representative government within the Ching realm.

Clearly, the Taiwan Republic arose prematurely on the Chinese scene. Unlike most republics the world over, this first Asian republic was not a product of a revolution or the outcome of an independence movement. Neither did its founders and supporters seek to bring about deep-rooted social and political change in Taiwan, nor advocate such fundamental concepts as equality, individual rights and the elective process necessary for a viable system of representative government. Only a few political innovations were introduced: a presidential office and a centralized administrative structure established on the provincial level; and parliamentary bodies created in both Taipei and Tainan. Otherwise, so-called republican government on the island amounted to a facade superimposed upon the existing Ching administrative framework. In all, the republic and its vestiges remained only temporary expedients on the part of desperate resistance leaders still loyal to Ching rule.

Studied outside of the Chinese context, this unprecedented republic resembles two other short-lived insular republics founded in Hawaii and the Philippines at about the same time. Both of those provisional republics were also created to fulfill specific political objectives. The Hawaiian Republic was founded in 1894 in conjunction with American annexation aims. The Philippine Republic, proclaimed in 1898, represented attempts by Filipino leaders to end Spanish rule and stave off an American takeover. The Taiwan Republic experienced different results than the Hawaiian Republic, for the American annexation scheme succeeded while the Taiwan resistance effort failed to reunite that island with its mainland base, that of imperial China. On the other hand, the fate of the Taiwan and Philippine republics were similar. Both helped to sustain armed resistance against foreign powers; then each ultimately failed and gave way to an alien colonial regime.

Notes to Chapter VII

1 Several scholars in Taiwan also have distinguished between the Sino-Japanese War and the subsequent Taiwan war of resistance. See the following articles dealing with the war literature of the period: Ch'en Han-kuang, "I-wei chih chan yu Chung-kuo shih-t'an" (The war of 1895 and the field of Chinese poetry), *T'ai-pei wen-wu*, IX, 1 (March, 1960), 90; and Liao Han-ch'en, "Chia-wu chih i tsai wen-t'an shang ti fan-ying" (Reflections of the 1894-95 war in the field of literature), *T'ai-wan wen-hsien*, VII, 1/2 (June, 1956), 93.

2 Such instructions were sent to Chang Chih-tung on May 15. Decrees with more explicit instructions were issued to Chang and other provincial officials on May 28 and June 2. *Ching Te-tsung shih-lu hsuan-chi* (Selections from the *shih-lu* of the Ching emperor, Te-tsung) (Taipei: Bank of Taiwan, 1964), II, 299, 302. Hereafter cited as *SLHC*.

3 *Ibid.*, p. 301.

4 Commissioner Li had been warned by H. B. Morse, the commissioner of customs at Tamshui, and others that it was unsafe for him to set foot on Taiwan, so angry were the inhabitants over the cession of their island. Hosea Ballou Morse, *Letter-books (1886-1907)*, MS (Houghton Library, Harvard), III, letter 1306. An account of the ceremonies carried out on shipboard is to be found in James W. Davidson, *The Island of Formosa Past and Present* (Yokohama, 1903), pp. 292-95.

5 Negative attitudes towards the republic on the part of Western observers appear in "Del Kemper, U.S. Consul, Amoy, to Edwin F. Uhl, Acting Secretary of State, June 21, 1895", *U.S. Consular Despatches, Amoy;* and A. Gérard, *Ma Mission en Chine (1893-1897)* (Paris, 1918), II, 102. Davidson, *op.cit.*, ch. 19, also makes disparaging remarks in his account of the republic.

6 For example, see Governor-General Kabayama's report contained in Sugiyama Seiken, *Taiwan rekidai sōtoko no chiseki* (Administrative record of Taiwan's successive governors-general) (Tokyo, 1922), p. 27.

7 These postwar occupation actions are mentioned in Hung Ch'i-sheng (I-chih), *Ying-hai hsieh-wang chi* (Record of those deserted in the great sea) (Taipei: Bank of Taiwan reprint, 1959), p. 21.

8 Davidson, *op. cit.*, p. 343.

9 These figures and a more detailed enumeration of the number of uprisings and armed conflicts that occurred in Taiwan during various periods appear in the following work compiled by the late Taiwanese demographer, Ch'en Shao-hsing: *T'ai-wan sheng wen hsien wei yuan hui* (Taiwan Provincial Historical Commission), comp., *Jen-min chih; jen-k'ou p'ien* (Records of the people; section on population), *T'ai-wan sheng t'ung-chih kao* (Draft gazetteer of Taiwan province), *chuan* 2 (Taipei, 1964), pp. 193-95. This draft gazetteer is hereafter cited as *T'ung-chih kao*.

10 As one witness described it, "bandits rose up like hair" about the island. Hung Ch'i-sheng, *op.cit.*, p. 2.

11 The slaughter of the Kwangtung troops is briefly dealt with in Wu Te-kung, *Jang T'ai chi* (Record of the surrender of Taiwan), reprinted in *Ke T'ai san-chi* (Three records of the cession of Taiwan) (Taipei: Bank of Taiwan, 1959), pp. 41, 42-43; and the action against the Hakkas in Hsieh Hsueh-yu, *"I-wei k'ang-Jih tsa-chi"* (Miscellaneous records of the 1895 resistance against Japan), *T'ai-pei wen-wu,* IX, 1 (March, 1960), 79.

12 The rivalry between the intendant, Liu Ao, and Liu Ming-chuan is treated with in the biography of Liu Ao, found in Lien Heng (Ya-t'ang), *T'ai-wan t'ung-shih* (General history of Taiwan) (Taipei, 1955, reprint), pp. 697-98.

13 Taipei, founded in 1879, served as the temporary provincial capital while Liu-Ming-chuan governed the island. Only in 1894 did the city gain official recognition as the permanent capital. *SLHC,* II 257.

14 Yao Hsi-kuang *Tung-fang ping-shih chi-lueh* (General account of Eastern military affairs) (Taipei: Wen-hai ch'u pan-she, reprint), p. 297.

15 I have attempted to show the various reactions of the Taiwan inhabitants to the war and takeover in Part II of an unpublished dissertation. Harry Jerome Lamley, *The Taiwan Literati and Early Japanese Rule, 1895-1915: A Study of their Reactions to the Japanese Occupation and Subsequent Responses to Colonial Rule and Modernization* (University of Washington, 1964), pp. 140-271.

16 The Taiwanese historian, Lien Heng, maintained that the island's total resistance force comprised over 300 battalions, with 360 men to each battalion. Lien Heng, *op. cit.,* p. 70. Many Chinese writers have followed this rather exaggerated claim. In contrast, just prior to the buildup only some 20 battalions reportedly were stationed on Taiwan. Yao Hsi-kuang, *op. cit.,* p. 272.

17 Ssu-t'ung tzu, *T'ai-hai ssu-t'ung lu* (Aggrieved report from the Taiwan sea) (Taipei, 1959, reprint), pp. 2, 4.

18 *Ibid.,* pp. 2,5; *SLHC,* II, 264.

19 *Ibid.,* p. 265.

20 *Ibid.,* pp. 267, 272, 274-75.

21 *Ibid.,* p. 275.

22 Biographical accounts of Tang and Liu are included in Lien Heng, *op. cit.,* pp. 781-85. Tang's own account of his activities in Indochina appear in his diary: Tang Ching-sung, *Ch'ing ying jih-chi* (Taipei, 1893).

23 For the instructions sent to Tang, see *SLHC,* II, 275. Tang's general criticism of Shao's incompetence appears in a memorial cited in *ibid.,* pp. 274-75.

24 Ssu-t'ung tzu, *op. cit.,* pp. 3, 5.

25 The ill-will between Tang and Liu, plus their encounter in Taipei, is dealt with in Lo Hsiang-lin, ed., *Liu Yung-fu li-shih ts'ao* (Draft history of Liu Yung-fu) (Taipei, 1957, reprint), pp. 238-40.

26 Ssu-t'ung tzu, *op. cit.,* p. 3.

27 *Ibid.*

28 *Ibid.* Lin Chao-tung's importance and wealth, viewed in conjunction with the rise of the Lin family of Wu-feng, are described in Johanna Menzel Meskill, "The Lins of Wufeng: The Rise of a Taiwanese Gentry Family," in Leonard H. D. Gordon, *Taiwan: Studies in Chinese Local History* (Columbia University Press, 1970), pp. 6-18.

29 One authority estimates that around 75,000 Chinese troops were sent to Taiwan during the Sino-Japanese War. Chen Han-kuang, *T'ai-wan k'ang-Jih shih* (History of Taiwan's resistance against Japan) (Taipei, 1948), p. 2. Tang Ching-sung claimed to have 150,000 troops under his command at the outset of the war. Davidson, *op. cit.*, p. 286. Besides this standing force, he probably counted the reserve and irregular units that had been enlisted locally.

30 *SLHC*, II, 279.

31 Characteristics of the *i-yung* battalions are briefly described by Ssu-t'ung tzu, *op. cit.*, pp. 3-4.

32 *Ibid.*, p. 4.

33 Chiu Ts'ung, "Ts'ang-hai hsien-sheng Chiu kung Feng-chia nien-p'u" *(Nien-p'u* of Chiu Feng-chia, Mr. Ts'ang-hai), reprinted in *T'ai-wan feng-wu*, IX, 4 (Oct., 1959), 46.

34 See Chiu's correspondence of this period reprinted in Chiu Lin, comp., "Chiu Feng-chia hsin-kao" (Drafts of Chiu Feng-chia's letters), *Chin-tai-shih tzu-liao*, no. 20 (June, 1958), esp. pp. 37 and 41.

35 Davidson, *op. cit.*, pp. 286-89.

36 Ssu-t'ung tzu, *op. cit.*, p. 4.

37 *SLHC*, II, p. 294.

38 Governor Tang did not receive a full account of the takeover of the Pescadores until March 27, when troops and civilians from these islands arrived in Taiwan and reported their loss. See the coded letter H. B. Morse sent to Robert Hart (No. 77, March 30, 1895), contained in the collection of maritime customs records (translated into Chinese), entitled *Chung-kuo hai-kuan yü Chung-Jih chan-cheng* (Chinese maritime customs and the Sino-Japanese War) (Peking, 1958), p. 219. Hereafter cited as *CKHK*.

39 Yao Hsi-kuang, *op. cit.*, p. 275. Other poor opinions of the Kwangtung troops appear in Yu Ming-chen, *T'ai-wan pa-jih chi* (Eight-day record of Taiwan), contained in the above cited work, *Ke T'ai san-chi*, p. 12.

40 Ssu-t'ung tzu, *op. cit.*, pp. 2-3.

41 For descriptions and appraisals of the Li Wen-kuei incident, see Yao Hsi-kuang, *op. cit.*, pp. 277-79; Lien Heng, *op. cit.*, p. 783; and Morse, *Letter-books*, III, letter 1290.

42 H. B. Morse reported that after the incident Admiral Yang changed to the side opposing the governor. Coded letter to Hart, no. 80 (April 23, 1895), *CKHK*, p. 222.

43 See, for example, Ssu-t'ung tzu, *op. cit.*, p. 11.

44 Morse commented on the evident "inaction of the governor" following the incident. *Letter-books*, III, letter 1290.

45 *SLHC*, II, 268.

46 Morse, *Letter-books*, III, letter 1244.

47 *Ibid.*, letters 1244, 1260.

48 *SLHC*, II, 289.

49 Ssu-t'ung tzu, *op. cit.*, p. 4. Lin may have advanced only this sum, as he was requested to do late in March, rather than the full amount. *SLHC*, II, p. 289.

50 *Ibid.*, p. 291.

51 *Ibid.*, pp. 298-99.

52 *Chang Wen-hsiang kung ch'uan chi* (Collected works of Chang Chih-tung) (Taipei: Wen-hai ch'u-pan-she reprint, 1963), IV, 2694. Hereafter

cited as *CWHCC.*

53 In this memorial Chiu is designated as the *i-yung* commander of all Taiwan. Wang Yen-wei, comp., *Ching-chi wai-chiao shih-liao* (Historical source material concerning foreign relations at the end of the Ching period) (Taipei: Wen-hai ch'u-pan-she reprint, 1963), *chuan* 109, 5a. Hereafter cited as *WCSL.*

54 *Ibid.,* 5a-b.

55 Excerpts from this cable, as well as remarks about it, may be found in the collection of telegrams and memorial drafts appended to Yu Ming-chen, *op. cit.,* pp. 20-21

56 Wu Te-kung, *op. cit.,* p. 2.

57 A translation of a placard written to incite the people against the Japanese appears in Davidson, *op. cit.,* p. 279. Another one which bitterly assails Li Hung-chang and other court officials is cited in Ch'en Han-kuang, *T'ai-wan k'ang-Jih shih,* pp. 34-36.

58 *WCSL, chüan* 110, 14b.

59 This particular petition is often referred to by historians since it represents a series of protest petitions submitted by *chü-jen* from all parts of China who were then in Peking preparing to take the metropolitan examinations. Actually, this Taiwan gentry petition was not entirely the work of such examination candidates, as has usually been asserted. Only three of the petitioners were *chü-jen.* The other two were Taiwan scholars who already held the *chin-shin* degree and were employed at the capital. Their petition is contained in Pei-p'ing ku-kuan po-wu-yuan (Peiping Palace Museum), comp., *Ching Kuang-hsu ch'ao Chung-Jih chiao-she shih-liao* (Historical sources of the Sino-Japanese negotiations during the Kuang-hsu reign of the Ching dynasty) (Taipei: Wen-hai ch'u-pan-she reprint, 1963), *chuan* 39, no. 3032 (appended), 35b-36b. Hereafter cited as *CSSL.*

60 *Ibid.,* 35b.

61 The memorial is contained in both *WCSL, chuan* 110, 14b-15a; and *CSSL, chuan* 39, no. 3038, 38a-b.

62 *WCSL, chüan* 110, 14b.

63 *Ibid.* The international law reference cited was called simply the *Kung-fa hui-t'ung* (Institutes of international law), *chang* (section) 286.

64 China's special envoy to Russia, Wang Chih-chun, then in Paris, had telegraphed Chang Chih-tung concerning the idea of a plebiscite as sanctioned by international law. *CWHCC,* IV, 2673.

65 *Ibid.,* p. 2687.

66 Chiu Lin, *op. cit.,* p. 44.

67 *North China Herald,* LIV, no. 1451 (May 24, 1895), 779. Here Chiu is referred to as the "Hakka chief, Ku Hung-kuk".

68 *CSSL, chüan* 39, no. 3010, 39b-40a.

69 *Ibid.*

70 Coded letter, Morse to Hart, no. 80 (April 23, 1895), *CKHK,* pp. 221-22; Ssu-t'ung tzu, *op. cit.,* p. 6.

71 Such disturbances and instances of mob action were reported by Western observers on the scene. See Morse, *Letter-books,* III, letters 1290 and 1298; Davidson's accounts printed in the *North China Herald,* LIV, no. 1451, 779; and the descriptions in his book, *op. cit.,* pp. 268-74.

72 *CKHK*, p. 222; and Morse, *Letter-books*, III, letter 1290. Instances of such intimidation of officials and wealthy inhabitants who sought to flee Taiwan are recorded in Hung Chi-sheng, *op. cit.*, p. 2; and Wu Te-kung, *op. cit.*, pp. 2, 41-42.

73 Morse, *Letter-books*, III, letter 1290.

74 *CWHCC*, IV, 2678.

75 Reports of this conference appear in a coded letter, Morse to Hart, no. 81 (April 26, 1895), *CKHK*, p. 223; Morse, *Letter-books*, III, letter 1290; and "Kemper to Uhl, May 14, 1895", *U.S. Consular Despatches, Amoy*.

76 *CWHCC*, IV, 2679.

77 Chang first mentioned the idea of such types of "bribes" to Tang on April 17, the day the treaty was signed. *Ibid.* pp. 2269-70.

78 Taiwan's foreign relations during this period are treated with in Kuo Ting-yee, *T'ai-wan shih-shih kai-shuo* (A Sketch History of Taiwan) (Taipei, 1954), pp. 219-25; and Wang Yun-sheng, *Liu-shih-nien lai Chung-kuo yu Jih-pen* (China and Japan over the preceding sixty years) (Tientsin, 2nd printing, 1932-34), *chüan* 3, 28-36. See also the telegraphed messages of Chang Chih-tung for this period contained in *CWHCC*, IV.

79 Lien Heng, *op. cit.*, p. 783. Tang later made brief references to this incident in his announcements concerning the founding of the Taiwan Republic,

80 Morse, *Letter-books*, III, letter 1298; and Morse's coded letter to Hart, no. 84 (May 17, 1895), 227.

81 This declaration is cited in *Cheng-shih chih; fang-shu p'ien* (Records of political affairs; section on defense), *T'ung-chih kao, chuan* 3 (Taipei, 1959), 215. It is also translated in Davidson, *op. cit.*, p. 278. However, the use of the expression "independent island Republic" for the term *"tao-kuo"* (island-state) makes this translation a misleading one.

82 *CSSL, chüan* 44, no. 3203, 27a.

83 *Ibid.*, no. 3219, 32a.

84 *SLHC*, II, 300.

85 F. Q. Quo, "British Diplomacy and the Cession of Formosa, 1894-95," *Modern Asian Studies*, XI, 2 (1968), 153.

86 Allegations that the court and provinces were behind the creation of an island-state in Taiwan were spread by the English and German legations. *SLHC*, II, 302.

87 H. B. Morse and James W. Davidson have left firsthand accounts of the Taiwan Republic, yet both seem to have been misinformed about its origins. Governor Tang alleged that orders or plans were sent from Peking. Both duly reported that this was so. Davidson, *op. cit.*, pp. 278-79; Morse, *Letter-books*, III, letter 1298.

88 *CWHCC*, IV, 2688.

89 Chang preferred the use of less radical terms, and steadfastly opposed the concept of popular rule. *Ibid.*, pp. 2688 and 2693. Finally, early in June after the war of resistance had begun, Chang suggested that Tang form an aristocracy based on enfeoffments and titles of nobility. *Ibid.*, p. 2698.

90 Chen's biography is contained in Ch'en Yen, *Fu-chien t'ung-chih lieh-chuan hsüan* (Selection of biographies from the Fukien gazetteer) (Taipei: Bank of Taiwan, 1964), II, 304-07.

91 *CWHCC*, IV, 2688.

92 Chen Hsin-te, trans., "T'ai-wan k'ang-chan Jih-fang tzu-liao" (Japanese sources on the Taiwan war of resistance), reprinted in Chung-kuo shih-hsüeh hui (Chinese Academy of Historical Studies), ed., *Chung-Jih chan-cheng* (The Sino-Japanese War) (Shanghai, 1956), VI, 454-55. Hereafter cited as *CJCC*.

93 Wu Te-kung, *op. cit.*, p. 35; Chen Hsin-te, *op. cit.*, pp. 454-55.

94 See the English translation of this announcement in Davidson, *op. cit.*, pp. 279-80; and Morse, *Letter-books*, III, letter 1298.

95 *North China Herald*, LIV (June 7, 1895), 863-64; Davidson, *op. cit.*, pp. 282-83; Yao Hsi-kuang, *op. cit.*, p. 282.

96 Wu Te-kung, *op. cit.*, pp. 34-35.

97 See, for example, Chiang Ch'uan, "Chiu Ts'ang-hai chuan" (Biography of Chiu Feng-chia), reprinted in the *T'ai-wan feng-wu*, IX, 4 (Oct., 1959), 35. Contemporaries who attributed the creation of the republic to Chen include: Wu Te-kung, *op. cit.*, p. 35; and Wang Sung, *T'ai-yang shih-hua* (T'ai-yang poetry talks) (Taipei: Bank of Taiwan reprint, 1959), pp. 26, 55.

98 Wu Te-kung, *op. cit.*, pp. 34-35; Liao Han-ch'en, "T'ai-wan min-chu-kuo tsai T'ai-pei" (The Taiwan Republic in Taipei), *T'ai-nan wen-hua*, II, 3 (Sept., 1952), 20.

99 Tang's report to the Tsungli Yamen is contained in *CSSL, chuan* 45, no. 3247, 3a. The visit of the long awaited French warship, the Beautemp-Beaupré, is treated in the article: G. Germain and Kao Kien-long, "En Marge Du Traite De Shimonoseki: Tractions du sujet de Formose (Avril-Mai 1895)", *Bulletin de l'Universite l'Aurore*, 3rd series, VI, 3 (1945), 510-12.

100 See Chen's telegram to his family on the mainland, cited in *Li Wen-chung kung ch'uan-chi* (Complete writing of Li Hung-chang), as reprinted in *CJCC*, IV, 364.

101 Chiu Tsung, "Hu huai lu," in his compilation, *Ch'ien T'ai-wan min-chu-kuo i-chün ta-chiang-chün Ts'ang-hai hsien-sheng Chiu kung Feng-chia shih-hsüan* (Selections of poetry of the commander-in-chief of the former Taiwan Republic's reserve army, Mr. Ts'ang-hai Chiu Feng-chia) (Shanghai, 1935), pp. 151-52.

102 The fact that Chiu was not vice president, as many writers have asserted, has been shown by Tseng Nai-shih, "I-wei chih i Chiu Feng-chia shih-chi k'ao-cheng" (Investigations of traces of Chiu Feng-chia during the 1895 war), *T'ai-wan wen-hsien*, VII, 3/4 (Dec., 1956), 65-69.

103 Lo Hsiang-lin, *op. cit.*, pp. 238-40.

104 See Tang's cable to the *Tsungli Yamen*, dated May 26 (KH21/5/3), in *CSSL, chüan* 45, no. 3256, 6a. Elsewhere, I have argued that Tang avoided using terms that would convey the idea of full independence, although writers have often used such terms when treating with Tang and the republic. Harry J. Lamley, "The 1895 Taiwan Republic: A Significant Episode in Modern Chinese History," *The Journal of Asian Studies*, XXVII, 4 (August, 1968), 752.

105 Lien Heng, *op. cit.*, p. 68.

106 Brief descriptions of the tiger-flag are contained in the *North China Herald*, LIV (June 7, 1895), 863; and Davidson, *op. cit.*, p. 282.

107 *CSSL, chuan* 45, no. 3264, 7b.

108 Hosea B. Morse, "A Short Lived Republic (Formosa, May 24th to June 3rd, 1895)," *The New China Review*, I, 1 (1919), 28.

109 *CSSL, chüan* 45, no. 3264, 7b.

110 *Ibid.*, no. 3259, 6a.

111 Such rumors are reflected in the literature of the period. For example, a poem by a local scholar called Tang a king and his government a "confused three-day petty dynasty." Lien Hsiao-ching, "Huang Tsan-chün ch'i jen ch'i shih ch'i shih" (Huang Tsan-chun: his self, his affairs, his poetry), *Tai-pei wen-wu*, III, 1 (May, 1954), 103. A more recent work has preserved poetry and stories concerning Tang, his wife, and Chen Chi-tung which allege that the governor aspired to become a king or emperor of Taiwan. Mao-tun (Lu Tun), *T'ai-wan min-chu-kuo ti liang-wei ta tsung-t'ung* (Two presidents of the Taiwan Republic) (Hong Kong, 1949), pp. 14-15.

112 Ssu-t'ung tzu, *op. cit.*, pp. 6-7; Hu Chuan, *T'ai-wan chi-lu liang-chung* (Two recorded accounts of Taiwan) (Taipei, 1951, reprint), I, 90a-b. These appointments were as follows: Yu Ming-chen, Minister of Internal Affairs (superseding the provincial finance commissioner); Li Ping-jui, Minister of Military Affairs (superseding the provincial military secretariat or staff office that had functioned under the governor); and Chen Chi-tung, Minister of Foreign Affairs (a new office in Taiwan, housed at the Taipei *ch'ou-fang chu*).

113 Yao Hsi-kuang, *op. cit.*, pp. 282-83; Davidson, *op. cit.*, p. 281; Morse, *Letter-books*, III, letter 1306.

114 The members met to decide what to do about Commissioner Li Ching-fang who was about to arrive and transfer Taiwan over to the Japanese. *CKHK*, p. 233.

115 Morse, *Letter-books*, III, letter 1298.

116 These claims are discussed and judged dubious by Huang Chao-tang, a scholar who has made a careful study of the organization of the Taiwan Republic and its vestiges in Tainan from the limited sources available. See his recent book, *Taiwan minshukoku no kenkyū* (A Study of the Taiwan Republic) (The University of Tokyo Press, 1970), p. 163.

117 *Ibid.*

118 Chen had previously stressed these ideas when explaining the formation and influence of public opinion in imperial China to French readers. His discussion is contained in his most widely read work, *Les Chinois Peints Par Eux-Memes* (Paris, 1884). The phrases cited here are taken from the English translation: James Millington, trans., *The Chinese Painted by Themselves* (London, n.d.), pp. 79-80.

119 Hu Chuan, *op. cit.*, I, 90a-b.

120 Huang Chao-tang, *op. cit.*, pp. 161-62. After his inauguration as president of the republic, Tang attempted to induce the local officials to remain at their posts. He set May 27 as the deadline for them to decide whether to stay on or depart for the mainland. To those who remained, Tang promised double pay and rations. Yao Hsi-kuang, *op. cit.*, p. 280; Davidson, *op. cit.*, p. 281.

121 Morse, *Letter-books*, III, letter 1298; *CKHK*, pp. 230-31; Davidson, *op. cit.*, pp. 281-82.

122 The silver presidential seal bestowed upon Tang had been made in Mengchia. On the day of the inauguration a procession of local dignitaries formed in that port town, and wended its way through the streets before entering Taipei city by the West Gate and proceeding to the governor's *yamen*. See the recollections of that event by Taipei old-timers, published in

the *T'ai-pei wen-wu*, II, 1 (April, 1953), 8-9.

123 This was Yao Hsi-tung, apparently an expectant intendant from Tientsin, whom Tang had previously sent on missions to the mainland. *CKHK*, p. 227. See also Ssu-t'ung tzu, *op. cit.*, pp. 6 and 7.

124 Chen Hsin-te, *op. cit.*, p. 455.

125 *CWHCC*, IV, 2687-88.

126 Ssu-tung tzu, *op. cit.*, p. 2.

127 Governor Tang was instructed by an imperial edict to shift Liu's forces to this area. *SLHC*, II, 291.

128 Ssu-t'ung tzu, *op. cit.*, p. 16. Some accounts allege that, early in June, Tang issued Liu instructions to hasten to Tainan and take custody of the vacant Taiwan brigade-general post. Lo Hsiang-lin, *op. cit.*, p. 240.

129 Ssu-t'ung tzu, *op. cit.*, p. 16.

130 Wu Te-kung, *op. cit.*, p. 51; Lo Hsiang-lin, *op. cit.*, p. 248.

131 Wu Te-kung, *op. cit.*, p. 50.

132 *North China Herald*, LV (Nov. 1, 1895), 729; and Wu Chih-ch'ing, "T'ai-wan chan-cheng chi" (Record of the Taiwan war), *Chin-tai-shih tzu-liao*, no. 28 (1962), pp. 91-92.

133 For accounts of the issuance of stamps and currency in Tainan, see *Ibid.*, p. 92; *North China Herald*, LV (Nov. 29, 1895), 909-11; and Lai Chien-ming, "T'ai-wan min-chu-kuo yu-piao" (Stamps of the Taiwan Republic), *T'ai-nan wen-hua*, II, 3 (Sept., 1952), 34-46.

134 Lo Hsiang-lin, *op. cit.*, pp. 249-50.

135 See the introduction to the oath Liu administered to representatives of the Tainan inhabitants and defense forces (discussed below). Chen Hsin-te, *op. cit.*, pp. 450-51.

136 I Shun-ting, *Hun nan chi* (Taipei: Bank of Taiwan reprint, 1965), p. 6.

137 *Ibid.*, p. 16; and Wu Chih-ching, *op. cit.*, p. 92. Both of these witnesses were critical of the Tainan parliament and its members.

138 Chen Hsin-te, *op. cit.*, pp. 450-54.

139 Lo Hsiang-lin, *op. cit.*, p. 242.

140 Chen Hsin-te, *op. cit.*, p. 451.

141 For details of Liu's departure and his narrow escape from the Japanese aboard ship, see Lo Hsiang-lin, *op. cit.*, pp. 262-69.

142 Examples of Liu's harsh treatment of the gentry and merchants in the Tainan area are reported in Wu Te-kung, *op. cit.*, p. 70.

143 The two and a half divisions included the Imperial Guards, the Second Division, and reserves from the Osaka Fourth Division. Davidson, *op. cit.*, pp. 353-54. The number of Japanese troops sent to Taiwan during the war varies in different accounts. Chen Han-kuang sets the figure at 70,049, including the coolies. See his *T'ai-wan k'ang-Jih shih*, p. 52.

144 Estimates of the units and number of troops that made up the total defense force during the war, including the local volunteer units that arose during the second and third phases, vary considerably. Chen Han-kuang estimates over 120,000 troops. *Ibid.*, p. 2.

145 Davidson claims that altogether both sides lost over 12,000 men as the result of wounds and disease. His figures indicate that the casualties caused by disease were extremely high. The Japanese lost 4,642 men in Taiwan due to sickness. Another 5,246 were confined to hospitals in Taiwan, and 21,748

more were sent back to Japan for treatment. His figures are usually followed by Japanese authors, while Chinese writers tend to set Japanese losses at a higher figure. See Davidson, *op. cit.*, pp. 364-66; and, for example, the table which Chinese translators appended to the book by Sigiura Wasaku, reentitled *Ching-mo Jih-chun kung T'ai chi* (Record of the Japanese military attack on Taiwan at the end of the Ching period) (n.p., n.d.), p. 115.

146 The suffering of the civilian population in Taiwan is not well documented. Some idea of the chaos and deplorable conditions of the time may be gained from the vivid poetry written by local scholars during the period, as well as from the few written accounts of the conflict. Some of the epidemics that raged in Taiwan during and after the war are mentioned in Ogata Toketoshi, comp., *Shisei gojūnen Taiwan sōsō shi* (The history of the inauguration of Taiwan's initial fifty years of rule) (Taihoku, 1944), pp. 183-84.

147 Tang's last several days in Taiwan are described in the diary kept by Yu Ming-chen, *op. cit.*, pp. 13-14.

148 Ssu-t'ung tzu, *op. cit.*, p. 11.

149 *Ibid.*

150 Wu Te-kung, *op. cit.*, p. 53.

151 Ssu-t'ung tzu, *op. cit.*, pp. 13-14. This anonymous author praises Prefect Li and his resistance effort, and claims the local inhabitants led him to a nearby port town when Changhua fell. He does not mention the battle of Pa-kua Mountain, nor the fighting in Changhua city.

152 Davidson, *op. cit.*, p. 325.

153 A short biographical sketch of Wu Peng-nien is appended to Chen Han-kuang, *op. cit.*, pp. 175-76.

154 *Ibid.*, pp. 174-75.

155 *Ibid.*, pp. 177-78.

156 *Ibid.*, p. 178.

157 See Wu Te-kung's concluding remarks in his account, *Jang T'ai chi*, p. 75.

158 Brief accounts of the limited revenue available at Changhua and Tainan are given in Ssu-t'ung tzu, *op. cit.*, pp. 12 and 16.

159 Wu Te-kung, *op. cit.* p 57; *North China Herald*, LV, no. 1478 (Nov. 29, 1895), 910.

160 Wu Te-kung, *op. cit.*, pp. 47, 51; Ssu- t'ung tzu, *op. cit.*, p. 12.

161 Wu Te-kung, *op. cit.*, p. 52. On the whole, relations between Li and the bureau managers were not harmonious, according to Wu who served as one of the managers. These gentry sometimes acted on their own initiative to secure revenue and reinforcements for the mid-island region.

162 *Ibid.*, pp. 50-51; Huang Chao-tang, *op. cit.*, p. 165.

163 This gentry figure was the *chin-shih* degree holder, Hsu Nan-ying, who commanded Tainan's *tuan-lien* force as well. Hsu's activities during the war and his escape to the mainland after Liu Yung-fu's departure are described in Hsieh Hsueh-yu, *op. cit.*, pp. 75-76, 79.

164 *Cheng-shih chih; pao-an p'ien* (Records of political affairs; section on peace preservation), *T'ung-chih kao, chüan* 3 (Taipei, 1959), p. 171.

165 Wu Te-kung, *op. cit.*, pp. 62-63.

166 *Ibid.*, p. 51; Hsieh Hsueh-yu, *op. cit.*, pp. 76, 79.

167 For example, see Hung Chi-sheng, *op. cit.*, p. 12.

168 Wu Te-kung, *op. cit.*, pp. 55, 62-63.

169 Wu Chih-ching, *op. cit.*, pp. 94-103.

170 Appeals addressed to Chang from both Li and Liu are to be found in *CWHCC*, IV, pp. 2709, 2713, 2715. Chang replied by way of the governor-general at Foochow. *Ibid.*, p. 2713. In addition, Li and Liu sent personal aides to solicit help from Chang and other officials in central and southern China. Wu Te-kung, *op. cit.*, p. 52; I Shun-ting, *op. cit.*, pp. 7-16; and Wu Chih-ching,*op. cit.*, pp. 92, 94-97.

171 Wu Te-kung, *op. cit.*, pp. 52-53, 55.

172 Chen Han-kuang, *op. cit.*, pp. 133, 146-47. The Changhua gentry managers even requested relief rations from the *pao-chia* bureau in Chia-i. Wu Te-kung, *op. cit.*, p. 55.

173 The war and turbulence in the north are described vividly in Davidson, *op. cit.* chapt. XX, 291-312.

174 *Ibid.*, p. 312; Sugiyama Seiken, *op. cit.*, pp. 28-29.

175 Chen Han-kuang, *op. cit.*, pp. 97-98.

176 *Ibid.*, p. 96; Davidson, *op. cit.*, p. 312.

177 *Ibid.*, pp. 324-25, 353.

178 These various defensive units that entered the second phase of the war are dealt with in Ssu-t'ung tzu, *op. cit.*, pp. 11-12.

179 *Ibid.*, p. 12.

180 Wu Te-kung, *op. cit.*, p. 47.

181 *Ibid.*, pp. 48-49, 52-55.

182 *I-min* bands of this type were active in Taiwan at least by the latter part of the eighteenth century when such local protective forces operated during the Lin Shuang-wen uprising. Huang Tien-chuan, "Ching Lin Shuang-wen chih pien chung ti i-min shou-ch'eng" (A partisan leader's insignia during the Lin Shuang-wen uprising of the Ching period), *T'ai-wan feng-wu*, XVI, 3 (June, 1966), 27-30.

183 Wu Tang-hsing had warned that as "slaves of the Dwarfs", all fields and property, as well as each person and every chicken, dog, ox and pig would be taxed, while everyone would have to wear different clothes and speak a strange language. Wu's announcement is cited in Chen Han-kuang, *op. cit.*, p. 80.

184 For details concerning Wu T'ang-hsing and his force see *Ibid.*, pp. 78-80; and Wu Te-kung, *op. cit.*, pp. 42-43, 51-52.

185 Tseng Nai-shih, "Wu Tang-hsing shih-chi k'ao-cheng" (Verification of the traces of matters concerning Wu Tang-hsing), *T'ai-wan wen-hsien*, IX, 3 (Sept., 1958), 45, 49-50.

186 Davidson, *op. cit.*, pp. 331-32; Chen Han-kuang, *op. cit.*, pp. 116-18.

187 *Ibid.*, p. 121.

188 This noteworthy battle has been described by a number of writers. The battle itself is dealt with in Davidson, *op. cit.*, pp. 336-39. For details concerning the fall of Changhua and Lukang, see Wu Te-kung, *op. cit.*, pp. 59-62.

189 Chen Han-kuang, *op. cit.*, pp. 129-31; Davidson, *op. cit.*, pp. 339-41, 358.

190 The defensive units as well as the Japanese forces on hand for the third phase of the war are listed in Chen Han-kuang, *op. cit.*, pp. 132-42.

191 Wu Chih-ching, *op. cit.*, p. 93.

192 Davidson, *op. cit.*, pp. 353-54.

193 *Ibid.*, pp. 358-59; Chen Han-kuang, *op. cit.*, pp. 143-47; Sigiura Wasaku, *op. cit.*, p. 91.

194 Davidson, *op. cit.*, pp. 353, 354-56, 359-61.

195 *Ibid.*, pp. 357-58.

196 Hsieh Hsueh-yu, *op. cit.*, pp. 75-76, 77.

197 Kabayama's proclamation, addressed to the inhabitants of Tainan and dated October 27, 1895, is contained in Wakumoto Otokichi, comp., *Nisshin-eki Taiwan shi* (History of Taiwan in the Sino-Japanese War) (Taihoku, 1930), pp. 177-78. Subsequently, on November 18, after it seemed that control had been gained over the southernmost *hsien* of Hengchun, the Governor-General issued a more formal pacification announcement. Sugiyama Seiken, *op. cit.*, p. 27.

198 The activities of partisan bands over these years are recorded in the *Ke-ming chih: k'ang-Jih p'ien* (Records on revolution; section on resistance to the Japanese), *T'ung-chih kao, chuan* 9 (Taipei, 1954), pp. 28-78. A briefer and more contemporary account of the postwar resistance against the Japanese is to be found in Hung Chi-sheng, *op. cit.*, pp. 21-45.

199 This expression is contained in the sixth and final letter of Liang's "Yu T'ai-wan shu-tu" (Letters of travel in Taiwan), in Liang Chi-chao, *Yin-ping-shih ho-chi* (Complete collection of the Yin-ping Studio) (Shanghai, 1936), *chuan chi*, V, 205.

200 In August and September, 1895, a group of local resistance leaders in northern Taiwan proposed to reestablish the republic in their occupied area. They recognized Liu Yung-fu (who was still in Tainan) as president and sought to make I Shun-ting, a Hunanese scholar serving Liu, the vice president. I Shun-ting, *op. cit.*, pp. 19-21. Some two years later, in May, 1897, local leaders of remnant partisan bands attempted to restore the republic. Their pronouncements indicate that the republic still signified an anti-Japanese and pro-Ching spirit. Tseng Nai-shih, "Chung-hua min-tsu i-wei k'ang-Jih shih tao-lun — chien wei 'min-chu-kuo' chu-shuo cheng-wu" (Instructive remarks concerning the Chinese people's 1895 resistance to Japan — together with corrections of what has been said about the "Republic"), *T'ai-wan wen-hsien*, VI, 3 (Sept., 1955), 20-23.

201 Hung Chi-sheng, *op. cit.*, pp. 39-40.

202 Davidson, *op. cit.*, pp. 209-10, 213.

203 *Cheng-shih chih; fang-shu p'ien, loc. cit.*, p. 166.

204 A description of the weapons, new and old, used by the defenders of Taiwan is provided in Davidson, *op. cit.*, pp. 286-89.

205 A few scholars in Tainan were stirred to emulate the resistance spirit that Cheng Cheng-kung had manifested against the Ching. Two young scholars attempted to resort to arms to drive away the Japanese. Hsieh Hsueh-yu, *op. cit.*, p. 78. Hsu Nan-ying also expressed pro-Ming sentiment in a poem. Hsu Nan-ying, *K'uei-yuan liu-ts'ao* (Remaining drafts of Kuei-yuan) (Taipei: Bank of Taiwan reprint, 1962), p. 30.

206 Hsieh Hsueh-yu, *op. cit.*, p. 75.

Select Bibliography

Davidson, James W., *The Island of Formosa Past and Present* (Yokohama: Kelly & Walsh, 1903), chapters 18-22.

Lamley, Harry J., "The 1895 Taiwan Republic: A Significant Episode in Modern Chinese History," *The Journal of Asian Studies*, XXVII, 4 (August, 1968), 739-62.

——————, "The 1895 Taiwan War of Resistance: Local Chinese Efforts against a Foreign Power," in Leonard H. D. Gordon, *Taiwan: Studies in Chinese Local History* (Columbia University Press, 1970), 23-77.

Morse, H. B., "A Short Lived Republic (Formosa, May 24th to June 3rd, 1895)," *The New China Review*, I, 1 (March, 1919), 23-37.

Quo, F. Q., "British Diplomacy and the Cession of Formosa, 1894-95," *Modern Asian Studies*, XI, 2 (1968), 141-54.

Woodside, A. B., "Tang Ching-sung and the Rise of the 1895 Taiwan Republic," *Papers on China* (East Asian Research Center, Harvard University), XVII (Dec., 1963), 160-91.

Chapter VIII

Taiwan's Japanese Interlude, 1895-1945

BY HYMAN KUBLIN

O n April 17, 1895, after three weeks of hard bargaining, representatives of China and Japan affixed their signatures to the Treaty of Shimonoseki. For all practical purposes, the Sino-Japanese War, which had broken out in the summer of the preceding year, was brought to a close. Among other provisions, the peace treaty called upon China to cede the island of Taiwan (Formosa) to victorious Japan. The formal transfer took place on June 2 aboard a Japanese ship anchored in Keelung harbor. Taiwan remained a part of the Japanese Empire until the end of World War II in 1945, when it was restored to China.

The acquisition of Taiwan marked the opening of a new stage in the still brief history of Japanese empire-building. In the early years of the Meiji Period (1868-1912) several insular territories — the Bonin, Kurile, and Liu-chiu Islands — had been peacefully absorbed into the Japanese imperial domain. To all of these island groups in her maritime frontier the Empire of Japan had claims to sovereignty of greater or lesser validity. Japan's acquisition of Taiwan, however was the result of totally different circumstances; the great island was the prize of Japan's triumph in battle. From the point of view of the Japanese, Taiwan, unlike the islands "gathered in" during the early Meiji era, was an alien land inhabited by peoples who could only be designated *gaijin* (foreigners).

The Japanese scholar, Takekoshi Yosaburo, underscored how sharply the annexation of Taiwan departed from the precedents of Japanese history. In his monumental account of Japan's venture into colonialism in Taiwan, written in the opening years of the twentieth century, he noted:[1] "The 17th of April, 1895, is a day

long to be remembered by us, because on that day the people and
territory belonging to another nation were transferred to our rule, a
fact never before met with in all the twenty-five long centuries of
our national existence. . . ." The fact that they were viewed as
alien intruders by the people of Taiwan was unmistakably
impressed upon the Japanese from the moment of their arrival on
the island. Far from being welcomed, they were greeted with hails
of gunfire.

Epochal in her national history as was the acquisition of the
island of Taiwan, the Japanese government had apparently not
weighed carefully the implications of the act before or during the
negotiations at Shimonoseki. Carried away by pride in their
overwhelming military victory, most of Japan's leaders took it for
granted that the best interests of the nation would be served
thereby. Surely they had no clear or concrete notion of how their
national interests would be furthered by possession of Taiwan and,
more important, what type and degree of national commitment
would be entailed to insure that these interests be advanced.
Several years were to pass before the Japanese finally decided
what to do with Taiwan and how the island might promote the
well-being of the mother country.

In the meantime, the tone and character of initial Japanese
rule over Taiwan were set by the circumstances under which the
original takeover of the island from the Chinese took shape.
Having encountered stiff armed opposition upon their arrival, the
Japanese were enraged by this blatant defiance of imperial
authority. The resistance forces in the northern part of the island,
largely organized by the infant Republican government of Taiwan,
were quickly smashed but the more formidable opposition in the
south was not overcome for many months. And after that, several
more years of military and police action were required before the
Japanese government could consider the island subdued and
tranquillized. When it ultimately tallied up its casualties, it grimly
realized that its losses in many a battle of the Sino-Japanese War
itself had been much smaller.[2]

The Japanese thus had good grounds to believe from the very
outset of their occupation of Taiwan that an overriding problem
would be the enforcement of obedience to their authority. It was
doubtless not mere chance that their senior administrative officials,
or governors-general, were, until the end of World War I, men

eligible to carry the symbolic sword of the warrior. The practice was started when Kabayama Sukenori, a rear-admiral in the Imperial Japanese Navy, took up his appointment in June, 1895. After serving a full year, he was succeeded by Lieutenant-General Katsura Taro who held the office for a bare four months. He was followed as Governor-General by Lieutenant-General Nogi Maru-nosuke who ruled Taiwan for the next seventeen months.

A review of the terms in office of the first three Japanese Governors-General of Taiwan makes it clear that military charac-teristics were paramount in their administrations. To be sure, all of them made some efforts to organize a new and more efficient system of civil administration. Hoping to stimulate local economy, studies of the conditions and needs of the island's farming, mining, and manufacturing sectors were made, and thought was given to the development of sources of revenue for the government. But when all is said and done, it cannot be gainsaid that what prevailed was essentially a system of military rule. To this day Chinese and Japanese historians, as might be expected, disagree as to the degree of severity of this rule. But it is generally agreed that the not too fine hand of the soldier and policeman was easily discernible in a broad range of the island's affairs.

As the third year of the occupation of Taiwan by Japan neared its end, the government in Tokyo was gripped by disappointment over its maiden colonial venture.[3] It was not simply that the Chinese and aboriginal peoples continued to resist the imposition of Japanese rule. Perhaps more discouraging, there seemed to be little prospect of the island ceasing to be a financial drain upon the hard-pressed home government. To the Meiji oligarchs in Tokyo, such considerations loomed ever larger with the passage of time. Colonialism without profit could be tolerated, many of them believed, but colonialism at a financial loss was inexcusable.

To some Japanese political leaders, who had initially welcom-ed the acquisition of Taiwan as their country's membership card in the world's "colonial club," the setbacks in Taiwan seemed all the more galling. Here apparently was confirmation of the commonly held view of the mighty Western Powers that "pushy but really backward" Japan was not qualified to assume the responsibilities of colonialism. Such tasks, it was frequently and condescendingly maintained by Western spokesmen, were best entrusted to the indisputably "civilized powers." Hence it now appeared that not merely the success of Japan's colonial venture was at stake; of transcendent importance was the question of Japan's national honor.[4]

A drastic change in Japanese policy for Taiwan got under way in the spring of 1898 when General Nogi was superseded by Lieutenant-General Kodama Gentarō. A soldier of proven administrative ability, he held this post as Governor-General until April, 1906, while serving concurrently in other positions of the highest responsibility in the Japanese government and army. Under General Kodama's supervision, Taiwan was steadily transformed into a model colony, so much so that Japanese thereafter were to cite his record of achievement as incontestable proof of Japan's qualification as a colonial power.

Perhaps the wisest move made by General Kodama as a colonial administrator was the appointment of Gotō Shimpei as his chief civil administrator. In time he was given the prestigious title of Chief of Civil Administration. Gotō was a doctor and, relatively young as he was at the time of his appointment, he had already acquired considerable experience in the field of public sanitation and hygiene. During the Sino-Japanese War, his training and ability in this area were used advantageously by the Imperial Japanese Army. From the moment he became a colonial official in Taiwan he commanded not only the admiration but the full confidence of General Kodama.

It was Gotō who devised the various policies for the overall administration and development of Taiwan. Scientist in spirit in his approach to civic problems, he was also a pragmatist. His ultimate interests in Taiwan was of course primarily to serve the national interests of Japan. But he believed that such ends could best be achieved by solving Taiwan's problems in Taiwan's terms. His Taiwan policy was to give due consideration to Taiwanese traditions, values, and customs. As a result, even his most daring innovations, more likely than not, had a touch of the familiar to the Taiwanese eye.

Fortunately for the Kodama-Gotō team, it set to work at a time when local armed opposition to Japanese rule was tapering off. While efforts at pacification were not abandoned, the suppression of "bandits" was increasingly looked upon as a police rather than a military operation. Emphasis was thus placed upon the extension of civil government and more attention was devoted to civil affairs. For a while top priority was given to the recruitment of personnel for colonial service in Taiwan.

In the selection of high-level adminstrators and technicians Gotō himself played an active role. Previously many Japanese adventurers, opportunists, and ne'er-do-wells had flocked to Taiwan to seek "golden opportunities" in the burgeoning colonial administration. Under Gotō, standards for the employement of officials and personnel for the colonial service were tightened. Conditions of employment were also raised in order to attract and retain qualified and committed personnel. To the Kodama-Gotō administration may be credited the foundation of a corps of career colonial civil servants in Taiwan.

Japanese personnel, enlisted for or assigned to service in Taiwan, were fed into the colonial. administrative apparatus. Like the army and navy commands, which always enjoyed certain independence and had a rationale and function distinctly their own, Taiwan also enjoyed a civilian colonial hierarchy. Generally speaking, it existed on three levels: the central colonial government, situated in Taipei (Taihoku), was headed by the Governor-General; the regional administrations functioned in the various prefectures into which the island was divided; and the lower local level political machinery which operated in the numerous towns and villages. From the point of view of the Taiwanese, this interlocking administrative system meant the injection of an official Japanese presence into every level of island life.

To expedite the work of the official representatives of Japanese authority, communication and transportation facilities were steadily improved and extended. The telegraphic system, which had earlier been set up by the Chinese government, was enlarged and efforts were made to increase the efficiency of the postal system. New roads were built and a start was made in the extension of old and construction of new railroad lines. It goes without saying that these developmente benefitted both the island's economy and defense.

From the moment they took occupation of Taiwan in 1895 the Japanese were uncertain about the size of the island's population. Even the Chinese had no knowledge of exactly how many people resided in the island province. At the time of the Japanese takeover, it was generally assumed that the inhabitants of Taiwan numbered more than 2,000,000. The new Japanese colonial authorities were eager to learn the size of the island's population but it was appreciated that no reliable census could be taken until Japanese control had been extended throughout the island and a proper administrative apparatus had been set up. These goals having been achieved by the Kodama-Gotō regime, an official census was taken in 1905. It revealed a population of almost 3,000,000, 95 per cent of Chinese origin.

Once the practice of census-taking was initiated, the Japanese repeated it at regular intervals in the following years. After 1905 the next official population count was taken a decade later. In the era after 1915, censuses were taken at five-year intervals, the final one in 1940. By the end of Japanese rule in 1945, it was estimated that the population of Taiwan had surpassed 6,000,000. In other words, the population of Taiwan increased steadily during a half century of Japanese rule; the annual rate of growth from the 1920's on was more than 2 per cent.

The major reason for the unbroken growth of Taiwan's population between 1895 and 1945 was not so much the rise in the birth rate as the sharp drop in the death rate. The Japanese colonial government set to work at a very early time to improve public sanitation and hygiene. The staggering losses incurred by their occupation forces from local disease stirred Japanese authorities to take positive action in this area. From modest beginnings the Japanese moved ahead to exterminate such "killers" as plague and cholera, and to control malaria. "The whole approach of the Japanese to the problem of disease in Taiwan," a historian observed,[5]

> was an austere one. They avoided every possible expense in equipment and physical facilities, and depended on intensive use of all the administrative resources at their command.
>
> In slightly over a decade the authorities almost eradicated plague as a major disease, through strict vigilance for suspected cases of infection, rigorous quarantine regulations, and careful inspection of incoming ocean cargoes for infected rats. Cholera was similarly prevented from spreading by incessant search for suspected afflictions and quarantine of identified cases. . . . By unremitting and energetic insistance. . . .the Japanese managed to prevent any larger epidemic outbreak of malaria during their stay in Taiwan.

As plague, cholera, and malaria waned as hazards to life and health, their place was taken by other diseases as the major contributors to fatalities on Taiwan. Respiratory ailments and enteric disorders constantly remained rife. Upper class Chinese and most Japanese residents in Taiwan were generally able to avoid those conditions of living which *ipso facto* facilitated the likelihood of exposure to infection by these ailments. The same, however, could not be said of the poorer and uneducated Chinese. Their incidence of infection continued to remain high year after year.

A critical project launched by the Japanese in Taiwan in 1898 was a land survey. Essentially it was designed to furnish a sound basis for levying taxes, the land tax being the major source of revenue for the government. The Japanese had quickly discovered that the traditional land-owning and land-tax system prevailing on Taiwan was far more complex than the one used in Japan itself. From the standpoint of the Japanese colonial authorities, the system posed unnecessary problems in assessing and collecting taxes. While the Japanese generally respected Taiwanese traditions and customs in carrying out their survey, the final result was a sharper definition of ownership of the lands placed upon the official tax registers.[6] And the increase in revenue from land taxes assisted greatly in bringing about the achievement anxiously sought by the Japanese: financial self sufficiency for colonial Taiwan.

One of the most radical innovations of the Japanese authorities was the establishment of a modern police system. Inasmuch as Army troops were entrusted with the primary responsibility of upholding law and order, during the early years of the colonial administration, the function of the police was somewhat ambiguous. In 1898, however, shortly after Kodama and Gotō assumed direction of Taiwan affairs, steps were taken to reorganize the police establishment. It seems clear that they envisaged a role and responsibility for the police essentially different from what had prevailed before. Under Kodama and Gotō the mission of the military was sharply delimited and the policeman became in effect, a key colonial functionary on the prefectural and, particularly, the town and village level.[7]

As in all personnel matters Gotō enlisted recruits for the Taiwan police force with great care and deliberation. Among other inducements, the prospective policemen were offered excellent wages. Once in Taiwan they were put through a well conceived training program lasting for many months. After completing his training, the policeman was sent into the field to take up his duties. In addition to Japanese colonial police personal, positions on lower and local levels were open to the Taiwan Chinese.

The ordinary policeman in the new system had a broad variety of duties. "Under Gotō," it has been said,[8]

> the police became the backbone of regional administration. In addition to regular policing duties, the police supervised the collection of taxes, the enforcement of sanitary measures, and works connected with the salt, camphor, and opium monopolies. They were also responsible for the movements of aborigines and the illegal entry of Chinese immigrants. They superintended road and irrigation improvements, introduced new plant specimens to the farmers, and encouraged education and the development of local industries. They also instructed the people in the complexities of land registration and the purchase and sale of government bonds and stocks, and preached the gospel of frugality.

This police system lasted until the fall of 1920. It was then overhauled by Den Kenjirō, the first civilian Governor-General of Taiwan. The main thrust of Governor Den's reforms was to require policemen to concentrate their energies strictly upon police matters. Administrative responsibilities, which had previously consumed much of their time and effort, were reassigned to other functionaries in the colonial government. This reform was unfortunately not successfully implemented. Though further efforts were made in the following years to achieve Governor Den's aims, the policeman's activities extended far beyond law enforcement until the very end of the Japanese colonial era.

When in 1906 General Kodama and, then, Dr. Gotō gave up their posts of leadership in Taiwan, both could take deep satisfaction from their record of achievement during their eight years of office.[9]   In general, the island had been pacified, an administrative structure essentially civilian had been set up, the island's economy had been stimulated, and a good start had been made upon many projects designed to raise the quality of island life. These many improvements were manifest to both Taiwanese and Japanese. But what was cause for special satisfaction to both Kodama and Gotō was their success in promoting the finances of this colony to a self sufficient basis.

During the first few years of Japan's occupation of Taiwan, expenses for administering the island had sharply outrun revenue. In addition to having to pay for the maintenance and operations of its military forces, the Japanese government had found it necessary to subsidize the colonial regime to the extent of millions of *yen* annually. During the years of the Kodama-Gotō administration, the financial drain upon Japan was gradually eliminated. Not only were tax revenues sharply increased but funds for economic development and expansion were acquired through the floatation of bonds sold in Japan as well as in Taiwan.

In the decade after the retirement of Kodama and Gotō various projects which they had initiated began at long last to show signs of success. Until the opening years of the twentieth century the principal military or para-military activity of the Japanese administration had been the suppression of armed resistance by the Taiwan Chinese and the liquidation of what was called banditry. Thereafter the colonial administration was able to devote increasing attention and resources to the problem of tranquillizing and controlling the aborigines. Inhabiting the eastern half of Taiwan, a rugged mountainous and densely forested region, these tribesmen had continued to resist Japanese encroachment into their "home lands" as bitterly as they had opposed the advance of the Chinese for several hundred years.

The tribesmen of Taiwan, particularly those who dwelt in the northeastern quarter of the island, had long been held in fear by the Chinese settlers. It was not simply their custom of head-hunting which terrified the Chinese who intruded into the border areas. Perhaps more so was the readiness of these "savages" to fight desperately in defense of their land which they considered their own. They were hostile towards "homesteaders" who sought since time immemorial arable lands in the foothills of the mountains and they did not hesitate to attack woodsmen who risked their lives to obtain valuable timber in the tropical forest. But in the later years of the nineteenth century a frequent target of their assaults were the collectors of camphor. Since the highly valued camphor trees, from which camphor and camphor oil were obtained, were found mainly in areas which the tribesmen traditionally regarded as part of their domain, the increasing intrusions of the Chinese camphor workers from the western plains more and more exasperated them.

To cope with the perennial danger of attacks by tribesmen, the colonial government adopted the tactics which had basically been customary in Ching times. This was to construct and maintain a long border-guard line along the "frontier." Consisting of a chain of outposts manned by armed "border guards" (Japanese, *aiyu;* Chinese, *aiyong),* they were usually formidable enough to repel raids by the aborigines into the zones of "civilization." Though the border guards were commanded by Japanese officers, largely specially trained policemen, the rank and file was composed of Taiwan Chinese and an occasional "civilized savage." For obvious reasons the border guards ususally depended upon the cooperation and assistance of Chinese communities and settlers in the frontier regions.

The border-guard line was not considered a static fortified position. It was periodically moved forward, extended, and consolidated in the face of resistance from the aborigines. The ultimate aim was to force the tribesmen into delimited areas, comparable to the Indian reservations in the United States, where they would be isolated and controlled. Then, it was hoped, the aborigines could be induced to give up their warlike ways, especially their head-hunting practices, and settle down to the life of peaceable farmers. But by the beginning of World War I not much headway was made in achieving these goals. [10]

It is doubtful that the Japanese ever achieved total success in subduing the tribesmen. While many of them were, to be sure, killed or hammered into submission, thousands of others persisted in their defiance. In time the colonial authorities resorted to new methods of control and conquest. For instance, the border-guard line was for long stretches made up of barbed wire fences, often electrified. In the 1920's and 1930's, it is reported, the Japanese made use of airplanes to bomb and harass troublesome tribesmen. Nevertheless, despite the continued resistance to the advancing border guards the aborigines were compelled to abandon extensive tracts of territory, part of which was then given over to farming, timbering, and mining enterprises.

As areas in the foothills of the mountain ranges of eastern Taiwan became exploitable, the production of one lucrative commodity in particular began to increase. In the final decades of Chinese rule and during the early years of Japanese sway the international demand for camphor began to rise steadily.[11] Since Taiwan was one of the few, and perhaps the best, source for this commodity, it was in an excellent position to profit from the situation. As early as 1898 the production and sale of Taiwan camphor were controlled through government monopoly. As camphor producers were enabled to penetrate into many former tribesmen-controlled areas, the amount of camphor obtained for export into the world's markets rose. Not until the 1920's, when it became possible to produce synthetic camphor at competitive prices, did the profits of the Taiwan industry level off and decline.

Before she acquired Taiwan, Japan had had little to do with the island and its peoples. But China's surrender of the island occurred during a critical era in the history of Japan. Since the Meiji Restoration of 1868, Japan's population, which had been stable for about one hundred and fifty years, had begun to rise steadily. While the production of food had also increased, it seemed by the end of the nineteenth century that the time was rapidly approaching when Japan would no longer be self sufficient in food supply. There is no doubt that increasing imports of agricultural products from Taiwan helped relieve Japan's anxieties and spared her much of the need to import these commodities from lands outside of the Empire. Until the end of Japanese rule Taiwan continued to be a major supplier of foodstuffs to Japan.

The most important agricultural produce of Taiwan under both the Chinese and Japanese was rice. At all times more arable land on the island was given over to the cultivation of rice than any other plant. During the Japanese period, when statistics became more detailed and reliable, the acreage given over to rice production was reported to be more than 50 per cent of the island's cultivated land. At an early moment the Japanese colonial authorities encouraged the expansion of rice acreage; for about twenty five years much of the increased production was exported to China where it found a ready market. Exports to Japan rose sharply only after World War I. It seems that the average Japanese did not particularly care for the Taiwan varieties of rice, considering them to be inferior. Only when types of rice favored by the Japanese palate were introduced for Taiwan cultivation did exports to Japan start to rise sharply. Thereafter Japan ordinarily imported 50 per cent or more of the Taiwan rice export.

Taiwan's second most important crop was sugar cane. It had been raised on the island for hundreds of years. Soon after their arrival the Japanese began to study the circumstances of sugar production. In Taiwan sugar they observed a possible solution to a problem in their national economy. Since the Japanese consumed substantial quantities of sugar each year but only produced a pittance themselves; vast amounts had to be imported each year. In fact, sugar was one of the major imports of Japan and required the outlay of a large amount of foreign exchange. A sharp increase in the supply of sugar produced within the Empire would surely improve the not too satisfactory foreign trade picture.

To assess Taiwan's potential for increased sugar production Dr. Gotō called upon Dr. Nitobe Inazo, one of Japan's preeminent agricultural economists. The resulting report, entitled the *Taiwan Sugar Policy*, was finally submitted to Governor-General Kodama in 1901. ". . .Dr. Nitobe recommended," in this epochal report,[12]

> that the irrigated area and the area under cultivation be increased through various measures of encouragement, assistance, and direct government action, the establishment of sugar research stations, and the introduction of improved varieties of sugar cane, while other recommendations were made concerning sugar manufacturing.

The proposed Taiwan Sugar Policy was quickly accepted and its recommendations were put into effect. Improved varieties of sugar cane were transplanted from Java and Lahaina in Hawaii, and Taiwan producers were given grants and subsidies.

Few of the changes introduced into the life of Taiwan by the Japanese during their half-century of rule were more successful than Nitobe's sugar policy. Measuring their achievement during the period extending from 1905-1906 to 1938-1939, Andrew J. Grajdanzev wrote on the eve of World War II:[13]

> In thirty-three years the area under sugar cane increased almost four times, total production twelve times, and the yield per *ko* [2.377 acres] 2.7 times.
>
> In 1939 the Japanese Empire occupied seventh place among producers of sugar and fourth place among producers of cane sugar. The Japanese sugar industry became a factor of world importance. It is true that Japan exports very little sugar, but her

absence from the world market as a purchaser is of considerable importance.

There can be no doubt as to the importance of sugar cane cultivation and of the sugar industury in Taiwan and the degree of success achieved by the Japanese government and Chinese cultivators.

In the twentieth century several other agricultural products were grown with increasing success. Pineapple had long been cultivated on the island mainly for local consumption. The Japanese encouraged its cultivation and over the years a mounting volume of the annual crop was exported to Japan. Bananas too had been raised in Taiwan for centuries but not until the Japanese appeared upon the scene did they become an important export. Both pineapple and bananas, it should be noted, were generally raised on land not suitable for rice and sugar cane. Under the Japanese the production of jute rose modestly. The cultivation of two staple crops, sweet potato and tea, occupied the attention of many farmers. Taiwan tea had for many years been in demand in the lands of East Asia; in the twentieth century the island's black, *oolong* (aromatic), and *pouchong* — competed with bananas for third place, after rice and sugar, in Taiwan's list of major agricultural exports.

Before 1914 agriculture had dominated the economy of Taiwan. The volume and value of the output of industry, fishing, forestry, and mining, had been relatively inconsequential. Industry alone assumed a more important place in the economy of Taiwan with the passage of time. (By the beginning of the Pacific War in 1941 industrial output accounted for more than 40 per cent of the value of Taiwan's total production). Only agriculture contributed a higher percentage.

From the beginning of Japanese rule the principal sector of industry consisted mainly of food-processing. Most important were sugar refining and the canning of pineapple, which in time accounted for more than 70 per cent of the value of Taiwan's industrial output. Over the years methods of sugar refining and pineapple-canning were constantly improved. From about the time of World War I more and more attention was paid to the production of chemicals and fertilizers most of which were used locally.

In 1915, the Japanese completed the second decade of their rule over Taiwan. It was mainly the Chinese settlers in Taiwan, those who could remember the days when the island was under the rule of the Manchu dynasty, primarily people thirty years of age and older, who appreciated the many changes that had taken place. And here and there a Japanese colonial civil servant, who had come to Taiwan during the early years of the occupation, would now marvel at the contrasts between "Taiwan then and now." To the "old timers," whether Chinese or Japanese, one of the most startling of the many changes that had occurred was in the composition of the population. With the passage of each year since 1895 the "average age" of the islanders had shrunk. In a society and culture where age was highly respected, more and more of the population had to be classified as youthful. What kind of political consciousness would the Taiwan "youth" develop? To what political issues, if any, would this younger set respond?

During the first decade of the twentieth century, reformist and revolutionary movements appeared upon the political scene in imperial China. All were to a greater or lesser extent critical of the leadership of the Manchu government. Possibly the most radical of these movements was that spearheaded by Dr. Sun Yat-sen's *T'ung-meng Hui* which aimed at the overthrow of the Manchu dynasty and the establishment of a republic. But despite the fact that the Taiwan Chinese had no love for China's Manchu rulers, they do not seem to have become involved in any of the revolutionary campaigns directed against them. Perhaps a major reason for their passivity is that revolutionary leaders made no concerted effort to enlist their support.

No Chinese was more sensitive than Dr. Sun, during the closing years of the Manchu dynasty, to the existence of Chinese communities outside the "Middle Kingdom." Much of his political and financial support was derived from *hua-chiao* (overseas Chinese) groups in such places as Indochina, Singapore, Hawaii, and Canada. Dr. Sun was well aware too that the Japanese government raised no great difficulties for revolutionary groups organized among the many Chinese students attending universities in Japan, notably in Tokyo. Since these student revolutionaries were largely the "arm-chair" variety and were transient residents in Japan, Japanese authorities rarely were perturbed by their activities. But Dr. Sun most likely realized that he could not engage in revolutionary agitation among the Taiwan Chinese without arousing alarm among Japanese authorities. From their point of view, Taiwan Chinese were neither transient aliens nor immigrants of recent provenance but were, since 1895, subjects of His Imperial Majesty, the Meiji Emperor. As subjects of the Japanese Empire, they were expected to behave properly in their political thinking and action.

To exercise effective control in the maintenance of law and order, and in other related matters, the Japanese took steps in 1898 to revive and strengthen the traditional *pao-chia* (Japanese *hoko*) system. This local community organization was introduced into Taiwan in the eighteenth century from the mainland. Employing the principle of mutual responsibility, the *pao-chia* played a valuable role in ferreting out criminals, in performing various police functions, and in implementing communal tasks. Languishing during the later years of Chinese rule, it was overhauled while Liu Ming-chuan served as Governor (1885-1891). When military gave way to civilian rule in 1898, the *pao-chia* system was assigned a multitude of responsibilities. In case of need, this network of household organizations, extending through-out the island, could be used by the Japanese authorities to detect and report activities of Chinese revolutionaries and political organizations.

If the Japanese had no need to be apprehensive of Chinese revolutionaries and were confident of the means to cope with them if the occasion arose, it was nonetheless clearly demonstrat-ed that they could not always control Japanese "trouble makers." In November, 1914, Itagaki Taisuke, an eminent Japanese political leader and veteran of libertarian causes, visited Taiwan. In short order he organized the *Dōka-kai*, or Assimilation Society. Itagaki's purpose was clear-cut; he wanted to hasten assimilation of the Taiwan Chinese by the Japanese. A barrier to this end, he believed, was the preferential treatment in Taiwan of the Japanese and the discrimination, direct and indirect, manifested by the colonial regime against the native population. There was basically nothing seditious or even politically dangerous about the *Dōka-kai*. Nevertheless, it was viewed suspiciously by colonial authorities and in February, 1915, the organization was quietly suppressed.

A strong believer in assimilation, at least for a while, was Lin Hsien-tang, a wealthy and politically alert Taiwan Chinese. He was strongly influenced some years before World War I by advice given him by the distinguished scholar, Liang Chi-chao. It would be wise, counseled Liang,[14] for the Taiwan Chinese "to ape the ways of the Irish in fighting against England, namely to work with enlightened Japanese leaders to check the power of the colonial government and reduce its oppression in Taiwan." Lin was to bear these words in mind constantly during the course of his long political career.

Lin is well known in the history of modern Taiwan for his efforts to promote the education of his fellow islanders beyond the elementary level. He believed that the school system establish-ed by the Japanese had many limitations. With the inauguration of colonial rule the Japanese started to organize a system of schools to replace the scattered educational institutions that had grown up with little planning under the Chinese government. The Japanese had spent the entire period from 1870 to 1895 to construct the foundations of a modern education system in Japan and they were familiar with the many problems entailed. An explanation of the ultimate decisions made was presented by Takekoshi Yosaburo. "Immediately on the acquisition of Taiwan," he stated,[15]

> our authorities gave much thought to the subject of education, being anxious to educate the inhabitants in conformity with the policy which has been so often advocated as the best for developing a newly acquired territory — first educate the people. Our educational authorities, however, were confronted with a difficulty which they did not know how to avoid. Should they give the people a practical scientific education and thus enable them to better themselves, have more comfortable homes and make more money; or should they give such an education as would assimilate them with us, Japanese? If the latter course be adopted, then little time or energy can be devoted to teaching the practical sciences, and the idea that education is simply a means of enabling a man to earn more must be banished from their minds. . . . In 1896, when civil administration was introduced, the authorities at first adopted the assimilation idea. . . .In these, [the new schools] Japanese was made the principal subject of study. . . .

However, the educational system and its purposes were modified in the following years, and opportunities for study in the government schools beyond the elementary level were made available.

In addition to the school system established by the colonial regime for the Taiwan Chinese and the aboriginal tribesmen, there were several other types of schools. Numerous communities maintained their own schools in which the traditional style of Chinese education was offered. And the Japanese maintained a special system of schools, principally in the cities and larger towns, designed for the education of the children of Japanese residents in Taiwan. While the Taiwan Chinese were not excluded from these schools, only a small number ever attended them. In these schools opportunities were available to study beyond the elementary level, in advanced units that were comparable to the middle and higher schools of Japan. Chinese who hoped to prepare for careers requiring a consummate knowledge of the Japanese language attempted to secure entry into these schools.

Japan adopted a policy of compulsory elementary education as early as 1872. No serious effort, however, was ever made to introduce a similar policy into colonial Taiwan until the late 1930's. It is clear that the majority of children of school age never attended school during the Japanese colonial era. During the decade of the 1930's official statistics reveal that less than 50 per cent of Chinese youngsters were in school. And of these boys and girls only a fortunate few were able to advance beyond the primary grades to get more than six years of schooling.

Thanks to the prodding of men like Lin Hsien-tang the first middle and higher schools for Chinese students were established during the World War I period. A small number of Chinese students also managed to gain entrance to one or another of the few vocational schools on the island. And before the end of World War I pathetically few Taiwan Chinese were fortunate enough to go to college or university. Those who did studied mainly in institutions of higher learning in Japan at which the majority of them sought legal or medical training. Only an occasional Taiwan Chinese succeeded in getting a university education in China, Europe, or the United States.

At the end of World War I, a longer period of political and intellectual ferment set in throughout Asia. In the Far East Japanese, Chinese, and to some extent Korean life and society bubbled with change and innovation. It would be misleading even to imply that Taiwan was shaken by this tide of change. But that the island was touched by unprecedented ripples of restiveness is undeniable. Certain it is that the immediate postwar years marked a watershed in the history of modern Taiwan.

Leading the way in the agitation for liberal political, social, and legal changes were Taiwanese university students in Japan. It is worth noting that these young men, primarily coming from the wealthiest sector of Taiwan society, were all born after the Japanese annexation of the island. During their adolescent years they had, because of the incessant changes and innovations promoted by the Japanese colonial authorities, been made constantly aware of the fact that theirs was a society and way of life in transition. While it was not too difficult to predict what the many changes were leading to, these university students had caught glimpses, actual and theoretical, of alternative political and social goals in Japan itself.

Taiwanese university students in Japan, much like other young men and women attending institutions of higher education throughout the Far East, did not escape exposure to the nationalistic and ideological currents set in motion by World War I. The ideas which inspired the participants in the May 4th Movement in China and the *Mansei* Movement in Korea were, *mutatis mutandis*, the thoughts which fired many a Taiwanese — and Japanese — student in Japan. In addition to being inspired by liberal, and perhaps democratic ideas emanating from the West, the Taiwanese university student was moved by many of the political institutions and practices of Japan itself. For all the criticism that many Westerners may have leveled against the Japanese political and social system, it was doubtless still obvious to the Taiwanese student that there were fundamental differences between the arbitrary colonial regime under which they were reared and the government in Japan. At a minimum, the Taiwanese student must have been aware that in Japan a constitutional, parliamentary system of government prevailed and that the large majority of Japanese citizens enjoyed suffrage rights. Such factors must be kept in mind when assessing the nature of the "demands" and goals of Taiwanese political activists during the post-World War I decade.

As early as 1918 Taiwanese students in Tokyo organized an association known as the *Dōmei-kai* to champion reforms in their homeland. One of their first targets was some of the draconian laws enforced by the colonial government. In the following year this group began to issue a monthly publication called *Taiwan Ching-nien* (Taiwan Youth). It is likely that the idea for this type of journal was inspired by the example of the increasingly well-known *Hsin Ching Nien* (New Youth), a political and intellectual magazine of the *avante garde* which had been launched in Shanghai several years before. The purpose of *Taiwan Youth* was especially to urge the "Japanese government to conform to the Wilsonian spirit of the era by granting Taiwan greater democratic representation."[16] Several years later this publication was changed to a weekly and, simultaneously, an unsuccessful attempt was made to transfer it to Taiwan.

The obstacles to setting up publication of *Taiwan Youth* in Taiwan itself underscore the policy of the Japanese colonial authorities towards newspapers in general. No newspaper could be published in Taiwan without the express permission of the colonial authorities, and no more than one paper was to be authorized for any city. Newspapers, moreover, had to be published in Japanese, though for a while they were allowed to publish a column in Chinese. As late as 1932 only four newspapers were published in Taiwan; in that year the weekly *Taiwan Ching-nien*, transferred to Taiwan only a few years before, was allowed to be published as a Chinese-language daily, the *Taiwan Shin Min-Pao*. But shortly before the outbreak of the Sino-Japanese War in 1937, it was compelled to suspend publication. Thereafter only the Japanese-language newspapers were allowed to be published.

At the end of World War I, it was not only Taiwanese university students in Japan who pressed for reforms in colonial administration. In Taiwan itself a small number of leaders in business and professional life also made known their desire for political and social change. Lin Hsien-tang was outstanding in this respect. In 1921 he founded the *Taiwan Bunka Kyọkai* (Taiwan Cultural Association) which urged the need for moderate reforms in the colonial regime and the metropolitan government in Tokyo. It became standard procedure for this group to submit petitions to the Imperial Diet. It called, above all, for home or self rule, through the election of a parliamentary assembly, for power to review the annual budget, and, understandably, for restrictions upon the authority of the Governor-General. The outcome of this clamor was the grant of a few minor concessions. But to the end of their rule the Japanese never relaxed their firm grip upon the governing of Taiwan.

If organizations like the Taiwan Cultural Association, whose political objectives and tactics were generally moderate, could not make much headway in the 1920's, groups of a more radical character were even less successful. In this respect the record of the Marxist-oriented *Taiwan Musan Seinen-kai* (Taiwan Proleterian Youth League) is enlightening. Making its appearance in 1926, it attempted to spread its ideas among intellectuals and particularly workers. After a brief period of life, it slowly faded away. In the late 1920's a pioneering labor union comprised mainly of public transportation workers, and more radical in words than in deeds, was founded. After conducting several strikes, annoying to the colonial regime, the union was suppressed. For the remaining years of the Japanese colonial era, the labor scene in Taiwan was practically devoid of any unrest.

Despite the ripples of political and intellectual restiveness in Taiwan during the decade after World War I, public peace was almost never seriously disturbed. Some writers have attributed this state of affairs to a dislike of violence by the Taiwan Chinese of this generation. This conclusion amounts to saying that, since Taiwanese did not engage in violent political actions during these years, they must have disliked violence! Other writers have stressed the efficiency of the Japanese colonial police. There is probably considerable truth to this observation. Thus, an "histori-an. . .reports over 8500 annual political arrests from 1895 to 1910, 6,500 annually in the 1920's and 3,400 annually in the 1930's, but few of the rebels were executed or given long prison terms."[17] What these statistics may perhaps suggest is that, despite the fact that the political climate was more restive than ever before during the 1920's the police actually made fewer political arrests annually during this era. Why? It is possible that, while many Taiwanese may have had grievances during these years attributable to colonial rule, these were likely not grave enough to drive them to radical political action or violent protest.

A major reason why most Taiwanese did not display overt political antagonism towards their Japanese rulers in the immediate post-World War I period may well have been their flourishing economic condition. During the 1920's just about every sector of the island's economy showed impressive indications of growth. This is well revealed by the following statistics of the gross value of production in the main sectors of the Taiwan economy.[18] The percentage of the total gross value of each sector is also shown:[19]

Gross Production in Taiwan

	1921	1929
	(millions of yen)	(millions of yen)
Agriculture	201.3	301.9
Fishing	9.6	21.0
Forestry	10.7	13.9
Industry	130.9	246.8
Mining	10.3	14.8

Percentage of Total Gross Value

	1921	1929
Agriculture	55.5	50.4
Fishing	2.6	3.5
Forestry	3.0	2.3
Industry	36.1	41.3
Mining	2.8	2.5

Actually the increases in production, that is, in the value of production, of most areas of the economy were not sharp but rather modest and steady. About 40 per cent of the increase of the total gross value of production in 1929 is creditable to the substantial rise in the output of sugar. At the beginning of the 1920's decade a drastic decline in the production of sugar occurred and full recovery was not achieved until about 1925. By 1929 output was almost doubled and the largest output to date was recorded.

An excellent barometer of the mounting economic and business activity of Taiwan during the post-World War I years is the trend of foreign trade. The increases in the volume and value of exports and imports were literally astounding, as may be noted from the following statistics:[20]

Taiwan External Trade   (in Millions of *yen*)

	Export	Import
1896-1900 (average)	14.6	18.1
1911-1915 (average)	63.0	56.6
1916-1920 (average)	158.1	117.0
1921-1925 (average)	205.3	136.8
1926-1930 (average)	252.0	186.8

A detailed analysis of these general statistics reveals the following trends and shifts in Taiwan's relations with her principal trading partners:[21]

| | Exports | | | Imports | | |
| | *(in 1,000s of yen)* | | | | | |
	1896-1900	1911-1915	1926-1930	1896-1900	1911-1915	1926-1930
U.S.A.	659	5,689	4,866	957	1,252	3,413
Great Britain	1	877	1,053	1,326	2,340	3,083
China	9,182	3,864	19,529	6,771	6,970	25,893
Japan	2,860	49,122	215,210	4,888	40,071	127,666

During this period from 1896 to 1930 Japan's share of Taiwan's export trade rose from 19.6 per cent to 85.5 per cent. Japan's share of Taiwan's imports increased from 27 per cent to 68.3 per cent. China's share of Taiwan's exports declined from 63.1 per cent to 7.8 per cent, while her share of Taiwan's imports fell from 37.4 per cent to 13.8 per cent.

The continuous expansion of Taiwan's external trade, especially after the close of the First World War, was facilitated by and at the same time stimulated the growth of the island's principal ports. Prior to 1895 the main ports of Taiwan were Tamshui,(Japanese, Hobe) in the northwest corner of the island and Anping (Japanese, Anpei) on the southwest coast. Even before China surrendered the island to Japan, Tamshui was being ignored and steps were being taken by the local government to improve the harbor of Keelung (Japanese,Kürum). When Japan occupied Taiwan, work to develop the port of Keelung was continued. In 1912 the third development program of a series of five was inaugurated. When it was completed in 1929, Keelung harbor was equipped to handle more than half of the island's external trade.

Keelung's development as the major port of Taiwan was favored by the Japanese for many reasons. It was advantageously situated with respect to the city of Taipei which had been selected by the Japanese government as the administrative seat, or capital, of Taiwan. In the area around Keelung, moreover, were located the principal coal mines of the island. Though not of first-rate quality, this coal was usable by many of the steamships which called at Keelung. In time coal was to become an important export commodity. Keelung, finally, was situated much closer to Japan and Shanghai, markets for many of the island's exports and sources of many of its imports.

Another major port developed by the Japanese was Kaohsiung (Japanese, Takao) on the southwest coast; old Anping lies a short distance to the north. In the late nineteenth century Kaohsiung was little more than a sleepy fishing village. By the end of World War I it had sprouted into the second busiest port in Taiwan, handling more than 40 per cent of the island's import and export trade. For many years thereafter a comparable volume of trade passed through the port of Kaohsiung. As the city steadily grew into one of the foremost industrial centers of the island, it flourished as the site of refineries to process imported petroleum. Because of its oil refineries, port facilities, and numerous factories Kaohsiung was heavily bombed from the air in World War II.

In addition to lavishing expenses on the development of Keelung and Kaohsiung, the Japanese devoted great attention to Taipei, capital of the colonial regime. It was connected by railway with both nearby Keelung and Tamshui. A railroad from Taipei extended southward along the coast for about two hundred miles to Kaohsiung. A larger part of the island's Japanese inhabitants lived and worked in the capital. Many of the old buildings and edifices of the Chinese era were preserved by the Japanese for many years and, with the new and modern public buildings and offices, Taipei long continued to have a unique appearance among the urban communities of Taiwan.

Not many foreigners (westerners) lived in Taiwan during the Japanese colonial period. In many respects, this state of affairs was little different from the situation before June, 1895. A handful of Catholic and Protestant missionaries continued to proselytize and look after their "flocks" who congregated mainly in the cities and larger towns.[22] A few foreign consuls, looking after their country's commercial interests, resided in the "Foreign Quarter" of Taipei but were frequent visitors to Keelung and Kaohsiung. An occasional curious traveler from Japan or a Westerner engaged in a world tour debarked at Keelung and appreciative tourist guides soon arranged for them to gawk at and take photographs of "tame aborigines."[23] What Westerners knew about Taiwan in the years after World War I was derived from the occasional travelogue published in Europe or the United States.[24]

Visitors to Taiwan, coming on from Japan rather than
Shanghai or Hong Kong, had the opportunity in Taipei to get
first-hand information about one of the most commonly discussed
practices ("evils") of Asia, namely, opium-smoking. What interested
the ordinary tourist is that the Japanese authorities in Taiwan,
unlike many other governments in the Orient, were carrying on a
long-range program to eliminate the practice of opium-smoking.
Launched not long after the Japanese annexation of the island, the
results were beginning to become significantly evident after more
than a full generation of implementation.

During the peace negotiations at Shimonoseki Li Hung-
chang, in attempting to deflect the Japanese demand for the
cession of Taiwan, had pointed out the problems of opium-smuggl-
ing and opium-smoking. The Japanese negotiators had undaunt-
edly responded that they were equal to the challenge. But after
they had floundered about for several years the colonial authorities in Taiwan ruefully admitted that new approaches were
essential if the widespread problem of opium-smoking were to be
brought under control.

Starting with the administration of Gotō, Japanese policy
towards opium-smoking followed the principle of attrition rather
than abolition. From this time on, opium-smokers were required
to register with the government. Thereafter they were permitted
to obtain their habitual ration from an official agency at a fixed
price. A crackdown was instituted against opium-smugglers, and
illegal handlers of opium throughout the island soon felt the heavy
hand of the law. In an effort to discourage the development of
opium-addiction among the young, educational programs were
carried out continuously in the growing school system. At the
same time the police, working with the *pao-chia* system, were
assigned responsibility for enforcing the laws concerning opium
handling and smoking.

In the initial registration of opium-smokers in 1898 licenses
were applied for by 95,449 addicts. It is safe to assume that not all
the users of opium on Taiwan made themselves known to the
appropriate officials. Despite the fact that new addicts were
frowned upon by the government 119,991 opium-smokers were
registered with the government ten years later. But in 1926 the
number of registrants dropped to only 31,434. Most of these
registrants, officials were careful to point out, were over fifty-five

years of age. How successful the Japanese policy finally was may be guaged from the fact that there were only 10,788 registered opium-smokers in 1938. The Japanese Opium Monopoly set up many years before had obviously proven its worth.

Fifty years ago visitors to Taipei were urged to visit the local Botanical Garden which boasted a magnificent collection of the island's tropical plants and flowers. Prominently displayed were samples of Taiwan's orchids, which have since become highly admired by horticulturists around the world. The Taihoku (Taipei) Imperial University was opened in 1928, and soon became one of the island's showpieces. During the seventeen years it continued under Japanese administration, its student body remained quite small.[25] Japanese students, usually the sons of local residents who could not afford to attend a homeland university, ordinarily outnumbered the Chinese by more than two to one. The faculty too was almost exclusively Japanese. (Several teachers colleges were also established by the Japanese in Taiwan. Their students, largely Japanese, underwent training as staff for island schools).

In the late 1920's the political climate, which had been somewhat moderate for about a decade, began to change in Japan. As the so-called "liberal twenties" started to peter out, liberal, democratic, and radical movements and activities soon came into official disfavor. Simultaneously the Japanese government which had been pursuing policies of cooperation in international affairs, began to veer towards an increasingly nationalistic course. The backwash of these shifts was quickly felt throughout the Japanese Empire, including of course Taiwan.

The steady shift in Japanese policies in Taiwan which set in about 1928 was not noticeable principally in the realm of political affairs. The native people of Taiwan had long since become accustomed to a greater or lesser degree of governmental arbitrariness. By the 1930's, it may be assumed, the Japanese had every reason to believe that their policemen and armed forces were more than adequate to handle any threat to public peace that might arise. As a matter of fact, as has been seen, the number of political arrests made annually reached an all-time low during this decade.

In addition to having confidence in its police and military establishments, the Japanese government had no reason to believe that its colonial administrative officials would be unable to deal appropriately with challenges to imperial authority. By the early years of the Japanese Showa era (1926 - - - - -) the colonial administrative system had had some thirty years of experience in directing Taiwan affairs. Various changes had been made since the days of Kodama and Gotō and by the late 1920's the Japanese government was reasonably certain that no major reorganization or overhauling of administrative practices would be called for in the foreseeable future.

At the apex of the colonial government in Taiwan was, as has been seen, the Governor-General, who received his appointment from the Emperor himself. During the half century of Japanese colonial rule the average term of office of the governors-general was a little more than two years. This official possessed an awesome authority and when it was combined, as it frequently was, with his powers as commander of the military forces on the island, he was in effect one of the most powerful functionaries in the Japanese Empire. About a half dozen ministries and many more bureaus and offices, mainly staffed by Japanese bureaucrats and technicians, were assigned primary responsiblity for on-going administrative affairs. The chiefs of these administrative departments were the "staff officers" of the Governor-General. Conspicuously absent from high-level administrative positions were the Taiwan Chinese.

After World War I, provision was made for the establishment of an advisory council for the Governor-General. Its members, numbering forty or so, were appointed for two-year terms by the Governor-General, who could also dismiss them arbitrarily. The members of the council were selected from the ranks of high civilian officials and military officers who were ordinarily Japanese. The council had no real power; its advice was accepted or rejected, as he saw fit, by the Governor-General.

The prefectural governments were an administrative step lower than the central government in Taipei. Their system of rule was modeled basically upon the pattern of the central colonial government. While the local governors were of course responsible to their superior in Taipei, within their administrative bailiwicks they were the epitome of imperial authority. In addition to the prefectural organizations, the poorer and less developed areas of the island were set up as districts for administrative purposes. On Taiwan these districts were located in the eastern regions of the island.

Other levels of administration were established by the Japanese to oversee purely local concerns. In addition to county governmental machinery, the larger cities and towns were supervised closely by Japanese administrative officials. It was mainly on these levels that the Taiwan Chinese were permitted to participate in their own administration. No one, however, whether Chinese or Japanese, had any illusions about the repository of ultimate power.

In retrospect, it seems fairly obvious that the most meaningful changes in Taiwan in the decade before the outbreak of the Pacific War were those related to economic and military affairs. The impact of the Depression which began to engulf Japan after 1928 is easily measured in the decline in economic production which characterized just about every sector of the island's economy. The gross value of the output in agriculture, industry, fishing, and forestry dropped off steadily; only mining registered regular increases in the gross value of production during the early years of the Depression. A fairly good barometer of economic happenings during the era from 1927 to 1936, when a recovery was well under way, is the annual production of the all-important sugar.[26]

Sugar Production, 1927-1936

1927	411,140 (tons)
1929	789,328
1930	810,484
1931	989,048
1933	633,724
1934	647,724
1935	965,652
1936	901,679

By 1935 the worst of the depression had passed and output in many sectors of the economy had started to surpass previous all-time Taiwan records. Equally important was the establishment of new types of industrial enterprises and the production gains scored in certain technically complex industries. Neither the output of coal nor of oil increased significantly in the 1930's but since Taiwan's needs for coal were very modest, they were easily met by the island's mines. As for oil, it was largely imported and refined by the facilities at Kaohsiung. Despite the island's good potential for the generation of hydroelectric power, as late as 1933 production did not exceed 40,000 kilowatts. In 1934, however, the Japanese completed a monumental engineering project which resulted in a major increase in the supply of hydroelectric power.

Many a visitor to Sun Moon Lake (Japanese, Jitsugetsu-tan; Chinese, Jih-yüeh Tan) in the foothills of the mountains in central Taiwan is, even today, unaware that the beautiful body of water is artificially made. The lake, more than 2,000 feet above sea level, was created by tunneling water from sources much higher in the mountains. The descending water is then used to generate electric power: in the 1930's this amounted to 200,000 kilowatts. No hydroelectric station in the entire East Asian area, with the exception of Japan itself and Manchuria, could equal this output for many years. Much of the power was fed into factories engaged in the production of manganese, aluminum, and chemicals.

In the decade after the onset of the world Depression Japanese international trade was subjected to a variety of political and economic pressures. Most alarming to Japan were the restrictions, in the form of tariff barriers, imposed upon the admission of her exports into the markets of many nations. Since Japan's economic well-being was heavily dependent upon foreign trade, her political and military leaders bitterly denounced the tariff policies of the antagonistic powers. In order to cope with the crisis Japan made some basic modifications in her own external trade practices. Most notable were the steps she took to bind her imperial overseas territories economically closer to her. This is well seen in the experience of Manchuria, Korea, and Taiwan. Since such Japanese trade policy was best illustrated by the example of Taiwan, let us see how the island fared in its trading relations with Japan in the decade before the outbreak of World War II.

In the following table the value of Taiwan's exports to Japan during key years of the period, 1930-1939, are set forth.[27]

Exports from Taiwan to Japan
1930-1939

1930	215,210,000 *(yen)*
1936	358,895,000

1937	410,259,000
1938	420,104,000
1939	509,745,000

From these statistics it is apparent that during the period in question the *yen* value of Taiwan's exports to Japan rose steadily. During this same period Taiwan's exports to areas brought under Japanese political and military control also inched gradually upward. What this means is that by the end of the decade of the 1930's Taiwan's export trade was carried on overwhelmingly with the Japanese Empire and satellite regions. Simultaneously, exports to the United States, the European powers, and the Asian colonial areas of the European powers practically disappeared. (Similar trends are evident in the export trade of Korea and "Manchukuo" during these years). Perhaps as much as 80 per cent of the commodities shipped out of Taiwan consisted of the traditional types of foodstuff that had long been the mainstay of its export trade.

Insofar as Taiwan's imports during the 1930's are concerned, increasingly they were obtained from Japan and areas under her control. The relevant statistics are given below. [28]

Imports into Taiwan from Japan
(1930-1939)

1930	127,666,000 *(yen)*
1936	243,832,000
1937	277,895,000
1938	327,950,000
1939	357,608,000

As in the case of exports, so too Taiwan's best trading partner for imports was Japan. In 1930 about 70 per cent of the colony's imports came from the Japanese Empire. In the following years the percentage moved steadily upward so that by the end of the decade it exceeded 90 per cent. From outside the Empire Taiwan imported primarily those goods and raw materials which were not otherwise available.

It is obvious that during the years 1930-1939 Taiwan sold much more to Japan than it purchased, and the island colony enjoyed constantly a "favorable balance of trade." Japan would of course have preferred to ship more goods, mainly manufactured products, to Taiwan but the matter was scarcely critical. In the first place, since the trade between Japan and Taiwan took place within the framework of the *yen* bloc, no inordinate problems were raised for the government in Tokyo. Secondly, it should be borne in mind that Japan's imports from Taiwan went a long way towards enabling her to fulfill larger imperial objectives. Since about 1914 Japan had had to import increasing amounts of foodstuffs each year to feed her growing population. She preferred to acquire as much as possible of these needed foodstuffs from sources within the Empire. During each year of the 1930's rice and sugar comprised between 60 to 70 per cent of Taiwan's exports to Japan. In fact, Taiwan was one of the principal suppliers of these two staple foodstuffs and, as such, relieved Japan of the need to expend foreign exchange in purchasing these items outside the Empire. Finally, when the Japanese government considered its trade balance with Taiwan, it was viewed in the final analysis as only one item in the overall pattern of trade with all areas of the overseas Empire. In this overall picture, Japan enjoyed a favorable balance of trade.

Despite the fact that military affairs began to figure more prominently in Japanese imperial policies, especially after 1931 when Japan invaded Manchuria, the impact was not felt directly in Taiwan for many years. Whatever hopes Japanese expansionists may have had for extension of the Empire after the Mukden Incident, they did not entail advances to the south. Until the eruption of the Sino-Japanese War in July, 1937, the attention of Japanese military and foreign policy-makers was riveted upon Manchuria, Inner Mongolia, and North China. The build-up of the Japanese military establishment at home and on the continent was primarily a mission of the Japanese and, secondarily, of the Korean and Manchurian industrial systems. As late as the time of the Marco Polo Bridge Incident it does not seem that the Japanese authorities saw any compelling need to assign Taiwan a role in the imperial scheme of things essentially different from what it had played since the days of the Depression.

Not long after the initial clashes between Chinese and Japanese troops at Lukouchiao (Marcho Polo Bridge) the struggle slowly spread into central eastern and then South China. In these circumstances the Japanese army, navy, and air force began to exploit the strategic locale of Taiwan. More and more it was looked upon as a fortress and arsenal, as a staging base, for military operations against obstreperous China. A buildup of military and naval facilities slowly got under way. Port installations at Kaohsiung, Keelung, and Tainan were improved and extended, while airfields for the use of the Navy and Army Air Forces were enlarged in the vicinity of these cities.

The value of Taiwan as a staging base for Japanese offensive operations was made crystal clear to the world during the opening days of the Pacific War in December, 1941. As one facet of its overall plan to overrun the colonial areas of Southeast Asia the Japanese High Command launched an assault by carrier-based aircraft against American naval and air bases in Hawaii. Within hours after the execution of this daring thrust the Philippines were taken under attack. The initial critical blows, upon which the success or failure of the subsequent amphibious assaults by Japanese troops depended, were struck by Army and Navy planes based on Taiwan. When these aircraft blitzed American air installations on the northern Philippine island of Luzon, achieving results beyond the highest expectations of the attackers themselves, the success of the Japanese sweep over the Philippines, Malaya, and the East Indies was assured.

After the outbreak of World War II in the Pacific, Taiwan was shielded for several years from the agonies of battle. To be sure, its agricultural and industrial output was counted upon by Japan to assist in the maintenance of her forces temporarily or permanently stationed on the island. Exportable surpluses shipped to Japan were valued more so that ever before. Taiwan was also used as a training camp for army troops who were to be used in campaigns in the jungle areas of the Southwest Pacific. Japanese ships, laden with cargoes of raw materials from the lands of Southeast Asia, were provided with air cover against attacks by American submarines, by aircraft based on Taiwan. And large amounts of military supplies for Japan's forces in Southeast Asia were distributed from storehouses on the island. With all this beehive of activity it was still difficult for the people of Taiwan to understand that a war of unprecedented proportions was raging throughout the Pacific and much of East and Southeast Asia until the closing months of 1944. It was then that the island first began to experience the fury of the conflict.

With the fall of the Mariana Islands in the western Pacific to United States amphibious forces in the summer of 1944 Taiwan began to loom large in the analyses of American naval strategists. The United States plan to cut the Japanese wartime empire in half by a bisecting attack across the central Pacific seemed to be entering its final stage. The successful completion of this operation, it was believed, would not only isolate Japanese military forces in the Southwest Pacific but would also sever the vital supply lines between Japan and Southeast Asia. In American strategy councils, consequently, proposals were made for an American assault against Taiwan and perhaps related landings on the coasts of mainland China.

Taiwan was spared from such a pounding when the aforementioned military strategy was opposed by General Douglas MacArthur, supreme commander in the Southwest Pacific Theater of Operations. He called instead for a gigantic campaign to recover the Philippines, a maneuver which got under way in October, 1944, when landings were made at Leyte in the central Philippines. To forestall air raids by the Japanese from airfields outside the area of the Philippines, American aircraft hit Japanese airfields in Taiwan among others. Such air attacks were to be carried out periodically during the remaining months of the war. Since selective rather than mass bombings were made, the destruction in Taiwan was localized. Some of the principal targets were military and industrial installations at Taipei, Keelung, Tainan, and Kaohsiung, the last city doubtless suffering the heaviest damage.

During the battle for the Philippines the desperate Japanese defenders introduced a "secret weapon" which they hoped would enable them to turn the tide of the war. Before the Philippine campaign had run its course Japanese *kamikaze* pilots inflicted heavy damage upon American ships but did not succeed in turning defeat into victory. When the outcome of the battle was clear beyond a shadow of doubt, the Special Attack Force, as the *kamikaze* units were called, was ordered to fall back to stations in Taiwan. With her forward echelons in the Southwest Pacific isolated and neutralized, Japan's first line of defense against the advancing American forces consisted of the island bastions of Iwo-jima, Okinawa, and Taiwan. To help in the defense of these islands, especially the latter two, the Japanese Navy depended heavily upon *kamikaze* pilots "trained" on Taiwan.[29]

While Japan was devising measures to defend Taiwan to the last man of its garrison, plans on the Chinese side were afoot to divest her of control of the island. For many years the Nationalist government of China had been too preoccupied with mainland problems to concern itself with Taiwan. In 1940-1941, however, it was impressed upon China's wartime government in Chungking that some Chinese in Taiwan believed they had a major stake in the struggle against Japan. Though it had been known for some time that only sporadic resistance was being waged against the island's colonial rulers, evidence seemd to be mounting that the anti-Japanese activists among Taiwan Chinese were beginning to take a united stand.

In the spring of 1940 it was announced that the Federation of Taiwan Revolutionists had been founded. Composed of a small number of anti-Japanese organizations, some of whom had for several years engaged in sabotage in Taiwan, the Federation pledged to continue the struggle to disrupt Japan's war effort on the island. The Federation also began to publish a newspaper, the *Taiwan Hsiengang*, to publicize its ideas and activities.[30]

A momentous proposal affecting the future of Taiwan was made towards the close of 1943. In November President Franklin D. Roosevelt of the United States, Prime Minister Winston Churchill of Great Britain, and President Chiang Kai-shek of the Republic of China convened in Cairo to discuss plans for the future prosecution of the war against Japan. Their major political decision was enunciated in the historic Cairo Declaration.[31]

> The several military missions have agreed upon future military operations against Japan. They covet no gain for themselves and have no thought of territorial expansion. It is their purpose that Japan shall be stripped of all the islands in the Pacific which she has seized or occupied sonce the beginning of the first World War in 1914, and that all the territories Japan has stolen from the Chinese, such as Manchuria, Formosa (Taiwan), and the Pescadores, shall be restored to the Republic of China.

Here, for the first time, the restoration of Taiwan to the Republic of China was explicitly set forth as a war aim of the Allied Powers against Japan.

In 1943 the Nationalist government of China also set up a

Taiwan Provincial Headquarters, presumably in Chungking. This move revealed succinctly the direction of thinking of Nationalist China's leaders with respect to Taiwan. Despite the urgings of Taiwan revolutionaries the Nationalist government remained reluctant "to establish a Taiwan Provisional Government in preparation for the recovery of the island."[32]

The promise of the Cairo Declaration was reiterated in the final wartime pronouncement of the Allied leaders. On July 26, 1945, President Roosevelt and Prime Minister Churchill, "with the full concurrence of President Chiang Kai-shek" who was not present, issued the Potsdam Declaration. "The terms of the Cairo Declaration," it was stated in Article 9, "shall be carried out...."[33]

A few weeks later the world heaved a sigh of relief when the Empire of Japan announced its surrender. It was decided by General MacArthur, Supreme Commander of the Allied Powers, that the Republic of China would accept the surrender of the Japanese military forces in Taiwan. Almost 200,000 troops, comprising the Japanese 10th Area Army, laid down their arms on the island, and together with thousands of officers and men in the Japanese Navy and Air Force, were shortly thereafter repatriated. In addition, thousands of Japanese civilians, mainly members of the erstwhile colonial administration, were evacuated to their homeland. In the months after the surrender a few hundred of the some 30,000 Taiwanese, staying in various parts of the former Japanese Empire and officially designated as "displaced persons," were repatriated.

Several years elapsed before the government of Japan officially and legally gave up the sovereignty over Taiwan which it had acquired by the Treaty of Shimonoseki. This was done in the Treaty of San Francisco of 1952 in which the Allied Powers and Japan formally concluded arrangements for peace. In this treaty Japan abandoned legal title to Taiwan. A separate instrument of peace was negotiated between Japan and the Republic of China.

From a very early moment in Japan's history as colonial sovereign of Taiwan, and for many years thereafter, the question was often raised in Japan as well as abroad as to her success or failure as a colonial power. Since the end of World War II Chinese and especially the younger generation of scholars in Japan have frequently raised the issue. As may quickly be surmised, verdicts have ranged the spectrum from unqualified approval to blanket condemnation. Considering the widely varying criteria that have over the years been adduced to assess Japan's "success or failure as a colonial power," it is not surprising that nothing aprroximating a consensus has emerged. Nor does it seem likely that general agreement on so controversial a matter will ever be achieved.

Other questions aside, how did Japanese of the pre-1945 era, particularly those who were in a position to make an intelligent judgment, appraise their country's record of rule in Taiwan? In this respect, it must be borne in mind, most Japanese — whether politician, military leader, colonial administrator, or intellectual — held in common a basic premise. According to this belief, Taiwan, from the moment of its transfer from Chinese to Japanese sovereignty, was an integral part of the Greater Japanese Empire. As such, the interests and welfare of the island were subordinate to those of the Empire of which it had become a constituent component. Taiwan was not deemed to have a *raison d'être* independent of its sovereign, symbolized by His Imperial Majesty.[34]

When General Kodama was appointed Governor-General of Taiwan in 1898, he succeeded, with the assistance of Gotō Shimpei, in formulating a colonial policy for Taiwan.[35] For all practical purposes this policy was not altered during the remaining years of Japanese rule of the island. Its central objective, in the short run, was to make Taiwan financially self sufficient; Taiwan was to pay its own way within the Japanese Empire. The practice of the metropolitan government furnishing subsidies for the administration and development of its colony, as had been customary during the early years of its transfer from China, was to be terminated as quickly as possible. To the extent that this aim was realized, the Japanese were to characterize their record in Taiwan as successful. That the financial drain upon Japan ceased during the first decade of the twentieth century was a source of deep satisfaction to Japan's political leaders.

The correlated and long range Japanese colonial policy in Taiwan was to insure that the island contribute to the larger national interests of the mother country. During practically the entire colonial era this meant that, on an economic level, Taiwan was to serve as a provider of needed agricultural commodities, notably foodstuffs, for Japan; in return the island colony was to function as a market for Japanese goods and services. During the later years of Japanese rule especially Japan's leaders were commonly convinced that the broader imperial interest was being substantially advanced by their island colony in the tropics. While to be sure the maintenance of a large military establishment and garrison on Taiwan, particularly after the outbreak of the Sino-Japanese War in 1937, entailed heavy expenses for the home government, this was viewed as a necessary outlay for the Empire as a whole.

Japan's achievement in promoting the economic development of Taiwan has invariably been discussed in laudatory terms. It is not difficult to see why the colonial administrators of other powers were impressed by, at least, the technical aspects of Japan's accomplishments. It is true that many Taiwan people benefitted, directly and indirectly, from these accomplishments. Considered in the simplest but most fundamental way the Taiwan people generally attained a much higher standard of living under Japanese rule than they had as subjects of Manchu China. But when one gets to the heart of the matter, it may be said that this result was a coincidental outcome of otherwise different primary colonial aims. In short, Taiwan and not the Taiwan people represented the greatest concern of Japan.

In addition to Japanese opinions, estimates of the nature of Japan's colonial record in Taiwan are available from the Taiwanese side during the entire period of Japanese rule. That many Taiwanese throughout the period of 1895-1945 were less interested in the material aspects of the Japanese colonial record and more concerned with the harsh spirit of Japanese rule is clear. Some Taiwan people of every generation living under Japanese colonialism found courage to vent their dissatisfaction in one way or another. "In the first 20 years after 1895," a recent report notes,[36]

> no less than twenty-one anti-Japanese uprisings occurred in Taiwan. The movement continued unabated throughout the years. As late as 1930 a major uprising broke out among the Chinese and aborigines and it took the Japanese civil and military authorities months to suppress it. Since 1915, Chinese and aborigines in Taiwan have used political means in their fight against the invaders. No less than 138 political organizations were formed for the restoration of Chinese rule over the island.

These evidences of anti-Japanese activity should be understood for what they essentially were: "votes of no-confidence" in Japanese rule and expressions of disdain for Japan's colonial achievements.

Admittedly an overwhelming number of Taiwanese did not overtly display whatever antagonism they may have privately felt toward their alien imperial rulers. The tight controls exercised by the police discouraged open opposition, while the close supervision of the press made the expression of critical or seditious sentiments well-nigh impossible.

Despite this, it must be admitted that, while most Taiwan Chinese were gladdened by the prospect of returning to the fold of their fatherland when the curtain fell on World War II in the Pacific, they did not always think too unkindly of their departing Japanese rulers. Many a Taiwanese, to be sure, did not find it difficult to muster up grievances and complaints against his former imperial overlords. And, yet, numerous islanders in all walks of life had fared well under Japanese domination. Perhaps it would not be unfair to say that any number of the islanders looked upon the departing Japanese in 1945 as wardens unacceptable but used to, who should best be sped on their way homeward.

Notes to Chapter VIII

1 Takekoshi, Yosaburo, *Japanese Rule in Formosa*. trans. by George Braithwaite (London, 1907), p. 12.

2 As Takekoshi reported, "Our losses in the whole campaign were as under, *viz*.:—

Died in Formosa of Disease 4,642
Sent to Japan for treatment 21,748
Remaining in hospitals in Formosa 5,246
Killed in battle (officers and soldiers) 164
Wounded (not fatally, officers and soldiers) .515

Unhappily His Imperial Highness Prince Kitashirakawa succumbed to an attack of malarial fever. . . .The Chinese losses are impossible to ascertain, but it is said that no less that 7,000 dead were actually found on the field." *Ibid.*, p. 91.

3 Some Japanese officials actually proposed that Japan get rid of her "white elephant" by selling it to another power.

4 "We have, it is true," wrote Gotō Shimpei, "emerged victorious from the recent war, but the world still doubts our colonizing ability." Gotō, in the Preface to Takekoshi, *op. cit.*, p.vi. As for Takekoshi himself, he too addressed a few remarks on the sensitive issue. "Western nations," he stated, "have long believed that on their shoulders alone rested the responsibility of colonizing the yet unopened portions of the globe, and extending to the inhabitants the benefits of civilization; but now we Japanese rising from the ocean in the extreme Orient, wish as a nation to take part in this great and glorious work." *Ibid.*, p. vii.

5 George W. Barclay, *Colonial Development and Population in Taiwan* (Princeton, 1954), pp. 136-137.

6 For some details see: E. Patricia Tsurumi, "Taiwan under Kodama Gentarō and Gotō Shimpei," Harvard University, East Asian Research Center, *Papers on Japan*, IV (1967), pp. 112-113; 124.

7 A useful study of the development of the Japanese police system on Formosa is: Chen Ching-shih, "The Police and *Hoko* Systems in Taiwan under Japanese Administration (1895-1945)," Harvard University, East Asian Research Center, *Papers on Japan*, IV (1967), pp. 147-176.

8 Tsurumi, *op. cit.*, pp. 117-118.

9 Patricia Tsurumi makes the following incisive comparison of Kodama and Gotō: "In the works which deal with the administration in Taiwan from 1898 to 1906, one is struck not only by Gotō's fund of ideas, his ability and initiative, but also by the fact that among those who knew both Gotō and Kodama in their Taiwan days, Kodama is almost invariably remembered as the greater man. A soldier who not only tolerated but actively supported civilian rule, a superior who made no speeches when his subordinate advised him not to, [he was]. . . a general who chased politicians all over Japan. . ." *Ibid.*, p. 137.

10 Accounts of Japanese struggles with the aborigines comprise a large part of the popular literature written in the West before 1930. For an official

version designed for the edification of Westerners, consult: Government of Formosa. *Report on the Control of the Aborigines in Formosa.* Taihoku, 1911. This brochure is copiously illustrated.

11 Camphor had a variety of industrial uses. It entered into the manufacture of celluloid and smokeless gunpowder. It was also an ingredient in various drugs and salves. Many insect repellants used in the household contained camphor or camphor oil. In recent years natural camphor has been replaced industrially by synthetics.

12 Andrew J. Grajdanzev, *Formosa Today* (New York, 1942), p. 58. For further details on the introduction of the Taiwan Sugar Policy see: Kitasawa, Sukeo. *The Life of Dr. Nitobe* (Tokyo, 1953), pp. 43-48.

13 *Ibid.,* pp. 59-60.

14 Quoted in: Douglas Mendal,*The Politics of Formosan Nationalism* (Berkeley, 1970), p. 22.

15 Takekoshi, *op. cit.*, pp. 295-296.

16 Mendel, *op. cit.*, p. 21.

17 W. G. Goddard, cited in Mendal, *op. cit.*, p. 22.

18 Grajdanzev, *op. cit.*, p. 90.

19 *Ibid.,* p. 90.

20 Garjdanzev, *op. cit.*, p. 142.

21 *Ibid.*, p. 143.

22 In Taiwan, as in mainland China, the missionaries were deeply interested in education at all levels. The Presbyterian Seminary in Tainan was one of the better institutions of college caliber founded in Taiwan in the pre-World War II period.

23 For many years after World War I travelers in the Japanese Empire were usually "armed" with T. Philip Terry's invaluable *Terry's Guide to the Japanese Empire, Including Korea and Formosa* (Boston, 1914, 1920, and 1928). Travelers in search of a thrill in Taiwan were informed of the following on pages 783-784 (1920 ed.): "An excursion to a village of reclaimed savages can be made by conferring with the hotel manager and obtaining a police escort."

24 The travelogues on Taiwan written by Westerners between 1921 and the outbreak of World War II are listed in: Yuan Tung-li, *China in Western Literature* (New Haven, 1958), pp. 664-665. It will readily be noticed that almost all of the listed works were written in the 1920's; very few of the books date from the 1930's.

25 Taihoku Imperial University, it has been noted, "was organized to promote research rather than teaching, its classes were small, and Taiwanese students were not readily admitted." Barclay, *op. cit.*, p. 68.

26 Statistics extracted from Grajdanzev, *op. cit.*, p. 98.

27 Statistics extracted from Grajdanzev, *ibid.*, p. 143.

28 Statistics extracted from Grajdanzev, *ibid.*, p. 143.

29 For data on the *kamikaze* units see: R. Inoguchi, *et.al. Divine Wind: Japan's Suicide Squadrons in World War II* (New York, 1970), *passim.*

30 Grajdanzev, *op. cit.*, p. 179.

31 Text in: Chinese Ministry of Information (comp.). *China Handbook, 1937-1945*, rev. and enlarged with 1946 Supplement (New York, 1947), pp. 128-129.

32 *Ibid.*, p. 34.

33 Complete text in *ibid.*, 129-130.

34 A notable exception during the pre-World War II years was the highly respected Professor Yanaihara Tadao. In his well-known study, *Teikoku Shugi-ka no Taiwan* (Taiwan under Imperialism), published in 1929, he revealed his sympathy for the plight of Taiwanese.

35 See especially: Chang Han-yu and Myers Ramon H., "Japanese Colonial Development Policy in Taiwan, 1895-1906: a Case of Bureaucratic Entrepreneurship," *Journal of Asian Studies*, XXII, no. 4 (August 1963), pp. 436-437.

36 Chinese Ministry of Information (comp.). *op. cit.*, p. 34.

Select Bibliography

Barclay, George W., *Colonial Development and Population in Taiwan* (Princeton: Princeton University Press, 1954).

Chang, Han-yu and Myers, Ramon H., "Japanese Colonial Development Policy in Taiwan, 1895-1906; a Case of Bureaucratic Entrepreneurship," *Journal of Asian Studies*, XXII, no. 4 (August, 1963), 433-449.

Chen Ching-chih,, "The Police and *Hoko* Systems in Taiwan under Japanese Administration (1895-1945)," Harvard University, East Asian Research Center, *Papers on Japan*, IV (1967), 147-176.

Grajdanzev, Andrew J., *Formosa Today: an Analysis of the Economic Development and Strategic Importance of Japan's Tropical Colony* (New York: Institute of Pacific Relations, 1942).

Katsura, Taro, and others, "Formosa," in Alfred Stead (ed.), *Japan by the Japanese: a Survey by Its Highest Authorites* (New York: Dodd, Mead, 1904).

Kublin, Hyman, "The Evolution of Japanese Colonialism," *Comparative Studies in Society and History*, II, no. 1 (October, 1959), 67-84.

Lamley, Harry J., "The 1895 Taiwan Republic: a Significant Episode in Modern Chinese History," *Journal of Asian Studies*, XXVII, no. 4 (August, 1968), 739-762.

Mancall, Mark (ed.)., *Formosa Today* (New York: Frederick A. Praeger, 1964).

Report on the Control of the Aborigines in Formosa. Issued by the Bureau of Aboriginal Affairs, Government of Formosa (Taihoku: Bureau of Aboriginal Affairs, 1911).

Takekoshi, Yosaburo, *Japanese Rule in Formosa*. trans. by George Braithwaite (London: Longmans, Green, 1907).

Tsurumi, E. Patricia, "Taiwan under Kodama Gentarō and Gotō Shimpei," Harvard University, East Asia Research Center, *Papers on Japan*, IV (1967), 95-146.

Uhalley, Jr., Stephen, "The Taiwanese in Taiwan" in Joseph M. Kitagawa (ed.), *Understanding Modern China* (Chicago: University of Chicago, 1969), 163-184.

Chapter IX

Taiwan's Movement into Political Modernity, 1945-1972

BY RICHARD L. WALKER

espite the attention to political dynamics and political development in many of the newly emergent countries of the world, particularly in Africa and Asia, the image of an unchanging Taiwan, or Government of the Republic of China (GRC), has persisted. This is a remarkable fact, given the acknowledged economic dynamism and rapid movement into other aspects of modernization on an island which in 1972 had a population greater than any of almost three-quarters of the world's countries. By most of the standards set forth in the literature on political development produced in the 1960's and early 1970's, the GRC was a politically developed country in 1972.

Perhaps the image of an unchanging Taiwan comes from the fact that so many of the initial political leaders who participated in moving the GRC to Taiwan were still active and in power in 1972. This included the redoubtable Chiang Kai-shek who in March 1972 was re-elected to the Presidency of the National Government for his fifth six-year term at the age of eighty-four. But beneath the façade of seeming consistency and continuity in Taiwan (some critics call it stagnation), formidable changes have taken place. Politically many of them portend future developments which deserve attention.

When on December 10, 1949 Chiang Kai-shek arrived in Taipei from the Chinese mainland — still technically in "retirement" from the Presidency which he did not reassume until March 1 the following year — the political and other fortunes of the Chinese Nationalists were at lowest ebb. As seen from Taipei at that time, the situation could hardly have been worse. With regard to international status, the United States in its famous August *China*

White Paper had written off the Nationalists' cause.[2] A follow-up
Department of State policy guidance paper of December 23, 1949
had advised American diplomats to prepare for the fall of Taiwan
to the Communists.[3] The words commonly used at that time to
describe the Nationalist cause were "discredited," "corrupt,"
"reactionary," and "hopeless." Certainly the morale of those
Nationalist leaders who straggled into Taiwan beginning in 1948
and through 1950 was all but shattered. The Taiwan they came to
had been bombed during World War II, production was down,
inflation was rife, housing and other facilities were far from
adequate, and there seemed no way to handle the more than
million immigrants who became an almost intolerable burden. As
Neil H. Jacoby, in his very balanced assessment *U.S. Aid to
Taiwan*, points out:

> When U.S. economic aid to the Republic of China was
> resumed in the latter part of 1950, after the outbreak of the
> Korean War, the Nationalist government in Taiwan was in a critical
> financial and economic position. Food, clothing, and basic
> necessities of living were in short supply, as a consequence of
> wartime losses of production facilities and a rapid increase in
> population by natural causes and inflow from mainland China.
> Heavy military spending on defense had created huge deficits in
> the Chinese budget. Price inflation was threatening to repeat the
> tragic sequence of events that contributed to the Communist
> takeover of mainland China. During 1950, the Chinese government
> lost about $90 million in convertible currencies, reducing its
> foreign exchange resources below a minimum level. There was
> widespread popular unrest, which could have impaired the
> stability of the government as well as the military and economic
> viablity of the country.[4]

Perhaps the worst part of the whole situation in Taiwan was
the overall psychological attitude and outlook of the government
leaders as well as the people in those early days. Top leaders of the
ruling Kuomintang (KMT) were searching for justifications for
their losses on the mainland. There was a tendency to latch on to
any political scapegoat and to blame each other as well as their
foreign allies for desertion or selling out. Political attitudes tended
to polarize and were filled with distrust. Communism, which had
been successful in China, was seen more and more as a totally
implacable force and contagious virus with which no one seemed

able to cope. Grumblings or discontent could be and often were interpreted to be part of a Communist plot, and those who were unwilling to accept the KMT-run government policies were all too frequently viewed as tools of a Communist conspiracy. In an atmosphere where insecurity feeds upon and begets further insecurity, distrust and suspicion grew. Unfortunately, a number of articulate and energetic leaders, whose talents could have been used constructively, channeled their energies into a negative and emotive anti-Communism. This was an enthusiastic part of the political atmosphere in the 1950's, but by the 1970's it had worn thin and younger leaders were demanding more positive causes.

To add to the problem, the wounds of the violence which began on February 28, 1947 (referred to in Taiwan as the *Erh-erh-pa* or 2/28) were still fresh and bitter. In the period following the formal Japanese retrocession of Taiwan to the GRC on October 25, 1945, the Nationalist performance in Taiwan had been miserable. The first governor appointed to administer the province, Chen Yi, and his underlings treated it as conquered enemy territory rather than as a part of liberated China. There is little question that their rule was corrupt, predatory, and oppressive and led to the February and March uprisings in 1947 triggered by a black-marketing incident. In suppressing the uprising unnecessary violence and killing by Chen's troops created an antagonism between the Taiwanese and Mainlanders which has proved deep and long-enduring.[5] It was perhaps natural that the KMT leaders, whose situation was desperate anyway, should have found Communist plotting in the background of the incidents. But such rationalization could hardly extirpate a resentment which was still intense when the government for the whole of China descended upon Taiwan in December 1949. Of all the problems they had to face, how the KMT could bring back a positive attitude and willingness to cooperate with some enthusiasm on the part of an alienated, discontent local population was possibly the greatest.[6]

Of course, the fact that numerous Taiwanese had to be moved around or evicted from Japanese-abandoned homes and properties where they had established squatters' rights in order to accommodate VIP's from mainland China only exacerbated the problem. In the midst of their insecurity and what may have seemed to be desperate last throes, the GRC leaders naturally imposed a blackout on discussion of Mainlander-Taiwanese relations. The enforced silence only tended to exaggerate the problem.

Making Taiwanese-Mainlander relations an unmentionable topic subsequently led also to frequent oversimplifications on the part of outside observers of the Taiwan political scene. They have failed to note, for example, the continuing division between northerners and Yangtse Valley Chinese among those who came from the mainland. Again the Taiwanese are far from a homogeneous group. The "Min-nan" (south of the Min River) people who settled on the island from Fukien during the 17th to the 19th centuries have usually separated in clannish manner into two major groupings — those who came from Changchou and those whose ancestors came from Chuanchou. The Hakka people who came to Taiwan from Kwangtung province during the latter part of that period spoke a different language and were frequently involved in communal conflict with their Amoy-speaking fellow Chinese, both before and during Japanese occupation. Among the Min-nan people those from Changchou have generally been more political-ly active. If we exclude the roughly 2 per cent of Taiwan's population who are aborigines (probably the only true Taiwanese), the Amoy or Min-nan (also called Hokkien), roughly divided in half between Changchou and Chuan-chou people, constitute approximately 85 per cent of the Taiwanese, and the Hakka account for about 15 per cent. Divisions in language and custom, family and clan loyalties, and different patterns in urbanization and economic activity make generalization about the "Taiwanese" far less accurate than many observing the Taiwan scene would normally suppose.[7]

Yet another problem confronted the Nationalists as they looked to what could only seem to be a bleak future in 1949. They based many of their claims for support in the world against the Communists on a contention that they stood within the framework of Sun Yat-sen's ideology for a democratic future for China. The leaders of the National Government, therefore, were pressed to claim that they were engaged in active democratic processes, and yet this they could not be within a crisis situation. What was labeled a "period of national emergency" during the course of the "Communist rebellion" was to become a protracted excuse for delaying many measures for democratic reform and freedom and thus the KMT was too often in the position of claiming to be something it was not and of being able to be called to account for failures to create an open society. Further, in those bleak days the group who came to Taiwan were for the most part those who had had contacts with the West — many of them Christians who had fled from the Communists. The expectations which their friends, and particularly the missionaries who joined them in Taiwan, raised for them were for the most part unrealistic, given the situation they faced.

On the other hand, despite such drawbacks in so grim a condition the Nationalists did possess a number of assets upon which they could call if the situation ever stabilized itself in Taiwan and a period of security could be guaranteed. One of these was the desperate determination to prove they *did* have a capability to move China into the modern world. This was bred of a realization that their future would depend on how well they performed, a realization also that they could hardly be worse off.

Secondly, as many observers pointed out, Taiwan is a small place — less than 14,000 square miles — and for an area of this size the Nationalists were able to bring to bear a rather formidable amount of talent from the whole of the Chinese mainland. Many of those who came to Taiwan had party, government and industrial experience as organizers and administrators. They were uniquely qualified for the most part to fill the top posts which the Japanese during their rule had arrogated unto themselves and which had been left vacant when more than 300,000 Japanese had been sent home at the end of the war.[8]

Further, despite wartime damage the Japanese had created an infrastructure for political as well as economic development. The communications and administration net which the Japanese had set up including some initial experiments in the 1930's with "self-government" and a relatively good start on basic education made it possible for the Nationalists, given the energy which they must display, to make significant progress. Here again, their nationalism and their ethos of insecurity prevented them in the early years from acknowledging any of the contributions of the Japanese half-century.[9] This attitude in 1949 and 1950 only tended to reinforce negativism on the part of the Taiwanese, some of whom forgot the intensity with which they had maintained their "Chineseness" during the Japanese occupation.

Yet another asset was the fact that the Nationalists, in moving to the rather austere conditions in Taiwan, had been able to shed many of the opportunists who bore so much of a responsibility for the miserable failure on the mainland. The more than one million civilians who, in addition to almost half a million military, came to Taiwan represented some of China's most sophisticated scholars and competent technicians. They were united by a feeling that something requiring great energy and dedication would have to be done.

Then, too, during the long war years and even subsequently, Chiang Kai-shek himself had been a leader around whom a great number of people could rally. There was little question that all who had repaired to the embattled small island were grateful to have a leader like Chiang. His followers were in a process which became self-perpetuating, to build his image and make him into almost a superman. In later years friends and supporters were embarrassed by the slogans throughout Taiwan which pronounced him the "Saving Star of the Chinese People," but in 1949 there was an obvious effectiveness in this kind of personalization of leadership and association with a man who had proven during the war years that he was a man of destiny.[10]

By 1972 it was only too obvious that the long range assets had won out over the forbidding problems of the Taiwan scene of 1949. The contrast between the Taiwan to which the United States in a dramatic about-face pledged aid and security following the start of the Korean War in June 1950 and the Taiwan of 1972 was manifest in practically every field. To begin with, the population had more than doubled from 7,397,000 at the end of 1949 to 15,069,000 at the end of March 1972. Despite this doubling of population, per capita income had increased by more than five times so that at the end of 1971 it stood at $329, and the gross national product or the economy of the GRC was expected to surpass seven billion US dollars in 1972.[11] Other changes included an increase, as a result of a successful land reform, from 38 per cent full-owning farmers to 77 per cent and a decline in tenancy from 36 per cent to 10 per cent. (Part-owners declined from 26 per cent to 13 per cent.) In the twenty-two years industrialization had proceeded apace and with it had come urbanization and a relative decline in the farming population of an island which for the most part under the Japanese had been little more than a large garden. Where there had been six institutions of higher learning in 1950, there were ninety-two in the academic year 1970-1971. Taiwan had very few foreign visitors in 1950, but it was a major center of tourist trade expecting to have more than 650,000 international visitors in 1972. All of these changes were bound to make political life in Taiwan in the 1970's quite different from the 1950's.[12]

The important point which has been all too often forgotten or overlooked in studies of the Taiwan scene is that the remarkable progress in social, educational, economic and other fields could not have been possible without *political* direction and thrust from a capable élite. The GRC under the one-party rule of the KMT has been characterized by a group of modernizers who were able to see the interrelationships of all aspects of life on the island. The same KMT leaders who managed to maintain a stable currency in Taiwan (in contrast to the disastrous inflationary spiral which helped to spell Nationalist doom on the Chinese mainland) and who worked with intensity on the modernization and industrialization of the economy were political leaders and Party members as well as economic and planning experts. The work of the Sino-American Joint Commission on Rural Reconstruction (JCRR) in the Land Reform Program and in building a formidable network of Farmers' Association was a political as well as an agricultural activity. To attempt to disassociate social and economic development from the politics of modernization in Taiwan would be to deny the role of such people as the author and a major instigator of the successful agrarian policies as Governor and later Vice President and Premier, Chen Cheng, or the able Chairman of the Council for International Economic Cooperation and Development and subsequently also Vice President, and Premier (until May 1972), C. K. Yen, or the Minister of Economic Affairs and later Minister of Finance, K. T. Li. It was the presence of a large group of people of this calibre that lent a continuity to the political processes in Taiwan, a continuity which stood in marked contrast to some of the violent fluctuations in policies and regimes in other developing countries.

It is this continuity in leadership at the national level which has tended to obscure some of the major political changes which have taken place in the politics of Taiwan within all of the major areas which can be singled out as significant and distinguishing features of Nationalist rule. These features, some of which have also lent a surface gloss of harmony through which relatively few newsmen and observers have been able to penetrate, have had both positive and negative aspects. There are several such features which are deserving of some examination if we are to understand the development and operation of the political system in Taiwan.

I
Kuomintang Rule

Despite the polite nod which is given to two small groups in Taiwan, the Young China Party and the China Democratic Socialist Party, Nationalist China is run exclusively by the Kuomintang. The GRC is a one-party system, and since the establishment of the "temporary" capital for all of China in Taipei, every major political movement and decision has been made by the Party prior to initiation by the government. Cabinet appointments, for example, are as a matter of course approved by the Party prior to formal governmental confirmation. When Chiang Kai-shek arrived in Taiwan in December 1949, his temporary retirement from his governmental position as President did not prevent him from continuing to work in his position as *Tsung-tsai* or Director-General of the KMT, and no one had any doubt that he was running the show.

In those bleak early days one of the most important first moves by the Nationalist leaders was an attempt to breathe some life back into the KMT. The party, founded by Sun Yat-sen and going under the name Kuomintang (National People's Party or Nationalist Party) since 1912, had been reorganized with the aid of Soviet advisers in 1924 and had maintained in the intervening quarter of a century, despite attempts at reform and democratization, many of the monolithic features of the Communist Party of the Soviet Union which had served as a model for the reorganization.[13] The KMT had access to state funds for its activities and high-ranking KMT members received deference and rewards in a manner which had encouraged corruption and abuse in China during and immediately after World War II. With a long experience in handling the Party and with the full powers his position as Director-General gave him, Chiang was in a position to promote and demote members and leaders in the government at will. In

July 1950, Chiang established a 16-member Central Reform Committee to take over the functions of the Central Executive Committee of the party and to carry out a reform program which he had himself helped to draft. Behind the platitudes which filled the document could be discerned a general thrust which he intended for the KMT to give to their rule in Taiwan.

In his own explanation of the Reform Program Chiang stated that his responsibilities could not be performed "if Party comrades do not realize their past mistakes and unite. . . ." He urged that the Party "continue the five-thousand-year-long history and culture of the Chinese nation and further develop them into a resounding bell . . .   We must make Taiwan the basis for rebuilding a free China . . .   To achieve this we must thoroughly reform our Party, reorganize the revolutionary structure, re-activate the revolutionary spirit . . . "[14] Such themes became standard for KMT members in the years which followed. During the period until the convening of the Seventh National Congress of the Party, October 10-20, 1952, the Central Reform Committee had organized and reorganized the KMT's machinery in Taiwan and expanded membership through a recruiting campaign in all the counties and cities of Taiwan. The drive for new members among the local population became a continuing feature of KMT policy. Party membership grew from 282,000 in 1952 to 667,000 in 1963 (approximately one out of every nine inhabitants of voting age).[15] At the Seventh Congress the KMT reverted to rule by a Central Committee which has since been maintained. The eighth Congress of the Party met in Taipei in October 1957, the Ninth Congress in November 1963, and the Tenth Congress, which expanded the Central Committee to 99 members met in March-April 1969. By the time the Tenth Congress convened the new KMT headquarters building in Taipei had been completed. Its size and central position in the city were an indication of the dominant role of the Kuomintang.

Throughout Taiwan the KMT has developed its own well-disciplined Party cellular structure. Since on the average membership guarantees a better than 75 per cent chance of election at the local level, a preponderant number of those standing for office are KMT members. In many respects the Party function and performance at the local level in Taiwan could be said to bear a resemblance to the one-party system which existed in the American South in the pre-Eisenhower days. In Hualien County *(Hsien)* on the eastern coast of Taiwan, for example, forty-three of the fifty-three candidates for thirty-four seats in the County Council in the election of 1968 were KMT members. Many of the Party recruits have taken their membership on a *pro forma* basis, and this has been a matter of constant concern among leaders. The election became almost the equivalent of a primary in a one-party Southern county in the United States.[16]

Because the KMT is all-China in emphasis and focus, it has not been surprising that the Mainlanders have tended to dominate key positions. On the other hand, the Party's numerous activities — organizing demonstrations, political education sessions, pro-government publicity campaigns, and domination of the media — have probably had an important part in the national (as opposed to provincial) political socialization process in Taiwan. It would be difficult for the adults in Taiwan or for the students (and in 1972 more than one-quarter of the population was in school) to avoid contact with the phrases and symbols which interpret the Party's national goals and policies. Although numerous social improvement and welfare campaigns also occupy Party attention at the local level and enlist the support of the now preponderantly Taiwanese membership, the key positions in the KMT headquarters at all levels are still dominated by the dedicated followers of the Director-General who came to Taiwan from the Chinese mainland. In Hualien County in 1968, for example, all but one of the section chiefs of the County KMT headquarters were Mainlanders and all but two of the thirteen branch chiefs throughout the county were Mainlanders. Following the Tenth Party Congress, however, more emphasis was placed upon raising Taiwanese to positions of importance in KMT affairs. The reorganization of the Central Committee on May 15, 1972 saw three of the top sixteen positions filled by native Taiwanese.[17] At the time of the Tenth KMT Congress it was announced that Taiwanese participation was 10.2 per cent higher than at the Ninth Congress, and at the Second Central Committee meeting a year later (March 1970) a firm decision was taken to increase the number of younger Taiwanese entering into the top Party positions.

In the two decades between the Seventh Congress of the KMT in October 1952 and the reorganization of the Central

Committee in May 1972 it has been possible to discern some significant shifts in policy beneath the unchanging surface of the slogans, the authoritarian structure, and the continuing political monopoly by the mainland Chinese. In the first place, a mere reading of the Party pronouncements and manifestos indicates obvious new directions in activities and items of attention. Apparently, over the years the top leaders have had serious discussions about the role which the KMT could play as a bridge between Mainlanders and Taiwanese, and they have taken Taiwanese discontent as an issue deserving of priority attention — though it has not been, of course, discussed overtly. The KMT has conducted an almost never-ending series of campaigns calculated to improve its image as a center for popular participation and support.[18] The Party sponsors in some areas a once-a-year campaign for aiding the poor during which time activists make clear KMT and government identity in their concern for social improvement and progress. At the local level Party headquarters accumulate "chits" for free food as well as for medical and dental services which can be dispensed on an emergency basis as a supplement to state-provided services. A reading of recent KMT documents also reveals an increase in attention to civilian and local Taiwan problems in contrast with earlier emphasis on military preparedness for the "counter-attack" (the term has shifted to "mainland recovery") , the world anti-Communist campaign, and an overwhelming concentration on mainland problems.[19]

A second shift, which obviously lies behind the changed focus of attention, has been the result of the passing from the scene of many of the top Nationalist generals in the armed forces, who were, of course, also top Party members. The growing proportions of the civilian component in the Party, and particularly their concerns with practical matters of trade, investment, and other economic policies, were bound to be reflected in the deliberations of the Party councils which determine national policy. This was probably best symbolized by the replacement of General Chen Cheng as concurrent Vice President and Premier with Yen Chia-kan after Chen died. The process of civilianization of the Party has probably also been hastened by the explicit policy of recruiting younger members as full-time functionaries to the headquarters at all levels. Thus, although the unchanging visage of the *Tsung-tsai* and the same blue-and-white paintings of KMT slogans seemed to dominate the Party scene and gave the surface impression of limited change, the KMT in the 1970's was hardly the same organization it had been two decades earlier.

Despite such shifts in Party makeup and attention, however, some of the features of the KMT have remained unchanged. It has retained under Chiang Kai-shek its structure of democratic centralism which has made possible arbitrary decisions on promotions and demotions, and frequently at the whim of the leader. It has continued to insist on and stress secrecy with regard to its deliberations and, since these are all too frequently concerned with governmental operations, this reinforces a certain arbitrariness and authoritarianism which can impede positive responses among the membership. And perhaps most serious of all, the KMT, as was the case in mainland China, has had difficulty in recruiting and retaining intellectuals. In Taiwan the intellectuals — and this would include writers, professors, artists, and scientists as well as some of the brightest college students — have generally resisted the discipline of the Party and have preferred to remain as outside critics. Perhaps one of the chief shortcomings of the KMT one-party rule has been its inability to recruit the sort of intellectual talents which could hasten the process of modernizing its structure.

II
Official Ideology

Closely connected with KMT rule in Taiwan have been the doctrines of its founder which have been elevated to the status of an official ideology. The *San Min Chu I* or Three Principles of the People of Dr. Sun Yat-sen had probably been vaguely heard of by some of the Chinese in Taiwan during the Japanese occupation of the island, but with retrocession the political doctrines of Dr. Sun became a part of the whole education and life of the people — and on an intense basis. For more than a quarter of a century the *San Min Chu I*, its symbols, its interpretations, its identity with the Chinese people, the songs associated with it, and slogans derived from it have been a main part of the process of political socialization in Taiwan. The impact should not be underestimated!

Though Sun's ideology (and the subsequent cult build around the "Father of the First Republic in Asia") has been criticized as rather thin fare by Chinese intellectuals and by outside critics, it had by 1945 been worked into a fairly well standardized and organized basis for legitimizing the Nationalist government, providing goals for the people, and enabling Mainlanders and Taiwanese alike to identify with the Chinese state. By 1972, more than 80 per cent of the population in Taiwan had gone to public schools where every day they sang the National Anthem whose first words begin, "*San Min Chu I*, that which our Party honors." They studied required courses about the *Kuo-fu*, Father of the Chinese Republic, and his Three Principles of the People; they saluted the national flag and learned that its three colors represent those Three Principles; they learned the phrases which identified China with Sun's party and with their own future. Sun's *San Min Chu I* actually represents fairly neatly the themes which modern students of nation-building have concluded to be a necessary part of an associated ideology: nationalism, democracy, and people's livelihood. The last of the three has been variously translated and interpreted as "socialism" or policies of a "welfare state," but in recent times in Taiwan with the emphasis on development of private enterprise, it has come to be interpreted more generally in terms of a better life for the people.[20]

Within the framework of an official ideology all of the accouterments of a modern nation state have been extended in almost saturation proportions throughout Taiwan. National holidays bring forth long programs on radio and televison about *San Min Chu I*, parades display the national symbols, and all government policies and pronouncements are couched in terms of how they contribute to the program laid out by Sun Yat-sen. Further, because the official Nationalist ideology does not reject the Chinese Confucian past, it does draw some reenforcement from Chinese pride in a distinguished history.

It is, of course, easy to overestimate the impact of Sun Yat-senism in Taiwan. Some Taiwanese have maintained that by monopolizing the interpretation of *San Min Chu I* the Mainlanders are merely using it as a tool for control. More serious perhaps is the criticism that is directed against the intellectually stifling effect of an official ideology. Party hacks often become self-appointed censors of unorthodox thoughts, and this all too frequently serves to alienate further some of the original or brilliant minds which reject the *San Min Chu I* as unsuited for the complicated problems of modern China. As one observer of the scene in Taiwan noted in 1968:

> Most youths have become cynical about Kuomintang ideology, and although young men continue to join the Party, they do so for personal advancement. Politically, they adopt attitudes of escapism or quiescence, seldom commitment. In the long run, this can only undermine the party's vitality.
>
> Today, the effects of the Kuomintang's alienation of the intellectuals are largely invisible, but they are sure to be felt eventually. Yet it is hard to know what the Kuomintang ought to do about the situation, for it is truly caught in a dilemma. The fundamental rationale for its existence and its rule of Taiwan compels it to resist liberalisation, and especially direct criticism. But the resulting policy of cultural conservatism does nothing to promote the KMT as a political party which can produce the magic formula to win the battle for the hearts and minds.[21]

This is, of course, the reaction of a Western intellectual who would in all likelihood underestimate the extent to which a process of political socialization has taken place as a result of an extended period of exposure to an official ideology. The real question may well be whether the Nationalists can succeed in presenting the obviously better living conditions in Taiwan to the average citizen as a result of the implementation of *San Min Chu I.* In the case of the Land Reform, it seems that they have to some extent succeeded. One further item worth noting in this connection is the possibility that as the KMT broadens its base with an increasing number of technical modernizers, the ideology could become more flexible and the challenge of adjusting some of its Chinese-based concepts to a computerized and jet-age society more intellectually attractive.

Meanwhile, however, it is possible that whereas an official organizing ideology may be of inestimable value for a politically underdeveloped society, in a politically much more sophisticated Taiwan, with, for example, more than 200,000 students in institutions of higher learning in 1970, its utility for national development may be passing the point of diminishing returns and it may be encouraging an undermining skepticism. Certainly the relatively modest achievements of the Kuomintang's "Cultural

Renaissance" in the second half of the 1960's raised some doubts about its ability to link culture and ideology.[22] Nevertheless, those who run for political office in Taiwan and those who seek support for their projects, however diverse, still invoke Sun Yat-sen and *San Min Chu I.*

III
Two-Tiered Government

A third distinctive feature — and a persistent problem — of the Taiwan political scene has been its dual government. In many respects this may represent a unique political phenomenon in history. Since the establishment of the "temporary capital" of the GRC in Taipei in December, 1949, the island has supported the claimant government for the whole of the China mainland, including some skeletal administrations for mainland provinces. The National Assembly, elected and selected on the China mainland in 1947, had in turn elected Chiang Kai-shek as President for his first six-year term of a permitted two terms according to the Constitution adopted on Christmas Day 1946. Other National institutions included the five Yuan, or separate branches, of the government organized according to Sun Yat-sen's concept of a Five-Power Constitution. Of all these — Legislative, Judicial, Control, Examination, and Executive — only the Executive Branch was to undergo a process of meaningful renewal during the more than two decades in exile in Taiwan. The other four branches faced the problem of how to maintain activity, and indeed respect, for personnel who were suffering from geriatric desuetude.

Over the years it became necessary to suspend some of the provisions of the Constitution during the "emergency." The Judicial Yuan, not surprisingly, ruled that the provision against a third term for the President should be suspended. This made possible Chiang's reelections even up to a remarkable fifth term on March 21, 1972. But age and time had taken its toll on the National Assembly. Of an original National Assembly of 2,961 members in 1947 only 1,316 were present to vote for the fifth term.[23] These included, interestingly enough, fifteen who had been newly elected from Taipei (made a national level independent city with status equal to a province in 1967) and Taiwan. But the problem of attrition in the nationally elected bodies remained serious. Though eleven new members were added to the Legislative Yuan by special elections held for Taipei and Taiwan in 1969, and regulations were promulgated in July 1972 for the election of fifteen new members from Overseas Chinese communities, the Legislative Branch membership, even when those in residence abroad joined, was still little more than half the original size of 759.[24]

National level institutions of the GRC under the control of the KMT have set all major policies which have involved the inhabitants of Taiwan. In the first two decades the monopolization of national level offices by the Mainlanders tended to accentuate already existing divisions and tensions. The top positions in the military, in the security services, in the customs service, in the various ministries of the Executive Yuan, and in numerous other national bodies have been sinecures for Mainlanders. Gradually, however, a number of these offices have been allowed to lapse as the incumbents died. In the 1960's increasing efforts were made to bring Taiwanese into positions in the National government. With the naming of the President's elder son, Chiang Ching-kuo, as Premier in the spring of 1972, a dramatic turn was made toward the conciliation of Taiwanese demands for a greater voice in national policies. Six Taiwanese were named to cabinet level posts. The new Premier also named two Taiwanese as Provincial Governor of Taiwan and Mayor of Taipei Special municipality.[25]

Undoubtedly a major problem for the two-tiered government has been the drain on scarce resources occasioned by an unnecessary bureaucracy. Further, there have been complaints that holders of national governmental offices have used their political positions to extort favors and squeeze by delaying signature or "chops" (seals) on necessary papers.[26] This has occasioned frequent drives over the years for cutting red tape, especially when the self-importance which could be created by delay in authorizations seemed to be standing in the way of economic progress.[27]

One result of the constant attention to the politics of the GRC and its national-level concerns over more than two decades has been to accelerate the education of the people in Taiwan to world issues and problems. National level, as well as local, newspapers, radio and TV give extensive coverage to world affairs — international conferences, the United Nations, sporting events, etc. The KMT's *Central Daily News*, as well as such other widely circulated provincial newspapers as the *Chung-kuo Shih-pao (China Times)* and *Lien Ho Pao (United Daily)*, use the second person pronoun in headlines and stories to refer to the GRC in such a manner as to aid the process of national identification.

Of course, the fact that all males in Taiwan have been subject to a tour of military service in a country which maintains the sixth largest standing armed force in the world has also helped with the process of national consciousness and political integration among the people in Taiwan. In company grade ranks and below, the composition of the armed forces represents accurately the distribution of the population among Mainlanders, Hakka, and Min-nan peoples. The information and education programs of the armed forces and their relatively modern standards of mechanization, sanitation, and training have also had an impact which deserves closer study. Certainly one of the major achievements of the Nationalist government was its program of vocational rehabilitation for the servicemen who came from the Chinese mainland and were subsequently retired. It was Chiang Ching-kuo who ran this program, and its wide-ranging activities undoubtedly gave him insights into a great number of the problems at the local level.

Naturally a great number of contradictions were bound to develop between the demands by a national level government (responsible for military security and international status) and the provincial and local governments, primarily concerned with problems of education, social standards, or rural development. It was necessary at the outset that national policies take into account Taiwan's own particularly pressing needs. The work of the Sino-American Joint Commission on Rural Reconstruction (JCRR) is a good example of a national governmental program focused almost exclusively on Taiwan. It, like the many agencies involved in channeling United States aid to Taiwan between 1951 and its termination in 1965, had to be handled at the national level since it involved cooperation with and dealing with a foreign government. Yet JCRR's work, whether organizing farmers' associations, planning fertilizer distribution, or developing cooperatives, was almost exclusively local.[28] The question of whether to pursue actively a family planning program for Taiwan was an issue of national policy, yet only Taiwan — with one of the most pressing population to land ratios in the world — could be affected. The military needed manpower and the national goal of mainland recovery made opting for family planning a sensitive political issue, yet the local scene demanded it.[29]

Over the years such problems have been worked out with a trend which gives increasing role and attention to local governmental organs. Probably the key to the trend is to be found in the increasing development of funding and personnel for the provincial and local governments. In 1950 the Taiwan provincial budget amounted to approximately US $9.16 million; in 1959 it had grown to US $77.77 million; but for fiscal 1972 it was a formidable US $472.50, and that did not include the Taipei City budget which had been separated and independent beginning in fiscal 1968. The handling of funds of this size was bound to concentrate much more attention on the politics of the local scene in Taiwan.[30]

Very little attentioin has been devoted, unfortunately, to the processes of local political development in Taiwan. While it is true that the Land Reform Program, the work of the JCRR, and the four-year industrial plans linked to building infra-structure in the island have been studied and have elicited generally favorable comment from the outside world, the program for building administration and popularly elected representative bodies at the local level has been virtually ignored. Of course an obvious reason has been that the politics and events at the national level — debates in the Legislative Yuan, membership in the United Nations, relations with Japan or the United States, the activities of Chiang Kai-shek — have been on the surface more dramatic and newsworthy. But as a part of its Reform Program in 1950, the KMT announced that development of democratic local representative institutions in Taiwan would have a high priority, and there is a positive story of achievement on that score which deserves more attention.[31]

Beginning with the first election for *hsien* or county councilmen in the east coast county of Hualien on July 2, 1950, the sixteen counties and five cities of Taiwan have regularly gone to the polls to elect magistrates, majors, councilmen, and representatives to the Taiwan Provincial Assembly. The smaller townships *(chen* or Market towns and *hsiang* or administrative villages) have at the same time elected their own representative councils and chiefs. Voter participation among the electorate has been high and the election campaigns during the permitted ten days prior to the elections have been spirited. All citizens of twenty years with at least six months' residence in the constituency are able to vote. The major task of the popularly elected assemblies, which is generally taken quite seriously, is to handle budget problems. Since city and county budgets, within an area of increasing prosperity, also increased rather markedly, allocations and priorities have been debated upon and taken seriously by elected representatives, who also take their other representational tasks as important. It is worth noting that KMT candidates were generally more successful in the rural counties. In the 1964 elections more than 75 per cent of the elected officials and representatives were KMT candidates. Increasing political involvement by rural residents in Taiwan is a reflection of the training provided by the farmers' associations in their deliberative gatherings and the encouragement given as a result of the land reform.[32]

Studies of the political system at the local level in Taiwan reveal that by the beginning of the 1970's firm patterns for active political participation and responsibility had been established. The people in the village-towns, counties and cities of Taiwan are conscious of the importance of representation and participation. The assemblies are now accepted and vital for the functioning of local government and their members take their prerogatives and functions seriously. It is worth pointing out that the representative pattern of politics in Taiwan is reinforced by numerous official and unofficial organizations ranging from Rotary clubs to rural cooperatives.

While the trend toward increasing political activity and participation at the provincial level and below is quite clear in Taiwan, the fact remains that the major concerns and budgetary allocations are in the hands of a predominantly Mainlander elite who think, work, and act in the name of China. Because the outside world, including those many scholars and students from the West who have sought training in things Chinese, must perforce give attention to national policies and, for example, deal with the national Foreign Affairs Police, it is natural that the politics, cliques, gossip, policies, and personalities in Taipei, rather than some of the solid building of a viable provincial political

system from the provincial capital in Taichung, should have
received preponderant attention. In the long range future of
Taiwan itself, however, the development of a standardized and
relatively stable political infrastructure may prove to be one of the
major accomplishments of a quarter century of a more conscien-
tious and responsive Nationalist rule following the disastrous
events of 1947.

The tension created between the two levels of government has
required subtle political handling. Too much attention to Taiwan
and the aspirations of the local inhabitants at the provincial level
of government could be interpreted as a nod in favor of Taiwan
Independence. Too much energy and expenditure devoted to tired
and illusory slogans of twenty year vintage could widen the
Mainlander-Taiwanese rift which some observers still felt was of
unmitigated intensity in late 1971.[33] Thus policies and programs
which in effect bring the two levels of government together go for
the most part unannounced and unhearalded so that outer
appearances can be maintained. In the wake of diplomatic
setbacks in 1971 and 1972, one observer noted:

> Officially, the government is adhering doggedly to the dogma
> that it is the only legitimate authority for the Chinese nation and
> that one day there will be a return to the Mainland. But in actual
> practice, this concept is being soft-pedaled. The government is
> pragmatically pursuing more immediate concerns — survival,
> prosperity, domestic cohesion. Or as one observer put it: "This
> government professes to be the government of China but it is
> behaving more and more as the government of Taiwan."[34]

IV

Military Emergency

During the whole of the Nationalist period in Taiwan the
island has never lived under peacetime conditions. At the same
time the political and economic modernizers were attempting to
bring some of the high ideals of Sun Yat-sen into reality, the
"emergency" of a continuing war with the Communist forces on
the Chinese mainland — an "emergency" handled and accepted by
the KMT and the numerous military-political leaders in its top

ranks from Chiang Kai-shek on down — placed restrictions on freedom of action, imposed censorship on the press, and led to incidents which proved embarrassing to those very Nationalist officials who were attempting to prove that the GRC was indeed the hope for a democratic future for all of the Chinese people.

During the early years there was ample reason for the insecurities felt by the Nationalist leaders. They had been "burned" by some of the "liberal third force" leaders who had defected to the forces of Mao Tse-tung. Their situation in Taiwan seemed tenuous in the extreme, though with the signature of a mutual security treaty with the United States in 1954 some of their reasons for worries on the military side of the problem seemed alleviated.[35] That there was still a military civil war situation, however, was dramatized for all of the residents of Taiwan during the Off-Shore Islands Crisis of 1958 and the sustained bombardment of Quemoy and Matsu by the Communists — a bombardment which continued with symbolic shelling every other day in the years which followed to remind the world that the issue between the Nationalists and Communists had not been settled.[36]

The military emergency and serious nature of the challenge from the overwhelmingly greater forces in mainland China have led to a pattern in politics which has seriously impeded the growth of many aspects of the democratic freedoms pledged by Sun Yat-sen and the Constitution. A great number of outside critics of Nationalist rule in Taiwan, some of them motivated by the politics of the Taiwan Independence Movement, others by the fascination with the grandiose experiments by the Chinese Communists, have tended to zero in on the undesirable features of a continued period of martial law to the exclusion of positive aspects of political construction which have taken place.[37] There have also been a number of cases which have attracted international attention to the detriment of the GRC claims to represent a democratic future for China — Lei Chen, Li Ao, Peng Ming-min, and the Yuyitung brothers became *causes celebres* among anti-KMT specialists in the West.[38] Obviously on Taiwan the continuing threat by the Communists to "liberate" the island has led to a garrison state mentality on the part of many of the leaders and certainly Chiang Kai-shek foremost among them.

The manifestations and operation of the security system in

Taiwan have surely been a drawback to democratization. There is a well-organized system of surveillance together with informers. Security Police are a familiar feature on the landscape. In a society where the armed forces number more than half a million, approximately one out of every twelve adults is directly involved in national defense and concerns for external and internal security. Censorship has also been a standard feature of the state of "emergency" during the "Communist rebellion." Many who have followed the Nationalist cause with some sympathy have urged a relaxation of some of these undesirable features, but the KMT's knowledge of and experience with their Communist enemies have led them to distrust a society too permissive for the emergency.

The militarism connected with the emergency has also been a distinctive feature of the Nationalist period in Taiwan. Many of the aspects of military discipline have entered into the civilian side of political life — parades, mass organizations and demonstrations, uniforms, and military phraseology. Here, too, it is possible to discern both positive and negative features as far as the modernization and political development in Tawian are concerned.[39]

Of course, with the economic — and particularly the sophisticated industrial — development of Taiwan there was a marked decline in some of the preoccupations with military and security matters in the latter 1960's. The security forces were obviously not large enough to carry out a surveillance role over hundreds of thousands of tourists, industrialists, and businessmen. The extensiveness of Taiwan's interconnections with the outside world was already an indication that some of the sensitivities of the 1950's were fading. President Chiang Kai-shek reflected this in his annual October 10th (the Chinese National Independence Day) messages by shifting emphasis from military confrontation to political and economic competition. Nevertheless, the continuing state of war with the government of Mao Tse-tung helped in major measure to place limits on dissent from or opposition to official policies and interpretations within the GRC.

V

Custodial Role

A fifth distinguishing feature of the political system which has developed in Taiwan has been the emphasis on the island's function as the custodian of Chinese culture. Especially during the early years, when the Nationalists were joined in the flight to Taiwan by some of the finest scholars from the China mainland and when some of the Maoist zealots were actively threatening to "destroy the old" society and culture *in toto*, Nationalist leaders latched upon their mission as connected to the saving of China's cultural tradition for the world. This led to the elevation back to position of high esteem some of those very Confucian traditions which Sun Yat-sen had himself felt would have to be done away with if China were to become modernized.[40]

The KMT's view of its "sacred obligation" to preserve China's cultural heritage has had mixed results. Sometimes it has led to Party interference in academic institutions and to enforced interpretations of China's past history and culture. This has all too often led in turn to harrassment and to further alienation of the very intellectual support which the Nationalist cause sorely needed over the years. It has also led to attempts, sometimes of questionable validity, to present top Party leaders as carrying on the tradition of the scholar-officials of China's dynastic past. Chiang Kai-shek himself was all too frequently presented in Taiwan as the personification of the first scholar of the land, and his speeches and messages to the people in Taiwan were couched in the four-character platitudes of Confucian morality. The Party has assumed obligations to lecture the society in Taiwan on precepts of traditional morality when often its members are guilty of violation of those very precepts or when the precepts are difficult to relate to an increasingly urbane and modernized society.[41]

On the other hand the policy of custodial obligation has lent wider perspectives to the political scene in Taiwan and has provided values and activities which have aided in smoothing internal divisions. While much of the curriculum in the *Kuo-min Hsueh-hsiao*, national schools, could be criticized for its failure to provide relevant instruction for vocational goals, the subjects stressed throughout the system related to the Chinese tradition, Chinese history, and traditional morality. Further, the conduct of all classes in *Kuo-yu* (the national language — Mandarin Chinese) for more than a quarter of a century was bound to hasten the process of political socialization.[42]

As a national-level government the GRC provided support for a national Academy of Sciences (Academia Sinica) where much of the scholarship and work was within the Chinese tradition with high standards and where Mainland and Taiwanese researchers worked in amicable cooperation. The National Palace Museum, perhaps the world's greatest collection of Chinese historical and cultural treasures, became not only an attraction for Taiwan's tourist industry but was a center for regular tours by students from educational institutions around the island. Examinations for entrance into the system of higher education in Taiwan also put emphasis on traditional Chinese culture and history. Again, it is worth pointing out that the GRC developed a program for bringing students from the Overseas Chinese communities in Southeast Asia to Taiwan for a traditional Chinese-style education. The presence of Overseas Chinese students was viewed as helping the Nationalists maintain their symbolic position in the struggle with the Communists on the Chinese mainland.[43]

The custodial theme, and the institutions and policies connected with it over the years, have had political repercussions which have probably been inadequately appreciated and are deserving of closer study. The National Language Movement, the use of national symbols and historical traditions in the schools, the emphasis on the importance of the Chinese cultural tradition: such items have also contributed to the political climate in Taiwan. Among the student population commonalities in social and political perspectives are the rule: they are overwhelmingly Chinese, whether Taiwanese or Mainlander.[44] Tensions are obviously still there, but by the 1970's they had become predominately provincial-type tensions within an accepted national culture. That this was the case constituted no small achievement for the Nationalists.

Obviously the Nationalists were successful in presenting their Communist antagonists as a threat to a shared culture. As a member of the Editorial Board of the *New York Times* noted in the spring of 1972:

> The drift in thinking both among the island's twelve million Taiwanese and its two million mainland Chinese, who dominate the government, is toward a coming-together to face a common danger. Both are moving toward a "Chinese, but separate"

position. The Taiwanese are turning away from an independence goal that, if achieved, could only be defended with American military support. The mainlanders are abandoning dreams of going home to retake power. There is a trend toward small country-mindedness.[45]

The concept of Taiwan's custodial role for China's traditional culture has enabled a number of economic and social modernizers an increased flexibility. Their argument is that when their fellow Chinese across the Taiwan Strait are able to escape from the Marxist-Leninist-Maoist political system and wish to adjust China's traditions to the demands of the space age, Taiwan will have much to contribute. Needless to say, Nationalist leaders utilized a regular influx of refugees from mainland China over the years to help underscore such a theme.

*   *   *   *

Such major features of the political system as outlined above have, in general, combined to present an outward appearance of an almost unchanging political monolith. Yet, in the case of each of these features we have noted factors of change beneath the surface. In an age of rapid transport and communications, of rapid industrialization and the spread of the benefits of economic development, political modernization and change can be expected. It would be a mistake to search for political change only in structural terms. Yet even a favorably disposed analyst of the Taiwan scene, Dean Neil Jacoby in his pioneering study of *U.S. Aid to Taiwan*, tended to equate structural persistence as equivalent to political stagnation. He noted, for example, "In contrast to its rapid social and economic development, Taiwan experienced little basic change in its political structure during 1951-65."[46] On the other hand, his conclusion pointed toward non-structural changes in Taiwan's politics which could be perceived taking place in later years:

> By 1965, it was clear that, if Chinese government policies failed to cope with the problems of urbanization, political lag, an inadequate educational system, and the "brain drain," these problems would tend to generate increasing social friction and discontent. In particular, intelligent moves were needed toward more political accommodation among the various groups on the

island, in order to give everyone an equal opportunity to
participate in the government of Free China and, thus, to relieve
the tensions created by economic and social changes.[47]

Obviously, given the number of beneath-the-surface political
changes already mentioned, some GRC leaders were well aware of
the problems to which Jacoby was pointing when he surveyed the
impact of a fifteen-year United States aid program (regarded as
one of America's most successful). The dynamics and success of
the economic and social programs in Taiwan had indeed set loose
political pressures which needed to be accommodated. Obviously
the political structure has not changed, but within the limitations
which it imposed — and in some cases owing to the motivation and
centralized direction provided by an unchanging structure — it is
possible to discern certain significant political trends which were
in operation in the early 1970's. Some of these point toward
further political modernization and development in Taiwan and
indicate its potential sources.

First, and important because it is people rather than structures
who actually comprise government, political direction in Taiwan
began passing to a young élite with different perspectives. The
transition was orderly and made possible new policy emphases. As
J. Bruce Jacobs noted in 1971, "Analysis of personnel changes in
recent years shows that new persons, generally younger and better
educated than their predecessors, are beginning to participate in
the political system."[48] In the numerous appointments announced
following election of Chiang Ching-kuo as Premier by the
Legislative Yuan on May 26, 1972, it became quite clear that the
Executive Branch of the National Government and the Provincial
Government would be run by an appreciably younger group. The
older Nationalist generals and Party seniors, while still important,
were passing from the scene of active direction and administration.
Premier Chiang's new appointments were predominantly civilians
and technically competent experts. The emphasis of their background was obviously on Taiwan and its economic modernization
as opposed to a military and ideological security concentration on
the part of those who were being replaced.

A second major thrust in the political development in Taiwan
was the increasing involvement of Taiwanese in top positions,
national as well as provincial. It is possible that the activities of the

leaders of the Taiwan Independence Movement in Japan and the United States over the years pressured Nationalist leaders to make concessions.[49] It is also possible that more than a few years were needed to train Taiwanese for positions of political and administrative responsibility. Formosa was desperately short of administrative and technical expertise when the Nationalist Government moved there. Whatever the motivation, it was quite clear in 1972 that the Taiwanese were being given a stake in the GRC, that the KMT was broadening the base of its support. We have already noted the increased number of Taiwanese appointed to national executive positions by Chiang Ching-kuo.

In the trend toward engagement of Taiwanese Chinese in active political participation, the naming of Hsieh Tung-ming as Taiwan Provincial Governor in May 1972 was a significant step. Not only was Hsieh the first locally-born governor — he had been speaker of the Taiwan Provincial Assembly — but in contrast to his immediate predecessors, a civilian. The two prior governors had both been Military-Security leaders, protégés of Chiang Kai-shek, and members of the rapidly-dwindling first class of the Whampoa Military Academy.[50] The appointment of the young Chang Feng-hsü as Mayor of the province-level city government of Taipei bespoke equally of new directions in politics in Taiwan, the beginnings of which had been apparent in the preceeding years.[51]

A third major thrust in the political development, as we have noted, has been the increasingly active role of local political organs. The appointments made by Chiang Ching-kuo and by Provincial Governor Hsieh from among the local population were preponderantly those who had had successful experience in government at the local level in Taiwan. Although elected provincial and county assemblies still have difficulty in competition with the appointed officials and bureaucrats at their level, they have shown increased tendencies toward providing direction and a restraining influence upon the administrative officials. Local self-government has become one of the major aspects of political life in Taiwan, one which has deserved more attention from the outside world. Elections and representational functions are taken seriously, participation is active and wide, and the trend is to regard experience at the local level as apprenticeship for service at higher level.[52]

A fourth political trend in Taiwan and in the modernization of its politics represents a problem which comes out of the Chinese tradition: increased bureaucracy. In large part because the national government has been engaged in four-year economic development plans, because it owns and manages some of the national industries, such as sugar, because it engages in international affairs as a great power with a formidable military force, bureaucracy has been an especially persistent problem for Taiwan, and sometimes, as has been the case for other governments around the world, an impediment to imaginative policies and actions. Government employees at the national level had reached a total of 260,000 in 1970. According to the *Taiwan Statistical Data Book for 1971*, governmental employees at all levels, including servicemen, in 1970 constituted 27.4 per cent of the more than five million employed in Taiwan. Despite frequently announced policies to reduce the number of governmental employees, numbers and the percentage have continued to grow.[53] Parkinson's Law is not strictly a Western phenomenon.

A fifth trend, clearly perceivable in the publications and governmental activities in Taiwan has been the necessary concern of the GRC with an increasing range of problems which have accompanied economic modernization. For example, in 1970 there were 819,104 motor vehicles registered in Taiwan. This compared with only 10,710 in 1952. Obviously new demands were being placed upon the political infrastructure in terms of standards for licensing or traffic control (another boon to growth of bureaucracy, some opined). Such prodigious growth in vehicles brought with it the necessity to establish special traffic courts in four major Taiwan cities in March 1969. Again, authorities in Taiwan showed themselves responsive to concerns and trends throughout the world regarding the environment and pollution problems — yet another symptom of Taiwan's close relations with larger world political trends.

Despite continuing constraints on political dissent, and despite structural rigidities and authoritarian practices, the developments in political life in Taiwan, seen from the vantage point of the 1970's, pointed in the direction of increasing pluralism and flexibility. With the passing of the older élite and the rise of the very top positions of those who have been responsible for Taiwan's social and economic progress, the way was open for further political development and modernization.

While we might wish that many of the manifestations of Taiwan's movement into political modernity had occurred earlier, the direction offers hope that the Nationalist leaders (Mainlanders and Taiwanese alike) can match the model for agrarian reform and economic development which they offer in competition with their Communist rivals with a politically modernized system which is equally competitive. A key remaining unanswered question is whether this can be accomplished within the framework of a single party system, for there seems little doubt about continued KMT political dominance in the future.

Notes to Chapter IX

1 Political scientists in the West only recently began to break away from a parochialism in the interpretations of political development in other societies. They began to appreciate some of the necessary structural antecedents for modernization, including communications, interest articulation, interest aggregation and the development of political culture. The Little Brown Series in Comparative Politics including Gabriel A. Almond and G. Bingham Powell, Jr., *Comparative Politics: A Developmental Approach* (1966), Lucian W. Pye and Sidney Verba, *Political Culture and Political Development*, and Richard R. Fagen, *Politics and Communication* (1966) have added valuable concepts and a new (if cumbersome) terminology to the field. David E. Apter, *The Politics of Modernization* (Chicago: 1965) and Myron Wiener, "Political Integration and Political Development," *The Annals*, Vol. 358 (March, 1965) have also contributed important concepts. Much of the literature on political development during the latter part of the 1960's and early 1970's owes a debt to the pioneering work of Karl Deutsch and Harold D. Lasswell. It is worth noting that apart from some beginnings by Wei Yung, "Political Development in the Republic of China on Taiwan," in Hungdah Chiu, Ed., *China and the Question of Taiwan: Documents and Analysis* (forthcoming) and Hung-chao Tai, "The Kuomintang and Modernization in Taiwan," in Samuel P. Huntington and Clement H. Moore, Eds., *Authoritarian Politics in Modern Society: The Dynamics of Established One-Party Systems* (New York 1970) relatively little work has been done on the political development in Taiwan within the framework of the new political analysis and terminology.

2 The Department of State's *The China White Paper* of August 1949 has been reprinted with a new "Introduction" by Lyman P. Van Slyke (Stanford University Press, 1967).

3 82d Congress, 1st Session, *The Military Situation in the Far East* (The MacArthur Hearings), pp. 1667-1772.

4 Neil H. Jacoby, *U.S. Aid to Taiwan: A Study of Foreign Aid, Self-Help and Development* (New York: Frederick A. Prager, 1966), pp. 29-30.

5 The August 1949 *White Paper* contained a report from the then American Consulate in Taipei describing the ineptitude of the Nationalists early period of return to Taiwan (pp. 923-938). Douglas Mendel, *The Politics of Formosan Nationalism* (Berkeley: University of California Press, 1970), Chapter 2, "Revulsion Against Early Nationalist Rule," pp. 26-41 and particularly George H. Kerr, *Formosa Betrayed*(Boston: Houghton Mifflin, 1965), pp. 61-377 give highly critical and at times somewhat emotive descriptions of the Nationalist performance. In retrospect it seems clear that the Nationalists did not really care enough about Taiwan in those first two post-war years to send the talented people the situation required. They were, after all, primarily concerned with their major war against Mao Tse-tung's forces on the China mainland. It is also to be doubted whether they had adequate personnel. There is need for a study which sets Nationalist policies in Taiwan against the background of demands placed upon the leaders in mainland China. Frequently Chiang Kai-shek was assigned blame for incidents and policies over which he could only have had peripheral concern or knowledge. This would certainly apply to the early situation in Taiwan.

6 This was clearly understood by Chen Cheng, who replaced the civilian Wei Tao-ming as Taiwan's third governor in December 1948. It was he who initiated the land reform program which gave the then preponderant peasantry at least a small vested interest in the continuance of the Nationalist rule. See Chen Cheng, *Land Reform in Taiwan* (Taipei: China Publishing Company, 1961).

7 For several years the leaders of the Taiwan Independence Movement in Japan and the United States have published journals which have presented the question as a simple Taiwanese-Mainlander situation. The journal published in Japan, *Taiwan Youth*, for example bore the Amoy dialect transliteration of the four Chinese characters on its cover, *Taiwan Chenglian*. Some Hakkas who saw this commented to me on their resentment and pointed out that the Hakka reading of the four characters would be *Tôy Vān Chiáng Ngiān*. It is worth noting that the preponderant number of the leaders of the Taiwan Independence Movement, which has caused no little amount of sensitive defensiveness and overreaction among Nationalist leaders, are from the Changchow faction of the Min-nan group. Communal violence and constant tension, especially between the Hakka and Hokkien peoples was a constant concern both before and during the Japanese occupation of Taiwan. When a research team from the University of South Carolina worked on a local political development project in Haulien *hsien* in 1967 and 1968, one of the major contributions of the popular Magistrate K'o Ting-hsuan frequently mentioned by people throughout the *hsien* was his work in smoothing relations between the two groups who were just about equally divided there. Older people told tales of communal violence between the two groups in earlier years. A good indication of how clearly outside scholars really perceive some of the diversity in Taiwan and the political importance of it lies in how they handle the tensions between Hakka and Min-nan peoples. Neither Kerr nor Mandel (see Note 5), who have presumably made a close study of Taiwan politics, treat the subject in their volumes.

8 For fairly balanced treatments of these early years and their problems see Joseph W. Ballentine, *Formosa: A Problem for United States Foreign Policy* (Washington, D.C.: Brookings Institution, 1952) and Fred W. Riggs, *Formosa Under Chinese Nationalist Rule* (New York: Macmillan, 1952). See also Richard L. Walker, "Taiwan's Development as Free China," *The Annals*, Vol. 321 (January 1959), pp. 122-135.

9 On some aspects of the Japanese development of Taiwan see George W. Barclay, *Colonial Development and Population in Taiwan* (Princeton: Princeton University Press, 1954) and Andrew J. Grajdanzev, *Formosa Today: An Analysis of the Economic Development and Strategic Importance of Japan's Tropical Colony* (New York: Institute of Pacific Relations, 1942). The latter volume, produced during the intensity of anti-Japanese feeling during the early part of the war, attempts to argue the oppressive nature of the Japanese colonial policies, but the facts given tend to substantiate a relatively large amount of energy, talent and resources plowed into the island.

10 For some of the highly critical comments which the personality cult built up for Chiang Kai-shek has evoked see Mark Mancall, Ed., *Formosa Today* (New York: Frederick A. Praeger, 1964), esp. pp. 16-17. The thirteen contributors to this volume, edited with a clearly one-sided bias, leave the reader with the impression that practically nothing has been accomplished or has gone right in Taiwan. Graduate students who spent research time in

Taiwan and who read the volume as an introduction to political and social problems there prior to departure found it difficult to believe that the volume was describing the same place where they were doing their research work.

11 *News From China*, Chinese Information Service, New York, April 28, 1972 and *Free China Weekly*, 12.51, Taipei, December 26, 1971.

12 For a good overall appraisal of progress in Taiwan, together with balancing criticisms of aspects of political life, see the special supplement to the London *Times*, Tuesday, December 9, 1969 entitled, "Taiwan, a Special Report." The annual *Taiwan Statistical Data Book* published by the Council for International Economic Cooperation and Development of the Executive Yuan in Taipei is a source of valuable and reliable information. Its bald figures offer a rather dramatic evidence of development.

13 Still the best account of the Soviet role in the KMT structure is Ts'ui Shu-ch'in, *Sun Chung-shan yü Kung-ch'an Chu-i (Sun Yat-sen and Communism)*, (Hong Kong: The Asia Press, 1954).

14 Milton J.T. Shieh, *The Kuomintang: Selected Historical Documents, 1894-1969* (New York: St. John's University Press, 1970), p. 211.

15 Hung-chao Tai, "The Kuomintang and Modernization in Taiwan," p. 425. The KMT has been reluctant in recent years to publish membership data.

16 This concern has been expressed in KMT documents and in interviews with local party leaders in Taiwan, particularly in 1967 and 1968 when the University of South Carolina and the Free University of Berlin were interviewing as a part of a joint research project on local political development in Taiwan.

17 The new reorganization (see the *Central Daily News*, May 16, 1972) undoubtedly represented the impact of Chiang Ching-kuo who had just been named the new Premier.

18 Hung-chao Tai, "The Kuomintang and the Modernization of Taiwan," p. 428 mentions some of these.

19 Note, for example, the change in accent in the documents produced in Milton Shieh, *The Kuomintang: Selected Historical Documents, 1894-1969*.

20 For a summary discussion of the nation-building role of ideologies see Harvey G. Kebschull's introduction to his selections on the subject in *Politics in Transitional Societies* (New York: Appleton-Century-Crofts, 1968), pp. 101-111.

21 "A Correspondent," "Hearts and Minds," *Far Eastern Economic Review* (Hong Kong), August 29, 1968, p. 435.

22 For a critical appraisal of Taipei's attempt to match the Communist Cultural Revolution in mainland China with a Cultural Renaissance in Taiwan see Warren Tozer, "Taiwan's 'Cultural Renaissance'," *The China Quarterly*, No. 43, July/September, 1970, pp. 81-99.

23 *New York Times*, March 22, 1972.

24 The problem of attrition because of age is dealt with in Yung Wei, "Political Development in the Republic of China on Taiwan." See also J. Bruce Jacobs, "Recent Leadership and Political Trends in Taiwan," *The China Quarterly*, No. 45, January/March, 1971, pp. 133-136.

25 *The China Post* (Taipei), May 30, 1972, The elder son of Chiang Kai-shek prior to becoming Premier had had extensive experience and close contacts with the Taiwanese in his various military and security capacities. He was frequently pictured as being "close to the troops," and it is possible that

he is much more sensitive about the need to relieve tensions than his father, who as an elder statesman was, according to one high official, constantly reassured that the Mainlander-Taiwanese tensions were exaggerated by critics in an attempt to discredit the good works of the Nationalists.

26 Aspects of bureaucratic interference by some Mainlander officials with Taiwanese enterprisers and red tape are discussed by Allan B. Cole, "Political Roles of Taiwanese Enterprisers," *Asian Survey*, 7. 9, September 1967, pp. 645-654. The author himself observed some of the aspects of the process which Cole describes while serving a Fulbright year in Taiwan. It took three full days of dickering and 26 "chops" to import an automobile even after all the official approvals had been obtained.

27 Shortly after assuming office in June 1972, Chiang Ching-kuo announced a stringent set of reforms designed to cut down on official entertaining, influence peddling and squeeze. His record, which included rather stringent measures in Shanghai to halt the inflation before the Nationalist collapse on the mainland, made his drive on some malpractices more credible than prior drives against red tape.

28 For a good summary of JCRR's accomplishments over a more than twenty-year history see *JCRR: Its Organization, Policies and Objectives, and Contributions to the Agricultural Development of Taiwan*, Taipei, 1970. The JCRR *Annual Reports* are also a source of valuable information (reliable) on agrarian developments in Taiwan.

29 J. Bruce Jacobs, "Recent Leadership and Political Trends in Taiwan," p. 148, summarizes the population control dilemma which was finally officially solved by cabinet approval in 1969. He points out: "The advocates of birth control won permission to institute a non-governmental programme by arguing ingeniously and ingenuously that the military could not actually be planning to delay recovery of the Mainland until babies now being born could serve as soldiers." It is within the framework of such argumentation, much of which displays no small amount of originality and intellectual ability, that many policies have been reversed in Taiwan. Surface appearances are maintained; the dynamics are beneath the surface where some of the currents of change are strong indeed.

30 Annual proposed budget figures are published by the Taiwan Provincial Government, Taichung. For the 1972 figure, *News From China*, China Information Service, New York, July 1972.

31 A project on "Local Political Development in Taiwan," carried on jointly by the Otto-Suhr Institute of the Free University of Berlin and the Institute of International Studies of the University of South Carolina beginning in 1967 has revealed the value of work to be done on political development at the local level in Taiwan. Mr. Ulrich Grundler of the Free University of Berlin, for example, presented a paper at a colloquium in South Carolina reporting on his work in analyzing the Taiwan Provincial Assembly (April 25, 1970). The author presented a preliminary report on findings by the South Carolina group in Hualien Hsien at a regional meeting of the Association for Asian Studies in Durham, North Carolina, January 27, 1968, entitled "Local Political Development in Taiwan's Frontierland."

32 Aspects of KMT performance in local elections are discussed by Hung-chao Tai, "The Kuomintang and Modernization in Taiwan," pp. 419-423. Frank Bessac, "The Effect of Industrialization Upon the Allocation of Labor in a Taiwanese Village," *Journal of the China Society* (Taipei), Vol.

VI (1969), p. 13 states that the Land Reform has had wider political and social impact than is generally appreciated. He feels there has been "greater participation by a wider spectrum of individuals in politics than before." Bernard Gallin, who has done valuable anthropological field work in Taiwan and whose books are among the most valuable insights into the rural scene in Taiwan, has discussed some of the initial destabilizing effects of the Land Reform and popular education in Taiwan and pointed to the initial problems of replacing respected rural gentry with younger opportunists in some cases: "Rural Development in Taiwan: The Role of the Government," *Rural Sociology*, 29.3, September 1964, pp. 313-323.

33 See the dispatch by Takashi Oka in the *New York Times*, September 26, 1971, based upon his discussions with disaffected Taiwanese.

34 Joseph R. L. Sterne, "Taiwan Finds Limbo Has Bright Side," *Baltimore Sun*, June 17, 1972.

35 Albert Ravenholt, "Formosa Today," *Foreign Affairs*, July 1952, pp. 612-624 dealt sympathetically but realistically with the problems occasioned by the military crisis and attendant insecurities at an early period. He noted, "For the great majority of Chinese on Formosa the fearful feature of this situation is the lack of legal protection for the ordinary citizen." (p. 620).

36 For two reporters' description of the Offshore Islands and the every-other-day shelling see DeWitt Copp and Marshall Peck, *The Odd Day* (New York: William Morrow, 1962).

37 An example of the extremes to which negative attitudes can go is Mark Mancall's "Introduction: Taiwan, Island of Resignation and Despair," in the volume which he edited, *Formosa Today*. Mancall writes with seeming persuasiveness of "Intellectual and moral stagnation" (p. 28) under a system which he labels "submerged totalitarianism." Readers of his selectively edited work would come to a conclusion that not only had there been no political progress but that economic and social progress in Taiwan were equally absent. Kerr, *Formosa Betrayed* and Mendel. *The Politics of Formosan Nationalism* are equally committed to presenting the thesis that the KMT can do nothing right. What is worth noting, however, is that the continuing state of "emergency" and martial law has provided critics of the GRC with ample examples of political oppression and authoritarianism for polemical writing. The "hosannas" sung by such committed Nationalist supporters as W.G. Goddard hardly strengthen the case. See his *Formosa: A Study in Chinese History* (Ann Arbor: University of Michigan Press, 1966), esp. 168-221.

38 The detailed negative comment on the Lai Chen case has been digested by Mancall (*Formosa Today*, pp. 38-41). He calls it a "good example" of KMT repression; certainly it was an example of political ineptitude in handling a sensitive political case. The cases of Li Ao, Peng Ming-min, and the Yuyitung brothers were discussed in detail in the Hong Kong Chinese press with harsh criticisms levelled against the Nationalists even by their supporters. See "Hearts and Minds" in the *Far Eastern Economic Review* (Hong Kong), August 29, 1968, pp. 434-435 and J. Bruce Jacobs, "Recent Leadership and Political Trends in Taiwan," pp. 149-154.

39 An aspect of modernization in Taiwan which has long been deserving of study is the role of the armed forces. Many of their contributions have been positive, though an expanded civic action program could improve on the image. See J.J. Johnson, *The Role of the Military in Underdeveloped Countries* (Princeton: Princeton University Press, 1962) and Harry Walter-

house, *A Time to Build: Military Civic Action Medium For Economic Development and Social Reform* (Columbia, South Carolina: Institute of International Studies, 1964).

40 Obviously the role of Taiwan as a repository for Chinese culture has been an important item to feature in materials sent abroad by the Government Information Office in Taipei. Over the years its regular publications, such as the monthly *Free China Review*, have featured articles stressing the custodial theme. The theme is also reinforced for diplomatic staffs and foreign residents in Taiwan by invitations to attend traditional ceremonial occasions such as, for example, the regular yearly early morning ceremonies at the Confucian temple in Taipei on Confucius' Birthday (also Teachers's Day) September 28.

41 These points are elaborated upon at some length in Warren Tozer's article, "Taiwan's 'Cultural Renaissance': A Preliminary View," cited in Note 22 above. Tozer's point about the paradox faced by the KMT in promoting democratic concepts while at the same time endorsing aspects of traditional Confucianism which were paternalistic is well taken. (p. 98).

42 Bernard Gallin, "Rural Development in Taiwan: The Role of the Government," pp. 320-322 discusses some of the destablizing effects of the national school program, particularly the division in the society between those who go on to middle school and those who are left in the villages of Taiwan with a low functional literacy. The Taiwan Provincial Government approached this problem with an extension of the required amount of schooling from six years to nine years in 1969. The nine-year compulsory schooling, requiring formidable investment in plant and teacher training, was encountering numerous difficulties in 1972.

43 On the program for the Overseas Chinese students, Neil H. Jacoby, *U.S. Aid to Taiwan*, p. 186, remarks: "The major purpose was political—to offer an alternative to education in Communist China. While the program was successful, it did not have the intent or effect of contributing to the development of Taiwan per se."

44 Sheldon L. Appleton, "Taiwanese and Mainlanders on Taiwan: A Survey of Student Attitudes," *China Quarterly*, 44, October/December 1970, pp. 38-65 notes the common Chineseness of social and political attitudes.

45 Robert Kleiman, "Taiwan Without Tears," *New York Times*, May 8, 1972.

46 Neil H. Jacoby, *U.S. Aid to Taiwan*, p. 111.

47 *Ibid.*, p. 173.

48 J. Bruce Jacobs, "Leadership and Political Trends in Taiwan," p. 133.

49 President Nixon's visit to mainland China and his joint communique with Chou En-lai of February 28, 1972 did much to undercut the fervor of the Taiwan Independence Movement (TIM). For a committed interpretation of the movement see Douglas Mendel, *The Politics of Formosan Nationalism* (Berkeley: University of California Press, 1970). Another volume reflecting the position of the TIM is Lung-chu Chen and Harold D. Lasswell, *Formosa, China, and the United Nations* (New York: St. Martin's Press, 1967). Chen has been represented as the Minister of Foreign Affairs of the World United Formosans for Independence.

50 See J. Bruce Jacobs, "Leadership and Political Trends in Taiwan," p. 149.

51 Hung-chao Tai, "The Kuomintang on Modernization in Taiwan," p. 429; see also especially Mark Plummer, "Taiwan: The New Look in Government," *Asian Survey* IX (January, 1969), pp. 18-22 and "Taiwan: Toward a Second Generation of Mainland Rule," *Asian Survey* X (January, 1970), pp. 18-24. Jacobs (pp. 141-142) also discusses the trend toward greater involvement of the Taiwanese in the political system on the island.

52 These generalizations are based upon the finding of the researches described in note 31.

53 Yung Wei, "Political Development in the Republic of China on Taiwan," note 95, and Council for International Economic Cooperation and Development, Taipei, *Taiwan Statistical Data Book*, 1971, pp. 7-8.

Selected Bibliography

Ballantine, Joseph W, *Formosa: A Problem for United States Foreign Policy* (Washington: The Brookings Institution, 1952)
>An early appraisal of the problems of Nationalist rule in Taiwan and initial accomplishments.

Chen Cheng, *Land Reform in Taiwan* (Taiwan: China Publishing Company, 1961)
>An official description of successful land reform in Taiwan which relates the measures to Kuomintang doctrines.

Chen Lung-chu and Lasswell, Harold D., *Formosa, China and the United Nations* (New York: St. Martin's Press, 1967)
>A legally argued appeal for Taiwan independence with harsh criticisms of Mainlander rule in Taiwan.

Cole, Allan B., "Political Roles of Taiwanese Enterprisers," *Asian Survey*, 7.9, September, 1967, pp. 645-654.
>A critical account of some of the problems confronting Taiwanese businessmen when dealing with Nationalist officials.

Gallin, Bernard, *Hsin Hsing, Taiwan: A Chinese Village in Change* (Berkeley: University of California Press, 1966)
>A balanced and detailed study of political complications and changes in a Hakka village in west-central Taiwan. Primarily sociological in focus, the volume nevertheless offers valuable political insights.

Gallin, Bernard, "Rural Development in Taiwan: The Role of the Government," *Rural Sociology*, 29.3, September 1964, pp. 313-323.
>A discussion of some of the rural effects of the land reform and the national education program.

Goddard, W. G., *Formosa: A Study in Chinese History* (Ann Arbor: University of Michigan Press, 1966)
>A panegyric treatment of Nationalist rule in Taiwan, sufficiently uncritical to cast doubt on its legitimate points.

Jacobs, J. Bruce, "Recent Leadership and Political Trends in Taiwan," *China Quarterly*, 45, January, 1971, pp. 129-154.
>A scholarly and balanced appraisal of political changes in Taiwan, 1969-1970.

Jacoby, Neil H., *U.S. Aid to Taiwan: A Study of Foreign Aid, Self-Help, and Development* (New York: Frederick A. Prager, 1966)
>A detailed and detached study of U.S. assistance programs to Taiwan over a fifteen year period.

Kerr, George H., *Formosa Betrayed* (Boston: Houghton Mifflin, 1965)
>A polemic against Nationalist rule derived from the author's bitter experiences during the early period.

Mancall, Mark, Ed., *Formosa Today* (New York: Frederick A. Prager, 1963)
>A collection of thirteen pieces which argue that under Nationalist rule Taiwan is a cultural and political desert. The obvious bias tends to raise doubts about the many legitimate criticisms.

Mendel, Douglas, *The Politics of Formosan Nationalism* (Berkeley and Los Angeles: University of California Press, 1970)
> Anti-Nationalist and pro-Taiwan Independence Movement arguments.

Riggs, Fred W., *Formosa Under Chinese Nationalist Rule* (New York: Macmillan, 1952)
> A good balanced early treatment.

Tai Hung-chao, "The Kuomintang and Modernization in Taiwan," in S.P. Huntington and C.A. Moore, Eds., *Authoritarian Politics in Modern Society, The Dynamics of Established One Party Systems* (New York: Basic Books, 1970)
> A realistic appraisal of the problems and achievements of the KMT in Taiwan.

Wei Yung, "Political Development in the Republic of China on Taiwan," in Chiu Hungdah, Ed., *China and the Question of Taiwan: Documents and Analysis* (Forthcoming)
> A sympathetic yet balanced account of Taiwan's political development.

Chapter X

Economic Development of Taiwan

BY ANTHONY Y.C. KOO

Introduction

Taiwan has returned in 1945 to the status of a Chinese province. It was then an under-developed colonial economy. The industrial sector built largely during World War II was small and foreign trade was chiefly or oriented towards Japan. Most of the productive capacity in agriculture and industry was in disrepair. Yet within the twenty-five year period, 1945-1970, Taiwan has achieved and maintained an economic growth rate that had few parallel in history. This is impressive especially since Taiwan started with a rampant inflation and has little natural advantage in the way of abundant mineral or energy resources.

There are several recent studies on the economic structure of Taiwan detailing the various aspects of its achievement to date [attached reference list: 2,3,4,5,6,7]. In order to avoid duplication this paper will be selective in its approach and we shall begin in Section I with a brief review of Taiwan's economic heritage. Sections 2-4 will concentrate on three milestone which in our view laid the foundation for Taiwan's economic development. They are: price stabilization through monetary reform and fiscal restraints (Section 2); careful programming and use of U.S. aid fund (Section 3); and balanced growth of agriculture and industry through land reform (Section 4). The record of overall economic achievement will be reported in Section 5 and that of the foreign trade sector in Section 6. A look at Taiwan's economy in the seventies and beyond in Section 7 concludes the paper.

I
Economic Heritage

Immediately after World War II, Taiwan's economy was at its lowest ebb if not at a standstill. The sudden withdrawal of Japanese nationals from the island created a vacuum of technical personnel and skilled supervisors. The shortage was not completely solved until the large scale arrival of refugees from mainland China in the late forties. But the influx was without its liability, as the economy was suddenly confronted with a larger population in relation to its immediate resources. After the fall of mainland to the the Chinese Communists, Taiwan was further handicapped by the urgent necessity to reorient its export market from mainland China to other parts of the world. In order that the reader may better understand the economic heritage of Taiwan, the present section presents an elaboration of this general statement of the problem.

The strategy of development when Taiwan was under the control of Japan (1895-1945) was to emphasize agriculture, especially in the production of rice and sugar cane. These were then in great demand in Japan. With an assured export market, enough foreign exchange was generated so that the development was financed with little or no foreign capital.

To this end, the Japanese Government encouraged a continuous inflow of Japanese technical and professional personnel to Taiwan. Taking into account the professional talents of such immigrants, commerce and communication people stood out as the largest single group at the beginning. In the decade of 1910-1919, agriculture and fishery headed the list with nearly a net inflow of 18,000 persons. The lead switched during the 1920's to civil servants and professionals with nearly 17,000 net immigrants. The sequence roughly corresponded to the pattern of initial investment in social overhead of road and harbor construction and establishment of basic business organizations. Then came the time of intensive agriculture development and general expansion of demand for government and other professional service.[1]

The work directly related to rice production was promotion of water conservation and seed improvement. Water conservation, in general, means both irrigation and flood control. The need for irrigation arises out of the uneven distribution of rainfall during the year, plus its yearly variation. The acuteness of the water problem is most clearly illustrated in the area south of Ta-an-chi. During the winter season the average monthly rainfall is less than forty millimeters, while it is above 200 millimeters in summer. If conditions were left to nature, the timing of seeding and planting of crops would have to depend on the rainfall. Lateness in getting any significant amount of water from rainfall often delays the planting to a degree which reduces crop yields. The biggest percentage increase in irrigated land took place in the 1920's when more than 10 per cent of newly irrigated and drained land was added. In absolute figures, its big increase in irrigated acreage (single and double paddy) took place in the 1930's with the completion of the huge Chianan irrigation developments in the western-central part of the island. All the double-paddy land out of the total paddy land reached a high of 74 per cent in the 1930's with an average of 60 per cent in the period of 1920-1960.

The work of seed improvement of Chailai rice, a local variety, was started as early as 1899. The most notable achievement of the research, however, was the introduction and adaptation of Ponlai rice to the local conditions in Taiwan. Beginning in 1926, when a new breeding method was discovered, the planting of Ponlai rice gradually moved from the high plateaus to the sea-level areas, thus making possible the spread of Ponlai rice fields from northern Taiwan to the south and from one crop to more than one.

In addition to seed selection, the application of fertilizers contributed greatly to the increase of the yield of rice. The intensive use of fertilizer and the popularization of Ponlai rice seemed to move hand in hand, and represented a major break-through in rice production, an innovation of the greatest import-ance for the Taiwan economy. There remained the job of quick dissemination of knowledge. Fortunately, keeping farmers inform-ed of improved methods was undertaken early through an extensive network of agricultural associations.

The efforts described above were reflected in rising rice yields per hectare. It increased from an average of 1,280 kilograms in the 1900's to 1,930 kilograms in the 1930's. Japan, being the chief beneficiary, imported 76,000 metric tons of rice a year in the former period, or 14 per cent of total production, and 576,000 metric tons a year, or 46 per cent of the total production in the 1930's. This means Japan took practically all the rice export from

Taiwan. In terms of export percentage, Japan took 84 per cent in the 1900's with an increase to 99 per cent in the ensuing three decades, as shown in Table I.

Table 1

Average Rice Production and Exports to Japan
by Decades

Year	(1) Output (1,000 MT)	(2) Exports to Japan (1,000 MT)	(3) (2)/(1) Percentage	(4) Exports to Japan as Percentage of Total Exports
1900-09	543	76	14.0	84.0
1910-19	690	119	17.2	98.6
1920-29	787	250	31.7	99.8
1930-39	1,258	576	45.8	99.4

Source: *Economic History of Taiwan During the Period of Japanese Control* (in Chinese), Vol. 1.

(Bureau of Economic Research, Bank of Taiwan, 1958), pp.37, 140-41, 147-48.

In 1902, the Sugar Industry Encouragement Act was promulgated under which various forms of subsidy were to be given to the sugar-cane producers for expenditures incurred in developing sugar-cane plantations, irrigation and drainage of sugar-cane fields, breeding of better species, and introduction of fertilizers, etc. Other measures included the free grant of government land for sugar-cane plantations and the availability of low interest rate loans for financing exports. The result of such efforts was impressive. In the forty-year period beginning 1902, the planting area increased from 16,029 hectares to 107,676 hectares, or an increase of 67.2 per cent. The output of sugar-cane increased from 409 million kilograms to 4,159 million kilograms, or an 1,012 per cent increase. The per hectare yield rose from 25,572 kilograms to 38,628 kilograms, a 5 per cent increase.

From 1894 to 1944, sugar production in Taiwan increased from 55,253 metric tons to 327,199 metric tons or by 592 per cent. The sugar export from Taiwan increased from 25,927 metric tons in 1901 to 243,650 metric tons in 1944, or by 935 per cent. In 1901 the sugar export to Japan was 48 per cent of the total output and in 1944 it was 75 per cent as shown in Table 2.

Table 2

Average Sugar Production and Exports to Japan
by Decades

Year	(1) Output (MT)	(2) Exports to Japan (MT)	(3) (2)/(1) Percentage	(4) Exports to Japan as Percentage of Total Exports
1894-1900	43,361	n.a.	—	—
1901-1910	98,274	65,409	71	93
1911-1920	249,735	216,211	98	92
1921-1930	552,807	478,587	87	97
1931-1940	950,179	845,798	92	95
1941-1945	840,672	564,827	67	84

Source: *Economic History of Taiwan During the Period of Japanese Control* (in Chinese), Vol. 1.

(Bureau of Economic Research, Bank of Taiwan, 1958), pp. 79-80

The picture of agriculture changed drastically just before the end of the war. First there was a shortage of rural labor; this was coupled with the lack of assistance from the government and neglect of irrigation facilities. Then the output of fertilizer was reduced to less than 5 per cent of its peak output of 1939 and its supply to the farmers trickled. Furthermore, the requisition of rice by the Japanese to meet the military demand dampened the production incentive of the farmers. In 1945 agriculture production amounted to only 48 per cent of the output of the pre-war normal year 1937. Mining, forestry, fishery and livestock production indices all fell below the 50 per cent mark of 1937.[2]

The industrial section of Taiwan was small to start with. The more important ones were cotton yarn, fertilizer, cement and camphor. In 1945 the output of cotton yarn was about one-third of the peak output; fertilizers down to about 5 per cent; cement, 6 per cent; camphor, 4 per cent. The details together with the production figures for other industrial output were shown in Table 3. On top of the production decline was the sudden upsurge of population. It was slightly above six million in 1946. In the five years 1946 through 1950 it reached 7.55 million,[3] an increase of

24 per cent or the largest increase in any five year period in Taiwan. Furthermore, the mainland immigrants brought their liquid assets, thus aggravating the demand for goods and services in the local market.

Table 3

Production of Principal Industries at 1945-46
Compared with the Peak Year

(1) Industry	(2) Unit	(3) Peak Output	(4) Year	(5) 1945	(6) 1946
Electric Power	1,000 KWH	1,195,327	1943	357,033	472,002
Paper	MT	19,094	1940	2,553	1,941
Coal	MT	1,182,635	1940	—	450,324
Fertilizer	MT	11,538	1939	400	3,204
Cement	MT	303,348	1944	18,620	97,269
Cotton Yarn	Kg.	540,000	1943	149,664	410,182
Sulphric Acid	MT	12,950	1939	—	600
Camphor	MT	1,965,885	1935	64,500	472,893
Tobacco	Kg.	1,859,280	1943	417,595	537,499
Crude Oil	KL	22,827	1939	2,170	2,531
Salt	MT	465,210	1938	67,751	217,128
Sugar	MT	1,374,043	1939	—	86,074

Source: *China Hand Book* (Taipei: The China Handbook Editorial Board, China Publishing Co.,1951) pp. 222-227.

II
Battle Against Inflation

During the period when Taiwan was under the control of Japan, the currency system of Taiwan was gradually integrated with that of Japan. The integration was complete by 1911 to the extent that the money in Taiwan could be converted into Japanese currency at a one-to-one exchange rate. This removed the exchange rate problem for Japan in trading between the two. In addition, the monetary arrangement required banks in Taiwan to keep their gold reserves in Japan. Unfortunately it was not returned to Taiwan as reserves for all currency then in circulation.

This situation, of course, made the goal of price stabilization in Taiwan harder to achieve in the post-war years.

On May 22, 1946, the Bank of Taiwan was authorized to issue 5,330,593,000 Yuan "taipi," a new currency limited in its circulation only to Taiwan. "Taipi" could be converted into "faipi", the currency of mainland China, at a fixed exchange rate of thirty yuan faipi for one yuan "taipi." There was no reserve for "taipi," the amount of issuance was subject to the approval of the Central government. In the following six months, the pre-restoration bank notes of Taiwan were redeemed at a one-to-one ratio to "taipi." The purpose of authorizing Taiwan to have its local currency was to insulate it from the rampant inflation on mainland China which went from bad to worse. Accordingly, the Taiwan Provincial Government was authorized to adjust the exchange rates between "faipi" and "taipi" on the basis of the price levels in Shanghai and Taipei. During the brief period from June 13 to August 18, 1948, the exchange rates were adjusted seventy-four times, starting with one "taipi" to ninety-two "faipi" to a ratio of one to 1,635. The ensuing "gold yuan note" monetary reform on mainland China was short-lived. On March 31, 1949, the exchange rate between "taipi" and "gold yuan note" was three to one. Two months later the ratio changed to 1:2,000.[4] In spite of the frequent exchange rate adjustments, the "taipi" was over-valued in terms of the Shanghai-Taipei price levels with the consequent large-scale transfer of funds from the mainland to Taipei. When the Central government moved from the mainland to Taipei, the Bank of Taiwan was instructed to finance the government's budget deficit. The deficits were financed chiefly by borrowing from the Bank of Taiwan which played a dual role of commercial and central bank and by directly increasing the issuance of notes. Following the huge issuance of "taipi" was a concomitant price rise at an annual rate of 776 per cent in 1947, 1,144 per cent in 1948 and 1,189 per cent up to June 1949.

A program for monetary reform was announced by the Provincial Government on June 15, 1949 with the backing of four categories of assets from the Central Government:

(1)   The public enterprises taken over the the Central Government from the Japanese nationals after World War II were transferred to the Taiwan Provincial Government.

(2)   The Central Government repaid in terms of gold and

commodities for the loans made by the Bank of Taiwan.

(3)   800,000 ounces of gold was appropriated, and

(4)   a loan of US $10,000,000 was made to the Provincial Government.

The new currency, known as New Taiwan dollar (NT$), was backed by one hundred per cent reserve in the form of gold, silver, foreign exchange and export commodities with a ceiling of NT 200 million. The exchange rate was set at NT$5 for US $1, and the old currency "taipi" was called back at the ratio of 40,000 yuan "taipi" for one NT dollar.

The reform faltered because the money supply kept on rising steadily under the pressure of financing the budget deficit of the Central Government and the need for rehabilitation of the government owned public enterprises. By June, 1950 the currency ceiling was reached. The continued financing of government deficit required raising the limit from that originally set by NT$50 million. In February, 1951 the construction of power plant facilities called for another extra limit issuance of NT$95 million. After that there was no limit for note issuance. To strengthen the confidence of the people in the currency, the monetary authorities instituted a program of purchase and sale of gold and foreign exchange to the public which was quickly abandoned after a net sale of 1.45 million ounces of gold and US$6.6 million. In the meantime, the wholesale price with June 1949 as base (100) surged up to 180 by the end of 1949 and rose to over 240 in the Spring of 1950.[5] A serie of upward revisions of official exchange rates took place. By July 11, 1950, the rate was NT$10.35 to US$. The foreign assets of the Bank of Taiwan were exhausted by the spring of 1951.

The situation seemed desperate but was by no means hopeless because of two factors which inspired confidence in the future of the economy. First is the resumption of United States aid in July 1950 after the outbreak of the Korean war, and the second is that the land reform program was well underway. Each topic will be treated separately in Sections 3 and 4.

In this section we shall center upon the battle against inflation on the financial front. A series of measures were taken. The Bank of Taiwan followed a more restrictive credit policy after early 1951 which resulted in a decline of loans to the public enterprises. In addition, a concerted effort was made to sell government bonds and lottery tickets which yielded about NT$250 million during 1951. Transfer of profits in the form of interest and dividend payments from the government-owned enterprises was stepped up. In the 1949-1951 period, a total of NT$182 million was paid in the form of interest and dividends. The more significant move on the part of the monetary authority was the recognition that under the highly inflationary situation the public could not be expected to accept or hold assets having long maturities. They started in March 1950 to offer deposits of one, two and three month maturities paying extraordinarily high nominal rates of interest. They were known as preferential interest rate deposits. The rate of interest offered in March 1950 was 7 per cent a month, compounded monthly to 125 per cent annually. Preferential interest rate deposits in the banking system rose spectacularly from NT$2 million early in 1950 to NT$164 million by September. A year later, September 1951, it increased to NT$538 million. In April 1952, the government began a series of steady reductions in the rate of interest paid on deposit approximately one-half a percentage point every two months. A year later, in April, the government introduced one-year deposit certificates at a monthly rate of 3 per cent. The rise in deposits continued and reached NT$28 million in June 1953, because as the rate of inflation slowed down (the average wholesale price rose 9.7 per cent from 1952 to 1953), savers were able to obtain a higher real return even at a lower nominal interest rate.

We can find another financial indicator of public confidence in the currency by examining the money income ratios in selected years. Money has the dual function of being a store of value and a means of payments. If the ratio of real cash balance to real national income rises, it reflects an increase of confidence in the currency and *vice versa* if the ratio declines. In an inflationary period, people will usually hold some money for transaction purposes but certainly not as a store of value. In 1937, considered a pre-war normal year in Taiwan, the ratio of total cash balance to national income was about 0.27. It rose to 0.83 in 1944 because of rationing and non-availability of goods at that time. The record of the ratio for the post-war period is shown in Table 4. The lowest ratio of 0.047 was reached in 1949. The rise was slow but steady since 1952. It reached 0.142 in 1968. The hard battle against inflation was at last won but not without substantial assistance of the United States aid on the side, which will be the subject of the next section.

Table 4

Changes of the Money-Income Ratio
in Selected Years

(1) Year	(2) Ratio of Real Cash Balance to Real National Income (both at 1964 Constant Prices)
1947	0.107
1948	0.069
1949	0.047
1950	0.065
1952	0.055
1954	0.071
1956	0.078
1958	0.091
1960	0.088
1963	0.098
1965	0.119
1967	0.126
1968	0.142

Source: Fu-chi Liu, *Essays on Monetary Development in Taiwan*
(Taipei: China Committee for Publication Aid and Prize
Awards, 1970), p. 35.

III
United States Aid

The United States aid to Taiwan played many a role — social, military, and economic. The story is told elsewhere. What we propose to show in the present paper is its impact on price stability by financing government budget deficit, contributing to building infrastructure, and bringing badly needed foreign exchanges to cover the import surplus.

Both the revenue and expenditure for the Central and Provincial governments were steadily rising during the decades of the fifties and sixties. The budget deficit, nevertheless, remained because of military expenditures which formed 85 to 90 per cent of the national government outlays. In Table 5 the consolidated

Table 5

Consolidated Revenues and Expenditures of the Central and Provincial Governments in Taiwan, 1951-1964

(in millions of NT$)

Item	1951	1952	1953	1954	1955	1956	1957	1958	1959	1960	1961	1962	1963	1964
Domestic Revenue	1,515	1,983	2,484	3,028	3,950	5,097	6,056	6,881	8,333	9,420	10,124	11,378	13,406	15,057
Total Expenditures	1,981	2,852	3,317	4,788	5,359	6,491	8,102	9,001	10,544	13,806	14,006	16,256	17,101	18,252
Foreign Grants	92	751	805	1,488	1,246	1,063	1,564	1,358	1,914	3,556	2,911	2,962	2,818	2,142
percent grants/deficit	20	86	97	85	86	76	76	64	87	81	75	67	76	67
Financing Deficit after foreign grants														
Domestic Borrowing and Change in Cash Balance	374	118	28	272	163	34	-7	254	65	416	344	1,125	245	691
Foreign Borrowing	—	—	—	—	—	297	489	508	232	414	627	791	632	362

Source: N.H. Jacoby, *U.S. Aid to Taiwan* (New York: F.A. Praeger, Publisher, 1966), p. 283.

budget of the Central and Provincial governments are shown. There was a deficit every year; it ranged from NT$466 million in fiscal year 1951 to NT$3,195 million in fiscal year 1964. The U.S. grants to cover the deficit moved up also steadily over the period. It was NT$92 million in 1951 and NT$2,142 million in 1964 maintaining a grant to deficit average ratio of 75 per cent. Without going into details, the procedure of the Aid program is that the major part of the aid-financed commodity imports were "paid for" by the Chinese government with the deposit of new Taiwan dollars in segregated accounts which were under either United States government, Chinese government, or joint control. The essential effect of these local currency transactions was to require the Chinese government to reduce its monetary claims against local reserves. Most local currency funds were generated from the sale of commodities supplies by "PL 480 Title I" commodities and commodities financed by Defense support. About one-third of the aid-generated local fund was used for military support and the remaining two-thirds for development purposes.

One of the aid achievements which has a direct bearing on the economic development is to build infrastructure, that is, to foster agricultural and human resources, leaving the industrial develop-ment largely to private enterprises. The improvement of transpor-tation and communication facilities and the provision of adequate and inexpensive electric power are prerequisites to rapid indus-trialization. The benefits of building multi-purpose dams for irrigation and power generation go beyond the supply of electri-city for household and industrial needs. Attention should be called to the fact that about 25 per cent of the economic aid went to investment in human resources. Indeed it is a common shortcom-ing in thinking that development is too large in terms of investment in concrete things and too little in terms of investment in persons. This shows itself especially in the deficiency in public health programs and in education programs. As for public health, we have seen in advanced countries that measures for the improvement of diets and for the elimination of debilitating diseases can considerably increase productivity. And as for education, we have seen that in addition to the contributions to technical and higher education, financial assistance were given to agricultural research and agricultural extension.

The program of economic aid to agricultural and land reform was largely made through the Sino-American Joint Commission for Rural Reconstruction (JCRR). The money from JCRR for land reform was timely and served as a catalyst for many projects. The major item of support by JCRR in land reform has been the land-to-the-tiller program. Next are its supports for the 37.5 per cent rent reduction and, to a minor extent, the sale of public land. The details of each program will be covered in Section 4. In addition, JCRR's activities included supplementary measures to land reform such as rural health, forestry and soil conservation, livestock production, water use and control, fisheries, rural electrification and communication, etc. For the years 1951-1961 JCRR appropriated US$6.8 million plus NT$275 million (at 1949 prices) for all its major projects.

During the early fifties, annual exports ranged between $100 and $125 millioi [Table 6]. Annual imports, including those financed by aid, ran more than double this amount, despite very tight import controls. The import surplus ran on the average $100 million a year [Tables 6 and 7]. About 90 per cent of the import surplus was aid-financed. Another way of expressing the importance of United States aid-financed imports is to say that they constituted slightly above 40 per cent of the total imports during the period. The percentage fell consistently over the years; it fell below 40 per cent in 1957 and was down to 36 per cent in 1960, 11.9 per cent in 1965 and 1.1 per cent in 1969.[6] In the meantime, exports expanded. Exports started to rise in 1957 and the momentum was sustained through 1968. While higher world prices for sugar were partly responsible, exports of industrial goods were the primary contributors to the rise. They included textiles, metals, machinery, chemicals, and plywood. In terms of international balance of payment, the situation changes very favorably after 1962. During 1963, Taiwan exports rose to nearly equal to non-aid imports and the trend continued with some accumulation of foreign exchange reserves.

In short, United States aid was important, among other reasons, to the industrial development of Taiwan because the program of aid was shaped in accordance with the urgent needs of the time. Take the provision of foreign exchange to finance the import surplus as an example. Industrial projects as a whole require more capital equipment. In view of the limited resources

Table 6

Composition of Exports, Selected Years, 1952-1968
(in millions of US $)

Year	Total	Crude Agricultural Products		Processed Agricultural Products		Industrial Products	
		Value	Percentage in total	Value	Percentage in total	Value	Percentage in total
1952	111	32	26.9	82	68.3	6	4.8
1955	133	39	29.5	84	62.8	10	7.7
1960	174	19	10.7	97	55.4	59	33.9
1965	496	116	23.4	152	30.7	228	45.9
1968	842	109	13.0	173	20.6	559	66.4

Source: Bank of Taiwan Reports, Various years, Taipei, Taiwan.

Table 7

Composition of Imports, Selected Years, 1952-1968
(in millions of US $)

Year	Total	Capital Goods		Agricultural & Industrial Raw Materials		Consumption Goods	
		Value	Percentage in total	Value	Percentage in total	Value	Percentage in total
1952	206	27	13.1	153	74.2	26	12.7
1955	190	35	18.6	135	71.2	19	10.2
1960	252	69	27.5	159	63.0	24	9.5
1965	555	164	29.5	349	62.7	43	7.8
1968	1,026	362	35.2	589	57.4	76	7.4

Source: Bank of Taiwan Reports, various years, Taipei, Taiwan.

of the island for the manufacture of capital equipment, Taiwan, as the other underdeveloped areas, will have to import a large portion of such equipment. The question of capital provision is consequently not merely a matter of savings; it is also a problem of the balance of payments. The inflow of foreign capital was extremely limited in the fifties averaging 2.5 million U.S. dollars a year for 1952-1959.[7] Thus it is not possible to suppose that the difficulty can be overcome by the inflow of external capital. The amount of capital accumulation that can be financed from the domestic savings is liable to be more limited than would be apparent if one considers saving potential alone.

IV
Land Reform Since Retrocession

The scarcity and uneven distribution of farmland has long been the most serious problem encountered by the farmers in most parts of China. Taiwan is no exception. The pressure of population on land was held in check when the doubling of the population was almost matched by a commensurate increase of the farmland from 1905 to 1945. Tenancy conditions never received as much attention as they deserved during the period of Japanese control when, in fact, available evidence seem to suggest that the tenancy problem became increasingly more serious. There had developed a land tenancy system under which the average farmland rental was kept at approximately 50 per cent of the total annual main crop yield. It ran as high as 70 per cent in the more fertile areas. In addition, there was an arrangement known as "iron-clad" rent, by which, irrespective of good or bad harvest or of natural disasters, the tenant was required to pay a certain amount of rent. There was also a rent on farm by-products, payable in some cases in the same ratio as the regular rent. Only a very few lease contracts were either written or for specified periods of time. Instances of sub-leasing by tenants to other tenants were also common. This led to a commutative form of exploitation. Extortions in the form of security deposits, guarantee money and payment of rent in advance were also prevalent. The picture of these tenants on the eve of land reform was bleak indeed.

Land reform in the rural area of Taiwan proceeded by stages, of which rent reduction was the initial one. Arrangements for implementing the program started in January, 1949, and actual enforcement began in April. It limited farm rent to a maximum of 37.5 per cent of the total main crop yield. The figure 37.5 per cent was arrived at by taking one quarter of the total annual yield as the tenant's share and then dividing the remaining three quarters equally between landlord and tenant.

At the same time, all extra burdens such as advance rent payments and security deposits were abolished. The revision of farm lease contracts was carried out as part of the procedure for negotiation according to the regulations for rent reduction. All farm lease contracts were written in this way. It was further provided by law that the lease period should not be shorter than six years. Contracts for private farmland under lease that had been duly revised by June, 1949, totaled 377,364. The figure marked the formal completion of the major phase of the rent reduction program.

The second stage of the reform began with the sale of government land acquired after World War II from the Japanese nationals. When the island was under Japanese administration, land was set aside for Japanese immigrants, Japanese industrial firms and enterprises, such as the various sugar companies and Taiwan Colonization and Settlement Corporation which were large landlords. All this land, together with that owned by individual Japanese nationals and the various levels of government, was taken over by the Chinese Government in 1945 and thus became public farm land. It totaled 181,490 *chia* (one *chia* = 0.999 hectare or 434,981 acres), of which 41 per cent was paddy field and 59 per cent dry land.

In June, 1951, the approval of the "Regulation Governing the Implementation of the Sale of Public Land to Help Establish Owner-Farmers in Taiwan" marked another milestone in land reform in Taiwan. Approximately 100,000 *chia* were made available for distribution, with preference given to the present tenant cultivators. The actual sale took place by stages, and there were six successive sales including the first in 1948 which was carried out by an executive order before the formal legislation. The amount of public land which any one farm family was permitted to purchase was limited to 0.5 to two *chia* of paddy and one to four *chia* of dry land. The range in size of the land is necessary in order to account for the differences in the categories and grades of land in various parts of the island so that a reasonable level of living can be assured for the average farm family.

The correct appraisal of the land value was important to the success of the program. The criterion adopted for the calculation of the land value was 2.5 times the annual main crop yield per *chia* of each grade of cultivated land. It was a good approximation of the market price of land, which was ten times the farm rent of the public land.

The Land-to-the-Tiller Act was formally promulgated in 1953. Three basic ideas underlaid the act: (1) to help tenant farmers acquire land ownership without increasing their financial burden; (2) to protect the interests of the landlords; and (3) to convert landholdings into industrial holdings. It was only natural that the present tenant cultivator should be given preference as the prospective buyer of the land compulsorily purchased and resold by the government. The interest of the landlords was protected in two ways: the price of farm land offered by the government for resale was calculated on the same basis as that of farm land compulsorily purchased from landlords, namely, 2.5 times the total amount of the annual main crop yield for the respective land grades. To safeguard their livelihood during the transition period, provision was made for the retention of three *chia* of medium-grade land by individual landlords and, to ensure that the money paid to them for the land would be used profitably, measures were taken to transfer state-owned corporations to private ownership by offering government stock for sale to private investors.

The completion of the successive states of land reform increased the area of farmland under the cultivation of owner-farmers. By area, 55 per cent of the farmland belonged to owner-cultivators in 1948. The percentage increased steadily over the years and became 82.9 per cent in 1953, 8.49 per cent in 1956 and 85.6 per cent in 1959. Along with the wider distribution of land ownership, there was a reduction in the size of holdings. Data are available only for selected years. Ten per cent of the 1952 land holdings were below 0.5 hectare and 15 per cent between 0.5 - 0.99 hectare. In 1955 the corresponding percentage figures were fourteen and twenty-one, respectively. To summarize the pattern, 25 per cent of the land holdings in 1952 were below 1.0 hectare, while in 1955, the figure was 35 per cent.

One contribution of the land reform to economic development can be measured in terms of the earnings of foreign exchange from the export proceeds of the agriculture products and indirectly through processed agriculture commodities. Annual exports of the agriculture products ranged from $7 million (U.S. dollars) in 1950 to $40 million in 1955, and the processed agriculture products from $63 million in 1951 to $125 million in 1957. Expressing the export proceeds of the agriculture and processed agriculture products in the percentage of the total, it was 18.6 per cent, on the average, for the former and 66.7 per cent for the latter in the period of twelve years.

Those who believe that the resources devoted to the land reform programs could have served the cause of development faster if they were channeled to industrial projects instead, have over-simplified the problem. Even if one can achieve a higher discounted income through the industry first policy, there is the question of uncertainty over the future. However, in terms of cost, the foreign exchange resources constitute the major effective constraint in making the initial choice between various investment alternatives. On that score land reform in Taiwan (broadly defined) in the form of rationalization of holdings, a good extension service, equitable distribution of yield between the owner and tenant, a tax and subsidy scheme giving incentive to increased outputs, and some credit facilities on reasonable terms seemed to have exerted less of a strain on the balance of payments than industrial development would for the period under consideration.

There is another aspect to the thesis that the opportunity cost of land reform is low. If by capital formation we mean the use of any current resources that add to future output, certainly significant fractions of outlays incurred by the owner-cultivators on the educatioin of their children, improvement of their health, and even a living, insofar as they contribute to their greater productivity, should be included under capital. Then, a broader base of economic development has been laid by the land reform than we realize in view of the size of the rural population affected. In fact, Kuznets went further. According to him, the need for physical stock of capital can be met "by substituting training and education of human beings and the improvement in the whole fabric of social organization for machines."[8] In making the above remarks, we do not deny the importance of physical capital accumulation for economic development, we seek only to redress the possible downward bias in assessing the contribution of land reform to capital formation.

The expansion of agricultural output necessitates some increase of farm output, including those from the industrial sector. In Taiwan, they were materials consisting chiefly of pesticides and chemical fertilizer. A 1957 farm income study shows that farmers spent 22 per cent of their total farm expenditure on fertilizer, which was the largest item of expenditure. Of the total, about two-thirds were supplied domestically.

The farmers' purchases of household goods from the non-agriculture sector also rose. The increase, which was more than double in the decade from 1950 to 1960, is attributable partly to the rise of the farm income and partly to a percentage distribution of consumption expenditure between the farm and non-farm products. In 1950, the farm families divided their consumption expenditure almost equally between the two sectors, while in 1960 they spent 40 per cent of their total income on farm products as against 44 per cent on non-farm products.

Although a precise relationship between an increase of demand for consumer goods and a concomitant increase of investment through the working of the acceleration principle cannot be firmly established, one must admit the stimulant effect of the expansion of agricultural output in creating markets for the products of potential new industries.

V

Economic Achievements of the Domestic Sector

No simple index will be adequate to describe the economic achievements in Taiwan for the last two decades. The best one can do is to show a set of figures which taken together might project a picture of achievement. We divide the story into two main parts. In the present section, we shall center upon the domestic sector. The achievement of the foreign sector will be detailed in Section 6.

In 1952, the national income of Taiwan was NT$34,307 million (at 1964 prices) and increased to NT$125,134 million in 1968 at a compound growth rate of more than 8 per cent per annum. Because of the rapid increase in population, a more appropriate indicator of the improvement of economic well-being should be in per head terms. The per head income in 1952 was NT$4,221 in 1952 and the comparable figure for 1968 was NT$9,167 (both in 1964 prices), or it grew at a compound rate of more than 6 per cent per annum. The details are shown in Table 8 together with the annual rate of growth for both sets of figures.

It is of interest to note that the share of private consumption in national income increased at a slower rate than that of gross fixed capital formation [Table 8]. Taking 1952 as the base year,

Table 8

National Income, Income Per Head, and Capital Formation at 1964 Prices

Year	National Income NT$ (million)	Growth rate %	Income per head NTS	Growth rate %	Capital Formation NTS (million)	Growth rate %
1952	34,307	11.48	4,220	7.93	6,037	33.36
1953	36,572	6.60	4,334	2.69	6,661	10.34
1954	38,312	4.76	4,379	1.03	7,331	10.06
1955	41,801	9.11	4,605	5.15	6,123	16.48
1956	43,709	4.56	4,655	1.09	7,301	19.24
1957	46,814	7.10	4,831	3.79	7,450	2.04
1958	49,185	5.06	4,899	1.41	8,767	17.68
1959	52,963	7.68	5,078	3.64	10,396	18.58
1960	56,148	6.01	5,203	2.47	12,566	20.87
1961	60,779	8.25	5,452	4.78	14,248	13.39
1962	64,324	5.83	5,588	2.50	14,898	4.56
1963	72,356	12.49	6,089	8.96	15,784	5.95
1964	84,686	17.04	6,909	13.48	19,248	21.95
1965	89,613	5.82	7,096	2.71	25,451	32.23
1966	96,661	7.86	7,439	4.83	28,464	11.84
1967	105,528	9.17	7,936	6.88	34,153	19.90
1968	125,134	18.58	9,167	15.51	40,612	18.91

Source: Hsing, Mo-huan, *Industrilization and Trade Policies in Taiwan*, p. 273 and p. 277.

private consumption rose at a compound rate of slightly above 7 per cent while gross capital formation at a rate of 10 percent per annum for the period of seventeen years. Alternately expressed, the share of gross capital formation in national income has steadily gained in importance. It almost doubled from 1952 to 1965-1968.

Comparing the growth rates of agriculture and industrial sectors, the latter leads the former by a wide margin. The value of the gross domestic product of the agriculture sector was NT $15,323 million in 1952 but not quite doubled to NT$30,459 in 1968 (in 1964 prices), while that of the industrial sector was NT$4,264 million and NT$31,228 respectively for comparable years. Similarly the gross capital formation in the agricultural sector was NT$1,353 million in 1952 and NT$4,198 in 1968; the same figures for the industrial sector was NT$1,536 million and

NT$14,708 million in 1952 and 1968. However, in terms of the number of economically active persons, the agricultural sector still dominates the industrial sector. In 1968, there were 2,144 thousand persons in the agricultural as compared with 510 thousand persons in industry. The shift in relative importance between the two sectors in the economy can best be expressed in terms of the percentage distribution of gross domestic product, capital formation and economically active population [Table 9]. In 1952 about 42 per cent of gross domestic products originated from the agriculture sector, and 12 per cent from industry. Their contributions were roughly even, slightly over 23 per cent each by 1968.

Table 9

Gross Domestic Product, Capital Formation and

Economically Active Population, Selected Years 1952-68

Year	Gross Domestic Product		Capital Formation		Economically Active Population	
	Agriculture	Industry	Agriculture	Industry	Agriculture	Industry
	(NT$ Million at 1964 Prices)				(Number 1,000 Persons)	
1952	15,323	4,264	1,353	1,536	1,792	236
	(41.78)	(11.63)	(22.41)	(25.44)	(61.04)	(8.09)
1955	17,174	7,006	1,141	1,808	1,812	258
	(38.39)	(15.66)	(18,63)	(29.53)	(59.88)	(8.53)
1960	19,139	11,855	1,817	3,805	1,877	333
	(30.74)	(19.04)	(19.21)	(21.89)	(56.13)	(9.96)
1965	26,096	19,612	3,535	8,708	2,017	400
	(25.94)	(19.40)	(13.89)	(34.57)	(53.72)	(10.65)
1968	30,459	31,228	4,198	14,708	2,144	510
	(23.33)	(23.92)	(10.92)	(36.22)	(49.44)	(11.76)

Source: Hsing, Mo-huan, *Industrialization and Trade Policies in Taiwan.*

Note: Numbers in the parentheses indicate percentage distribution of gross domestic product (or capital formation, economically active population as the case may be) among agriculture, industry and the other sector. The percentage does not add up to 100 because of omission of the other sector.

The capital formation in the industrial sector was slightly ahead of the agricultural sector. They were 25 and 22 per cent respectfully. By 1960 the former was almost twice that of the latter, *i.e.*, 31 per cent versus 14 per cent. The lead increased to more than 3.5 times in 1968. With regard to the percentage distribution of the economically active population, there was a decline of 12 per cent in the agricultural sector for 1952-68 [Table 9]. However, the decline could not entirely be attributable to the expansion of employment in the industries where share increased less than 4 per cent for the same period. In other words, the bulk of workers went to the other or the service sectors where there was an increase of the economically active population in percentage distribution terms by 8 per cent.

VI
The Foreign Trade Sector

Foreign trade stimulates growth in many ways, of which economic specialization is only one. Through specialization we gain additional income, knowledge of production, and, in general, technology and capital grow together. We shall begin with a quantitative assessment of the trade expansion of Taiwan.

Taiwan exported US$111 million worth of goods in 1952 and US$842 in 1968, a compound growth rate of over 11.3 per cent a year. The total value of imports also grew. It went from US$206 million to US$1,026 million for the same sixteen year period, roughly at a compound rate of 11.1 per cent a year, which is slightly below the growth rate of exports. The record is impressive and can be shown in another way. We can express the value of exports and imports in percent of gross domestic products. We find that the value of exports contributed to 8.6 per cent of the gross domestic products in 1953, and rose to 26.9 per cent in 1959. The same percentage share of value of imports to gross domestic product was 13.8 in 1953 and 27.9 in 1959.[9]

To identify the sources of growth of exports and imports, we have to disaggregate the total value of exports and imports. For exports, the sub-categories are crude agricultural products, processed agricultural producrs and industrial products [Table 6]. For the period 1952-1968, the industrial products completely dominated the growth; it went from US$6 million in 1952 to US$559 in 1968; the agriculture products also rose in exports but nowhere close to the industrial products. Of the industrial products, several items stood out. There were hardly any exports of textiles, electrical, metal and wood products in 1952, but each occupied a significant percentage in the distribution of industrial exports in the 1965-1968 period. For textiles, it was 19.35 per cent, metal and metal products 14.49 per cent, wood and wood products 11.02 per cent and electrical products 5.31 per cent [see Table 10]. One interesting facet of the relative decline in exports of agricultural products is the decline of sugar and rice, which were the two major items in the early fifties. For 1952 the value of sugar was 58 per cent of the total exports and rice 19 per cent, making a combined total of 77 per cent. The combined percentage hovered around 75 up to 1957. It went steadily downward ever since; dipped to 55 per cent in 1959; about 30 per cent in the early sixties, 22 per cent in 1965 and almost about 5 per cent in 1969. Of this combined value of sugar and rice exports, the rice exports constituted less than 0.5 per cent. The decline of the value of sugar, among others, is due partly to the unfavorable sugar price in 1962 and 1964-1969, which we shall turn to later in the section.

The rapid rise of imports was expected. Largely through import control, the increase of imports of consumption goods was held to a minimum [Table 7]. It was US$26 million in 1952 and rose to US$76 million in 1968. In terms of percentage of total imports, it actually declined in the same period from 12.7 per cent to 7.5 per cent in 1968. Similarly the percentage of raw materials imports declined relative to total imports although the absolute value rose. The bulk of the import increase was due to the imports of capital goods, from a moderate US$27 million in 1952 to US$362 million during the sixteen years.

Following the change in the composition of the exports and imports was the geographical reorientation of the sources of supply and destination of exports. In the early fifties more than half of the exports went to Japan, about 5 per cent was destined to U.S. and another 5 per cent to Western Europe and Canada combined. In 1959 Japan's share was down to 16 per cent while the U.S. took about 36 per cent of the exports; Western Europe and Canada combined another 10 per cent. Taiwan's exports to

Table 10

Percentage Distribution of Major Industrial Exports

(per centage shares)

Year	Food	Textile	Wood and Wood Products	Paper and Paper Products	Chemical & Chemical Products	Petroleum & Coal products	Non-metallic Mineral Products	Electrical Products	Metals and Metal Products	Others
1952	93.63	n.a.	0.06	0.12	0.20	0.16	0.34	0.34	0.82	4.33
1953-6	89.91	1.17	0.57	0.46	0.89	0.33	0.40	0.01	2.36	3.91
1957-60	75.57	7.38	2.91	1.26	2.08	1.15	1.87	0.26	3.40	4.12
1961-4	45.00	15.46	8.82	1.50	4.91	3.22	4.77	0.89	7.87	7.59
1965-8	24.70	19.35	11.02	1.35	4.90	2.19	3.77	5.31	14.49	12.92

Source: Hsing, Mo-huan, *Industrialization and Trade Policies in Taiwan.*

the rest of Asia remained about the same, roughly in the neighborhood of one fourth of the total exports [Table 11].

Table 11

Percentage Distribution of Exports and Imports by Regions
Selected Years 1954-69

	Exports (destination)					Imports (origin)				
	Japan	USA	Asia	Europe & Canada	Others	Japan	USA	Asia	Europe & Canada	Others
1954	53.9	4.8	28.3	4.4	8.6	30.3	52.4	4.7	4.0	8.6
1955	60.6	4.3	22.8	3.8	8.5	30.9	47.0	5.9	5.1	11.1
1960	37.4	12.5	32.7	4.8	12.7	34.6	40.8	8.8	6.9	8.9
1965	31.1	20.0	26.0	9.5	13.5	37.1	34.3	10.6	7.2	11.6
1969	16.1	35.9	22.3	9.6	16.1	40.6	27.7	11.4	7.4	12.9

Source: *Taiwan Statistical Date Book, 1970.*

The geographical reorientation of the imports is as noticeable as that of exports. In 1954, more than half of the total imports came from the United States, it was reduced to a little more than a quarter of the total imports, that is, the reduction is in the order of almost one half. In the mean time, Japan's share increased by 10 per cent, *i.e.*, an increase from 30 per cent in 1954 to 40 per cent in 1969. Similarly, the imports from Western Europe and Canada combined rose from 4 per cent to 7.4 per cent in the same period. For the reader who is interested in a more refined measure of the geographical concentration of Taiwan's exports and imports, an index of concentration is needed because of the technical nature of concentration indexes; they are relegated to the footnote.[10]

There are many ways to show the gains from foreign trade. A more common indicator is the net barter terms of trade expressed as a ratio of unit value index of exports to unit value index of imports. A worsening (improvement) of the net barter terms of trade reflects a larger increase (decrease) in the import prices from the base year than in the export prices. Consequently, it takes a greater volume of exports to exchange for an equivalent volume of imports than in the base year. In this sense, the gains from trade suffer a reduction as compared with that of the base year. The net barter terms of trade of Taiwan (with 1961 as the base year) are shown in Table 12. One notes that the terms of trade moved closely with the index of sugar prices [shown in column 3 of Table 12], because of the undue weight given to sugar in the unit value of exports.[11] As the percentage of sugar in total exports declined to less than 5 per cent in recent years, the compilation of the unit value index of exports should reflect this decline in order to make the net barter terms of trade a more accurate measure of the change in economic welfare through foreign trade.

Table 12

Net Barter Terms of Trade & Index of
Sugar Prices, Selected Years 1952-68
1961=100

Year	Unit Value of Exports		Unit Value of Imports P_m	Net Barter Terms of Trade P_x/P_m
	P_x	Index of Sugar Prices		
1952	130.3	—	114.1	114.2
1955	127.7	115	114.7	111.3
1960	98.2	92	100.9	95.4
1965	97.2	83	100.2	97.0
1968	100.6	79	103.9	96.9

Source: Koo, A. Y. C. , *The Role of Land Reform in Economic Development — A Case Study of Taiwan.*

VII
From the Seventies on and Beyond

Whatever Taiwan economy has accomplished is now a matter of record. Students of economic development are bound to wonder whether the past rate of accomplishments can be repeated and the upward momentum sustained from the seventies on and beyond. Such a question deserves some thought and we should not avoid it by saying that the future is unpredictable and that predictions are hazardous. What we prepare to do below is to list a few key factors that will influence the future course of development.

Looking forward to the standard of living and employment picture in the decade ahead, we shall review the growth of population. The rate of growth of the population has been uneven depending upon the period chosen. It was 1.7 per cent (compound rate) from 1901-1944; 4.1 per cent 1946-1960 and 2.2 per cent from 1901-1960.[12] Even if we take the net reproduction rate of one, *i.e.*, if the fertility rates at Taiwan were to drop immediately to levels of about two children per family, the population would be about 60 per cent higher in 2030 than in 1968.[13] The reason is that Taiwan has a prior history of higher fertility level above replacement. The composition of its population is young with a relatively large percent in the young child bearing ages. Although each young couple may have fewer children, yet there are so many of them that the result is a large number of babies, and the population continues to grow. Of course, no one expects Taiwan's birth rate to fall so rapidly. One way to examine the consequence of different trend possibilities is to ask how much Taiwan's population would grow, if its vital rates converge to those of Japan at various times in the future — 1978, 1988, 1998, etc. The later the date selected the more gradual will be the rate of decline of population growth. Japan has been taken as the reference point because it is an Eastern Asian country with reproduction rates close to the replacement level. Table 13 below illustrates that Taiwan's pupulation would grow to some place between 22 and 30 million, depending on how rapidly the age-specific rates fall to the replacement level characteristic of Japan. The difference between the two figures is in how rapidly the change occurs, because birth rates in Taiwan have been falling fairly consistently since about 1959. For example, attaining the Japanese rates by 1988 instead of 1978 means that the maximum population will be reached about five years later and about 2.6 million larger. The government policy does not set such long-run goals. However, even with a rather vigorous family planning program which is under way, it would be remarkable if the net reproduction rate of one were reached in 1978.

Table 13

Projected Populations for Taiwan, Assumbing Its
Vital Rates Converge to Japanese Levels at
Various Future Dates

Year Taiwan Assumes Recent Japanese Vital Rates	Projected Taiwan Population (in Millions)			Maximum Population Number (in Millions)	Year
	1988	2008	2028		
1973	17.9	21.2	22.7	22.7	2033
1978	18.4	22.0	23.7	23.8	2033
1988	19.6	23.8	26.1	26.4	2038
1998	20.3	25.4	28.8	29.4	2048

Source: Avery, R., and R. Freeman, *Implications of Fertility at Replacement Levels for Taiwan*, p. 8.

Counter to the increase in population is the improvement of the quality of manpower. The increase of per head income and the improvement of the nutritional quality of food intake usually go together. To be specific, both rural and urban per head rice consumption suffered a slight decline from 1956 to 1969, while for the same period per head consumption of pork (from 15.65 to 24.8 kg), poultry, meat (from 1.32 to 1.70 kg) and milk products (from 1.45 to 8.44 kg) greatly increased.[14] Along with better nutrition and better health is the extension of the period of free education from six years to nine years beginning in 1969 and the growing strengthening of vocational training. The emphasis is reflected in the increase in expenditure on "education, science and culture" from about 8 per cent to 15 per cent of the total government budget between 1953 and 1968. In percentage terms of gross national product, it was about 1.5 per cent and 3 per cent for the respective years. Since better health and better education make possible the fullest and optimum use of human resources, an economic policy that contributes to this end has laid a foundation for a productive society.

Agriculture will continue to exert weight in the employment picture, notwithstanding its declining importance in the value of output. Thus the study of farm size and land productivity takes on added significance as a basic economic problem of a densely populated underdeveloped area such as Taiwan. Surprisingly, the evidence on yields on a per *chia* basis during the four recent years indicates that land holdings below 0.49 *chia* enjoyed the highest productivity per unit of land for both the first and second crops.[15] The result should be interpreted with care and should not be used to minimize the general unfavorable consequences on productivity that fragmentation will entail. The argument that a division of farm land into smaller units would cause a decline in productivity is based on the assumption that there are economies of large-scale production. The assumption may be valid in industrialized countries such as the United States and has been put forth occasionally as an argument against agrarian reform on the grounds of a possible loss of land productivity. The data in Taiwan do not bear out this contention. The finding, however, should not be interpreted as a denial of the importance of the scale of the agricultural unit. It simply means that the optimum scale of agricultural output is difficult to define precisely because of the diversified conditions in many lands.

In fact, the redemarcation of land in Taiwan was a part of the agrarian reform program aimed at bringing about a more economical utilization of land in order to achieve the goal of reducing production costs and increasing yields without necessarily enlarging the farm units. Even after the land-to-the-tiller program, factors still exist that prevent the full development of the land potential. They are poor drainage and inadequate irrigation, undesirable division of farm lots in irregualr shapes, the dispersed nature of the farm land owned by the same farmer, and shortage of good farm roads for transporting fertilizers, produce, farm machinery, and equipment.

As a preparatory step to the implementation of a long term continuing project, a demonstration redemarcation of farm land was put into effect in 1961. A total of 3,362 hectares of farmland was redemarcated. The immediate benefit of the project can be expressed in terms of increased land productivity. According to the reports of several districts, such as Yunlin, Taichung, and Changhua, the rice productivity has been increased by 25 per cent. The contributing factors are: first, accessibility of farms to roads enables the farmers to increased use of organic fertilizers from compost piles by as much as three to five times. Second, better irrigation and drainage facilities make control of water in the field feasible, thus increasing the efficiency of the fertilizers and decreasing the loss of crops through poor drainage. Third, consolidation of scattered pieces of land not only increases the production area but also makes possible deep plowing by farm machinery.

Even though the size of holdings might exert no immediate bearing on land productivity in Taiwan, what is its long-run impact on the potential and continued productivity of land (in terms of savings and investment in farm improvement)? In a survey study of farm savings in Taiwan for the period 1953-1967 and the savings-investment behavior of farm holdings of various sizes, one might get the impression that the cultivators of smallest holdings, *i.e.*, 0.5 hectare and below, were the lowest in all categories of savings, and the amount increased as the holding sizes became larger.[16] Insofar as the impact on potential land productivity is concerned, savings-investment in farm improvement should be our prime concern. For a more meaningful comparison on this score, one must convert the figures under the section entitled Farm Improvement to a per hectare basis, *i.e.*, we should divide the actual figures in the class interval 0.5 hectare and below by 0.25; those in 0.5-1.0 by 0.75 and so forth. The figures so calculated show that farmers of small holdings in the first two class intervals invested more money in farm improvement per hectare, *i.e.*, NT$5,500 and NT$5,611 respectively than those in the medium and large holding categories (NT$4,891, NT$5,135 and NT$5,350 respectively). In view of their continued relatively larger investment in farm improvement, it is doubtful that the land productivity of small holdings will materially deteriorate to that of large holdings in the near future.

Direct control of private industries through licensing has been in existence since the very beginning of retrocession of Taiwan to China. The criteria for granting or withholding licensing have been so varied as to include exportability of products, need for foreign exchange in importing necessary intermediate products, capital requirements and technical feasibility. An extreme form of restriction is the indefinite suspension of the granting of licenses of establishing certain businesses. For example, in the early 1950's, a ban was placed on new factories producing flour, vegetable oil, knitted goods, aluminum products, etc. Since then the restrictions were modified and partially replaced, but a new form of restriction was introduced. Self-manufactured content has been required of new factories producing tillers, refrigerators, air conditioners, televisions and automobiles since 1961 and 1962. Consistent with the restrictions in the establishment of new factories is a system of import and exchange controls. The original intent of the system was to conserve foreign exchange. But the control mechanism remains long after the reason for having it has since disappeared. Because some goods are entirely prohibited or permitted to be imported at a small quota, the restrictive nature is much more severe than the nominal and effective rates of tariff which in many instances are extremely high, especially for consumer goods.[17]

It is well known that a tariff on the intermediate goods designed to protect domestic producers of the goods will at the same time raise the cost of the producers using the imported intermediate goods as imputs. To offset such hidden "taxes" on certain producers, a system of tax rebates was initiated to subsidize the producers of goods for exports. Since its inception in 1951 and 1952, its scope has undergone continuous expansion. By 1967 more than 6,000 exportable goods were blanketed with a total tax rebate of NT$2,320 million.[18] Apart from the tax rebate, exporters were subsidized by the Bank of Taiwan's interest rate on export advances in terms of foreign currencies which are much more favorable than those charged to other private enterprises. The net of all the measures might result in a net subsidy to the domestic products but the red tape involved in applying for rebates and subsidies of various forms must be time consuming. As a counter measure to that, the Statute for Foreign National was promulgated in 1954 and later extended to cover local investors. Many tax benefits were also accorded to specified productive enterprises including a five year tax holiday and a 10 per cent reduction of business tax where appropriate. Side by side with these special tax benefits for certain new enterprises, the Kaohsiung Export Processing Zone was created in the late sixties. The privileges enjoyed by the approved industries in the zone consists of freedom from quantitative controls of exports and imports, exchange control, import duties, commodity and business taxes and business income taxes for five years.

The basic question is not whether such an elaborate fiscal

incentive system worked. It did. The issue is whether the same objective of encouraging exports and investment could be accomplished more efficiently or at less cost. Because of the general equilibrium nature of all fiscal measures, a policy designed to increase the incentive for higher output, productivity and rate of investment will have to lie in a fiscal reform program that has an overall view of the economy. An optimistic note in this respect is the formation of the Taxation Reform Commission in 1969. Steps are in motion for a comprehensive review of fiscal and taxation policies with a view to rationalization and simplification. Pending the complete overhaul of the fiscal system, a partial equilibrium approach based on the first and second feasible best policies would be beneficial to the economy. Under the scheme, one first defines the goal function, specifies the constraints and then maximizes the goal subject to the constraints.

According to one example worked out in detail, the goal function of setting the fertilizer price is to maximize the net foreign exchange earnings of rice exports reduced by the value of fertilizer imports.[19] The constraints will be that the rice collection for the government from the rice-fertilizer barter and agricultural tax should be no less than a certain specified minimum. The singling out of the fertilizer-rice barter for discussion is not without good reason. We believe that there will be tangible impacts on agricultural input stemming from such rationalization of price ratios. Where domestic distortion of the factor market exists, the potential benefit that might be derived from a first feasible best policy could be appreciable.

The greater the foreign market the greater the possibilities of specialization and expansion of foreign trade. The size of the foreign market depends upon the tolls, the tariffs, the quotas and the prohibitions of other countries, especially those of the advanced nations. Taiwan is no exception and the extent of her dependence on foreign trade is quite vulnerable both because of its large share in national income and the limited range of export products. As we are all aware, any specialist is likely to suffer if the demand for the service in which he specializes diminishes. Demands are altering all the time, because taste changes or because new techniques or new goods render the old skill obsolete. If the specialist cannot turn his hand to something else, he may suffer a severe loss of income. This also applies to an economy as a whole;

the greater the specialization, the greater is the need for flexibility in resources utilization. In the long run, the terms of trade of a country are a matter of good fortune and the capacity to enter new industries and to quit the old. No one can do much about luck, but if a country has the capacity to shift its resources in response to changes in demand, the terms of trade will tend to be favorable despite average luck. [20]

In conclusion, in a resource scarce and labor abundant economy such as Taiwan, the task to continuously improve the standard of living of the people by sustaining a high rate of economic growth is not an easy one. Thus, the achievement in Taiwan so far is truly remarkable in view of the constraints. In the last analysis, however, short of a reduction of birth rate and development and mastery of modern and advanced techniques of production, the problem of sustaining rapid economic growth will be a constant challenge. Fortunately, it is being squarely met on both fronts: Family planning and improvement of the quality of labor force on the one hand and promotion of new technology industries on the other. The outcome of this concentrated effort deserves our foremost attention because of the implications beyond Taiwan. The struggle, if successful, will be a beacon of hope and a source of inspiration to all who are faced with the same kind of economic problems as Taiwan.

Notes to Chapter X

1 *Statistical Abstract of Taiwan Province During the Fifty-One Year Period* (in Chinese) (Taipei, 1946), Table 95.

2 *Monthly Economic Review*, Bank of China, Oct., 1951.

3 *Household Registration Statistics of Taiwan*, Department of Civil Affairs, Provincial Government of Taiwan. Figures refer to year-end population excluding armed forces.

4 Chuan-how Chu, "The Records of Money Issuance of Taiwan," *Quarterly Journal of Bank of Taiwan* (Taipei, Taiwan), Vol. 17, No. 4, Dec., 1965, p. 162. *The Historical Financial Data of Taiwan* (Taipei, Taiwan, 1953), Economic Research Department, Bank of Taiwan, pp. 7-8.

5 Liu, Fu-chi, *Essays on Monetary Development in Taiwan* (Taipei: China Committee for Publication Aid and Prize Awards, 1970), p. 12.

6 Kuo, S. W. Y., *The Economic Structure of Taiwan, 1952-1969* (Taipei: Graduate Institute of Economics, National Taiwan University, 1970), p. 73.

7 Hsing, Mo-huan, *Industrialization and Trade Policies in Taiwan* (Taipei: The Institute of Economics, Academia Sinica, Mimeograph Series No. 2), p. 290.

8 S. Kuznets, "Taiwan A Theory of Economic Growth" in R. Lekachmen (ed.) *National Policy for Economic Welfare at Home and Abroad* (New York: Doubleday and Co., 1955), reprinted in S. Kuznets, *Economic Growth and Structure* (New York: W.W. Norton and Co., 1965), p. 36.

9 Kuo, S.W.Y., *The Economic Structure of Taiwan, 1952-1969, op.cit.*, p. 70.

10

Coefficients of Trade Concentration

| Period | Exports | | Imports | |
	Commodity	Geographical	Commodity	Geographical
1952	61.98	54.75	27.74	—
1953-6	62.81	50.52	29.75	53.13
1957-60	53.25	43.97	32.64	53.68
1961-4	35.45	39.02	30.00	50.81
1965-8	31.99	38.71	30.06	50.15

Source: Liang, Kuo-shu, "Trade and Policy in Taiwan, 1952-65," Conference on Economic Development of Taiwan, Taipei, 1967, pp. 256-8; for years 1965-8, see Hsing,Mo-huan, *Industrialization and Trade Policies in Taiwan, op. cit.*, p. 159. For the method of calculation, see A.O. Hirshcman, *National Power and hte Structure of Foreign Trade* (Berkeley, University of California Press, 1945).

11 Kuo, S.W.Y., *The Economic Structure of Taiwan, 1952-1969, op. cit.,* pp. 78-80.

12 Ho, Yhi-min, *Agricultural Development of Taiwan, 1903-1960* (Vanderbilt University Press, 1969), p. 45.

13 Avery, R., and R. Freeman, *Implications of Fertility at Replacement Levels for Taiwan* (Working Paper No. 5, 1970, Population Studies Center, University of Michigan, Ann Arbor, Michigan), p. 8.

14 Chang, Te Tsu, *Long-Term Projections of Supply, Demand and Trade for Selected Agricultural Products in Taiwan* (Taipei: The Research Institute of Agricultural Economics, College of Agriculture, National Taiwan University, 1970).

15 Koo, A. Y. C., *The Role of Land Reform in Economic Development—A Case Study of Taiwan* (New York: F. A. Praeger, 1968).

16

Sum of Farm Saving-Investment 1953-67
Classified According to Size of Holding

(Unit: 1952 NT$)

Size of Holdings (in Hectare)	Farm Improvement		Durable Goods	Education
	Actual	Per Hectare*	Actual	Actual
0.5 and below	1,375	5,500	9,308	1,940
0.5 — 1.0	4,208	5,611	10,396	2,242
1.0 — 1.5	6,114	4,891	14,531	3,882
1.5 — 2.0	8,986	5,153	24,102	5,081
2.0 and above	13,326	5,350	25,599	6,875

Source: T.C. Shih and W.H. Lai, *A Study of Farm Savings in Taiwan* (in Chinese) Special Studies No. 10 (Taipei, Academia Sinica, June, 1970) p. 11.
*Calculated by the author

17 Liu, Fu-chi, *The Effective Protective Rates Under the Existing Tariff Structure in Taiwan* (in Chinese) (Taipei: Taxation Reform Commission, January, 1970).

18 Hsing, Mo-huan, *Industrialization and Trade Policies in Taiwan, op. cit.,* p. 213.

19 The farmers in Taiwan get commercial fertilizers from the government agencies in exchange for rice. The system was initiated in 1948 and is still in practice. The barter ratio is set by the government each year in accordance with the type of chemical fertilizer.

In order to determine the extent to which the barter ratio deviates from one that expresses the relative international prices, estimates were made for ten chemicals, based on the figures of 1960. We find that the existing barter price for fertilizer is higher in terms of rice than the ratio based on the market prices of rice and fertilizers. Take the 1959 barter ratio for example. The difference expressed in percentage terms range from 11.2 above the market price for calcium super phosphate to 33.3 above for ammonium sulphate. Using the fertilizer consumption pattern of 1959, we estimate the amount of rice collected under the existing barter ratio and compare it with that collected under the market ratio. The excess of the rice collected under the former ratio over that of the latter is 101,000 metric tons of rice. At the price ratio of NT$1,000 per metric ton, we arrive at a total value of about NT$404 million in one year's barter transfer between rice and fertilizer. See Cf. Koo, A. Y. C. *The Role of Land Reform in Economic Development—A Case Study of Taiwan, op. cit.*

The arbitrarily high price of fertilizers naturally deters its application to rice growing under the assumption of rational behavior (profit maximization) on the part of the farmers. It should be emphasized that although the comsumption of commercial fertilizer per land area has surpassed the pre-war years, the comsumption per crop area, however, is still below the pre-war level. In 1936-40, it was 0.446 metric ton per crop hectare, while in 1956-60, it was 0.432 (See Ho, Yhi-min, *Agricultural Development of Taiwan, 1903-1960, op. cit.*, p. 81). Recently steps have been taken to narrow the difference between the arbitrary and the world prices of fertilizers. The gap, nevertheless, exists because there exists an institutional constraint on the pricing of fertilizers, namely, the government needs to collect a given amount of rice annually to feed the armed forces and civil servants. If the government stays out of the fertilizer-rice barter deals, it may have to raise the agricultural land tax on rice output collected in kind. The land tax has been another means of meeting the rice needs of the government.

For the first feasible formulation, see R. C. Hsu, "First-Best and Second-Best Policies of Taxation on Traded Imports — The Case of Fertilizer Pricing in Taiwan, 1950-66," paper presented at the Economics Society of Michigan, April, 1970 in Detroit, Michigan.

[20] Kindleberger, C.P., *The Terms of Trade: A European Case Study* (MIT Press and John Wiley and Sons, 1956), p. 306. "Luck may find a country with fixed resources engaged in the production of commodities which are in good demand (Belgian iron and steel, Swedish timber) or in bad demand (Italian marble, French wine), but flexibility provides a guarantee of reasonable terms of trade."

Select Bibliography

1. Avery, R., and R. Freeman, *Implications of Fertility at Replacement Levels for Taiwan*, Working Paper No. 5, 1970, Population Studies Center, University of Michigan, Ann Arbor, Michigan.
2. Ho, Yhi-min, *Agricultural Development of Taiwan, 1903-1960* (Vanderbilt University Press, 1966).
3. Hsing, Mo-huan, *Industrialization and Trade Policies in Taiwan* (Taipei: The Institute of Economics, Academia Sinica, Mimeograph Series No. 2, no date).
4. Jacoby, N. H., *U.S. Aid to Taiwan* (New York: F. A. Praeger Publishers, 1966).
5. Koo, A. Y. C., *The Role of Land Reform in Economic Development — A Case Study of Taiwan* (New York: F. A. Praeger, 1968).
6. Kuo, S. W. Y., *The Economic Structure of Taiwan 1952-1969* (Taipei: Graduate Institute of Economics, National Taiwan University, 1970).
7. Liu, Fu-chi, *Essays on Monetary Development in Taiwan* (Taipei: China Committee for Publication Aid and Prize Awards, 1970).
8. _____, *The Effective Protective Rates Under the Existing Tariff Structure in Taiwan* (in Chinese) (Taipei: Taxation Reform Commission, Jan. 1970).

Chapter XI

Taiwan: A Modernizing Chinese Society

BY YUNG WEI

One of the major foci of research among social scientists in recent years has been the study of the process of modernization in the developing nations in Asia, Africa, and Latin America. Several factors have contributed to the development of this kind of interest among social scientists. First of all, the change of status of many areas in Asia and Africa from former colonies of western nations to that of independent states has generated much attention among political scientists in the process of nation-building of these newly independent peoples.

Other than the political scientists, the economists became interested in the developing nations as testing grounds for various competitive theories or models of economic development. Sociologists and anthropologists, on the other hand, are interested in the developing nations as social laboratories where rapid, persistent, and sometimes drastic social changes are taking place and where they can conduct research to investigate the process of transformation of a society from the traditional to transitional or modern social systems.

As a result of the interest shown and the resultant research conducted in the developing nations and areas of the world after the Second World War, we have substantially increased our knowledge in connection with the process of the development of political institutions, the changes of social structure, and the process of economic improvement of many non-western societies.[1] Most of the social scientists had hoped that the developing nations would be able to gradually transform traditional societies with low living standards to modern societies with a higher level of economic development and a greater degree of social and political stability.

Yet events that have occurred in the developing nations after the Second World War have been rather discouraging. Except for a few successful examples, most of the developing nations have not had significant achievement in their efforts toward modernization. In many cases, there even seems to be a trend toward more traditional and tribal practice, less political stability, and lower standards of living for the people in the developing nations. The negative effect of the modernization process has been so prevalent as to necessitate a political scientist to coin a term "political decay" to refer to the unhappy experience of many developing nations.[2]

Of the few developing nations that have been fortunate enough to have made significant progress toward modernization, the Republic of China on Taiwan stands out as a distinct example. In addition to the much discussed economic miracle achieved in Taiwan in recent years, the orderly and highly successful land reform and the rapid transformation of Taiwan from primarily a rural community into an industrialized and urbanized society has also caught the attention of many social scientists interested in the development process of non-western nations. Why have the Chinese people on Taiwan been able to make rapid gains in developing the island into an industrial economy while many other countries with much more resources have failed in similar efforts? What has been the role of land reform in modernizing the Chinese society on Taiwan? To what extent did educational advancement help the development process? Finally, what kinds of impact did the rapid industrialization and urbanization have on the social structure and social attitude of the people on Taiwan? These are some of the questions which have been frequently asked by scholars interested in the modernization process in the Republic of China on Taiwan in the past two decades.

Needless to say, answers to the above questions will not only lead to an understanding of the transformation of Taiwan from a rural society to a modern industrialized economy, but also will shed much light on the modernization cases of many developing nations of the world. For this reason, a growing number of social scientists in the West have gradually become interested in the study of the modernization process of Taiwan and its impact on the traditional socio-cultural patterns of the Chinese society on that island. With mainland China so far shutting its door to social research by western scholars, Taiwan has gradually become the social laboratory wherein social scientists can still conduct free inquiry on social changes in the Chinese settings.[3]

It is, therefore, the purpose of this essay to examine the process of modernization of the Chinese society on Taiwan since it was restored to be a province of the Republic of China in 1945. Discussions in the essay are organized into five major parts. The first part of the essay is devoted to the clarification of the term "modernization." The second part presents a brief review of various stages of modernization of Taiwan since 1945. The third part investigates the various aspects of the modernization process on Taiwan, including population changes, land reform and its socio-economic impacts, educational progress and its influence, social and cultural integration, and the communication "revolution." The fourth part of the essay deals with the impact of the modernization process on the social structure, social attitude, and the behavior patterns of the people. Finally, in the fifth part of the essay, an effort will be made to identify the major factors contributing to the rapid modernization process on Taiwan in the past two decades. The significance and the implications of the achievements of the government and the people of Republic of China to the modernization efforts of other developing nations will also be examined.

Given the broad perspective of this essay and the limited supply of hard empirical data (except in economical development) on the modernization process of Taiwan in the past twenty-five years, it is needless to say that this study represents at best a preliminary effort on the part of this author to tackle the subject. The purpose of this study is more to call the attention of western social scientists to this rapidly modernizing society on Taiwan and identify some of the major areas of investigation rather than presenting conclusive findings in each of these areas. The completion of the latter task would have to wait until more empirical data have been collected by the social scientists in, hopefully, the not too distant future.

I
Modernization: A Clarification of the Concept

Prior to the discussion of the modernization process on

Taiwan, a clarification of the concept of "modernization" is necessary. A quick survey of literature of modernization leads one to find that among the terms used by the social scientists, "modernization" is probably the least defined, or to put it more accurately, the most diversely defined. It means different things to different people. For the economists, "modernization" often equates "industrialization" and the accumulation of material wealth. For the sociologists, it is frequently used to describe the process of increasing social mobility, urbanization, and the secularization of social structures. As for the political scientists, especially those in western nations, "modernization" is usually used to refer to higher political participation and the decline of traditional political influences or groups.

Although all the above usages by economists, sociologists, and political scientists have all touched upon the content of what is generally considered as the process of modernization, none of them provides us with a perspective broad enough to embrace the various dimensions of modernization phenomenon. To cope with this problem Eisenstadt, a sociologist, has summarized the modernization process into basically two aspects: structural characteristics and the adaptiveness of sociocultural systems. Among the structural characteristics, Eisenstadt said, are economic specialization, urbanization, the increase of social mobility through the spread of formal education, the breakdown of ascriptive criteria, the development of highly differentiated political structure, the weakening of control of traditional political elites, the spread of political participation, the differentiation of cultural and value systems, and the growth of a widespread communications work.[4] The other aspect of modernization is the process of sustained growth and change through the development of a sociocultural and political system that is able not only to generate continuous change but "is also capable of absorbing changes beyond its own institutional premises."[5]

In a more recent work, Eisenstadt further elaborated and clarified the process of modernization as the emergence of social forces or conditions which facilitate or impede such process of growth, including the development of an institutional structure capable of absorbing change.[6] In regard to the development of indices for the measurement of modernization, Eisenstadt directs the reader's attention to the concept of "social mobilization" developed by Karl W. Deutsch.[7] The term "Social Mobilization" was coined by Deutsch to refer to "a process in which major clusters of old social, economic, and psychological commitments are eroded and broken and people become available for new patterns of socialization and behavior."[8] The indices which Deutsch has suggested to measure social mobilization include: percentage of the population that had been exposed to significant aspects of modern life through demonstration of machinery, buildings, consumer goods; contact and response to mass media; change of residence; moving into urban areas; increase of education; change from agricultural occupations; and growth of per capita income.[9]

From the writings of Eisenstadt and Deutsch, we may differentiate three dimensions of the modernization of a society. First, there is the materialistic dimension. This is the more visible and concrete aspect of modernization which is closely associated with the installations of industrialization or their products. Factories, railroads, telegraph systems, automobiles, airplanes, radios, televisions, and many other symbols of industrialization have often been considered as the indicators of modernization. This is especially true to the less educated and less sophisticated sector of the population of an underdeveloped nation.

The second dimension of modernization is found in the development of institutions which are indispensable to the maintenance of a modern society. Thus, the institutional dimension of modernization involves the establishment of modern government administration, an efficient banking system, an independent legal system, and an educational system which is available to most members of a society. Without the existence of these important institutions, a society can hardly sustain its progress toward the production of more material goods. The sudden departure of European technicians and the collapse of the management which resulted in the paralysis of manufacturing and mining installations after the independence of certain African nations, such as the Belgian Congo, was a clear case in point.

The third dimension, which is probably the most important dimension of modernization, lies in the thought and behavior of the people of a society. Modernization has been pictured as a process in which individual members of a society are faced with vital choices. "To be modern means to see life as alternatives, preferences, and choices."[10] Ostensibly, the choices seem to be made in the arena of economic systems, political structure, and social institution. Yet a close look reveals that the choices are actually made by every individual of a modernizing society between various sets of values, norms, and attitudes of the traditional and modern socio-cultural systems. In this respect, modernization means the adoption of a "rationalist and positivist spirit"[11] and the rejection of a resigning, withdrawn, and fatalistic mode and attitude toward life.

A modern man is a person who is this-worldly, willing to face the challenges posed by a changing social and material environment surrounding him. He no longer attributes the success or failure in his life to supernatural forces or to the circumstances of the society, but to his ability or inability to change and control the environment to achieve his goal. Thus a modern man is a man with the urge to achieve, or, to use the term coined by David C. McClelland, the "achievement motive."[12]

When a society has a substantial portion of its population, especially the educated elite, possess the urge for achievement, economic development will be much more probable than in a society in which the people have a low need for achievement.[13] In a less specific language but broader theoretical scheme, Max Weber earlier also made similar statements in his now famous treatise on the Protestant ethic and Capitalism.[14]

The writings of the above mentioned scholars all point to one thing, that is, modernization, at a deeper level, is to be found in the mode of thinking and the behavior patterns of the people of a society. When a society is composed of individuals with positive attitudes toward life, a high need for achievement, and an inclination to accept challenge and change, the emergence of modern institutions and the production of material goods will be the logical result. On the other hand, even if a traditional society succeeds in artificially transplanting the formal institutions as well as industrial installations from another society but is unable to change the mentality and the behavioral patterns of its people, it remains a traditional, or pre-modern society.

For this reason, the author of the present essay will try to investigate not only the process of industrialization, urbanization, and other aspects of economic development on Taiwan but also will examine the changing values and behavioral patterns of the people on the island as a result of rapid industrialization and economic development. It is the conviction of this author that only through probing into the attitude and behavior of the individuals caught up in the modernization process can we obtain a deeper and more penetrating understanding of this complex phenomenon.

II
Modernization on Taiwan: The Historical Background and the Stages of Post-War Developments

Pre-1895 Development of Taiwan

From a historical perspective, modernization on Taiwan today represents a continuous effort of the Chinese people to adjust to and to overcome the problems produced directly or indirectly by the intrusion of the West into East Asia. The military confrontation between Cheng Cheng-kung (Koxinga), a Ming loyalist in the early Ching period, and the Dutch colonists in 1661 which resulted in the defeat of the latter in December of that year symbolized the Chinese effort to retain the island under Chinese rule against the encroachment of western powers. Although the major goal of Cheng Cheng-kung and his son was to develop Taiwan into a military stronghold against the Manchus on the Chinese mainland, their short-lived rule of twenty-two years on Taiwan did fulfill an important mission, that is, to make Taiwan an important settlement of the Chinese people.[15]

In 1683, the Ching government launched a successful attack against Cheng's force on Taiwan, defeated the Ming loyalists, and incorporated Taiwan into the domain of the Ching Empire. Since then, for more that 150 years, the Ching government did not pay much attention to the development of Taiwan.

The military adventures of the French and the Japanese in Penghu and Taiwan in the nineteenth century, however, greatly changed the policy of the Manchu court from that of benign negligence to that of active concern. From the 1870's onward, a succession of able governors of Fukien Province made significant efforts to improve both military defense and the socio-economic conditions of Taiwan. In 1877, Taiwan became a province of Ching China at the request of a group of reform-oriented Chinese officials.

Under the capable administration of an enlightened governor, Liu Ming-chuan "postal service, telegraph lines, railroads, and sea ports were developed. . . . Mining of sulfur was begun. . . . Coal mining in northern Taiwan and gold mining in the east were [also] developed."[17] Thus, by the time it was ceded to Japan in 1895, Taiwan had already become one of the most modernized areas in China.

The Japanese Rule on Taiwan (1895-1945)

The fifty years of Japanese rule on Taiwan, from 1895 to 1945, was typified by rigid political control and significant economic development. Politically, the Japanese colonial administration on Taiwan relied primarily on Japanese police and officials to rule the people of the Island.[18] The Chinese people on Taiwan were prevented from participation in politics even at the village level. "On the social plane, Japanese superiority was asserted and enforced with many forms of discrimination to keep the Chinese populace subordinate."[19] "The arbitrary nature of this kind of rule obviously bred contempt and discontent," observed a Japanese scholar.[20]

In the economic arena, the Japanese colonial government made extensive efforts to develop Taiwan so that it could supply the Japanese Empire with agricultural products and serve as a market for Japan's industrial products.[21] Significant improvements of health facilities on Taiwan were made, which resulted in rapid population growth—a doubling of the people on the Island between 1905 and 1940.[22] Transportation and communication networks were also developed to link the northern and southern as well as the eastern and western part of Taiwan. Production of rice, tea, and sugar rose far above the pre-Japanese period, owing partly to the development of irrigation systems and the introduction of modern methods. The Japanese, however, never seriously intended to develop heavy industry on Taiwan.[23] Apparently, the Japanese would like to see that Taiwan continually looked to Japan for supplies of heavy equipment so that the former would always rely upon the latter for further development of its light industries.

Throughout the fifty-year Japanese rule, the Chinese population remained a dominated racial group. Efforts were made by the Japanese government to assimilate the Chinese on Taiwan into

Japanese cultural patterns. But except in a few isolated cases, most of the Taiwanese "remained essentially Chinese in their social and political outlooks as well as in their ancestry"[24] when Taiwan was returned to China in 1945. The fifty-year rule of Japan, nevertheless, did leave its marks on Taiwan in terms of making Taiwan a more modern society by Asian standards. In comparison with their own compatriots in other provinces of China in 1945, the Taiwanese enjoyed a relatively higher standard of living typified by the existence of running water, electric light, paved highways, and public health service in many rural towns and villages.

It must be pointed out, however, that the bombing by United States air forces toward the end of the Second World War did extensive damage to the industries, harbor facilities, and transportation systems on Taiwan. The last-ditch effort made by the Japanese to support their war by the rationing of food, conscription of large numbers of Taiwanese into the military service, and the tight control of commercial activities in general, led to serious dislocations in the socio-economic conditions on the Island.[25] Thus, when Taiwan was restored to China on October 25, 1945, it was a depleted island badly in need of all kinds of assistance to help it recover from the destruction of war.

The Stages of Modernization on Taiwan after 1945

The process of modernization on Taiwan after 1945 can be roughly divided into four major stages or periods. The first period, which lasted from 1945 to 1949, was a period of restoration and readjustment. After Japan returned Taiwan to China in 1945, a total of approximately 480,000 Japanese governmental officials, military men, and civilians left the island for Japan.[26] Among the departed Japanese were some 20,000 technicians and managers, 40,000 officials, and 10,000 professional workers.[27] The departure of such a large number of skilled personnel naturally led to a series of problems in various parts of the Taiwanese society, such as government administration, transportation, and industries. Commerce on the Island was at a very low level. Serious food shortages occurred. Outlaw elements who had been turned loose by the defeated Japanese law enforcement authority constituted a serious threat to the maintenance of security on the Island.

The above problems were further amplified and intensified by the incompetent rule of the first Chinese Governor-General in Taiwan which eventually led to a wide-spread rebellion by the Taiwanese against the Nationalist authority on February 28, 1947. Reports on the so-called "Erh Erh Pa (February 28) Incident" vary to a very great extent, dependent on the attitude of the authors toward the Nationalist Government as well as the sources they have used.[28] But one thing is sure, the incident left a deep scar on the relationships between the Mainlanders and the Taiwanese on the Island, which has been utilized by the so-called "Formosan Independent Movement" as one of the major rallying points for support.[29]

While the situation was bad for the Nationalists on Taiwan in 1947, their position on the Mainland was not better. Within two years, the Chinese Communists succeeded in occupying most of the areas of Mainland China. In late 1949, the Nationalists moved the seat of the national government from mainland China to Taiwan. Most political observers believed that it would be a matter of time before the Chinese Communists would take over the Island.[30] The situation in and outside of Taiwan at the time seemed to support their observation. The Nationalist armed forces which had retreated from the mainland to Taiwan were disorganized and badly in need of weaponry and supplies. The economy was threatened by inflation caused, among many other things, by the sudden influx of some one million refugees from the mainland.

Yet several events which occurred in 1950 brought drastic changes in the domestic as well as the external environment of the Chinese Nationalist government in Taiwan. First, the resumption of the presidency by Chiang Kai-shek early that year provided the Nationalists and the people on the Island a rallying point of unification and allegiance. Moreover, the breaking out of the Korean War on June 26, 1950 led to a quick change of United States policy toward Taiwan—from one of "let the dust settle" to that of genuine concern. The Seventh Fleet of the United States was ordered by President Truman to patrol the Taiwan Straits. Military aid and economic assistance also began to arrive in Taiwan. A sense of security and stability was thus gained by the government and people on Taiwan.

The years 1950 to 1958 represented a period of reconstruction and development for the government and people on Taiwan.

Several important measures were adopted by the Government of the Republic of China (GRC), which contributed greatly to the transformation of Taiwan from a basically rural economy with some light industry into a more industrialized economy. First, there was the vital decision by the government to fully carry out a land reform on the island. The land reform started with the reduction of land rent to a maximum of 37.5 per cent of the annual main crop. This was followed by the sale of public farm land to the landless tenants. Finally, a "Land to the Tiller" program was implemented. Contrary to the violent "land reform" carried out by the Chinese Communists on the mainland, in which the landlords suffered innumerable difficulties, the "Land to the Tiller" program was carried out peacefully with the landlords receiving due compensation for the land they gave up for redistribution to the tenants. In essence, the GRC purchased the land from the landlords in exchange for land bonds and stock shares in government owned enterprises. The land thus obtained was redistributed among the tenants who were required to pay back the price of the land to the government in a period of ten years.[31] This land reform has become the most important ingredient of the support enjoyed by GRC among the Taiwanese population. It has also been an important step toward further economic development on the Island.

Other than the land reform, the government's initiation and implementation of the first "Four Year Plan" in Taiwan was another important development in this period. In contrast to many developing nations whose leaders tried to jump from a rural economy to heavy industrial development, the leaders of GRC took a cautious and gradual course in developing the economy of the island. Emphasis was placed on increasing agricultural output along with the strengthening of consumer-oriented light industries. A slogan, "use agriculture to nourish industry, then use industry to develop agriculture," was advocated. Further development of electricity sources, fertilizer, and other light industries such as glass, cement, and textiles were encouraged. The plantation of sugar cane, bananas, and other economic crops were also stressed. This balanced plan for the economic development of Taiwan, which was followed by three successive "Four Year Plans" of similar orientation, has proven to be extremely successful in developing the limited natural resources of the Island.[32]

In addition to land reform and economic development, the GRC also devoted itself to the development of self-government at the local and provincial levels on Taiwan and to the expansion of educational facilities on the island. Self-government was practiced in Taiwan since 1951. The most important development of provincial self-rule was the inauguration of the Provisional Taiwan Provincial Assembly on December 11, 1951, which replaced the former Provincial Council of Taiwan. Eight years later, in August, 1959, GRC promulgated the Organic Law of the Taiwan Provincial Assembly and the Provisional Taiwan Provincial Assembly became the first Taiwan Provincial Assembly.[33] All members of the Provincial Taiwan Assembly, the county magistrates, and mayors, have been elected by popular vote, with the exception of the Governor of Taiwan who has been appointed by the Executive Yuan of the National Government.[34]

The implementation of self-government by the GRC during the 1950-1959 period gave the people of Taiwan an opportunity to participate in the political decision-making process at the local and provincial level, which contrasted sharply with the extreme restriction on political activities of the people of Taiwan under Japanese rule. With the realization of land reform and the improvement of living conditions of all the people in Taiwan, there was a constant increase of interest in political activities as evidenced by the high turn-out rates in the elections held in Taiwan. This was especially true in small towns and rural areas.[35] A sense of political efficacy as well as an identity with the goal of the political system among the populace of Taiwan was thus achieved.

In regard to educational advancement, the GRC made import-ant strides during this period. The government not only fully fulfilled the constitutional requirement to give free and compul-sory education to practically every school-aged child in Taiwan, but also substantially increased the number of high schools as well as colleges and universities on the Island. The Ministry of Education, with economic support from the United States, also made a major effort to attract overseas Chinese students to attend colleges in Taiwan. The result was a gradual decrease of overseas Chinese attending colleges and universities on Mainland China and a steady increase of Taiwan-trained educators, engineers, and other professional workers in the overseas Chinese communities, which helped retain the loyalty of many overseas Chinese toward the GRC.[36]

With the improvements achieved and confidence gained during the 1950-1959 period, the Chinese people on Taiwan moved into the new period of 1959 to 1965. This was a period of rapid increase of industrialization and transformation of Taiwan from a rural to an industrial, urban-oriented society. During this period, the people of Taiwan experienced unprecedented economic growth and social progress. Starting from 1960, the inflation which had plagued the post-Second World War economy of Nationalist China was effectively arrested. Since that year, the price level has an average annual increase of less than 2 per cent.[37]

In 1963 and 1964, Taiwan experienced, for the first time since the pre-war period, a balance of trade.[38] Moreover, the composition of exports became increasingly different from that of pre-1959 periods. In 1959, manufactured goods other than processed foods made up only 12 per cent of the total value of export. This figure rose to 29 per cent in 1960, and again to 40 per cent in 1964.[39]

Owing to rapid economic development, a structural change took place in the Taiwan economy. The agricultural sector decreased from 37.7 per cent of the total national output in 1952 to 32.5 per cent in 1960. Whereas on the other hand, the industrial output increased from 17.9 per cent to 24.7 per cent during the same period. A marked increase in the private sector of the economy also occurred in 1960, growing from 42 per cent in 1952 to 57 per cent in 1960.[40]

One of the important devices used by the GRC to further boost industrialization and export during this period was the establishment of the export processing zone in Kaohsiung, a major port in southern Taiwan. Within a short period of its formal establishment, a large number and amount of investment from foreign firms and overseas Chinese started pouring into the export processing zone, which not only provided new jobs for local workers but also introduced new technical know-how to the indigenous industries.[41]

Furthermore, a marked increase of income was achieved by the Taiwan farmer who had paid off all the land loan to the government in 1963. This led to the demand for more consumer goods, which in turn helped the development of the light industries of the Island. The combination of all these factors produced a record annual economic growth (GNP) of 10 per cent between 1961 and 1968.[42] So well was the economy of Taiwan doing in 1964 that the United States decided to stop the economic aid to Taiwan the next year, a rare occurrence in the history of American aid to the developing countries after the Second World War.[43]

With the cessation of economic aid from the United States in 1965, Taiwan entered into a new stage of modernization and development. Before this, it was a development depending heavily on foreign economic aid and assistance. From now on, the government and people of Taiwan must rely primarily on their own to fulfill the unfinished task.

Although economic aid from the United States Government ended in 1965, American dollars continued to flow into Taiwan in the form of "concessional loans" and investment from private firms.[44] Investment from overseas Chinese grew at a very fast rate. As a result, rapid economic growth continued. This rapid pace of economic development was evidenced in the mushrooming of factories in the country-side and of the high-rising office buildings, resort hotels, and apartments in the cities.[45]

Other than economic and industrial growth, the government and the people of the Republic of China also made headway in the areas of health, social welfare, and education. By 1968, epidemic disease was practically eradicated from the Island. Social security (insurance) was extended to government employees, laborers, fishermen, and sugar cane farmers. Free and compulsory education was further extended from six to nine years with an average attendance ratio of 97.3 per cent among children and youth of school age.[46] A significant increase of life expectancy of the people in Taiwan was achieved, from forty-one years for men and forty-six years for women in 1940, to sixty-five years for men and sixty-nine years for women in 1967.[47]

Starting in 1969, the fifth four-year plan was put into implementation. This plan gives special attention to the development of electrical power, transportation, and more advanced industries requiring skilled labor and capital. Shipbuilding was now given a high priority, for this industry tends to serve as an impetus for the development of other heavy industries. Also, a contract was signed with an Austrian firm to build a large scale steel plant in Taiwan. In the area of power supply, a nuclear-power electrical plant was planned to be built in the northern tip of Taiwan.[49]

Despite the setbacks the Republic of China has suffered in its relations with other nations in 1970 to 1971, such as the recognition of Communist China by a series of nations following the example of Canada, as well as the seating of the delegation of Communist China in the United Nations, economic and social progress in Taiwan persisted.[50] According to a recent report released by the Ministry of Economic Affairs, the annual growth rate for Taiwan was 11.1 per cent in 1970 and 11.4 in 1971, which were actually higher than previous years.[51] The per capita income reached 329 U.S. dollars, as compared to 292 in 1970, and 267 in 1968. The total foreign trade of the ROC approached 4 billion dollars,[52] which nearly equates the total foreign trade of Communist China. This achievement is made more significant when one is reminded that the population of Communist China is fifty-three times that of Taiwan; and its territory more than 264 times.

The success of the modernization efforts achieved by the government and people of the Republic of China in Taiwan during the twenty-two years between 1949 and 1971 becomes evident when we compare certain crucial data on the social and economic development of Taiwan with those of the United States, Japan, and other developing nations of Asia. As data in Table 1 demonstrate, Taiwan leads Thailand, the Philippines, Ceylon, and Burma in almost all socio-economic indices; although it falls behind the United States and Japan with a substantial large margin. Its high growth rate renders hope for a gradual narrowing of the gap.

Today, the people of Taiwan enjoy a standard of living second only to Japan in East and Southeast Asia.[53] The modernization process of Taiwan, in actuality, was more dramatically demonstrated, not by its current achievements, which are still modest by Western standards, but by the amazing pace with which it was accomplished. Table 2 shows that between 1953 and 1968 the people of Taiwan were able to increase industrial production to more than seven times that of 1953. They were also able to boost the number of construction activities more than seventeen times. The per capita income rose to more than five times that of 1953.

Table 1

Data on the Level of Social and Economic Development of the Republic of China
as Compared with other Developing and Developed Nations

Countries	Per Capita National Income	Annual Rate of Economic Growth[2]	Population Per Physician	Infantile Mortality[3]	Per capita Energy Production & consumption[4]	Calories Intake	Rate of Population Increase (%)[5]
Republic of China	US. $ 267[1]	10.4	2,540	20.6	816	2,520	2.9
Burma	67	—	9,580	88.7	57	—	—
Ceylon	132	3.9	4,060	47.7	114	2,170	2.4
Philippines	250	4.6	1,390	72.0	248	2,000	3.5
Thailand	137	—	8,550	33.5	198	2,140	3.1
Republic of Korea (South)	163	8.5	2,360	—	555	2,240	2.5
Japan	1,122	10.3	910	14.9	2,515	2,460	1.1
U.S.A.	3,578	5.0	650	22.4	10,331	3,200	1.2

1. The newest figure is US $329 achieved in 1971.
2. Average annual rates of growth of real gross domestic product at market prices in the 1960-68 period.
3. Death of infants under one year of age per 1,000 live birth in 1967.
4. Coal equivalent in kilograms.
5. Average annual rate of growth between 1963 and 1968.

Data Source: U.N. Statistical Yearbook, 1969; U.N. Demographical Yearbook, 1969; and UNESCO Statistical Yearbook, 1968.

Table 2

Selected Index of Social and Economic Progress on Taiwan Between 1953 and 1968

INDEX	YEAR							
	1953	1962	1963	1964	1965	1966	1967	1968
Crude Birth Rate (%)	4.66[1]	3.74	3.63	3.45	3.27	3.24	2.82	2.93
Crude Death Rate (%)	0.94	0.64	0.61	0.57	0.55	0.54	0.55	0.55
Infantile Mortality[2]	33.7	29.1	26.4	23.9	22.2	20.2	20.6	—
Industrial Productions[3]	36	91	100	120	140	161	188	228
Number of Constructions Activities[4]	62	90	100	121	450	699	852	1,079
Per Capita National Income Growth (in US $)	55	130	151	168	185	199	221	267

1. The Birth rate of 1952; that of 1953 is unavailable.
2. Death of infants under one year of age per 1,000 live birth.
3. Take the figure of 1963 as basis for comparison.
4. Same as above.

Date Source: Data on the crude birth rate are taken from *China Year book, 1969-1970* (Taipei: China Publishing Co., 1970), p. 104; data on per capita national income in the years of 1953, 1962 and 1964 are computed from New Taiwan dollars from data in *Industry of Free China* (March, 1960), p. 38; and *Industry of Free China* (Feb., 1969), p. 54; all other data are from *U.N. Statistical Yearbook, 1969*.

In the same period, the crude birth rate, crude death rate, and infantile mortality showed significant decline, reflecting the marked inprovement of the living conditions of the people on Taiwan.

III

Modernization on Taiwan: An Examination of Its Various Aspects

Having reviewed the various stages of modernization in Taiwan, we are now ready to look into the different aspects[54] of modernization on the Island after the end of the Second World War. Five aspects of the modernization process on Taiwan have been selected to be discussed here. They are: population change, land reform, educational progress, communication "revolution," and social and political integration.[55]

Population Change

The population of a nation can be both an asset and a liability to its drive for modernization. Generally speaking, a young (but not too young), educated, and moderately increasing population tends to lend support to the modernization effort of a society. On the other hand, a dense, uneducated, and rapidly increasing population tends to hinder the chance for modernization of a nation.[56]

In terms of population change in Taiwan in the past twenty-two years, several distinct features can be discerned, some of which are favorable to social and economic development while others are not so favorable. The first distinct feature of the population of Taiwan has been its rapid growth. In fact, the growth of population of Taiwan has been one of the fastest in the world. The total population of Taiwan in 1900 was estimated to be two million persons; this figure was increased to three million in 1905, and four million in 1940.[57] After Taiwan was restored to China at the end of the Second World War, rapid population growth continued under the Chinese Nationalist rule. By 1952, the population figure of the island reached 8,128,000. The number was further increased to 10,792,000 in 1960, and to 14,833,012 in 1970.[58]

The large population of Taiwan, which is crowded in its limited territorial size, produces the highest population density record of the world.[59] The newest figures show that the population density of Taiwan was 1,063 per square mile in the total area, and 4,414 per square mile in the cultivated areas.[60]

Table 3

Population Density and Natural Increase Rate on Taiwan (1952-1968)

End of Year	Density (per sq.m.)[1]	Birth Rate (% of total pop.)	Death Rate (% of total pop.)	Natural Increase (% of total pop.)
1952	586	4.66	0.99	3.68
1956	677	4.48	0.80	3.68
1959	751	4.12	0.72	3.39
1960	777	3.95	0.70	3.25
1961	803	3.83	0.67	3.16
1962	830	3.74	0.64	3.10
1963	856	3.63	0.61	3.01
1964	884	3.45	0.57	2.88
1965	910	3.27	0.55	2.72
1966	936	3.24	0.55	2.69
1967	956	2.85	0.55	2.30
1968	1000	2.93	0.55	2.38

Data Source: *China Yearbook, 1967-70, op. cit.*, p. 104.

[1]Computed from density per square kilomile.

The great population increase was mainly created by the high birth rate of the population of Taiwan, coupled with the gradual decrease in the death rate resulting from the improvement of health conditions. This high natural increase of population of Taiwan has led to a population composition in the shape of a pyramid, with the younger people constituting the majority of the population. For instance, in 1970, individuals with an age of 19 or less constituted 54 per cent of the total population of Taiwan.[61]

In comparison with the age composition of Japan, the United States, and France, that of Taiwan has been the youngest.[62] In this regard, the population structure of Taiwan lies between those of the underdeveloped areas and those of the developed nations, revealing the transitional nature of the modernization process of Taiwan.

Other than rapid population growth and high density, another distinct feature of the population of Taiwan has been its high social increase. By "social increase," it is meant the increase of population of a certain area which is not due to natural increase, such as a higher birth than death rate, but is a result of migration of population into areas from other geographical units. In the case of Taiwan, social increase has been a very important element of population increase on the Island. As a matter of fact, except for the 210,000 aborigines of Malay origin, nearly all the 14.8 million inhabitants on Taiwan are either immigrants from the Chinese mainland themselves or are offsprings of immigrants.[63] Of the 14.6 million inhabitants of Chinese origin, two distinct groups can be differentiated. The larger group, which is generally referred to as the "native Taiwanese," are the offsprings of earlier Chinese migrants who came to Taiwan from Fukien and Kwangtung provinces of southern China. Although the Chinese from these two provinces started migrating to Taiwan as early as the fourteenth century, the largest waves of migration occurred during the seventeenth century.[64]

Of the 14.8 million population of Taiwan, approximately 86.4 per cent are identified as the "native Taiwanese."[65] The rest are the "Mainlanders," refering to the newer immigrants who came to Taiwan from mainland China after the Second World War. They came to Taiwan in large numbers and from all parts of mainland China in 1949 when the Chinese Communists took over the mainland from the Nationalists. Among the newly arrived mainlanders were many government officials, industrialists, businessmen, professors and teachers, engineers, and officers as well as soldiers of the armed forces.[66] The sudden arrival of some one million mainlanders in Taiwan in 1949 constituted for a short while a serious burden to the social and economic institutions of Taiwan. But the Mainlanders, especially the highly educated and trained elite, have made significant contributions to the social, economic and political development on Taiwan throughout the past twenty-two years.

In addition to rapid population and high social increase, another important feature of population change in Taiwan has been the accelerated urban growth. When Taiwan was returned to China by Japan in 1945, it was already a more urbanized place than many other provinces of mainland China. In addition to many smaller cities and towns, Taipei, Keelung, Taichung, Tainan, and Kaohsiung were the five bigger urban centers, each with a population of more than 100,000. As the population of Taiwan increased at a phenomenal pace and as the Island became more industrialized, these bigger urban areas attracted great numbers of people from the rural areas. A study covering the population increase during the 1950-1965 period revealed that a much higher ratio of population increase occurred in metropolitan and industrial centers than in the rural and frontier regions.[67]

As Table 4 clearly shows, while the population of Taiwan increased from 7,557,000 in 1950 to 12,822,000 in 1965, the biggest increase was found in the metropolitan and industrial areas. This big increase of population in the metropolitan and industrial areas has led to a change of percentage of these areas in the total population of Taiwan from 25.2 per cent in 1950 to 31.3 per cent in 1965. On the other hand, the percentage of rural and agricultural areas dropped consistently throughout this period, from that of 70.8 per cent in the total population in 1950 to that of 62.2 per cent in 1965.

Owing to the rapid urban growth, the population of the City of Taipei increased from 325,919 in 1947 to 1,174,883 in 1966, or an increase of 260 per cent. During the same period, the population of four other major cities of Taiwan, Keelung, Taichung, Tainan, and Kaohsiung, also had a dramatic increase, ranging from 140 per cent to 270 per cent. Yet, the population increase of Taiwan during the same period amounted to only about 100 per cent, as compared to that of 1947.[68]

Having examined some of the important features of population change in Taiwan, some reflection on its relation to the process of modernization is in order. Looking from the vantage point of modernization, the dense, rapidly-growing and quickly urbanizing population of Taiwan is both a blessing and a burden. For instance, the predominance of young people in the population composition of Taiwan provides the growing economy and

Table 4

The Population of Metropolitan Areas
and Hsiens (Counties) by Industrial Type, 1950-1965

Areas by Industrial Type	Population (in Thousands) End of the Year								Per Cent Change		
	1950		1955		1960		1965		1951-55	1956-60	1961-65
	%	(N)	%	(N)	%	(N)	%	(N)			
Metropolitan	17.7%	(1,338)	19.6	(1,767)	20.6%	(2,257)	21.8%	(2,799)	32.1	27.7	24.2
Industrial	7.5	(569)	7.9	(725)	8.7	(950)	9.5	(1,219)	27.5	31.0	28.2
Rural Mixed	25.4	(1,917)	24.6	(2,258)	24.4	(2,673)	23.8	(3,051)	17.8	18.4	14.2
Agricultural	29.6	(2,246)	28.6	(2,617)	27.7	(3,041)	26.7	(3,423)	16.5	16.2	12.6
Predominantly Agricultural	15.8	(1,197)	15.2	(1,389)	14.4	(1,577)	13.7	(1,760)	16.0	13.6	11.6
Frontier	3.8	(290)	4.1	(372)	4.2	(467)	4.4	(569)	28.0	25.6	22.0
Total	100%	(7,557)	100%	(9,127)	100%	(10,965)	100%	(12,822)	20.8	20.1	16.9

Data Source:
Paul K. C. Liu, "Population Redistribution and Economic Development in Taiwan, 1951-1965," in *Conference on Economic Development of Taiwan* (Collection of Papers) (Taipei: China Council on Sino-American Cooperation in the Humanities and Social Sciences, Academic Sinica, 1967), p. 202.

industry with a large reservoir of labor force. It also, however, constitutes an acute demand for employment which the Taiwanese economy has not yet been able to satisfy fully, resulting in a high ratio of unemployment.[69]

Other than unemployment, another problem created by a high birth rate and a young population has been a large ratio of dependent population among the people of Taiwan. For instance, in 1964, for every one hundred productive persons between the ages of fifteen and sixty-five, there were ninety dependents. The ratio is estimated to drop to seventy-three for every one hundred in 1974, but will increase again to seventy-six in 1989.[70] The existence of such a high ratio of dependent population naturally was a burden to the social and economic development of Taiwan.

Birth control was first advocated by private agencies and by The Sino-American Joint Commission of Rural Reconstruction (JCRR), and was later accepted by the government as a necessary means to counter the rapidly growing population. A Committee For Family Planning was established within the organizational framework of the Bureau of Public Health of the Taiwan Provincial Government to promote the methods of birth control. Judging from the gradual decrease of birth rate of the population of Taiwan (see Table 2), we may conclude that the effort of government and private agencies to promote birth control has achieved some significant effects.[71]

The fast pace of urbanization of the population of Taiwan also has had its good and bad effects on the socio-economic conditions of Taiwan. According to many theorists, urbanization is closely associated with the process of modernization.[72] Daniel Lerner, for instance, pointed out in his study of the modernization process of the Middle East nations that increasing urbanization tends to raise literacy, which in turn will increase media exposure and lead to wider and extensive economic and political participation.[73] Karl Deutsch also used urbanization as a basic indicator for "social mobilization," a phenomenon which he believed to be the prerequisite for political development.[74]

Although we cannot be completely certain that the rapid urbanization in Taiwan was the primary cause which led to the acceleration of economic development, the expansion of population in the cities did create more demand for the construction of housing projects, expansion of public facilities, and the upgrading

of the educational institutions. It also brought the labor force
released from the rural areas closer to the factories and commercial establishments in the urban centers. Besides, exposure to the
mass media and the increased interaction between people in the
cities made exchange of opinions and ideas much easier than in the
rural regions, which in turn has contributed to the knowledge of,
and the desire for, the higher living standards enjoyed by people of
modern nations.

All of the above developments associated with urbanization
have undoubtedly functioned as catalysts for social progress and
economic development. But, while urbanization has helped the
process of modernization in Taiwan on the one hand, it also has
created many problems for the Island on the other. The
inadequacy of public facilities such as parks, libraries, public
swimming pools, the increasingly serious problem of traffic
congestion, the expansion of slums, the rising juvenile delinquency[75] and suicide rate,[76] and more recently, air and water
pollution, have become common problems for the bigger cities on
Taiwan, especially Taipei.[77]

The GRC has been very much aware of the problems created
by the rapid urbanization. Various measures have been taken to
lessen the problems generated by the urbanization process.
Educational institutions, police departments, and private agencies
together have launched many programs to reduce and prevent the
problem of juvenile delinquency in the cities.[78] To handle the
problems of slums and lack of public recreational and sanitary
facilities, an island-wide community development project has been
adopted and implemented since 1968. Aiming at the improvement
of living conditions in Taiwan, especially in the urban centers, the
project has led to the building of low cost housing units for the
poor people in the cities, the construction of public roads and
parks, and the establishment of public baths in many localities all
over the island.[79]

The Taiwan Provincial Government has also made long-range
plans for a balanced development between large metropolitan
centers and small-size satellite towns. The final goal is to maintain
the growth of urban centers at a more reasonable level so that the
city government could have the needed time and resources to solve
many of the pressing problems associated with urban population
growth.[80]

Land Reform

Of all the post-war developments in Taiwan, the single most important is probably the implementation of successful land reform by the GRC. Uneven distribution of land in the rural areas has been one of the major reasons of local unrest in China for many centuries. The concentration of large amounts of land in the hands of landlords who lived off the rent paid to them by the poor tenants has been a phenomenon that has frequently been exploited by various rebellious political groups to rally support from among peasants to oppose the ruling authority in China. The Chinese Communists, for example, have used "land reform" as a major instrument to agitate the landless peasants of China to oppose the Nationalist government.[81]

The Chinese Nationalists also realized the importance of the land problem in China. As a matter of fact, one of the basic goals of the Republican Revolution led by Dr. Sun Yat-sen was to equalize land ownership.[82] Yet because of various factors, such as the wars with warlords, the invasion by Japan, the continuous harassment by the Chinese Communists, and the resistance of conservative elements within the country, the Chinese Nationalist government was not able to carry out fully the land reform programs envisioned by Dr. Sun Yat-sen on the Chinese mainland. It was not until the Nationalists retreated to Taiwan that they were able to fully implement the various programs of land reform embedded in the *Three Principles of the People (San Min Chu I).*[83]

The prime mover behind the land reform on Taiwan was the late Vice-President Chen Cheng, who was the Governor of the province in the early 1950's. The JCRR also played an important role in carrying out the various programs of land reform.[84] Moreover, the ruling political party, Kuomintang, also contributed to the success of the land reform by mobilizing the party personnel in the rural areas to iron out resistance from the local political leaders whose interests often overlapped with the land-owning strata of the rural socio-economic structure.[85]

This is no place to give a detailed account of the processes of land reform in Taiwan.[86] Nevertheless, several important features of the land reform in Taiwan should be noted. First, it was a gradual and peaceful reform. The land reform in Taiwan went through a three-stage process which began with the reduction of land rent, and was followed by the selling of public land, and eventually consummated with the "Land to the Tiller" program. Contrasted with the brutal treatment of landlords by the Chinese Communists in mainland China, the GRC never intended to wipe out the landlords as a "class." Instead, the government tried to win voluntary cooperation from the landlords so that coercive measures could be avoided in implementing the various programs of land reform.

A second important feature of the land reform in Taiwan was to be found in the government's effort to avoid generating antagonism between the landlords and tenant farmers. For instance, during the period of land rent reduction, the GRC established numerous Farm Tenancy Committees in 1952 to settle disputes between the landlords and tenants. The function of the Farm Tenancy Committee was basically to mediate and to bring about reconciliation between the landlords and farmers in order to prevent the disputes from developing into legal suits through which the relationship between the landlords and tenant farmers could be seriously damaged.[87]

Another important feature of land reform in Taiwan has been the provision of compensation to the landlords by the GRC. According to the Land-to-the-Tiller Act, the landlords who had turned their land over to the government to be redistributed among the former tenant farmers were compensated by receiving 70 per cent of its value in land bonds and 30 per cent in government enterprise stock shares. These two kinds of bonds were to be paid in equal installments spreading over a period of ten years and bearing interest of four per cent per annum.[88] This policy of adequate compensation for the landlords practiced by the GRC was again a sharp contrast to the categorical confiscation of the land of landlords by the Chinese Communists.[89] By adopting this policy, the government was able to win the sympathy and support of most of the landlords in Taiwan. It also had a desirable side effect, i.e., the assimilation of the capital of the landlords into economic and industrial development.

The peaceful land reform conducted by the GRC has had a profound and long-lasting effect on the modernization process in Taiwan. The most conspicuous effect of land reform has been the improvement of the livelihood of the former tenants. According to the findings of social surveys conducted by Martin M. C. Yang and Hung-chin Ts'ai, there were marked improvements in the economic conditions of the former tenants. Not only were the new land-owning farmers able to substantially increase their income after the land reform, they also developed new patterns in household expenditures.

Prior to land reform, the former tenant farmers spent most of their income for food, clothing, and other basic daily necessities. Ten years after the reform, the farmers spent a higher percentage of their income on other "luxurious" categories such as health care, improvement of the farm building, running water and electricity, educational expenses for the children, and recreational activities.[90] Most of the former tenants, when asked to compare their living conditions before and after the land reform, indicated that there was significant improvement of their livelihood after the land reform.[91] The replacement of thatched roof houses by brick houses in the rural areas, the improvement of clothing of members of the farming families, the increasing ownership of bicycles, and later the replacement of bicycles by motorcycles in the countryside, have been concrete evidences testifying to the improved living conditions in Taiwan's rural areas.

If material progress has been a significant indicator of the success of land reform in Taiwan, the change of social status and social attitude of the Taiwanese farmers is even more important to the modernization process. Before the land reform was implemented, tenant farmers had low social status in the rural areas. The landlords in Taiwan, like landlords in most parts of traditional China,[92] enjoyed higher status and played a leading role in the decision-making process at the village level. The tenant farmer usually played a passive role in village activities and were submissive to the landlords in all important issues.

After land reform, the landlords lost much of their influence and status in the rural areas, partly because of the relative improvement in the socio-economic condition of the former tenants and partly because of a gradual decline of interest in the rural regions after giving up the bulk of their land holdings to the tenants. The former tenant farmers, on the other hand, were greatly encouraged by their newly acquired status as land-owning farmers and showed a marked increase of interest in participating in community affairs providing a drastic contrast to the diminishing community interest among the former landlords.[93]

Table 5

Changes in Community Interest Among Tenants, Original Owners, and Landlords After Land Reform in Taiwan

Rural Groups	Increase	No Change	Types of Change Decrease	Never Interested	No Answer	%	(N)
Former Tenant, now owner	20.80%	66.80%	8.64	—	3.76	100	(1,250)
Current Tenant	20.80	51.60	2.40	20.00	5.20	100	(250)
Original Owner	29.20	46.00	10.40	14.00	0.40	100	(250)
Former Landlord Ordinary	9.20	54.60	34.36	—	1.84	100	(489)
Large	8.00	49.33	42.67	—	—	100	(75)
Total (N)	(436)	(1,383)	(340)	(85)	(70)		(2,314)
Total %	18.80%	60.00%	14.60%	3.60%	3.00%		100%

Data Source:　Martin M. C. Yang, *Socio-Economic Results of Land Reform in Taiwan* (Honolulu: East-West Center Press, 1970), pp. 363-364.

This increase of community interest among the land-owning farmers led to a higher participation in community organizations as well as in the political process on the Island. According to the research conducted by Martin M.C. Yang and Hung-chin Ts'ai, the former tenants (now land-owning farmers) showed a significant increase of participation in community organizations such as farmer's association, the farm-tenancy committee, the irrigation association, the public construction control board, and the neighborhood-heads' association.[94] Participation in these community organizations served as a training ground for the involvement of former tenants in the political process of Taiwan. Increasingly, the former tenants, who had already acquired some experience with public affairs in various community organizations, are entering into races for village heads, delegates to the village and town councils, and other political positions at the local level. However, in comparison with the level of political participation of the former landlords, that of the former tenants is still low and could become higher in the future.[95]

One of the most significant impacts of land reform on the people in rural Taiwan is to be found in their attitude toward education. Before land reform, the farmers in Taiwan usually considered education beyond six-year elementary school a luxury for their children. Some parents even prevented their children from going to elementary school so that the children could lend them a helping hand with the farm work. This attitude and practice has ceased to be the case in Taiwan. In Yang's study, it was found that before land reform less than 63 per cent of the former tenants' households sent all their children to elementary school; this figure was increased to 92 per cent after land reform.[96]

A more drastic change, however, was found in the attitude of the former tenants toward education beyond the elementary school level. For instance, it was pointed out by M. C. Yang in his study that most of the former tenants ceased to be satisfied with merely an elementary school education for their children. Many of the farmers felt that they should send their children to junior and senior high schools, and even to universities and colleges.[97] As a result, there was a steady increase in the number of farmers' children entering high schools, vocational schools, and institutions of higher learning.

Although land reform has led to the improvement of living conditions, the expansion of community interest and political participation and the elevation of the educational level in the rural areas of Taiwan, it has also created some problems for the rural community. Foremost among the problems of the post-land-reform rural areas has been the exodus of farm population into the cities. Several factors have contributed to the development of this process. First, the former landlords who had given up their land in the countryside became interested in business and industrial activities in the urban centers. Second, the prosperity brought about by land reform led to the accumulation of capital among the more well-to-do farmers. These farmers got involved more and more in investing in industries and business and eventually moved their residence to the cities. Third, owing to the rise of educational level of the rural population, many of the children of the farmers were able to obtain white-collar jobs in the civil service, schools, business, and other professions in the cities. Finally, the higher wage for jobs in the city constituted another major attraction for rural youth to seek employment in the urban areas.[98]

The loss of rural population to the cities has led to serious shortage of man power in the rural areas, especially during the harvest seasons. To recruit the needed help, the farmers must pay much higher wages to hire temporary workers from other villages or towns, a phenomenon that did not exist before the land reform. Because of the decrease of economic returns from agricultural activities, many farmers would like to sell their lands and invest the capital in business or industrial activities, which has led to a drop of land value in the rural areas.[99]

The afore-mentioned problems or rural Taiwan have caught the attention and generated great concern among political leaders in Taiwan, especially those in the ruling Kuomintang. A "Guide Line for Agricultural Policy" was adopted by the GRC in November, 1969, which was followed by a more complete plan, "The Guidelines of Rural Construction at the Present Stage," promulgated by the Kuomintang.[100] Among the measures embedded in these two policy statements are included: enlargement of unit farm management, the mechanization of farm work, the stabilization of the price of farm products, and the strengthening of farm organizations.[101]

Whether the implementation of the above measures would lead

to the stabilization of farm economy is now heatedly debated among agricultural experts, economists, and law-makers in Taiwan. Judging by the experience of most industrialized nations, what is now happening to the Taiwanese rural communities seems to be a painful but unavoidable process of transition. The emphasis should probably be placed not upon how to prevent or to deter this kind of change from a rural to an urban society, but to minimize the undesirable side-effects and to protect, as much as possible, the farmers who are caught in this process of transition from rural to more industrial and more urbanized society.

Educational Progress

In any modernizing society, education always plays an important role. To be literate is the foremost and basic prerequisite for a person's understanding and experience of, and participation in, the modern way of life. Consequently, the raising of the literacy rate among the population of a nation through universal education has been given top priority by the leaders of the developing nations. It is through popular education that the modernizing nations seek to transmit various kind of scientific knowledge to the people. In addition to the transmittal of scientific knowledge, education also performs the functions of socialization and integration by generating a common identity among the people and by joining them with the ruling élite in a united endeavor towards modernization.[102]

In most developing nations, the rise of literacy through the expansion of education is closely related to urbanization. Generally speaking, ". . . increasing urbanization has tended to raise literacy; rising literacy has tended to increase media exposure; increasing media exposure has 'gone with' wider economic participation (per capita income) and political participation (voting)."[103] In other words, increase of literacy through the urbanization process is essential to achieve a higher level of "social mobilization" as described by Karl W. Deutsch.[104]

In Taiwan, three factors acted together to bring about a rapidly rising level of education among the population. The first two factors, or causes, have been land reform and the urbanization process. The impact of these two factors upon the rising aspiration for education among the people in Taiwan has already been discussed. A third factor, which is no less important than land reform and urbanization, has been the conscious effort made by the GRC. The Constitution of the Republic of China clearly stipulates that "expenditures of educational programs, scientific studies and cultural service shall not be, in respect of the Central Government, less than 15 per cent of the total national budget; in respect of each province, less than 25 per cent of the total provincial budgets; and in respect of each municipality or *hsien* (county), less than 35 per cent of the total municipal or *hsien* budget."[105] This constitutional provision has served as the guideline of educational expenditure and has a positive influence on the development of educational facilities and programs at all levels in Taiwan.

We may measure the post-war educational progress in Taiwan by comparing the number of schools and students enrolled at all levels of educational institutions. As shown in Table 6, the educational systems of Taiwan have undergone a fantastic process of expansion between 1944 and 1970. The expansion has been most impressive at the level of higher education. For instance, the number of institutions of higher learning increased from five to seventy-five; and the number of students increased from 2,174 to 138,577, an increase of sixty-four times! Similar expansion is also found in the number of schools and students at the high school level. Even the number of elementary schools and students has been more than doubled. As a result, the percentage of school age children enrolled in elementary schools has risen from 71.3 per cent in 1944 to 97.9 per cent in 1970.

In 1968, GRC adopted a most important measure in the field of education. This is the extension of "basic education," i.e., free and compulsory elementary education, from six years to nine years. By implementing this measure, the government was able to significantly raise the level of education for the people of Taiwan and to generate a larger reservoir of better educated man-power to meet the demand for more skilled labor and higher personnel in future economic development.[106] In terms of education and research development at the higher level, a long-term science development program was adopted by the national government, which led to the establishment of the National Science Council. Under the able direction of Dr. Ta-yu Wu, the National Science Council has played an active and highly important role in science

Table 6

Educational Progress in Taiwan (1944-1970)

Level of Education Numbers of Schools and Students	1944	1970	The Extent of Expansion[1]
College Education			
Number of colleges and universities	5	75	15 (times)
Number of students	2,174	138,577	64
High School Education			
Number of Schools	75	778	10.4
Number of students	46,521	960,956	23
Elementary Education			
Number of schools	1,097	2,176	1.98
Number of students	898,424	2,165,645	2.42
Percentage of school-age children enrolled in elementary schools	71.3%	97.9%	

Data Source: *Essentials of the Taiwan Provincial Administration* (Taichung: Taiwan Provincial Government, 1971), pp. 3,4.

[1] Figures of 1970 divided by those of 1944.

education and research in the Republic of China.

With a strong backing from the national government, the National Science Council has taken various measures to raise the levels of science education and research in Taiwan, which include the strengthening of research facilities in various universities and colleges; the awarding of research fellowships to various university and college professors to promote original research; the engagement of overseas Chinese scientists (primarily in the United States) to go back to Taiwan to teach as visiting professors in the institutions of higher learning; and the sending of college professors and researchers of Taiwan to engage in advanced studies in the United States and Western Europe. Although meeting many obstacles and confronting various sorts of limitations, these programs initiated by the National Science Council have brought about a notable improvement on both the quality and quantity of science education and research on Taiwan. [107]

So far we have only dealt with the more obvious and concrete results of educational advancement in Taiwan. A more subtle but not less important function played by the educational systems in Taiwan has not yet been examined, that is, the function of political socialization. By "political socialization" is meant "the process by which people learn to adopt the norms, values, attitudes, and behavior accepted and practiced by the ongoing system."[109] When the GRC recovered Taiwan from Japan in 1945, it was faced with a two-fold task of political socialization. On the one hand, the government must re-socialize the adult Chinese population in Taiwan into embracing the cultural-political norms and systems of Republican China after the native population had been under Japanese rule for fifty years.

Another major task of political socialization immediately after the restoration of Taiwan to China was overhauling the education system left by the Japanese so that it would play the role of transmitting Chinese values, norms, and attitudes into the minds of children and youth of Taiwan. In this regard, the major instrument employed by the Chinese Nationalists has been the "Kuo-Yu Yung-Tung (National Language Movement)."[110] Essentially, the movement consisted of teaching standardized Mandarin both to the youth of school age as well as to the adult Taiwanese population at large. The prime mover behind this movement has been the "Executive Committee for the Promotion of the National Language (Mandarin)" which is under the jurisdiction of the Taiwan Provincial Government. In cooperation with the school system and other adult education agencies, the Committee supervised the promotion of Mandarin, the national speaking language, throughout the Island. By all indications, the "National Language Movement" has been a great success. For today in Taiwan, except in a few very remote areas, the overwhelming majority of the native population, especially those living in the cities, can now speak or at least understand Mandarin. The language barriers between the Taiwanese and the Mainlanders are thus largely eliminated, providing a common media of direct communication between the two groups.

Other than the "National Language Movement," the teaching of Chinese history and geography, including stories related to the Republican Revolution, the resistance of Japanese aggression, and the suppression and emergence of the Chinese Communists, constitutes another important part of political socialization in Taiwan. Judging by the findings of recent research conducted by western social scientists, it may be concluded that the education system of the Republic of China has successfully carried out the task of political socialization. For instance, in the research conducted by Sheldon Appleton, it was discovered that there is very little difference between the Mainlander and Taiwanese students in their socio-political perceptions and attitudes.[112] The research findings of Richard W. Wilson more or less yield the same results.[113] All these data lend support to the effectiveness of the education system of the Republic of China as agent of political socialization and integration. It also indicates the tenacious and persistent nature of Chinese culture in withstanding the penetration of other systems.

Although educational advancement in Taiwan has made significant contribution to the modernization of the Chinese society, it also has had its problems. Foremost among the problems of education in Taiwan is the pre-occupation among the people to push for more education without regard to their personal intellectual and financial capability and the actual need of the society. In other words, improvement of livelihood of the people in Taiwan and their rising literacy has led to an insatiable demand for more education for their children and themselves.

For many of the Chinese parents in Taiwan, the purpose of sending their children to elementary school is to prepare them to go to high school; and high school, for going on to colleges and universities. This tendency not only created an overly heavy demand for high school and college education which out-stripped the facilities, but also produced high school and college graduates beyond the employment capacity of Taiwan. Moreover, the highly competitive entrance examinations for high schools and universitites, which directly resulted from the lack of facilities to accommodate the large number of applicants, has become an ominous feature of the education system in Taiwan.[114]

There have been discussions among government officials and school administrators on the methods to improve the situation. The extension of compulsory education from six to nine years has partially solved the problem, at least at the level of elementary school to high school level.[115] Yet, given the limited facilities and resources for education, no solution is in sight for the excessive demand for higher education among the youth in Taiwan.

Other than the problem of extremely high demand for higher education which outstrips the facilities of the school system, another thorny problem of the education system in Taiwan has been the problem of "brain drain." By "brain drain," it is generally meant the loss of highly trained personnel from one country to another, generally from a less developed one to a more developed. According to figures released by the United Nations, between 30 June 1962 and 30 June 1967, 51,218 individuals immigrated into the United States from Taiwan, of which 7,343 were professionals, technical and kindred workers.[116] Among the 7,343 individuals, a substantial portion were Chinese students from Taiwan who took advantage of the 1965 immigration law and adjusted their status from "students" to "immigrants." Official tabulation given by the Ministry of Education of the Republic of China shows that 8,613 college graduates left Taiwan to pursue graduate studies in foreign countries between 1965 and 1969.[117] This number accounts for 22 per cent of the total output of college graduates during that period. Less than 5 per cent of them have returned to Taiwan after completing their studies in foreign lands.[118]

Various factors have contributed to this outflow of trained talent from Taiwan to the United States and other developed nations. Most of the research studies and government reports singled out the wage difference between the available jobs at home and those in the United States as the major reason for the "drain" of talent. But economic variables explain only part of the motivations of the "stayers." In a survey research conducted by this author, it was discovered that social, psychological, as well as political variables all have contributed to the lack of desire to return to Taiwan.[119]

The GRC has been very much concerned with the failure of many Chinese students to return to Taiwan after the completion of their studies in foreign countries. Both the Ministry of Education and the National Science Council have developed various measures to lure the highly trained Chinese talent in the West back to Taiwan. These measures include the subsidizing of the air and boat fares for returning students with graduate degrees, the invitation to foreign-based Chinese scholars to go back to Taiwan to teach in colleges as visiting professors with higher pay than regular professors, and the establishment of graduate research institutions with strong moral and financial support from the national government. These programs, coupled with the recent recession in the United States, has led to a gradual and moderate increase of western-trained students with science and technology degrees to Taiwan.[120]

Communication "Revolution"

One of the basic problems facing the leaders of the developing nations in their efforts toward modernization has been the difficulty of bridging the gap between elite and mass through social communication. Failure to penetrate into the hinter land and mobilize the peasants in the remote rural areas constitutes a major problem for the modernizing political elites. Whether a nation can develop efficient and common channels of communication not only determines its ability to transmit information and messages to, from, and between the masses, but also affects its degree of political integration.[121]

It has been pointed out by Richard H. Solomon that one of the basic problems faced by the Chinese Nationalists in their struggle with the Chinese Communists has been the former's failure to establish an efficient communication link between the peasantry and the established elite.[122] This weakness of communication links between the Kuomintang élite and the masses in the rural areas of mainland China was exploited by the Communists "both for destroying the effectiveness of the existing order and for building the [Communist] Party's own base of mass support."[123] When the Chinese Nationalists moved to Taiwan, they were determined not to repeat the mistakes which they had committed on the Chinese mainland in the area of political communication. Through the land reform processes, the GRC was able to establish various organizations in rural Taiwan, which, to a greater or lesser extent, performed the function of keeping the communication line open between the national and provincial governments on the one hand, and the rural communities on the other. Among these organizations are the farmers' association, the irrigation committee, and the association of fruit growers. Various programs sponsored by these organizations, such as the Farm Advising Program, the Home Economics Teaching Program, and the Rural Youth or 4-H Club Program sponsored by the farmers' association, played both the function of social communication and the function of agricultural innovation.[124]

Other than the various voluntary or semi-voluntary organizations in rural Taiwan, the Kuomintang also made conscious efforts to penetrate the rural as well as the urban communities by establishing party headquarters in important cities and "*min chung fu wu chan* (Stations for Serving the People)" in the villages, towns and wards within the cities. In addition to the tasks of recruitment of party members and organizational work, these party organs also performed the function of bridging the gap between government and party on the one hand, and offering public service such as providing social welfare, encouraging participation in village and town meetings, and promoting community development programs on the other.[125]

If community organizations and the various branches of the ruling party have played an important role of communication in Taiwan, the role played by the mass media in this area is even more outstanding. When Taiwan was under the Japanese rule, there was very tight control of mass media, especially newspapers and magazines in the Chinese language. The Japanese ruling authority kept a strict system of pre-publication inspection. As a result, when the Chinese Nationalists recovered Taiwan from the Japanese, there was not much of a mass media in existence in Taiwan save a few radio stations left by the Japanese. Restoration of Taiwan to Chinese rule brought about a sudden upsurge of all kinds of mass media, especially newspapers and magazines. Some of these early media of communication did not stand the test of time. But many survived and were joined by many other media of communication which were brought by the Chinese Nationalists from the Chinese mainland to Taiwan in 1949.[126]

As the government and people in Taiwan achieved a sense of security and as the socio-economic conditions steadily improved, a phenomenal growth of mass media occurred. According to the data released by the GRC, there are thirty-one newspapers, 1,227 magazines, eight-four radio stations, and four television companies in Taiwan.[127] The combined circulation of the newspapers exceeds 900,000 copies, which produces a record of one copy of a newspaper for every fifteen persons on Taiwan. As of June, 1969, there were 1,425,926 radio receivers in Taiwan, or more than one set for every ten persons. These figures of radio ownership and newspaper circulation are among the highest in Asia,. second only to that of Japan in the Far East.[128]

Before the emergence of television, the newspaper and radio played a leading role of mass communication. These two media have contributed to a great extent to the popularization of *"pai hua* (Vernacular written Chinese language)" as well as *"kuo yu* (Mandarin)" among the population in Taiwan; the former function was performed by newspapers; and the latter, by radio stations. The effort made by newspaper editors and radio station operators was vital in replacing the Japanese language by the Chinese in the early state of the post-war development of Taiwan. Later on, when the GRC was trying to carry out various programs for modernization such as the land reform, agricultural innovation, and educational advancement, newspapers and radio were in the forefront in the "selling" of these programs to the people of Taiwan and in rallying support from among the people for these grovernment projects.

Through the newspapers and radio stations, the people of Taiwan have been able to keep up with the important events at the local, national, and international level. According to the survey conducted by Chi-yin Chu, the ratio of people reading newspapers everyday in rural Taiwan is higher than those in rural areas near Manila, the Philippines, and the rural regions in Italy.[129] The people in rural Taiwan read newspapers for two major reasons: "To be informed about local, national, and international affairs," and "To increase one's knowledge (of modern life)."[130] A third major purpose of reading newspapers was for recreation. Despite the increased popularity of television, newspapers still remain the most important source of information on national and international affairs.[131]

Other than newspapers, radio broadcasting is another important medium of mass communication in Taiwan. Between 1953 and 1962, the number of radios in Taiwan increased thirteen times.[132] There is a radio in nearly every household in Taiwan. A major advantage of radio broadcast over newspapers as a medium of communication lies in the fact that it does not require literacy of the receivers to understand the content of the message. It is able to reach a wide and extensive audience, and is therefore very educational. Prior to the establishment of television stations in Taiwan, the GRC relied heavily on radio broadcasts to transmit important policy decisions and to introduce modern ways of doing things to the people of Taiwan, especially those in rural areas and in the aborigine regions high in the mountainous parts of the Island. According to a survey conducted by Chin-yao Ch'i in 1963, the most important reason given by the people of Taipei for listening to radio was for "news broadcasts." The second major reason for radio listening was for recreational programs such as music, songs, and broadcasts of dramas.[133] In comparison with the findings of Chu's research of newspaper reading habits in rural Taiwan, Ch'i's study on radio clearly shows that radio plays a somewhat more important role for recreation than newspapers.

Moreover, in Ch'i's study of radio listening, it was discovered that people of higher education and white-collar jobs tended to listen to news broadcasting more. On the other hand, those of lower education and blue-collar jobs tended to listen to recreational programs.[134] Another interesting finding of Ch'i's study was that radio broadcasts played an important function of social integration. It was discovered that although the broadcasting companies used both Mandarin (which is the national language) and Fukienese (which is the spoken language of the majority of Taiwanese), many of the native population enjoyed the programs broadcast in Mandarin. The degree of preference for Mandarin programs was positively correlated with the level of education and occupational status; and was negatively correlated with age. In other words, the more education a Taiwanese received, the higher his occupational status, and the younger his age, the more likely he would tend to enjoy Mandarin programs.[135]

The popularity of radio broadcasting reached its height in the late 1950's. Since then, its importance as a medium of mass communication has been gradually replaced by television. The first television station was established in Taiwan in February, 1962. Today, there are four television stations with a total number of 447,044 television sets in Taiwan. In the City of Taipei, there is a television set for every other family. As for the province of Taiwan, the figure is one set for every twelve families.[136]

The establishment of television stations in Taiwan brought the people of Taiwan into the audio-visual era of mass communication. Its impact on the entire population as a medium of communication can only be described as "revolutionary." In a matter of a few years, television has taken away a sizeable proportion of movie-goers, threatening both the movie industry and the movie theatres in Taiwan.[138] Television has also become increasingly a threat to newspapers, although to a lesser degree compared with that to the movie industry.[139] Even a casual observer cannot fail to detect the potential impact of television on the perception as well as the behavior patterns of the people of Taiwan. For watching television has become so important a part of daily life of the people in Taiwan that practically every restaurant, coffee house, barber shop and grocery store in the cities of Taiwan has a television set placed in the most prominent place in the shop.[140]

Owing to the shortness of the period of existence of television stations in Taiwan, there has not yet been vigorous empirical research on the impact of television upon the behavior of the people of Taiwan. There are, however, concrete survey data on the viewing habits as well as the attitude of the people toward various programs on the television stations in Taiwan. According to the study conducted by Chan Li, television has undoubtedly surpassed radio broadcasting, and is quickly catching up with newspapers, as a source of news and information.[141] When asked "What is the most reliable source of information?", the biggest percentage of respondents selected television, as opposed to newspapers and radio.[142] Li discovered in his survey, however, that people of higher education tended to have more trust in newspapers as a source of information; whereas on the other hand, farmers, workers, and housewives tended to have more trust in television than in newspapers and radios.[143]

A great deal of criticism has been voiced against the content of television programs by the people of Taiwan, especially from the more educated elite. Among the more frequent complaints are: too many commercials, too many unprocessed foreign television programs and movies, too many variety shows, too few cultural programs, and too much violence on the screen.[144] Because of the various criticisms of the existing programs on television, there have been suggestions to establish a public television station in Taiwan as well as to enact laws to regulate the proportions of different kinds of programs in the commercial stations.[145] The GRC has recently become concerned with the disproportionately high ratio of commercials and entertaining programs in the television. The Bureau of Cultural Affairs, for instance, recommended in a draft

Broadcasting (including television) Law that the following proportions for each type of program be observed by television stations:
news broadcasting and educational programs (no less than 20 per
cent), public service programs (no less than 10 per cent),
entertaining programs (no more than 50 per cent), and programs
of Chinese origin (no less than 60 per cent).[146]

The full impact of television on the modernization process of
Taiwan is yet to be measured. Yet, judging by the rapid increase of
television ownership among the people of Taiwan, the rising
preference for television as a major source of information, and the
increasing reliance upon television by the GRC as the major
medium of communication, it is safe to say that this medium will
have a profound effect on the thinking and behavior of the people
on that Island.

Social and Political Integration

One of the basic problems faced by the leaders of many
developing nations has been their inability to bring the various
social and political groups together to form a political community
with common identity and goals.[147] Whenever and wherever there
are significant and diversified social and political groups within a
political system, it is essential for the political elite of that system
to fully recognize the differences between these groups, and to try
to accommodate the demand and aspirations of each of these
groups so that violent, divisive courses of action can be avoided.
Failure in doing so has often led to tragic results for the nation
with multiple social and political sub-groups. The experiences of
India, Pakistan, Nigeria, and Indonesia are but a few of the more
notable examples. In most cases, nations which have failed to
reach an adequate level of social and political integration also have
either failed or suffered greatly in their efforts toward modernization.

In the case of Taiwan, one does not find the fundamentally
different ethnic, cultural, and religious groups as those existing in
India, Pakistan, Burma, and Nigeria. Except the 210,000 aborigines of Malay origin, which constitute less than 2 per cent of the
total population of Taiwan, the rest of the people on Taiwan are
practically all of Chinese (Han) origin. There are, however, two
important sub-groups that can be differentiated within the Chinese
population in Taiwan: the Taiwanese and the Mainlanders. As we

have previously pointed out in the section on population change on Taiwan, the Taiwanese constitute about 86.4 per cent of the population on the Island and are offsprings of earlier immigrants from mainland China. The Mainlanders, on the other hand, are the newer immigrants who came to Taiwan after the Second World War.

Although both the Taiwanese and Mainlanders are of Chinese origin, there are several discernible differences between them. First of all, the Taiwanese speak either a southern Fukienese dialect or the Hakka dialect of eastern Kwangtung; whereas the majority of the Mainlanders, on the other hand, use various versions of the Mandarin as their common spoken language. Second, the overwhelming majority of the Mainlanders live in the urban centers of Taiwan, as opposed to the Taiwanese who are more evenly distributed between the cities and rural villages. Finally, most of the Mainlanders are employed in jobs in national government, military, and academic circles. The Taiwanese, in general, are predominantly employed in agricultural, industrial, commercial and fishing sectors of Taiwan's economy.[148]

The above differences between the Taiwanese and Mainlanders naturally led to the creation of some kind of feelings of provincialism. This kind of feeling of provincialism, coupled with the inability of the GRC to recover the Chinese mainland, has led to the emergence of the so-called "Formosan Independence Movement "(FIM)."[149] The beginning of this movement can be traced back to February 28, 1947, when a group of Taiwanese rebelled against the Nationalist authority headed by Governor-General Chen Yi who had proved to be an incompetent administrator in the eyes of the people of this newly recovered territory of China.

Exactly what happened during the so-called "February 28 Incident" has been a subject of continuing debate between those who are favorably inclined to the GRC and those who are sympathetic to the "FIM."[150] Yet no one could deny the existence of a single fact, that is, blood has been shed among both the Taiwanese and Mainlanders on the Island during the "Feburary 28 Incident." The occurrence of this Incident at such an early stage of Taiwan's restoration to China was indeed most unfortunate. It has become an unhappy, though gradually fading, memory in the minds of the Taiwanese, which has been exploited by the "FIM" as one of their major appeals for support.

How much popular support the "FIM" enjoys among the people of Taiwan, like the nature of the "February 28 Incident," is subject to serious debate among scholars and journalists. For a while, the movement seemed to have some support among the overseas Taiwanese businessmen as well as Taiwanese students in Japan and in the United States. But as time passed and as hopes for the realization of an independent "Formosan Nation" increasingly dimmed,[151] the Movement gradually lost its steam. The return of Dr. Thomas Liao, leader of the "FIM" in Japan, to Taiwan in May, 1965, was a severe blow to the morale of the supporters of the Movement. Dr. Liao was pardoned by the Nationalist Government and is now the deputy chairman of the new Tsengwen Dam Commission.

Meanwhile, several important developments in Taiwan have led to a constant increase of assimilation and integration between the Mainlanders and Taiwanese. First of all, the successful "National Language Movement," which has been discussed previously in this chapter, has practically eliminated the communication barrier between the Taiwanese and Mainlanders. Nowadays, one can hardly tell the youngsters of these two provincial groups apart by listening to the way they talk, for both groups are speaking the Mandarin language with hardly any differences in pronunciation and intonation. This is especially true for the youth in the cities of Taiwan. The ability of the children of both the Taiwanese and Mainlanders to speak standard Mandarin has greatly facilitated the process of political socialization, which in turn has led to increased sharing of basic socio-cultural norms, values, and attitudes.[152]

Other than the "National Language Movement," a second factor for eliminating provincial feelings in Taiwan has been the narrowing of the gap between the Taiwanese and Mainlanders in terms of rural-urban divisions. As data in Table 7 show, between 1953 and 1965, the percentages of Taiwanese living in urban areas have increased from 53 per cent to 55 per cent. During the same period the rural Taiwanese population decreased from 47 to 45 per cent. The percentages of Mainlanders living in the cities, on the other hand, decreased from 89.5 per cent in 1955 to 83.5 per cent in 1965, which led to an increase of 6.5 per cent of the Mainlanders in rural Taiwan. This increase is made more significant when we realize that between 1955 and 1965, the Mainlander population in the cities has increased 70.8 per cent; but they had much higher increase of 213.5 per cent in the villages, and an even higher increase of 485.2 per cent in the aborigine areas high on the mountains. As a result, the division between the Taiwanese and Mainlanders along the rural-urban dichotomy has been substantially lessened.

A third important element contributing to social and political integration in Taiwan has been the economic progress achieved in the Island in the past some twenty years. The land reform, the rapid industrialization, and the overall economic advancement of the Island has generated a sense of pride among the people of Taiwan, Taiwanese and Mainlanders alike. Increasingly, more young Mainlanders have entered into business and industrial activities, which has brought about a gradual diminishing of the occupational differences between the Mainlanders and Taiwanese.

The decrease of language barrier, occupational differences, and urban-rural dichotomy has led to increasing inter-marriages between the Mainlanders and Taiwanese. This is especially true between the retired Mainlander soldiers and Taiwanese as well as aborigine girls, which has contributed to an increasing number of children of Mainlander-Taiwanese parentage.[153] In a survey of college studnets conducted by this author in Taiwan in July, 1971, it was discovered that the overwhelming majority of the boys and girls of either Taiwanese or Mainlander groups would have no objection to seeing their sisters or brothers marry members of the other group.[154] If this finding reflects the true feelings of the college students, then most likely there will be more inter-group marriages between the Mainlanders and Taiwanese in the future.

In addition to all the above-mentioned developments, another integrative factor of the population in Taiwan has been the willingness of the GRC to increase the extent of political participatioin of the Taiwanese. Through popular election at the city, county, and provincial levels, the Taiwanese have achieved absolute majority in the legislative and executive bodies of all these levels. In choosing candidates to represent the Party to run in local elections, the Kuomintang has tried to select Taiwanese who have already enjoyed popular support among the people in a particular locality. This pragmatic policy has enabled the Kuomintang to capture a large share of the elective offices at all levels of the Province.[155]

Table 7

Urban-Rural Distribution of Taiwanese and Mainlander in 1955 and 1965

Provincial Groups	Year	Urban Number	%	Rural Numbers	%	Total Number	%
Taiwanese							
	1955	4,345,090	53%	3,879,785	47%	8,224,875	100%
	1965	6,013,980	55%	4,893,564	45%	10,907,544	100%
Mainlanders							
	1955	763,224	89.5%	89,464	10.5%	852,688	100%
	1965	1,436,276	83.5%	284,528	16.5%	1,720,804	100%

Data Source: Based on Data in Table 40 in Tang-Ming Lee, *A Study on Social Increase of Population in Taiwan* (Taichung: Taiwan Population Studies Center, 1968), p. 69. In computing the population of urban areas, the figures of cities and towns are combined. Likewise, the population figures of counties and aborigine counties (San Ti' Hsiang) are combined to form the rural population.

In a special national election held in Taiwan in 1969, which was the first one ever held since the GRC moved to Taiwan in 1949, fifteen new members were elected to the National Assembly and eleven were elected to the Legislative Yuan. All of them were Taiwanese. At the time of this writing, the GRC is seriously considering having another national election in Taiwan to revitalize the membership of the legislative organs at the national level. This measure, if realized, would undoubtedly further increase and reinforce the mutual political identity between the Taiwanese and Mainlanders.

As the government of the United States is moving toward rapprochement and reconciliation with the Chinese Communists, and as the external environment of the Republic of China is facing increasing difficulties after its withdrawal from the United Nations, a sense of common destiny has been developed among the Taiwanese and Mainlanders.[156] Both groups have come to the realization that in the face of a rapprochement between their arch enemy and their major ally, there is little chance of survival save uniting as a single force to preserve Taiwan as a free society for themselves and their children.

For in the past twenty-five years, the people of Taiwan have united in building a society that is far more modern than the one in existence on the Chinese mainland. Despite all the claims made by the Chinese Communists on their various achievements, social scientists still find mainland China under the Communist rule primarily a poor, rural, and agricultural society with limited resources and benefits of modern living for the people to share. This is revealed by the low calorie and protein intake, low ratio of radio, telephone possession, low per capita income, and high percentage of people engaged in agricultural activities.

In comparison with Mainland China, Taiwan is a far more industrialized society, with much higher per capita income, calorie intake, and radio and telephone possession for its people. Given this kind of wide gaps between the society on Mainland China and that on Taiwan, it is inconceivable for the people of Taiwan to accept the authority of a communist regime which has thus far failed to demonstrate the superiority of their formula for modernization over the model that has been successfully tried out in Taiwan during the past twenty-five years. It is safe to say, therefore, that the primary concern of all the people in Taiwan,

Table 8

Mainland China Versus Taiwan:
A Comparison of Socio-Economic Indices

	Mainland China	Taiwan
Size of Territories under control (sq. miles)	3,700,000	13,945
Cultivated Land (sq. miles)	444,000	3,360
Population	750,000,000	14,833,012
Density (per sq. mile)	216	1,063
Density (per cultivated sq. mile)	1,800	4,414
Growth rates, annual	2.25%	2.2%
Adult Literacy	About 40%	83%
Labor Force	350,000,000	4,300,000
Agriculture	85%	43%
Industrial and other	15%	57%
Gross National Product	U.S. $ 8 billion	U.S.$ 6 billion
GNP per capita	$100	$329
Crude Steel per capita	33 lbs.	64.4 lbs
Telephones per capita	1:3,380	1:53
Radios per capita	1:145	1:10
Food: per capita daily		
Calories intake	1,780	2,670
Protein Intake	30	70

Data Sources: *Issues in United States Foreign Policy: No. 4. Communist China* (Washington, D.C.: Department of State, 1969), p. 14; *1968 Taiwan Demographic Fact Book* (Taichung, Taiwan: Department of Civil Affairs, Taiwan Provincial Government, 1969); *Facts About Free China* (Taipei, Taiwan: China Publishing Company, 1969); *China Year Book, 1969-1970* (Taipei, Taiwan: China Publishing Company, 1970); and Data reported by *Central Daily News* (Dec. 27, 1971), p. 1.

including both the Taiwanese and Mainlanders, is how to defend the fruits of their modernization efforts against the threat of the Chinese Communists.

Under the present circumstances, the members of the "FIM" are indeed caught in a difficult position. For one thing has become critically clear, the Chinese Communists will under no condition tolerate an independent "Formosan nation," and the United States, given her avowed intention of wooing Communist Chinese, is very unlikely to lend support to this separatist movement. There are indications that some of the leaders of the "FIM" have recently come to the realization that the political problem for the Taiwanese is really not that of "nation-building," but of political participation and political equality. With diminishing U.S. interest and influence in Taiwan and with a concomitant Chinese Communist political and military pressure on the Island, it is quite possible that the members of the "FIM" will seek reconciliation with the Chinese Nationalists. The Nationalists, on the other hand, may also be more willing than ever to welcome the former "FIM" members, who have given up their goal for independence, to join them in a common struggle against a powerful and determined enemy across the Taiwan Straits.

IV.

The Impact of Modernization Upon the Social Structure, Attitude, and Behavior of the People on Taiwan

A discussion of the modernization process in Taiwan would not be complete without an analysis of the impact of modernization on the social structure, attitude, and the behavior of the people on the Island. The process of modernization both reflects and affects the society wherein it takes place. As a dependent variable, the path, pace, and the degree of modernization are more or less determined by the value system, social structure, and political institutions of a society. As an independent variable, the modernization process shapes and molds the people of a society, injecting new values, norms, and attitudes in their minds and creating new patterns of social interaction.

Although empirical data on the changes in social structure, attitude, and behavior of the people in Taiwan are rather limited and fragmentary, it is possible to piece the scattered available data together and to present a preliminary report on the impact of modernization upon social change in Taiwan. The first major discovery by examining available data is that modernization has had a significant impact on the single most important social institution of the Chinese society on Taiwan — the family.

Traditionally, the ideal Chinese family has been the "extended family," with many generations of relatives living together. Although surveys conducted on Mainland China several decades ago already revealed that the "extended families" of China were gradually disintegrating,[157] the process seemed to be taking a much faster pace in today's Taiwan. There have been arguments that the "extended family" was a system that only existed in the landlord families, and not in the peasant families.[158] Yet research conducted by Martin M.C. Yang in Taiwan has shown that even the landlord's families are moving away from the "extended family" system.[159]

Among the major reasons for the decline of the "extended family" system are land reform and the urbanization process. In Yang's study, it was discovered that many of the families of the former landlords became either nuclear families or "reformed or revised families," meaning families with two generations or three generations, composed of grandparents, parents, and children. This change was caused primarily by the loss of socio-economic status of the landlords, which made it necessary for the members of the extended families of the former landlords to divide up their properties to become independent farmers, or to seek employment in industries, business and other occupations in the cities.[160]

Other than land reform, the urbanization process has been another important variable affecting the traditional families in Taiwan. It was found that the urbanization process tended to have a significant effect in reducing the size of the families in Taiwan. For instance, in a study conducted by Jean T. Burke in 1961, it was discovered that the average size of families in the small towns and villages was eight persons.[161] Another survey conducted by Robert M. Marsh in 1963 shows that 52 per cent of the families in Taipei had five to eight members.[162] In still another study made in the City of Taipei in 1967, it shows that the average size of the urban families in that city was 4.5 persons. Finally, according to the data released by the GRC in 1970, the average size of all the families in Taiwan was 5.6 persons.[163] By piecing these various data together, the influence of the urbanization process on the size of the families in Taiwan is clear indeed.[164]

Not only the size of the families in Taiwan has become smaller, the relationship between members of the families has also undergone some significant changes in recent years. Foremost of the changes has been the decline of parental authority. In the traditional Chinese family, the father or grandfather in a family enjoyed nearly complete authority in making important decisions concerning every member of the family. Yet this kind of vertical, one-way control has been subject to considerable challenges and changes in Taiwan in recent years.

For example, in Yang's survey on land reform, it was discovered that the relationship between father and son no longer corresponded to the patterns of authority (for the father) and submission (from the son), dictatorship and obedience, unreasonable demand and excessive tension. Instead, Yang found that although 64 per cent of the respondents still claimed that the father controlled all the affairs of his children, about 32 per cent believed that the father's authority no longer extended over all the affairs of his children. In other words, parents still hold considerable authority over the children, but it is much more moderate than before and is tempered with reason and restraint.[165]

In general, one finds that the relationship between the parents and their children has changed from that of near complete domination and control (of the children by the parents) to that of persuasion and discussion.[166] The adjustment to the new relationship naturally is more difficult for the parents than for the children. Many parents have complained that they were far more obedient and attentive to their parents than their children are to them today. Others have felt that they have been neglected by their married children, asserting that by having their son married, they have "gained a daughter-in-law, but have nevertheless lost the son."[167]

The younger generation, on the other hand, are not without their grievances. They argue that in a modern, industrialized and mobile society parents cannot treat their children as their possessions and entertain the idea of obtaining economic returns from their grown-up children. Instead, they deem that the parents should accept that raising children is an enjoyment in itself and that it is a social obligation for the parents to nourish and educate their children so that they can be good and useful members of a modern society.[168]

As a whole, the inter-generation conflict in Taiwan is not as serious as in other industrialized societies.[169] For example, Robert M. Marsh discovered that the people in Taipei, Taiwan, are more likely than their counterparts in Japan, Denmark, and the United States to aid their parents; they are also more likely to have their parents living with them.[170] The parents, on the other hand, are also inclined to aid their married children.[171]

In terms of marriage, most of the young people of Taiwan prefer "tzu-yu lien-ai (Free Selection)," meaning choosing their spouse by themselves.[172] Yet the majority of the young people in Taiwan still seek the opinion and consent of the parents when they come to the time for entering into marriage bonds. The fact that the overwhelming majority of the announcements of marriages in Taiwan are made in the names of the parents testifies to at least a nominal recognition of the authority of the parents in this area.

One of the primary reasons for the improvement of the status of the younger people in Taiwan is to be found in education. The youth of today's Taiwan are far more educated than their parents in terms of the formal education they have received in schools and in terms of breadth of knowledge of the modern society.[173] This puts them in a more equal position with their parents in a modernizing society wherein knowledge often means income and influence. Take the son of a farmer as an example. He learns the modern knowledge of farming from programs sponsored by the agricultural-extension service, and applies it to increase the production of his family lot more efficiently than his uneducated father. This leads to more income for the family and admiration from the neighbors. As a result, the father gradually yields decisions on farming methods to the son, and, not infrequently, gradually gives more opportunities to the son to express opinions on other matters of the family.[174]

Other than affecting family relations, increasing educational level was also found to be related to a decline of reliance among the people of Taiwan upon ascriptive standards in evaluating the socio-economic status of a person in a society. In a study conducted by Robert M. Marsh, the respondents were asked: "In deciding whether a person belongs to your social class (she-hu chieh-chi) or not, what do you think is most important to know: who his family is, how much money he has, what sort of education he has, what he believes about certain things, or what his occupation is?" To this question, 38 per cent of the Taiwanese chose occupation and another 29 per cent education. Only 3 per cent considered "family" most important.[175] Not only the Taiwanese in Taipei considered occupation and education the most important factors in determing a person's social status, they also tended to believe that "work and study" was far more important than "luck and pull or help from relatives or friends" in making a person successful in life.[176]

This kind of extreme emphasis on education, occupation, and other "universalistic" criteria for success in life has led, in one way or another, to a more egalitarian view toward other members of the society among the people of Taiwan, which has led to increasing social mobility in Taiwan. As a matter of fact, it was found that the rate of intergenerational occupational mobility among the Taiwanese is as high as that in more industrialized Japan and the United States.[177] Based on this finding, Robert M. Marsh concluded that the City of Taipei has a rather fluid social structure comparable to those of the cities in more advanced societies.[178]

The increasing emphasis on personal achievement and the high social mobility rate in Taiwan has significantly changed the outlook as well as the behavior of the people in Taiwan. First of all, a positive attitude towards life and towards the ability of the individual person to improve his life through self-reliance and self-effort has been developed among the people of Taiwan, including those in rural areas.[179] The people in Taiwan are found to be increasingly free from ignorance and superstitution as well as from the fear of natural calamities, authority of tradition, and experiences. They have become more "oriented to time present and future rather than towards the past."[180] They have also become aware of the importance of knowledge in the maintaining and gaining of social status.[181] Concomitantly, the respect for tradition, the reliance on intimate kinship relations, and the emphasis on ascriptive factors as means for improving a person's livelihood and status have declined.

What has happended, and is still happening, in Taiwan

probably can be summarized in two sociological concepts: the *Gemeinschaft* and *Gesellschaft*. According to Lucian W. Pye, human relations in the *Gemeinschaft* is pictured as highly affective, emphasizing the nonrational, emotional dimensions of man as to be found in the intimate relationship of the kinship groups, comradeship, and neighborliness. The relations in the *Gesellschaft*, on the other hand, are generally impersonal, affectively neutral, and emphasizing the "rational capacities of man by which he is able, first, to isolate and distinguish his goals of action, and then to employ, impersonally and deliberately, contractual arrangements as a part of strategies for optimizing his value."[182] Judging by these definitions, we may conclude that Taiwan is clearly moving quickly away from the Gemeinschaft-like society to the Gesellschaft-like society.

The changing from *Gemeinschaft* to *Gesellschaft*, or traditional to modern society, has not been without its prices for the people of Taiwan. The decline of parental authority and the gradual disappearance of extended families has made aging increasingly a problem. It also contributed to the rise of juvenile delinquency in Taiwan. The shift from an orientation of other-worldly to this-worldly has led to a decline of interest in religious practices, which has reduced expense for these activities.[183] But the shift also has led to more materialistic views and ways of life which, in many cases, are less satisfying than the traditional ways of life centered on religious beliefs and cultural activities.

The increasing social as well as geographical mobility has disrupted the social stability of the traditional society based on a more fixed, hierarchical social structure. Along with the decline of the authority and influence of the landlords and elders in the clan, conflicts between the members of rural villages are increasingly being brought to the court, causing more pain for the involved parties than solving them through mediation and conciliation which were widely practiced in the past.[184] Furthermore, increasing urbanization and social mobility also seem to have led to the increment of cases of mental disorder in Taiwan. For instance, in a fifteen year follow-up study conducted in Taiwan, it was found that there was significant increase of psychoneuroses. The rate of increase was the highest among the Mainlanders, followed by that of the migrant Taiwanese, with the original non-migrant residents having the lowest rate of increase.[185]

On top of all these problems, the exposure to western values and behavior patterns through mass media and direct contact with Westerners has led to noticeable changes in the values and behavior of the people of Taiwan, especially among the youth in the urban areas. The full effects are still to be measured by empirical studies. But the more conservative sector of the society has already pointed to the rising number of youngsters having long hair, wearing hippie-type clothing, and even taking drugs,[186] as clear symptoms of the undersirable effects of Western civilization.

All the above discussed changes and problems in the attitudes and behavior of the people of Taiwan have caused great concern among the intellectuals as well as government leaders. For most of the political leaders and Chinese intellectuals in Taiwan, the purpose of modernization is to preserve and enrich the content of the Chinese culture not to drastically change it nor to destroy it. Since the western nations are ahead of China in terms of modernization, it is necessary to import and borrow western technology and institutions from the West. Yet, in no case should this lead to the replacement of Chinese socio-cultural systems by Western civilization. This view is not only shared by the conservative and traditionally trained élite, but also by a sizeable portion of western educated intellectuals.[187]

The concern of the leaders and intellectuals in today's Taiwan over the pervasive influence and threat of western culture in many ways touches on a debate that has been waged in the intellectual circles of China for more than a century. More than a half century ago, Chang Chih-tung, a leading official-reformer of late Ching China, advocated that Chinese learning should be the "t'i (substance, essence)" and western learning should be the "yung (function, utility)." The implication was to use western technology, i.e., the "yung " to protect Chinese cultural heritage, i.e., the "t'i. " [188] The dilemma, however, has been that while it is possible to import and transplant western technologies to China, it is very difficult, at the same time, to keep the Chinese society free from the influence of western values, norms, and attitudes. This was the problem faced by the reformers of the late Ching China; and this is also the problem faced by the leaders of the Republic of China in Taiwan today.

To preserve the virtue of traditional Chinese culture and to counter the threat of both Marxist ideology of the Chinese

Communists and the "materialistic" culture of the Western world, the GRC, in collaboration with the leaders in the academic, religious, and cultural circles, have launched a *"wen-hua fu-hsing yun-tung* (Cultural Renaissance Movement)" in Taiwan.[189] The programs embedded in this movement include: encouraging good morals and customs through the use of mass communication media; developing tourism in order to help preserve historic sites and relics; planning and constructing stadiums, art galleries, music halls and other cultural facilities; promoting the "Guidelines for the Daily Life of the Citizens;" and the translation of Chinese classics from *"wen-yen* (classic Chinese)" to *"pai-hua* (modern Chinese)."[190] Only time can tell how successfully these programs can fulfill the function of preserving the Chinese traditional culture in Taiwan. But one thing is sure, the GRC will continue implementing the various programs in the "Cultural Renaissance Movement." At the same time, the modernization process of Taiwan will go on. It will undoubtedly bring more prosperity to the Island, and, at the same time, create new problems challenging the wisdom of the Chinese people in Taiwan in their efforts to pursue a higher standard of living as well as to preserve the Chinese way of life.

V

The Modernization Process on Taiwan:
Some Reflections and Projections

The purpose of the present essay has been to examine the process of modernization of the Chinese society in Taiwan since its restoration to China in 1945. Through the discussions in the various parts of the essay, the meaning of "modernization," the various stages of modernization in Taiwan, and the different aspects of modernization, including population change, land reform, educational progress, communication "revolution," and social and political integration, were examined one after another. Finally, the impact of modernization upon the social structure, social attitude, and the behavior of the people of Taiwan was assessed, using the available empirical data collected by social scientists through direct surveys on the Island.

Through the data and analysis presented in this essay, one can at least have a general view of the modernization process in Taiwan. Looking in retrospect, we may identify some of the more important contributing factors for modernization in Taiwan for the benefit of those who have raised the question: "Why were the people of Taiwan able to achieve a higher level of modernization while the peoples of many other developing nations have failed to do so?"

A. The Material and Institutional Foundations Laid by the Reformers of Late Ching China and the Japanese Colonialists

As we have pointed out in our discussion on the meaning of modernization, the development of basic facilities such as railroads, telegraph, and various power facilities is one of the important dimensions of modernization. Another dimension is to be found in the establishment of modern institutions such as banks, legal system, and modern administrational as well as educational systems. When the Chinese Nationalists recovered Taiwan from Japan, both of these two important foundations for modernization had already been developed to a considerable extent. As a result, the GRC was able to build toward modernization on an already developed infrastructure.

B. The Concentration of a Large Number of Science, Technology, and Administrative Elite in Taiwan After 1949

The migration of a large number of Mainlanders to Taiwan after 1949 provided the Island with an abundant supply of scientists, engineers, administrators, and entrepreneurs. Coming from various parts of China, they were really the elite, or the "cream" of the society of Mainland China. The overly high concentration of highly trained élite in Taiwan, for a while, created some problems of employment. But when the political and economic conditions gradually became stabilized, these people from the Chinese Mainland soon were able to join hands with the élite of the Taiwanese society in a common endeavor toward modernizing the Island.

C. The Economic Aid Provided by the United States

The large amount of economic aid given to Taiwan by the United States from 1951 to 1965 helped stabilize the currency of the Republic of China, provided the much needed capital for investment, and led to importation of technical know-how from the United States. In an indirect way, the Unites States economic aid also contributed to the political stability on the Island by restoring the credibility of the GRC in the economic area, thus leading to an increasing trust of the government by the people of the Island.

D. The Hardworking People of a Educated and Disciplined Society

Most of the Westerners who have visited and lived in Taiwan tend to agree that Taiwan has a highly industrious and dedicated people who are willing to work at an income which is much below those of the more developed nations. Diligence and perseverance may be the characteristics of all Chinese people, but the raised level of education further amplified these virtues and converted them into a tremendous push for modernization.

E. The Gradual and Balanced Development with its Emphasis Shifting from Agriculture to Light Industry, and then to Heavy Industry

The GRC has taken a cautious and gradual course for economic development. Emphasis was first placed on the increase of agricultural production. When this was achieved, light industries were able to develop and flourish with the support of a prosperous rural economy. It was not until light industries were fully developed that the government started investing in the high-cost heavy industries. In adopting this gradual and balanced policy of development, the Republic of China was able to avoid the mistakes of many developing nations and areas, including Communist China, whose leaders ventured into heavy industries with disastrous results at too early a stage in the process of economic development.

F. The Flexibility of the Political Elite in Adjusting Their Ideology to Local Conditions

The third principle of the Three Principles of the People, which is the official ideology of the Kuomintang, calls more or less for a kind of economy of democratic socialism. But the political leaders of the Republic of China in Taiwan were flexible enough to implement the land reform strictly according to the teaching of Dr. Sun Yat-sen, on the one hand, but took a more liberal attitude toward industrial development on the other by allowing the private sector of the economy to develop fully in Taiwan.[191] This was in sharp contrast to the leaders of Communist China who have more than once disrupted the regular process of economic development for ideological reasons, as occurred during the Great Leap Forward and the Cultural Revolution periods.

All of the above listed factors for modernization are supported, to a greater or lesser extent, by empirical data. There are other factors which may have contributed to the modernization process of Taiwan, but have yet to be examined by social scientists. For instance, what kind of effect did the continuous state of "crisis," created by the threat of Chinese Communists against Taiwan, have on the modernization process in terms of generating a sense of emergency among the people of the Island? Furthermore, what kind of impact did the two-layer governmental structure have on the modernization process of Taiwan? In other words, did the arrangement of having a national government which has more or less maintained a very low level of élite circulation, coupled with a local government with complete free competition for élite recruitment, help produce political stability which has greatly facilitated economic development on Taiwan? Only future research can give us a definite answer to these questions.

The story of success of the Republic of China in its modernization efforts has gradually caught the attention of an increasing number of developing nations in Asia, Africa, and Latin America. Although whether other developing nations can duplicate the experience of Taiwan is subject to debate, the achievements made by the Republic of China in the past twenty-five years have at least generated considerable interest. Many nations, for instance, have sent students and government officials to Taiwan to learn the process of land reform, agricultural innovation, rural development, and government administration from the Republic of China. In return, the GRC also has sent agricultural experts and teams, engineers, and medical doctors and nurses, to a sizable number of developing countries in Africa, Asia, and Latin America.[192] These personnel from the Republic of China have had an impressive record in helping the host countries and have won widespread friendship and admiration for their expertise as well as dedication.

By all indications, the progress made by the people of Taiwan toward modernization will continue at an even faster pace. Despite a series of setbacks suffered by the Republic of China in international politics, there has been little indication that this has seriously and adversely affected the process of economic development.[193] The extent of calmness and self-assurance demonstrated by the people of Taiwan after the seating of Communist China in the United Nations has left a deep impression on western observers.[194] It is safe to say, therefore, that with this kind of confidence and determination, the people of Taiwan will build an even more prosperous society on the Island in the near future, which will remain as a living testimony to the people of the world of what the Chinese people could achieve in an open, free, and competitive system.

Notes to Chapter XI

1 For example, see Daniel Lerner, *The Passing of Traditional Society, Modernizing the Middle East* (New York: The Free Press, 1958); David E. Apter, *The Politics of Modernization* (Chicago: The University of Chicago Press, 1965); Gabriel A. Almond and James S. Coleman (eds.), *The Politics of Developing Areas* (Princeton, N. J.: Princeton University Press, 1960); Max F. Millikan and Donald L. M. Blackmer (eds.), *The Emerging Nations, Their Growth and United States Policy* (Boston: Little, Brown and Co., 1961); P. T. Bauer and Basil S. Yamey, *The Economics of Under-Developed Countries* (Chicago: University of Chicago Press, 1957); and Bert F. Hoselitz (ed.), *Sociological Aspects of Economic Development* (Glencoe, Ill.: Free Press, 1960); and Eugene Staley, *The Future of Underdeveloped Countries: Political Implications of Economic Development* (New York: Harper and Row, 1954).

2 See Samuel P. Huntington, "Political Development and Political Decay," *World Politics*, 17 (April, 1965), pp. 386-430.

3 See Shao-hsing Chien, "Taiwan as a Laboratory for the Study of Chinese Society and Culture," in Shao-hsing Chien *et al., Four Articles on Population and Family Life in Taiwan*, Asian Studies Paper Reprint Series No. 2 (East Lansing, Michigan: Asian Studies Center, Michigan State University, 1967), pp. 1-8. Other than in its ready accessibility, another reason which facilitates social research in Taiwan is to be found in the abundant and continuous social and demographic data produced first by the Japanese and later by the Nationalist Chinese administrations. For a discussion of this, see Robert M. Marsh, "The Taiwanese of Taipei: Some Major Aspects of Their Structure and Attitudes," *Journal of Asian Studies*, 27 (March, 1968), pp. 571-584.

4 See S. N. Eisenstadt, *Modernization: Growth and Diversity* (Bloomington, Indiana: Dept. of Government, Indiana University, 1963), p. 5; cited in William H. Friedland, "A Sociological Approach to Modernization," in Chandler Morse *et al., Modernization by Design, Social Change in the Twentieth Century* (Ithaca, N. Y.: Cornell University Press, 1969), pp. 34-35.

5 Eisenstadt, *Ibid.*; Friedland, *Ibid.*

6 Eisenstadt (ed.), *Readings in Social Evolution and Development* (Oxford: Pergamon Press, 1970), p. 21.

7 *Ibid.*

8 Karl W. Deutsch, "Social Mobilization and Political Development," *The American Political Science Review*, IV (September, 1961), p. 494.

9 *Ibid.*, pp. 494-497.

10 David E. Apter, *The Politics of Modernization* (Chicago and London: The University of Chicago Press, 1965), p. 10.

11 Daniel Lerner, *The Passing of Traditional Society, Modernizing the Middle East* (New York: The Free Press, 1958), p. 45.

12 For a discussion on the "achievement motive," see David C. McClelland, *The Achieving Society* (New York: The Free Press, 1961), pp. 36-62.

13 *Ibid.*, p. 36.

14 See H. H. Gerth and C. Wright Mills (trans. and ed.), *From Max Weber: Essays in Sociology* (New York: Oxford University Press, 1958), pp. 302-322; and Reinhard Bendix, *Max Weber, An Intellectual Portrait* (Garden City, N. Y.: Doubleday & Co., 1960), pp. 49-79.

15 Tang-Ming Lee, *Li-lai Tai-wan Jen-kou She-hui Tseng-chia Chih Yen-chiu* (A Study on Social Increase of Population in Taiwan) (Taichung, Taiwan; Taiwan Population Center, 1968), p. 5; and Chiao-min Hsieh, *Taiwan, — Ilha Formosa, A Geography in Perspective* (Washington: Butterworth, 1964), pp. 149-153.

16 Taiwan was made into a province in 1887. See Hsieh, *op. cit.*, p. 155.

17 *Ibid.*

18 See Shinkichi Eto, "An Outline of Formosan History", in Mark Mancall (ed.), *Formosa Today* (New York: Praeger, 1964), pp. 43-58; also see Hsieh, *op. cit.*, p. 163.

19 John Fairbank, Edwin O. Reischauer, and Albert M. Craig, *East Asia, The Modern Transformation* (Boston: Houghton Mifflin Company, 1965), p. 759.

20 Eto, *op. cit.*, p. 57.

21 Hsieh, *op. cit.*, p. 163.

22 Fairbank, *et al.*, p. 759.

23 *Ibid.*, p. 760.

24 Sheldon Appleton, "Taiwanese and Mainlanders on Taiwan: A Survey of Student Attitudes," *China Quarterly* (Oct.-Dec., 1970), p. 56.

25 For a discussion of dislocations in the economy of Taiwan towards the end of Japanese rule, see *Taiwan Ching-chi Nien-piao (Annual Report on the Taiwan Economy)* (No. 4; Taipei: Bank of Taiwan, 1956), pp. 186-187.

26 Lee, *op. cit.*, p. 41.

27 Chien-sheng Shih, "Economic Development in Taiwan After the Second World War," *Weltwirtschaftliches Archiv*, Vol. 100, No. 1 (1968), p. 116.

28 For an official report prepared by the Chinese Nationalists, see *The Truth About the February 28, 1947 Incident in Taiwan* (Taichung: Historical Research Commission of Taiwan Province, 1967); for some opposite and highly critical accounts of the incident, see George H. Kerr, *Formosa Betrayed* (Boston: Houghton Mifflin, 1965), *passim;* and Douglas Mendel, *The Politics of Formosan Nationalism* (Berkeley and Los Angeles: University of California Press, 1970), pp. 31-41.

29 Most of the literature on the "Formosa Independence Movement" are produced either by the activists in the movement or by western scholars, journalists, and former diplomats who are highly sympathetic to the movement. As a result, opinions expressed in their work are often one-sided and highly critical of the Nationalist rule on Taiwan. For instance, see Mendel, *op. cit.*; also see Mark Mancall, *Formosa Today* (New York: Praeger, 1964); Lung-chu Chen and Harold D. Lasswell, *Formosa, China and the United Nations* (New York: St. Martin's Press, 1967); and Kerr, *op. cit.*.

30 See A. Doak Barnett, *Communist China and Asia, A Challenge to American Policy* (New York: Vintage Books, 1960), p. 389; also Mark Mancall (ed.), *Formosa Today* (New York: Praeger, 1968), p. 5.

31 For the process of land reform in Taiwan and its socio-economic impacts, see Chen Cheng, *Land Reform in Taiwan* (Taipei: China Publishing Co., 1961), pp. 66-81; and Martin M. C. Yang, *Socio-Economic Results of Land Reform in Taiwan* (Honolulu: East-West Center Press, 1970), *passim.*

32 See Sheppard Glass, "Some Aspects of Formosa's Economic Growth," in Mark Mancall (ed.), *Formosa Today* (New York: Praeger, 1964), pp. 68-90; Karl Brandt, "Economic Development: Lessons of Statecraft at Taiwan," *Orbis*, 11 (Winter, 1968), pp. 1067-80; Barnett, *op. cit.*, pp. 397-399; *Conference on Economic Development of Taiwan* (A Collection of Papers) (Taipei: China Council on Sino-American Cooperation in the Humanities and Social Sciences, Academia Sinica, June 19-28, 1967), *passim*; and *Industrialization in the Republic of China* (Taipei: Council for International Economic Co-operation and Development, 1969), p. 2.

33 For a description of self-government on Taiwan, see *China Yearbook, 1969-1970* (Taipei: China Publishing Co., 1970), pp. 159-168.

34 See Hung-chao Tai, "The Kuomintang and Modernization in Taiwan," in Samuel P. Huntington and Clement H. Moore (eds.), *Authoritarian Politics in Modern Society* (New York: Basic Books, 1970), p. 419; and Ch'ang-ch'uan Hsing, *T'ai-wan Ti-fan Hsuan-chu Chih Fing-hsi Yu Chin-tao* (An Analysis and Review of Local Elections in Taiwan) (Taipei: The Commercial Press, 1971), pp. 61-68.

35 Tai, *op. cit.*, pp. 416-419.

36 See *Chin-jih Chin Chung-Hua Ming-kuo* (Republic of China Today) (Taipei: Overseas Publisher, 1968), pp. 51-64; *China Yearbook, 1969-1970, op. cit.*, pp. 248-258; and Neil H. Jacoby, *U. S. Aid to Taiwan, A Study of Foreign Aid, Self-Help and Development* (New York: Praeger, 1966), pp. 166-167.

37 *Industrialization in the Republic of China, op. cit.*, pp. 4-5.

38 Ramon H. Myers, "Economic Development in Taiwan," in Hungdah Chiu (ed.), *China and the Question of Taiwan: Documents and Analysis* (to be published by Praeger in 1973), Chap. II.

39 *Ibid,*

40 *Industrialization in the Republic of China, op. cit.*, pp. 24-27.

41 *Ibid.*, pp. 33-34.

42 *Ibid.*, p. 3.

43 Jacoby, *U. S. Aid to Taiwan, op. cit.*, pp. 227-237.

44 Melvin Gurtov, "Taiwan in 1966: Political Rigidity, Economic Growth," *Asian Survey*, 7 (January, 1967), pp. 40-45.

45 For a report on the economic condition of Taiwan in 1970, see Hua Fei, "The Trend of Economic Development and the Economic Problem of Our Nation in 1971," *Hai-wai Hsueh-jen* (Overseas Intellectuals), Vol. 15 (Taipei: Ministry of Education) (August, 1971), pp. 2-6.

46 *Essentials of the Taiwan Provincial Administration* (Taichung: Taiwan Provincial Government, 1968), p. 3.

47 *Ibid.*, p. 15.

48 *Highlights of the Fifth Four-Year Economic Development Plan of the Republic of China* (Taipei: Council for International Economic Cooperation and Development, 1969), p. 304.

49 *Central Daily News* (Jan. 5, 1972), p. 1.

50 "Taiwan, Scorned by U.N., Still Has a Lot Going For It," *U. S. News and World Report* (Nov. 8, 1971), pp. 22-24.

51 *Central Daily News* (Dec. 27, 1971), p. 1.

52 *Ibid.*

53 Not counting Hong Kong and Singapore, for the special conditions of a near complete urban economy of these two areas.

54 The reason that we use the word "aspects," instead of "factors," or "causes," is due to the fact that sometime it is rather difficult to determine whether a particular phenomenon or process is a factor facilitating or accelerating the modernization process, or is in itself, a product of modernization. We shall, however, examine the factors of modernization in the latter part of this essay.

55 One of the important aspects of modernization in Taiwan, *i.e.*, the economic development, has not been selected here because of two reasons. First, it is covered by another chapter of the present book. Second, it has also been discussed to a certain degree in this essay in the section of the review of the stages of modernization on Taiwan.

56 For a discussion on the problems of rapid population growth and its negative effects upon the economic and social conditions of a nation, see J. Mayone Stycos, "Problems of Fertility Control in Underdeveloped Areas," in Larry K. Y. Ng and Stuart Mudd (eds.), *The Population Crisis, Implications and Plans for Action* (Bloomington, Ind.: Indiana University Press, 1970), pp. 58-71.

57 Hsieh, *Taiwan-Ilha Formosa, op. cit.*, p. 211.

58 *China Yearbook, 1969-1970, op. cit.*, p. 103; and *Central Daily News* (July 23, 1971), p. 3.

59 Not counting small, urbanized city-states such as Singapore, Malta, etc.

60 Computed from dividing the total population (14,833,012) by the total area of Taiwan, Penghu and the adjacent islets (13,945 sq. miles) and by the size of cultivated land (3,360 sq. miles).

61 *China Yearbook, 1969-1970, op. cit.*, p. 105.

62 Hsieh, *Taiwan, op. cit.*, pp. 218-219.

63 *T'ai-wan Kuan-fu Nien-wu-nien* (Twenty-Five Years After Taiwan's Restoration to China) (Taichung, Taiwan: Government Information Service, 1971), Part 19, pp. 58-59.

64 Hsieh, *Taiwan, op. cit.*, p. 149.

65 Lee, *A Study of Social Increase of Population in Taiwan, op. cit.*, p. 44.

66 *Ibid.*, pp. 44, 66.

67 See Paul K. C. Liu, "Population Redistribution and Economic Development in Taiwan, 1951-1965," in *Conference on Economic Development of Taiwan* (Taipei: China Council on Sino-American Cooperation in the Humanities and Social Sciences, Academia Sinica, 1967), pp. 199-299.

68 Kuang-hai Lung, *She-hui Tiao-chia yu She-hui Kung-tso* (Social Survey and Social Work) (Taipei: San-Ming Shu Chu, 1970), p. 110.

69 The ratio of unemployment rose constantly during 1951-62. In 1964, for instance, unemployment increased to between 450,000 and 500,000, representing about 10 per cent of the labor force. See Jacoby, *U. S. Aid to Taiwan, op. cit.*, p. 93.

70 *T'ai-wan Chih Jen-kou Yu Chia-t'ing Chi-hua* (The Population of Taiwan and Family Planning) (Taichung: Bureau of Public Health, Taiwan Provincial Govenment, 1967), p. 16.

71 Also see *Taiwan's Family Planning in Charts*, second ed. (Taichung, Taiwan: Population Studies Center, Taiwan Provincial Department of Health, 1967).

72 See Daniel Lerner, *The Passing of Traditional Society, op. cit.*, pp. 46. 60, 63, 66-67; and Deutsch, "Social Mobilization and Political Development," *op. cit.*

73 Lerner, *op. cit.*, p. 46; Raymond Tanter, "Toward A Theory of Political Development," (paper presented at the Midwest Political Science Convention, Chicago, Illinois, April 29, 1966), p. 18.

74 Deutsch, "Social Mobilization and Political Development," *op. cit.*

75 On the problem of juvenile delinquency in Taiwan, see Teng-fei Lin, "An Analysis of the Problem of Juvenile Delinquency in the Taiwan Areas," *Ta Hsueh (The Intellectual)*, Taipei, Taiwan (May, 1971), pp. 55-66.

76 See Ch'ang Kuei Lee, *Tzu-sha Ti Pi-chiao Yen-chiu* (A Comparative Study of Suicide — One of the Crucial Social Problems in Taiwan) (Taichung, Taiwan: Center for Social Research, Tunghai University, 1970).

77 In one respect, i.e., the crime rate, the bigger cities of Taiwan have something to boast of. Through the effort of an efficient police force, the government of the ROC has been able to keep crime in the cities of Taiwan at a much lower level than those of many other large urban centers of the world. This fact has frequently been observed and praised by western tourists who have travelled to Taiwan.

78 "The Problem of Juvenile Delinquency: Opinions of the Experts," *Ta Hsueh* (The Intellectual), 41 (May, 1971), pp. 28-54; and *T'ai-wan-Sheng She-cheng Ssu-cheng Kai-k'uang* (A Simple Survey of the Implementation of Social Policies of Taiwan Provincial Government) (Taichung, Taiwan: Bureau of Social Affairs, Taiwan Provincial Government, 1970), pp. 4-5.

79 *Essentials of the Taiwan Provincial Administration, op. cit.*, p. 15; *Tai-wan-Sheng She-cheng Kai-k'uang op. cit.*, pp. 15-16; and Hsiu-ju Liu, "Report of the Delegation of the Republic of China to the First Conference of Work Groups on Social Development, ECAFE," *She-hui Chien-she* (The Journal of Social Development), Taipei, Taiwan, 8 (March, 1971), pp. 6-14.

80 *Taiwan Kuan-Fu Nien Wu Nien, op. cit.*, Part 16, pp. 2-12.

81 The emergence of Mao Tse-tung to be the head of Chinese Communist Party was primarily due to his emphasis on the exploitation of rural problems to promote communist goals. For a basic communistic view of the peasant problem in China, see Mao Tse-tung, "Report on An Investigation of the Peasant Movement in Hunan," in *Selected Work of Mao Tse-tung* (Vol. 1; Peking: Foreign Language Press, 1965), pp. 23-59.

82 Chen Cheng, *Land Reform in Taiwan* (Taipei: China Publishing Company, 1961), pp. 10-17.

83 *Three Principles of the People* is the official ideology of the Kuomintang. It is composed of the Principle of Nationalism (*Min-chu Chu-I*), the Principle of Democracy (*Min-ch'uang Chu-I*), and the Principle of People's Livelihood (*Min-Sheng Chu-I*). The program of land reform is contained in the part on *Min-shen Chu-I*. See Sun Yet-sen, *San-Min Chu-I* (Three Principles of the people) (Taipei: Chung-Yang Wen-Wu Kung-Yin She, 1971), pp. 453-460.

84 Jacoby, *U. S. Aid to Taiwan, op. cit.*, pp. 171-173.

85 Tai, "The Kuomintang and Modernization in Taiwan," *op. cit.*, p. 428; also see Yung Wei, "Political Development in the Republic of China," in Hungdah Chiu, (ed.), *China and the Question of Taiwan: Documents and Analysis*, to be published by Praeger in 1973.

86 A brief discussion on the procedures of land reform on Taiwan has been

presented earlier in this chapter in the part on the stages of modernization on Taiwan.

87 Chen Cheng, *op. cit.*, pp. 33-35.

88 *Ibid.*, pp. 75-78.

89 For a comparison of land reform in Taiwan with that of the Communist land revolution on mainland China (from a Nationalist point of view), see Chen Cheng, *op. cit.*, pp. 112-130.

90 See Hung-chin Ts'ai, *T'ai-wan Lung-ti Kai-ke Tui She-hui Ching-chi ti Ying-hsiang* (The Socio-Economic Impact of Land Reform in Taiwan) (Taipei: Chai-Hsin Wen-Hua Chi-chin Hui, 1965), pp. 80-87.

91 Martin M. C. Yang, *Socio-Economic Results of Land Reform in Taiwan* (Honolulu: East-West Center Press, 1970), pp. 265-270.

92 See Hsiao-tung Fei, *Chinese Gentry, Essays in Rural-Urban Relations* (Chicago: The University of Chicago Press, 1953); and Chung-li Chang, *The Chinese Gentry, Studies on Their Role in Nineteenth-Century Chinese Society* (Seattle: University of Washington Press, 1955).

93 Yang, *op. cit.*, pp. 353-366; and Ts'ai, *op. cit.*, pp. 49-56; and Bernard Gallin, *Hsin Shing, Taiwan: A Chinese Village in Change* (Berkeley, California: University of California Press, 1966), pp. 112-117.

94 Yang, *op. cit.*, p. 356.

95 Ts'ai, *op. cit.*, pp. 76-77.

96 Yang, p. 373.

97 *Ibid.*, p. 378.

98 Wang Tso-Yung, *et. al.*, *T'ai-wan Ti-erh-tz'u Tu-ti Kai-ke Chu-I* (Suggestions for a Second Land Reform in Taiwan) (Taipei: Huan-Yu ch'u-pan-she, 1970), pp. 63-64.

99 Wu Fung-san, *Ching-Tien Ti Taiwan Lung-Ts'un* (Rural Villages of Today's Taiwan) (Taipei: Chih-Li Wan-pao-she, 1971), pp. 26-27.

100 *Ibid.*, pp. 17-18.

101 *Ibid.*, p. 18.

102 David E. Apter, *The Politics of Modernization* (Chicago: The University of Chicago Press, 1965), pp. 145-148.

103 Lerner, *The Passing of Traditional Society, op. cit.*, p. 46.

104 Deutsch, "Social Mobilization and Political Development," *op. cit.*

105 Article 164 of the Constitution of the ROC. See *China Yearbook, 1969-1970, op. cit.*, pp. 709-710.

106 *Essentials of the Taiwan Provincial Administration* (Taichung: Taiwan Provincial Government, 1971), p. 3.

107 Ta-yu Wu, "The Development of Science in Our Country in Recent Years," *Central Daily News* (Jan. 2, 1970), p. 4.

108 For discussion on the concept of "political socialization," see Herbert H. Hyman, *Political Socialization* (New York: Free Press, 1959); Kenneth P. Langton, *Political Socialization* (New York and London: Oxford University Press, 1969); Richard E. Dawson and Kenneth Prewitt, *Political Socialization* (Boston: Little, Brown and Co., 1959).

109 Roberta S. Siegal (ed.), *Learning About Politics, A Reader in Political Socialization* (New York: Random House, 1970), p. xii.

110 *Taiwan Kuan-Fu Nien-Wu Nien, op. cit.*, Part 19, pp. 58-59.

111 See Sheldon Appleton, "Taiwanese and Mainlanders on Taiwan," *op.*

cit.; Richard W. Wilson, "A Comparison of Political Attitudes of Taiwanese Children and Mainlander Children on Taiwan," *Asian Survey*, 8 (Dec., 1968), pp. 980-1000; and Richard W. Wilson, "The Learning of Political Symbols in Chinese Culture," *Journal of Asian and African Studies*, 3 (July-October, 1968), pp. 246-254.

112 Appleton, *op. cit.*, pp. 56-57.

113 Wilson, *op. cit.*, p. 998.

114 Jacoby, *U. S. Aid to Taiwan, op. cit.*, p. 167.

115 It must be pointed out however, that the nine-year free and compulsory education is not without its problems. For a discussion of this, see Pao-shih Lin, "An Over-all Review of the Implementation of the Nine-Year National Education," in *Che-i-tai Ch'ing-nien T'an T'ai-wan Wen-T'i* (Taiwan as the Young Generation Sees) (Taipei: Huan-Yu Tsu Pan She, 1970), pp. 130-142.

116 See U. N. General Assembly, "Outflow of Trained Personnel from Developing Countries," Report of the Secretary General, (Mimeo A17294) (Nov., 1968), p. 55.

117 According to a report in *The Asian Student* (Feb. 22, 1969), p. 3.

118 *Ibid.*

119 For a preliminary report on the findings, see Yung Wei, "Socio-Psychological Variables and Inter-Nation Intellectual Migration: Findings From Interviewing Returnees in the Republic of China," (paper presented to the Annual Convention of International Studies Association, Pittsburgh, Penna., April 2-4, 1970).

120 *Ibid.*

121 For a sample of discussion on the relationship between communication and integration, see Karl W. Deutsch, "Communication Theory and Political Integration," in Philip E. Jacob and James V. Toscano (eds), *The Integration of Political Communities* (Philadelphia and New York: J. B. Lippincott Company, 1964), pp. 46-74; Lucian W. Pye (ed.), *Communication and Political Development* (Princeton, N.J.: Princeton University Press, 1963); and Karl W. Deutsch, *The Nerves of Government, Models of Political Communication and Control* (New York: The Free Press of Glencoe, 1963), especially chaps. 9 and 10.

122 Richard H. Solomon, "Communication Patterns and the Chinese Revolution," *China Quarterly*, 32 (October-December, 1967), pp. 101-110.

123 *Ibid.*, p. 102.

124 Yang, *Socio-Economic Results of Land Reform in Taiwan, op. cit.*, pp. 389-396.

125 See Tai, "The Kuomintang and Modernization on Taiwan," *op. cit.*, p. 428.

126 *Taiwan Kuan-Fu Nien Wu Nien, op. cit.*, Part 20, pp. 1, 3-4, 9-10.

127 *China Yearbook, 1969-1970, op. cit.*, pp. 288-294. The data were based upon government survey conducted in 1969. At the time, there were only three television stations. The fourth television station was established in 1971.

128 *Ibid.*, pp. 288-293.

129 Chi-Yin Chu, *T'ai-wan Hsiang-ts'un Tu-che Tu-pao Hsi-kuan Tiao-ch'a* (A Survey on the Habits of Newspaper Reading Among People in Rural Taiwan) (Taipei: Chia-Hsin Cultural Foundation, 1964), p. 36.

130 *Ibid.*, pp. 33-35.

131 See Chan Li, "Wo-Kuo Tien-Shih Kuan-chung I-chien Tiao-ch'a (A Survey of the Opinions of Television Viewers in Our Country)," *Chung-san Foundation Bulletin*, Taipei, Taiwan (November, 1970), pp. 74,75.

132 Chin-yao Ch'i, "A Study of Radio Listening Habits of the People on Taiwan; also on the Relationships Between Radio-Broadcast Listening and Social Change," in Ch'i, *Collections of Papers on Politics, Law, and Journalism* (Taipei: Hai-Tien Tsu Pan She, 1966), p. 49.

133 *Ibid.*, pp. 32-50.

134 *Ibid.*, pp. 34-47.

135 *Ibid.*, pp. 50-51.

136 Chan Li, *op. cit.*, p. 51.

137 Despite the increasing threat from television, movie theatres in Taiwan still were able to attract a record number of audience. For example, an average person on Taiwan saw movies for sixty-six times in 1968, which was the highest figure in the world, according to the figure released by UNESCO.

138 See Yung Wei, et al., "Television and Daily Life," *Hai-wai Hsueh-jen* (Overseas Chinese Intellectuals), Taipei, Taiwan (March 1, 1960), p. 27.

139 Chan Li, *op. cit.*, pp. 75-78.

140 As observed by this author in 1970-71 when he was a visiting professor at a university in Taiwan.

141 Chan Li, *op. cit.*, pp. 74-75.

142 *Ibid.*, p. 75.

143 *Ibid.*, pp. 86-87.

144 *Ibid.*, pp. 91-100.

145 See Chan Li, "An Examination of Television System of Our Country," *Pao-hsueh Pan-yueh-kan* (Journalism Fortnightly), Taipei, Taiwan (Dec. 31, 1970), pp. 3-11.

146 *Ibid.*, p. 10.

147 For discussion on the concept of "political integration" as well as the relationship between personal identity and nation-building, see Karl W. Deutsch, *Nationalism and Social Communication, An Inquiry into the Foundation of Nationality* (Cambridge, Mass.: The M.I.T. Press, 1953), pp. 60-94; K. W. Deutsch, *Political Community at the International Level, Problems of Definition and Measurement* (Garden City, N. Y.: Doubleday and Co., 1954); and Lucien W. Pye, *Politics, Personality, and Nation-Building, Burma's Search for Identity* (New Haven and London: Yale University Press, 1962), pp. 3-58.

148 Tang-ming Lee, *A Study on Social Increase of Population in Taiwan*, *op. cit.*, pp. 66-75.

149 See Footnote 29 for literature on the "FIM."

150 See Footnote 28 for various accounts of the "February 28, 1947" Incident. It may be noted that the members of the "FIM" have deliberately tried to avoid using the term "Taiwanese," which is more commonly used in China, to refer to the natives of Taiwan. Instead, they have insisted on using the term "Formosans" which was first used by the Portuguese to call the inhabitants of the Island.

151 Even Douglas Mendel, an American political scientist who is highly sympathetic to the cause of the "Formosan Independent Movement" yielded to the fact that it is not feasible for the "Formosans" to gain "independence"

through revolution in the foreseeable future. See Mendel, *op. cit.*, pp. 242-245.

152 For a discussion on the socialization process on Taiwan, see the section on educational progress of this chapter.

153 Lee, *op. cit.*, p. 70.

154 Yung Wei, "Political Culture and Socialization on Taiwan: Findings from Interviewing College Students." (Unpublished research report).

155 Hung-chao Tai, "The Kuomintang and Modernization in Taiwan," *op. cit.*, p. 417; and Mark Plummer, "Taiwan: 'The New Look' in Government," *Asian Survey*, 9 (Jan., 1969), pp. 18-22.

156 See Louis Kraar, "Taiwan's Strategy for Survival," *Fortune* (Nov., 1971), pp. 125-131, 188, 193, 194.

157 See Pen-Wen Sun, *Hsien-tai Chung-kuo She-hui Wen-t'i* (Social Problems of Modern China), 4 vols. (Chungking: The Commercial Press, 1943), Vol. 1, pp. 51-54, 110-118.

158 Sun, *op. cit.*, pp. 61-68.

159 Martin M. C. Yang, *T'ai-wan T'u-ti Kai-ke Tui Hsiang-ts'un She-hui Chih-tu Yin-hsiang Chih Yen-chiu* (A Study of the Impact of Land Reform on the Social System in Rural Taiwan) (Taipei: China Committee on Sino-American Co-operation in the Humanities and Social Sciences, Academia Sinica, 1970), pp. 92-98.

160 *Ibid.*, p. 96.

161 Jean T. Burke, *A Study of Existing Social Conditions in the Eight Townships of the Shihmen Reservoir Area, including a Brief Analysis of the Impact of Irrigation and Benchmarks for Measuring Social Change*, Economic Digest Series No. 14 (Taipei: Chinese-American Joint Commission of Rural Reconstruction), p. 10.

162 Robert M. Marsh, "The Taiwanese of Taipei," *Journal of Asian Studies*, 27 (March, 1968), pp. 571-584.

163 *Essentials of the Taiwan Provincial Administration, op. cit.*, p. 2.

164 For the decline of extended family in urban areas, see Arthur F. Raper, "Urbanization and the Family," in Shao-hsing Chen *et al.*, *Four Articles on Population and Family Life in Taiwan* (East Lansing, Mich.: Asian Studies Center, 1967), pp. 25-39.

165 Yang, *Socio-Economic Results of Land Reform in Taiwan, op. cit.*, pp. 446-455.

166 In a recent survey conducted by the Bureau of Civic Affairs of the Provincial Government of Taiwan, it was found that close to 40 per cent of the college students chose "discussion of the problem with the parents," and around 15 percent selected "stick to my position," as the solution of differences between them and their parents. See *Ta-hsueh-sheng tui tan-chien Sheng-ho Huang-ching Ti K'an-fa* (The Opinion of College Students Toward their Living (Social) Environments) (Taichung: Bureau of Civic Affairs, Taiwan Provincial Government, 1970), pp. 31-32.

167 Chin-Han Chang, "Gaining a daughter-in-law, but losing the son—On the Intergenerational Conflicts in Modern (Chinese) Families," in *Che-i-tai Ch'ing-Nien T'an T'ai-wan Wen-ti, op. cit.*, pp. 156-162.

168 *Ibid.*, pp. 157-158.

169 *Ta-hsueh-sheng Tui Tang-chien Sheng-ho Huang-ching Ti K'an-fa, op. cit.*, p. 135.

170 Robert M. Marsh, "Taiwanese of Taipei," *op. cit.*, pp. 572-573.

171 *Ibid.*, pp. 574-575;

172 This was found in a survey conducted by the Nationalist Party in 1969. See *Chih-shih Ch'ing-nien I-pan Hsin-ni Ch'u-shih Tiao-ch'a Pao-kao* (A Report of the Survey on the General Psychological Inclinations of the Young Intellectuals) (Taipei: Fifth Division, Central Committee, Kuomintang, 1970), pp. 59-60.

173 Yang, *Socio-Economic Results of Land Reform in Taiwan, op. cit.*, pp. 454-455.

174 *Ibid.*

175 Marsh, *op. cit.*, pp. 576-577.

176 *Ibid.*

177 *Ibid.*, pp. 578-579.

178 *Ibid.*, p. 580. It should be pointed out, however, that high social mobility may not be a new phenomenon only in existence in the modern Chinese society on Taiwan. Ping-ti Ho, for instance, discovered rather high rate of mobility in the Chinese society of the Ming and Ching China. See Ping-ti Ho, *The Ladder of Success in Imperial China, Aspects of Social Mobility, 1368-1911* (New York: Columbia University Press, 1962), pp. 255-266.

179 For a discussion on the development of this kind of attitude among the "new farmers," see Yang, *The Socio-Economic Results of Land Reform in Taiwan, op. cit.*, pp. 521-533.

180 Norma Diamond, *K'un Shen, A Taiwanese Village* (New York: Holt, Rinehart and Winston, 1969), p. 108.

181 For the relationship between social status and the acquisition of information through mass media in a small, remote village in northern Taiwan, see Godwin Chu, "Impact of Mass Media on a Gemeinschaft Like Social Structure," *Rural Sociology*, 33 (June, 1968), pp. 189-199.

182 Pye, *Politics, Personality, and Nation-Building, op. cit.*, p. 34.

183 Burke, *op. cit.*, p. 16.

184 See Bernard Gallin, "Mediation in Changing Chinese Society in Rural Taiwan," in David C. Buxbaum, *Traditional and Modern Legal Institutions in Asia and Africa* (Leiden, Netherlands: E. J. Brill, 1967), pp. 77-90.

185 Tsung-yi Lin *et al.*, "Mental Disorders in Taiwan, Fifteen Years Later: A Preliminary Report," in William Caudill and Tsung-yi Lin (eds.), *Mental Health Research in Asia and the Pacific* (Honolulu: East-West Center Press, 1969), pp. 66-91.

186 See Su-P'e Li, Eng-king Yeh, et al., "Drug Misuse Among the Taiwanese Youth," *Hsin-ni Wei-sheng T'ung-shun* (Mental Health Bulletin) Taipei, Taiwan (Dec. 20, 1970), pp. 4-13.

187 For a sample of opinions, see Yuan-su Yen *et al.*, "Taiwan Under the Shadow of Western Civilization," in *Che I Tai Ch'ing-Nien T'an Taiwan Wen-T'i, op. cit.*, pp. 1-27.

188 For a discussion on the "T'i-Yung" Philosophy of Chang Chih-Tung, see Joseph R. Levenson, *Modern China and Its Confucian Past* (Garden City, New York: Doubleday and Co., 1964), pp. 82-105.

190 *Ibid.*, p. 85.

191 Tai, *"The Kuomintang and Modernization on Taiwan," op. cit.*, pp. 431-433.

192 For a discussion on the export of agricultural expertise from the Republic of China to African countries, see William Clifford, "Free China's Dirt Farm Diplomacy," *Lion*, 50 (Oct., 1967), pp. 30-32.

193 See Kraar, "Taiwan's Strategy for Survival," *op. cit.*

194 *Ibid.*

Contributors

GEORGE M. BECKMANN received his Ph.D. from Stanford University. He taught at the University of Kansas and Claremont Graduate School, and was a Visiting Associate Professor at Harvard University. Having served as Professor of Asian Studies and History, Director, Far Eastern and Russian Institute, and Chairman, East Asian Studies Faculty Group, University of Washington at Seattle, he is presently Dean of that University's College of Arts and Sciences. He is the author of *Imperialism and Revolution in Modern China, 1940-1950* and *The Modernization of China and Japan.*

PARRIS H. CHANG 張 旭 成 received his Ph.D. from Columbia University. He is presently Associate Professor of Political Science at Pennsylvania State University. He has done research at the Center for Chinese Studies, University of Michigan, and is the author of *Radicals and Radical Ideology in the Cultural Revolution* (1972) and numerous articles on Contemporary China.

CHIAO-MIN HSIEH 謝 覺 民 earned his Ph.D. from Syracuse University and is Professor of Geography at the University of Pittsburgh. He served as a research associate at Chinese Institute of Geography in Chungking (1941-1946), and at M.I.T. in Boston (1954-1956). He taught at Taiwan Normal University (1946-1947), Dartmouth College (1953-1954), and Catholic University of America (1956-1957), as well as the University of Leeds, England in 1964. His major published works include *Taiwan — Ilha Formosa* (1964), *China — Ageless Land and Countless People* (1967) and chapters in two books.

ANTHONY Y. C. KOO 顧 應 昌 received his Ph.D. from Harvard University and is Professor of Economics at Michigan State University. He taught at the University of Michigan from 1964 to 1967. Since 1968 he has been a member of Academia Sinica. He is the author of *Land Reform and Economic Development —A Case Study of Taiwan* 1966) and numerous articles on world economy and trade.

HYMAN KUBLIN earned his Ph.D. from Harvard University and is Professor of History at Brooklyn College of the City University of New York. He was Visiting Professor at the University of Delaware, University of California at Berkeley, and University of Hawaii, and is the author of *The Ruin of Asia (1963), Asian Revolutionary: The Life of Sen Katayama (1964), China (1968),* and *Japan (1969).*

TING-YEE KUO 郭 廷 以 studied at National South Eastern University and taught at Tsing-Hua University from 1928 to 1931, National Central University from 1932 to 1948 and Taiwan National University from 1949 to 1963. He was Visiting Professor at the University of Washington at Seattle. He has done research at Harvard University. From 1955 to 1970, he served as Director of the Institute of Modern

History, Academia Sinica of which he has been a member since 1968. He is now Senior Research Associate of the East Asian Institute at Columbia University. His major published works, all in Chinese, include, *T'ai-wan shih-shih kai-shou* (A Sketch History of Taiwan), *Chin-tai chung-kuo shih* (History of Modern China) and *Chung-kuo tung-shih* (A General History of China).

HARRY J. LAMLEY received his Ph.D. from the University of Washington, Seattle, and Associate Professor of History at the University of Hawaii. He taught at Taiwan Normal University from 1956 to 1958 and San Diego State College from 1964 to 1965, and is the author of "The 1895 Taiwan Republic: A Significant Episode in Modern Chinese History" published in the *Journal of Asian Studies* (August 1968).

CHAN LIEN 連　戰 earned his Ph.D. from the University of Chicago and is Professor and Chairman of the Department of Political Science at National Taiwan University. He taught at Wisconsin State University from 1965 to 1966 and the University of Connecticut from 1966 to 1968. He is the author of several articles published in learned and professional journals.

PAUL K.T. SIH 薛　光　前 earned his doctorate from the University of Rome in Italy and is Professor of Asian Studies and History, and Director of the Center of Asian Studies at St. John's University where he serves concurrently as Assistant to the President for International Studies and Education. He taught at Soochow University, China, and was a consultant to the National Science Foundation, Washington, D.C., from 1961 to 1971. He is the author of *Decision for China* and the editor of *The Strenuous Decade: China's Nation-Building Efforts, 1927-1937.*

RICHARD L. WALKER received his Ph.D. from Yale University and is James F. Byrnes Professor of International Relations, Director, Institute of International Studies, University of South Carolina. He taught at Yale University from 1950 to 1957, National Taiwan University from 1954 to 1955. His major published works include *The Multi-State System of Ancient China* (1953), *China Under Communism, the First Five Years* (1955), *China and the West, Cultural Collision* (1956), *The China Danger* (1966), *Prospects in the Pacific* (1972), as well as numerous articles on Chinese and international studies.

YUNG WEI 魏　鏞 earned his Ph.D. from the University of Oregon at Eugene and is Associate Professor of Political Science at Memphis State University in Tennessee. He taught at the University of Nevada from 1966 to 1968, and National Chengchi University, Taipei, from 1970 to 1971. He has done research at the Survey Research Center, University of Michigan, and is the author of *The Nature and Methods of Social Sciences* and the editor of *Communist China: A System-Functional Reader.*

Index

A

XYZ